# Maurice Duruflé

# Eastman Studies in Music

Ralph P. Locke, Senior Editor
Eastman School of Music

## Additional Titles on French Music and Organ Music

A complete list of titles in the Eastman Studies in Music Series,
in order of publication, may be found at the end of this book.

# Maurice Duruflé

## The Man and His Music

JAMES E. FRAZIER

UNIVERSITY OF ROCHESTER PRESS

First published 2007

University of Rochester Press
668 Mt. Hope Avenue, Rochester, NY 14620, USA
www.urpress.com
and Boydell & Brewer Limited
PO Box 9, Woodbridge, Suffolk IP12 3DF, UK
www.boydellandbrewer.com

ISBN-13: 978-1-58046-227-3
ISBN-10: 1-58046-227-8

ISSN: 1071-9989

**Library of Congress Cataloging-in-Publication Data**
Frazier, James E.
  Maurice Duruflé : the man and his music / James E. Frazier.
     p. cm. — (Eastman studies in music ; [v. 47])
  List of Duruflé's works: p.
  Includes bibliographical references, discography (p.   ), and index.
  ISBN-13: 978-1-58046-227-3 (hardcover : alk. paper)
  ISBN-10: 1-58046-227-8 (alk. paper)
  1.  Duruflé, Maurice, 1902–1986.  2.   Organists—France—Biography.
  3.  Composers—France—Biography.  I.  Title.
  ML416.D87F73 2007
  780.92—dc22
  [B]

                              2007009847

The publication of this book is made possible, in part, by generous grants from the
District of Columbia AGO Foundation and the Twin Cities Chapter of the American
Guild of Organists.

Frontispiece: Maurice Duruflé. Photograph by Seeberger, courtesy of the American
Guild of Organists.

Photograph at the beginning of chapter 12: Marie-Madeleine Duruflé. Photograph
by Seeberger, courtesy of the American Guild of Organists.

A catalogue record for this title is available from the British Library.

*To Jeffrey Wilson Reed
and Simon*

# Contents

# *Illustrations*

# *Foreword*

My very first experience with Maurice and Marie-Madeleine Duruflé goes back to the recital they performed at First Presbyterian Church in Fort Wayne, Indiana on September 20, 1966. As a young teen who had recently discovered the instrument and who was under the incomparable guidance of the Duruflés' host, Jack Ruhl, the evening proved to be a turning point in my life. The two major loves in my life, the French language and the organ, suddenly fit together in ways I'm still discovering today. It goes without saying that the playing was phenomenal. Who could have guessed that such virtuosity was possible on the organ? And then, the very elegant reception with both Monsieur and Madame autographing programs and providing me with my first earful of native French. Those two had cast a spell over that fifteen-year-old as they had much of the United States. I resolved to become her student, although at that point I couldn't imagine how such an opportunity would come about.

Many years later, in 1977, while a student of Marie-Claire Alain's in Paris, I was reintroduced to Mme Duruflé, who, after considerable coaxing, agreed to take me on. There followed an intensely rich two-year period where I recast my technique, and played the Duruflé works and many of the symphonic and neoclassical works for which Marie-Madeleine Duruflé was so justly famous. My study in Paris finished, we nonetheless continued to correspond, and every time I returned to Paris, I hurried to Saint Étienne-du-Mont to find her, usually during the 11:00 mass.

Although she always remained my august teacher, the relationship invariably matured, especially during the spring semester in 1992, when she accepted our invitation to be Artist-in-Residence at the University of North Texas, where I was Coordinator of Organ at the time. It was Marie-Madeleine who decided she would live in my simple apartment on Teasley Lane, for she wanted to speak French, and felt that the accommodations I had made for her in a sumptuous home south of Denton were entirely too lavish for her modest needs. Over those six months, what had been principally a student-teacher relationship evolved very quickly to intimate friendship. There was very little about the family and about her career that wasn't discussed in detail, although I knew better than to ask questions about Maurice's first wife.

All of this explanation is offered simply to clarify that my approach to Maurice Duruflé and his music was largely through her optic. I never studied directly with Maurice Duruflé, only speaking with him occasionally on the telephone when I called to check a lesson schedule or when Mme Duruflé was having the occasional toothache and didn't want to take the call.

There are many fine studies of the life and music of Maurice Duruflé available today, but none of them succeeds as well at relating a broader picture of the man and his music as does James Frazier's *Maurice Duruflé*. The author delves deeply into his subject and offers an embarrassingly rich tableau against which to bring to life Duruflé and his music. Duruflé's reticence and discretion are legendary both here and in France, and it is probably these sides of Maurice Duruflé's character that have contributed to the mysteries that surround him today, twenty years after his death.

Why was Maurice Duruflé so hesitant in acknowledging his composition lessons with Widor at the Conservatoire? True, Widor was viewed at this time as quite *passé*, and Duruflé's later style may have owed little to this training, but Widor, judging from the letter of recommendation he wrote to the priest of Saint Étienne-du-Mont prior to Duruflé's appointment there, appears to have been extremely supportive of his student. And then, there is the matter of the first marriage, long whispered about in the Parisian organ circles with a sort of twinkle in the eye, but, more significantly, accompanied by furtive explanations that the first wife was not mentally balanced and that Duruflé had no choice but to separate. For the first time, we learn in James Frazier's work that Lucette Bousquet was anything but unstable. She had a long, prodigious career as a pianist and teacher, forming the careers of several accomplished artists. As much as memories of this relationship seem to have pained the second family (the Chevaliers), there is absolutely no dishonor, especially in this day and age, associated with annulment and remarriage. James Frazier relates the story with great sensitivity and respect, and no one's reputation is remotely tarnished by recognizing the woman who was at Maurice Duruflé's side for at least fifteen years, the period during which he composed his undisputed masterworks.

The story of the *Requiem*, Op. 9, is fraught with even greater landmines, and I leave it to James Frazier to relate just what was involved during the Vichy Regime itself. I only wish to underscore Frazier's acknowledgment that original work on the war years was done by another American musicologist, Leslie A. Sprout, who first brought to light the important contributions made to French music during those bleak and empty years. Frazier offers considerable background and analysis of what it meant to be active in Paris at this time, and the various levels of involvement one might have with that regime *without* being cast as a sympathizer or even a traitor after 1945 as was Alfred Cortot. No, the fact that Duruflé accepted a commission in 1941 and was eventually paid by the Fourth Republic in 1948 in no way impugns his loyalty to France. It was surely a matter of subsistence during a long period when there was no money, and certainly no joie de vivre, but life had to go on during those horrendous years, and Maurice Duruflé had mouths to feed and rent to pay.

A close friend of mine confided to me some years ago that Maurice Duruflé's music was really quite second—rate. He identified several incongruities of style, especially in Opus 2, and, with a wave of his hand, dismissed the music, reminding me that one of our French colleagues had allegedly once said, "And finally, this music makes you feel good." To this admirer, who still shivers at passages in the Préludes (Op. 4 and Op. 5) or the intense drama of the Prelude and Fugue, "Them were fightin' words." Such is the old dichotomy identified during the eighteenth century by Rameau and Rousseau, both claiming nature as their raison d'être in art, but imparting extremely different meanings to it. I suspect for the more "scientific" musicologist and listener, there are those works that may not hold together as well as others, due to what just may be the residual influences of Widor and Dukas attempting to reconcile themselves in the same piece. In the case of Opus 2, Duruflé tried to unify those contrasting styles and sections with a strong tactus, and it seems to me that when those tempo relationships are observed, the *Scherzo* works extremely well. But I must confess to being a bit more on the Rousseau side of things. It was, after all, Jean-Jacques Rousseau who wrote:

> If your eyes fill with tears, if you feel your heart palpitate, if disturbances agitate you, if oppression suffocates you, [go to] work. . . . But if the charms of this great art leave you unaffected, if you have neither delirium nor ecstasy, if you find beautiful that which transports, dare you ask what is genius? Vulgar man, do not profane this sublime name. What would it matter to know it? You couldn't feel it.

And in Duruflé, there is exactly that: intense, searing feeling. Duruflé succeeds brilliantly in piercing the soul. The listener with any sensitivity whatsoever is never left unmoved. Bravo Maurice Duruflé, and my deepest thanks to James Frazier for relating the entire story of his life, times, and career with such devotion and sensitivity.

Jesse Eschbach
Chair of the Keyboard Studies Division
The College of Music
University of North Texas

# Preface

I have never wondered why I took up the writing of this book. From my earliest exposure to the music of Maurice Duruflé, when I was in college, I felt the most profound affinity for the man himself. Thus was set in motion a quest that led me to Paris as a Fulbright student. But only a few days after settling into my apartment on rue de la Sorbonne in May 1975, I learned that the Duruflés had been gravely injured in an auto accident. The mystery that I have always believed surrounded the man grew more vast because of their tragedy, and because I would never meet him.

Long after Duruflé's death, and after Mme Duruflé's recovery, I traveled considerable distances to hear her perform on her U.S. tours. In 1993, having played the Duruflé organ works for many years, I worked them up in order to play them all in a couple of coaching sessions with her in Paris. I had one lesson on the organ in their apartment, and the other in the church. Seven years later, on January 22, 2000, I attended her memorial service in Paris, rendering thanks, as it were, for a precious gift that I shall always treasure *de tout cœur*.

Having never met Duruflé himself, it was important that I visit the places where he lived, his home in Louviers and his three apartments in Paris. I walked the halls of the choir school in Rouen and those of the Conservatoire in Paris. I also visited his vacation home and his grave, both in Ménerbes, not far from Avignon.

In the writing of this book I have assembled myriad random pieces of Duruflé's life in the hope that the result is a faithful and coherent semblance of a man who was frustratingly elusive. I like to imagine that what I now cherish of him is somehow complete, or at least as complete as it will ever be for me. The book is a collection of the souvenirs I have amassed, a scrapbook, if you will, documenting an affair. It is also a diary of my heart, in a way, and a map of my own labyrinthine mind.

*Minneapolis, September 2006*

# *Acknowledgments*

I am privileged to have met family members and intimates of the Duruflés, along with some of their students and colleagues, and former choirboys of the Rouen cathedral school, who shared their memories, some of them poignant and some tragic, some of them humorous, some of them proud and noble, but all of them, in some way, sacred to me.

Paul Duruflé, the nephew and closest living relative of Maurice, graciously shared personal memories and important details and clarifications of his uncle's life, and provided previously unpublished photographs of Maurice's parents, brothers, and extended family, a few of which are reproduced here. It was through M. Duruflé that I was introduced to Patrick Bousquet, the son of Lucette Bousquet, Duruflé's first wife, who opened a door previously closed upon the woman who had shared Duruflé's life for fifteen years.

Éliane Chevalier, the devoted sister of Marie-Madeleine, founder of the Association Maurice et Marie-Madeleine Duruflé, and tireless promoter of the Duruflé legacy, shared helpful personal and professional information. Her sudden death, on August 13, 2001, was a tragic loss to the effort she had so selflessly advanced on behalf of her sister and brother-in-law.

Jean-Martin Chevalier, second cousin of the Chevalier sisters, arranged for my visit to Ménerbes, where the Chevalier family had a home and where Maurice and Marie-Madeleine vacationed. I spent a privileged afternoon chatting with the elderly Mme André Longueverne, a long-time intimate friend of the Chevaliers and the Duruflés, a distinguished woman frail of body but strong of mind and memory, whose home was adjacent to the Chevalier house and across the road from Duruflé's *pavillon*. Mme Longueverne had keys to the Chevalier house. Though it had sold, no one was living there, and all of the Chevalier effects were intact: the table and chairs before the fireplace in the *salle à manger*, with its antique chest, the furniture in the parlor, the upright piano, the little library of papa Chevalier, the pictures of Marie-Madeleine and Éliane on the walls, with their grandmother who first taught them piano. Mme Longueverne and I sat in the modest parlor and talked at length about the Duruflés and the Chevaliers, whom she revered with a nearly religious devotion, having known them for over four decades.

On January 15, 2002, I interviewed three former *maîtrisiens* of the Rouen cathedral, and heard their recollections of life at the school. The youngest of the three, Francis Pinguet, an organist and musicologist, was a chorister from 1953 to 1958. His book *Les Écoles de la musique divine* launched me on a solid course at the outset of my research.

Bernard Delaporte, then President of the Anciens élèves de la Maîtrise Saint-Évode, maintained close connections with the cathedral and the choir school. Equipped with skeleton keys, he gave me a cook's tour of the cathedral and every floor of the choir school, as well as the Salle d'État in the archbishop's residence, where Duruflé and his fellow choristers sang concerts before the cardinal.

André Levasseur was at the choir school during and after the Second World War. He helped haul the pipes of the Dupré house organ to the cathedral after Marcel Dupré bequeathed it to the cathedral. Following the war, Levasseur began commuting to Paris to study harmony and organ privately with Duruflé. He was organist at Notre-Dame des Anges in Bihorel, a suburb of Rouen, from the 1940s.

Laurence Reibel, the Attaché de Conservation du Patrimoine at the Musée municipal in Louviers, mounted a well-researched exposition on Duruflé early in 2002, through the opening months of the centenary of his birth. Mlle Reibel supplied me with copies of valuable civil documents from the Hôtel de Ville in Louviers.

Karen McFarlane was the Duruflés' American concert manager and devoted friend and confidant for many years. She generously photocopied reams of correspondence between her office and the Duruflés, which date from her predecessor Lilian Murtagh's days through the death of Mme Duruflé. These papers made a critical contribution to the chapter on the Duruflés' tours of North America.

Jesse Eschbach, who knew Marie-Madeleine Duruflé perhaps more intimately than any other American, hosted her during her residency at the University of North Texas, in 1992. I am indebted to him for his support of my research into sensitive areas. His love for the French organ tradition in general, and for the Duruflé legacy in particular, is accompanied by a scholarly regard for the truth. I am honored that he so readily consented to provide the foreword to my work.

The concert organist and pianist Rodger Vine, who became organist at the Arlington Street Church in Boston in 1974, was a virtual companion for the final two years in the writing of this volume, offering valuable insights and bits of information from his studies with the Duruflés. Beginning in September 1971 he coached with Duruflé on every piece of keyboard music he ever published, including the *Prélude, récitatif et variations* and the organ version of the *Requiem.*

I extend my gratitude to the Reverend W. Andrew Waldo, the rector of Trinity Episcopal Church, Excelsior, Minnesota, and to the parish choir, for the sabbatical given me in 2004, during which I completed much of the work on this book.

I am deeply grateful for the expertise and patience of my editors at the University of Rochester Press: Ralph P. Locke, Senior Editor for the Eastman Studies in Music; and Editorial Director Suzanne E. Guiod, who outdistanced themselves in their solicitude and exactness with regard to this book. My gratitude to, and respect for, Louise Goldberg, my copyeditor, is truly boundless. Apart from her exacting eye for detail, which one has a right to expect from a competent copyeditor, Dr. Goldberg's facility with the French language and her competence as a musicologist—which one has no right to expect from a copyeditor—made her the perfect person to see the manuscript through to publication. The refinements of this book are due largely to her scholarly care and precision.

I acknowledge my debt also to Barbara Owen for her assistance at the Organ Library of the Boston Chapter of the American Guild of Organists, and to Jörg Abbing, Marie-Odile Andrade, Felix Aprahamian, Anthony Baglivi, Frédéric Blanc, Suzanne Chaisemartin, James David Christie, Jean-Louis Coignet, Ronald Ebrecht, Michael Ferguson, Allen Hobbs, Marie-Louis Jaquet-Langlais, Sylvia Kahan, Robert Burns King, Ralph Kneeream, Olivier Latry, David Liddle, Eric Mairlot, Haig Mardirosian, Larry Palmer, Daniel Roth, Rollin Smith, Leslie A. Sprout, Kenneth Starr, and Frederick Swann for their contributions to my work as I was preparing this book. I am also grateful to a well-connected Parisian correspondent who provided valuable documents and helpful observations, including some publications and a few important scores that are otherwise unobtainable, but who wishes to remain anonymous. There were others who sent letters, shared their ideas, and otherwise contributed to this volume, to whom I remain deeply grateful. Thomas Chase, Jesse Eschbach, Charles Hackman, and Rodger Vine read the typescript, making corrections and offering many valuable suggestions. Any remaining errors are mine alone.

# Note

Except where noted, the translations from the French are by the author. Kirk Allison provided a running translation of Jörg Abbing's German work *Maurice Duruflé: Aspekte zu Leben und Werk*, and Cheryl MacInnes provided a translation of the Russian article "Slushaya Organistov."

Quotations from *The American Organist*, including excerpts from the author's articles in the November and December editions of 2002, are reprinted altered or verbatim by permission of *The American Organist Magazine*. Other portions of this volume first appeared in *Maurice Duruflé, 1902–1986: The Last Impressionist*, edited by Ronald Ebrecht; they are reprinted with permission of Scarecrow Press, Inc. Quotations from *Maurice Duruflé: Souvenirs et autres écrits*, edited by Frédéric Blanc, are reprinted by kind permission of the publisher, Séguier. And quotations from *Louis Vierne: Organist of Notre-Dame Cathedral*, by Rollin Smith, are reprinted by permission of Pendragon Press.

Efforts to locate the photographic enterprise Seeberger, in Paris, have been unsuccessful. For future editions, the author will be glad to make appropriate arrangements with the copyright holders if their identity becomes known. The same is true for other unidentified copyright owners.

# A Note to the Reader on Terminology

The Conservatoire national supérieur de musique is often referred to as the Paris Conservatoire, or simply the Conservatoire. It has gone through several name changes since its founding shortly after the Revolution. The collection of manuscripts, correspondence, memorabilia, and books that were in the Duruflé apartment during the writing of this book are identified as the Duruflé Papers. All correspondence between the Duruflés and their American managers is contained in the McFarlane Papers, housed at Karen McFarlane Artists in Cleveland, Ohio. Apart from a few missing letters, photocopies of this correspondence are in the possession of the author. The Bibliothèque nationale de France is abbreviated as BnF.

**The Association Maurice et Marie-Madeleine Duruflé** is often referred to as the Duruflé Association. Its website is located at http://www.france-orgue.fr/durufle/

***Bulletin*** refers to the *Bulletin de l'Association Maurice et Marie-Madeleine Duruflé*.

**ORTF** refers to the Office de radiodiffusion-télévision française.

***SAE*** refers to *Maurice Duruflé: Souvenirs et autres écrits*, edited by Frédéric Blanc.

***basse donnée***. A harmony exercise in which a bass line is to be harmonized.

***chant donné***. A harmony exercise in which a melody is to be harmonized.

***fugue d'école***. A model "school fugue" that was developed at the Paris Conservatoire in the nineteenth and twentieth centuries, the *fugue d'école* is different from the standard fugue in its prominence of the counter-exposition and of pedal point. The classic text is *Traité de la fugue* (1901) by André Gédalge.

***grand orgue***. The large organ in a gallery at the west end of a church or cathedral. The term (not italicized in this book) also refers to the bottom manual and primary division of a French organ.

***maître de chapelle***. Director of a choir at a church or cathedral.

***maître de chœur***. Same as ***maître de chapelle***.

***maîtrise***. A choir school attached to a church or cathedral.

*maîtrisien.* A chorister at a choir school.

*motu proprio.* A papal document (Latin: *of his own accord*) having the form of a decree, whose provisions are decided by the pope himself, without the advice of the cardinals or a council.

**opera or similar work.** This admittedly vague-sounding category attempts to indicate the actual meaning of various French phrases that occur in official documents regarding works composed under the system of governmental commissions to composers, phrases such as "œuvre théâtrale lyrique," "ouvrage lyrique musical," "opérette," or "musique de scène pour un ouvrage dramatique." Works that were considered bureaucratically acceptable in this category were ones that could conceivably be performed at one of France's opera houses (théâtres-lyriques), even if, often, they never were. They include one-act operas (e.g., Milhaud's *Médée*), ballets (e.g., Pierné's *Ondine*), and incidental music (e.g., Delvincourt's music for Sophocles's *Œdipe roi*). Others were complex works for symphonic and vocal resources, such as Gailhard's *Ode à la France blessée.*

**ordinary.** The traditionally choral portions of the mass which ordinarily remain unchanged from week to week. The complete ordinary includes the Kyrie eleison, the Gloria in excelsis, the Nicene Creed, the Sanctus and Benedictus, and the Agnus Dei.

*organiste du chœur.* The organist who accompanies the choir, usually from the choir area in the front of the church or cathedral.

*organiste titulaire.* A person who holds title as the principal organist, whose duty is to play the large organ in the gallery at the west end of a church or cathedral. The *organiste titulaire* has historically not accompanied singing, either by the choir or the congregation, but improvises and plays solo organ literature.

*orgue de chœur.* The small organ used to accompany the choir at the front of the church or cathedral.

*positif.* A division of pipes playable from the middle manual of a typical three-manual French organ.

**proper.** The traditionally choral portions of the mass which are variable so as to reflect the particular solemnity or feast day. The proper includes the Introit, the Gradual, the Tract, the Offertory, and the Communion.

*récit.* A division of pipes playable from the top manual of a typical three-manual French organ. Because the pipes are situated in a box having shutters that can be opened and closed, the division is said to be expressive.

**Second Vatican Council.** The council of Roman Catholic bishops that met at the Vatican from 1962 to 1965, giving authorization for mass in vernacular languages, with vernacular styles of music.

*suppléant.* A substitute who deputizes for the titular organist.

**titular organist.** See *organiste titulaire.*

**Trent, Council of.** The council of Roman Catholic bishops that met in Trent, Italy, from 1545 to 1563. The bishops commissioned the so-called Tridentine mass, sung in Latin to Gregorian chant, which was the universal norm until the Second Vatican Council.

**Voicing**. The process by which organ pipes are regulated so that they have a tonal color and power in proper relation to the rest of the organ. The aesthetic of an organ is determined in part by its voicing.

# Introduction

Among the greatest organists of the twentieth century, Maurice Duruflé was also the eminent composer of some of the most sublime repertoire ever composed for organ, orchestra, and choir. He was a teacher, a recitalist, a virtuosic improviser of impeccable pedigree, and a man of the church. The fact that his opus list, though small, has held an important place in the choral and organ repertoire for three-quarters of a century is testimony to the need for a biography such as this.

Early in the course of my research, it became clear to me that Duruflé was more complex than the hitherto published accounts let on, and that I would have to allow his complexities to coexist, presenting an account that had not been censored the way previous accounts had been censored. The hidden features of his life are no less a part of him than the features we have long esteemed.

Even in his memoirs, which were not published in a more complete form until 2005, Duruflé's own guarded account of his life is too sketchy for us to quicken a living impression of him. And to understand his life strictly through his career is to ignore a vast part of that life, for a fuller grasp of which we must also consider four areas of what may at first appear to be far-flung territory, specifically, the Roman Catholic liturgy and its evolution; the world of French choral music; the architectural heritage of France; and the country's bewilderingly complex political, social, and cultural history, within which Duruflé spun out his life and career. These four areas affecting his life have been ignored in the existing brief accounts. But they are germane to his multifaceted biography, as I shall here explain, giving brief attention to each.

The Roman Catholic liturgy plays so prominent a role in Duruflé's life that to ignore its triumphs and its tragedies in this narrative would be substantially to misrepresent Duruflé himself. The link between the liturgy and the music composed for it was a compelling consideration for him, and thus for the character of his music. And though that link is generally appreciated at a superficial level, it has not adequately been explored in studies of French organists from the early twentieth century, a period in the church's history when that link was beginning to dissolve.

Moreover, the formal training of the organist in France almost completely lacked any sturdy grounding in what is today called liturgical studies, by which a true understanding of the essential link between music and the liturgy can be achieved. Though Duruflé's early formation was more richly liturgical than that of his forebears and colleagues, his eventual disenchantment with the church proved that the link binding the music to the liturgy as he knew it had been broken, not only for him, but for most French organists of his generation.

The world of choral music is also featured in this biography, for two principal reasons. The first is that several choral societies in Paris, and one particularly renowned church choir, played a seminal role in the revival of early music in the first decades of the twentieth century, a role that has been sorely underestimated for how it advanced modern music. The Chanteurs de Saint Gervais, based at the church by that name, revealed medieval plainsong and Renaissance polyphony to the impressionable Debussy and Ravel, who were important influences in Duruflé's musical maturity, thus performing a truly inestimable service to modern music as late as the 1930s. And for that we must acknowledge the influence of this choir and others like it.

There were countless ordinary church choirs in Paris, to be sure, which were lackluster by comparison. For a realistic picture of these lesser choirs, I have referred to Joris-Karl Huysmans's acerbic descriptions of them, which he served up in his book *En Route* (1895), an account of his conversion to Roman Catholicism. Although Huysmans's work predated Duruflé by several decades, his description of these choirs helps explain how Albert Schweitzer could legitimately ask why it was so difficult to form good choirs in Paris. Indeed, the very mediocrity of most French choirs raises the inevitable question as to how it happened that Duruflé's renown as a composer should depend on his having written a major choral work.

Duruflé's conservatory training was as an organist and a composer, not as a singer or choral director, and until he produced the *Requiem*, in 1947, all his previously published works were for instruments. That the refined choral mastery and idiomatic vocal writing evident in the *Requiem* should issue from the pen of a composer with no professional vocal or choral experience as an adult, in a city known for its poor choirs, only raises our regard for the accomplishment that the *Requiem* represents.

How it came to be lies in the broad and exacting choral experience that Duruflé had as a boy chorister at the cathedral in Rouen. This is the second point that needs to be made about choral music in this biography. At least until his change of voice, Duruflé was a singer, and some of his greatest musical experiences as a youth were choral. Singing the Gregorian chant ordinaries and propers, and choral mass settings by Beethoven and the modern French masters, brought him a kind of intense joy that remained with him throughout his adulthood, even if good choirs in Paris were in short supply.

The third area, the architecture of medieval and Renaissance France, played a critical role in the way Duruflé heard and conceived music. He had a keen eye for architecture, and was captive to its allure. His father was an architect, and one of his brothers studied architecture and worked in the building trade. Duruflé's drawings include a sketch of a well-known flamboyant gothic staircase in Rouen, which obviously impressed him. He had the great fortune to spend his entire life singing and playing in architectural masterpieces from the middle and late gothic, and early Renaissance periods, in the three cities where he lived all of his life: Louviers, Rouen, and Paris. Over time, Duruflé's built environment brought him to an appreciation for musical architecture, evident in the strong architectural component of his compositions. The architectural mastery of Duruflé's œuvre was no accident, nor was it merely the result of his having studied composition with the likes of Louis Vierne and Paul Dukas, whose teaching stressed the importance of sonic architecture.

The love-hate relationship between church and state in France is quite unlike that of any other country. Indeed, the national psyche of France has influenced the music of the French church in a way that eludes easy grasp by anyone not born into it. This is the fourth area to be included in this life of Duruflé. The music of the church has been influenced, sometimes positively and sometimes negatively, by shifting sociopolitical and cultural forces. Because the church was at odds with the secularist Third Republic, for example, there was a growing urgency among the hierarchy and church musicians of that era to promote a music that was distinctly countercultural and ecclesiastical in tone, free of secular and republican values and the clichés of opera and ballet. Chant and polyphony therefore enjoyed a heyday in the first half of the twentieth century. But during the Vichy era, when the Nazi-run government befriended the church, that same ecclesiastical music, in an astonishing turn of events, won the favor of the government, which deemed it not only beneficial for French culture, but appropriate for a country on its knees after the humiliation of national defeat. The French organist has therefore felt torn by a divided allegiance: he is at once a servant of the church and a servant of French culture and identity.

It was exactly this aforementioned ecclesiastical music that so many of the French clergy came to believe was out of step with their congregations beginning in the late 1940s. When the Second Vatican Council finally gave its imprimatur to indigenous, vernacular music, in 1963, the French clergy saw classically trained church musicians as the enemy, because they continued to defend a style of music that had successfully isolated itself from secular culture. Duruflé became disillusioned with the direction church music was taking, at least in part because the clergy had so effectively scuttled the music to which he had been attached since his childhood. These, then, are the four areas woven into the context of Duruflé's life and work.

Paris was a hotbed of creative activity when Duruflé settled there as a young man, at the start of the roaring twenties. His first apartment, where he lived while a student at the Conservatoire, was on rue de Douai, on the right bank, in a neighborhood of music students and prominent musicians who lived there because of its proximity to the Paris Conservatoire and the concert halls. In fact,

Duruflé's flat was only two blocks from the apartment and studio of Nadia Boulanger, who, at that very time, was teaching the first of many prominent French and American musicians who would study with her over the ensuing decades, Aaron Copland and Virgil Thomson among them. Duruflé is not known to have availed himself of her salons, or to have met these American composers. His physical proximity to Boulanger's residence, coupled with his emotional distance from it, are typical of the privacy he would prefer into adulthood, and a token of the many opportunities he declined.

Duruflé's second apartment was on rue Dupuytren, just off boulevard Saint-Michel in the sixth arrondissement. At the time he was commuting to Paris for lessons with Charles Tournemire, the ground floor of this small building housed the American Sylvia Beach's first manifestation of Shakespeare and Company, an English-language poetry center. Before Duruflé moved there, in the early 1930s, Beach had moved the shop around the corner to rue de l'Odéon. The new shop was more spacious, the address was easier for customers to find, and it was there that Shakespeare and Company enjoyed its renown. Beach had visits from George Gershwin, Erik Satie, Francis Poulenc, Ezra Pound, F. Scott Fitzgerald, Ernest Hemingway, Aaron Copland, and Virgil Thomson, among many others from the literary and musical avant-garde.

It is not unreasonable to expect a budding young composer to find this society of native French and English-speaking writers and musicians alluring. And some did. The high-strung and abstract Jacques Benoist-Méchin, for instance, who was studying composition at the nearby Schola Cantorum at the time, was an intelligent young man with a knack for poetry and an interest in philosophy. He struck up a friendship with George Antheil and, in fact, played Antheil's *Ballet mécanique*[1] on a player piano to a small audience at the Paris Conservatoire.[2] He also performed his own works on the piano in Sylvia's shop, and he wrote a number of books.[3]

Another young French musician making the acquaintance of American expatriate musicians was Duruflé's own friend, the organist André Fleury, who met Virgil Thomson and even collaborated with him. Two months after he premiered Duruflé's *Scherzo*, Fleury played the premier of Thomson's *Variations and Fugues on Sunday School Hymns*. Fleury had these early contacts with American composers in a way that Duruflé never did.[4]

Whether Duruflé ever knew or cared that the once-dingy *rez-de-chaussée* below his flat on rue Dupuytren had such a pedigree will never be known. Ultimately, of course, it does not matter to his biography, except that his avoidance of the avant-garde writers, musicians, poets, and philosophers who were flocking to Beach's shop just around the corner from his flat is another indication of the extent to which he preferred his own isolated company, demonstrating that his retiring nature would typify his adult life as it had his boyhood.

To be fair, however, it must be said that when Duruflé moved to Paris, the mood in the capital at the start of the 1920s was not kindly disposed to young provincial organists who were more interested in church music than in the antics of Les Six, or the literary and musical avant-garde meeting at Shakespeare and Company. Duruflé was a timid man, and his world was set quite apart.

Duruflé's life was full of contradictions. Despite his strong choral background as a youth, for example, he never held a parish post as *maître de chapelle*. He conducted countless performances of his own works, but refused to conduct the works of other composers. He accepted only one important commission that came to be published, but he declined any number of other commissions. He had a vast organ repertoire, but in a recital career that spanned more than forty years, his programming was conservative and repetitious, and he never programmed what most musicians would consider new repertoire. Moreover, in North America at least, he performed few of the historically important works that he had studied with Tournemire and Louis Vierne, for the performance of which he could rightly claim authority.

Furthermore, Duruflé published no books or treatises of any sort. He was a brilliant improviser, but he published nothing about improvisation. Skilled at orchestration and transcription, he published nothing on these subjects. He taught harmony at the Paris Conservatoire for twenty-seven years, but he published no *traité d'harmonie*. He had the enviable thirty-year experience of performing with the greatest orchestras of Paris, under the world's greatest conductors, but he left no memoirs of those experiences. If any organist was ever in a position to write with authority on the relationship of the organ to the orchestra, and on the orchestral character of the organ, Duruflé was, but he wrote little on these subjects. Only on the role of plainsong in the Roman Catholic liturgy, and on the proper character of liturgical music, did he publish a number of articles. He wrote others on the subject of organ design, his tours of Russia and the United States, his studies with Tournemire and Vierne, and the organ concerto of Francis Poulenc. But his memoirs cover only his childhood and teen years. What he does *not* say in his publications holds as much interest as what he *does* say.

There have been other troublesome lacunae in the career of Maurice Duruflé that are the result, partly, of changing sociopolitical forces. One of them is the result of the hiatus in musicology pertaining to the two world wars. It is only recently that historians of music and art have given their account of the First World War. "Scholars of cultural forms or institutions have often interrupted their narrative at 1914 and continued in 1918, leaving a hiatus of four and a half years. As [art historian] Elizabeth Kahn has pointed out, art history and World War I never met, until recently."[5] The same is true with regard to the Second World War. Only recently have musicologists begun to study the relationship of the Vichy government to the careers of French composers. Their discovery, in 2002, that Vichy commissioned Duruflé to compose the *Requiem* stirred considerable misunderstanding, denial, and even hostility among the day's prominent Parisian organists.

Research for this biography was hampered by several other factors. The choir school of the Rouen Cathedral, where Duruflé was a chorister for seven years, was closed in 1977, and no archives remain, either in the city library, or at the cathedral, or in the diocesan archives.[6] Likewise, the archives of the Fondation Singer-Polignac contain nothing, neither photographs, letters, or other documents,[7] relative to Duruflé's performance of the Poulenc Organ Concerto.

A composer's life is, to some extent, described by, or contained in, his opus list. Duruflé's small output was, in its own way, another complication to the research, because the bulk of it represents only about thirty of his eighty-four years. It is specious, of course, to draw a composer's biography on his works alone, but there is no doubt that we learn something about a composer by exploring how his style developed, how his musical interests changed, and how his œuvre reflects the vagaries and caprices of his life. His opus list is too small to support such a study.

Duruflé had two open secrets which assumed a sensationalist character over the years, looming over more important matters with an ill-proportioned prominence. These are his partial baldness, which led to his use of a toupee all his life, and the existence and identity of his first wife. He discussed neither of these in public, and preferred that no one else do so either.

Duruflé kept secrets because he chose to. And he kept the darker features of his life close to his chest, even in some instances bending the truth about them, thus restricting what the public could know about him. That many of his family, his colleagues, and students, and now the association established to perpetuate his legacy, have tried to keep the same secrets is an expression of their enduring fidelity to his memory.

But it is not the task of the historian to keep secrets, and certainly not when those secrets have substance to bear upon the biography of a great man. Exactly where to draw the line between the personal and the professional aspects of Duruflé's life is not always easy to assess, because the two are tightly intertwined. As a rule, biographers err on the side of discretion unless disclosure significantly advances their thesis. In any case, unsubstantiated rumors and strictly intimate details from the life of Duruflé find no place in these pages.

Because he published so little music, there is a tendency to hope for an unpublished masterpiece lurking among his personal effects, or for just several more notes that he put together on some staff paper. Likewise, because his secluded life lacked high drama, every small-town recital he played assumes an outsized importance. So we seek other satisfactions. Let us say, simply, that if there is an essential truth about the life of Maurice Duruflé, it lies in its minute intensities, like the world in a grain of sand. Why struggle to find other masterpieces and high drama that simply don't exist, when a single piece like the *Prélude et fugue sur le nom d'ALAIN* provides a vista upon the man that is as broad and deep as it is high?

I have written this portrait of Maurice Duruflé from a distinctly North American perspective. The tours of North America that he made with his wife

Marie-Madeleine were an important part of his career. Moreover, Duruflé's world renown is in large measure the result of his fame among English-speaking audiences.

After Éliane Chevalier died, Frédéric Blanc succeeded her as president of the Association Maurice et Marie-Madeleine Duruflé. He was living in the Duruflé apartment throughout the course of my research—Mlle Chevalier gave him lifetime use of the apartment—and was the custodian of the Duruflé Papers and other effects that remained there. With rare exceptions, no one besides Blanc was privy to those important documents, which no doubt comprise correspondence, photographs, a library, and manuscripts that would open important perspectives on Duruflé's life. Unlike Mme Marcel Dupré, who submitted her husband's manuscripts to the Bibliothèque nationale de France, M. Blanc declined to surrender the Duruflé works to that institution, where they would be available to researchers, and denied access to them by historians and musicologists. Duruflé scholars may well hope that they are given free access to them in the future.

There are a few dissertations on Duruflé in French. The two that hold particular relevance to a biography of Duruflé are those by Philippe Robert (1977) and Laurent Ronzon (1996). A large portion of Robert's work was printed, with helpful additions, in a 1991 issue of *Cahiers et mémoires* (a supplement to the journal *L'Orgue*, no. 45), along with minor errors and major omissions. Most of Robert's work on the *Requiem*, the *Messe* "*Cum jubilo*," and the four motets, which appears in his dissertation, was omitted from *Cahiers et mémoires*, as were the sections on the orchestral and chamber works. The unpublished dissertation by Ronzon is the only one to document Duruflé's study and teaching at the Paris Conservatoire. Elements of Ronzon's work are published here for the first time. Both dissertations contain valuable material regarding Duruflé's teaching career and early professional life, but little about the man himself or his later performing and composing career.

There are many more dissertations in English. Of these, none deal with Duruflé's biography in any concerted way, although the brief biographical sketch provided by Herndon Spillman at the beginning of his 1976 dissertation, "The Organ Works of Maurice Duruflé," reflects good research and was the best in any language for many years—but it was never published and is no longer available.

The chapter "In Gregorian Mode," that I wrote for the book *Maurice Duruflé, 1902–1986: The Last Impressionist*, edited by Ronald Ebrecht and published in 2002, was due some three years before I finished my research. Ebrecht wanted to publish his book during the centennial of Duruflé's birth, and to ensure that it would precede Frédéric Blanc's impending publication of Duruflé's writings and memoirs, which finally appeared in 2005. The latter book contains Duruflé's memoirs, numerous articles, some letters, and interviews, some of which present interesting new details, but much of which was already published in journal articles elsewhere. The German work *Maurice Duruflé: Aspekte zu Leben und Werk* (2002) was regarded by its author, Jörg Abbing, as the first comprehensive biography of Duruflé, which it was at the time, but it leaves out important elements of his life and career. The present volume is thus the most comprehensive biography of Maurice Duruflé in any language.

But as thorough as I have tried to be in the writing of this book, it cannot claim to be an exhaustive account. I therefore put my work forward with a certain reticence, realizing that it may in time require reevaluation in light of the materials housed—at least for now—in the Duruflé apartment on place du Panthéon. While these parameters have been a disappointment to me, I have stopped where I must, and will leave the rest to researchers who come after me. May this modest contribution to Duruflé's legacy redound to his enduring honor and lasting esteem.

# Chapter One

# *Duruflé's Childhood and Early Education*

Like many another quaint Norman town, Louviers[1] was typical for the half-timbered houses and shops that leaned with precarious medieval charm over its cobblestone streets, a small and pleasantly situated industrial town. But by its enchanting site on twenty-one shallow branches of the river Eure, Louviers distinguished itself from other Norman towns, the factories of its flourishing textile trade straddling those streams in the manner of an industrial Venice.

The modest home of the Duruflé family stood at the northeast edge of town, at 59, rue du Quai,[2] next to a café, where several streams of the river converge on their way north to the Seine. Charles and Marie-Mathilde lived there with their sons Henri, Marcel, and Maurice. Across the street from the family's nondescript two-story row house, which stood directly on the street, was a grocery store, and next to it a butcher. The train station was a five-minute walk from their home, eastward across the river.

The late-medieval church of Notre-Dame was the architectural and religious heart of town and was the church attended by the Duruflé family. The edifice stands just a few blocks south of their home, its squat tower visible from their front door, and has a sense of grandeur that belies its relatively small size. A tower originally stood above the crossing, but when Maurice was nearly four years old it was felled by a serious storm. The ravages of time and the bombardments of war have blackened the whitish stone; its north side is tinted green with moss, and its south yellowed by the sun. The stonework of the exterior south flank is riotously ornate, the product of its late gothic aesthetic. It was in this church that Maurice Duruflé discovered his vocation as a musician.

Astride one of the Eure's streams a block east of the church is the old convent of the Pénitents de Saint François, constructed in 1646 as a Franciscan monastery. It was closed during the Revolution but subsequently housed a boys' school and then a prison. Today it is the home for the École municipal de Musique Maurice Duruflé, established in the 1980s.

On January 11, 1902,[3] the mayor of Louviers penned the first formal account of the birth of Maurice-Gustave Duruflé in a florid narrative for the town's civil records, reporting that he was born at 6:15 in the morning to Julien-Charles-Amédée Duruflé and Marie-Mathilde Prévost.

A native of Thiberville (Eure), Marie-Mathilde was born on September 10, 1876, and Charles, a native of Elbeuf-sur-Seine (Seine-Inférieure), was born on December 17, 1864. The couple were married on September 10, 1895. Charles and Marie-Mathilde were a quiet couple, "very reserved, very untalkative, very uncommunicative, and very modest."[4] Maurice was the youngest of their three boys and the only one to be born in the new century. The eldest, Henri (b. 1896), was six years old, and the middle boy, Marcel Joseph (b. 1898), born in Caudebec-les-Elbeuf, was four when his baby brother was born. They were a pious family and they never raised their voices. Without an automobile, they traveled little and they never took vacations.

Louviers had several sporting clubs open to young boys. Maurice enjoyed swimming, in fact he became a very good swimmer,[5] and he probably swam in the canal de la Villette, one of the man-made branches of the river Eure. He also enjoyed fishing and bicycling. It was an act of national allegiance to play or sing in town choruses and bands.[6] Louviers boasted several such amateur music societies when Maurice was a boy. Louviers even had its own "anthem," "Sur la route de Louviers," a suggestive song that had been part of local lore since the eighteenth century, when it grew up among road crews.

Maurice's father, Charles, was self-employed as an architect-artisan and is believed to have built houses.[7] He also had a passion for music. Although he was not himself a musician in the practical sense of the word, he had a pronounced musical taste and he made solid judgments about music. Charles owned a small instrument called a harmoniflûte, a one-stop harmonium that had been in his family for some time.[8] Young Maurice attended high mass at Notre-Dame with his parents and brothers on Sundays, and would return home to play on the diminutive instrument the chants he had just heard sung by the choir, including the pseudo-Gregorian *Credo* of Henri Dumont.[9]

When Maurice was nearly five years old, Charles saw to it that his son began taking private piano lessons with Madame Poussin, the best-known piano teacher in Louviers. Once a week the young boy also attended her solfège class with a dozen other children, accompanied by their mothers. Mme Poussin presented her piano students in monthly recitals, attended by the students' families. Duruflé later recalled that "these family get-togethers had a great advantage for the pupils, that of testing them before the public and of stimulating them."[10] At one of the gatherings, his teacher asked the young Maurice what an accidental was in music. He replied, "It's when you fall off the stool." The laughter of the audience caused him to blush with shame.[11] At the end of the year Poussin would organize a public concert and award prizes. Maurice was given a *prix de piano* at a recital on July 27, 1907, when he was five-and-a-half years old. In addition to his piano studies, Maurice also learned to play the clarinet. Among other hobbies, he enjoyed stamp collecting and sketching, and in time he became an avid photographer.

Maurice attended the boys' school on the opposite side of town from his home. His monthly report cards indicate that he excelled in most subjects. On his report card for November 1909,[12] for instance, when he was seven years old, his teacher gave him mostly high marks.

| | |
|---|---|
| Assiduousness | 10 |
| Conduct | 9 |
| Orderliness, tidiness | 10 |
| Homework | 6 |
| Lessons | 8 |
| Application | 10 |
| Writing | 9 |
| Drawing | 9 |
| History | 9 |
| French composition | 10 |

In her written comments, Maurice's teacher made note of his remarkable aptitude for drawing, but indicated he was weak in arithmetic. His grade-point average was nine on a scale of ten.

The subject of music was not mentioned on Duruflé's report card, but the French government had been promoting music education in the nation's public schools since 1872, to strengthen secular values dear to the republic. The crusade to teach "proper" songs led to the distribution of songbooks and the incorporation of singing lessons into the curriculum of the elementary schools. The movement gained momentum toward the end of the century in an effort to "inculcate a sense of the fatherland, of civilization, and of moral ideals."[13] Through their singing lessons, young French children learned a republican patriotism and a sense of national duty.

After about four years of private piano lessons, Maurice's parents realized he had developed as far as he could with Mme Poussin, so when he was nine years old they began taking him by train into Rouen for music lessons with Jules Haelling (1869–1926), a former pupil of Alexandre Guilmant at the Paris Conservatoire.[14] Haelling was titular organist of the cathedral and a teacher at the cathedral choir school, known as Maîtrise Saint-Évode.[15] After several months of lessons, Haelling urged Maurice's parents to enroll him in the *maîtrise*, as choir schools were then called,[16] which they proposed to do on Easter day in 1912, but without telling their son. Charles had only suggested they take a trip to Rouen, to discover some of the riches of the capital of Normandy, and see its famous monuments and its magnificent cathedral. It would be an exciting trip for the young boy. Perhaps his parents wanted to avoid a scene from their son, afraid that if he'd known of their plans, his resistance would weaken their resolve to leave him in Rouen.[17] Charles embraced Maurice and said to him, "You're going to live in this beautiful house now, where you will work on music. I'll come to see you every Sunday."

Years later, Duruflé recounted that his father's action was as effective as it was emotionally disastrous, and that his father had no idea just how traumatic his "imprisonment" would be, after such a gentle family life at home. He suffered very much by his separation from his family.[18]

The school property was dark and dank, and the medieval wall that separated the school from the street was so grim that townspeople pitied the boys for living in what looked like a prison (see Fig. 1.1). Duruflé wrote: "This school, located on a site next to the cathedral and the archbishop's residence, completely surrounded by a huge wall oddly reminiscent of a prison, held my curiosity, but nothing more. The whole was rather sad and austere."[19] On that first night in the dormitory, the *maître de chapelle* of the cathedral, Canon Bénard, found Duruflé sobbing in his bed and went to console him.

> He made me see a glimpse of the joys that were awaiting me in this beautiful house, the study of religious music, the attendance each Sunday at the magnificent cathedral ceremonies where the Maîtrise sings for high mass and vespers; and then one day I would play the organ like my classmates. A great page was opened before me, or rather a real book whose first page was particularly bitter. Indeed, if I had found upon my arrival at this prison a guardian angel, I made the acquaintance of the torturer the next day. I say "the torturer" appropriately. To be precise, he was the director. Out of respect for his memory, I shall keep his name [Canon Bourgeois] to myself. Then began for me this orderly and monotonous life of the boarding school, very hard when one is ten years old, knowing he will see his parents again in the pleasant family home only every three months, on school holidays. A regimen of life which no doubt prepares you marvelously for the one awaiting you one day in the barracks, but it came a little early.[20]

It took some time for Duruflé to acquaint himself with his confreres in his new surroundings. "My timidity paralyzed me to such an extent that I didn't say a word to my neighbors for several days, like a cat that hides itself under a piece of furniture when it's forced to change houses."[21]

Away from home, as he was, for nearly all of his teen years, Duruflé gradually became estranged from his brothers, and particularly from Henri, who planned to become an architect, like his father. With the financial support of his *marraine*[22]—because his parents were putting what little money they had to Maurice's expenses in Rouen—Henri went to Paris in 1914 to study architecture at the École des Beaux-Arts, but in the spring of 1915 he was mobilized by the army. He described his war experience thus: "When you're eighteen years old and somebody puts a pistol in one hand and a dagger in the other, and makes you drink a quarter of a liter of rum with some ether, and orders you into the trench to kill German soldiers, you ask yourself what you could have done to a good God to deserve this."[23] Henri's life was disrupted by three and a half years of war in the infantry, the trenches, and the mud, and by a year of occupation. He was unable to resume his studies after the war, and instead worked in Le Havre in the building trade. In 1924 he became director of a branch of the business in Lisieux.[24]

There were several reasons that Henri might have come to resent Maurice. The latter left home at ten years of age, to live what Henri probably perceived as a

Figure 1.1. Rue Saint-Romain, Rouen. Street scene showing the front of the choir school (on right). Etching by Hedley Fitton, 1908.

privileged life. Soon thereafter Maurice was spared having to serve in the army during the First World War because he was too young, while Henri had his life's ambition and his hopes for the future dashed by his deployment to the front. Maurice then enrolled in the world's finest music conservatory while Henri had no choice but to make do with a more humble employment than the distinguished one he envisioned for himself in architecture. Their mutual animosity followed them into adulthood. When the Second World War came, Maurice was too old to be sent to the front. And after the death of their mother, on December 13, 1950, he and Henri had a disagreement about their inheritance.[25]

Little is known about the middle brother, Marcel Joseph, but he "was probably jealous of his younger brother Maurice because he was unable to pursue his own studies. He probably had a very violent conflict with him."[26] Marcel was mobilized in 1917 and was later institutionalized in an asylum in Quatre Mares, a village near the little town of Neubourg in Normandy, perhaps as a result of his war experience. The family never talked about Marcel and he never married. He was later institutionalized in a psychiatric hospice in Louviers, and died there on October 31, 1935, when he was thirty-seven years old.

In effect, Duruflé lost his two brothers long before they died. His departure to Rouen when they were in their teens, and then his move to Paris, wedged a geographical separation among them that only enforced their emotional distance, a fact that was certainly a source of heartache for him throughout his adulthood.

# Chapter Two

# *Life at the Cathedral Choir School*

Little is known about the choir school prior to the fourteenth century,[1] when chapter records dated November 13, 1377 refer to a *maîtrise* of four altar boys directed by a maître named Médard. In the twelfth century a document concerning mass on Christmas day delegated the intonation of the *Gloria in excelsis* to boys positioned in the upper galleries of the cathedral.

Like the four hundred other choir schools in France,[2] known at that time by the name *psallette*, the school in Rouen was closed during the Revolution toward the end of the eighteenth century. After the reopening of the country's churches, in 1802, the *maîtrise* was reborn in the Cour d'Albane, a cloister at the northwest corner of the cathedral close. In 1806 eight boys were taken in by competition, and by 1851 there were twenty-six choristers. Toward the end of the century the school moved to a building on the east side of the cathedral's north transept, situated on the medieval rue Saint-Romain. Cardinal Sourrieu inaugurated the "new" facility, naming it after Saint Évode, the sixteenth bishop of Rouen (d. 550).

In Duruflé's day, the Maîtrise Saint-Évode was among the more prominent schools in the city.[3] Along with the choir schools at the cathedral in Dijon and the basilica in Nantes, it was one of the greatest choir schools in all of France. The *maîtrise* drew young boys from among Rouen's working class and middle class alike. Until the Second World War, it functioned mostly as a private school whose students received their *certificat d'études* at age fourteen, but who seldom went on to secondary studies. Some, however, pursued careers in music.[4]

In 1918, toward the end of the First World War, a virulent strain of influenza spread across Europe, killing more people worldwide than did the war itself. The Spanish grippe, as the epidemic was often called, struck in places where hygienic conditions were bad, among gatherings of people in close quarters, such as depots, barracks, and choir schools. There was a great deal of uncertainty as to its causes and preventions, and as to how the disease was spread.

Rouen was not spared the ravages of the pandemic; 206 people died in October at its height,[5] one of whom lived on rue Saint-Romain. At the choir school, as former *maîtrisiens* remember hearing about it, the boys' heads were shaved as a preventive measure. The shaving of Duruflé's scalp with an unsterile implement is alleged to have caused the patchy baldness for which he wore a toupee the rest of his life.[6]

The choirboys took their recreation in a playground on the east side of the school, enclosed by the wall on the north, the archbishop's palace on the east and the cathedral itself on the south. A fourteenth-century chapel once stood on the site of the playground, where Joan of Arc was condemned to death on May 29, 1431. The only vestige of the building is the empty stone frame of a large gothic window rising up out of the wall, looming over the playground.

In addition to their music studies, the boys took classes in French, mathematics, geography, history, science, Latin, and Greek.[7] General classroom instruction was given "by a layman, a former Jesuit, not unpleasant except for his squared beard," in a room that Duruflé described as "rather sad." A man of severe appearance, the teacher "always troubled me for he stammered horribly. When I heard him say 'Du-Du-Duruflé' I was terrified."[8]

Maurice dressed differently from the other boys, wearing baggy knickers, or plusfours, instead of the short pants worn by everyone else. His fellow choristers remembered him for his timidity and his baldness, a child withdrawn into himself. But in the refectory, charged with distributing bread to the tables, Maurice sometimes played the clown.[9]

The choristers followed a rigorous, virtually monastic regimen:[10]

| | |
|---|---|
| 6:00 | rising |
| 6:30 | prayer in common |
| 7:00 | breakfast |
| 7:30 | class, in general subjects |
| 9:30 | rehearsal, study of chant with Abbé Bénard |
| 12:00 | lunch |
| 12:30 | recreation |
| 1:30 | rehearsal |
| 2:30 | class |
| 4:00 | recreation |
| 4:30 | class, alternating solfège and piano |
| 6:00 | another choral rehearsal |
| 7:00 | dinner |
| 8:30 | bedtime, except on Tuesdays and Fridays, when there was a rehearsal with the choir men |

The boys were allowed some leisure time and a relaxation of the schedule on Thursday afternoons, when there were no classes. In his free time, Duruflé produced a number of pencil sketches. One of them, from 1914, depicts the lacy staircase to the organ tribune at the church of Saint Maclou, just a block east of the archbishop's palace.

The staffing of Maîtrise Saint-Évode was largely self-perpetuating. Many of its alumni, some of them lay and some clergy, pursued advanced musical training in Paris and then returned as directors, as *maîtres de chapelle*, as organists, or as teachers of harmony, solfège, or piano. This was the case with most, if not all, of Duruflé's teachers.

The most beloved teacher at the school was Canon Adolphe Bourdon (1850–1928), known to the boys as "Papa Bourdon," who was both *maître de chapelle* and director of the *maîtrise* from 1881 until 1911. It was during his tenure that the choir school enjoyed a new golden age. He stepped down from these positions the year before Duruflé became a chorister, but served as temporary *maître de chapelle* during the war, and retained a close association with the school all through Duruflé's chorister years. He recognized and nurtured Duruflé's musical gifts.

"A remarkable musician, a prolific composer, [and] a former student of Gounod," Bourdon had a keen knowledge of Gregorian chant. "For the first time, we heard him speak of Dom Pothier, *maître de chœur* at Solesmes. . . . This was a true revolution in the liturgical chant practiced until that time at the cathedral, with its old plainchant and its square notes. It was an up-to-date presentation of this marvelous Gregorian chant with all its suppleness, its flight, its mystical radiance."

Abbé Bénard, the *maître de chapelle* during Duruflé's first two years, introduced much of the plainsong sung by the choirboys. He succeeded Canon Bourdon in 1911 and remained in the post until 1931, except when he was away during the war. Duruflé was fond of Bénard and thought him "absolutely delightful, an angel." Bénard "made us do some vocalizing, and we sight-read the separate parts of the motets that we were to sing the following Sunday in the cathedral. The study of plainsong, the ordinary, and the proper for Sunday. All of this was a revelation for me."[11]

In 1911, Canon Bourgeois, a former *maîtrisien*, succeeded the much-loved Canon Bourdon as director of the *maîtrise*, and was in charge of the school for the duration of Duruflé's residence there. The young chorister was contemptuous of Bourgeois and of the discipline he imposed upon the boys, and he believed Bourgeois should never have been assigned to the school. Many choirboys had "very bad memories" of him.[12] "This austere house," he wrote,

> could have been delightful for the forty little *maîtrisiens* who lived and worked there. Unfortunately there was the torturer. When I think that during the six years that I spent there, I never saw a doctor come when one of us was sick. It was the torturer who treated us himself with his phials. He even extracted our teeth. Moreover, there were dramas between himself and parents of the students because of this.[13]

After entering the school, Duruflé remained a pupil of alumnus Jules Haelling, with whom he studied organ, counterpoint, and harmony (using Théodore Dubois's treatise on harmony).[14] The young protégé said that he owed his earliest formation as an organist to this severe but good man, and to him Duruflé attributed his "very correct organ technique."[15]

A native of Alsace, Haelling became a chorister at Saint-Évode in 1879 and was only seventeen when he was named *organiste du chœur* in 1887.[16] He studied organ with alumnus Émilien Ledru before going on to study with Alexandre Guilmant in Paris. A published composer,[17] Haelling became the cathedral's titular organist in 1897. In his nearby home Haelling had an *orgue de salon* by Cavaillé-Coll-Mutin (see Appendix C, p. 262).

Haelling's assistant was alumnus Henri Beaucamp (1885–1937), who returned to teach at the school in 1904 after having studied with both Charles Tournemire and Louis Vierne in Paris. Beaucamp had the responsibility of ensuring that the boys practiced diligently before they were allowed to practice on their own,[18] using the eight pianos located on the top floor in small cells named for famous composers. Beaucamp surely recounted for the young Maurice his reminiscences of Tournemire and Vierne, who would later become his own teachers. A brilliant recitalist,[19] Beaucamp became the cathedral's titular organist upon the death of Haelling in 1926, a post he held until his own death in 1937.

Jules Lambert, the cathedral's young *organiste du chœur*, had been a chorister there between 1908 and 1915, and was thus Duruflé's senior by only about four years. A student of Haelling, he taught Duruflé harmony during the war years. Lambert also held the post of organist at the church of Saint Sever, across the river. Another elder contemporary of Duruflé, Raphaël Sarazue, taught him solfège.[20]

Choir rehearsals took place in the rehearsal hall with the trebles and the altos seated on either side of a grand piano, which was played by one of the older students who had finished his general subjects but was pursuing musical studies, as would eventually be the case with Duruflé. The boys sang new pieces to sol-fa syllables before adding the words. Twice each week, after dinner, they rehearsed with the choir men. "What intense musical joys for me," Duruflé wrote, "these ensemble rehearsals with soloists and choirs accompanied at the piano!"[21]

By about 1914, Gregorian chant was well established in the services of the cathedral, after its restoration by the Benedictines in Solesmes,[22] but the choir continued to sing works by Bach, Mozart, Haydn, and Beethoven, as well as modern settings of the mass, and motets, by Gounod, Franck, Saint-Saëns, and Fauré, among others. Whereas the choir school at the cathedral in Dijon, founded by Mgr. Moissenet (1850–1939), specialized in Renaissance polyphony, the *maîtrise* in Rouen specialized in works by modern French composers, although the Renaissance masters were sung there as well.

As exciting as Duruflé found all of the choral and organ music that surrounded him, he particularly loved the ceremonies themselves, which "absolutely cast a spell over me."

> The extraordinary environment of this cathedral . . . this splendor that was evoked as the liturgy unfolded, profoundly impressed me. These were, I can say, the best moments of my life as a chorister. I looked forward to feast days with an impatient joy. . . .
>
> Benediction of the Blessed Sacrament took on a particular solemnity. . . . We, the boys of the *maîtrise*, in white alb with our hoods pulled up, like monks in our little red

capes, were delighted to open the processional. . . . Then came the long line of major seminarians, the venerable cortege of titled canons in their rich hoods edged with white ermine and a large scarf also edged with white and grey ermine. . . . Then followed the clergy of the cathedral, and finally the canopy of red velvet sheltering the monstrance carried by the archbishop, and preceded by eight thurifers who incensed the Blessed Sacrament. . . . It is there, in this display of grandeur, in the midst of such great liturgical and musical riches, that I felt my vocation as an organist.[23]

Of all the ceremonies that took place in the imposing cathedral (see Fig. 2.1), "nothing was more grand," Duruflé wrote,

> than the singing of the *Christus vincit*, the choir of seminarians alternating with the choirboys, to which the *grand orgue* responded with its versets, while the archbishop, holding his crozier, was seated on a gilded chair before the altar, turned toward the faithful and surrounded by all the canons. The acclamations *Feliciter, Feliciter* filled me with enthusiasm.[24]

Sometimes referred to as the Carolingian acclamations, because of its association with Charlemagne,[25] the grandeur of the *Christus vincit* was indeed palpable and impressive (see Fig. 2.2). At the heart of the ceremony was the simple acclamation: *Christus vincit! Christus regnat! Christus imperat!* ("Christ conquers! Christ reigns! Christ rules!").

The cathedral had a four-manual *grand orgue* in the west gallery constructed by Merklin-Schütze in 1859–60.[26] The *orgue de chœur* was from the Ducroquet firm. As soon as he was judged proficient, Duruflé began playing the latter[27] for the nine-o'clock chapter mass one morning each week, and sometimes even substituted for Haelling at the *grand orgue*, his repertoire consisting of Bach, Franck, Widor, Guilmant, and Vierne.[28]

On the occasion of the awarding of prizes, the choirboys would present a concert of piano and choral music in the Salle des États in the archbishop's palace, an elegant eighteenth-century hall, for which the cardinal would sit in the front row of seats.[29]

The First World War was waged during four of Duruflé's years at the school, with Germany declaring war on France on August 3, 1914. Except for the general austerity, the restrictions on food, and the alerts at night, the war brought no grave disturbances to the routines of the school.[30] But the already spartan disciplines grew unusually severe. Duruflé recalled:

> Life became extremely hard, especially for the children that we were, who needed nourishment. The food restrictions were particularly hard. When our parents sent us a few parcels of bread, they were immediately intercepted by the torturer [Canon Bourgeois] and the addressees called to order. . . .
>     For this difficult period of the war, during which German planes favored us with serious bombardments at night, work continued at the *maîtrise*.[31]

Figure 2.1. Rouen Cathedral, view from the altar, showing the choir in the fore-
ground. Photograph courtesy of the Boston Organ Library.

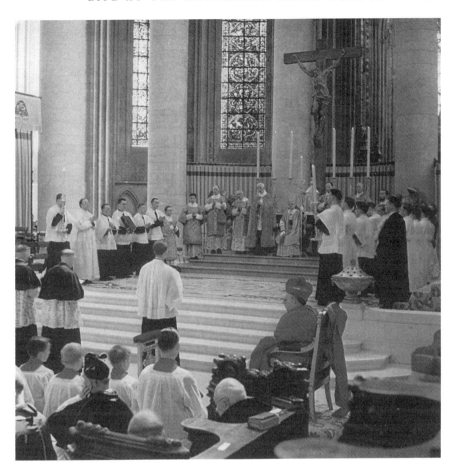

Figure 2.2. Ceremony of the *Christus vincit* at the reopening of the Rouen Cathedral in June 1956 following the Second World War, showing Cardinal Martin seated before the high altar. Photograph courtesy of Francis Pinguet.

During the alerts at night, the choir boys would wrap themselves in blankets, go to the darkened cathedral, and seek shelter in the base of the Tour Saint-Romain, in the protective niches of the baptistery.

Several teachers at the choir school were called into the army, including Jules Haelling, Abbé Bénard, and the young Jules Lambert. When Haelling was called up, the director of the school reassigned the teaching of harmony to Lambert, who said, "I kept Duruflé's first composition, from Christmas 1915. It was perfection."[32] In 1916, when Lambert himself went to the war, the fourteen-year old Duruflé took over for him at the organ of Saint Sever,[33] a parish on the other side of the river Seine, where Lambert was the organist. By the time of his return in 1919, Duruflé was an alumnus of the school[34] and helped out as rehearsal accompanist and organist. In the meantime he also became the organist at Saint André[35] in Mont Saint-Aignan, a suburb of Rouen.

In 1918, Jules Haelling urged the sixteen-year old Duruflé to take some courses in Paris to perfect his playing. But Duruflé's parents were worried about his going to the capital at his young age. The cost was also a concern for them, as they had two other sons to raise and educate. In the end they postponed his trips to Paris until the following year, when he was seventeen.

There were several fine amateur choral societies in Rouen, the most prominent being Accord Parfait, founded and directed by Albert Dupré (1860–1940), the father of Marcel Dupré. And Jules Haelling was the founder and conductor of the choral society La Gamme. From as early as his fifteenth year Duruflé had the opportunity to accompany La Gamme under Haelling's direction.[36] He also played solo organ repertoire for their concerts, including, for example, the *Marche religieuse* of Alexandre Guilmant (March 31, 1917), the Prélude from the Third Sonata of Guilmant, the *Marche pontificale* of Widor (March 23, 1918), the Prélude in B of Saint-Saëns, the *Prélude, fugue et variation* of Franck, and the Final from the First Symphony of Vierne (April 18, 1919).

In 1919, when the incumbent organist at his home church in Louviers died, Duruflé was appointed titular there, a post he would hold for roughly sixteen years. He considered the John Abbey organ excellent and he composed much of his music on it during his trips home from Paris.[37] Abbey constructed the thirty-six stop, three-manual organ in 1887, and enlarged it to 44 stops in 1894.[38] Its two cases were originally built for a Cistercian abbey in Bonport, where the cardinal and statesman Melchior de Polignac (1661–1742) had been abbot.[39] Upon the dissolution of the monasteries, in 1791, the instrument was moved to Louviers,[40] its unusually plain cases befitting the abbey's Cistercian aesthetic.

Duruflé played several recitals on the Abbey organ during his tenure.[41] On June 18, 1924 he played the Toccata and Fugue in D Minor, BWV 565, of Bach, the *Intermezzo* of Barié, the *Marche funèbre* and *Chant séraphique* of Guilmant, the Choral and Scherzo from the Second Symphony of Vierne, the *Troisième Choral* of Franck, and the Prélude in B of Marcel Dupré, giving some idea of the ambitious repertoire he had studied either with Eugène Gigout or, more likely, Vierne. He played recitals in Louviers again in 1925 and 1926.

Duruflé's musical formation at the Maîtrise Saint-Évode can be equated roughly to that of Paul Paray (1886–1979), an alumnus[42] who preceded Duruflé. Paray wrote:

> At the maîtrise in Rouen I had an early formation that was very solid, and I was extraordinarily well nurtured in music. . . . I began to learn the rudiments there, very difficult ear training, every day, and with my alto voice I sang the Renaissance masters: Victoria, Palestrina, Allegri, Schütz, all the great polyphonists . . . what a school! . . . having had at this maîtrise two exceptional teachers (the organist Jules Haelling and

abbé Adolphe Bourdon), even at age twelve, at the cathedral of Rouen, I managed to accompany the services at the organ, and at fourteen and fifteen years, I played all the works of Bach by heart! . . . All the chorals, the great fugues, the great preludes. What a school![43]

Paray served as titular organist at his home church of Saint Clément, just a few blocks from Saint Sever, and later became a composer and conductor of international reputation. He served as conductor of Concerts Colonne, the Paris Opéra, and Concerts Lamoureux. In 1936 he conducted the premiere of Duruflé's *Trois Danses*, and in 1947 he conducted the concert premiere of the *Requiem*. Paray later moved to the United States, where he was conductor of the Detroit Symphony Orchestra from 1952 to 1963.

Another alumnus, the baritone Camille Maurane, born in Rouen in 1911, had a distinguished singing career, and in the course of twenty years he sang more than fifty roles in opera, opéra-comique, and operetta. As a recitalist he was considered one of the better masters of the French style. A voice teacher at the Conservatoire from 1962 until 1981, in 1947 he was soloist for the radio premiere of Duruflé's *Requiem*, and in 1966 he sang for the premiere of his *Messe "Cum jubilo."*

Pierre Villette (1926–98), another native of Rouen, was a chorister at Saint-Évode under the direction of his cousin, Canon Robert Delestre (1901–93),[44] who was *maître de chapelle* there for over forty years, beginning in 1931. After leaving the school, he studied harmony privately with Duruflé in Paris, prior to his entrance into the Paris Conservatoire in 1941, whereupon he became a pupil of Paul Dukas and Marcel Dupré. But he continued studying privately with Duruflé.[45]

The decline of the Maîtrise Saint-Évode, in the 1960s and 1970s, was merely symptomatic of the cataclysmic shift in worldview that culminated with the juggernaut of the Second Vatican Council. The school simply could not survive modernity as a cloistered school that trained boys to sing Gregorian chant and choral music for the Latin mass. So it closed its doors in 1977.

# Chapter Three

# *Lessons with Charles Tournemire*

Maurice Emmanuel, the composer and musicologist who held a post as historian at the Paris Conservatoire from 1909 to 1936, played the crucial role in providing Duruflé an entrée to the Paris organ world. Emmanuel spent his summers at the country house he owned not far from Louviers, and was occasionally visited there by Charles Tournemire.[1] When Duruflé's father was called to do some architectural work on Emmanuel's property, he asked him for some advice about his son's musical future. Emmanuel was also a friend of Jules Haelling, who is said to have mediated the contact between the elder Duruflé and Emmanuel.[2] On the organ in Louviers, Maurice played for Emmanuel the *Prelude and Fugue in A Minor*, BWV 543, of Bach, which he had studied with Haelling. The Conservatoire professor suggested Duruflé do some preliminary study with Charles Tournemire in Paris before taking the entrance exam for the organ class at the Conservatoire.

Emmanuel and Tournemire were presently colleagues at the Conservatoire, as they had earlier been colleagues at Sainte Clotilde, where Tournemire had been titular organist since 1898, and where Emmanuel was *maître de chapelle* from 1904 to 1907. So in 1919, through Emmanuel's contact, Duruflé met Tournemire, the Conservatoire's *professeur d'ensemble instrumental*. Tournemire took him on as one of his rare private students.

A native of Bordeaux, Charles Tournemire (1870–1939) began early studies at the Bordeaux Conservatoire, and at the age of eleven won first prize in a piano competition. For three years he studied organ technique, repertoire, composition, and improvisation with César Franck at the Paris Conservatoire, and in 1891 he won a *premier prix* in Widor's organ class.

Tournemire accepted as students only those in whom he was genuinely interested. He did not teach technique, because he expected his students already to be technically proficient. Duruflé's fellow student Jean Langlais declared him a poor teacher and said he hated giving lessons,[3] and Duruflé believed that he had little pedagogical ability.[4] Duruflé commuted to Paris twice each week for his lessons with Tournemire,[5] giving piano lessons in Louviers to help cover the cost of his new studies.[6]

Duruflé took his lessons in Tournemire's home,[7] a fifth-floor apartment at 4, rue Milne-Edwards, a short street due north of the Arc de Triomphe, and just a few blocks inside what was then the city's western periphery. Tournemire owned an *orgue de salon* of nine stops by Charles Mutin.

The young organist was deeply impressed but intimidated by his new teacher. "This quick-witted, good-natured man had a very exuberant and high-strung temperament, passing abruptly from calm to fury—all of which frightfully intimidated me. However, my first lessons always ended in an atmosphere of confidence and cheerfulness."[8]

Duruflé's lessons with Tournemire followed a course of study similar to that of the organ class at the Conservatoire: "the accompaniment of a Gregorian antiphon followed by a short free improvisation on the same theme, a *fugue d'école*, and a free improvisation in the form of a classical sonata first movement built on a single theme, then a prepared piece."[9] The prepared pieces generally went well, and fugue went without upset, because Tournemire "was not particularly attracted to this austere and scholastic form of improvisation. He carried it out himself in a very free manner. . . ."[10] But Duruflé's improvisations often provoked a stormy response from the impatient Tournemire. He would push Duruflé aside and embark on an inspired improvisation on the same theme he had given his student, form mattering little to him.

On the subject of improvisation Tournemire taught that a long preparatory study of harmony, of counterpoint above all, and a heavy dose of fugue and of orchestration, are essential to the serious student.[11] He recalled that with César Franck "there was not a question of any formula, or of any trick effects, but only of poetry, emotion, and imaginative richness."[12]

In his *Précis d'exécution de registration et d'improvisation à l'orgue* (1936), Tournemire gave the following advice about improvising in concert, as Langlais remembered it: "First, you create an atmosphere. . . . Then you introduce a theme. This is followed by a massive crescendo, reaching a climax in a large, dissonant chord on full organ, followed by a long silence, followed by a second dissonant chord (all to frighten the audience!). Then one concludes quietly on the Voix céleste."[13]

Duruflé often made arrangements to be in Paris on Sunday mornings to hear Tournemire play for the high mass at nine-thirty and for the low mass at eleven o'clock. He was in awe of Tournemire's success at improvisation. "As soon as his right foot was free, he swiftly placed it on the pedal, ready to transmit to it again the jolts of his excitable and impulsive temperament. The privileged listeners who heard him, who saw this phenomenal man before his keyboards, will never forget the emotions that they owe to him."[14]

Duruflé noted the liturgical character of Tournemire's improvisations at Sainte Clotilde:

Tournemire never played from written music at Sunday mass. With the book of Gregorian chant always on the music rack, opened to the liturgical office of the day, he improvised throughout the entire mass, with an interruption only for the reading of the gospel and the sermon. That amounted to a half-hour of music. I hasten to add that this half-hour of music was always inspired by the Gregorian themes of the day and reflected the different portions of the service. It was not a concert, but a genuine musical commentary on the liturgy.[15]

Duruflé wrote that the church's magnificent Cavaillé-Coll

responded marvelously to [Tournemire's] enticements, to the flights of his imagination, by turns poetic, picturesque, whimsical; then impassioned, tumultuous, raging, then peaceful, mystical, ecstatic. Carried away by the music that sprang forth spontaneously from his fingers, he could no longer control his reflexes. He had departed elsewhere. When he played upon the récit, he would close his eyes at the same time as the expression box. During a crescendo, he could be seen becoming animated little by little, emphasizing with an involuntary grimace a particularly dissonant harmony. Then as he reached the tutti, at the reentrance of the themes in pedal octaves, he suddenly stood on the pedal keyboard for several measures, to the great astonishment of his guests, all the while continuing to improvise. He rarely finished the *sortie* on full organ. He generally preferred a conclusion in softness and ecstasy. All organists knew the following anecdote: One Sunday, after Tournemire had finished his *sortie* very quietly on a récit bourdon, one of his guests discreetly moved close to his ear, intending to do him a favor, and said to him in a low voice, "Maître, this is the *sortie*." The Maître suddenly glanced at him and calmly replied, "Well, my dear friend, sortez."[16]

When asked how he conceived his role as an organist, Tournemire replied that it was strictly based upon the liturgy, inspired by the splendor of the texts of the service and the "Gregorian lines which are, in the words of [Joris-Karl] Huysmans, the 'airy and moving paraphrase of the immobile structure of cathedrals.' "[17] Inspired by the singing of the monks at the abbey in Solesmes, which he himself had visited,[18] Tournemire held that the profession of church organist was a sacred institution, whose principles and values he expressed in the unpublished book which he wrote toward the end of his life, "On the high mission of the church organist."

Tournemire's improvisations boasted a freedom which his composed works lacked. Duruflé observed that his teacher's magnum opus, the *L'Orgue mystique*, a series of organ suites for the liturgical year, "does not recall his improvisations at all. . . . I'm not saying I don't like *L'Orgue mystique*, but in his improvisations there was a spontaneity, an impulse that we don't feel in *L'Orgue mystique* which smacks of labor. . . . One senses the work at the desk."[19]

In his early years, Tournemire wrote that his preferred forms were the prelude, the fugue, the choral and, above all, the Beethoven variation.[20] But Duruflé recalled that Tournemire later favored the free form above all others.[21] He abandoned "the great architecture [and] the fine 'sculpture' of the organ" in favor of paraphrases, titled sometimes *Paraphrases-Carillons, Fantaisies, Chorals,* or *Guirlandes alleluiatiques.*[22]

Duruflé studied the organ works of Franck with Tournemire, who had studied them with Franck himself, Tournemire's predecessor at Sainte Clotilde. Duruflé's authority with regard to Franck, as a disciple once removed, later bore fruit, not only in his inspired and nuanced playing of the Franck works, but in his edition of Franck's *Trois Chorals*, whose importance will be discussed below.

Duruflé's trips to Paris grew longer and longer because he felt that something besides his own lessons was necessary if he was to be fully prepared for the entrance examination for the organ class in October of 1920. He wanted to hear the finest organists in Paris and to acquaint himself with its symphony orchestras.

Early in 1920, after Duruflé had been studying with Tournemire for only a few months, Tournemire asked him to substitute for him at Sainte Clotilde so that he could devote all of his time to composition (he had already begun work on *L'Orgue mystique*). Tournemire generally played for mass and vespers only on Sundays and feast days,[23] and left weddings and funerals to his students, giving them the entire fee, which was considerable at the bourgeois parish.[24] Duruflé was therefore able to retain his post as titular at Notre-Dame in Louviers, while taking on the additional duties in Paris.[25]

For Duruflé it was a privilege and an incomparable joy to play the Cavaillé-Coll organ at Sainte Clotilde. "The works of Franck there took on a sincerity of expression unknown to me until then. Nowhere else had I sensed this perfect communion between the timbre of the stops and the music. . . ."

> The organist who has the good fortune to play Franck at Sainte Clotilde experiences total satisfaction. What could be more beautiful, more authentic than the wonderful trompette harmonique on the récit for playing the *adagio* of the *Troisième Choral* or the first variation of the *Premièr Choral*? What could be more tender than the delicious hautbois of Cavaillé-Coll to express the naïveté, the gentleness of the *Prélude, Fugue et Variation* or the charm of the *Pastorale*? What more ideal sonority can one desire than that of the full récit to render a thought that was inspired by these very colors? . . . The quality of this récit is like a miracle. Without doubt, a number of technical reasons contributed to this. The dimensions of the expressive box; its remarkable responsiveness and its perfect progression; the placement of the box at the very rear of the case; the large sonorous space surrounding the box on all sides, giving it an extraordinary resonance; finally the acoustics of the church and, above all, the genius of the organ-builder, all this brought about the miracle.[26]

But Duruflé's service at Sainte Clothilde came to an abrupt end.

> I left Tournemire in 1930, I left him even earlier, or rather I didn't leave him, it was he who sent me walking! . . . I wasn't able to replace him at Sainte Clotilde one day when I had a conflict; . . . I likewise had a wedding in Louviers—I went to Tournemire's home very embarrassed, very sheepish, to tell him: "Maître, I'm sorry but for once I cannot fill in for you." He threw me out the door (laughs). He was like that.[27]

In another turn of events, Tournemire decided to terminate his lessons with Duruflé, probably in the spring of 1920, throwing the latter into "a real panic. Indeed, I was attached with great affection to this generous, enthusiastic man, to this fascinating musician. On the other hand, I did not feel at all ready for the entrance exam at the Conservatoire."[28]

Despite their sometimes rocky relationship, Duruflé remained devoted to Tournemire, dedicating a composition to him, playing movements from his *L'Orgue mystique* in both service and concert, transcribing five of his improvisations from recordings, engaging him as consultant on organ projects, and even sharing the bench with him in Louviers. As late as 1977, he acknowledged, "I have never forgotten anything that I learned from my cherished Master, Charles Tournemire."[29]

From the very beginning of their relationship, however, Tournemire was evidently less than fond of Duruflé. Though they continued to have professional dealings until Tournemire died, the latter expressed his dislike of Duruflé, not only to him directly, but privately to other organists, and, indeed, to his other students, as we shall see below.

Tournemire's second wife, Alice Espir, whom he married in 1934, and whom Jean Langlais considered deceitful and manipulative,[30] was no more fond of Duruflé than was her husband. Duruflé, however, was successful in making arrangements with her, after her husband's death, to transcribe his five recorded improvisations.

Duruflé studied with Charles Tournemire for less than a year, beginning in October of 1919 and ending probably in the spring of 1920. With the entrance exam for the Conservatoire organ class still five or six months away, and feeling depressed, he sought the help of Louis Vierne,[31] to whom he was presented by the organist Georges Jacob.[32] Duruflé already professed great admiration for Vierne, and knew how he had successfully prepared numerous candidates for admission to the Conservatoire.

# Chapter Four

# *Lessons with Louis Vierne*

When Duruflé moved to Paris, around the time he began studying with Louis Vierne, he took an apartment at 50bis, rue de Douai,[1] on the right bank, not far from the Paris Conservatoire. It was a famously musical neighborhood.[2] In fact, Duruflé's flat was a mere two blocks north of the apartment on rue Ballu where Nadia Boulanger (1887–1979), one of the greatest musical pedagogues of the century, had lived since 1904. Her beloved sister and composer Lili died in 1918, but Nadia remained there until her death in 1979, hosting her Wednesday musical salons for countless French and American students, including Aaron Copland, Melville Smith, and Virgil Thomson.

Boulanger certainly knew of Duruflé by 1930,[3] and from as early as 1935 he played the organ for the memorial masses that Nadia arranged to be said for her sister at the Boulangers' parish church, La Trinité, for the annual remembrance of her death on March 15. Apart from a cessation of the services during the war, they continued for nearly sixty years.

Duruflé began playing for these services probably as a consequence of Boulanger's falling out with Olivier Messiaen, who had previously played for them as the organist at Trinité. For the service in 1934, Messiaen played a Bach choral at the beginning, but otherwise improvised from start to finish, for which Boulanger sharply reproached him. He defended himself in a letter to her, adding with insolence: "I remain sorry about your disappointment and understand very well that a program—even super magnificent—will always seem to you unworthy of the memory of your sister!" There was always "a kind of muted but courteous antagonism between them, established on a certain mutual regard."[4] One year, after Duruflé had married Marie-Madeleine Chevalier, he sent his wife in his place. Boulanger was at first uneasy about the substitution, but was reportedly pleased with Mme Duruflé's playing.[5]

Now settled into his first Paris apartment, Duruflé could more easily pursue his studies with Louis Vierne (1870–1937), arguably one of the greatest organists of his generation. A native of Poitiers, Vierne was born with a congenital cataract condition. "He could see very little. He had to hold the page an inch or so in front of his face, and even then it was difficult. It was the same way when he wrote. He had to use strong spectacles and an enormous pencil in order to write notes on the page."[6]

In 1881, the young Vierne became a resident at the Institut des jeunes aveugles,[7] where he studied organ with the blind Louis Lebel (1831–88) who was also the organist at Saint Étienne-du-Mont and a former pupil of Jacques-Nicolas Lemmens. After Lebel's death, Vierne studied with Adolphe Marty, who was also blind. He subsequently studied with César Franck, at the Paris Conservatoire, though only for the last year of Franck's life, and was in the same class as Tournemire. Vierne also studied with Charles-Marie Widor, becoming Widor's assistant at Saint Sulpice in 1892, and was an assistant to Widor and Alexandre Guilmant at the Conservatoire. From 1912, he taught at the Schola Cantorum. He became titular organist at Notre-Dame Cathedral in 1900, where he remained until his death at the console, in 1937.

Vierne was out of the country while Duruflé was commuting to Paris for his lessons with Tournemire, and he did not return until April 12, 1920,[8] having been in Switzerland since 1916 for treatment of his glaucoma. Duruflé could not have begun his lessons with Vierne much before the end of April. He there-fore had no more than about five or six months of study with Vierne before he successfully passed the entrance exam into Eugène Gigout's organ class at the Conservatoire, in October. Duruflé continued studying with Vierne while he was in Gigout's class, but it is not clear just how long that study lasted. The date appears nowhere. But it is likely that his friendship with Vierne, and his solici-tous care for him, repaid itself with occasional coaching sessions even as late as 1935, when Duruflé played Vierne's Sixth Symphony at Notre-Dame.

Forced to sell his organ and his apartment on avenue du Maine before going to Switzerland, Vierne lived briefly at the Hôtel Lord Byron, on the rue Lord Byron, after he returned to Paris. In 1920[9] Madeleine Richepin (1898–1962), a former student at the Paris Conservatoire, who would become his amanuensis, friend, travel companion, registrant, and fellow performer, found a modest apartment for him on rue Saint-Ferdinand, a block up from the Avenue de la Grand Armée, where he would live the rest of his life.

"Without an acceptable *orgue de salon* of his own—Vierne had a poor instru-ment in his apartment until 1926—he had to teach for about six years on the instruments of various churches and in the homes of former students who had organs."[10] Duruflé took his lessons in such salons, and occasionally also at Notre-Dame.[11] His friend and fellow student Henri Doyen took his lessons on the stu-dio organs of Mlle Cartier, Georges Jacob, and Maurice Blazy, among others, on various studio organs at the shop of Cavaillé-Coll-Mutin, on avenue du Maine, and even at Salle Gaveau and Salle Pleyel. Vierne occasionally gave lessons also at the American Cathedral of the Holy Trinity. Duruflé himself must have taken his lessons on some of these organs before 1926, when Vierne purchased an instru-ment from Cavaillé-Coll-Mutin, after which he was able to teach from his home.[12]

Duruflé gives a vivid account of his first encounter with Vierne.

I went to 37, rue Saint-Ferdinand where he lived in a modest apartment. He received me in a salon where there stood, side by side, a magnificent Pleyel grand piano and an awful electrified two-manual organ built by Convers. I found there a delightful, warm-hearted man who was very prepared to make me work. What a relief, what comfort for me! With deep emotion I looked at this beautiful face with its fine features, to which blindness lent an expression of intense inner life. His eyes, partly open, looked up from time to time towards the sky as if to search there for light.[13]

In both temperament and teaching, Vierne differed dramatically from Tournemire. The latter was unfriendly,[14] impulsive, and volatile, while Vierne was serene and rational, a more classic spirit. Duruflé wrote that "Vierne's temperament was always the same. You could find him in the same mood in which you left him. That was a pleasant change, because when you went to Tournemire, you never knew what awaited you."[15] Vierne was "very kind and affectionate. He was very encouraging."[16] Duruflé wrote:

> Vierne's teaching was entirely different from Tournemire's. . . . He had a much more classic mind, more rational: thus, the study of fugue with him took on a rigorous form. The countersubject had to be thought out and played just as if it were written down. The episodes were to have an essentially polyphonic style, the tonal construction had to be logical. . . . Free improvisation had to be equally disciplined both in the exposition of the themes and in the management and length of the developments. For execution, one found Vierne to be the perfect technician, the student of Widor, founder of the French organ school.[17]

Vierne was influenced by three masters: Widor, Guilmant, and Franck. From Widor he inherited the care for impeccable, noble, and vibrant performance. From Guilmant he learned the rational use of the timbres of the organ, especially mutations and mixtures. And from Franck he learned to develop, with consummate skill, the practice and constant care for musical architecture, and for melodic themes almost always chosen with success.[18] Vierne has been called "the carpenter and architect of sound."[19]

What Vierne learned from his studies with Franck may be gleaned from what we know of Franck's teaching, who placed emphasis on improvisation at the expense of technique and repertoire. Franck himself left scant evidence about his manual technique, but sources indicate his use of the thumb glissando, 5–4–5 fingering for an ascending passage in the right hand, and finger substitution to ensure legato within Bach works. As for the pedal, the few sources indicate his use of a mixed toe-heel technique. Otherwise, Franck was not "a proponent of systematic training in the matter of technique, as understood to include manual and pedal exercises."[20]

But Vierne also studied the organ with Charles-Marie Widor (1844–1937), who introduced the technique and methodology of the Belgian Jacques-Nicolas Lemmens to his teaching of organ at the Conservatoire. Duruflé considered Vierne the perfect technician at the console.

> Vierne knew how to make his organ [at Notre-Dame] sing admirably. His playing was of a perfect precision of attack, and his phrasing was very personal. His slender and

sinewy fingers, his flawless posture, without useless gestures, bestowed upon him an ease and an uncommon naturalness. . . . Although Vierne was nevertheless of an average height, he managed without difficulty to master this large console. He skillfully yielded to its demands and adapted his playing and his style to the imposing character of this instrument, which was unique in all the world.[21]

The principal feature of the Lemmens technique was his insistence on a precise legato, made possible, in the manuals, by finger substitution and thumb glissandos. For the pedal he insisted on a similarly exact legato, which assumed a good toe-to-toe technique but took toe-heel pedaling as its point of departure. Lemmens made greater use of the heel than did his predecessors in organ methodology. For difficult passages, he recommended two kinds of substitution in the pedal, the first in which one foot substitutes for the other, and the second in which the toe and heel of each foot substitute for each other. While it was distinctly Belgian and French, the Lemmens method depended on German models in significant ways, particularly for what, in that era, was considered the authentic tradition of playing Bach. At the same time, it took for granted a decidedly pianistic technique.

Vierne gave precise instructions about the organist's movements.[22] He guarded against useless and unsightly gesticulations, because even the smallest unjustified movement represents a loss of time and effort. If the student is diligent at slow, conscientious practice, he taught, even virtuosic pieces can thus be mastered without difficulty. The fingers should not be stretched out over the keys, but must attack them with precision and sharpness, yet without any hardness that would aggravate the noisy mechanism. The fingers should be kept rounded. Legato, he advised, results from the instantaneous transfer of pressure from one finger to another. An infinitesimal failure produces either a gap or a blur; one must connect notes clearly for a true technique. One's knees must be kept at right angles to the pedal board in order for the torso to retain its upright posture. One should never play with a flat foot, but with the inner side of the sole. The toes were to be kept in constant contact with the ends of the black notes, without ever playing the white notes from behind, except during substitution or crossing.

Tournemire wrote of Vierne that he "had acquired in full the pure technique of Lemmens, transmitted by Widor."[23] Although little has been said about it in commentaries published about Duruflé, there can be no doubt that Vierne passed the Lemmens technique and method along to his student. Duruflé himself wrote that Vierne's teaching was situated in the tradition of Widor.[24]

Vierne held the strict view that one should not try to imitate the dynamics and colors of the orchestra when one plays the organ.[25] Especially for playing Bach, all nuance of timbre remains completely subordinate to the structure of the piece. As for the playing of Bach fugues, Vierne strictly advised against the use of reeds, asking, "Would you double four-part polyphony in an orchestra with trumpets and trombones?" He encouraged the well-nuanced use of the swell box in playing Bach, but never to produce accents.[26]

For three-manual organs with two expressive divisions, Vierne demonstrated how one could orchestrate a smooth crescendo that was idiomatic for the organ:

> Begin on the récit *pp* with the foundations; add the foundations of the positif, open the expressive box of this manual a bit (if it possesses one); introduce the mixtures and reeds of the récit; add the foundations of the *grand-orgue*; open the positif box halfway; open the récit box completely, then that of the positif; finally, introduce the mixtures and reeds of the *grand-orgue* as well as those of the pédale to arrive at *fff*.[27]

Vierne wisely warned that these effects were not appropriate when playing early music, except with careful discretion.

Vierne would often have his students play on the piano the rapid passages from an organ piece they were working on, or even the entire piece, the better to insist on cleanness and precision, articulation, line, and impeccable tempo, such as he did with the *Pièce d'orgue* (*Fantasia* in G Major), BWV 572,[28] of Bach, or his own *Divertissement* and *Postlude* from the *Vingt-quatre Pièces en style libre.*[29]

If Duruflé's lessons were like those of his friend Henri Doyen, he had to do homework in counterpoint and play the examples several times at his lessons, play a verset or organ interlude he had written on a liturgical theme proposed by Vierne, and play at least two pages of a work by Bach, and two pages from one of Vierne's pieces in free style.

Duruflé studied the works of Franck with Vierne, as he had with Tournemire; it would be interesting to know how Vierne's approach differed from Tournemire's, and how the two coalesced in Duruflé. And since Vierne had studied four of Widor's later symphonies with the composer himself,[30] one wonders if Duruflé had the benefit of learning any of Widor's works under Vierne's tutelage.[31] Widor, after all, was among Vierne's favorite composers.[32]

According to Duruflé, Vierne composed and improvised in a single style, unlike Tournemire.

> [Vierne's] improvisations recalled his *Symphonies*. With him the composer and the improviser were the same musician. Just as in his *Symphonies*, the "writing" of his improvisations was very carefully done. He excelled in four- and five-voice polyphony. He loved to let the marvelous ensemble of fonds 8 sing in this form of writing. . . . The service generally ended with a large improvised symphonic fresco in which the form was always clear, the thematic construction solid, and the registration in good taste. There were no picturesque effects, no useless details, but broad melodic lines with carefully planned sonorities. From his master Widor he had retained this decorative style, this classical rigor that characterized the organist of Saint Sulpice. But as a former pupil of Franck, he added to it a melodic richness, an expressiveness and a personal harmonic warmth which classed him instead in the line of the last romantics. An aesthetic of this type was admirably suitable to the environment of Notre-Dame. Vierne had so identified himself with the grandeur of the setting, he had so blended with it, that he became the soul of his cathedral.[33]

Vierne had enormous respect for Gregorian chant. "Look at Gregorian chant," he was quoted as saying, "certainly the greatest musical work of all time: it never shouts. Its melodies, which have the great merit of being anonymous, are always serene. The *Requiem* Mass doesn't whimper; noëls don't laugh."[34] Nevertheless Vierne's interest in plainsong was less pronounced than Tournemire's, and he never heard the singing of the monks at Solesmes.[35] Henri Doyen speculated whether Vierne might have improvised differently, or even written a work based on Gregorian melodies, if he had become a regular visitor of Solesmes.[36]

Vierne considered Duruflé "the most brilliant and the most original of the young generation of organists . . . a first-class performer, and an improviser with abundant and varied imagination. Utterly sensitive and poetic, he has a rare, perceptive gift for composition," and observed that Duruflé's tryptich on *Veni Creator* "is now in the repertoire of every artist capable of playing it and in the libraries of the others."[37] He wrote:

> [Duruflé's] music attracts attention by its absolute freedom, by its complete rejection of any system displayed arbitrarily for its own sake, by its great depth of thought and by a solid construction that in no way hampers its emotional expansion nor its attention to detail. This art reveals an intense inner life expressed in the most adequate means with rare sensitivity.
>
> His sometimes daring modernism is fully justified by the nature of the emotions he means to translate. That is infinitely rare.[38]

Vierne had substitutes cover for him at Notre-Dame when he was away on tour, and he depended on them more and more as his health became increasingly precarious in the 1930s. Although some writers claim that Duruflé filled in for Vierne on Sundays[39] until 1931,[40] it is likely that Duruflé remained only until 1930, when he was dismissed by the clergy at Notre-Dame, all the while remaining titular at his church in Louviers.

The first time he played the organ at Notre-Dame, Duruflé

> experienced a feeling verging on fright because of its exceptional power. . . . Like a sea captain on his bridge, [the organist] breathes in the great open sea. The sensation is absolutely exhilarating. He has the illusion that someone else is playing, for he is aware of himself as both performer and listener. . . . Such an exceptional arrangement is very enriching for the organist. . . . Indeed, since the positif case no longer constitutes a screen to the hearing of the whole organ and of its sound balance . . . he can divide himself in two and become his own critic. While his fingers are on the keyboard, his ears are below the tribune, among the other listeners, which prompts him to alter his playing fundamentally and to register accordingly. As for the instrument itself, the memory I have of it is marvelous. Its sound was extremely beautiful because most of its stops were from Cavaillé-Coll. . . . The tutti, with its extraordinary bombarde 32 in the pedal, had an incomparable majesty and splendor, suited to the size of Notre-Dame, which is not inconsiderable. The same goes for all the foundations. The harmonic flutes were the most beautiful that Cavaillé-Coll ever built.[41]

Nevertheless, the console presented considerable challenges to the performer. Duruflé wrote:

> And yet, what a console. Good heavens! Five keyboards, the highest of which was unfortunately the récit. The expression [i.e., the swell mechanism] was controlled by means of a spoon-shaped pedal, with only two intermediate notches. It was placed all the way to the right, beyond the pedalboard. One can imagine the not very comfortable position of the organist having both hands on the récit, his left foot on the low C of the pedal, and his right foot on the spoon [pedal]. It was practically necessary to resign oneself to playing with the box either open or closed.[42]

Little is known about the repertoire Duruflé played at Notre-Dame, or the style of his improvising, except that the clergy thought his music too modern,[43] and the *maître de chapelle* in particular considered his playing "too subdued, too distant, and too polished (*ciselée*) for the vast vessel of the cathedral," as compared with "the great sound frescoes in the style of Vierne or Saint-Martin [which] were more suitable."[44] In fact, the cathedral authorities were dissatisfied enough with Duruflé's work that they evicted him, probably sometime during the first three months of 1930.[45] In fairness to the young organist, however, it must be added that Duruflé was undoubtedly an innocent victim of Vierne's deteriorating rapport with the clergy, who objected to the atmosphere created by the crowds of people that congregated in the organ tribune when Vierne was on duty. At those times, Vierne's friend, Madeleine Richepin, reigned in the tribune, which the clergy believed resembled more "the wings of a theater or a salon full of gossip than an integral part of a church."[46]

The organ at Notre-Dame needed work as early as 1912,[47] but it was not repaired until 1932, meaning that for all of his years as a student and *suppléant* of Vierne, Duruflé played the instrument in its compromised state. His premiere of Vierne's Sixth Symphony at Notre-Dame, in 1935, may well have afforded him his first opportunity to explore the repaired instrument and to experience firsthand the work of organ builder Joseph Beuchet, whose firm would be awarded the contract for the organ at Saint Étienne-du-Mont three years later, in 1938.

Duruflé developed a deep and abiding affection for Vierne that would continue until the latter's death at the console in Notre-Dame Cathedral in 1937, with Duruflé standing at his side. The two men had similar life experiences. Both had failed marriages. Both lost brothers prematurely. Both suffered physically, Vierne through his blindness and Duruflé through the many maladies that beset him in his final decades. And both men had been separated from their families at a very young age, to be quartered in institutions. Like Duruflé, Vierne recounted "the many impressions that overwhelmed [him] when [he] was thus separated from family life, and confined with strangers."[48] And Duruflé's music, like Vierne's, betrays a life lived profoundly and intensely, shoulder to shoulder with life's darker side.

# Chapter Five

# *The Conservatoire Student*

Although the Conservatoire records indicate that Duruflé was formally admitted to the school on September 12, 1919,[1] it was not until October of 1920 that he played his entrance exam for Eugène Gigout's organ class, performing for a jury comprising Gigout, Charles Tournemire, and André Marchal.[2] Tournemire is quoted as having said of Duruflé: "He will surely be a *premier prix*, in the style of Marchal."[3] At age eighteen, Duruflé became the youngest in Gigout's class of ten students, the oldest being thirty-six.[4]

According to contemporary reports, Gigout "played [the organ] in a very clean style, which did not prevent him from performing the music of Franck with great intensity. As an improviser he is reported to have been eclectic, but was drawn particularly to classicism."[5] According to Fanny Edgar Thomas, writing for *The Musical Courier* in 1894, Gigout was "one of the most fertile and original masters of that art in the city, indeed being so proclaimed by [Camille] Saint-Saëns, that exacting critic."[6] Gigout concertized widely in France, Switzerland, Catalonia, and England, and in the course of sixty years he inaugurated some fifty instruments. At the home of Bérenger de Miramon he performed with harpsichordist Wanda Landowska.[7]

When he was thirteen years old, Gigout studied composition at the École Niedermeyer, in Paris, with Saint-Saëns, and was an organ student of Clément Loret, a former pupil of Lemmens. In 1863, he was appointed organist at Saint Augustin in Paris, a position he held until his death. In 1885, he established the École d'Orgue, d'Improvisation et de Plain-chant, and became professor of organ at the Conservatoire in 1911. Gigout gave the first performance of Franck's *Choral* in A Minor. He published a revised edition, with his own *Avertissement*, of the *École d'orgue* by Jacques-Nicolas Lemmens. With good reason it can be assumed that Gigout taught Duruflé according to the Lemmens method, as had Haelling and Vierne before him. Indeed, Gigout was said to have taught his students to play Bach according to the "true Bach tradition," as the French understood it.

Gigout was considered, by some at least, to have been on the cutting edge of certain aspects of organ design and practice, so much so that he can be said to have anticipated the neoclassical movement in organ design, of which Duruflé would soon become an ardent promoter. Concerning French reeds, for example, the Alsatian organist Albert Schweitzer wrote that he and Widor believed them too strong and dominant, an artistic handicap, and were of the opinion that "we must go back to the building of reeds which do not dominate the whole instrument, but harmonize with the foundation stops and the mixtures, and to a certain extent only beautify them. Gigout holds the same opinion."[8]

As for the swell box, it was gaining increased usage as the century wore on, particularly among the students of Gigout. Schweitzer commented that a limited but frequent use of the device was found in Franck and the early works of Saint-Saëns, where it provides some emotional expressiveness which the organ otherwise lacks, but that it triumphs in the later works of Guilmant and Widor. "To their pupils, and no less to the pupils of Gigout, it has become flesh and blood."[9]

Schweitzer described two schools of French organ playing, as regards the pedals, and again he notes Gigout's position on the subject. The older school, not directly influenced by German practice, included Boëly, Chauvet, and César Franck. The younger generation, which betrays German influence, included Saint-Saëns and Gigout. Gigout, he wrote, "stands all alone in this school. He is the classicist, who has attained a pure organ style. He has something of Handel's manner. His influence as a teacher is outstanding, and his playing marvelous."[10]

Duruflé's low regard for Eugène Gigout has had the unfortunate effect of diminishing our own respect for the latter's stature as an organist and teacher. In his few uncomplimentary remarks, Duruflé asked rhetorically:

> What can one say about the teaching of Gigout, the professor at that time? He was a kind man. His teaching was very traditional, based almost exclusively upon the study of the *fugue d'école*, which gave his courses a very austere atmosphere. Maintaining the countersubject in the course of the fugue was not obligatory. This made things much easier. Performance was downright boring, without any study of registration. Free improvisation took a form of the first movement of sonata form with only one theme which had no relationship with classical allegro. It was a hybrid form in three parts whose first and third parts had rather the character of an andante. The central development was more animated.[11]

Gigout's successor in the post, Marcel Dupré, by contrast, began imposing two themes, and demanding that the countersubject be kept strictly throughout.[12]

In 1976 Duruflé's friend André Fleury[13] was asked whether Gigout was progressive in his teaching methods. He replied, in the same vein as Duruflé, "Not at all. He was rather pedantic and old-fashioned."[14]

> He didn't say much about interpretation, and if worse came to worst we did not ask very much, because we were studying with Vierne besides. The young girls liked *père* Gigout very much, the young men a little less. In any case, he was very good, he was an excellent man. But what he did seemed to us so outdated. Nevertheless, sometimes, I heard him improvise not so badly; there were some thirds in contrary movement, a nice counterpoint, some imitation.[15]

Duruflé considered Gigout a decisively lesser influence upon him than Vierne and Tournemire.[16] Having continued his private lessons with Vierne through the two years he was in Gigout's organ class,[17] Duruflé attributed to Vierne, not Gigout, his success in the competitions.[18] Duruflé remarked many years later, "I always regretted not being able to work with Dupré. I would much rather have worked with him than Gigout, who was a fine man, but that is all."[19] Duruflé said that Dupré, "who is called the Liszt of the organ, caused performance technique at the organ to advance considerably to a level of virtuosity unknown before him, thanks to his works. It resulted in new sonic effects. A whole generation of today's organists who had been his students benefited from this evolution."[20]

Duruflé received three awards during his study with Gigout. For the organ competition in June 1921, he received *premier accessit*,[21] and in June 1922 he was awarded the prestigious *premier prix*. He also received the *Prix Alexandre-Guilmant*, an award of 500 francs designated by Guilmant to be given each year to the first native or naturalized French student named winner of the *premier prix d'orgue*.

After Duruflé completed his work with Gigout, Maurice Emmanuel, who kept abreast of his work, "strongly advised me to remain at the Conservatoire to take the classes in writing there. Indeed, I had rather little experience in this discipline. I had simply finished the harmony treatise of Dubois with Jules Haelling at the *maîtrise* in Rouen, then done some work in counterpoint with Tournemire in order to be able to tackle improvisation in fugue."[22] Emmanuel advised Duruflé to study harmony with Jean Gallon, "a remarkable master," which he did for the next two years, from 1922 to 1924.

Jean Gallon (1878–1959) was on the Conservatoire faculty from 1919 until 1949. As a student, he studied harmony with Albert Lavignac and composition with Charles Lenepveu. He was *maître de chapelle* at Saint Philippe-du-Roule from his teen years and later wrote several treatises on harmony.

The young Duruflé revered Gallon[23] profoundly and had great affection for him, describing him as "the most prestigious of all the professors of harmony. The warmth, the enthusiasm that flowed out of this rich, powerful, generous, and affectionate nature gave incomparable influence to his teaching. With the gifts he possessed he could have had a career as a composer. He preferred to sacrifice it to his harmony class which filled out his whole life."[24]

Gallon's class enforced high standards for Duruflé, and brought him new discoveries, to which he readily responded. He felt inferior to his fellow pupils, being dazzled by their work. He described his experience with *basses données* and *chants donnés*.

*Basses données* in the polyphonic style of Bach with subject, countersubject, imitations, return of the theme in different voice parts, always accompanied by the countersubject. It was a true preparatory work for the writing of fugue. We were very far from the treatise of Dubois. The *chant donné*, to which I felt particularly drawn, was likewise a surprise for me by the distinction of its harmonization and the perfection of its realization. The work of the chorale whose theme was always by Bach took on a special value because it depends on the study of real harmony. Contrapuntal writing was very meticulous with regard to the melody of each part, which left far behind our old harmonizations in struck chords.[25]

Duruflé received the *second accessit* in harmony in June 1923, and in May 1924 he received the *premier prix*.[26] One of his student works, based on a *basse donnée*, was published in 1924 by Heugel. While naive, it nevertheless betrays skill and an incipient imagination.

Upon completing his work with Gallon, Duruflé again took the advice of his mentor Maurice Emmanuel, who "never lost sight of me. . . . 'You must continue,' he said to me. 'Go study fugue with [Georges] Caussade. Then present yourself for the class in accompaniment.'" Duruflé followed Emmanuel's suggestion and took two courses simultaneously, but he later came to regret it. "It was an error on my part to want to pursue two classes simultaneously, especially a class as difficult as that of piano accompaniment. I had to sacrifice my work on fugue to devote myself entirely to the other."[27]

Duruflé studied fugue and counterpoint with Georges Caussade (1873–1936),[28] who taught counterpoint at the Conservatoire from 1905, and fugue from 1921. In his memoirs Duruflé wrote that Caussade was "a remarkable professor of fugue, broad-minded, having a faultless musicality with an analytical mind for writing which was miraculous. With such a man possessing a pedagogical sense to an extreme degree, the study of fugue was fascinating."[29]

In June 1928, Duruflé received the *premier prix* in fugue, writing on a subject of Henri Rabaud, director of the Conservatoire. For the execution of this exam the students were closed in a room from six in the morning until 11:30 at night, with no access to an instrument or didactic works. All the first-prize winners' compositions were published in 1928 by Heugel. Duruflé's work bears no title, but can be called *Fugue* in C Minor for practicality sake, or *Fugue on a Theme of Rabaud*.

From 1923 to 1926 Duruflé studied piano accompaniment[30] with Abel César Estyle, about whom the sources are virtually silent, apart from the fact that he was born in 1877. In his memoirs Duruflé mentioned only that Estyle "was an excellent man, at once gruff and a bit timid. He had been the chorus director at the Opéra for a long time."[31]

In his memoirs Duruflé wrote about his first day in the class:

> I confess that until that day I had never seriously opened up an orchestral score with all its transposing instruments apparently written in different keys, but which, transcribed at the piano, had to sound in the real tonality. As the orchestration was written on pages of about twenty-five to thirty staves one above the other, this presented a particularly arduous difficulty of reading. Moreover, questions of piano technique presented themselves to me, as I had studied organ more than anything else.[32]

At the end of his first year in Estyle's class, Duruflé won *second accessit* in the competition, in June 1924.[33] At the end of his second year, he won *premier accessit*, in

June 1925.[34] At the end of his third year in the class, "after unremitting work," Duruflé won *premier prix*, in June 1926. He also received the *Legs Nicodami* (Nicodami Legacy), "a yearly pension for life of five hundred francs bequeathed by Mme Ravinet, the widow of M. Nicodami, former professor at the Conservatoire."

In 1925 Duruflé entered the composition class of Charles-Marie Widor (1844–1937), the redoubtable composer, conductor, and organist of Saint Sulpice. Widor was César Franck's successor as professor of organ at the Conservatoire, and Théodore Dubois's successor as professor of counterpoint and fugue. He left the teaching of organ to become professor of composition in 1905, a post he held through 1927, at which time he was named *professeur hono-raire*.[35] Duruflé entered Widor's class when the latter was eighty-one years old, and remained his pupil for over two years (1925–27).

But for some reason Duruflé flatly denied he had been a pupil of Widor: "I knew Widor the last year that he was professor of composition at the Conservatoire. I was not his student; I was a student of Paul Dukas who was his successor."[36] In fact, Duruflé received two prizes in composition while he was a student of Widor, one in 1926 and another in 1927,[37] and in both cases the official Conservatoire records identify him as a student of Widor. Moreover, on October 4, 1929, Widor wrote to the priest at Saint Étienne-du-Mont recommending him for the post there, and identifying him as "my former student (at the Conservatoire)."

In his later years, Widor was lax about his teaching duties, and while he continued teaching the composition class, "he was content to coast along, frequently arriving late, after gossiping with [Isidor] Philipp in the adjoining class."[38] Indeed, beginning in 1927, when Widor was named *professeur honoraire*, Henri Libert (1869–1937) was Widor's teaching assistant at Fontainebleau. Libert had also been Widor's assistant for his composition and fugue classes at the Paris Conservatoire, from 1896 until 1905.[39] In later years, Widor entrusted the teaching of fugue to Ganay.[40] One can assume that if Widor was not teaching the composition class himself (as, for instance, around the time he had cataract surgery early in 1929),[41] his substitute, whether it was Libert, Ganay, or someone else, would have taught the subject and used the methods that Widor approved. In any case, the announcement of Duruflé's prizes in composition appeared not only in the *Annuaire officiel du Conservatoire national*, but also in *Le Courrier musical et théâtral*, with Widor identified as his professor.[42]

Tournemire, Vierne, Messiaen, and Langlais had also studied composition with Widor, and apparently Widor did not have an effective relationship with them. One authority says that Tournemire and Vierne never attended his lectures.[43] Widor's involvement with the Institut de France, the elite guardian of French culture, may have been a psychological barrier to his students.[44] He might well have seemed too worldly, witty, and fashionable a socialite for his young students.

Furthermore, in his own compositions and in his improvisations at Saint Sulpice, Widor showed minimal interest in the plainsong revival that profoundly captivated Duruflé. As professor of the organ class, Widor did occasionally select plainsong themes for his students' improvisation exercises.[45] But when he assumed the post as professor of composition, Widor inherited an entrenched tradition which "concentrated exclusively on the techniques of operatic writing," a legacy which he was unable to discard because of its importance in preparing students for the Prix de Rome.[46] Vierne conjectured that Widor may have been under the illusion that he could broaden the spirit of the prize and reduce the importance of the Prix de Rome in the course.

Occasionally Widor tried to make his students write symphonic music, for example, but most of his time was spent serving up the "Cantata" and the "Chorus," in preparation for the examination for the Prix de Rome. In the composition class he had to reckon with the students in rival classes and keep his own at the same level.[47]

Duruflé would have had little interest in an approach to composition that focused on opera. The prestige of the Prix de Rome led many another organist to pursue its laurels, however, and a number of prominent organists were recipients over the years, including Nadia Boulanger, Henriette Roget,[48] Rolande Falcinelli, Gaston Litaize,[49] Jean-Jacques Grunenwald, Marcel Samuel-Rousseau, and Paul Pierné (the cousin of Gabriel Pierné).

In January 1926, Duruflé was among Widor's six students taking the semester exam in composition, and was identified as an aspirant. He presented his *Pastorale* for organ to the jury. In May 1926, he took the final exam, no longer identified as an aspirant. He composed his work on the first five measures of the bass entrance in the *Credo* from Bach's Mass in B Minor, BWV 232, titling the composition *Pièce pour orgue sur le thème du Credo*.

In June 1926, Duruflé received *second accessit* for the competition in composition, being identified as a student of Charles-Marie Widor. For the exam in January 1927, he presented his *Méditation* for organ[50] to the jury. From the Fondation Fernand-Halphen, named for a former Conservatoire student who died defending France, Duruflé received 1200 francs for his piece, by far the largest monetary award given on that date. For the examination in April 1927, Duruflé wrote a *Pièce* for organ on a theme by Raoul Lapavia.

For the competition in June 1927, Duruflé was awarded *second prix* for his *Triptyque* for piano, along with two monetary awards. The Fondation Fernand-Halphen gave him 1200 francs. He also received the *Prix Lepaulle*, named for Céleste-Émilie Julliard-Lepaulle, in the amount of 708 francs, an award given each year to a young musician who composed during the year "une œuvre quelconque remarquable."[51] It remains to be determined whether Duruflé's *Pièce* for organ or the *Triptyque* for piano was that "remarkable work." Duruflé was still identified as a student of Widor.

Widor retired from the Conservatoire in October 1927, when he was nearly eighty-four years old.[52] In January 1928, a sixty-three-year old Paul Dukas (1865–1935) succeeded him, and zealous students flocked to him for the next seven years.[53]

As with the earlier professors Duruflé chose to study with, the recommendation as to a teacher of composition came from Maurice Emmanuel who "was always watching from the wings. He said to me, 'Now you should enter the composition class of Paul Dukas.' In this new subject not only was I a novice but I knew nothing about it. I had never been tempted by composition."[54]

Duruflé wrote in his memoirs that Dukas "made a great impression among his students, first by his personality as a composer, and also by a severity, a coolness upon first contact which concealed a man, to tell the truth, who afterward disclosed himself full of kindness and concern."[55] Indeed, Dukas's later correspondence and conversations bear witness to the zeal with which he followed the careers of his former students. Duruflé was among them.[56]

Dukas studied counterpoint and fugue at the Conservatoire and was a friend and fellow student of Debussy in the composition class of Ernest Guiraud. Dukas impressed his classmates by his sure musical judgments and his rather distant manner. He lived simply, in a kind of semiretirement, and at a distance from the world.

Even in his first significant work, the youthful Symphony in C Major, Dukas's personality clearly revealed itself in the work's inner energy and concentrated force of feeling, his love of rhythm, his impassioned taste for order and musical architecture, and his acute sense of expression and instrumental color.[57] Soon thereafter, his *Variations, interlude et finale sur un thème de Rameau* demonstrated anew the essential features of his writing: his sense of logic, of construction, and of organization. His *Ariane et Barbe-bleue* was praised as a progressive but classically fashioned work, and some critics saw it as following the lead of Debussy's *Pelléas et Mélisande.* The work brought him international acclaim.

Like other composers of his day, Dukas held an interest in the rediscovery of early music, including eighteenth-century French music. In his articles and reviews he expressed his admiration for Palestrina, Monteverdi, Rameau, and Gluck. One of his pupils said that the music of Johann Sebastian Bach figured prominently in Dukas's course. Dukas collaborated with Fernand Lamy in 1913 on the edition of a suite of ballets taken from *Les Paladins* of Jean-Philippe Rameau.[58] While he never studied with Franck, one detects in his cantata *Velléda* the influence of the master, whose style Dukas had studied.[59]

Like his colleague Claude Debussy, Dukas was influenced by the Chanteurs de Saint Gervais, the Parisian choir conducted by his friend Charles Bordes, which played a decisive role in the revival of Renaissance polyphony and Bach. Their concerts "obtained for [Dukas] frequent occasions to discuss the great masters of this distant era, Josquin des Prez . . . Orlandus Lassus . . . Clément Jannequin."[60] Dukas credited Palestrina with "wresting music from the scholastic monstrosities to which it was then condemned and restoring it to what it must be: an art of pure expression." He wrote that Palestrina "coordinated with genius all the elements of sparse beauty that jumped out in their works and kneaded them with a powerful hand into a form whose austere magnificence still strikes us with amazement. He thus appears to us as the living personification of the first age of music. . . ."[61]

After 1907, Dukas's works became more and more serious and he hesitated to have them performed. Being a perfectionist, he destroyed a number of his manuscripts, and nearly destroyed the manuscript for *La Peri*, the *poème dansé* that helped to establish his reputation. After its success had won him a preeminent place among the great modern French composers, Dukas confined himself to almost total silence and did not finish any of his larger projects after 1912. He had a high ideal of craftsmanship, he was extremely self-critical, and he had a small output.

Duruflé's debt to Dukas has usually been described in terms of his instincts for orchestral coloring. But he was also in debt to Dukas—an eminent cartesian, an impeccable architect of sound[62]—for his skills at architecture and organization. This influence upon Duruflé has perhaps been underestimated. Louis Vierne is rightly credited for much of Duruflé's early sense of order, particularly in comparison with Tournemire, but Dukas's sense of architecture did not go unnoticed by Duruflé.

Asked what it was about Dukas that inspired his students, Duruflé replied that he was so severe as to be discouraging. "But in the end everything he said was of such interest that we would listen, of course, our ears wide open to everything he said."[63] As to whether Dukas insisted that his students study the masters, such as Bach, or that they develop their own language, Duruflé replied: "He always advised us to search for our own language. He did not impose on us a style of writing music."[64]

Olivier Messiaen indicated that "Dukas taught me structure, that is, the right formulation of a work, but more importantly, he taught me to orchestrate."[65] Messiaen was already surprising his fellow students by the works he brought in. Duruflé wrote that "it was there that we heard for the first time his *Préludes* for piano and his symphonic poem *Les Offrandes oubliées*."[66] Dukas did, however, urge his students to depend on their inner ear for composition and to write without the piano. Duruflé confessed that he was never able to succeed at it.[67]

In January 1928, the very month that Dukas succeeded Widor, Duruflé took the composition exam for Dukas's class, submitting his *Scherzo* for organ,[68] which won him 1200 francs from the Halphen foundation. In May 1928, the students in the class were closed in a room from six in the morning until eleven in the evening to write a composition on one of four themes. Duruflé wrote a *Pièce* for organ on nine measures of allegro in four sharps. He was the only winner of the *premier prix* for the competition in June 1928. He wrote in his memoirs that he obtained the award for his Trio for flute, viola, and piano (i.e., the *Prélude, récitatif et variations*). *Premier accessit* was awarded to André Fleury and *second accessit* to Olivier Messiaen. For his work, Duruflé was given a monetary award of 600 francs by the Fondation Fernand-Halphen. He also received his second *Prix Lepaulle* in the amount of 708 francs.

It has generally been assumed, and justifiably so, that Duruflé studied with Dukas only for the five months or so before he won the *premier prix* in composition in 1928. But in fact he continued to study composition even after winning the prize.[69] Indeed, a photograph of Dukas's composition class in 1930 includes Duruflé,[70] illustrating that Duruflé actually studied with Dukas for over two years. Overall therefore, Duruflé studied composition for at least five years, beginning first with Widor in 1925, or perhaps with his substitute, and then with Dukas until at least 1930.[71]

After completing his other courses, Duruflé began studying orchestral conducting, the only subject at which he was frankly unsuccessful. His professor was Philippe Gaubert, the conductor of the distinguished Société des Concerts du Conservatoire. For his first conducting exam, in March 1931, Duruflé conducted the *Rédemption* of César Franck, receiving too low a score for him to be admitted to the competition. A year later, in April 1932, he took his last examination, conducting Mozart's Overture to *The Magic Flute*. The jury for that test was required to vote for a maximum of six students that would be admitted to the competition. Duruflé was graded seventh, the only student not permitted to compete. He considered himself a poor conductor the rest of his life.

Apart from his conducting classes, Duruflé had a stellar career during his twelve years at the Conservatoire, receiving at least one award at the end of every academic year, including five *premiers prix*, one *second prix*, two *premiers accessits*, and three *seconds accessits*, for a total of eleven awards. Conservatoire regulations did not allow students to continue beyond their thirtieth year of age, so in 1932 Duruflé's student career came to an end.[72] He had already been the titular organist at Saint Étienne-du-Mont for two years.

About three months after his last examination, Duruflé married Lucette Andrée Simonne Bousquet, whom he knew from Louviers. The marriage took place on August 30, 1932, in a civil ceremony in the eleventh arrondissement of Paris.[73] On the same day there was a religious ceremony at the church of Sainte Marguerite, in the same arrondissement, where Lucette was living at the time and where she would return after their divorce.

Lucette was four years younger than Maurice. Her parents, natives of Louviers, were married in 1905 but soon moved to Elbeuf-sur-Seine. On April 16, 1906, they were visiting her maternal grandfather at his home in Louviers. It was there, on that date, that Lucette was born.[74]

Lucette's father is said to have been in the plumbing business, and in that capacity he had professional dealings with Charles Duruflé in Louviers. For undetermined reasons, Duruflé's parents were vigorously opposed to the marriage of their son with Lucette.[75]

Having first studied piano with Maurice, Lucette later coached under the famed pianists Marguerite Long and Lucette Descaves and became a respected teacher of piano and solfège in her own right. She was said to be particularly fond of Chopin, Mozart, Liszt, Beethoven, and Bach, but she also taught modern

French composers, including Ravel, Poulenc, and Satie.[76] After the divorce, she taught from her home on avenue Philippe Auguste, near the place de la Nation, in the eastern part of the city.[77] Among her students[78] were the pianists Olivier Greif, Frédéric Wurtz, Myriam Birger, and the sisters Katia and Marielle Labèque, all of whom subsequently enjoyed international careers.

It is uncertain whether Duruflé was already married when he moved to the left bank, to the apartment at 8, rue Dupuytren. In any case, the couple lived there for about six years, until 1938. In that year Duruflé moved to place du Panthéon,[79] probably with Bousquet, as the two continued visiting his extended family as a couple at least as late as the early 1940s.[80]

Duruflé's marriage to Bousquet lasted for fifteen years,[81] but their relationship deteriorated fairly early on. Bousquet confessed to having suffered a great deal, and surely the same can be said of Duruflé. But according to her son Patrick Bousquet, "there was a great musical complicity" between them. In 1943 they visited Duruflé's brother Henri and his family in Lisieux, and played "some wonderful piano concerts" in the parlor. Duruflé composed most of his greatest works while he was married to Bousquet, including the *Suite*, the *Prélude et fugue sur le nom d'ALAIN*, the *Andante et Scherzo*, *Trois Danses*, and much of the *Requiem*.

The couple were granted a civil divorce on June 26, 1947,[82] but the ecclesiastical annulment, declaring the marriage null in the eyes of the church, was not confirmed until June 23, 1953, some six years after the civil divorce. On August 4 of that year, the church declared Duruflé free to remarry.[83] Patrick Bousquet writes, "My mother accepted the annulment to allow Maurice, who . . . was very observant, to remarry in the church. . . ." According to the son, some letters written by Duruflé to his mother in the 1960s admitted that he "regretted his past attitude."[84]

After Duruflé married Marie-Madeleine Chevalier, in 1953, his marriage to Lucette became an open secret and remained so long after his death, for reasons that are not altogether clear.[85] Conjecture that the divorce and annulment were cause for public disgrace became increasingly unlikely as the decades wore on, as did the theory that the existence of the first marriage somehow diminished the second, or that the existence of Bousquet constituted a menace to the life and career of Chevalier. It could be that the open secret merely outlived its original purpose of letting go the past; it could also be that some deep-felt secret of Duruflé will never be known.

# Chapter Six

# *Duruflé's Distinctions*

While he was still a student at the Conservatoire, Duruflé won two important competitions sponsored by Les Amis de l'Orgue, one in 1929 and the other in 1930. The first assured his renown as an organist and improviser, and the second established his reputation as a composer of distinction.

Upon the urging of Vierne,[1] Duruflé participated in the competition in organ performance and improvisation that was sponsored at the Église de l'Étoile,[2] in June of 1929, by Les Amis de l'Orgue, the association of professional organists established in 1927. For the preliminary round the contestants had to perform the *Toccata, Adagio, and Fugue*, BWV 564, of Bach, and improvise an ornamented choral on "a theme from the Catholic liturgy." They then had to improvise a symphonic paraphrase on the same theme, in a form of the contestant's choice. For the second round the contestants had to be prepared to play any of eight pieces,[3] including the fourth trio sonata of Bach, the *Choral* in E Major of Franck, the first movement of Widor's *Symphonie gothique*, the third part of Tournemire's *Triple Choral* and the final movement of Vierne's Third Symphony.[4] It was the last-named piece that the jury asked of Duruflé. Then he was asked to play an *improvisation symphonique*, including a prelude and fugue on a given theme, and then a free improvisation on two given themes in the form of an *Allegro, Adagio, and Finale*. Serving on the jury were Vincent d'Indy,[5] Charles Tournemire, Louis Vierne, Joseph Bonnet, Alexandre Cellier, and André Marchal.[6]

Duruflé was named the winner on June 29 and was awarded the prize of 5000 francs. Louis Vierne, who undoubtedly took considerable pride in his pupil's success, remembered Duruflé's "blazing organ competition" as the event that established him as an organist and improviser.[7] It was indeed a monumental achievement.

The following year, Les Amis de l'Orgue sponsored a competition in composition, on June 20, 1930 at the Institut des jeunes aveugles. A preliminary round eliminated nine contestants, including André Fleury. Joseph Ermend-Bonnal, Henriette Roget, and Duruflé proceeded to the final round, all of whom had been students of Tournemire, a fact that put the maître in an awkward position as a member of the jury.

In advance of the contest, Tournemire made it perfectly clear in private correspondence with Ermend-Bonnal that he favored the latter's entry over those of Roget and Duruflé. He had a particular fondness for Bonnal and he was lavish in his praise for the score Bonnal submitted. Above all, he did not want Duruflé's submission to win first prize. On June 12, Tournemire wrote to Bonnal:

> I myself find that your work[8] is "grandiose." The beginning, on a Basque theme (your own, perhaps) is of an incomparable freshness. It is all done naturally. Your *Toccata* is full of force, of power (There is too much Franck in your work. It's not necessary to do Franck today. It doesn't wear well!!!) G[abriel] P[ierné], the author of *Bouton d'Or*, President of the Jury (!), member of the Institute (!!!) found it overlong—Ibert, Boulanger, Roussel, Bréville, etc., had the same opinion. I protested in vain. Bonnet, I rather believe, will vote for you. As for me, my vote is absolutely firm. My only fear is that the majority have fallen for Duruflé! But this isn't mathematical. No. 3 is Mlle Roget, winner of this year's *premier prix* in organ. But she's a beginner. Here then, all 3 are my students and they're going to fight against each other?
>
> You, you are a master. Besides, you have the age for great things. Your work has given me great joy. You've written a masterpiece.[9]

Norbert Dufourcq[10] assisted Duruflé at the console for his performance of the *Prélude, adagio et choral varié sur le Veni Creator*. As *Le Ménestrel* reported, "It was obvious, at all events, that one of [the contestants] distinguished himself quite clearly from the other two."[11] Duruflé was declared winner of the first prize of 3000 francs, to the disappointment, surely, of Ermend-Bonnal, but of Tournemire as well.[12] Duruflé probably never learned of his betrayal by Tournemire. Serving on the jury were Gabriel Pierné, Nadia Boulanger, Joseph Bonnet, Pierre de Bréville, Alexandre Cellier, Claude Delvincourt, Jacques Ibert, Adolphe Marty, Achille Philip, Albert Roussel, Louis Vierne, and Charles Tournemire.[13]

Duruflé went on to win other prizes. In 1936 he secured the *Prix de la Fondation Blumenthal pour la pensée et l'art français*. Established in 1920 by Florence Blumenthal and her husband Georges, an eminent New York financier, the Blumenthal Foundation was established to promote French thought and art. The prize was awarded to a painter, sculptor, writer, or musician for a work submitted to a jury; it included a monetary award.[14]

According to a brief notice in *Le Courrier musical et théâtral*, in 1922, the prize was made every two years by an American committee. "The conditions of this prize are particularly difficult: candidates [in music] must, indeed, present two symphonic works to a jury. . . ."[15] Many of France's most esteemed musicians, writers, and artists have been recipients of the prize.

On December 6, 1935, *Le Ménestrel* published an announcement of the forthcoming competition, noting that the winner would receive 20,000 francs paid in two annual installments. Duruflé's award is curiously undocumented, and he never referred to it in articles or interviews. Even the Duruflé Association had to speculate about it, guessing that the award was for his *Trois Danses*, Op. 6,[16] which was premiered in 1936. This is the most likely possibility. Armand Machabey, however, having mentioned Duruflé's earlier published works in general, and the *Suite*, the orchestral *Sicilienne*, and the *Trois Danses* in particular, wrote that ". . . these works . . . are given official recognition by the Prix Blumenthal."[17] *La Revue musicale* noted only that the award was "for the music" of Duruflé.[18]

In 1954 Duruflé was named Chevalier de la Légion d'Honneur,[19] a distinction of enormous prestige in France. In 1966 he was elevated to the rank of Officier de la Légion d'Honneur. The decoration was created in 1802 by Napoléon Bonaparte to honor civil and military service.

In 1956 Duruflé was the first to be awarded the *Grand prix musical du Département de la Seine*.[20] In 1958 he was named Chevalier des arts et lettres, and in 1966 he was made an Officier des arts et lettres.

Duruflé twice won the *Grand prix du disque*. In 1959 he earned the distinction for his conducting of the *Requiem*, with his wife as organist.[21] In 1962 the couple won the prize for their recording of his organ works.[22]

In 1961 Pope John XXIII designated Duruflé a Commander in the Order of Saint Gregory the Great. The citation in the Vatican's official publication, *Acta Apostolicae Sedis*, of November 1961, reads as follows, in a translation from the Italian: "With Notes of the Office of State, Holy Father John XXIII, happily reigning, deigned to confer . . . the Title of the Order of Saint Gregory the Great, civil class . . . on 17 November 1961, upon Sgnr Duruflé Maurizio."[23]

The Order of Saint Gregory the Great was founded by Gregory XVI, in 1831, and is bestowed on "persons who distinguish themselves for conspicuous virtue and notable accomplishment on behalf of Church and society, regardless of their religious belief" or nationality.[24] One is presented for the award by the bishop of the candidate's diocese, who addresses it to the Secretary of State, who in turn submits it to the pope's attention.

The 1970 edition of Duruflé's *Suite*, Op. 5, included a fiche indicating that the papal designation was awarded him for "l'ensemble de son œuvre de musique religieuse," that is, for the whole of his religious music. But in correspondence with Nadia Boulanger, Duruflé specified that the award was in acknowledgement of the *Requiem*.[25] The Duruflés went to Rome for the awards ceremony at the Pontifical Institute of Sacred Music.

In 1969 Duruflé was named Officier de l'order national du mérite.[26] And lastly, in 1979, he was awarded the Prix René Dumesnil by the Académie des Beaux-Arts of the distinguished Institut de France.

Chapter Seven

# The Contested Successions at Notre-Dame and Sainte Clotilde

Duruflé was not always successful in obtaining the church posts he applied for. In 1928, the organist post at the church of Saint Vincent-de-Paul, in the tenth arrondissement, became vacant after the tenure of Alexandre Georges (1850–1938).[1] In a letter dated March 3, 1929, Louis Vierne recommended to the archbishop of Paris that he consider as a candidate the twenty-seven year old Duruflé. "I would like, Your Eminence, to recommend still another of my pupils: Monsieur Maurice Duruflé, the winner of the *premier prix* in organ at the Conservatoire, and likewise an exceptional organist, is also a musician with special qualities . . . not only a gifted, charming, young artist of pure Catholic sensibility, but likewise . . . a person who commands his *métier* to the highest degree."[2] Duruflé was not named to the post, which went instead to René Kopp, *suppléant* to Alexandre Georges, who was deputy head of the department of accounting of the Compagnie du Nord.

Duruflé's success at being named to Saint Étienne-du-Mont, in 1929, may be hailed as something of a coup, by virtue of his still being a student, until we recall that Saint Étienne-du-Mont had little musical distinction at that time. Its *grand orgue* was in a deplorable state, its *orgue de chœur* was a tubular pneumatic, its choir was undistinguished, and the legacy of the church's titulars was no match for those at Notre-Dame, Sainte Clotilde, Saint Sulpice, the Madeleine, Saint Augustin, or La Trinité. But for a man with Duruflé's appreciation for architecture, the post was not without some personal satisfaction for him. Nevertheless, there could be no guarantee that Saint Étienne-du-Mont would interest him very far into the future.[3]

So in 1937, having been the titular at Saint Étienne-du-Mont for some eight years, he sought the position at Notre-Dame after the death of Louis Vierne, and in 1939 he was a candidate at Sainte Clotilde, after the death of Tournemire. But in both instances the clergy, after being dissuaded from holding competitions, appointed other successors.

Early in 1936, Vierne wrote a letter to the cardinal expressing his wish that his successor be chosen by competition, not by appointment of the cathedral chapter. In his letter to the cardinal, Vierne indicated that he is "entrusting sealed copies of this letter to Monsieur l'Archiprêtre de Notre-Dame and to the president of Les Amis de l'Orgue, requesting that its contents be made known only after [his] death."[4]

Vierne feared the chapter would appoint the aristocrat, Léonce de Saint-Martin (1886–1954), considered an inferior organist at the time, who had studied with him from 1923 to 1930.[5] Vierne hired him as his assistant in 1924, only to dismiss him in April 1930. But the clergy virtually forced Vierne to reinstate him. Saint-Martin remained in the post until Vierne's death.[6]

Saint-Martin attended none of the prestigious music schools in Paris. A former pupil of the blind organist Adolphe Marty and of Albert Bertelin (1872–1951), he had been *organiste du chœur* at Saint François-Xavier. In 1919 he was named titular organist at Notre-Dame des Blancs-Manteaux. While studying with Vierne, in 1920, he began substituting for Marcel Dupré, in the latter's capacity as Vierne's official deputy at the cathedral. Marcel Dupré inaugurated Saint-Martin's house organ in 1922, and in 1936 and 1937 Saint-Martin recorded a series of fifty-three weekly radio broadcasts for Radio-France on his instrument.

By unwitting premonition, the chapter of Notre-Dame told Vierne that his recital slated for June 2, 1937, the 1750th of his career, would be the last public recital permitted in the cathedral. The concert proved to be the last of his life as well, for he died at the console, with Duruflé at his side to assist with registration.[7] Besides Duruflé, Vierne was attended in the tribune by a Jean Fellot and his wife, and by Madeleine Richepin and her husband, Dr. Lucien Mallet.[8] Duruflé gave these accounts of Vierne's death:

> When he began to play [his] *Stèle pour un enfant défunt*, his fingers clutched the keyboards. He had barely lifted his hands when he collapsed on his bench, afflicted by a stroke. He was expected to improvise on the theme of the "Salve Regina." But instead of this final homage to the Virgin of Notre-Dame, we heard a long pedal note. It was his foot which pressed upon the pedal and which would never lift itself again.[9]

> Some might have said the organ emitted a sinister groan. Nobody will forget, on this tragic evening, the distraction that seized everyone in the audience at that moment, the anxious waiting in front of the hospital where his body had just been transported, the last glimmers of hope that we persisted in guarding all the same, then the horrible news, the anguish, the tears, the sobs that were perceived here and there in the courtyard, on a desolate night.[10]

According to one account, "Duruflé quieted the pandemonium by courageously finishing the recital before a stunned audience."[11]

Vierne's Requiem Mass at Notre-Dame, on June 5, was strictly liturgical, with the Gregorian melodies sung by the choirboys and the organ being silent. Madeleine Richepin did not attend the funeral, perhaps because of the ill will shown Vierne by the cathedral chapter.[12] Duruflé maintained a close professional relationship with her thereafter. In fact, after she isolated herself from the society of Vierne's acquaintances, Duruflé remained her only link with the organ world,[13] along with the publisher Henry Lemoine, who was under contract to publish all of Vierne's hitherto unpublished works.[14]

After Vierne's death, Béranger de Miramon Fitz-James, president of Les Amis de l'Orgue, opened the envelope containing Vierne's letter, and disclosed its contents to his organist colleagues. Assuming that the chapter would accede to Vierne's expressed wishes, and that a competition would be held, four organists declared themselves candidates for the position: Maurice Duruflé, Jean Langlais, Gaston Litaize, and Jehan Alain.[15]

But there would be no competition. The chapter was disinclined to accede to Vierne's wishes, and some of the clergy enjoyed a social acquaintance with Saint-Martin. So on June 6, the day after Vierne was buried, the chapter unanimously appointed Saint-Martin as cathedral organist.[16]

Equipped with Vierne's letter, Miramon Fitz-James divulged to the organists of France Vierne's expressed wish that there be a competition. He promptly drafted a petition addressed to the Archbishop of Paris, the chapter, and the cathedral administrator, and had it signed by "fifty-five professionals representing the French organ school, including every great living French organist." Duruflé was among the signatories to the petition.

On June 14, many of the signatories gathered at the École César-Franck to hear the chapter's response to the petition and to decide on a course of action. They requested an audience with the cardinal who met on July 17 with Henri Busser, president of the Union des maîtres-de-chapelle et organistes, and Miramon Fitz-James. The cardinal insisted "he could not oppose the decision of the chapter to name the organist of its choice."[17] The decision was irrevocable.

The chapter's action was not kept from the broader public. Indeed, it became public knowledge, and both the clergy and Saint-Martin took a lashing from the French and foreign press. Robert Bernard wrote a blistering accusation in *La Revue musicale*, charging the clergy with favoritism and injustice and declaring Saint-Martin's appointment a mockery of one of the most renowned sanctuaries in Christendom.[18] Duruflé himself published nothing on the subject.

The succession at Sainte Clotilde followed nearly as convoluted a course as that at Notre-Dame, though it was less dramatic and less public. When Charles Tournemire drowned at Arcachon, his seaside getaway near Bordeaux, on November 3, 1939,[19] perhaps by suicide, Duruflé was already ten years into his tenure at Saint Étienne-du-Mont and could lay no claim to a "foot in the door" at Sainte Clotilde. Although his chances were excellent, as they had been at Notre-Dame, events took a different turn.

According to Jean Langlais, Tournemire summoned him to his side on June 14, 1939, having fallen ill after prostate surgery. He told Langlais, in the presence of Mme Tournemire, that he wanted him to be his successor at Sainte Clotilde and that his will would so stipulate. "I have just been operated on. I have seen death very near, and I have realized that one thing is very close to my heart before my death—my succession at Sainte Clotilde."[20] Tournemire asked that Langlais keep the information secret until his death, whereupon he would find the wish expressed in his will.

After her husband's death, Mme Tournemire refused to acknowledge his verbal codicil and Langlais never knew for certain whether or not Tournemire ever wrote his request into the will. Mme Tournemire denied that her husband left any mention of it. As Ann Labounsky has noted, "The moody Tournemire could easily have changed his mind or could equally have added a note, which was either set aside intentionally or lost by mistake."[21]

According to the only other known documented report,[22] a competition was organized with the approval of Canon Verdrie, the curé of Sainte Clotilde, and with Les Amis de l'Orgue designated as the *comité organisateur*. Several interested candidates were prevented from competing, owing to the war, so the date for the competition was postponed, more or less indefinitely. With peace increasingly elusive, however, a date for the contest was finally set for December 20, 1941, over two years after Tournemire had died.

Jean Langlais persisted in his belief that Tournemire wanted him as his successor, and he said as much to his friends Litaize, Fleury, and Duruflé, all of whom were contestants for the post. The three subsequently withdrew from the competition, wanting to honor the alleged wishes of Tournemire. The only remaining contestants were Daniel-Lesur and Antoine Reboulot, who, with Langlais, were given practice time at Sainte Clotilde. But on December 14 Norbert Dufourcq, on behalf of Les Amis de l'Orgue, wrote a letter to Langlais informing him that Daniel-Lesur and Reboulot had both decided against competing and that Canon Verdrie had therefore cancelled the competition.

On March 2, 1942 Verdrie wrote to Langlais to explain that, despite his high regard for him, Langlais's relative youth—he was thirty-five—prevented his being named to the post without a competition. Verdrie had received counsel in this regard not only from the archbishop, but from Mme Tournemire who advised that, although her husband expressed his preference for Langlais, he understood all along that his successor would be designated by competition. Conceding that he could not wait any longer for the end of the war, Verdrie appointed Joseph Ermend-Bonnal to succeed Tournemire, having obtained de Miramon's recommendation of this "great musician, great Christian, highly worthy of general esteem and of your tribune." At the same time, the priest wrote, Langlais might expect to succeed Ermend-Bonnal, who, by virtue of his advanced age (he was sixty-two), would probably retire in a few years.[23]

Despite the furor raised among organists over the cancelled competitions at Notre-Dame and Sainte Clotilde, there was apparently slight precedent for competitions. In April 1939, Albert Bertelin (1871–1952), a former composition student of Widor, published an article in *La Petite Maîtrise*[24] in which he gives some history of the practice in Paris of appointing organists by jury. Bertelin wrote that Widor believed Vierne the right man to succeed Eugène-Michel

Sargent at Notre-Dame, in 1900. The latter had no *suppléants*,[25] according to Bertelin, so there were no organists with an advantage. But any candidate with a recommendation from Widor had every likelihood of winning the post.[26]

The need for a competition developed, Bertelin relates, when there arose the candidacy of an unnamed organist of considerable renown. According to Bertelin, it was then that Widor proposed there be a competition by jury. Widor was confident that this particular contestant was too well known to risk the possibility of losing to a jury. The contestant did, in fact, withdraw from the competition. Widor rounded up a few musicians from the Institute to constitute a jury, serving himself as president. Vierne was named to the post from among five finalists.

In Bertelin's view there was no other precedent for the jury selection of titular organists. He wrote, "The nomination of organists, in the churches of Paris, has always been made directly by the curés of the parishes. No one has ever dreamed of forming a jury to appoint a candidate. . . ."[27]

As if to settle any lingering doubt about the place of competitions, Cardinal Emmanuel Suhard, in 1943, declared competitions the norm in those Paris churches whose organs are monuments of artistic organ building.[28] He went so far as to define the content of the competitions. Suhard also reminded the clergy of their duty to rely upon experts in the selection of titular organists, and noted that in too many churches the clergy are disconcertingly lax about music for divine worship.

But the regulations came too late to be of any relevance to Duruflé's career. He published no memoirs about the transition at Sainte Clotilde, and we can only surmise how this second reversal might have affected him.

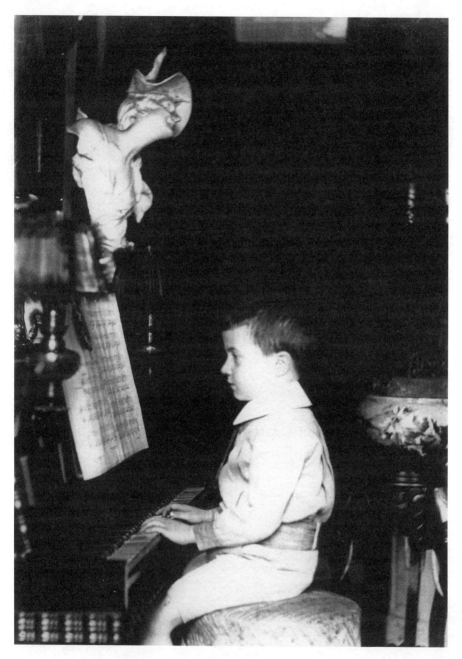

Figure 8.1. Young Maurice at the instrument in his family home. Photograph courtesy of Paul Duruflé.

# Chapter Eight

# *Duruflé's Performing Career*

Duruflé began his career as a touring recitalist at a fairly young age. Among the earliest signs that his career had promise were the recitals he presented in 1923, when he was twenty-one years old, at the cathedral of Saint Pierre in Lisieux, at the college of Saint François de Sales in Évreux (1925), at Notre-Dame in Orbec (1928), and at Saint Taurin in Évreux (1929). In the ensuing years he developed a wide range of professional relationships with his colleagues and with performing organizations in Paris.

On April 20, 1928 he played what can probably be counted his Paris debut recital, at the Institut des jeunes aveugles,[1] in a series of four recitals sponsored between February and May of that year by Les Amis de l'Orgue. Though billed as a private performance for the association, the recital was reviewed in the press. His program featured the premieres of the Molto adagio from Suite No. 35 of Tournemire's *L'Orgue mystique* and the Paraphrase from the third Suite.[2] The review appeared in *Le Courrier musical et théâtral*: "M. Maurice Duruflé proved himself a brilliant and sensitive performer of Frescobaldi, Grigny, J. S. Bach, Franck, Vierne, and Tournemire. He demonstrated the benefits that a strong school education can confer in broadening one's innate gifts of taste and feeling."[3]

His touring assumed a more ambitious scale in 1931, when he toured the south of France, performing on March 3 at the cathedral in Monaco, on March 4 at the cathedral in Nice, and, on March 6 at Sacré-Cœur in Menton. In Nice, and probably in the two other cities as well, he played the *Prélude, adagio et choral varié sur le Veni Creator*.[4] It was surely through Duruflé's friendship with Louis Vierne and Madeleine Richepin that this brief tour was arranged. Richepin's mother had a villa near Menton, on the French Riviera, and Vierne vacationed there.

Among Duruflé's many professional associations, the earliest (apart from Les Amis de l'Orgue) was with the Société nationale de musique, founded in 1871 by Camille Saint-Saëns and Romain Bussine, whose aim was to promote French music. Dubbed "the cradle of the magnificent renewal of our French music," the society routinely extended calls for scores from the composers among its membership, of works that had not already been performed publicly.

On January 12, 1929, the organization played host to the premiere of Duruflé's Opus 3, the *Prélude, récitatif et variations*. Duruflé himself performed for

Figure 8.2. Maurice, age 15, at the Abbey organ, Notre-Dame, Louviers, 1917. Photograph courtesy of Paul Duruflé.

Figure 8.3. Duruflé at his parents' home in Louviers. Photograph courtesy of Paul Duruflé.

the Société twice in the next two years. On May 31, 1930, he played two Franck works in the concert hall of the Hôtel Majestic, and on May 16, 1931, he played his *Prélude, adagio et choral varié sur le Veni Creator* in the Salle de la Société des Concerts at the former Conservatoire.

In December of 1929, Duruflé was elected to membership on the executive committee of the Société, along with Olivier Messiaen, Georges Dandelot, Maurice Emmanuel, and Jacques de la Presle,[5] serving under the presidency of Vincent d'Indy. Among other members of the committee were Nadia Boulanger, Simone Plé, Claude Delvincourt, Jacques Ibert, Paul Le Flem, and Max d'Ollone. In 1933 Duruflé was elected to another term that ended in 1936, when he rotated off with Robert Casadesus and Albert Roussel.[6]

Duruflé participated in a concert performance of fourteen pieces from Tournemire's *L'Orgue mystique*, given on April 25, 1932, at Sainte Clotilde by several young organists, for which he played the Prélude and Fugue from the Suite for the XVe Dimanche après la Pentecôte.[7] The others were Litaize, Langlais, Messiaen, Fleury, and Noëlie Pierront. The reviewer in *Le Ménestrel* was effusive in his praise of their performances, but what particularly pleased him was that *L'Orgue mystique* was attracting the attention of young organists.[8]

Two years later, in 1934—despite their earlier contretemps—Tournemire had regard enough for Duruflé that he dedicated his Suite No. 41 of *L'Orgue mystique* "à mon élève Maurice Duruflé, organiste de Saint Étienne-du-Mont à Paris." Moreover, Duruflé and Tournemire were on the Commission des orgues, they served on several juries together, and in 1926 Tournemire agreed to serve as consultant for the work that Cavaillé-Coll-Convers did on the organ at Duruflé's home church in Louviers. He subsequently shared the bench with Duruflé for the inaugural recital.

Duruflé was occasionally called upon by his colleagues to play the premieres of their new works. He played the first performances of Joseph Ermend-Bonnal's *Symphonie media vita* in 1932, Vierne's Sixth Symphony in 1935, Poulenc's Organ Concerto in 1938, and Charles Koechlin's Three Sonatines for organ in 1939.

Duruflé also had a long association with the mezzo-soprano Hélène Bouvier, who sang the radio and concert premieres of his *Requiem*. She appeared in subsequent performances of the work as well, and was featured on the recording under Duruflé's direction. Bouvier made her Paris Opéra debut in the role of Dalila in 1938, and in fact sang the role for the complete recording of Saint-Saëns's opera *Samson et Dalila*. She also appeared with the orchestras Colonne, Lamoureux, Pasdeloup, and the Société des Concerts du Conservatoire, singing all the great oratorios, including the Passions of Bach and Handel's *Messiah*.

On March 12, 1930, Duruflé was among the distinguished guests attending a festive banquet in honor of the promotion of Louis Vierne to the Legion d'Honneur.[9] The soirée ended at the home of the vice-president of Les Amis de l'Orgue, Comte Christian de Berthier, where Marchal, Duruflé, and Fleury played works by Vierne on his *orgue de salon* by Merklin.[10]

Duruflé had a long and cordial relationship with Les Amis de l'Orgue. He made numerous appearances under their aegis, the earliest being a concert on the salon organ of Berthier in 1938.[11] He made at least ten appearances for the organization between the 1953–54 season and that of 1972–73.[12] He also served on the jury for a number of competitions sponsored by the organization.[13]

On June 3, 1935,[14] Duruflé played the first complete performance in France of Vierne's colossal Sixth Symphony at Notre-Dame, the fifth concert in the 1934–35 season of Les Amis de l'Orgue. Vierne referred to his "joy . . . in the matchless interpretation of my *Sixième Symphonie* played in its entirety by Maurice Duruflé. It was perfection itself, and I was deeply moved."[15]

Composed while Vierne was visiting the villa of Madeleine Richepin's mother, in Cap-Martin on the French Riviera, the manuscript of the work is dated "Roquebrune, 15 juillet–15 septembre 1930." The published edition (Lemoine) is dedicated to New York organist Lynnwood Farnam,[16] "in memory of my much lamented friend," and is dated "Menton, juillet-septembre 1930."[17] Farnam died on November 23, 1930, shortly after Vierne had completed the symphony. Though published in 1931, the work as a whole was not premiered in France until Duruflé played it at Notre-Dame Cathedral in 1935.

Of the Sixth Symphony Bernard Gavoty wrote that Vierne

ponders this work facing the sunny sea, becoming exhilarated from the sea spray of the Mediterranean, then completely full of latinity and of delicate perfume from the pleasant shore, returns to his paper haunted by the play of the waves: still he is careful to keep their iridescent reflection on his work, for he has a horror of imitative music, as is obvious in a letter addressed to [Gavoty] on August 20, 1930: "he who reproduces the noise of the sea for himself is an idiot; he who creates the atmosphere of the sea to serve as a frame for his dream is an artist."[18]

In 1937, the year of Vierne's death, Duruflé wrote that in the Sixth Symphony, "where we feel a soul ravaged by anguish. . . . Louis Vierne left us what was the drama of his life, tormented by moral and physical suffering. In the sublime *Aria* . . . , of a poignant and almost despairing strain, doesn't it seem that the composer sensed his destiny? Moreover, he had a very particular affection for this page."[19]

Carl Weinrich played the work on February 7 and 8, 1932 at the Church of the Holy Communion in New York City, where he succeeded Farnam, and this performance has been incorrectly identified as its world premiere.[20] The North American premiere was actually played by the French organist Mlle Renée Nizan who toured the United States and Canada late in 1931, and gave the premiere of the work in Canada. She was surprised "to find it on all the music racks" of North America.[21] Nizan also played the symphony's Scherzo and the Final at the Trocadéro in 1932.[22]

Duruflé wrote program notes for the work at the bidding of Rollin Smith.[23] The notes constitute a rare glimpse of Duruflé's approach to the genre:

*Symphony VI* (like the second, fourth, and fifth symphonies) is constructed in cyclical form. The same theme, presented under a different rhythmic aspect in each of the five movements gives the symphony a stylistic unity and solid construction so characteristic of the personality of Louis Vierne.

In the initial *Allegro* the chromatic writing, characteristic of the composer, displays his rigor and severity.

With the *Aria* we reach the pinnacle of the work. In this long melody that expands and recurs ceaselessly, the composer confides a secret to us—a rending appeal, a pathetic cry springing from his heart. Perhaps Louis Vierne saw in this page the evocation of the fatal destiny that pursued him throughout his life.

The *Scherzo*, although wishing to jest, neither succeeds in finding a true gaiety nor makes one forget the somber nightmares that haunt the *Aria*. Instead, the composer, with a sparkling verve, depicts the diabolical giggles of grimacing gargoyles.

The *Adagio*: a profound meditation, an eloquent lyricism, a romantic exuberance.

In the *Final*, above a fierce rhythm of timpani played in the pedals, is displayed a scintillating theme in the brilliant tonality of B major. After the agonizing pages that precede [it], one senses the composer's enthusiasm has returned. In the peroration that concludes the *Final*, the cyclical theme is heard a last time.[24]

Vierne gave the autographed manuscript of the Sixth Symphony to Duruflé, whose widow retained the manuscript until seven years after her husband's death. On June 26, 1993, at the urging of Jesse Eschbach, Mme Duruflé gave the manuscript to the department of music of the Bibliothèque nationale, accompanied with this note:

> This Sixth Symphony was offered by Louis Vierne to my husband, Maurice Duruflé, in gratitude for the considerable work that he had done in meticulously correcting the proofs. The registrations and annotations are in the hand of my husband.
> I am happy to make a gift of this work to the Bibliothèque Nationale.

Vierne made the general plan for a seventh organ symphony in C, to be dedicated to Duruflé, but left no sketches.[25]

Duruflé was becoming increasingly well known across the channel, though his reviews were not always favorable. Having first performed in England in 1938, under the aegis of the Organ Music Society, he returned in 1949, for a recital on September 22. Recalling Duruflé's first visit, a reviewer noted that his Bach style was merely workaday, while his presentation of the modern French repertoire was charming.

> Duruflé has a sense of the beautiful in registration, a fine judgment for rhythm and the handling of organ tone . . . , and, unlike many foreign players, he can (usually) remember whether he has left the swell-box open or not. . . . Not only is his organ style [in his own compositions] well-nigh perfect (his spacing of chords is a model, and one regrets only his occasional over-elaboration, which makes some passages almost unplayable on organs different from his); but he shows the real inspiration in long stretches of sustained writing, as in the Prelude on "Veni Creator." He has moreover the rare faculty of making a *whole* work every time, so that even a detached Scherzo appears to us, not as a handful of pretty bits and pieces, but complete, with its individual style consistently carried out, and seen, as it were, in the round.[26]

Duruflé enjoyed a long personal friendship with Henri Doyen, a former *maîtrisien* of the choir school at Notre-Dame, Paris, and subsequently a student of Vierne. A fellow student of Duruflé's at the Conservatoire, Doyen was ordained a priest and served as canon musician at the Soissons cathedral. The Duruflés performed and recorded on the Gonzalez organ at the cathedral, making no secret of their affection for this neoclassic instrument. For a concert in Soissons on June 6, 1964, Duruflé performed, among other pieces, Tournemire's *Triple Choral* ("not heard since the war, it was for many a stunning revelation"[27]).

Duruflé served on many juries, not only at the Paris Conservatoire and for Les Amis de l'Orgue, but also in Haarlem and Munich, where candidates he described as *très intéressants* performed for large enthusiastic audiences. For the Concours international d'orgue of Munich, in 1955, Duruflé served on the jury with Flor Peeters. The Belgian reported that after one of the contestants had played a piece by Max Reger, Duruflé commented that it had *trop de notes* ("too many notes"). When he subsequently noticed that his own Toccata had been programmed by one of the contestants, he told Peeters that it would be best not to ask for that piece because it too had *trop de notes*.[28]

Duruflé was asked by the American Guild of Organists to adjudicate the first-ever competition in improvisation to be sponsored at its national convention in Philadelphia in 1964.[29] Starting in 1966, the Duruflés were invited to participate on juries for the Conservatoire in Nice by its director, Pierre Cochereau.

For master classes in North America, Duruflé agreed to hear performances only of his own works and those of Franck and Vierne, but not those of Bach, Tournemire, or Dupré. The correspondence with his managers provides no insight into his refusal to hear these composers' works. Perhaps he intuited that his own approach to Bach was out of step with current fashion, and unlike so many Americans he probably never had the occasion to study the Dupré works with the composer. But his refusal to hear the works of Tournemire is perplexing, in view of the fact that he studied the *Triple Choral* with the composer, as well as parts of *L'Orgue mystique*, and transcribed his five improvisations.

Duruflé played countless recitals across France, including a number that were inaugural events celebrating new organs or organs newly rebuilt and enlarged. For example, he inaugurated the organs at Pont-Saint-Pierre (1926), Hermival-les-Vaux (1929), Villiers-Bretonneux (1932), Saint Marcel in Laon (1933), Saint Clément in Rouen (1936), and Saint Martin in Liévin (1936). He played inaugural recitals on the newly restored organ by Victor Gonzalez at the Palais de Chaillot in Paris in 1941 and the instrument at the cathedral in Lisieux in 1943.[30] In 1955 he inaugurated the neoclassic organ for the church of Saint Augustin in Deauville.[31] In 1962, he and his wife dedicated the Isnard-Cavaillé-Coll-Boisseau organ of Saint-Salomon-Saint-Grégoire in Pithiviers. In 1966, the couple played the inaugural recital of the restored organ at Valréas. And in June of that year, they inaugurated the restored organ at the cathedral in Angoulême.[32]

Unlike many of his teachers, colleagues, and students, Maurice Duruflé was never a soldier during the Second World War, and he never suffered wounds or participated in the Resistance against the German occupiers. He was mobilized, in 1939, however, to serve in the army post office as organist for the Administration des Postes et Télécommunications et de la Télédiffusion (PTT),[33] which did little to advance his career.

German planes bombed Duruflé's home town on June 10, 12, and 13, 1940. The resulting fires destroyed a good part of the city. Notre-Dame was largely unscathed, but its organ suffered damage.[34] Duruflé served as consultant for the complete restoration of the instrument, and in 1942 he played its inaugural recital, with the assistance of the titular organist, Mlle Simonne Bouvier. The organ builder Joseph Beuchet (diplômé des Maîtres du chant françaises de Paris) participated as a singer.

Duruflé's life was touched directly in several ways by the events of the Liberation. His nephew Paul recounts[35] that in August of 1944 his uncle was arrested for several hours, purportedly for having innocently drawn a crowd by giving a piano lesson that was audible through a window.[35]

On Saturday, August 26, 1944, the day after the liberation of Paris, well over a million people lined the parade route from the Arc de Triomphe to Notre-Dame Cathedral. Though the service at the cathedral was to be a victory *Te Deum*, the church hierarchy had been so discredited by its support of Vichy that General de Gaulle refused to permit Cardinal Suhard to attend.[36] Nor did the cathedral organist, Léonce de Saint-Martin, play for the service. Indeed, he was away from the cathedral for four of the war years, and was reproached for having his photograph taken at the side of some German organists in military uniform.[37] Whatever the reason for Saint-Martin's not having played for the *Te Deum* at Notre-Dame, either because of his personal sympathies[38] or merely because of his association with France's premier cathedral, Duruflé was invited to play the organ instead,[39] implying his political innocence.

But outside the cathedral, the Forces françaises de l'intérieur began firing at the towers. Members of the Jewish platoon concentrated on the north tower, by which access was obtained to the organ tribune. Inside, policemen and soldiers trying to protect de Gaulle shot up into the vaulting of the cathedral, bringing down chunks of masonry. Members of the congregation threw themselves to the floor, or tried to hide behind pillars, or under chairs.[40] Despite the mayhem, De Gaulle walked forward up the aisle to the high altar where the service was to begin. Duruflé, on the other hand, was unable to make his way inside the tower stairs because it was blocked by armed guards.

Not long before the war's end, on February 5, 1945, while he was in the process of composing the *Requiem*, Duruflé's father died in Louviers of the grippe he had caught at the burial of a nephew gunned down during the summer of 1944 by an allied airplane.[41] Duruflé was deeply attached to his father, who was buried in the Louviers cemetery.[42]

After the war had ended, Duruflé wrote a letter to his good friend André Fleury, probably in 1945, describing his work at the Conservatoire, at home, and at the church:

> At the Conservatoire an abundance of candidates in all the classes, probably due to the end of hostilities. There will be few winners . . . but this gives me additional work, and as for me, I realize it is to the detriment of my personal work, which is absolutely non-existent. It is true that in my refrigerator[43] it is totally impossible for me to produce a measure. And then the absence of an instrument at my church hardly stimulates me, and I devote myself especially to my teaching. My class at the Conservatoire interests me very much.[44]

After the war, Duruflé had professional dealings with the dancer and choreographer Janine Solane, whom he first met in 1938.[45] Invited to participate in a recital that he would be playing at the Palais de Chaillot, she choreographed a dance, calling it *Sermon de Fra Savonarole*, composed for a piano piece by Liszt, which she wanted transcribed for the new organ. Duruflé was completely opposed to the adaptation[46] but finally conceded and agreed to play it. As if to atone for what she called her heresy, Solane also choreographed a solo to be danced to Duruflé's performance of the Franck *Pastorale*.

Before she made Duruflé's acquaintance, Solane had choreographed a piece for Bach's "Werde munter, mein Gemüthe" (from Cantata 147) in a piano transcription. She asked Duruflé to play the piece on the organ. As she told it, "His musical honesty could not accept such an arrangement." Urging that it would really not constitute musical treason, she prevailed and he consented. The piece is known as "Jesu, joy of man's desiring" in the English-speaking world.

In 1941 Solane completed her choreography for Bach's "little fugue in G minor for organ [BWV 578]," giving her another opportunity to work with Duruflé. But she wanted to "stretch" the five wonderful chords at the end. "You understand, Mademoiselle," Duruflé said, "the tempo has been set. One can not, all of a sudden, slow it down at the end." She knew he was right, and yet she needed it to slow down. He wouldn't hear of it. "It's very beautiful, Mademoiselle, but it isn't possible." She wasn't sure what happened—perhaps it was the charm of Marie-Madeleine at work on her behalf—but at the last rehearsal he gave her the five chords slower as she wanted them. "How I admire this man!"

Lastly there was the work Solane titled *Saint Sébastien sous les flèches*—Saint Sebastian under the arrows—to be danced to Bach's "Wenn wir in höchsten Nöthen sein."[47] She waxed rhapsodic about Duruflé's performance. "I let myself go, secure about the music he was giving me, emanating from this so-inspired artist, master of his measured touch, completely under the control of an expression as intense as it was intimate, navigating the keys in complicity with the multitude of stops." To have worked with Duruflé—this exceptional being, she called him—was for her a favor from heaven.

In the decade of the 1960s, Duruflé and his wife embarked upon a number of recording projects. Many of them were of considerable magnitude, either by virtue of the number of works to be recorded, or because they involved large orchestras. The list is exhausting.

Duruflé recorded his *Requiem* in 1958, with orchestra. The couple recorded works by Vierne and Tournemire in Soissons and at Saint Étienne-du-Mont, in 1960 and 1961. In 1961 and 1962 they recorded Duruflé's complete organ works on the same two instruments. In 1961, Duruflé was the organist for the recording of the Poulenc Organ Concerto at Saint Étienne-du-Mont. In 1963 he was the organist for Georges Prêtre's recording of the Saint-Saëns *Organ Symphony* at Saint Étienne-du-Mont. In November of that year, the couple began their recordings of the major Bach works at Soissons, to be completed in July 1965. In the same year, Duruflé's four motets were recorded by the Chorale Stéphane Caillat. In 1966 he played the organ for a recording of works for organ and cello with cellist André Navarra. Also in 1966, the Duruflés' joint recital at Saint Thomas Church in New York City was recorded live, and in Saint Louis, Missouri, they recorded for the King of Instruments series of the Aeolian-Skinner Company. In September 1967, they recorded an eclectic repertoire at the National Shrine of the Immaculate Conception, in Washington, DC. In 1968 the Orchestre national recorded the *Trois Danses*. In 1969, Mme Duruflé recorded works by Louis-Claude Daquin and Louis-Nicolas Clérambault at Saint Sauveur, Le Petit-Andely. And in 1971, the Chorale Stéphane Caillat and the Orchestre national recorded the *Messe "Cum jubilo."* Duruflé was the organist for lesser recordings prior to and after the 1960s, but that impressive decade was devoted to all the major recording projects he and Mme Duruflé ever undertook.

Duruflé had many opportunities to accompany or work with the better choral organizations in Paris, including the choir of Saint Eustache, the vocal ensemble of Nadia Boulanger, the boychoir known as Les Petits Chanteurs à la Croix de Bois,[48] the Chorale Philippe Caillard, the Chorale Stéphane Caillat, the Quatuor vocal à camera, the radio choirs, the choir of the Société des Concerts, the Chorale de l'Université de Paris, the Chorale Yvonne Gouverné, the Chorale Élisabeth Brasseur, the Choral Amicitia, La Psallette des Petits Ceciliens, and Les Petits Chanteurs de Versailles.

From this random account of his professional activities outside the church and the Conservatoire, it becomes clear that Duruflé's reputation as a solitary organist, composer and teacher reflects only part of his busy life, another part of which was given to a wide public through a range of concert performances.

# Chapter Nine

# *The Orchestral Musician*

Duruflé had the rare distinction of having performed with the finest orchestras of Paris over a period of many years. His first such experience took place on November 14, 1930, at Salle Pleyel in a performance of *Carnaval* (1892), by Alexander Glazunov, presented by the Orchestre symphonique de Paris with the Russian choirs of Vlassof.[1] Two months later, on January 11, 1931, he played for a performance of *Israel in Egypt* by George Frideric Handel, given by the Concerts Pasdeloup. In the same year he was the organist for a performance with the Symphonie de la Préfecture de Police, given in the Salle of the former Conservatoire.[2] In 1933 he played the organ for performances of the J. S. Bach *Magnificat*, BWV 243, and the *Messe solennelle* of Franz Liszt at the Concerts Pasdeloup. His first appearance as soloist for the Saint-Saëns Symphony No. 3, the *Organ Symphony*, was with the Orchestre symphonique de Paris on February 5, 1933, at the Salle Pleyel, under the direction of Pierre Monteux.

Duruflé was for many years the house organist for the orchestra of the Paris Conservatoire, the Société des Concerts du Conservatoire. The oldest orchestra in Paris, the Société was long considered the best in the city. Duruflé's first season with the orchestra was in 1939–40, succeeding Georges Jacob, and his first appearance was probably on December 4, 1938, when he would have been needed to play *organo ad libitum* for the first French performance of Karol Szymanowski's *Stabat Mater*, and the organ continuo for Bach's Cantata 55: *Nun ist das Heil*, under the direction of Charles Münch. The first time he was featured as a soloist with the Société was during the war, on December 22, 1941, when he played a repeat performance of the Poulenc Organ Concerto, under Münch's direction.

Duruflé and Marguerite Roesgen-Champion played harpsichords for the Société's performance of Bach's *Art of Fugue*, BWV 1080, in 1943, under the direction of Münch. In 1946 at the Palais de Chaillot, Duruflé was organist for the orchestra's performance of the Bach Mass in B Minor, BWV 232, with the Choral Amicitia, conducted by Jean Constantinesco. In 1964 the orchestra recorded the Saint-Saëns Symphony No. 3, with Duruflé as the organist under Georges Prêtre at Saint Étienne-du-Mont. This is the only known recording by the Société des Concerts for which Duruflé was the featured soloist. But he also played the organ part in the orchestra's recording of Honegger's *Une Cantate de Noël*,[3] a rather more interesting score for the organist than that of Saint-Saëns.

In 1952, at the Palais de Chaillot, he was the organist for a recording of Florent Schmitt's *Psaume XLVII,* under conductor Georges Tzipine, with the Chorale Élisabeth Brasseur, and for the 1958 recording at Saint Étienne-du-Mont of the Schmitt *Psaume* and Vierne's three settings of *Angelus.*

The Société played the premiere of Duruflé's *Scherzo,* Op. 8, on November 17, 1940, under the direction of Münch,[4] and repeated the work at the Edinburgh Festival in 1949. In 1944 they played his transcriptions of four Bach chorales, and in 1951 they performed his *Requiem* at the Théâtre des Champs-Élysées, with the Chorale Élisabeth Brasseur, under the direction of André Cluytens.[5]

Among the staples in the orchestra's repertoire, Duruflé, by virtue of his being house organist (and perhaps also harpsichordist and celesta player, as the need dictated), can be assumed to have played for the *Requiem* of Fauré (1939, 1941, 1943, 1944, 1952, 1954, 1958)[6] and for many major works of Bach, including (besides the Mass in B Minor mentioned above) the Magnificat in D (1939, 1941, 1942), the *Christmas Oratorio* (1940, 1945), the *Saint Matthew Passion* (1941, 1944, 1954) and the *Missa Brevis in G* (1956), with many other performances of the *Orchestral Suites* and the *Brandenburg Concertos,* and a number of cantatas. He is likely also to have performed the Beethoven *Missa Solemnis* (1941, 1945, 1950), the Brahms *Ein Deutsches Requiem* (1957), *Le Martyre de Saint Sébastien* of Debussy (1941, 1942, 1944, 1947), *L'Apocalypse selon Saint Jean* of Jean Françaix (1942), Honegger's *La Danse des morts* (1941, 1942)[7] and his *Roi David* (1951, 1955), Monteverdi's *Orfeo* (1941, 1946), the Mozart *Coronation Mass* (1942, 1947, 1951) and the Mozart *Requiem* (1941, 1945, 1946, 1949), Florent Schmitt's *Psaume XLVII* (1941, 1947, 1948), Ottorino Respighi's *Pines of Rome* (1942, 1946), the Schubert Mass in A-flat (1939) and the Mass in G (1941, 1960), *Also sprach Zarathustra* of Richard Strauss (1953, 1959) and the final scene from Strauss's *Salome* (1947).

While the organ parts in many of these works are insignificant—in fact, many are merely incidental, ad libitum, simple basso continuo, or are played on a harmonium—Duruflé's experience as house organist for the Société for so long illustrates the extent to which he was exposed to a wide swath of orchestral literature. But this was not the totality of his orchestral experience. He also had a fruitful relationship with the other fine orchestras in Paris, including the Concerts Colonne. In 1936 Paul Paray conducted both the orchestra's premiere of Duruflé's *Trois Danses* and the first concert performance of the *Requiem,* on December 28, 1947, with the Chorale Yvonne Gouverné and organist Henriette Roget. The orchestra played the *Requiem* again in 1950, with Gaston Poulet conducting and Colette Aymonier the organist.

Duruflé also enjoyed a long relationship with the Orchestre des Concerts Lamoureux, whose regular home was the Salle Pleyel. On March 5, 1938, the orchestra played Duruflé's *Trois Danses* under Eugène Bigot's direction. In 1945 Bigot conducted Lamoureux's premiere of Vierne's *La Ballade du désespéré,* in its orchestration by Duruflé, with soprano Marcelle Bunlet, and in 1949 he also conducted a performance of Duruflé's *Requiem*. Duruflé was the organist, in 1953, for the orchestra's recording of the Fauré *Requiem*, with conductor Jean Fournet. In 1958 Duruflé himself conducted the orchestra in a performance of his own *Requiem*, with Mme Duruflé as the organist. The orchestra's recording of the work, in the same year, also under the composer's baton, won the *Grand Prix du disque* in 1959. And in 1966, Jean-Baptiste Mari conducted the Lamoureux orchestra for the premiere of the *Messe "Cum jubilo,"* with baritone Camille Maurane and the Chorale Stéphane Caillat.

Duruflé also played with the orchestra of the Concerts Pasdeloup, an orchestra established by conductor Jules Pasdeloup to present *musique moderne de l'époque* ("contemporary music"). Pasdeloup played the first performance of Duruflé's orchestration of Vierne's *Soirs étrangers*, Op. 56, in 1944, under the direction of Jean Clergue, with cellist Georges Schwartz. And they performed Duruflé's *Requiem* in 1949, with the Chorale Brasseur.

Duruflé is known to have performed at least once for the Société triton, an organization that lasted from 1932 to 1939. He was organist, in 1937, for a performance of several motets by Florent Schmitt,[8] namely, *Hymne à Saint Nicolas de Lorraine, Ave Regina, De profundis, Virgo gloriosa,* and *Laudate Dominum,* with the Quatuor vocal à camera.[9]

The Orchestre national presented the radio premiere of Duruflé's *Requiem* on November 2, 1947, under the direction of Roger Désormière. In 1951 Duruflé played for that orchestra's performance of Honegger's *Roi David*, under the composer's direction. They also played the premiere of Duruflé's *Andante*, from Opus 8, in 1952, under the direction of Henri Tomasi. In 1968 the orchestra recorded the *Trois Danses*, and in 1971 the *Messe "Cum jubilo,"* issuing them on a single recording, along with the *Quatre Motets*.

Duruflé's long affiliation with superb orchestras sharpened his aptitude for orchestral writing and coloring. It equipped him to compose for the organ and the orchestra with the ear of a seasoned symphonist, an orchestrator who knew well how to match particular timbres to particular musical passages, giving an orchestral character to his works for organ. Duruflé wrote of orchestration that "if the work of composition is often discouraging, here it becomes fascinating. It's only a question of choosing the instruments, of mixing the timbres, of realizing the writing, although this choice had already been sketched in the course of composition. It is a joy of an intellectual order, perhaps, but a real joy."[10]

Duruflé's affection for the orchestra influenced his organ compositions and their registration. In a questionnaire sent to young organists in 1936, he made the following remarks:

> One of the most appealing things about the organ, the most seductive perhaps, is the wealth of its colors and the study of their combinations. The particular pleasure that the organist feels in focusing on registration can alone be compared to that of the

composer before a page of an orchestral score, with the advantage for the former that he can hear it immediately, whether it seems good to him. If the orchestra offers richer expressive qualities and more varied and subtle color combinations, the organ, by contrast, possesses across the expanse of its range an incomparable sonorous equilibrium. In instrumentation the musician must, alas, take into account the technical potential of each instrument; in the organ he possesses each color, from its lowest limit to its highest, with a perfect homogeneity. But let us not press this comparison any further.[11]

In his 1941 comparison of the organ and the orchestra, Duruflé wrote about certain cautions:

One must not be mistaken about [the organ's] true aesthetic. It is compared too often to the orchestra, with which it has only a very distant relationship, simply that of the diversity of timbres. One cannot ask of it a form of sensitivity that it does not have because of the very nature of its sonority. One cannot ask of it too great a quickness of shading, a strengthening of sound on a rhythmic accent or on an expressive note, its expression box being able to give only progressive effects of distance or of connection to a sound that always maintains at its source the same pressure and the same intensity. But to understand and to love the organ, one must appreciate precisely this sound that lasts, which can go on indefinitely, always unchanging; one must like the timbre for itself, stripped of all vibration that would risk impairing any of its beauty; one must like this reserve, this modesty in the expressive tone that finds other ways to express itself.[12]

Duruflé's many transcriptions and reductions attest to the fluidity with which he approached orchestration and registration, organ parts often being transferable to the orchestra, and vice versa, a skill enhanced by his long association with the many fine orchestras of Paris.

# Chapter Ten

# *The Poulenc Organ Concerto*

In 1938 and 1939 Duruflé was the soloist for the two premieres of Francis Poulenc's Concerto for organ. The experience brought him into brief contact with the Princess Edmond de Polignac, one of the greatest music patrons of the time. Moreover, the greater popularity of the concerto on this side of the Atlantic has lent a singular importance to Duruflé's having played the premieres, which one critic described as "one of his most important assignments."[1] But given the rocky course of the concerto's genesis, it is surprising the premieres ever came to pass.

The Princess Edmond de Polignac (1865–1943) was the American heiress to the Singer sewing machine fortune. Born Winnaretta Singer, she had a Paris salon that was the center of artistic and musical life between the wars. She showcased Fauré and Debussy, and commissioned new works from the major composers of her day, including Satie, Ravel,[2] Stravinsky, de Falla, Jean Françaix, Igor Markevitch, and Poulenc. From Poulenc she commissioned two works, the Concerto for two pianos and the Concerto for organ. The princess was herself a pianist and organist, having studied the latter with Eugène Gigout[3] and Nadia Boulanger. Her second husband, Prince Edmond de Polignac, thirty years her senior, was a descendant of the Cardinal Melchior de Polignac.[4]

Beginning in 1933, Nadia Boulanger became the princess's advisor for new commissions and for the concerts presented in her salon. Polignac's commission for an organ concerto was made through Boulanger, in the autumn of 1934,[5] and was originally offered not to Poulenc, but to Jean Françaix.[6] Françaix found himself too busy with other projects[7] and suggested Poulenc, who accepted the commission enthusiastically.[8]

On September 16, 1934, the princess wrote to Poulenc offering him 12,500 francs, half of what he wanted for the commission.[9] In the same month, Boulanger wrote to Poulenc, telling him of her delight about the concerto, hoping to chat with him about "the possibility of writing a work that the princess could eventually play, perhaps with a quartet or piano!"[10]

A month later, in October 1934, Poulenc wrote to the princess's niece, Marie-Blanche de Polignac: "You must already know that I'm writing a concerto for organ and string orchestra for your aunt. I'm amused at the craziness of it and I already have many ideas." Poulenc signed a contract with Durand on October 21, 1935, stipulating that the firm would pay him 4000 francs.[11] His insecurities as a composer were particularly evident in his production of the organ concerto. Unlike some of his other work, which came to him with astonishing rapidity, the organ concerto was more typically laborious for him. His delays in finishing the work presented problems for the Princess Polignac and Boulanger, and caused him no little stress.

The fact that the published score indicates the work was composed in April–August 1938, at Anost, near d'Autun, has been the source of ongoing confusion about the dating of the concerto. The fact is that a first version of the work was nearly finished in 1936.[12] Writing on April 30 of that year, Poulenc explained to Marie-Blanche de Polignac: "The Concerto is nearing the end. It has given me a lot of trouble, but I trust that it is fine as it is and that it will please you. This is not the amusing Poulenc of the Concerto for two pianos but rather a Poulenc on his way to the cloister,[13] very fifteenth-century, if you will."[14]

On June 17, Poulenc wrote to Igor Markevitch, "My Organ Concerto that I'm finishing has cost me a lot of tears because I constructed it with some new materials."[15] In a letter of August 1936 to Marie-Blanche de Polignac, Poulenc wrote that he had been working very hard on his "serious and austere concerto" that was "of a very new trend."[16]

For some reason, Poulenc had second thoughts about the work that he had nearly completed. In September 1936 he wrote to Boulanger, "Here I am . . . searching for the 1/6 of the concerto that was unsuccessful this spring. I hope to obtain it from on high. . . ." He asked when the two of them could meet "to see together the organ of the *Litanies*[17] before the organ of the concerto."[18] In November he wrote to Boulanger and asked her to tell the princess that "the concerto is not a myth, that I'm ashamed, but I won't deliver it to her until it is perfect, with this *imperfect* perfection that is mine."[19] In the same letter he told her, without elaboration, "I leave you complete freedom for the organ part."

Four months later, in March 1937, Poulenc wrote to Suzanne Latarjet that he had finished the concerto. But correspondence on the subject of the concerto virtually ceased for the next fourteen months. Poulenc evidently was not comfortable submitting the work in its present state. Nevertheless, Polignac planned a soiree for January 1938, at which a chamber opera by Françaix and Poulenc's organ concerto would receive their premieres.[20] After a return trip from London, however, the princess fell ill and decided to postpone the soiree until June.

On May 24, Polignac wrote to Poulenc, saying that she wanted to believe the work is finally finished, asking the make-up of the orchestra, and expressing her hope that it be performed on June 20 along with the work of Françaix.[21] In his response to her at the end of May,[22] he wrote that he had never had such difficulty finding his means of expression. He begged her not to program the concerto for the 20th, and this for several reasons: there was barely enough time to copy the material; and changes in the organ part would certainly have to be made, besides the long and delicate process of registering the organ. And, what is of capital importance in a biography of Duruflé, he writes, "It will also be necessary to find an organist and to rehearse it."[23] One month from the projected premiere, and still no decision had been made as to the organ soloist.

Poulenc insisted that Polignac arrange for some string players to read through the work for the two of them and Nadia one afternoon at the end of June, in private. The session would be, as he wrote, "the proof of my success or my mistake."[24] The princess acquiesced, and the concert was rescheduled for June 30, but the delay did not provide sufficient time. Jean Françaix's *Le Diable boiteux*, commissioned by Polignac, received its private premiere on that date, but the organ concerto did not.

Poulenc finally completed the concerto at the end of July 1938 and played the work for the princess in her atelier on August 4.[25] In September he delivered the completed score to her at her residence in Venice.[26] The manuscript bears the inscription: "dedicated very respectfully to the Princess Edmond de Polignac by her faithful musician Francis Poulenc. October 1938."

As early as July, arrangements had been made by Boulanger and Anthony Lewis of the BBC to include the concerto in a concert to be presented by the BBC in London, on November 4, along with the British premiers of Françaix's *Le Diable boiteux* and Stravinsky's "Dumbarton Oaks" Concerto. But "either it was not ready in time or the princess refused to allow its performance since the salon premiere had not yet taken place."[27]

On December 10, 1938, the princess wrote to Poulenc setting dates for the rehearsals and performance: "So it will be Friday—rehearsal Thursday morning with M. Duruflé and rehearsal Friday morning. . . . I am very proud of my concerto."[28] None of the above documents indicates when Duruflé was approached to play the organ part, but this letter suggests that the date of the premiere was not finally settled until the week before.

After the long saga of its composition, the *avant-première* of the concerto, under the direction of Nadia Boulanger, thus took place on December 16, 1938, in the atelier of the Princess Polignac.[29] After a suite by Henry Purcell, a sonata by Bach, and some songs by Poulenc, sung by their dedicatee Marie-Blanche de Polignac, Duruflé played the Cavaillé-Coll organ[30] as the soloist for the grand finale of the evening.[31]

Poulenc's concerto is the only work in the organ repertoire to have had its birth in the Paris salon of Polignac, and it was the last of the pieces commissioned by her. It received little attention at the time. *Le Figaro*, for instance, which often published articles and guest lists for concerts in her salon, made no mention of the performance.[32] But a critique did appear in a special number of *La Revue musicale*,[33] in which the reviewer referred to "an interesting Concerto for organ by Francis Poulenc brilliantly interpreted by M. Maurice Duruflé. We will have the occasion to speak of this work again, when it is given in a public concert, and to praise its high and manly inspiration. Written in a very bare style, it uses technical means issuing directly from the language of J. S. Bach."[34]

Despite his involvement with the concerto, Duruflé never became a part of the princess's circle. She courted composers, not performers,[35] and it is possible she never had any personal contact with him.[36] Duruflé was, in fact, "simply the hired help for the occasion."[37]

One may legitimately wonder whether Boulanger and Polignac ever considered commissioning a work from Duruflé himself. Duruflé's *Trois Danses*, premiered two years earlier,[38] had established his public credentials as a composer to be reckoned with, but he was not among the celebrated composers of the avant-garde.

Duruflé was also the organist for the public premiere of Poulenc's concerto at the Salle Gaveau, which followed the *avant-première* by six months. While practicing in the hall, Duruflé encountered a number of problems with the organ. The work of Charles Mutin of the Cavaillé-Coll firm, he described it as "a rather poor instrument, certainly one unworthy of such a work."[39] In a letter to Poulenc on June 13, a week before the performance, Duruflé wrote:

> The organ needs a serious overhaul. I called on Gonzalez for Thursday 2:30 and M. Bret with him; we will see what can be done. I will work there until 4:30. If you are back in Paris, I would like to have your advice on the registration after Thursday.
>
> For Monday, I'm afraid I can't make our appointment at 5:15, because I will be on the jury for fugue at the Conservatoire at 2:00 and this could end at 4:30 or after 5. With this uncertainty, I wonder if it wouldn't be prudent for us to plan another meeting with you and Désormière to adjust the sonorities. I will be free Monday morning or Saturday all day. Note that I may be at Gaveau at 5:15, but I do not want to risk having you wait.
>
> Since the organ possesses 4 free combinations, just one registrant will suffice. Do you know the name and address of the one who assisted me so well at the Princess Polignac's?[40]

The public premiere of the concerto then took place at a different venue from the *avant-première*, on a different organ, and with a different orchestra and conductor. Roger Désormière conducted the Orchestre symphonique de Paris on June 21, 1939 at a La Sérénade concert in the Salle Gaveau, with Duruflé as organist.[41]

The composer was lauded by a full house, and some music critics acclaimed the work one of Poulenc's most successful.[42] Norbert Dufourcq acknowledged that Duruflé played "with his usual mastery," but gave the work a rather tepid review over all, counting it a fault that the work proceeds without breaks between the sections.[43] In 1970, Harry Halbreich wrote that the first performance was received with indifference.[44]

In July, shortly after the public premiere, Poulenc wrote to Nadia Boulanger comparing the private and the public performances. "Désormière was perfectly correct but you had also the heart and the lyricism, and God knows that my music has need of it."[45]

Poulenc also confessed to some disappointment with the concerto. While his new songs to texts by Apollinaire attained their end, as did the *Quatre Motets pour un temps de pénitence*, he wrote, "The Concerto, on the other hand, was a little disconcerting and boring, let's say the word. The French do not like the organ. This is certain."[46]

Poulenc was asked whether he conceived of the concerto as an instrumental work for the church, in the manner of a concerto da chiesa, or as a concert work, in which "the organ is used only by virtue of its tonal resources, making no allusion to its nature as an ecclesiastical instrument." He replied that "it occupies an important place in my work, in the margin of my religious music. It is not a concerto da chiesa, properly speaking, but by limiting myself in the orchestra, to strings alone and three timpani, I rendered the performance of it possible in the church."[47]

Despite Poulenc's protestations that he did not know organ technique, Duruflé wrote that, in examining the work, he "quickly perceived that [Poulenc] had understood perfectly the essence of the organ and that his writing for this instrument was irreproachable,"[48] a fact that was surely helped by his hearing Marcel Dupré improvise at Saint Sulpice almost every Sunday.[49] Duruflé also commended Poulenc's wise use of the orchestra.

> Few composers before Poulenc had risked writing for organ and orchestra. It is well-known how difficult it is to combine and reconcile the two entities due to . . . their almost incompatible sonorities. The sensitive nervosity of the strings, the poetry of the woodwinds and horns, and the brightness of the brass . . . seem at odds with the mélange of organ sound: cold, distant, inaccessible, an impenetrable realm. . . . The solution was simple and Poulenc understood it intuitively. All the wind instruments of the orchestra were simply suppressed while the organ, wind instrument par excellence of considerable resources, could assume their parts. He conserved the string ensemble, relegating to it all the expressive writing, all the musical sensibility of the score. Likewise, he retained the timpani to insure rhythmic life. . . . From this results an absolutely orchestral writing, of perfect equilibrium, astonishing presence and a resultant sonority of homogeneity, suppleness, diversity, and extraordinary cogency. This method, both new and very personal, is a milestone in organ history, one which several symphonic composers have not hesitated to follow and to master.[50]

Before the score of the concerto was published, by Salabert in 1939, Poulenc asked Duruflé to meet with him at the organ of Saint Étienne-du-Mont to discuss the registrations.[51] Poulenc would describe the kind of sound he was looking for in each section and Duruflé would recommend the stops that would produce the desired effect. Poulenc asked him how to achieve "that sort of tedious drone" that church organs often have.[52] Duruflé wrote:

> At a certain passage of the organ part (page 7) he said to me: "See, here I want a neuter [*sic*] timbre, do you know if this sonority can be expressed on the organ?" I proposed the Fonds 8′. "That's it, that's exactly it," he said, delighted. The Cromorne of page 16 (in the left hand) he accepted with joy. He then gave me numerous indications on the interpretation of his work.[53]

The published score thus acknowledges Duruflé's assistance: "The registration was established with the assistance of Monsieur Maurice Duruflé."

Poulenc sent a copy of the newly published score to Duruflé in November 1939, with the dedication: "For my dear Duruflé with my affection and my gratitude. Fr. Poulenc—1939." Duruflé replied on November 22: "I thank you with all my heart for sending your magnificent concerto, as well as for the kind lines that you added to it. It gives me very great pleasure. When will I have the joy of playing it again? Let's hope this dreadful war will not last!"[54]

In February 1961, Duruflé was organist for the recording of the work[55] at Saint Étienne-du-Mont, with the Orchestre national, Georges Prêtre conducting.[56] To Henri Hell, on March 2, 1961, Poulenc wrote that "Pathé-Marconi professes to be delighted with the recordings. The organ at Saint Étienne is superb and the rehearsal without orchestra was ravishing. It appears that the balance is good. It was difficult."[57]

And in a letter to Pierre Vidal, dated March 15, Poulenc wrote, "The *Gloria* and the new recording (superb) of the Organ Concerto should in theory be out by Easter. You will hear the organ of Saint Étienne-du-Mont under the fingers of Duruflé—it's fantastic!"[58]

Duruflé said that Poulenc was not present at the recording because he was out of the country on tour. He had given his directions to conductor Georges Prêtre, for whom Poulenc professed the deepest esteem, and to whom he entrusted the performance of his orchestral works.[59]

The recording was, as Mme Duruflé recalled, "a great success around the world," and the first to be made on the new organ at Saint Étienne-du-Mont.[60] The disc, according to her, delighted audiences with the sonorities of Duruflé's instrument and the extraordinary acoustics of the church. No one, she said, had heard the sound of "our organ" in other countries.[61]

Poulenc was evidently pleased with Duruflé's performance of his concerto. In fact, Poulenc wrote a letter to Duruflé around Christmas 1962, in which he makes a passing reference to a projected recording of the concerto for the BBC, for which he wanted Duruflé to be the organist. Above all, Poulenc begged to be spared an English organist. "You are *the only one* [emphasis in original] to play according to my heart. Have you heard the recording with Münch? It's good, but it's missing something. It is this something that I would love so much to see you bring to the English, who are too puritan for my music. Try to arrange this."[62]

Though Charles Münch did not conduct the premiere of the concerto, which was Poulenc's original intention, he became one of the work's greatest champions. Münch conducted the third performance of the work, on December 21, 1941, at the Palais de Chaillot, with Duruflé and the Société des Concerts. He gave it another hearing on Chaillot's reconstructed organ during the 1944–45 season, again with Duruflé as the soloist.

Thereafter, however, interest in the concerto waned in France, and in fact was superseded by its popularity in North America. In 1978, Henri Hell wrote:

This concerto has for a long time been a popular work abroad, notably in the United States where it is listed regularly in the programs of the great symphonic associations. In France it is almost unknown. Since the performance conducted by Münch, the concerto for organ has seldom been played. Is this by virtue of the moderate taste of the French for the organ, or rather is it necessary to incriminate the unusual character of this concerto in the work of Poulenc?[63]

Münch went on to conduct the work in New York, on January 25, 1947, with the New York Philharmonic and its organist, Édouard Nies-Berger.[64] But the work had its American premiere, in 1941, at the Germanic Museum on the Harvard University campus in Cambridge, Massachusetts, with organist E. Power Biggs.[65]

# Chapter Eleven

# *Professor of Harmony at the Paris Conservatoire*

Duruflé was affiliated with the Paris Conservatoire, in one capacity or another, for fifty years, beginning in 1920 when he entered the organ class, and ending in 1970 when he resigned as professor of harmony. Even during the hiatus of approximately ten years between his last student exam and the first class he taught in harmony, he served on Conservatoire juries, performed with the Conservatoire orchestra, and was a substitute organ teacher.

Duruflé's earliest experience as a teacher at the Paris Conservatoire was in his unofficial capacity as substitute for Marcel Dupré in the organ class. In 1942 he filled in for Dupré and taught a number of soon-to-be-prominent organists, including Suzanne Chaisemartin, Marie-Claire Alain, Pierre Cochereau, and Marie-Madeleine Chevalier.

In his memoirs Duruflé wrote about his relationship with Dupré. The elder man

> bore an almost familial affection for me, for both of us were Normans. . . . He followed the course of my studies ever since my time at the *maîtrise*. . . .
>
> I did not lose an occasion, of course, to attend all the concerts of this prestigious organist.[1] I would encounter him often in the hallways of the Conservatoire, where he always favored me with a nice smile. One day, in 1942, I believe, he made me an unexpected proposal. "My dear Duruflé," he said to me, "I must soon leave again for the United States for a tour of six months. Would you agree to substitute for me in my organ class during my absence?" I was at once astonished and very flattered. Indeed, I was not his student. I did not feel myself worthy to accept this honor. At his insistence, I had to accept.[2]

Dupré's students particularly enjoyed playing the Franck works for Duruflé because he had studied them with Tournemire, a student of Franck. They studied his own compositions with him as well,[3] and valued the times when he was substituting. Marie-Claire Alain wrote that by accepting their questions and comments Duruflé was less intimidating than Dupré.[4] Whereas Dupré insisted on a rigorous tempo, with little variation allowed in the way of shaping and *rubato*, they appreciated Duruflé's greater flexibility. The ambiance was more relaxed:

they dared risk some musical freedom and could tackle less traditional reper-toire.[5] Duruflé taught his students how to learn.[6]

Duruflé's earliest efforts to join the Conservatoire faculty on an official basis were unsuccessful. He applied for two posts that opened in 1937, but in both instances he lost to other candidates. The first was in April for the position as professor of instrumental solfège, for which Duruflé placed second out of six candidates. The second vacancy was for a professor of vocal solfège, which opened in October. Duruflé placed second among five candidates.[7]

In 1943 the position for a professor of harmony[8] became vacant. Dupré urged Duruflé to apply for the post, and in October of that year he was successful in his bid. He was forty-one, it was wartime, his marriage was in decline, he was working on the *Requiem,* and, given the straits of the French economy, the addi-tional salary was a welcome supplement to his salary at Saint Étienne-du-Mont.

Duruflé had long been drawn to the teaching of harmony. He wrote in his memoirs: "Indeed, I have always taken an avid interest in the teaching of har-mony. This instruction is above all a science, science at the service of music, it goes without saying, but relying on realities, that is to say on some principles of writing that were brought to their perfection by J. S. Bach. This explains, I think, why the teaching of harmony is possible while that of composition is not."[9]

Initially Duruflé taught the *cycle supérieur,* but in 1949 he began teaching a *classe de premier cycle* as well.[10] He taught fourteen hours per week: Tuesday, Thursday, and Saturday afternoons, from 2 o'clock to 6 o'clock p.m., and on Mondays for two hours. He was so often fifteen minutes late for class that his stu-dents dubbed him "quart d'heure Duruflé" ("quarter-hour Duruflé").[11] His class-room was on the third floor of the building, in the Salle Pierné,[12] where his classes had to compete with the sounds of instrumentalists from neighboring rooms. Former students recount that he never looked at his watch while teaching, and often finished more than an hour later than the official quitting time.

Duruflé rode his bicycle to the school, wearing a hat, even during his last year there, when he was sixty-eight years old. He thus presented a picturesque image over the years, with his hat, his black leather briefcase stitched with fine beige thread in his hand, and his pants legs held up with the clips customary at the time, shuffling his bike through the entrance hallway to the courtyard, at the foot of the monument to the dead.

He would greet his students with a powerful handshake and then sit promptly at the piano, with his class seated in a circle around him to study the work set before him. "He played slowly, measure by measure, the homework of a pupil. Sometimes he would call out, 'Oh no . . . not that!' "[13] One day he was reviewing someone's homework that was "marred by a serious gaffe in the writing." Duruflé reportedly took mischievous pleasure in replaying the offending pas-sage before asking the unfortunate composer, "And you find this beautiful?" The pupil, flushed with embarrassment, replied in the negative. Duruflé retorted, "Then why did you write it?"[14] According to one student, Duruflé gave few compliments to his pupils, and sometimes, through a mix of frankness and cautious reserve in his manner of expression, there was an awkwardness in the comments he gave, sometimes discouraging the fragile ego of the student in question.

For the *cycle préparatoire*, Duruflé used Théodore Dubois's *Traité d'harmonie* (1921) and gave his pupils sometimes as many as seventeen exercises that they worked on at home, harmonizing either *chants donnés* or *basses données*. He adhered to the typically French tradition that was observed at the Conservatoire,[15] insisting on a rigorous observance of the rules of technical harmonic writing and urged his students to do their work away from the piano, so as to train their inner ear.

Duruflé's approach to the rudiments of harmony was typical in that it followed the usual procedure of describing the functions of six chords, six-four chords, dominant sevenths, and the like. He conceived the degrees of the scale in three categories, referring to them as good degrees (the tonic, the subdominant and the dominant), normal degrees (the super tonic and the submediant), and bad degrees (the mediant).[16]

For the *cycle supérieur*, Duruflé gave the students two new exercises every week, usually a *basse donnée* and a *chant donné*, taking them from various competitions from the Prix Halphen, from other professors, or even from persons outside the Conservatoire, such as Florent Schmitt, Max d'Ollone, Henri Dutilleux, and Robert Schumann. Only occasionally did he give his students texts of his own writing. In addition to standard exercises, Duruflé had his students harmonize popular melodies to introduce them to the concept of modality.

Duruflé wrote in his memoirs:

> The *chant donné* has always especially attracted me. The search for style, the color of the harmony, the density of the writing, the discipline of the realization, all these problems that present themselves in each of the texts . . . give to this instruction a never-ending variety. The work of realizing the bass, which must develop for the student the sense of thematic construction; the observance of the rules of writing, more strict than in the melody; and finally a certain gift of melodic invention that must manifest itself and that the melody requires to a much lesser extent, all of this reveals a greater or lesser predisposition for composition in the student. . . . This teaching gave me profound joy during my twenty-seven years in this class.[17]

Duruflé's approach in the *cycle supérieure* was to focus on a particular concept, so that one year it was Bach and the next year it was Schumann, perhaps, or Mozart, Chopin, Fauré, Debussy, or Ravel. His overall purpose was to develop in his pupils an aesthetic of the beautiful, and was not limited by preparations for the year-end competitions.[18] Over time, the students absorbed what they called "un style Duruflé": a writing style influenced by the organ; by Bach, Fauré, and Ravel; and by a modal language.[19]

Compared to his teaching of the beginning students, the students in the *cycle supérieur* found "his teaching [to be] more relaxed, adapted to the personality of each student, beginning at the moment when there are no more mistakes."[20] His eschewing of a treatise for his advanced students followed from his belief that the rules of harmony were to be learned from the scores of classical composers. His students knew they were being exposed to a tradition that went back to the teaching of Fauré, and were proud to be a link in that tradition. Marie-Claire Alain, a student in the class from 1944 to 1946,[21] said, "Each time I reread the homework that is in my possession from the class, I admire his knowledge of harmony and of linear counterpoint, inspired by vocal writing. This skill at elegance in its simplicity, present in Fauré's music, we found again in Maurice Duruflé, in his teaching as well as in his compositions."[22]

Daniel Roth had great memories of Duruflé's instruction:

> We worked with him on a *basse donnée* in the style of Bach, a polyphonic exercise as introduction to counterpoint study, and a *chant donné* in the style of the German romantics; above all in the style of Schumann, whom he much honored—likewise with the great French [composers] from Franck to Ravel. Sometimes we remained for many minutes at one measure in order to find a perfect solution for a modulation . . . a good bass voice, a beautiful soprano. . . . He was a terrible perfectionist.[23]

Over one hundred young people studied harmony with Duruflé during his tenure.[24] "The students who left his class to go into the course in counterpoint were renowned as the strongest, as they had the habit of excellent writing."[25] He was as demanding with them as he was with himself,[26] and fulfilled his responsibility to their formation and their preparation for the competitions.[27]

Duruflé stood in defense of his students when he felt they had been treated unfairly by the administration. In 1948 the jury awarded no first prize to the contestants in the women's competition.[28] Duruflé objected that the rules had been administered without considering the circumstances, and that the musical material given them was conceived in other than classical terms: there were changes of meter, tonal ambiguities, and elements from popular traditions, thus contravening the classical formation of the Conservatoire.[29] Duruflé therefore proposed a relaxation of the disciplinary measures that would otherwise have fallen to the women. Giving his assent to Duruflé's proposal, Claude Delvincourt, the director of the Conservatoire, granted the women a year of supplementary studies.

With uncharacteristic boldness, Duruflé on several occasions agitated for changes in grading procedures at the Conservatoire. From as early as 1948 he urged that students be protected from unfairly subjective grading in the competitions, whereby a single member of the jury could, through favoritism, submit a grade that was excessively high (or low). As a result of his protests, the system was reformed so as to reflect more fairly the overall work of the competing students.

When Delvincourt authorized the inclusion of a jazz fragment in the 1951 competition in harmony, Duruflé's response was vehement. He wrote to him, saying that all of the harmony professors objected on the grounds that none of them had prepared their students to harmonize in a jazz style. Duruflé acknowledged that nearly all of his students failed as a result. Duruflé's objection was twofold: he questioned whether it was appropriate for jazz to be introduced into the curriculum of the harmony classes in the first place; but secondly, if it was to be included, he asked to be notified in advance of the coming school year, so that the teachers could prepare their students accordingly.

Duruflé supported the teaching of writing based on the tradition founded by Bach and developed by Debussy (with *Pelléas*), Ravel, Dukas, Stravinsky (with *L'Oiseau de feu* and *Le Sacre du printemps*), and by Messiaen (with his *Préludes* for piano and the *Turangalila Symphony*). These men, Duruflé believed, were not anarchists; they relaxed the rules without breaking them.[30] He opposed the efforts of the avant-garde to depart from the traditional curriculum.

If Duruflé's success as a professor of harmony can be measured by the prizes won by his pupils, his success cannot be denied. Nearly a third of his students, thirty-two of them, were recipients of the *premier prix*, including Marie-Claire Alain, Francis Chapelet, Pierre Cochereau, Xavier Darasse, Jean Guillou, Philippe Lefèbvre, Catherine Meyer, Odile Pierre, Daniel Roth, and Claude Terrasse.[31]

Although he sometimes cited personal reasons for leaving,[32] Duruflé's departure from the Conservatoire in July of 1970 was the result, in part, of his disenchantment with the new directions taken by the Conservatoire in the harmony curriculum. He retired from the post at age sixty-eight, disillusioned with the Conservatoire just as he had become disillusioned with the musical reforms in the church.

## Chapter Twelve

# *Marie-Madeleine Chevalier*

By virtue of their intimate partnership, first of all as husband and wife, but also as musical colleagues, Maurice Duruflé and Marie-Madeleine Chevalier came to be regarded as a single, complementary entity. He provided the music that became her career, and she was his foremost interpreter. The difference that each made to the other was incalculable, such that neither could have made as profound an impact alone, outside of their alliance. This is not to deny the virtues and gifts of each, but merely to assert that by their companionship they constituted a miracle of collaboration. It is impossible to imagine what Duruflé's influence as a composer would have been without his wife, the organist, who gave perfect expression to his compositions, or what Chevalier's career would have been without her privileged access to him, to his organ, and to his music. She taught his private organ pupils before they advanced to study with him. She spoke for him, and, it must be said, she protected him from the public and was a keeper of his secrets.

Jeanne Marie-Madeleine Chevalier was born on May 8, 1921, in Marseilles,[1] on the Mediterranean coast. Her parents, Auguste-Marie Chevalier and Suzanne Chevalier-Rigoir, intended originally to name her Marie-Madeleine Jeanne, but because she was born on the feast of Jeanne d'Arc they decided to reverse the names to Jeanne Marie-Madeleine. She was, nevertheless, always known as Marie-Madeleine.

In 1927, when she was six years old, the Chevaliers, a devout Catholic family of amateur musicians, moved to the small town of Cavaillon, in Provence, where her maternal grandparents lived. Auguste and Suzanne raised their daughters Marie-Madeleine and Éliane in an artistic environment. Mr. Chevalier, in fact, was fond of Gregorian chant and Renaissance polyphony.

When she was six years old Marie-Madeleine began studying piano with her grandmother, Claire Rigoir. Mme Rigoir took note of her prodigy's "natural virtuosity, memory, perfect pitch, and her facility with sight-reading." Her charge would play in minor keys pieces that were in the major, finding that "it is nicer this way." She would cross hands, playing the bass part with the right hand, and the treble with the left.

At age seven Marie-Madeleine was playing extracts from the sonatas of Mozart and Beethoven, and began writing her first pieces for piano. Some of her compositions were influenced by the pieces she was playing on the piano, such as

Marie · Madeleine Duruflé

Beethoven's *Marche funèbre*. At age eight she was accompanying local instrumentalists. By age nine she was also writing works for the organ.

In October 1931, when Marie-Madeleine was ten years old, the Chevalier family moved to Paris and stayed for eight months, giving their daughter access to excellent teachers. There she studied Bach, Debussy, and Ravel with the pianist Marie Dhéré,[2] who prepared students for entrance into the piano class at the Conservatoire. Dhéré sent the young prodigy to Mme Samuel-Rousseau, who taught the solfège class at the Conservatoire, where Marie-Madeleine studied with her *hors-concours* (i.e., as a special student). Mme Samuel-Rousseau often took her to her husband's harmony classes.

Chevalier was also introduced to Jacques Ibert, for whom she played some of her own compositions and some by him. Ibert, who was director of the Villa Medici in Rome, said to her, "Like me, you will be a Prix de Rome."[3]

Marie Dhéré took Marie-Madeleine to attend the annual mass organized at the Église de la Trinité by Nadia Boulanger in memory of her younger sister Lili. Olivier Messiaen was the newly appointed titular organist at Trinité, and it is likely that the impressionable ten-year old heard his improvisations at that mass. After the service, Marie-Madeleine composed a *Pièce d'orgue* (April 1932), called such by her mother, though the piece is for piano, along with another piano piece, *Sérénité*, which is dated May 8, 1932 (her eleventh birthday).

Because of the worsening economic climate, Marie-Madeleine's father lost his job, forcing the family to return to Cavaillon in 1932, and giving the young girl the occasion to compose *Le Retour au mas* (June 1932). Soon thereafter the curé of the cathedral of Saint Véran, in Cavaillon, asked Marie-Madeleine to play the organ for a wedding. Several months later, he named the eleven-year-old the titular organist at the cathedral, whose instrument dated from the seventeenth century.[4] She later confessed:

> Do I dare mention one indiscretion that my eleven years will surely excuse? At the time I knew nothing about organ music or the conduct of the service. Apart from my improvisations, the *Well-Tempered Clavier* formed the basis of my repertoire. I gradually discovered the compositions proper to our instrument[5] and threw myself thoroughly into methodical work. My parents took turns tirelessly at the levers for the bellows, the instrument not then being supplied with electric winding.[6]

Marie-Madeleine's prowess began to be known throughout the region. For a piano recital on June 28, 1933, at the Palace-Théâtre in Cavaillon, when she was twelve years old, she played two of her own pieces, along with a *Fantaisie* and an *Impromptu* of Chopin, and *Giddy Girl* of Jacques Ibert.

At age twelve she began studying in nearby Avignon with the piano teacher Mme Nourrit, who gave her advice about technique, taught her about sonority and touch, and imparted a warmth of interpretation kept in check until then by her natural reserve. Even after she became a well-known organist, Marie-Madeleine said that Marie Dhéré and Mme Nourrit taught her everything she needed to know for her career.

Mme Nourrit urged Marie-Madeleine to study at the Conservatoire d'Avignon, which she did from 1933 to 1935.[7] In only one year, when she was thirteen, she won the *premiers prix* in solfège and piano. In the following year she received the *premier prix* in harmony, having studied the subject with Édouard Charles.

In 1938, the seventeen-year-old Chevalier met Marcel Dupré for the first time, an event of seminal importance in her life, as it opened opportunities that would transform her future as an organist. Dupré played a recital at the church of Saint Agricol in Avignon, attended by Marie-Madeleine. Édouard Charles presented her to Dupré, who agreed to meet with her. Dupré told her, "You will enter my class in October and will have your *prix d'orgue* at age 20." At the end of their brief conversation, Dupré said to her, "Write to me and I will meet with you at my home in Meudon after my long trip to America, in May 1939."[8]

The date for their meeting in Meudon, on the outskirts of Paris, was set for May 10, 1939. Accompanied by her mother, the young Marie-Madeleine was greeted with a simplicity that the Chevaliers found astonishing for so great a personage as Dupré. The maître subjected her to a thorough examination, including ear training, piano, sight-reading, the harmonization of a Bach choral, and the accompaniment of some Gregorian chant.[9]

But because of the approaching war, the prodigy was unable to relocate to the capital. She spent all the war years in virtual isolation in Cavaillon, waiting and tutoring herself in music. Musicians who were displaced by the war occasionally visited the Chevalier home. Marie-Madeleine would sight-read the accompaniments for some of these excellent musicians. Though the Chevalier home was not heated, and though she had chilblains, with her skin cracked from the cold, she played great piano music for hours into the evening, from memory in the dark, often wearing gloves. Or she and her sister would lock themselves in the church, making music until curfew, and then rush home, fearful of the patrols.

Increasingly well known around Provence, Mlle Chevalier, when she was about fourteen, began teaching piano, solfège, and organ, "bitterly resigned to being a piano teacher in a small provincial town. But she nevertheless practiced the organ diligently."[10] Her sister Éliane conducted the Choral Saint-Véran at the cathedral in Cavaillon, which occasionally presented public concerts featuring repertoire by Franck, Debussy, and Handel, for which Marie-Madeleine was the accompanist.

In 1945, when the war ended, Mlle Chevalier moved to Paris by herself, this time to stay.[11] After renewing her acquaintance with Dupré, she sent a postcard to her family back home, writing, "Marvelous interview surpassing all my hopes. Marcel Dupré more charming, more kind than ever, kept me almost two hours. He found me to be making very, very great progress. He had the most fatherly, complimentary, thoughtful, and courteous words that you could dream about . . ."[12]

For her first year of private study, Dupré entrusted her to his student Jeanne Demessieux,[13] the composer and organist of prodigious and legendary talent, with whom she also studied counterpoint and fugue.[14] The brilliant attacks and releases at the organ, especially the *deuxième mouvement* of the finger on release, were taught to Marie-Madeleine by Demessieux, who first brought it to her attention in the Toccata in F, BWV 540, of Bach.[15] Some years after Demessieux died, Mme Duruflé wrote a brief evocation of her former teacher, saying that

> despite her slender appearance, she possessed a strength of character that was out of the ordinary.
>
> Gifted with an unparalleled organ technique, she could play from memory, without apparent effort, the entire classical organ repertoire and a great part of the contemporary.
>
> Even with her high heels, she had a prodigious pedal virtuosity; this almost without moving.[16]

At the same time as her studies with Demessieux, Mlle Chevalier took a *petit cours* at Dupré's home in Meudon, with several other students. She heard his masterly performances and observed his brilliant technique, his skillful improvisations, and his posture at the organ. He was demanding but kind, always encouraging and full of humor.[17]

After completing the private preparatory course, she passed the exam for Dupré's organ class at the Paris Conservatoire, on January 15, 1947. Dupré described her as an "excellent student—great musical facility."[18] When Dupré was away on tour during the 1947–48 academic year, Maurice Duruflé substituted for him. In 1947, he took Mlle Chevalier on as his assistant at Saint Étienne-du-Mont, the same year his *Requiem* had its premiere, and the same year he divorced Lucette Bousquet. On May 6, 1947, Mlle Chevalier was awarded the *premier accessit* in the organ competition.

In 1949 Duruflé was again supplying for Dupré's organ class,[19] when he wrote these evaluations of Chevalier:

> *Notes of Duruflé, January '49*
> *Chevalier an excellent student*
> *A very hard-working musician*
> *Has made remarkable progress*

In May of that year he provided the following notes:

> *Notes class May '49*
> *Chevalier*
> *Remarkable student. Gentle*
> *Very responsible*
> *Constant progress*

On June 4, 1949, Mlle Chevalier won the *premier prix* in the organ competition, along with three other students: Françoise Renet, Jean Costa, and Jean Bonfils. It was the first time in the history of the Conservatoire that *premiers prix* were awarded to four contestants.[20] She was commended not only for her interpretation of the repertoire, but for "a feat that only Olivier Messiaen accomplished several years before, 'the great mélange,' counterpoint of the greatest complexity, improvised in her paraphrase of the Gregorian."[21]

Only a few months before her death, Mme Duruflé compared Dupré's style of teaching with that of her future husband, saying that

> Maurice Duruflé had a musical uniqueness which we liked to take advantage of. Indeed, when we wanted to play Franck, Dupré did not say much to us, not liking that we added anything to it. He did not like people who did too much with it. M. Duruflé was extremely good to make us play this music. There was a direct line between him and Franck that passed through Tournemire. This interested us very much. It was interesting for us to have two professors with very different conceptions and personalities. . . .
>
> It can be said that Duruflé had an absolutely perfect technique. The difference from Dupré is that, always under the influence of Franck, [Duruflé] had a very great freedom of interpretation.[22]

Mme Duruflé once told of an experience she and her sister Éliane had with Duruflé in 1945,[23] before she entered the Conservatoire.[24] Duruflé invited them to go with him to hear his brilliant harmony student Pierre Cochereau[25] improvise at the church of Saint Roch, where he was the organist. Mme Duruflé-Chevalier remembered that ". . . we had spent an unforgettable evening, in the half-light of the church, listening to these waves of extraordinary music falling from the vaults."[26]

In 1949, Mlle Chevalier began substituting for Marcel Dupré at Saint Sulpice, while she was still assisting Duruflé at Saint Étienne-du-Mont. From time to time, she also substituted for Paul Lecourt at Saint Bernard-de-la-chapelle,[27] for André Fleury at Saint Augustin, for Gaston Litaize at Saint François-Xavier, for Rolande Falcinelli at Sacré-Cœur, for Jeanne Demessieux at Saint Esprit, as well as at the churches of Saint Jean-Baptiste in Grenelle and Saint Pierre in Neuilly. She also returned to Cavaillon occasionally to play recitals, as she did in 1951, and for two concerts following the restoration of the Cavaillon cathedral organ under her husband's consultation.[28]

Shortly before her marriage to Duruflé, in 1953, Mlle Chevalier participated in the prestigious Premier concours international Charles-Marie Widor at the Festival de Lyon-Charbonnières,[29] competing for the Charles-Marie Widor award[30] in organ performance and improvisation. The competition was established by the eminent pianist Ennemond Trillat, director of the Conservatoire de Lyon, who was a friend of Widor.[31]

The competition took place at the Lyon Conservatoire, where the contestants were required to play from memory a program from the works of Bach, Franck, Widor, and a modern composer, and to pass several rounds of improvisation. The elimination round involved the performance of one of the pieces from the program and an improvisation on a *thème libre*. For the final round, the contestants had to play their complete program and improvise a fugue and an *Allegro symphonique* on two themes by Marcel Dupré. There were six finalists: Marie-Claire Alain, Janine Corajod, Bernard Havel, Xavier Dufresse, Norman Proulx, and Mlle Chevalier. The first prize of 400,000 francs went to Chevalier, who later repeated her program for the public, including the improvisations.[32]

For a number of years, Chevalier had known Duruflé only professionally and they had never courted, so it came as a complete surprise to her when he proposed marriage.[33] She went sleepless for three nights, during which time she came up with three questions for him, on whose answers her response would hinge. The first was this: Will you let me practice my religion (and go to Mass as frequently) as I wish? Second: Will you respect my political opinions? And third: Do you like animals, and cats in particular?[34] Chevalier expected a definite Yes to all three questions before she would consent to marriage. Evidently his answers met her expectations.

But the church's annulment of Duruflé's marriage to Lucette Bousquet was another necessary condition before their own marriage could take place. Mlle Chevalier's Catholic piety would never countenance her marrying a man who was still married in the eyes of the church. But the annulment took a number of years to process, because the Vatican was inundated with the task of settling the marital status of hundreds of couples whose men had not returned from the war.[35] The delayed annulment of Duruflé's first marriage, confirmed by the Vatican on June 23, 1953, exactly six years after the civil divorce, was thus responsible for the delay of their marriage.

On September 12, 1953, the couple were wed in a civil ceremony in the 18th arrondissement, where she was living at the time.[36] He was fifty-one years old and she was thirty-two. A religious ceremony followed on September 15 at Saint Étienne-du-Mont, for which Marcel Dupré was the organist.[37] The couple's desire for children would remain unfulfilled.[38]

During the period of their engagement, Chevalier was contacted by some prospective American sponsors who invited her to play in the United States. She declined, saying she was engaged and could not travel.[39] If she had consented, her American debut would have occurred a decade before it eventually took place, in 1964.

Her first joint recital with her husband took place at the Église du Cœur Eucharistique in Paris, with baritone Camille Maurane, in December 1953, only three months after their marriage.[40] They appeared in countless joint recitals thereafter. Mme Duruflé also played solo recitals in Paris as in the provinces

(Saint-Rémy-de-Provence, Cavaillon, Avignon, Carpentras, Vire, Mende, Lyons, Senlis, Bordeaux, Marseilles, and Belfort).

Mme Duruflé's musical tastes were similar to her husband's. Sharing his predilection for the neoclassic style of organ design, Mme Duruflé was, as she wrote, "a generous eclectic, welcoming every pursuit of the beautiful in all its fullness, whatever the ideal may be. I acknowledge an equal admiration for Cavaillé-Coll and Gonzalez, without preferring Notre-Dame and Saint Sulpice to Saint Merry and Saint Eustache."[41] But she renounced electronic organs as ridiculous forgeries.

She played a vast repertoire, from the piano works of Chopin, Mozart, Debussy, and Ravel, to organ works of all periods. But she acknowledged a particular passion for the great romantics, including especially Liszt and Franck. Among the more modern composers, she was fond of Vierne, Dupré, Ibert, and of course, the works of her husband. Only for atonal and serial music did she confess an abhorrence.

In 1959 Mme Duruflé composed *Six Fables de La Fontaine* for unaccompanied women's choir in two or three parts, dedicating them "à ma sœur Éliane Chevalier," who commissioned the work. Published by Durand in 1962, the six fables[42] attest to the composer's fondness for animals. They are entitled:

> *La Grenouille qui veut se faire aussi grosse que le boeuf* (*The Frog That Wants to Make Himself as Big as the Ox*; two-part)
> *Le Coq et la perle* (*The Rooster and the Pearl*; three-part)
> *Le Renard et les raisins* (*The Fox and the Grapes*; two-part)
> *Le Loup et l'agneau* (*The Wolf and the Lamb*; three-part)
> *La Cigale et la fourmi* (*The Cicada and the Ant*; three-part)
> *Le Corbeau et le renard* (*The Crow and the Fox*; three-part)

She actually composed the set for her sister's children's choirs at the Lycée Colbert, where she taught music.[43] Its first professional performance was given on May 20, 1964, in the auditorium of the ORTF by the Maîtrise of ORTF, under the direction of Jacques Besson.[44]

On May 7, 1971, Mme Duruflé had the privilege of playing for the concert to honor Dupré presented at Saint Sulpice by his faithful friends and former pupils, which included a performance by the parish choir of Dupré's *De profundis*. Olivier Messiaen attended the program, and wrote that the ceremony

> was so beautiful. . . . After the performance of one of his greatest works for choir and organ, each former pupil of Marcel Dupré, from the very earliest to the very latest, came to speak a text of homage to his master. All the testimonials concurred in deepest esteem, in truest affection. It was like the granting of some celestial *premier prix*.
> No one thought that twenty-three days later he would leave us so abruptly.[45]

Mme Duruflé was as troubled by the musical implications of the Second Vatican Council as was her husband. She addressed the subject of innovations in the liturgy four years before the document on the sacred liturgy was promulgated by the council:

> Permit me to say that I remain attached to the observance of the strictest tradition and that certain novelties recently inaugurated in the matter of liturgy seem perfectly incomprehensible to me. A mass completely sung or recited in French makes me suffer, and the use of the vernacular seems contrary to the Dogma of the Universality of the Church. On this point we owe fidelity to the *Motu proprio* of Saint Pius X.[46]

Although she most often played the choir organ for high mass, which allowed her to hear her husband improvise, at the *grand orgue* she customarily played a written piece for the offertory, an improvisation during communion, and a free development for the *sortie* (based on the "Ite missa est,"[47] for example).[48] Mme Duruflé understood her duty as a church organist to be a servant role: to comment upon the progress of the liturgy, providing what she called "musical incense."

Her devotion as a Roman Catholic was widely known. She recited the rosary frequently, even on tour, finding the meditative state restful.[49] She attended mass almost daily in Paris, where she usually went to the evening weekday liturgy. She read the writings of Dom Guéranger, the *Histoire d'une âme*, and the lives of the saints. After her death, this prayer, written in her hand, was found between the pages of her copy of Thomas à Kempis's *The Imitation of Christ*: "Lord! I am going to sleep (to work, to rest . . .) but my soul keeps you company. Its activity will rest (or will apply itself) during this work (sleep, rest . . .) but all my powers will remain under your estate, and my heart will keep you as its most steadfast and tender love."[50]

On May 29, 1975, the couple were returning to Paris from their vacation home in Ménerbes, driving in heavy rain on a highway in Livron, just south of Valence, when they were hit by an intoxicated driver in a Mercedes taking a curve from the opposite direction at 150 km per hour. He lost control of his car, crossed the median, crashed into the Duruflés' Renault 4L, and was killed upon impact. Maurice and Marie-Madeleine were critically injured, he being thrown from the car onto the highway with both legs broken, and she sustaining serious breaks to the shoulder, pelvis, and ribs, with wounds to her scalp.[51] They were rushed to a hospital in Valence for emergency surgery, but it was not equipped to treat them adequately. Mme Duruflé said later that her husband suffered so much pain that "it would have been better if he had died in the accident."[52]

Several hours after the accident, Marie-Madeleine's sister Éliane consulted with surgeons and physicians of their acquaintance, in Paris, who had them transported to the capital by ambulance. There the renowned surgeon Robert

Judet performed surgery on both of them. It is thanks to him that Duruflé did not lose his legs, because physicians in Valence had proposed amputation.[53]

The couple were then taken to a convalescent facility on the Norman coast, Le Centre de rééducation et de réadaptation fonctionnelles, situated in Granville. In this seaside haven, a popular tourist resort located on the rocky promontory that forms the bay of Mont Saint-Michel, the Duruflés spent the next ten months, receiving thalassotherapy[54] and recovering from their injuries. Marie-Madeleine underwent two operations, one on her shoulder, and another on her hip, in September and November of 1975. At the end of March 1976, the couple returned to Paris,[55] having already spent about seven million francs for the operations, the clinic, and the ambulances.[56]

During the Duruflés' absence from Paris, they were replaced in their duties at Saint Étienne-du-Mont by the American-born Sarah Terwilleger Soularue.[57] But on March 22, Mme Duruflé was approached by some Americans who told her that there was no organist to play for mass and urged her to play. Unsure as to whether she could still do so, it took her a half hour to negotiate the staircase to the organ loft. Finding it a miracle that her hands could do the work,[58] she thus resumed her regular Sunday morning duties, playing for the 9:30 and 11 o'clock masses,[59] where the congregation could "still hear some of the most extraordinary organ playing in the world." Her student Dennis Keene described what he heard during her improvised toccatas for the *sortie*:

> The astonishing fire and passion she displays each week during these postludes always attracts a large group of amazed listeners under the organ case. . . . The playing exhibited all the trademarks of her career: the legendary technique, the clarity of attack and release (!), the exceptional sense of rhythm, the disciplined, profound musicality, and, above all, that remarkable "internal flame" so well known by her audiences.[60]

Mme Duruflé resumed limited local concertizing in the spring of 1976,[61] and she and her husband were well enough to take a vacation that year.[62] As early as 1977, she had resumed teaching at home. Among her students, in the winter of 1977, was Mr. Keene, who wrote, "Mme Duruflé would help her husband into the kitchen, where he would listen to my lessons. Later she would pass on his comments."[63] In May of that year, the couple played for a recital at Saint Étienne-du-Mont in observance of the fiftieth anniversary of the founding of Les Amis de l'Orgue, and in May 1979 they played a recital jointly in Granville.[64]

Duruflé also resumed some limited teaching. His American student Rodger Vine, who had studied with him before the accident, returned afterward for some lessons in September 1978. Duruflé walked normally, as if there had never been an accident, despite the continuing pain in his legs. Moreover, his spirits were higher than before the accident.[65]

From another perspective, his former student Dorothy de Roij observed that "Duruflé, who in any case was already a very quiet person, was even more shy after the terrible accident. And one saw him scarcely at all. As I visited him once in Paris, he did not allow it to be seen how badly it was going for him. He held his composure."[66]

The couple both required additional surgery. By January 1978 Duruflé had had surgery seven times and his wife was about to undergo her sixth operation.[67] She had further surgery in February 1979,[68] and again in the summer of 1994, when she had two operations on her left shoulder.[69] She would require still further surgery in the coming years. Despite her own compromised health, Mme Duruflé devoted her time and solicitude to her husband's care throughout the eleven years left to him after the accident. In this she had the devoted support of her sister.

The couple's injuries were often underestimated. Their friends and devotees in North America began inquiring about future tours not long after the accident, evidently unaware of the extent of their injuries. In September of 1977, Karen McFarlane wrote to them suggesting a tour in 1979 or 1980. Frederick Swann asked that their first concert, whenever it should be, take place at the Riverside Church in New York. McFarlane consented to his request,[70] and on October 24 the Duruflés themselves consented as well, though they could not predict when they would be able to travel. Duruflé himself never crossed the Atlantic again.

Mme Duruflé's health was a continuing source of concern for her. In April of 1986, two months before her husband died, she wrote to Karen McFarlane: "I am overwhelmed with worry and work. My life is hard and difficult. My husband, so infirm, [can] no longer walk or do anything, nor any longer sign [his name]. As for me, some days after your trip in June [to Paris] I began to suffer intensely from sciatica. This makes ten months, then, that it has persecuted me."[71] After her husband died, she wrote to McFarlane:

> I have the consolation of having obtained for my husband, so cruelly afflicted, the gentlest life possible, as was his custom, keeping him at home, caring for him myself, at the cost of very great effort. I lifted him, I supported him when he was collapsing, I hardly slept for four years.
>
> He was wonderfully patient and kind, but a little unaware in my regard. He didn't realize that I was suffering a great deal too. I watched him waste away little by little, all his faculties failing; it was dramatic. However, I tried to maintain my serenity, and even my cheerfulness, happy when I saw him smile. . . .
>
> But I sensed that I was "falling apart." I suffer so much that it is sometimes very difficult for me to put my foot on the ground. The lower part of my spinal column is damaged, my hips arthritic.[72]

Five months after her husband's death, Karen McFarlane wrote to Mme Duruflé informing her that the committee planning the 1988 Houston convention of the American Guild of Organists had extended an invitation for her to perform.[73] Mme Duruflé told McFarlane she would have to have surgery for a prosthesis, and wrote, "How can I know in what physical state I will be in June '88? How can I take it on, at the risk of going back on my word at the last minute? No, I can't do it!"[74]

Early in 1987, the same year she was named Officier des arts et lettres by the Ministère de la culture, Mme Duruflé was on antibiotics and was still in need of a prosthesis for her left hip, suffering so much, she wrote, that she was unable to leave her apartment.[75] Her father died in the following year.

A considerable improvement in her health enabled her, between 1989 and 1994, to accept concerts in Paris, where she performed at Notre-Dame, Saint Eustache, the American Cathedral, Saint Étienne-du-Mont, and at the theater organ of the Gaumont Palace at the Pavillon Baltard, a nineteenth-century exhibition hall and theater just east of the Bois de Vincennes.[76] She also appeared in the provincial cities of Toulouse, Nîmes, and Pont-l'Abbé (where she made a recording).[77]

Mme Duruflé wrote a letter to Karen McFarlane, on May 27, 1989, announcing her intention of accepting three major engagements in the United States, her first since 1974. First, she accepted Dennis Keene's invitation to participate in a festival tribute to her husband, from November 12 to 19, 1989, in New York City. Secondly, she agreed to play for the June 1990 national convention of the American Guild of Organists in Boston. And, finally, she accepted Jesse Eschbach's proposal for her to be artist-in-residence at the University of North Texas.

The Tribute to Duruflé, in New York, was the first retrospective anywhere of Duruflé's complete œuvre, including the chamber, orchestral, choral, piano, and organ works,[78] presented at the Church of the Ascension, the Manhattan School of Music, and the Riverside Church. At the latter venue, Mme Duruflé performed the complete *Prélude, adagio et choral varié sur le Veni Creator*,[79] the *Scherzo*, and the *Prélude et fugue sur le nom d'ALAIN*. The Ascension choir and the men from Riverside performed the choral works. The Manhattan Symphony performed the orchestral works, under the direction of Ransom Wilson. The pianist couple Rémy Loumbrozo and Arianna Goldina played the then unpublished version of *Tambourin* for one piano, four hands. And McNeil Robinson and John Walker performed the organ works not played by Mme Duruflé herself.[80]

Regarding the national convention of the American Guild of Organists to be held in Boston, in 1990, Karen McFarlane told Mme Duruflé that the committee planned their program believing she would not be able to come. But William Self, who had nothing to do with the convention and had no authorization to do so, invited her to participate. The committee was, of course, delighted with the turn of events.[81]

She opened her sixty-minute recital at Trinity Church, Copley Square, with J. S. Bach's *O Mensch, bewein' dein' Sünde gross,* BWV 622, then played works by Buxtehude, Franck, Dupré, Tournemire, and the *Prélude* from her husband's *Suite,* Op. 5, and the *Prélude et fugue sur le nom d'ALAIN.* In a review of this recital, the Boston *Globe* reported that "the bold authority in her playing is matched by fantasy, color, imagination and humility . . . an inspiring demonstration of what still is possible anymore when great gifts are matched by equal dedication."[82]

Her performance at the convention was the centerpiece for a short tour. Arriving in Washington, DC, on June 6, she appeared first at National City Christian Church, then in Burlington, North Carolina, and then she flew to Boston for her two (identical) recitals at the convention. After the convention she appeared at First Methodist Church in Evanston, outside Chicago. All of the sponsors requested an improvisation, and she agreed to improvise if the audiences requested an encore. Her hosts were advised that she still could not walk even moderate distances, making wheelchairs necessary at the airports. The concerts were generously spaced over a period of nearly a month, designed thus to avoid unnecessary fatigue. She returned to Paris on July 2.

For her residency as visiting artist at the University of North Texas, during the spring semester of 1992, the terms specified weekly one-hour lessons for ten private students, three public master classes, and one faculty recital, in return for which she would receive $20,000. Mme Duruflé played her recital and the second of her master classes in conjunction with the school's fourth organ conference, on February 26–29, 1992, which was entitled "The Rise of Neo-Classicism— Its Impact on Organ Literature and Organ Building in Paris of the 1930s." Her recital and the master class featured works by Dupré, Tournemire, Vierne, and her husband.

Mme Duruflé also accepted sixteen engagements between March 6 and June 21,[83] appearing in the following places: Houston; Wichita State University; Corpus Christi and Galveston, Texas; Duluth, Minnesota; Texas Christian University in Fort Worth; Lincoln, Nebraska; Prairie Village, Kansas; the Crystal Cathedral in Garden Grove, California; Saint Paul's Roman Catholic Cathedral in Saint Paul, Minnesota; Shadyside Presbyterian Church in Pittsburgh; Haddonfield, New Jersey; Lancaster, Pennsylvania; the Cathedral of Mary Our Queen in Baltimore; New Britain, Connecticut; and Denton, Texas.[84]

For her visit at the Crystal Cathedral, Frederick Swann, the church's organist,[85] arranged for a recorded interview with the church's pastor, Dr. Robert Schuller. When Swann

told her that Dr. Schuller wanted to interview her, and gave her some possible questions, she teased me with "wicked" (her term) answers that she intended to give. When the interview happened, she was, of course, the perfect model of a sincere Catholic lady and spoke in hushed tones. At one point where she thought the camera was not on her, she turned and winked at me—but the camera caught her. It was edited out before appearing on TV.[86]

For the American tour that proved to be her last, Mme Duruflé returned to North America in the fall of 1993, for appearances from October 3 through November 21, in Stamford, Connecticut; Worcester, Massachusetts; the University of Michigan; Akron, Ohio; River Forest, Illinois; Interlochen, Michigan; the Cleveland Museum of Art; Cincinnati, Ohio; Winnipeg, Manitoba; San Antonio and Lubbock, Texas; Spelman College in Atlanta, Georgia; Burlington, North Carolina; Sarasota, Florida; and New York City. Her last Canadian recital was at Westminster United Church in Winnipeg, on October 31, 1993, and her last in the United States was at the Church of the Ascension in New York City, on November 21, 1993.

Mme Duruflé continued to be in demand by audiences and schools in North America after her 1993 tour, and she expressed some interest in returning in 1994 or 1995,[87] but these trips were not to be. Early in 1994, Thomas Murray, in his capacity as organist on the faculty of the Yale Institute of Sacred Music, inquired whether she would be available to spend a week at Yale, sometime between October 1994 and April 1995, "teaching some individual lessons, perhaps a masterclass of some sort or a lecture, perhaps a recital."[88] Nothing came of it.

While Mme Duruflé was in residency in Texas, in 1992, Sarah Soularue terminated her duties as *suppléant* at Saint Étienne-du-Mont and was replaced by Hervé Morin. Upon the latter's death by suicide, in 1996, the pastor at Saint Étienne-du-Mont named Thierry Escaich and Vincent Warnier co-titulars.[89] Their contracts specified that Mme Duruflé retained the right of first refusal and could play whenever she chose. She continued playing for the 11 o'clock mass at her own discretion, but by 1998 was playing only twice per month.[90] As a last and fitting tribute to her career as an organist, in 1998 Mme Duruflé was awarded the Médaille vermeil of the city of Paris.

Marie-Madeleine Duruflé-Chevalier was referred to by many as the *grande dame de l'orgue*. Her stunningly virtuosic and formidable technique became legendary in North America with the recital she played for the national convention of the American Guild of Organists meeting in Philadelphia in 1964. It was a technique that, though it shrank not from the most demanding passages, was always the servant of a musical and poetic finesse. She had a superior and incisive intellect, which allowed her control over the most complex and densely designed organ works. Her interpretations and improvisations alike were characterized by clarity of thought and a profound sensitivity. With her husband, she was widely regarded as the last exponent of the great romantic tradition of French organ playing that had begun with Franck and reached full flower with Widor and her teacher Dupré, founded as it was on sturdy French pianism. She played with an electric sense of rhythm that was not, however, mechanical or metronomic.

Compared with her husband's playing, hers was dynamic, his more lyrical. In an interview for the *New York Times*, in 1989, she allowed that her husband was a great organ virtuoso, but after they married she worked more than he did. Often he would say to her, "you play the most difficult pieces, and I play the interpretative pieces.' "[91]

An interesting anecdote reveals the extent to which Mme Duruflé was a virtuoso of the organ art. Rodger Vine heard her play Vierne's *Carillon de Westminster* one Sunday as a postlude at Saint Étienne-du-Mont. He asked if there wasn't something "different" about it. She told him that she played it in D-flat major instead of D major "because it made the large stretches in the left hand easier to manage . . . it was a 'good exercise' in transposition!"[92]

Mme Duruflé taught organ privately, but she also taught at the Schola Cantorum for several years, leaving the post because she was given too many students.[93] With her pupils she counseled slow, repetitive practice, which, though laborious, should at the same time be enthusiastic and optimistic,[94] and she would delay organ lessons, if necessary, until a student had worked on piano technique. She often asked her students to play scales before they tackled repertoire, and recommended the fifty-one Exercises of Brahms and the *Études* of Chopin in particular.[95]

For her beginning pupils, lessons always began with "pure technique," for which only the fingers mattered, not the music or the style. They would play a chorale from the *Orgelbüchlein* of Bach, slowly counting sixteenth notes and attacking each note with energy for what she called the *premier mouvement* ("first movement"). But it was the precise and energetic release of the note, the *deuxième mouvement* ("second movement") that she considered so important. In fact it was the basis of her legendary playing.[96]

It was a fundamental principle of Mme Duruflé's that her students practice on a silent keyboard, with no stops drawn. When the organist of Chester Cathedral, Roger Fisher, showed her the practice organ he was constructing, "she implied that I should not bother with the pipes, as I could already do all the practice I needed."[97] She followed her own advice. The Chopin piano étude that she occasionally played as an encore, Opus 10, no. 4, in C-sharp Minor, she would practice at Saint Étienne-du-Mont on Sundays, on a silent organ during the homily at the second Mass (having dutifully listened to it at the earlier mass).[98]

Duruflé and his wife noted on their American tours that Americans played too freely. According to Mme Duruflé one should play in tempo, and reserve rhythmic freedom for the truly great moments in the music. She added that neither Dupré nor her husband used the kind of excessive rubato that they heard from foreign organists playing French repertoire.[99]

Mme Duruflé had a southern charm characteristic of Provence. She loved to laugh and she loved making others laugh. Unlike her husband, she was vivacious and she loved being with people. She had a playful sense of humor, the joie de vivre that her husband lacked, and she left countless memories of an infectious temperament among those who hosted her on her tours. Frederick Swann tells the following story from her visit to Garden Grove, California in 1992:

> She developed [a] special attachment to my black cat "Otto," and he to her. I arrived home one evening to find her seated at the dining room table putting small yellow post-its on her music to indicate pistons. I heard her say "One for me, one for you." When I came into the room, Otto was stretched out full length in front of her, more covered with post-its than her music! . . . and completely happy with the attention she was giving.[100]

Indeed, Mme Duruflé had a warm place in her heart for little creatures, wherever she found them. Once, before giving a lesson at the organ of Saint Étienne-du-Mont, she opened her bag and took out several little pieces of cheese. Not a snack for herself and her student, she advised, the victuals were a meal she had brought for the little mouse that lived in the organ loft.[101]

She and her husband were guests of honor at the Saint Wilfred's Club[102] in New York City on one of their earlier tours. Having just visited Riverside Church, where Frederick Swan was the incumbent, and where Virgil Fox had been his predecessor, Mme Duruflé told her assembled colleagues that they had "just returned from the Riverside Zoo. The organists were a Fox and a Swan, and there was a serpent on the organ."[103]

Toward the end of her life, Mme Duruflé dealt with an unrelieved series of maladies that weakened her already compromised state. Early in 1996 she wrote, "My life is very difficult right now!!"[104] Eventually she moved to her sister's apartment on rue Ordener, in the eighteenth arrondissement, near Sacré-Cœur. She was sick with pneumonia early in 1997, and then was weakened by shingles. She was able to vacation in Ménerbes during the summer of 1999, but upon her return to Paris, in September, she fell and broke her wrist, whereupon she was moved to the Clinique médicale du Val de Seine in Louveciennes (Yvelines), where her husband had died some thirteen years earlier. There she died on October 5, 1999, at the age of 78.

A private funeral was held at Saint Étienne-du-Mont, followed by mass and committal on the afternoon of October 13 at the church in Ménerbes, with burial in the same simple grave where her husband, her parents, and her grandmother already lay.[105] A memorial service for the public took place on January 22, 2000, at Saint Étienne-du-Mont.

The poignant words that Mme Duruflé addressed to one of her American students, saddened that his year's study with her had come to an end, were as apropos at the time of her death: "Oh no, don't be sad. We have played the prelude to a friendship; we have all of life for the fugue."[106]

# Chapter Thirteen

# *Overview of Duruflé's Compositions*

Duruflé's success as a composer lies in the finesse with which he yoked objective craft and religious inspiration in a rarefied utterance unique in his day, in the process proving the consanguinity of ecclesiastical music and the French musical tradition. For a full understanding of the reception of his œuvre, the two strains must be held in balance. Any effort to evaluate his work by drawing on one without the other does a disservice to the uniqueness that was his.

Decades of critics have described Duruflé's craft in countless ways. When Claude Chamfray told Duruflé in 1956, "We are accustomed to considering you as a symphoniste classique," and asked him if the epithet was appropriate, Duruflé replied, "One cannot know himself. The critic is more capable of giving an opinion on this question than I am." By 1980, however, he would agree with Norbert Dufourcq that the designation was appropriate, inasmuch as he had written preludes and fugues, variations, and toccatas, which nevertheless had romantic elements as well.[1]

Strictly from the perspective of craft, Dufourcq wrote in 1977 that Duruflé's works are "considered and weighed with skill and conscientiousness; everything takes place with the supreme balance of one who possesses mastery; never anything too prominent, too harsh or too striking. Grandeur can know refinement, and refinement is always proof of taste."[2] A choir director at Notre-Dame put it this way in 1986: "[Duruflé] always knew how to retain something apollonian in his expression, a kind of relentless elegance without slackening or sloppiness, a dynamism, a rhythm that was striking but never over-excited."[3]

In 1957, the music historian Paul Huot-Pleuroux included Duruflé among the era's greatest symphonists and composers of opera, whose celebrated oratorios, masses, psalms, and motets were the glory of early twentieth-century French music. And like Honegger, Stravinsky, Florent Schmitt, and André Caplet, he wrote, Duruflé showed no disdain for the concert hall, despite his predilection for sacred music and music for the organ.[4]

In 2004, when asked what she believed characterized the art of Duruflé and of his musical and spiritual message, Marie-Claire Alain replied that "it is a perfectly honest art. . . . He did not seek to innovate; he was searching only to be sincere with himself."[5] And because he had something honestly to say, Duruflé's compositions do not sound dated. Attempting to qualify the style of his work, Rolande Falcinelli wrote in 2004:

> It is rather difficult because it isn't modern, but it isn't old-fashioned either. It is the distinctive feature of certain musicians who truly have something to say without caring about fashion. His music is very pure, very simple, but without those flaws of certain pages of Widor that are dated. So I have the impression that Duruflé's music will not carry these scars; it will not become dated.[6]

Nevertheless, numerous critics have pointed out that Duruflé was a conservative composer. Marie-Claire Alain, for instance, wrote, "He was not an innovator but a traditionalist. At a time when [Jehan] Alain and Messiaen broke all preconceived ideas, Duruflé evolved and amplified the old traditions, making them his own."[7] She noted further that "at the end of the 1940s it was very difficult to write what one was thinking. The dodecaphonic method was invading the air waves, and every composer who was not writing according to the serial technique was taken to be old-fashioned."[8]

With the more extreme forms of contemporary music Duruflé exhibited little patience. "Here a tone, there a tone—that was it. And they call that music."[9] In a discussion of avant-garde organ music on the radio he heard Pierre Cochereau describe organists who play with their elbows: "It would be better for them to use their buttocks because their buttocks have a wider range." Duruflé responded, "I found this very good."[10]

Duruflé once asked rhetorically:

> Are we moving toward a total destruction of our musical civilization? . . . [We talk about] *musique concrète*, aleatoric music, repetitive, experimental, electro-acoustic music, music of our times, a new language, research, etc. Despite so much research, we still seem to have found nothing. If this so-called contemporary music is to be that of tomorrow, why then maintain writing classes in our conservatories?[11]

Asked why he wrote in a relatively conservative language, Duruflé replied, "It is because I have always been surrounded by Gregorian chant, which is of course rather traditional."[12] Later in his life Duruflé had second thoughts about the pervasive influence that Gregorian chant had upon his compositions, and regretted having confined himself to a musical language based, as strictly as it was, on the modality of Gregorian chant.[13] He commented that

> As I have always been under the spell of Gregorian chant, I might say myself that it has sometimes even appeared somewhat tyrannical. Even as it puts one under its spell, it can be perhaps a little too confining, a little—how can I express it—too limiting of my harmonic field, if one could put it that way. But really, I don't want to say anything negative against Gregorian chant, just the opposite. I am very grateful because it has given me great joy in my career as an organist and composer.[14]

Some critics from later in the century, like Ned Rorem, failed to appreciate Duruflé's affection for plainsong. Rorem wrote of the *Requiem*:

> The music doesn't merit the attention. (Well, maybe once.) It's at all times gorgeous, but over-solemn and soundtracky. Like Les Six, without the camp or control, or like Messiaen without the outrageous harmonic sedition. The *Requiem* is slow from start to finish, using Gregorian chant exclusively for its tunes. Well, with Gregorian chant you can't lose. But neither can you win. The melody is inherently appealing, but impersonal by definition. Duruflé is Gregorian chant in thirds. He is to Poulenc as [Francesco] Cilea is to Puccini: The same thing but less good.[15]

Duruflé was always several steps behind the avant-garde, which accounts for the fact that his compositions were rarely thought modern. The first wave of musical modernism, preceding the First World War, appeared with the likes of Arnold Schoenberg's *Pierrot lunaire* (1912) some fourteen years before Duruflé completed his first major work, the *Scherzo*, in 1926. Even Tournemire was experimenting with twelve-tone writing, in his *Sept Chorals-Poèmes d'orgue pour les sept paroles du Christ*, in 1935, while Duruflé, his younger student, was writing *Trois Danses*. And when the second wave of modernism was launched, after the Second World War, Pierre Boulez, Karlheinz Stockhausen, and John Cage were giving composition an entirely new name while Duruflé was writing a *Requiem* that reminded listeners of Fauré.

By contrast, Duruflé explained how the innovations of Debussy and Ravel remained within the tradition:

> Debussy and Ravel incontestably caused traditional writing to evolve. Among their innovations, we can cite parallel chains of chords, rising or falling, consonant or dissonant, which, regarding the last named, abolish by the same fact the law restricting resolutions of sevenths. We can also mention multiple unresolved appoggiaturas, forming independent chords, which have considerably enriched our harmonic vocabulary. But these innovations, and this relaxing of the rules, remain in the tradition.[16]

Duruflé's opposition to experiments with nontraditional harmony placed him in a moderate position, one consistent with reason, and with a respect for the past, but with a generous regard for the future. His objection to the "schismatic" techniques of avant-garde composers, which ruptured the tradition as he understood it, inevitably accounted for his being labeled a conservative.

The source of Duruflé's compositional style is debated. Some find it in Gabriel Fauré, who is credited with preparing the way for Paul Dukas, Maurice Ravel, and Florent Schmitt, masters of the movement that issued forth from Debussy. Bernard Gavoty, for instance, referred to "the Fauré-like subtlety of Maurice Duruflé,"[17] and called him "the Fauré of the organ."[18] Similarly, Marie-Claire Alain wrote that Duruflé "found inspiration in Debussy, in Ravel (for the orchestration of his *Trois Danses*) and above all in Fauré of whom he loved the fluid writing and modal spirit."[19]

Duruflé himself felt differently about the matter. When asked about the influence that the harmonic language of Ravel, Debussy, and Fauré had upon him, he replied, ". . . above all Ravel, and Debussy, naturally. Less Fauré. I like Fauré less than I like Ravel or Debussy."[20] He admired Ravel's *Daphnis et Chloé, Le Tombeau de Couperin,* and *Ma Mère l'oye,* and Debussy's *La Mer,* singling out his *Prélude à "L'Après-midi d'un faune"* as Debussy's masterpiece.[21] But he never pointed to any work of Fauré as bearing influence upon him.[22]

By Duruflé's own estimation, the greatest influence upon him was Ravel. In his memoirs he commented favorably upon the music scene in the late 1920s, after Fauré and Debussy had both died.

> 1928. An exciting time for French music. Ravel, Roussel, Dukas, Schmitt, then Honegger, Poulenc. The center of attention was focused on Ravel. The first performance of a work by him was an event awaited by the entire music world. . . . Ravel surprised sometimes by his harmonic daring. But the classic form that he adopted bore witness to the respect he had for tradition. He was felt to be the master of his thought. The evolution was natural. . . . I had the privilege of attending several first performances of Ravel. . . . These were *Le Tombeau de Couperin,* the [Piano] Concerto in G . . . [and] *La Valse.* . . . I am happy to have lived at that exciting time.[23]

Ravel's approach to orchestration is evident in Duruflé's *Trois Danses,* but the *Sicilienne* also betrays a considerable debt. Ravel's musical alphabet appears in Duruflé's *Prélude et fugue sur le nom d'ALAIN,* and Duruflé's use of block chords in parallel motion is like Ravel's, as is his use of third-related harmonic transitions. Duruflé used quotations from Ravel in exercises with his harmony students. Moreover, Duruflé believed that, even though Ravel composed nothing for the instrument, he "knew the organ very well," basing this insight on the fact that Ravel imitated the sound of the cornet in his *Boléro,* where, in one passage, a piccolo plays the "tierce" above a melody while a flute plays the "nasard."[24]

Lionel Rogg argued: "Maurice Duruflé occupies in the literature for organ a place rather comparable to that of Maurice Ravel in connection with the piano: a writing of perfect limpidity, a harmony as subtle as it is personal, an innate sense of the resources and of the instrumental limits charactering their art, impregnated with refined sensuality."[25]

At the same time, Duruflé acknowledged that Debussy was a significant influence on him, if less so than Ravel.[26] As noted above, he considered the *Prélude à "L'Après-midi d'un faune"* Debussy's masterpiece.[27] Though he never specified exactly how he believed he was influenced by Debussy, the influence of the latter's harmonic language is conspicuous in Duruflé's work, a fact universally acknowledged. Debussy's use of the tritone, for instance, made its way to Duruflé through Ravel. Duruflé specifically noted the likeness of his Opus 8 *Andante* to Debussy; in fact he thought it was *too* influenced by Debussy.[28]

Duruflé disagreed with some historians on the role Debussy played in French composition. In his memoirs he wrote:

OVERVIEW OF DURUFLÉ'S COMPOSITIONS ❦ 101

Debussy, whom certain avant-gardists have described as a revolutionary for their own purposes, was the opposite of a revolutionary. He threw out nothing. He simply stretched the rules. He didn't break the glass; he simply opened the windows. Paul Dukas wrote in 1902, on the subject of the first performance of *Pelléas*: "The harmony of Debussy, about which some shouted over the perpetual breach of the rules, is only the brilliant stretching of the principles." [*Les Écrits de Paul Dukas sur la musique*][29]

The case has been made that Duruflé, a disciple of Debussy once removed, was an impressionist, or as Herndon Spillman was the first to propose, "one of the last impressionists."[30] In fact, the first book ever devoted to Duruflé, *Maurice Duruflé 1902–1986: The Last Impressionist*, takes this claim as its point of departure, or, as reviewer Haig Mardirosian suggests, its debatable premise.[31] One would expect, from its title, that the editor would have undertaken as his primary project to prove, firstly, the thesis that impressionism is a legitimate term in music; secondly, that it can be applied to Duruflé; and finally, that Duruflé was its last proponent. Editor Ronald Ebrecht, however, confines discussion of the subject to only two paragraphs in the preface, where it inadequately addresses all three points.

Early studies of impressionism delineated parallels between color and sound, it is true, such that a connection could be seen between impressionism in art and impressionism in music. The critic Camille Mauclair suggested, for instance, that "light is used in Impressionist painting in the manner that a theme in music is symphonically developed." He continues, "The landscapes of Claude Monet are in fact symphonies of luminous waves, and the music of Monsieur Debussy, based not on a succession of themes but on the relative values of sounds in themselves, bears a remarkable resemblance to these pictures. It is Impressionism consisting of sonorous patches."[32] But the word impressionism, as a musical term, began as a pejorative, and Debussy considered it "a useful term of abuse." In 1887, he submitted his orchestral piece *Printemps* for the Prix de Rome competition. Instead of a prize, however, he received a letter of rejection from the Académie des Beaux-Arts:

Monsieur Debussy . . . has a pronounced tendency—too pronounced—toward an exploration of the strange. One has the feeling of musical color exaggerated to the point where it causes the composer to forget the importance of precise construction and form. It is to be strongly hoped that he will guard against this vague impressionism, which is one of the most dangerous enemies of truth in works of art.[33]

The term nevertheless began to appear in music reviews in the 1890s and has been part of the lexicon ever since, bearing a definition that, however much it has been debated, has proven useful in discussions on the subject.

What does the term mean, and if its use is valid in music, is it valid with reference to the music of Duruflé? Musical impressionism, begun as a reaction against the excesses of romanticism, departed from the traditional major-minor system of diatonicism, and looked to medieval precedent in its use of parallel chord progressions, adopting such exotic whole-tone and pentatonic scales as could be heard in non-European music. It featured fresh-sounding chords containing dissonant ninths valued more for their individual sonorities than for their relation to one another, with dissonances that are unprepared and unresolved. Instruments were exploited for their color value. Unlike romantic precedents that sought to depict an event, place, or object, impressionist pieces aimed to symbolize their emotional impact, rather the way Monet's paintings of the Rouen cathedral are less paintings of the building as such than of its emotive atmosphere.

Ebrecht bases his thesis on five qualities presented by Michel Fleury in *L'Impressionisme et la musique*.[34] Impressionism in music, writes Ebrecht, has the following qualities, all of them having to do with harmony:

harmony preeminent over counterpoint
harmony usually nonfunctional
harmony favoring the pleasure of the ear
nuanced, unsettled harmony
suggestive rather than declamative [sic] harmony[35]


But Ebrecht makes no attempt to demonstrate how any of these qualities is germane to Duruflé, and, as Haig Mardirosian points out, he overlooks certain important attributes of Duruflé's music. Whereas counterpoint is incidental in Debussy, for example, it is a rigorous component of Duruflé's works. Moreover, it would be difficult to make a case that harmony takes precedence over counterpoint in Duruflé, certainly not to the extent that form ever suffers in any of his works. And harmony virtually always serves functional purposes. Mardirosian writes:

If much of [Duruflé's] music does reflect a Debussy-like penchant for known structures moving in parallel streams, it also reflects Ravel's restraint and neo-functionalism. Where a parallel chord stream points to a cadential target, that goal often has a specific and important place in the tonality of the movement in question. The concluding strain of the Prelude from the Op. 5 *Suite*, for instance, provides simple evidence. The chord stream, actually a stream of 6/4s in middle voices between the pedal E-flat and the augmented soprano melody, clearly wends its way from a tonic E-flat minor to a minor dominant on B-flat and back. While that hardly qualifies as a leading-tone-driven demand for resolution, it does acknowledge hierarchy and, at the very least, modalism.[36]

Mardirosian also notes that Duruflé qualifies as a harmonist, or a modalist in the manner of Fauré, who was not an impressionist. While "Debussy's harmony and timbre stretched well past European boundaries, and his music can be considered the beginnings of a challenge to Western tonality where whole-tone and pentatonic scales spawn not only melodies but harmony," Duruflé rarely leaves

Western bedrock triadicism.[37] And though Duruflé shared the techniques of Debussy and the orchestration of Dukas, Mardirosian doubts he would "measure up against the deeper mind-set, purposes, and objectives of Impressionism."[38] Whether Duruflé was or was not the last impressionist will likely remain a matter of continuing debate. Further consideration of the subject is beyond the scope of this book, but several recent dissertations tackle the matter in some detail.[39]

While there is common consent that Duruflé was influenced by the harmonic language of Debussy, little has been made of the influence of another feature of Debussy's musical language, namely, his well-developed concept of arabesque,[40] whose influence upon Duruflé was conspicuous and fundamental. If Debussy's notion of arabesque is crucial to an understanding of his art, as François Lesure has written,[41] the same is true of the art of Duruflé. And through a consideration of arabesque we are ultimately drawn to a discussion of the religious inspiration of Duruflé's œuvre.

By arabesque, Debussy meant that "capricious and sinuous line which had its origin in the motifs of stylized plants in Greek, Byzantine, Arabic and Persian ornamental art,"[42] whose evidence he perceived in disparate kinds of music, from plainsong, by way of Bach, to Javanese music. Debussy said of Bach's Brandenburg Concerto in G Major,[43] "We find here almost intact his 'musical arabesque.' . . . The primitives—Palestrina, Vittoria, Orlando di Lasso etc. all made use of this divine 'arabesque.' The polyphonists discovered its principle in Gregorian plainsong, and fortified its frail traceries with a solid counterpoint."[44]

Debussy first heard the music of the "primitives" in Rome, in 1885. But eight years later, he found it in Paris.

> It was at Saint-Gervais, a church where some intelligent priest took it into his head to revive some of that extremely beautiful sacred music of olden times. They sang an *a cappella* mass by Palestrina—marvelously fine. This music, although written in a very strict style, appears entirely white. The feelings are not conveyed by screaming (as has happened since) but by melodic "arabesques." It is achieved by the contours and by these arabesques intertwining to produce *melodic harmony*: something that now seems to be unique.[45]

For Debussy, arabesque is, in the view of Françoise Gervais, first of all, more or less independent of the harmony that accompanies it. Secondly, it is ornamental, in a rather broad sense, a characteristic inherent in the curves and countercurves of the lines. And thirdly, it is conjoint, meaning that it moves mostly stepwise, rather than by skips.[46] Referring to the Gregorian-inspired lines of Duruflé's *Requiem*, Seth Bingham described arabesques without actually using the word: "they move stepwise within narrow limits in a sort of rhythmic recitative with many repeated notes. Still the melodic design is clear, the flow of words natural and unforced."[47] Duruflé was influenced in the matter of musical arabesque also by his teacher Charles Tournemire, whom Olivier Messiaen called "the master of arabesque."[48]

Given that Duruflé's father was an architect, and his brother aspired to architecture, it is no surprise that Duruflé himself had an innate aptitude for arabesque in architecture. His pencil sketches include a depiction of the vegetative tracery of a flamboyant gothic staircase. His built context in Louviers, Rouen, and Paris was dominated by masterpieces of late gothic and early Renaissance architecture, which featured floriated finials and buttresses, a flamboyant porch, a looming traceried window without its glass, lacy staircases at Saint Maclou (see Fig. 13.1) and the canon's staircase at the Rouen cathedral (see Fig. 13.2), and a lithe and supple *jubé*, with coiled stairs and an elegantly columned triforium at Saint Étienne-du-Mont (see Fig. 13.3), to name only a few conspicuous examples, all of them arabesques in stone.

Arabesque is so prominent a feature in Duruflé's œuvre that it can be identified as a specifically "duruflèsque" compositional device. Indeed, it plays a prominent role in the *Prélude* on *Veni Creator*, in the *Prélude* and the *Sicilienne* from the *Suite*, in the *Scherzo*, in the *Prélude* on the *introit* for Epiphany, the *Prélude et fugue sur le nom d'ALAIN* and in the *Introit*, the *Sanctus*, and, to a lesser degree, the *Libera me* from the *Requiem*. In Opus 3, the *Prélude, récitatif et variations*, the arabesques in the flute and viola parts predominate in the *Prélude*, the *Récitatif*, and the first variation; they appear elsewhere less conspicuously. In Duruflé's transcriptions of Bach, the most prominent feature, both of *Werde munter, mein Gemüthe* (from Cantata 147) and *Ertödt uns durch dein' Güte* (from Cantata 22), is the arabesque in triplets in the first instance, and the sixteenth-note arabesque in the second.

Duruflé's proven architectural aptitude and his gift for musical arabesque arise from a single source in his experience of life. Because in him there is an architectural arabesque parallel to the musical, we may use the languages of architecture and music alike to describe how Duruflé's œuvre constitutes a kind of sacramental system, as we shall see. And in this way arabesque engineers the religious characteristics of Duruflé's œuvre. A remarkable fact indeed.

The ultimate effect of the late gothic and early Renaissance aesthetic in architecture is one of transparent solidity, like that of glass. The architect's quest was to make solid stone diaphanous, so that it would look supple, fluid, and weightless, permitting the passage and movement of light. The effect was achieved largely through the use of tall arches, narrow columns, generous glass, and thinly cut tracery, all of these a challenge to gravity, as it were, and, above all, a medium for light. All of these are architectural metaphors for musical arabesque.

The essential premise of a sacramental system is that divine life abides in the material world. By the right and proper manipulation of physical stuff, whether by an architect, a composer, or a priest, and whether the material be stone, glass, musical line, or bread and wine, the world of experience becomes a scrim,

Figure 13.1. Spiral stairs to the organ tribune, Saint Maclou, Rouen. Photograph by the author.

Rouen, A. Le Brument. 55 Quai Napoléon                    Imp. Lemercier, Paris

Cathédrale *(Escalier de la Bibliothèque)*

Figure 13.2. Flamboyant stairs to the canons' library (14th Century), north transept of the Rouen Cathedral, near the choristers' entrance to the cathedral.

Figure 13.3. Processional with the Blessed Sacrament, Saint Étienne-du-Mont, view from the west, showing the spiral stairs to the *jubé*. Engraving by T. Turnbull.

through which a more true light or life, as one prefers, is experienced and attained. Stone and musical arabesque, no less than bread and wine, when handled skillfully, intentionally, and with the right authority, do indeed have the capacity at once to reveal and to conceal a kind of light.

Though music is ephemeral and aural, it is no less capable of luminosity, if analogously so, than glass or stone, or bread and wine. This is precisely why music, in order to be liturgically suitable, must be construed by the composer and mastered by the performer in such a way that it can be "seen through," giving it a sacramental verity. To say that Duruflé's œuvre constitutes a kind of sacramental system, then, is to say that he handled the "stone" of musical arabesque, and employed a diaphanous type of construction, such that it allowed for the passage of a kind of light. In this way, his work bears the attribute of luminosity universally attributed to it. It remains for the listener to label the experience musical or architectural, and religious or aesthetic.

Because of its sacramental aptitude, Duruflé's work bears strong liturgical marks, found in its formal teleology and processional drive, or a sense of destiny. In other words, his works have a clear beginning, a development, and a conclusive end, with a logical and inevitable progression driving ahead from the one to the other. Seth Bingham noted this feature in the *Sanctus* of the *Requiem*. After quiet three-part chords for women's voices, he observed, and a considerable build-up of woodwinds, horns, and strings, there follows a steady increase in choral volume, with more and more instruments added, swelling to a peak of "great brilliance" at *in excelsis*. A decrescendo leads directly to a single brief statement of the *Benedictus*. "The total effect, perhaps intended by the composer, is that of a procession coming from far off, arriving in full splendor, passing and disappearing in the distance."[49]

This drive accounts ultimately for the eschatological dimension of Duruflé's work, meaning that it looks forward to the end of time. It is just this facet of Duruflé's œuvre that is studied by Père François Marchal in his unpublished dissertation, "Écouter le *Requiem* de Maurice Duruflé (1902–86) en théologien: Découvrir dans une œuvre de haute composition musicale l'exercice d'une intelligence de la foi sur le mystère des fins dernières."[50] Duruflé expressed himself on this very subject:

> This *Requiem* is not an ethereal work that sings about detachment from earthly concerns. It reflects, in the immutable form of Christian prayer, the anguish of mankind before the mystery of his final end. It is often dramatic, or filled with resignation, or with hope, or with terror, like the very words of Scripture that serve as the liturgy. It tends to translate human sentiments before their terrifying, inexplicable, or consoling destiny.[51]

Although Duruflé and Messiaen both produced works redolent of their Roman Catholicism, Messiaen's œuvre is less liturgical and more mystical than Duruflé's. Many of his works are either a contemplation of abstract and static theological concepts, such as the Trinity and the Blessed Sacrament, or meditations on moments in the life of Christ (the nativity, the ascension), or on the glorified Christ or the Holy Spirit. Messiaen wrote: "A number of my works are dedicated to shedding light on the theological truths of the Catholic faith."[52] Much of Messiaen's œuvre thus enjoys a mystic stillness, a contemplative stasis, as if arrested in time.[53] This is true even for a boisterous piece like *Les Yeux dans les roues*, from *Livre d'orgue*, a ferocious *perpetuum mobile* that begins out of nowhere and goes nowhere. The same cannot be said of Duruflé's work, which is processional.

Given its liturgical and sacramental dimensions, Duruflé's œuvre can be considered the culmination of the movement toward sacrality that spanned much of the nineteenth century and the first half of the twentieth. As Paul Huot-Pleuroux put it, Duruflé lived and composed during the third and last period in the revival of a religious aesthetic after the French Revolution.[54] His nurture and long career in the church equipped him as one of its greatest proponents, and certainly its last. Huot-Pleuroux names Duruflé alongside Caplet, Milhaud, Honegger, Poulenc, and Langlais as the diverse representatives of that era.

Having considered the craft and the religious inspiration of Duruflé's work, we turn now to their synthesis, about which the British music critic Felix Aprahamian wrote: "[Duruflé's] music uses two streams—the modality which derives from his liturgical background as an organist, and the harmonies that colour the compositions of his seniors, Debussy, Ravel and his own master, Dukas."[55] And he summarizes: "The synthesis effected by his music results in a language which, although old-fashioned by serialist standards, has its own personal accent."[56] Similarly, Roger Nichols properly claimed that Duruflé's effort was even "forward-looking in trying to reconcile two apparently incompatible languages."[57]

Francis Poulenc said as much in an interview during the 1950s. Asked his opinion of the young French school, namely Duruflé, Litaize, Langlais, Jehan Alain, and so on, as to whether they "manifest a beautiful renaissance of the religious art in France after the crisis of spectacular and theatrical music of the romantics and the slightly saint-sulpician[58] music of the franckistes," Poulenc replied, "Yes, I applaud without reserve the works of Duruflé. Litaize and Langlais are also very talented, and how gifted was Jehan Alain!"[59] Poulenc was speaking from the perspective of both compositional craft and religious inspiration.

Philippe Ronzon claims that it was through his use of Gregorian chant that Duruflé enriched musical vocabulary by composing in a "double tradition" of modal writing, that is, "the modal aspect peculiar to French works since the end of the nineteenth century as a solution to post-Wagnerism, and the aspect of plainsong, the beginning of Western music in the middle ages. Through this tradition, he realizes a synthesis combining the alpha and the omega of music in France."[60]

Duruflé was apparently not the first to yoke plainsong with modern harmony. It has been reported that in 1887 Théodore Dubois, professor of harmony at the Conservatoire, "accompanied some verses of the *Magnificat* with the then 'new' harmonies à la Claude-Achille Debussy, using organ stops that evoked the unresolved succession of dominant ninths, elevenths, and thirteenths."[61] But Duruflé was "one of the first to use this compact form of chord played with only one hand and, by this fact, 'condensed' in a range almost always shorter than an octave." From this emerges Duruflé's "perpetual *friction of the second*" caused by his use of sevenths and ninths, appoggiaturas, and added sixths, seconds, and tritones.[62]

Even in his works that did not quote plainsong Duruflé adhered to a modal style that was faithful to French harmonic tradition. He said in an interview: "I believe that I have continued to be sufficiently influenced by the modal style as in my *Trois Danses*, you see, that have nothing to do with Gregorian chant. Yes, I think that I have been very much influenced by modal style. . . . In the *Suite* for organ, I believe that I have never been able to escape completely from the modal style."[63]

Duruflé, however, did not compose in a strictly modal style. He noted that Tournemire "is modal in spirit but not to the letter. In the letter he has some rather strong harmonies. He is not a hundred percent modal; he is so only in spirit. He's right about that."[64] So it was also with Nicolas de Grigny, whose works contain elements of both modality and tonality admirably blended into one harmonic language.[65] Like de Grigny and so many of Duruflé's predecessors in impressionism, including Debussy,[66] Ravel, and Dukas, the compositions that Duruflé came to write enjoyed that same admirable mix of modality and tonality.

If his affection for modal writing consigned Duruflé to a conservative camp vis-à-vis the secular avant-garde, how does he compare with his predecessors in church music? Of all of his immediate forebears, namely Widor, Gigout, Vierne, and Tournemire, none would feature in a history of French music outside the church. But all of them bore significant influence upon Duruflé in an area of his career that was uppermost to him, namely, the field of sacred music.

Compared with these men, Duruflé is seen to be the progressive that he was, at least during the 1930s and 1940s. He espoused the Solesmes method, which Widor had largely dismissed. He used chant more enthusiastically than did Vierne, in a compositional guise that reflected his greater sympathy with the church. Gigout's classically conceived works, precisely because many of them were inspired by the cause for sacred music, were more conservative harmonically than Duruflé's works and showed no influence from Debussy or Ravel. And, while Tournemire's work was deeply influenced by the Solesmes school, Duruflé incorporated it into his own with a far superior sense of musical architecture. Moreover, he undertook his task with a deliberation and an intentionality lacking in his colleagues Langlais and Dupré. In these diverse ways, Duruflé advanced sacred music a step forward into the future.

If Duruflé's musical language can be characterized by a single affect, we may say it is serious, or severe, in the style of Franck and Palestrina. The latter's work is serious in that it was among the most objective and impersonal of all the continental composers writing in the polyphonic style of the Renaissance. Duruflé's work is similarly objective and impersonal, both in his choice of musical materials, and in their distance from the circumstances of his life. Consider especially his four Palestrinian motets. Franck's work is serious in comparison with the trivial, secular fare typical of the church music that preceded him, and Duruflé's work was the culmination of the serious movement thus begun by Franck.

At the same time, if Franck's work was severe by virtue of its *gravitas*, it was no less lyrical for that. And if Palestrina's was severe by virtue of its impersonal objectivity, it was nonetheless poetic. So too are Duruflé's works both lyrical and poetic. Bernard Gavoty characterized the great improvisers of the time, describing Tournemire as full of imagery, Vierne as lyrical, Dupré as architect, and Marchal and Duruflé as poets.[67]

In a rare disclosure of the inner workings of his mind, Duruflé described the process of composition by which this *gravitas* and this poetry emerged through his pen. He describes an altered state, one bearing a remarkable similarity to ecstasy, and rather different from the kind of inspiration often invoked by composers. He wrote:

> I don't believe very much in what is called "inspiration," this sort of state of grace that one imagines he feels at times, without any personal effort. I believe rather in work by elimination, slow, difficult and often disheartening work, but which can in the end bring about a kind of splitting of oneself, a trance during which thought can succeed at getting out of the body, a body whose presence is no longer felt. It can also happen that at this point one has the sensation of writing as if the solution were being dictated. This strange and fleeting sensation, which is from the domain of the subconscious, can be precisely aroused only by a constant effort of eliminating everything that seems unacceptable. At least this is what I believe.[68]

Duruflé was a meticulous composer. Writing was a slow and tedious process for him. Like Ravel, "he had to tear his music out of himself bit by bit." He was intensely critical of his works and he returned to them many times over the years to make revisions. His fellow pupil at the Conservatoire, Henri Doyen, who remembered Duruflé's first drafts, wrote that they had more erasures than pencil marks.[69] He threw a lot of his work away[70] and he wrote a number of pieces that were never published. Mme Duruflé said that "Maurice is very hard on himself."[71]

It has been said that the music of Maurice Duruflé needs no explanation because its "purity, firmness and grace know the way to our heart."[72] While this is true, there is, at the same time, a sense in which his music evades such explanation. As Christoph Martin Frommen has written, "It is difficult to describe Duruflé's music with words. It is not directly intelligible, and from this fact it purports to be, above all, a real-life experience, and for all those who have experienced it, it remains very vivid in the memory."[73]

Duruflé's work is, to a great extent, objective and self-referencing. His compositions are not picturesque or descriptive, not occasional, not revelatory of his passions or his loves, or of events or persons in his life.[74] Nor are they ideological, political, or sentimental. There is no swarm of locusts in Duruflé's work, as there is in that of Jean Langlais.[75] As Claude Rostand wrote, "Maurice Duruflé . . . is not among those who embroider to excess literary, moral or even metaphysical glosses on their scores, and this is so much the better. He contents himself to say what he has to say merely by means of the message on his music paper."[76]

But this is not to suggest that Duruflé's works lack meaning, or that by virtue of their objectivity they lack a personal dimension. On the contrary, their meaning is too rich to be limited to one meaning only, and too broad to be timebound or dated. It is precisely because of their objectivity that they can so easily be "entered into" by a wide range of listeners, without regard for the circumstances of Duruflé's life or those of the listener.

Duruflé was as much a transcriber as he was a composer. His transcriptions reflected not an attempt to have one idiom imitate another, but rather a breadth of conception that welcomed multiple expressions of the same musical idea. His original works are fewer in number than his combined transcriptions, versions, orchestrations, and reductions of existing works (both his own and those of others). From this perspective, the words of the orchestral conductor, Charles Münch, could well be attributed to Duruflé: "The organ was my first orchestra."[77]

Duruflé gives us some notion of the fluidity of his thinking about color in the organ and the orchestra, and how some music transfers well from the orchestra to the organ, and some does not. He contrasts Johann Sebastian Bach with César Franck:

Bach himself . . . seems to allow some liberty in the choice of timbres, for he transcribed for the organ several of his works for violin and for harpsichord, as well as numerous movements from his cantatas. The six chorale transcriptions [Schübler] are an example. The same is true for the Fugue in D Minor, taken from a sonata for solo violin, the Sinfonia to Cantata 146 for harpsichord or organ, and the four Concertos by Vivaldi written for violin and orchestra. In Franck's case, on the contrary, melody predominates over texture, as it does in most works by nineteenth-century composers. Franck's organ works may be performed only upon the organ, and with the registrations indicated by the composer. It is impossible to transcribe them for another instrument without changing their character.[78]

Duruflé left no doubt as to which orchestral instruments he believed did or did not transfer well to the organ.

It's impossible to transcribe for the organ the sonorities of the string orchestra. . . . It can give an illusion of the winds, the brass, and the woodwinds. But the strings! You absolutely cannot transcribe the sonority of the strings for the organ. There's a vibration in the strings and a warmth of tone that you don't find on the organ, which is itself rather cold. It's an absolutely different aesthetic. It has no relationship because of the strings.[79]

Whether we regard "coloration" as an orchestral feature or as a feature of the organ as a "color machine," Duruflé's organ compositions betray a fine-honed sense of coloring. Olivier Soularue writes:

We find with these three composers [Olivier Messiaen, Jehan Alain, and Duruflé] the particularly demanding concern for the right tone color, for the clever combination of timbres. Exploring a region that is at the opposite extreme of pure music, created without regard for timbre, of which the polyphony of J. S. Bach represents the summit, this French school of composer-organists thinks of itself as heir to the impressionism of Fauré, Debussy, and Ravel. Maurice Duruflé is the one who pushes this detail of orchestration the furthest. In his works for organ, the many registration indications are all as important as the musical text. It is not unusual for him to ask of the performer a great many changes of registration in a short fragment of several measures, obliging the latter to integrate these sometimes acrobatic maneuvers into his playing in the same way as the notes of the text.[80]

Indeed, Duruflé fully explored the capabilities of the organ and the human hand. He understood what they could do, and he exploited their limits to the fullest. As difficult as many passages are in his works, they are always idiomatic for the hand and the instrument.

It may surprise organists to learn that when asked whether he preferred writing for the organ or the orchestra, Duruflé replied without hesitation: the orchestra. But "it is certain that after the orchestra my preferences are for the organ."[81] Beyond these two mediums he harbored a fear of approaching other genres.

It is to the organ and the orchestra that I feel the most drawn. It seems to me, indeed, that these two worlds of sound, being inexhaustible, as it were, offer rich possibilities of renewal. The piano literature contains so many masterpieces that I feel incapable of adding anything further to an already long list. The string quartet equally causes me deep apprehension and it is with terror that I consider writing a melody, after the accomplished melodies left in this genre by Schubert, Faure [sic], or Debussy.[82]

Was Duruflé crippled by the excellence of his role models? We can only speculate as to the direction his œuvre might have taken if he had ventured further into other genres: into piano repertoire, for instance (consider his unpublished *Triptyque* for piano and the transcriptions of *Trois Danses*), or song repertoire (like the *Pie Jesu*), oratorio (of which the *Requiem* could be considered a type), symphony (in the style of *Trois Danses* or the *Andante et Scherzo*), chamber music (like his early trio), organ concerto (in the spirit of Poulenc),[83] or even vernacular liturgical music (consider *Notre Père*), all of which he dismissed for various reasons.

Of all his organ works, Duruflé's favorite was the *Prélude et fugue sur le nom d'ALAIN*. After that he favored the *Prélude, adagio et choral varié sur le Veni Creator*, and then the *Prélude* from the *Suite*. After that, he did not know, but he liked the *Toccata* the least.[84] Surely he considered the *Requiem* his greatest work.

Duruflé spawned no school of composition. He had no self-proclaimed disciples, apart from Pierre Cochereau, a fact which further confirms that he was the culmination of an era, and that his style of composition had run its course by about 1950. Some composers have essayed pieces in the style of Duruflé, or composed works in homage to him,[85] but these hardly constitute a school.

# Chapter Fourteen

# *Duruflé's Compositions*

## *Their Genesis and First Performances*

During his years as a harmony and composition student at the Conservatoire, from 1924 through 1928, Duruflé wrote ten compositions identified in the Conservatoire records of examinations and prizes now housed at the Archives nationales. Three of them were published. If it were any other composer under scrutiny, student works would probably draw little or no attention in a biography. In Duruflé's case, because of his small opus list, the hope that he may have written other worthy pieces that remain unpublished ignites interest in his student works, an interest supported by the fact that one of these pieces, the *Scherzo*, was published in a performance edition.[1] As to the whereabouts of the original manuscripts, the sources vary. At least some of Duruflé's published works are held by the Durand publishing house;[2] the unpublished works undoubtedly remain among the Duruflé Papers.

In 1924, Duruflé wrote an untitled work on a *basse donnée* by J. Morpain. Published that year by Heugel in four-part open score, the piece will interest historians, but it does not merit publication in a performance edition. In 1926, he composed a *Pastorale* for organ and a *Pièce pour orgue sur le thème du Credo* as well as the Op. 2 *Scherzo* for organ. In 1927 he wrote *Méditation* and *Pièce*, both for organ. In 1928 he composed another *Pièce* (a Fugue in C Minor), on a subject of Henri Rabaud, which was published by Heugel in four-part open score, in 1928, under the title *Fugues à 4 parties des élèves ayant remporté le Premier Prix aux Concours de Fugue* (1928). Because the piece was not published in a performance edition, and because it remained unknown until 2004, it was probably never performed, perhaps not even by Duruflé himself.[3] Despite its harmonically conservative nature, the work is extremely well crafted, bearing a refined, Bach-like sense of architecture, and reflects an advanced musical genius. It merits publication in a performance edition and wide performance in concert venues. The piece is perfectly idiomatic for the organ.[4]

Duruflé's *Triptyque: Fantaisie sur des thèmes grégoriens*, Op. 1 (1927), for piano, is dedicated to Vierne and remains unpublished.[5] Duruflé commented about it: "The piece is not really bad, because I had a *second prix* in composition with it.

Inasmuch as I had a *second prix* in composition, it was not for tossing in the basket. But this didn't make it worth publishing."[6] It was surely with an eye toward possible publication that Duruflé revised the piece in 1943.

## *Scherzo*, Op. 2

Duruflé's first work to be published in a performance edition was the *Scherzo*, Op. 2, for organ, whose dedicatee is Charles Tournemire. In his memoirs, Duruflé wrote that he composed the *Scherzo* in 1926, not under Widor's guidance but Tournemire's. Duruflé wrote:

> Maurice Emmanuel, who had known about my momentarily broken relationship with Tournemire, strongly recommended that I go see him again. I found him again with joy, and it is under his direction that I undertook the composition of a *Scherzo* for organ. After much effort, after a lot of touching up, I succeeded at finishing my first work. I dedicated it to him out of gratitude for all I owe him. It was with this *Scherzo* that I was admitted to the entrance exam for the class in composition in 1926.[7]

Other sources date the *Scherzo* to 1928. The copy of the score used by André Fleury to play the premiere in 1928 bears the dedication "To my dear friend André Fleury, very cordially. M. Duruflé—February 3, 1928."[8] The following note also appears on Fleury's score: "Examen de Composition—Janvier 1928."[9] Indeed, the examination took place on January 25, 1928 (the same month Dukas took over Widor's composition class), and the *Scherzo* won Duruflé the cash prize from the Fondation Fernand-Halphen.[10] The work was published in 1929.[11]

While it is possible that they are two distinct pieces, it is more likely that the 1928 *Scherzo* is merely a revision of the earlier work, considering Duruflé's penchant for revision.[12] Indeed, the earliest version of the work is considerably different from later versions. This reading of the situation, however, raises the question as to how Duruflé, in any legitimate way, could have used essentially one piece both for an entrance exam in 1926 and for a composition exam in 1928. Without access to the manuscripts there can be no resolution of this quandary.

The first public performance of the piece was given by Fleury on March 15, 1928,[13] at the Hôtel Majestic, an elegant Renaissance palace located a few blocks south of the Arc de Triomphe. The mediocre organ at the Majestic, however, was hardly worthy of the *Scherzo*. Indeed, Norbert Dufourcq described it as "an abominable organ . . . a pneumatic organ."[14]

In a lesson with one of her students, Mme Duruflé

pictorially described the atmosphere of the work and its seemingly incongruous "scenes." She suggested that the performer relax as though asleep and dreaming at the beginning, then to consider the first fragments of the scherzo theme as the passing wings of sprites, who then wake the slumberer and entertain with their dances. She sang the lilting theme of section B with a cheerful "la, la, la-la, la, la" and otherwise summoned a characterized interpretation of the piece.[15]

It has been suggested that the *Scherzo* was inspired by Dupré's *La Fileuse* from his *Suite bretonne* (1924), and perhaps also by Dukas's *Sorcerer's Apprentice*, an orchestral scherzo (1897).[16]

## *Prélude, récitatif et variations*, Op. 3

In 1928, Duruflé wrote the *Prélude, récitatif et variations*, Op. 3, for flute, viola, and piano,[17] dedicating the work to the memory of Jacques Durand, who died on August 22 of that year. Durand had studied at the Paris Conservatoire where he developed lasting friendships with Dukas and Debussy, who were themselves classmates and friends. Jacques succeeded his father as head of the publishing firm Durand & Cie, Duruflé's primary publisher. In his memoirs Duruflé wrote that he obtained a *premier prix* for this piece, referring to it as his Trio.[18]

The musicologist Armand Machabey commented that this work "reveals to what extent Duruflé had freed himself from the scholastic . . . in order to get in touch with universal forms."[19] Maurice Imbert called it "the work of beautiful substance, thought, and construction."[20] Ian Wells observed that the theme of the variations, "or something derived from it, features in an improvised prelude and fugue on a theme of Duruflé that Marcel Dupré broadcast from Meudon at Christmas 1949, the prelude being of particular interest as it treats the theme in a way comparable to Dupré's well-known G minor prelude."[21]

Opus 3 received its first hearing in the Salle Chopin at Pleyel on January 12, 1929,[22] under the aegis of the Société nationale, and was published in the same year. The performance was given by flutist Marcel Moyse, whom Tournemire once described in a review as "the foremost [flutist] in the world,"[23] with violist Maurice Vieux and the celebrated pianist Jean Doyen.[24] Duruflé occasionally played the piano part himself, as he did in Rouen on June 25, 1932, and in Louviers at the Eden-Théâtre, on November 11, 1932.

## *Prélude, adagio et choral varié sur le Veni Creator*, Op. 4

Duruflé's Opus 4, the *Prélude, adagio et choral varié sur le Veni Creator*, is a vast encomium to the Holy Spirit, being based completely upon phrases of the Gregorian plainsong hymn appointed for second vespers on Pentecost. Duruflé dedicated the work to Vierne with *affectueux hommage*, around the same time Vierne composed his own triptych, the first movement of which, Matines, he dedicated "à mon cher élève et ami Maurice Duruflé." Duruflé played the first (private) performance of the work for the Amis de l'Orgue competition in

1930, and gave the first public performance for the Société nationale de musique, at the Salle du Conservatoire on May 16, 1931. Earlier that year he played the work for several recitals on the Riviera. He played the work again at Sainte Clotilde on March 22, 1934.[25]

In his observations about this work, Andrew Thomson points out that the composition bears some formal resemblance to Vincent d'Indy's *Istar*, "a novel set of orchestral variations in reverse order, concluding with the theme itself."[26] Comparing the *Prélude* with the Adagio, Norbert Dufourcq characterized the former as "truly written for the keyboard," but the latter as "the orchestral type."[27] From a different perspective, Gwilym Beechey noted that the *Prélude*, like the Op. 2 *Scherzo*, "might be a compressed orchestral score with its many and frequent changes of manual and tone colour."[28] In any event, the orchestral nature of this work, particularly of the first two movements, places considerable demands upon the performer, which is surely one reason that so many organists play only the variations in recital.

But an observation by André Fleury about internal inconsistencies triggers a question about the dating of the various parts of the work, suggesting that it was composed in two stages. Fleury writes: "The first two movements of the *Veni Creator* are pure masterpieces. As for the Choral varié, one cannot put it at the same level."[29]

For lack of information to the contrary, critics have generally assumed that Duruflé wrote the entire Opus 4 specifically for the contest in composition sponsored by Les Amis de l'Orgue in 1930. Some have noted that the style of the *Prélude* and the Adagio is oddly more advanced compositionally and harmonically than the Choral varié, the first two movements reflecting Duruflé's study with Dukas in a way that the Choral varié does not. As a result, some hold that the Choral varié is a weak conclusion to the first two movements.

Duruflé originally called the set *Variations sur l'hymne "Veni Creator,"* in the plural, and played them as such at a recital in Louviers on October 18, 1926.[30] André Fleury wrote that the set "was written for an examination at the Conservatoire,"[31] meaning that Duruflé composed them as a student of Widor.[32] Three and a half years later, he used the variations as the final movement of a three-movement work for the competition hosted by Les Amis de l'Orgue in 1930. The guidelines[33] called for unpublished works consisting of three movements in the form of either *musique pure*, or *fantaisie*, or *musique à programme*. Duruflé composed the *Prélude* and the Adagio so that with the variations he would have a work of three movements eligible for the competition. It suited his purposes to rename the variations, giving them the singular title: Choral varié.[34]

It is of considerable interest that the Choral varié[35] and the *Scherzo*, works of very different compositional idioms, were composed in the same year, the latter under private tutelage with Tournemire, the former during Duruflé's formal study at the Conservatoire, probably with Widor. So even though Duruflé's 1927

*Triptyque* is numbered Opus 1, it was written after Opus 2 and part of Opus 4. The *Prélude, adagio et choral varié sur le Veni Creator* was first published in 1930.[36]

## *Suite* for Organ, Op. 5

Duruflé's next opus number is the Op. 5 *Suite* for organ (*Prélude, Sicilienne, Toccata*), dedicated "à mon Maître Paul Dukas." The work is dated 1932[37] and was first published in 1934.[38] Duruflé played the premiere of the *Prélude* on February 22, 1932, at Saint Merry, but the first performance of the complete work was given by Geneviève de la Salle at the church of Saint François-Xavier, on January 23, 1935. Duruflé himself played the British premiere in a performance for the Organ Music Society at Christ Church Woburn (London), on November 8, 1938.[39]

Norbert Dufourcq wrote that Duruflé's personality is evident in the *Prélude*, but that "the imprint of Vierne is obvious in the *Sicilienne* and the *Toccata*, as to the choice of themes above all."[40] Noting the influence of Vierne and Dukas, Andrew Thomson points out that the *Suite*

> leaves behind the inward-looking Gregorian world of Tournemire for Vierne's more rhetorical and secular idiom. That the latter's Sixth symphony was in his mind[41] during the Suite's composition is borne out by two marked similarities—the striking B flat pedal-points with which Duruflé's *Prélude* and Vierne's fourth movement (both in E-flat minor) commence, and the crashing B-major chords with added sixths in the concluding bars of both works. On the other hand, Duruflé's finely wrought and entirely individual sound world—of a textural clarity by no means always achieved by Vierne's chromatically saturated and hard driven quasi-orchestral invention—is itself a tribute to Dukas.[42]

Moreover, the *Prélude* shows the influence of Dukas's "underrated and neglected piano sonata (composed 1899–1900) where the first movement is also in E-flat minor and whose feelings are similarly somber, dark and even gruesome in their expression."[43] One wonders whether Duruflé found inspiration for the descending theme of the *Prélude* in the identical line (transposed) in Franck's *Final*, namely, the repeated left-hand line found in the fifth measure after the key change to six sharps: D♯–C♯–B–G♯, with the upper E sometimes played, sometimes implied.

Of all his major works, Duruflé considered the *Prélude* the easiest to play, along with the variations on *Veni Creator*,[44] and these are the two works he played most frequently in recital, identifying the former only as the *Prélude* in E-flat Minor and giving no indication of its being part of a suite. More than any of his other works, the second movement, the *Sicilienne*, betrays Duruflé's indebtedness to Ravel and Debussy. It also recalls the *Sicilienne* of Vierne, from his *Pièces de fantaisie*, composed in 1926.

Although Duruflé's *Sicilienne* stands alone, as do the other two movements, its pairing with the *Prélude* (without the *Toccata*) would seem unfinished, although Duruflé did play the two together in a recital in May 1934 at the home of Comtesse Christian de Berthier de Sauvigny, where he also played the Franck *Variations symphoniques*.[45]

By 1942 at the latest,[46] Duruflé had transcribed the *Sicilienne* for a small orchestra comprising flute, oboe, clarinet, bassoon, horn, and five-part strings. The work remains unpublished, and the author has found no mention of the work's having ever been performed. The manuscript is located in the Duruflé Papers.

As for the *Toccata*, most players consider the work a masterpiece. Gwilym Beechey, for example, wrote that it is "one of the best examples—if not *the* best and most satisfying—of the many French movements of its kind."[47] Duruflé, however, made no secret of the fact that he disliked the piece. "The first theme is very bad, then, [and] as the theme is the essential thing in a composition, the composition cannot be successful with a bad theme." Once challenged as to the fact that, since he published it he must have liked it at the time, Duruflé replied, "When you compose, you have to like what you've written at the time, otherwise you wouldn't write. . . . But when time has done its work, when time has passed, that is, some time after you've written it, you can certainly change your mind. I believe I'm not alone in this regard."[48] Mme Duruflé said to her husband about it, "I love the sauce very much even if you don't like it." He replied, "Yes, the sauce is there, but there's no beefsteak, and the beefsteak is the main thing."[49]

In his early years Duruflé refused to hear his students play the *Toccata* for their lessons. Later on, however, he was somewhat more accommodating, and he did occasionally hear the piece, though he had less to say about it than about his other works.[50] Neither he nor his wife ever recorded the *Toccata*. He did not want to hear her practice the piece, so she practiced it when she was in the church alone, or at home with the power to the organ turned off. Although she resumed practicing it in earnest after his death, she "had to stop because she was sure that he was watching her from heaven with a look of disapproval!"[51]

Some organists take liberties with the piece, which Duruflé did not like. Mme Duruflé remarked, "At the end of the *Toccata*, one finds a series of virtuosic chords. My husband did not like anyone to begin with a *rubato* followed by an accelerando. He had a horror of this effect of a train starting up."[52] For later editions, there was no cut in the development, as some have claimed was earlier suggested by Duruflé,[53] but in the edition of 1978 he did supply a completely different rewriting of the final measures.

In the *Toccata*, as elsewhere in his works, the indication "enlever les anches et les mixtures" means to remove the $2\frac{2}{3}'$ and $2'$ stops as well. Duruflé commented:

[w]hen Franck and Vierne indicated to add reeds, they implied pulling down the *appel d'anches*, which brought on the $2\frac{2}{3}'$ and $2'$ stops, as well as the mixtures. When you add

reeds to a division, generally speaking, you add the mixtures, cornets and other stops which accompany the reeds. Since the Cavaillé-Coll organ had such a great influence in France for such a long time, this tradition endured.[54]

The technical demands of the *Toccata* are formidable, as anyone who has tried to master the dense and widespread chords can testify. Duruflé had large hands and he found the difficult passages easier to maneuver than did his wife, whose hands were smaller. She made a few minor note-changes in order to reduce the spread, and occasionally suggested that her students do the same.[55]

Virgil Fox has been credited inaccurately with giving the American premiere of the *Suite*, which he performed from memory in 1956, at the Riverside Church, for the national convention of the American Guild of Organists meeting in New York City.[56] The work was already "much-played" by 1953, according to Seth Bingham.[57] Indeed, organist George Butler, as a student of George Faxon, played the work on his senior recital at Jordan Hall of the New England Conservatory of Music, on March 2, 1951, over five years before the performance by Fox.[58] It is remarkable that it took some twenty years for this marvelous work to be discovered by American organists.

## *Trois Danses,* Op. 6

Duruflé's turn to orchestral writing—with his *Trois Danses,* Op. 6—began as the result of a failed commission and the fact that he did not have easy access to a decent organ on which to compose. After describing the "sad story" of the organ at Saint Étienne-du-Mont in his memoirs, Duruflé wrote, "I redirected my activity as an organist to the orchestra."[59] Except for his *Messe "Cum jubilo,"* he began and completed all of his orchestral works, including the orchestral versions of the *Requiem,* during the period when the organ at the church was in disrepair.

In 1927, Paul Dukas introduced Duruflé to a playwright named Édouard Dujardin,[60] who asked him to write an orchestral work, some *musique de scène,* for a theater piece he had just written, which was to be performed in Paris.

> He wanted some background music . . . which would consist in evoking a savage dance. He gave me an example, making rhythmic gestures at full speed, accompanied by banging his fist on the table and roaring. I set to work and began a sort of Tambourin. But before going further, I took the precaution of playing this beginning for him. "This is not at all what I asked of you," he said to me. "It's too complicated." Briefly, the deal failed to come off, and we never saw each other again. Nevertheless, all work begun deserves reflection. I continued it and once it was finished I showed it to Paul Dukas, who encouraged me to orchestrate it; this gave me a chance for some profitable work. . . . I could finally submit my work to my Maître, who naturally made some very interesting critiques and recommended that I write a Suite of three dances. It was thus that I was led to writing the two others.[61]

The *Trois Danses* for orchestra (*Divertissement, Danse lente, Tambourin*), a masterful work of orchestral coloring and architecture, and a legacy of his study with Dukas, is dated 1932[62] and was published in 1939. It was performed at least five times within the first two years of its premiere on January 18, 1936, when it was presented at the Théâtre du Châtelet by the Orchestre Colonne under the direction of Paul Paray,[63] to whom the work is dedicated.

Of the set, Norbert Dufourcq wrote:

> Duruflé . . . pays tribute, beyond Debussy, to the supporters of the traditional form of the *Suite* by evoking through three choreographic *tempi* [the] steps and movement of a *commedia dell'arte* transported to a 20th century war cry, whose accents he tries to soften with a warm and luminous symphony. Nothing exaggerated in the *Trois danses*, nothing wanton: viril [*sic*] and spiritual music, as is that of Rameau, Debussy or Ravel. Duruflé sought a balance between form and emotion.[64]

The *Divertissement* is a classic scherzo with three refrains and two couplets. The intensely poetic *Danse lente* follows a free form. And the *Tambourin* is a rustic dance constructed in a traditional ABA form over an ostinato.

*Tambourin* was recorded in 1938 by the Concerts Lamoureux under the direction of Eugène Bigot, and was issued in 1944 as the eleventh recording in a series of forty representing an Anthology of Contemporary Music, a project of the Secrétariat général des Beaux-Arts and the Association française d'action artistique of the Vichy government.

It is astonishing, the extent to which the premiere of this work catapulted Duruflé into the limelight of the mainstream press and the broader public. The premiere of *Trois Danses* was received with accolades in the press by no fewer than seventeen reviews. Most of them saw the need to identify the composer as "the young organist of Saint Étienne-du-Mont," or something equivalent, to identify and place the composer who, by many, was previously unknown. By 1950 Claude Rostand could write that the work was "in the repertoire of all our symphonic associations."[65]

Ten days after its premiere, the piece was repeated, again by the Orchestre Colonne, but this time at the Poste-Parisien. It was subsequently played by Pierné in 1936 and then at the Conservatoire.[66] It was performed by Concerts Lamoureux in March 1938 under the direction of Eugène Bigot and at a Promenade Concert in London, in 1947.[67] For the first two decades of its existence, the *Trois Danses* was popular among the finest conductors and orchestras of the day, even in the United States. Paul Paray conducted the Detroit Symphony in two performances of the work, both times, however, omitting the *Divertissement*.[68]

French composers developed a particular fondness for the saxophone during the jazz era. In his *Trois Danses*, the jazz-suspicious Duruflé included a part for alto saxophone that attracted the interest of saxophonists. In 1943 Leduc published *Traits difficiles: Répertoire du Conservatoire national de musique de Paris tirés d'œuvres symphoniques et dramatiques pour tous instruments,* containing passages for the alto saxophone collected by Marcel Mule for study purposes.[69]

The work is rarely performed today, a circumstance that Duruflé may have foreseen in making several arrangements of it for piano. In 1961 he transcribed the *Tambourin* for solo piano[70] and published it in 1962. He also wrote a two-piano transcription of the complete set, which long remained unpublished.[71] The pianists Jean Doyen and Henriette Puig-Roget played the work from manuscript.[72] Duruflé was at first opposed to publishing the two-piano version

> because, you understand, when I set out to transcribe them from orchestra to piano there were many tremolos. In the orchestra the tremolo is a very beautiful thing, there's no doubt. And there are many kinds of tremolos, while at the piano you can't translate the orchestral tremolo. But you have to do it, precisely because the orchestral tremolo obliges you to do a tremolo at the piano, something that is not very pianistic. . . . I thought it was not worth publishing them.[73]

After her husband's death, Mme Duruflé, through her sister Éliane, gave sole performing rights for this manuscript copy to New York City residents Rémy Loumbrozo, a former solfège student of Éliane, and his pianist wife, Arianna Goldina.[74] The couple played the U.S. premiere of the work at Alice Tully Hall in Lincoln Center on March 4, 1989.[75] According to Éliane Chevalier, the two-piano version had been broadcast over French radio in the 1950s.[76] Loumbrozo and Goldina produced the premiere recording of the work in 1992.[77] Mme Duruflé said of their performance that it "corresponds exactly to my husband's own interpretation. It is moving, even the rests have a soul of their own. I feel that my praise cannot do justice to your playing."[78]

Loumbrozo and Goldina also own a photocopy of the manuscript version for one piano, four hands,[79] which they used for their performance of the *Danse lente* and *Tambourin* for the Duruflé retrospective at Riverside Church in November 1989. One reviewer described it as "a curiously successful piano four-hands version . . . [that] managed to avoid the thick textures that usually come with the four-hand genre."[80] Loumbrozo and Goldina, however, consider it "too crowded" and have said they will probably not play it again.[81] The couple consider the transcriptions idiomatic for the piano, except where the tremolos imitative of string tremolos are awkward, and where a long-held F, lasting about five measures, decays too early to have much meaning. Both transcriptions of the complete work, that for two pianos and that for four hands, one piano, were finally published in 1996. Duruflé's version for solo piano was published in 1997.

Duruflé apparently made no effort to transcribe *Trois Danses* for organ. One reason for this, as proposed by Wolfgang Reisinger,[82] may be that the transference of a secular orchestral work to an organ in a church seemed inappropriate to him. This may well be true, but Duruflé did not hesitate to write similarly secular works for the organ, such as the *Scherzo* and the *Suite*. For Duruflé the sacred and the secular coexisted in a blurred world. And this explains why, for him, the organ and orchestral worlds also blurred. The most compelling reason for Duruflé's not having transcribed it is that the work was simply too complex for the task, at least the two outer movements. *Danse lente*, however, has been transcribed for organ, and performed and recorded, by the British organist William Whitehead with the permission of the Duruflé Association—on the condition that it not be disseminated to third parties.[83]

## *Prélude et fugue sur le nom d'ALAIN*, Op. 7

In 1942 Duruflé composed what would become one of his most popular works, the *Prélude et fugue sur le nom d'ALAIN*, Op. 7, dedicating it to "Jehan Alain mort pour la France."[84] The promising composer and young organist Alain, Duruflé's friend and colleague, left the Paris Conservatoire in 1939, the same year he wrote *Litanies* for organ, whose theme Duruflé quotes in the *Prélude*. Duruflé was hesitant to identify Alain as "free spirited, optimistic, very joyful, happy," choosing instead to describe him as serious and introverted.[85] He died in the defense of France during the following year, according to this account:

> [On] June 20, 1940, the motorcyclist Jehan Alain was going on reconnaissance toward Petit-Puis,[86] near Saumur. At a bend in the road, a noise of boots came toward him. Time to throw his machine in a vineyard, to take over the hut of the wine grower for something to lean on, and he stood up to them. Sixteen Germans bit the dust before he himself was killed by a shot fired into his back at point-blank range. The enemy officer had final honors paid to his body.[87]

The composer played the premiere of Opus 7 at the Palais de Chaillot on December 26, 1942, as part of a series of monthly recitals presented during the 1941–42 season by Les Amis de l'Orgue on the newly restored Gonzalez organ at the Palais de Chaillot. The series was an effort to maintain enthusiasm for the organ during the war, at least in Paris, where organ recitals in churches had been curtailed.[88] Despite the extreme shortage of paper during and after the Occupation, the work was published in October 1943.[89]

In this work Duruflé followed the same procedure of assigning pitches to the alphabet as Maurice Ravel had used for his *Menuet sur le nom d'Haydn* (1910) for piano solo.[90] The scale in Duruflé's work is based on A, with a flatted B, providing an alphabet whose source is unknown, but whose implied harmony is pliable.[91] The only work that Ravel composed during a period of inactivity after his father's death, the minuet was written on commission for a musical homage published on the centenary of Haydn's death. Both Ravel's and Duruflé's alphabet-derived works were expressions of grief at the death of a male figure, in the first instance a father and in the second a friend.[92] Jehan Alain was memorialized in works by several other composers, including Langlais's *Chant héroïque*, Fleury's *In Memoriam*, and Dutilleux's orchestration of his *Prière pour nous autres charnels*.[93]

Arguably the most formally satisfying of all the Duruflé organ works, the *Prélude et fugue sur le nom d'ALAIN* is certainly the most frequently performed (after the *Choral varié sur le Veni Creator*). Duruflé's spelling of the name ALAIN provides the thematic material for both parts of the work. In the Prelude it generates an exuberant staccato arabesque that retains a certain seriousness despite its scherzo-like character. And in the fugue the name supplies a melancholy eighth-note subject that soon finds itself contrasted with a dazzling sixteenth-note second subject, the two together engineering a work of truly heroic dimension.

The author has seen no reference to the North American premiere of this piece.[94] But when asked whether she hadn't played the United States premiere of one of Duruflé's (unspecified) works, Marie-Claire Alain replied, "Yes, I played it from 1961 on, before Maurice and Marie-Madeleine made their first tour there. I achieved a moderate success; the public did not seem to realize the impact of this music."[95]

## Andante et Scherzo, Op. 8

In 1940 Duruflé revisited his Op. 2 *Scherzo* for organ, and transcribed it for orchestra, numbering it Opus 8. The transcription extends the development and omits the vignettes in the *da capo*, adding a complex six-against-four accompaniment in section C. Added glissandi produce a blurred effect similar to the effect of an ample acoustic.[96] He thus reimagined an existing work into a readily identifiable if somewhat different piece, with the result that Opus 8 could not be considered a version of Opus 2, in the manner of a reduction in reverse, for instance, or what might be called an agrandissement. There is no dedicatee for the Op. 8 *Scherzo*.

The first performance of Opus 8 was presented on November 17, 1940, by the Société des Concerts du Conservatoire under the direction of Charles Münch. The performance did not include the *Andante* that was appended to it later.[97] This was the first time any of Duruflé's works was performed by this renowned orchestra, whose organist he had been since 1939. The program on which the work was premiered was billed as a Festival Bach-Fauré, a fact that begs the question: how was Duruflé's *Scherzo* seen to be related to Bach and Fauré? The concert began with the latter's *Pénélope*, the orchestral suite *Pelléas et Mélisande*, and the *Cantique de Jean Racine*, and ended with J. S. Bach's *Cantate de la Croix*[98] and the Orchestral Suite in D.[99] Duruflé's *Scherzo* was performed between the Fauré and the Bach.[100]

In September of 1949 the Société des Concerts du Conservatoire went on tour for a week of performances at the Edinburgh Festival in Scotland, with André Cluytens conducting. Again the *Scherzo* was performed without its companion *Andante*.[101]

The *Scherzo*, Op. 8, was published in 1947, without the optional first movement. But when the *Andante* was published, as a completely separate publication, in March 1955, it appeared under the title *Andante et Scherzo pour orchestre*, Op. 8, I: *Andante*, the *Scherzo* of 1947 now serving as the second part of a bipartite work. Duruflé provided an optional bridge between the two movements so they can be played without interruption.

The *Andante*, completed on September 22, 1950,[102] is based upon themes from the *Scherzo* and is dedicated "à Henri Tomasi"(1901–71),[103] who conducted the premiere of the work on January 14, 1952, by the Orchestre national. It was performed again by Pasdeloup in January 1954 at the Palais de Chaillot, under the direction of Jean Fournet. The work had another performance in March 1955 by the Société des Concerts du Conservatoire under the baton of Georges Tzipine.

Describing the *Andante et Scherzo* as a luminous work, René Dumesnil says it is "admirably balanced, diverse in its unity, orchestrated with a suppleness" in which one recognizes a disciple of Dukas. The piece, he wrote, "is assured of a success that will only grow."[104] Duruflé himself, in a letter to Marie-Madeleine Chevalier the day he finished the *Andante*, wrote of the work: "I'm afraid I was influenced by Debussy for certain harmonies."[105] Duruflé, in fact, considered the piece *too* influenced by Debussy.[106]

In his review of the work, in *Opéra*, Bernard Gavoty took a different view. Although he considered the work marvelous for its *esthétique fauréenne*, he rendered what he called a light reproach for the way the *Andante* is joined rather artificially to the *Scherzo*, which he considered to be of a different style, emerging as an orchestration of a piece that was originally for organ. Gavoty claimed that Duruflé was unsuccessful at adapting the organ piece to the orchestra.[107]

Of all the reviewers, Gavoty, being an organist, had the advantage (or the disadvantage) of knowing the Opus 2 version of the *Scherzo*. He proposed that, were Duruflé to take his advice, the latter could compose an Allegro and a Final, adding them to the *Andante* and *Scherzo*, and have himself a complete symphony, of which Gavoty would have the honor of being the progenitor.[108]

In view of Duruflé's fondness for transcription, one could well wish that he had transcribed the *Andante* for organ so that it could be played in tandem with the *Scherzo*, Op. 2. Unfortunately the work does not lend itself easily to transcription, at least not for performance on a typical three-manual instrument of French design. Duruflé told his wife Marie-Madeleine that it is an orchestral piece, not an organ piece,[109] and Mme Duruflé insisted, in public at least, that if it could be transcribed, her husband would have done it.[110]

## *Requiem*, Op. 9

The next work in Duruflé's œuvre, the Op. 9 *Requiem*, is given full treatment in chapter 17.

## *Quatre Motets sur des thèmes grégoriens*, Op. 10

Duruflé composed and published the *Quatre Motets sur des thèmes grégoriens*, Op. 10, for unaccompanied chorus, in 1960, in four separate octavos, dedicating them to Auguste Le Guennant, the director of the Institut grégorien de Paris, whose counsel Duruflé had sought regarding the Solesmes rhythmic interpretation of Gregorian chant.[111]

The pieces were first performed at Saint Merry, on May 4, 1961, by the Chorale Stéphane Caillat.[112] Three of the motets are for SATB chorus; *Tota pulchra es* is for women's voices. In each case Duruflé constructed the voices around the Gregorian melody associated with the texts, as he had done with the *Requiem* and would later do with *Messe "Cum jubilo."* The craft and elegance of the motets, and the frequency with which they are sung, are testimony to Duruflé's success with small choral forms.

Though the motets have come to be sung during the mass, more or less at will, and though Duruflé indicated they could be sung during benediction of the Blessed Sacrament,[113] their texts are rooted in particular services from the liturgical year. All of them reflect some feature of Roman Catholic piety, namely, its petrine foundation (*Tu es Petrus*), its veneration of Mary (*Tota pulchra es*), its eucharistic devotion (*Tantum ergo*), or its Holy Week practices (*Ubi caritas*). All of the texts are drawn from the Tridentine liturgy still in use prior to the Second Vatican Council.

*Ubi caritas*, no. 1, scored for four-part mixed chorus, translates:

> Antiphon: Where charity and love abide, God is there.
> Verses:     The love of Christ has gathered us together.
>                Let us be glad and rejoice in him.
>                Let us fear and love the living God.
>                And let us love with a sincere heart.
> Antiphon: Where charity and love abide, God is there.
>                    (Author unknown [9th–10th century?])

This text was the eighth and final "antiphon" appointed to be sung at mass on Holy Thursday during the washing of feet,[114] an action that commemorates Jesus's washing of the feet of the apostles at the last supper.

*Tota pulchra es*, no. 2, is for three-part women's chorus. The text of this motet comprises the first three antiphons from second vespers for the feast of the Immaculate Conception, on December 8, namely, *Tota pulchra es*, *Vestimentum tuum*, and *Tu gloria Jerusalem*.

> Thou art all fair, O Mary, and there is no original sin in thee.
> Thy raiment is as white as snow, and thy face is like the sun.
> Thou art the glory of Jerusalem, the joy of Israel, the honor of our people.

Duruflé's inventive conflation of the three is foreign to vespers, and precludes the use of the motet in that context. The text bears the primary doctrinal import of the feast of the Immaculate Conception, namely, that Mary was conceived without taint of original sin. Inasmuch as the first antiphon is in the first mode, and the other two in the eighth mode, Duruflé's setting is complex and harmonically ambiguous, and the original chants appear in fragmented form. The scoring for women's voices alone highlights the marian character of the text.

The third motet, *Tu es Petrus*, no. 3, is for four-part mixed chorus. Its text lies at the heart of the petrine foundation of the Roman Catholic church:

> Thou art Peter, and upon this rock I shall build my church.
> (Matthew 16:18)

In the Tridentine liturgy, this text appeared a number of times in the course of the liturgical calendar, in various settings, suggesting its importance in Roman Catholic doctrine. At first vespers for the vigil of the feast of Saints Peter and Paul, which falls on June 29, *Tu es Petrus* was sung to the seventh mode setting upon which Duruflé based his motet.

The last motet, *Tantum ergo*, no. 4, for four-part mixed chorus, translates:

> Therefore we, before him bending,
> This great Sacrament revere;
> Types and shadows have their ending,
> For the newer rite is here;
> Faith, our outward sense befriending,
> Makes our inward vision clear.
>
> Glory let us give and blessing
> To the Father and the Son,
> Honor, thanks, and praise addressing,
> While eternal ages run;
> Ever too his love confessing
> Who from both with both is One.
> (Translation after John Mason Neale and Edward Caswall)

The rhymed and strophic Gregorian hymn *Pange lingua gloriosi corporis*, which is traditionally attributed to Saint Thomas Aquinas (1225?–74),[115] is the church's eucharistic hymn par excellence.[116] The two stanzas given here, usually referred to on their own as the *Tantum ergo* (the incipit), are the last two stanzas of that hymn. Of all the chants that Duruflé used for his four motets, only the *Tantum ergo* in its third-mode setting enjoyed a popular place in the repertoire of average congregations all over the Catholic world.[117]

The reason for its popularity is that these two stanzas of Aquinas's hymn were always sung during benediction of the Blessed Sacrament, a brief devotional service that for some Catholics exceeded in importance even the mass itself. In his memoirs about the liturgical routines of the Rouen cathedral, Duruflé singled out this service for particular mention.

But the original (and more authentically liturgical) use for the Gregorian hymn was at the end of the liturgy on Holy Thursday, when it was sung in its entirety.[118] The first four stanzas were sung after mass while the sacrament was transferred in processional to the altar of repose, usually a side altar set apart from the high altar. The final two stanzas of the hymn were sung when the processional reached the altar of repose.

Like the *Ubi caritas*, Duruflé's motet *Tantum ergo* enjoys a place in the repertoire of many North American choirs, some of which reserve it for Holy Thursday. Of the four motets, these are the two sung most often by choirs, just as their plainsong originals were sung for so many years by the Catholic faithful. Whereas the plainsong *Tota pulchra es* and the *Tu es Petrus* were never part of a congregational repertoire, so the choirs that sing the Duruflé motets have less liturgical need for these two of the four.

## Messe "Cum jubilo," Op. 11

Duruflé composed his last large work, the *Messe "Cum jubilo,"* Op. 11, in 1966 while he was in Ménerbes,[119] (see Fig. 14.1) and dedicated it "à ma femme." It is scored for unison baritone chorus and baritone solo, and incorporates the Gregorian mass ordinary known as *Cum jubilo*, including the *Kyrie, Gloria in excelsis, Sanctus*, a separate *Benedictus*, and the *Agnus Dei*,[120] and can be accompanied by large orchestra, reduced orchestra with organ, or organ alone. For its composition Duruflé sought the advice of Nadia Boulanger.[121]

Because the Gregorian setting is properly sung for masses honoring the Blessed Virgin Mary, performances of Duruflé's setting have often been associated with marian feasts, at least in France. Indeed, the first several performances of the work (except for the premiere itself) were given during the month of May, which Catholic piety associates with the Virgin Mary. Designated Mass IX, the Gregorian mass known as *Cum jubilo* was intended for any day celebrated in honor of the Blessed Virgin Mary. In practice, however, *Cum jubilo* was sung whenever desired.[122]

Like the *Requiem*, the earliest performances of Duruflé's *Messe* took place not in liturgical contexts, but in concert halls and in concert settings in churches. Thus the work was given its premiere, in the version for large orchestra, on December 18, 1966, at Salle Pleyel, by the Orchestre Lamoureux, directed by Jean-Baptiste Mari, and sung by baritone Camille Maurane and the men of the Chorale Stéphane Caillat.

Duruflé conducted another performance of the work by the same choir, with Mme Duruflé performing the solo-organ accompaniment, on May 16, 1967, at

Figure 14.1. Entrance to Duruflé's *pavillon*, Ménerbes. Photograph by author.

Saint Merry, for a concert featuring Bach and the école française.[123] The chorale also performed the mass in Bordeaux during the Mai Musical, in 1968.[124]

In November of 1968, the men of Stéphane Caillat's chorale sang "*Cum jubilo*" still another time, again at the church of Saint Merry, for which Duruflé was the conductor and Mme Duruflé the organist. The performance was sponsored by Les Amis de l'Orgue and by the association Una Voce, about which more will be said below.

Some proponents of the Latin liturgy advanced the theory that Duruflé composed "*Cum jubilo*" as a protest against the abuses that followed the Second Vatican Council, or in an effort to demonstrate that chant could be given a modern garb. Andrew Thomson conjectured that Duruflé wrote the work "perhaps as a defiant affirmation of a lost cause."[125] Although the theory has merit, Duruflé nowhere published comments to that effect, and his sister-in-law Éliane wrote, "No, it was not written in response to Vatican II."[126]

As with the *Requiem*, the version of *"Cum jubilo"* for full orchestra was the first to be written but the last to be published. The version for solo organ was published first (1967), owing to its greater practicality. The "réduction pour chant, orgue, et quintette à cordes, harpe, trompettes et timbales *ad libitum*" was published second, in 1971. In a prefatory note to the published score, Duruflé gives his rationale for this version: "The reduction for organ alone can seem insufficient in certain parts of this Mass where the expressive timbre of the strings is essential. This intermediate formula permits at the same time a lightening of the organ part, in blending it with, or opposing it to the other instruments." Finally, in 1972, the version for full orchestra was published, which Duruflé himself preferred.

Duruflé considered Messe *"Cum jubilo"* more difficult to perform than the *Requiem*.[127] Despite its being in unison, the work is not easy for the choir, and the temptation to designate it as "Gebrauchsmusik for liturgy"[128] ignores the challenges it presents. It is not deliberately simple, nor is it intended for amateurs.

From the perspective of its harmony, with its occasional bitonality and conflicting modalities, as Jeffrey Reynolds writes:

> The *Messe* is the most daring—and interesting—of Duruflé's choral music. . . . By virtue of its unusual performing forces, the *Messe "Cum Jubilo"* holds a special place not only in the composer's list of choral works, but in a list of all choral works of the twentieth century. The ability to sustain the listener's interest for such an extended work using only men's voices in unison and a single male soloist surely challenged Duruflé, as it would any composer. The answer to this challenge lay in Duruflé's ability to present the text of the Mass and its associated "Cum Jubilo" chants in a resourceful and creative manner.[129]

Commenting likewise on the work's more daring harmonies, Jörg Abbing observed that the opening chords in the *Benedictus* are completely in Messiaen's second mode of limited transposition, which Duruflé uses again in the *Agnus Dei*.[130]

Duruflé conducted the British premiere of Messe *"Cum jubilo"* on June 29, 1968, in the context of a high mass on the feast of Saints Peter and Paul at the Anglo-Catholic church of Saint Mary Magdalene, Paddington (London). Mme Duruflé was the organist. The use of an orchestra "was a necessary condition of the British premiere."[131] In a letter to Karen McFarlane, Duruflé mentioned that the performance was "très bonne. . . . I had at my disposal a remarkable chorus and orchestra."[132] Duruflé was subsequently invited to become affiliated with the Saint Mary Magdalene Music Society based at the church, and was even named its first president. After his death, Mme Duruflé succeeded him in the position.[133]

The Washington National Cathedral was the venue for the first performance of the work in the United States, also in 1968, where it was conducted by John Morehen.[134] Its first performance by the Duruflés in North America was given at Grace Cathedral in San Francisco on October 10, 1969. The New York premiere of the work was given at the Riverside Church ten days later, on October 20, also with Mme Duruflé at the organ and the composer conducting.

Duruflé eventually decided he preferred to have the baritone section sing the parts scored for baritone solo.[135] But realizing that the solo part lay high for baritones, he consented to adding some second tenors.[136] He proposed another alternative as well: a tenor soloist could sing the solo passage at rehearsal 17, or the baritone soloist could sing the small notes instead.[137]

## *Fugue sur le thème du carillon des heures de la cathédrale de Soissons*, Op. 12

Duruflé's *Fugue sur le thème du carillon des heures de la cathédrale de Soissons* was published in the collection *L'Organiste*, volume 50 (June 1962), "for the twenty-fifth anniversary of the death of Louis Vierne," by Éditions Musique sacrée, in a supplement to the journal *Musique Sacrée—L'Organiste*. It is dedicated "à Monsieur le Chanoine Henri Doyen, Organiste du Grand Orgue de la Cathédrale de Soissons, en amical souvenir." Doyen is said by some to have commissioned the work.[138] In his introduction to the volume in which this work appears, and for which he was editor, Doyen describes Duruflé's work as "lively and sprightly, in a minor mode that sometimes resembles Gregorian melody . . . always moving forward with seeming simplicity, always singing and responding with the ringing of joyous, numerous bells, in turn crystalline and shimmering, until the masterful ending on full organ. This is truly great art."[139] Duruflé played the first performance of this work in a recital at the Soissons cathedral on June 6, 1964, two weeks before he and his wife departed for their first American tour.

Evidently Duruflé was taken by the sound of the bells of Soissons cathedral, but he considered the melody of the *carillon des heures* a weak theme for an organ piece. Although it was not originally published as such, Mme Duruflé designated the work Opus 12, and its second edition, by Édition Europart-Music, published probably in 2000 under the auspices of the Duruflé Association, is so numbered.[140]

The newer edition is distinctly inferior to the original, with dynamic markings and registration and tempo indications typed on an old mechanical typewriter, and with caesuras written by hand, and sloppily so. The dedication to Henri

Doyen is retained, but there is no mention of the fact that the piece was first published as part of a collection to commemorate the twenty-fifth anniversary of the death of Vierne.

## Prélude à l'Introït de l'Épiphanie, Op. 13

The *Prélude à l'Introït de l'Épiphanie* appeared in 1961[141] in volume 48 of the series *Orgue et Liturgie*, under the direction of Norbert Dufourcq. Published by Éditions musicales de la Schola Cantorum et de la Procure générale de musique, the set appears without a publication date. The volume contains twelve *Préludes à l'Introït* for a random selection of Sundays and feasts, all of them solicited by Dufourcq. Duruflé's piece, perhaps actually commissioned by Dufourcq,[142] appears without an opus number, but Mme Duruflé identified it as Opus 13. By permission of the publisher it also appeared in *Music* magazine (the predecessor of the current run of *The American Organist*), in 1977.[143] Duruflé himself played its premiere at Saint Merry on May 4, 1961, on the same program at which his *Quatre Motets* were also premiered.

The two-page piece is a tightly constructed statement incorporating fragments of *Ecce advenit*, the antiphon from the Gregorian introit for the feast of the Epiphany:[144] "Behold the Lord the ruler comes, and kingdom, power, and dominion are in his hand." This work, like the others in the collection, has a liturgical purpose similar to that of the introits in Tournemire's *L'Orgue mystique*. At fifty-three measures, Duruflé's setting is four times longer than Tournemire's Introit for *Epiphania Domini* (vol. seven), which has only fourteen measures. A comparison of the vastly different compositional approaches taken by these two composers—maître and student—is instructive. Though they are settings of the same chant, Tournemire's is virtually formless, but much shorter than Duruflé's, while Duruflé's, though longer, is tightly and succinctly constructed.

## Notre Père, Op. 14

Duruflé's *Notre Père*, a setting of the Lord's Prayer in the vernacular, is a liturgical work intended to be sung during the mass. Unlike any of the movements from the *Requiem* or the *Messe "Cum jubilo"* it is brief enough to be practical for an ordinary Sunday liturgy. In fact, the piece was commissioned by a vicar of Saint Étienne-du-Mont,[145] and was composed and published in 1977, as Op. 14, when Duruflé was 75 years old. It is his only published setting of a text in French, and the only one intended for singing by a congregation in the vernacular liturgy, in which capacity it was used at Saint Étienne-du-Mont.

While it is true that the piece is not based on the plainsong for the *Pater noster* from the Latin mass, as Jeffrey Reynolds has pointed out, the melody has some characteristics of chant: "conjunct motion, limited ambitus, and syllabic text setting."[146] Moreover, the incipit (the words Notre Père) is set to the same pitches—do, re, mi, mi—as the Latin incipit (the words Pater noster).

The work was published by Durand, without an opus number, in two versions, one for unison voices and organ (published in 1977), and the other for four mixed voices *a cappella* (published in 1978).[147] Comparing the two versions, Dennis Keene, who gave their first performances in the United States,[148] preferred the one for unison voices, "for it seems simpler, less cultivated, more direct." Virtually homophonic and syllabic throughout, the piece is dedicated "à Marie-Madeleine Duruflé," whose designation of the work as Opus 14[149] is now commonly accepted. It is said by some sources that the work was in fact written by Mme Duruflé, with her husband's advice in the harmonization.[150] Ian Wells writes that Mme Duruflé "was asked by the clergy if Duruflé would set the Lord's Prayer in French for use in the parish mass. . . . Mme Duruflé-Chevalier replied that her husband could not sit at the piano for long enough to do so, but in order to try and encourage him she set the first part herself and gave him the impetus to complete it."[151] Jeffrey Reynolds writes that the version for unison voices and organ was made by Mme Duruflé and consists of the soprano line of the four-part motet with a simple organ accompaniment.[152]

Duruflé's setting of the *Notre Père* may have been his response to the ubiquitous setting by Nikolai Rimsky-Korsakov, in French, which in the late 1970s had achieved enormous popularity in the churches of Paris, inspired perhaps by its use at the church of Saint Gervais.

## Méditation

Around 1964 Duruflé composed a short three-page work for organ entitled *Méditation*, using a theme that would appear two years later as the opening melody in the *Agnus Dei* of his *Messe "Cum jubilo."*[153] This evocative work has neither opus number nor dedicatee and is not to be confused with his student work by the same title. It remained unpublished until after the death of Mme Duruflé, when, with her earlier authorization, Frédéric Blanc began playing the work, as he did on January 14, 2001, at Notre-Dame, Paris, for a performance that he considered the premiere,[154] discounting the fact that for years the Duruflés had performed the work during the liturgy at Saint Étienne-du-Mont. The first of Duruflé's works to be published posthumously, it is probably too slight a work for most concert performances, although Blanc suggests using it so. Published in 2002 by Durand, it is the last of Duruflé's works to appear in the catalog of this firm.

The quality of the posthumous publication of Duruflé's piece does not approximate the same impeccable standards of the works published under Duruflé's personal supervision, bearing mistakes as it does. Blanc notes that the

registrations are by Duruflé. He says nothing of the tempo and dynamic markings, but there is no reason to doubt they are Duruflé's as well. The errors, however, are Blanc's. He published some of the errata in 2003, but made further
errors in the process.[155]

## Duruflé's contribution to the *Soixante-quatre*
### *Leçons d'harmonie offertes en hommage à*
### *Jean Gallon par ses élèves*

Many of Jean Gallon's harmony students who received the *prix d'harmonie*
between 1919 and 1948 were invited to contribute short compositions to the
volume *Soixante-quatre Leçons d'harmonie offertes en hommage à Jean Gallon par
ses élèves* (1949), which was published by Durand in tribute to their harmony
professor.[156]

Duruflé's two-page contribution (p. 52) in open score has twenty-two measures and is based on a *chant donné*. Similar in character to the *Choral dorien* and
the *Choral phrygien* for organ by Jehan Alain, it is playable on the organ or
piano.[157] Wolfgang Reisinger points out that the work, in *stile antico* and ABA
form, is reminiscent of Duruflé's *Quatre Motets*, especially the *Ubi caritas*.[158]
Although this brief work was intended as a theoretical and analytical study, it has
come to be performed and even recorded in recent years.[159] In some sources,
especially on recordings of the work, Duruflé's offering is titled *Chant donné*
while in others it is identified as *Hommage à Jean Gallon*.

## Duruflé's Editions and Transcriptions: Vierne

Among the earliest of Duruflé's non-original works was his orchestration of
Vierne's *La Ballade du désespéré*, Op. 61, composed between August 24 and
September 30 of 1931, probably in disappointed response to the marriage of his
friend and companion Madeleine Richepin to the cancer specialist Dr. Lucien
Mallet (1885–1981).[160] Identified as a "poème lyrique" for voice and orchestra,
the sixteen-minute symphonic poem is dedicated to Richepin and was meant to
be sung by her.[161] Its brooding text is one last expression of Vierne's being, in
the words of Duruflé, "tormented by so many personal tragedies."[162] Vierne himself identifies the *Ballade* as "opus 61 and the last."[163]

The first page of the score indicates "orchestration de Maurice Duruflé
d'après les indications de l'auteur."[164] The work was never published in this version, but Vierne wrote a more practical version for voice and piano, dated
October 16, 1931,[165] which was published in 1947 as a "poème lyrique" for
tenor and orchestra or piano.

The work bears the following inscription:

Epigraph:
Here my task is finished . . . [ellipsis in the original]
My long and patient effort
Encloses my bitter destiny
In a supreme song of death.

*(16 October 1931* Louis Vierne)

The text of the *Ballade* is a poem by Henri Murger beginning "Qui frappe à ma porte à cette heure?" (Who knocks on my door at this hour?)[166]

In 1928, Vierne wrote a suite of pieces for cello and piano. *Soirs étrangers,* Op. 56, is a travelogue, of sorts, and comprises five movements evoking impressions of evenings in exotic places: *Grenade, Sur le Léman, Venise, Steppe canadien,* and *Poissons chinois.* It was not performed publicly during Vierne's lifetime, but was premiered nearly a year after his death, on May 17, 1938, by cellist Paul Bazelaire, with Bernard Gavoty playing the piano. Vierne had established a plan to transcribe the work for cello and orchestra, but the project was prevented by his death. Duruflé's orchestration of the piece, completed in 1943 and published in the same year by Lemoine, was premiered on April 23, 1944, at Concerts Pasdeloup.

In December 1928, Vierne improvised three works on the organ at Notre-Dame which he titled *Marche épiscopale, Méditation,* and *Cortège.*[167] The improvisations were recorded on 78 rpm discs by Odéon. Madeleine Richepin was there to assist him and she reportedly told Vierne about the time constraints on the discs. Vierne is quoted as responding, "What? Three minutes, thirty seconds per side? What do you want me to do in three and a half minutes? Oh, well, some pompous, Republican marches will do."[168] While the *Marche épiscopale*[169] and the *Cortège* are written in that vein, and represent distinctly lesser essays by Vierne, the *Méditation* is a profoundly poetic and lyrical work of sublime sentiment.

Vierne's student, Henri Doyen, was among the first to hear the recordings. He wrote:

> As I arrived one day for my lesson . . . the maître, obviously jolly with the little surprise he had in store for me, said point-blank as he offered me an armchair, "Sit there and don't move! Listen, pay attention, . . . Tell me what you think of it?" Then, going over to a machine that I had never seen before, he started it, and it was thus that I heard for the first time the *Marche épiscopale,* recorded some days earlier by the maître. . . .
> "So?" Vierne asked when the 78 was finished.
> "Cher maître, it's convincing: it only lacks Notre-Dame's two Suisses," I replied unhesitatingly (which perhaps later contributed to the choice of the title).
> The maître, utterly delighted with my response, then played me the other side of the disk entitled *Méditation*—so gentle that it made me think of Notre-Dame.[170]

Duruflé obtained the recordings on April 1, 1953, and in a letter to Marie-Madeleine Chevalier the next day he wrote:

It's rapture! This music puts you in a euphoric state that you can't imagine . . . What tender emotion, what sweet melancholy in the *Méditation*. Vierne possesses more than anybody in the world the art of making the organ sing, of leading a melody, of developing it with an inexhaustible breath, of varying it to great effect, of taking it up again under another form, and all of this, which is constructed and logical, like a written piece, blossoms with abandon, with a naturalness, a rare sensitivity. And what charm, what freshness in the modulations! Vierne knows how to reconcile the two extremes, that is to say, the rigor of logic and the fantasy of the imagination. He doesn't drop his theme for an instant. Nor does he forget the principal key in the course of his tonal escapes. He calls it back furtively with a delightful unexpectedness. And despite this continual presence of the intellect, he opens his heart wide.[171]

At the request of Mme Mallet-Richepin, executor to Vierne's estate, Duruflé reconstituted Vierne's improvisations, and published them in 1954 as *Trois Improvisations*.[172] His work was made possible by the directors and technicians of offico de Radiodiffusion-télévision française, which produced several discs from the original copy owned by Odéon.

Duruflé premiered the three works on April 5, 1954,[173] at Sainte Clotilde, in a recital sponsored by Les Amis de l'Orgue. To have heard Vierne "live," as it were, some seventeen years after his death, must have seemed ghostly to that first audience.

## Duruflé's Editions and Transcriptions: Tournemire

Like Vierne before him, Charles Tournemire recorded examples of his improvisations, in several recording sessions during 1930 and 1931,[174] and had them published by Polydor. Their given titles, their recording dates, and label numbers are as follows:

*Cantilène improvisée*, April 30, 1930 (Polydor 566 058)
*Fantaisie-Improvisation sur l'Ave maris stella*, April 30, 1930 (Polydor 561 061)
*Choral-Improvisation sur le Victimae paschali laudes*, April 30, 1930 (Polydor 566 060)
*Improvisation sur le Te Deum*, March 1931 (Polydor 561 050)
*Petite Rapsodie improvisée*,[175] November 1931 (Polydor 561 048)[176]

Daniel-Lesur and Bernard Schulé assisted Tournemire as registrants.[177] All of these recordings were made on the Cavaillé-Coll at Sainte-Clotilde before the 1933 alterations Tournemire made to the instrument.

A quarter century later, with the authority of Mme Tournemire,[178] Duruflé was at work transcribing her husband's improvisations. He also obtained authorization from ORTF and from Odéon. Duplicate discs had to be made from the copies in the archives, the matrices having been destroyed during the Second World War.[179] Duruflé published an explanatory note with the *Cinq*

*Improvisations,* which includes useful information for the performer. Writing on May 5, 1955, Duruflé told his friend André Fleury: "I'm in the process of reconstituting in musical notation some improvisations of Tournebroche,[180] who recorded them on discs in 1930. They're sensational! Exactly like those we admired so much. . . . I hope to give them their first performance at the inauguration of Saint Étienne-du-Mont . . . in October if everything goes as anticipated."[181]

The process of transcribing Tournemire's improvisations was tedious, more so than those of Vierne, because of their greater complexity. Duruflé said in an interview:

> I listened to them . . . especially at night because during the day there was noise, of course. . . . [A]nd in the passages that were difficult, because the recording was of a poor quality—at that time recordings produced a background noise—and the recording was not good, I had many hesitations, at those times I would slow it to half speed, instead of 78 rpm, and sometimes even a little slower. . . . It was a lot of work. . . . Tournemire improvised very quickly. He had a temperament that pushed him to improvise very quickly.[182]

The first performances of the reconstituted improvisations were played by Duruflé and his wife between 1956 and 1958, before the works were published. Mme Duruflé played the *Cantilène* and the *Te Deum* on April 7, 1956, at Saint Merry.[183] She presented the works again on June 7, 1956, for the inauguration of the new organ at Saint Étienne-du-Mont. Duruflé played the premiere of the *Petite Rapsodie improvisée* on January 22, 1957, at the Palais de Chaillot. And Mme Duruflé played the first performances of the *Ave maris stella* and the *Victimae paschali laudes* at Saint Étienne-du-Mont on June 3, 1958, for Les Amis de l'Orgue.[184] Although the premieres of these works took place in France, as did the improvisations of Vierne, it was in North America that Duruflé's reconstitutions met with enormous acclaim. By 1958 Duruflé had the improvisations published by Durand, dedicating them "en souvenir de mon Maître Charles Tournemire."[185]

The reconstitutions by Duruflé are not always faithful to the recordings. In correspondence with the author, Raymond Weidner wrote:

> When comparing the transcriptions to the score itself, one can see/hear differences: differences which, were I transcribing them, would have been done differently. As a matter of fact, when I performed Tournemire's improvisations, I played them more like the recordings rather than follow Duruflé's actual notes! Tournemire did maintain that it was easier to improvise than write out music because he could "play" far more notes when improvising than he cared to write down had he been composing.[186]

Marie-Madeleine Duruflé acknowledged the differences between the recordings and the transcriptions, explaining that her husband, with his skill for harmony and composition, altered certain passages that Tournemire, were he writing the pieces instead of improvising them, would certainly have handled differently.[187] Tournemire began the pedal cadenza of *Victimae paschali laudes*, for example, with a motif that he did not carry out, so Duruflé wrote what he believed his master probably intended.[188]

It is a fact of considerable interest, which has nevertheless escaped notice for more than a half century, that Tournemire was absolutely opposed to the reconstitution and publication of his improvisations. Several of his admirers had encouraged him to reconstitute them, including Joseph Bonnet.[189] The music critic for the *Times* of London, Felix Aprahamian, who knew Tournemire, wrote to him on January 31, 1936, asking whether Tournemire had yet committed the *Cantilène improvisée* to paper.[190] Tournemire replied, "You ask me if the *Cantilène* is published. But it never could be, since it was *only an improvisation* [emphasis in the original]."[191] When Tournemire went to London to play a recital in 1936, he also presented a lecture on improvisation, for which he played the discs he had recorded. Again Aprahamian urged him to transcribe the improvisations and have them published. Tournemire objected to the proposal, insisting that the works were intended as improvisations, not as pieces to be learned and performed by other organists.[192]

Eight years after their publication, Aprahamian wrote, in 1966, that the improvisations "are now available to players and have been made available contrary to the composer's expectations and probably contrary to his wishes as well."[193] It would be difficult to ascertain whether Duruflé or Mme Tournemire knew that Tournemire was opposed to the transcriptions, or whether she permitted Duruflé to transcribe them despite her husband's objections. In any case, Mme Tournemire and Duruflé shared the royalties from the publications.[194]

Contrary to common claims that *L'Orgue mystique* embodied Tournemire's improvisational style, Maurice and Marie-Madeleine Duruflé both considered his teacher's magnum opus to be different in style from his fabled improvisations, and less successful because they were less free. Mme Duruflé described *L'Orgue mystique* as "a bit stiff."[195] Duruflé's transcriptions, therefore, document a viewpoint that would otherwise have eluded proof after Tournemire's death. His labor of love provides scholars of *L'Orgue mystique* with a critical and essential foil for their studies.

In 1962 Duruflé published his own edition of Tournemire's *Triple Choral*, Op. 41, with "les indications de nuances, de registration et changements de claviers" as he learned them from his study of the work with Tournemire. In the manuscript of this work, dated November 1910,[196] Tournemire gives tempo and dynamic markings, and he indicates whether a passage is to be played on one manual or two, but he provides no registrational indications apart from the following generic notes given at the beginning of the piece:

The Fonds are to be used for the *Prélude*.
The First Choral will be played on a reed or the Fonds.

For the Second Choral, the player will introduce the reeds *mf* on the Récit. The Third Choral will be performed by means of two colors of particular gentleness, at the choice of the organist.

In his "révisions et annotations" of the work, published in 1962 by Schola Cantorum, Duruflé added indications from the score that he used for lessons with Tournemire, and took into account the particular characteristics of the Cavaillé-Coll organ at Sainte Clotilde.

Duruflé played the *Triple Choral* in a recital for Les Amis de l'Orgue at the Soissons cathedral, on June 6, 1964. He later indicated that the work had not been heard since the war, and that for many listeners it was "a stunning revelation."[197]

## Duruflé's Editions and Transcriptions: Franck

In 1957 Duruflé published his edition of the first volume of Franck's unfinished *L'Organiste, pour orgue ou harmonium*, "revised, fingered, and registered for organ by Duruflé," supplanting an earlier one by Tournemire. With regard to Franck's interpretive indications—tempo, nuances, ties, and detached notes—Duruflé scrupulously preserved the originals. Franck provided registrations only for harmonium; Duruflé's edition provides registrations also for pipe organ. As Carlton T. Russell wrote, Duruflé

> apparently felt that Tournemire's edition [published by Enoch, Paris] was not sufficient even for French organists, and thus made his lavish and even dearer one in 1957, still including only the fifty-nine pieces. As he states in his prefatory *notice*, he does follow more closely the first edition phrasing, thus correcting many of Tournemire's; and he does explain in detail the harmonium indications, as well as reminding the organist at the head of each piece if he should transpose either or both hands up or down an octave. Nonetheless, besides being heavily fingered and registrated [*sic*], this edition is above all aimed at French organists, who can read the text and (perhaps) pay the price.[198]

With his 1973 publication of Franck's *Trois Chorals*, in which he provided "révision et annotations,"[199] Duruflé entered the long-standing debate over the interpretation of Franck's organ works. Having studied the chorals with Tournemire, Duruflé "was an important representative of the Franck tradition as understood by Tournemire,"[200] because, as Duruflé pointed out, "Tournemire interpreted this music incomparably. He was privileged, he once told me, to perform the *Trois Chorals* on the piano at their first hearing, in private at the composer's home. Franck played the manual part and Tournemire the pedal part."[201] Duruflé's edition is all the more important, not only because Tournemire did not provide such an edition himself, but because the original edition, published by Durand (1891), was out of print. Moreover, Marcel Dupré published an edition in 1955 (Bornemann) which added phrase marks and ties, determined the precise rhythmic value of notes, deleted unnecessary ties, and used commas instead of Franck's fermatas, in the process substantially altering the original edition. Duruflé's edition had the advantage over Dupré's that it did not change any of the original text, neither its registration, its phrasing, its nuances, its tempo indications, ties, fermatas, the doubling of left hand and pedal notes, the distribution of polyphonic lines, the allotment of certain manual lines to the pedal, or even the engraving. And his additions appear in parentheses.[202] Further discussion about Duruflé's approach to the performance of Franck appears in chapter 20.

Duruflé's introduction to his edition of the Franck provides advice regarding the registration of the chorals, taking into account the peculiar tonal properties of the Cavaillé-Coll organ at Sainte Clotilde, especially the oboe, and the console design, which lacked récit-to-grand orgue and récit-to-pédale couplers. By the indication "anches" Duruflé reminds the performer that Franck intends the two-foot ranks, and the mixtures, to be drawn along with the reeds. In passages marked tutti, he cautions against adding 16' ranks from the récit, as Franck's instrument had no such ranks in that division.[203]

## Duruflé's Editions and Transcriptions: Bach

Duruflé wrote orchestral transcriptions for four organ chorales of Bach, and organ transcriptions for three movements from Bach's cantatas. The orchestral transcriptions are of *Nun komm, der Heiden Heiland*[204] and *O Lamm Gottes, unschuldig,* BWV 656, both from the Leipzig chorales, *Nun freut euch, lieben Christen gmein* (from divers chorales[205]), and *In dir ist Freude,* BWV 615 (from the *Orgelbüchlein*). The four transcriptions, which have never been published, were first performed in a program featuring the works of Bach, on December 23, 1944 at the Théâtre des Champs-Élysées, by the Société des Concerts du Conservatoire and conducted by Charles Münch. It would be instructive to compare Duruflé's approach to transcribing Bach organ works for orchestra with that of Leopold Stokowski, whose transcriptions of the *Toccata and Fugue* in D Minor, BWV 565, the *Toccata, Adagio, and Fugue* in C, BWV 564, and the Passacaglia and Fugue in C Minor, BWV 582, enjoyed renown through their performances by the Philadelphia Orchestra under his baton.

Duruflé wrote organ transcriptions of two movements from the cantatas of Bach. The first, *Werde munter, mein Gemüthe* (known in French as *Réjouis-toi, mon âme* and in English as *Jesu, Joy of Man's Desiring*) from Cantata 147, *Herz und Mund und Tat und Leben,* was first performed by Duruflé in the recital he presented at Palais de Chaillot on December 26, 1942. And *Ertödt uns durch dein' Güte* (French: *Mortifie-nous par ta bonté*) from Cantata 22, *Jesus nahm zu sich die Zwölfe,* despite its excellence, is unfortunately rarely played by organists. Both of these works were published. A third transcription remained unpublished during his lifetime: *Wachet auf, ruft uns die Stimme*, from Cantata 140, which Frédéric Blanc began performing by 2004.

## Other Transcriptions, Editions, etc., by Duruflé

Duruflé wrote an organ transcription of the *Prélude* to Gabriel Fauré's orchestral suite *Pelléas et Mélisande*, which Fauré dedicated to the Princess Edmond de Polignac. Frédéric Blanc began performing the piece several years after Mme Duruflé's death.[206]

Duruflé provided registrations for Jules Mouquet's two organ works titled *Deuxième Rapsodie* in G Minor (aeolian mode and phrygian mode [1914]), and his *Cortège* in A Minor (aeolian mode [1915–16]), published in 1953.[207]

For a 1966 Vogue Counterpoint recording of works for cello and organ, made at the organ of Notre-Dame d'Auteuil, Duruflé transcribed the *Adagio* of Albinoni, an *Aria* of Bach, Handel's *Largo, Intrada* by J.-A. DePlanes, and *Plainte* by Caix d'Hervelois. The cellist was the renowned André Navarra, winner of the *Grand prix du disque* in 1947.

Two years before his death, Duruflé wrote a brief preface for an elementary piano method entitled *Cours progressif de déchiffrage pour le piano: Débutant à élémentaire* (grade I to grade III), written by Catherine Meyer Garforth,[208] who won a *premier prix* during her study of harmony with him from 1961 to 1965.

Out of deference to her husband, Mme Duruflé maintained in public that he published everything he had written. In private she sometimes acknowledged that there were several works in manuscript whose publication she favored, but she wanted her husband's wishes honored as long as she was alive. Frédéric Blanc said she never made photocopies for anyone,[209] but gave him permission to publish the unpublished pieces after she died.[210]

Duruflé did the bulk of his composing at a time when his only steady income was from his church position, with stipends from his orchestral playing and probably modest royalties accruing from his few published works. While he completed the lucrative *Requiem* about four years into his tenure at the Conservatoire, he accepted the commission before he was employed there. To what extent Duruflé composed out of financial need is a matter of conjecture, but the theory is not without foundation.

Many reasons can be attested for Duruflé's small compositional output. Mme Duruflé said of her husband: "He composed slowly, with extraordinary awareness, not letting anything pass. And when a work was finished, he revised it again and again, meticulously. . . . He was also very busy with his career as a concert artist, as professor at the Conservatoire, and as organist at Saint Étienne-du-Mont and, during the summer, at the American Conservatory of Fontainebleau."[211] Mme Duruflé also pointed to his transcriptions[212] of the *Requiem* and of the *Trois Danses*, saying that all this represented an enormous amount of work. "This was not a 'production line' composer," she said. Duruflé himself explained that through the teaching of harmony he developed such a critical and exacting mind that he could no longer write.[213]

Duruflé also felt stigmatized by the radicalization of contemporary composition, having outlived the world he was writing for, and he saw little reason to continue composing in a musical language considered completely out of fashion.[214] Felix Aprahamian wrote that Duruflé's "timidity and extreme concern about what he sets down on paper, rather than painstaking researches in a new musical language, are responsible for so modest an output."[215] All the same, Duruflé regretted that he had written so little.[216]

In his dissertation about Duruflé's limited musical output, Wolfgang Reisinger posits the interesting theory, borne out by fact, that Duruflé lacked the inclination to transcribe his own organ improvisations.[217] He valued the transcriptions of other organists' improvisations, but he declined to transcribe his own. By virtue of their high quality, attested to by many who heard him improvise at Saint Étienne-du-Mont, this disinclination is greatly to be regretted.

When all is said and done, we are left to believe that Duruflé took seriously the maxim of Marcel Dupré: "Do not hurry to finish, and, still less, to let it be published."[218]

# Chapter Fifteen

# Duruflé's Role in the Plainsong Revival

It has often been observed that plainsong played a decisive role in Duruflé's formation and in his compositions, but it has not been pointed out that Duruflé actually played a role in its revival. While the centrality of plainsong emerged in his very first opus number, the unpublished *Fantaisie sur des thèmes grégoriens* (1927) for piano, and even earlier in a student work based on a Gregorian *Credo* (1926), plainsong was, for him, much more than one musical element among the many available to him. It was, rather, so much the pith of his existence that he raised the church's plainsong to an exalted place in the secular harmonies of modern French music, advancing the plainsong revival to its ultimate stage. Duruflé was not only a composer, in other words, but a reformer.

The church's effort to rid itself of banal secular influences and reappropriate the music proper to its worship began deep in the early years of the nineteenth century, and even earlier. After the French Revolution the musical practice of the church found itself in dire straits, and reformers took years to locate, research, revive, and experiment with the practice of plainsong so that it could effectively counter the republican tunes, the secular airs, and the trivial pomp that had become so popular in its wake. All of this was, in Duruflé's view, a "true revolution."

In the earliest decades of the revival, plainsong represented the church's alternative to the more popular forms of music that had entered worship after the Revolution. In most instances plainsong was an intrusion, an unwanted change in the familiar and the acceptable, and took upon itself the air of sacrality that put it in stark contrast with the more secular fare of the usual Sunday morning. It was perhaps no accident that this development took place in the same years that secularism and anticlericalism were rampant across France. Plainsong thus represented a church that was at defiant odds with the state.

Duruflé's birth in 1902, at the juncture of these two trends—just one year before Pope Pius X promulgated his reforms of church music and only three years before French law separated church from state—meant that his career would be played out in an atmosphere in which the church and the Third Republic oversaw a ferocious struggle of the sacred versus the secular. The two forces fought mightily against each other until the Second World War brought matters to a head and the church found itself on the losing side, along with the Vichy government.

Duruflé's formation in Rouen equipped him to bring the sacred and the secular into a respectful accommodation of each other, in a manner that was faithful both to the secular music of his era (at least initially) and to the church's official position on the subject of chant and modern music. In doing so, he accomplished two important things: he helped give an aural identity to the church that could be respected by French musical tradition, and he produced an aural equivalent to Joan of Arc, whose cult during the first half of the century represented the intractable détente of church and state. Duruflé's achievement was no less than this: he brought the ecclesiastical and musical reforms, begun a century earlier, to full flower, as one of the "revolution's" greatest advocates and partisans. And through his early exposure to the Solesmes method of chant in Rouen, as we shall see, and his later affinity for the modern harmonies of Claude Debussy, Maurice Ravel, and Paul Dukas, Duruflé would be well equipped to show plainsong compatible with the modern era.[1]

From our distant perspective, it is almost inconceivable that the French church ever lost touch with its musical roots in Gregorian chant, and did so to such an extent, indeed, that she forgot how to perform it. But after the medieval era, plainsong was gradually eclipsed all over Europe by new musical forms, including polyphony during the Renaissance, and, in the baroque, classical, and romantic periods by enlarged and bloated forms whose dubious liturgical value would fall under the scrutiny of the reformers.

The situation was exacerbated by the fact that, until the last quarter of the nineteenth century, stubborn Gallicanism ensured that France's liturgical and musical habits would be unique and distinct, not only from other countries, but from the Holy See itself, which it regarded suspiciously as a foreign power. A body of doctrine and practice that asserted the more or less complete freedom of the French church from the authority of the papacy, Gallicanism also ensured the independence of individual bishops and their dioceses from bishops in other dioceses. Even in the matter of Latin pronunciation, French bishops felt no need to pronounce the language as if it were anything but French. In these and in other ways the church in France represented a unique instance in the history of liturgical pluralism. Eventually Gallicanism begot a provincialism that entitled individual bishops to assume a nearly papal sovereignty over the liturgy and music in their own dioceses.

From as early as the sixteenth-century Council of Trent, to give an example, there existed in France the tradition of the organ playing "softly and meditatively" during the elevation. Although the Holy See's Congregation of Sacred Rites' Decree No. 3827 (May 24, 1894) forbade all singing during the elevation, it made no mention of the organ. So in France the organ was played during the elevation well into the twentieth century,[2] a practice that came to be appreciated as distinctly French, and one that would be explored to its fullest extent by Charles Tournemire.

The cathedral of Rouen posed another illustrative example of Gallicanism. In the eighteenth century, the vicar-general of the diocese, Urbain Robinet, revised the breviary to give it a stronger Gallican character, and in 1729 the breviary was adopted by the cathedral. By the time of the Revolution, the archbishop of Rouen had ordered a new method for singing chant in his diocese: *Nouvelle Méthode pour apprendre le plain-chant. Imprimé par ordre de Son Éminence Monseigneur le Cardinal de la Rochefoucault, Archévêque de Rouen. Spécialement à l'usage de son diocèse.*[3]

Gallican fervor was strong also in Paris. In 1741 the Abbé Jean Lebeuf (1687–1760), for instance, set forth the method of chant as it was sung in Paris (and elsewhere) in his *Traité historique et pratique sur le chant ecclésiastique: Avec le directoire qui en contient les Principes & les Règles, suivant l'usage présent du diocèse de Paris & autres.*[4]

But later on, Rouen and Paris also led the transition from Gallicanism to what is known as ultramontanism, the movement of the French church toward the centralization of authority and influence in the papacy, with the consequent fealty of individual French bishops to the See of Peter. The causes of this shift in worldview were complex and need not detain us here, except to say that the revival of plainsong was, in part, an effort to make the church in France "sound" more Roman and less French. To the extent that ultramontanism was successful, the French church effectively isolated itself from forms of music that were popular among the French citizenry, in the process appearing to restore its allegiance to a foreign power.

In 1855, in the spirit of ultramontanism, the chapter of Notre-Dame in Paris replaced the Parisian rite with the Roman rite.[5] The choir of Saint Sulpice was reorganized in the same year, with the avowed purpose of singing ecclesiastical music proper to the Roman church.[6] In like manner, in the following year, the archbishop of Rouen imposed the Roman liturgy throughout his diocese. In 1874, the Roman rite became mandatory in all the churches of Paris, including, of course, Saint Étienne-du-Mont.[7] And by 1875, all French dioceses had returned to the Roman rite,[8] over the objections of many French clergy.

The disarray of the church's liturgical music was only partly the result of a divisive Gallicanism. The rampant secularism brought further disarray with the Revolution of 1789, and more specifically with the so-called Directoire (1795–99), "a period of musical liberation . . . remembered for its patriotic balls and the creation of the Conservatoire de Musique." The church had become completely disenfranchised from its own music, and a general rupture in church life and practice thus ensued, with secular and nationalistic sentiment capturing the attention and the allegiance of loyal French citizens. The music historian Paul Huot-Pleuroux put it succinctly: "In the eighteenth century, religious music in France died."[9]

Some notion of the extent to which secular music had invaded the church can be gleaned from the publication, in 1786, of the anonymous work *Observations sur la musique à grand orchestre introduite dans plusieurs Églises & . . . sur l'admission de musiciens de l'Opéra dans ces Églises.*[10] In welcoming opera singers into its liturgy, along with music for large orchestra, the church was capitulating to the popular cry for operatic entertainment at mass. But the church could not successfully compete with the major productions now available to the middle class at the ballet, the opera, and the symphony. Religious music shamelessly ceded place to these increasingly popular genres.

In the meantime, the new opera, theaters, and concert halls became temples of a secular religion, with orchestras established to perform a music freed from the constraints of church and gentry. "Patriotic hymns had replaced motets, and military bands replaced the orchestras of the princes."[11] For many French citizens, these art forms became a religion that supplanted the music of the church.

For the nineteenth-century concertgoer Hermione Quinet, wife of historian Edgar Quinet, the orchestra of the Conservatoire exercised a priestly function: "I often forget that the Conservatoire is not a church, that the hundred musicians in the Société des Concerts live scattered throughout the twenty arrondissements of Paris and not in a seminary, that they are not a college of priests gathered before us to perform a holy service each Sunday."[12]

Others had the same experience as Mme Quinet. In *Le Peuple,* Jules Michelet wrote, "We have lost our gods!"[13] For Barthélemy-Prosper Enfantin, the theater was the church: "The Christian temples are deserted, the playhouses are filled with the faithful, the actor is taking the priest's place. . . . It is by the regenerated actor that the Christian will be saved."[14] The sentiment was summarized in *L'Artiste*: "In our nineteenth century, a century that no longer believes anything, music has become a kind of religion, a last belief to which society is clinging with all its might, exhausted as it is by dogmas and words."[15]

For the church the implications were catastrophic. The *maîtrises* had already been suppressed,[16] organs were in ruin, organists found employment outside the church, and the younger generation was not being trained in organ playing or church music. The technical skills needed to play an instrument equipped with multiple manuals and a clavier for the feet were effectively lost in France.

Some few church organists saw fit to counter the tide. When the seraphic César Franck emerged upon the scene, his music was perceived as "serious" by comparison with the prevailing secular and trivial fare. While he did not quote plainsong in his published organ works, which were intended for concert rather than for worship, he did improvise on plainsong melodies during the liturgy.[17]

But playing such as his was rare, and by no means typical. More characteristic of the times were the theatrical and frivolous styles that so pleased the general populace. Two organists who won considerable fame for the popular appeal of their music were Guillaume Lasceux, the organist of Saint Étienne-du-Mont between 1774 and 1819, and Louis-James-Alfred Lefébure-Wély, named organist at the Madeleine in 1847 and at Saint Sulpice in 1863. Both men specialized in storm scenes.

Some French composers who were writing opera and sacred music in the grand style recognized the church's predicament, and appreciated the ecclesiastical and liturgical relevance of the rediscovered music of the past. Charles Gounod, for instance, the composer of the operatic *Messe solennelle à Sainte Cecile*, in a letter to Charles Bordes, wrote: "Palestrina and Bach are, for us, the Fathers of the Church. It is important that we remain their sons."[18]

Even renowned composers with no connection to the church commented on the nature of music appropriate for worship, noting that it is primarily vocal, and that it is not trivial. Richard Wagner declared himself in this vein:

> To the human voice, the immediate vehicle of the sacred word, belongs the first place in the churches, and not to instrumental additions or the trivial scraping found in most of the church's pieces today. Catholic Church music can regain its former purity only by a return to the purely vocal style. If an accompaniment is considered absolutely necessary, the genius of Christianity has provided the instrument worthy of such function, the organ.[19]

The earliest efforts to revive sacred music followed fairly soon after the Revolution. With the Concordat of 1801, which virtually restored the powers of the Roman Catholic Church, Napoléon revived sacred music at the court, and in that year he reestablished the royal chapel, entrusting its care to Giovanni Paisiello (1740–1816), the Italian composer of opera. Even before the Revolution Paisiello had published a small book entitled *Essai sur la musique sacrée* (1787) in an effort to reform the church's music. In 1806, he initiated the Chapelle impériale with a performance by ten singers and twenty instrumentalists of a Mass in G Major. Paisiello was also charged with the reorganization of the *maîtrises* of Napoléon's empire, a fact that would have direct implications for Maurice Duruflé's early musical formation.

Among the next important efforts toward the revival of sacred music was the publication in 1818 of *Méthode de plain-chant, autrement appelé chant ecclésiastique ou chant grégorien*, by Alexandre Choron (1772–1834), which set the stage for the dramatic changes that would take a century to reach full flower.[20]

New schools were established to promote the revival and to train musicians in the performance of ecclesiastical music, including especially Choron's Institut royal de musique classique et religieuse (1817). Following a period of economic difficulty, the school was reopened in 1853 under the direction of Louis Niedermeyer (1802–61) and was named after him. In 1855, Niedermeyer published the *Méthode d'accompagnement du plain chant*. Gabriel Fauré (1845–1924), Léon Boëllmann (1862–97), and Eugène Gigout all studied at the École Niedermeyer, and Camille Saint-Saëns (1835–1921) taught there.

Choron and Niedermeyer both saw to it that religious music had an important place in their curricula, such that their students were exposed to the likes of

Josquin, Jannequin, Palestrina, Lassus, and Bach. In 1829 Choron published his *Corpus complet de musique d'Église à deux chœurs, avec orgue ad libitum, sans orchestre, choisi parmi les chefs-d'œuvre des plus grands maîtres.*[21]

In 1890 Charles Bordes, a student of Franck and a close friend of Paul Dukas, became *maître de chapelle* at the church of Saint Gervais, on the right bank. Two years later he founded the Association des Chanteurs de Saint Gervais, a choral society based at Saint Gervais,[22] whose programs featured the works of Palestrina, Vittoria, Allegri, Bach, and others, and whose works he published in an *Anthologie des Maîtres religieux primitives*, which contained twenty-two masses and 125 motets.[23]

Two years after that, on June 6, 1894, Bordes, Alexandre Guilmant, and Vincent d'Indy established a society named the Schola Cantorum, to advance the performance and dissemination of chant and early music. Guilmant was its president. The society had four objectives: a return to the Gregorian tradition for the performance of plainchant; the restoration of the Palestrina style to a position of honor as a model for polyphonic church music; the creation of a modern church music repertoire inspired by Gregorian and Palestrinian traditions and respectful of the texts and laws of the liturgy; and the improvement of organ repertoire from the standpoint of its union with Gregorian melodies and its suitability for use in church services.[24] The society's new magazine, *La Tribune de Saint-Gervais*, began regular publication in January 1895, under Bordes's direction, and featured articles relevant to the reforms.[25]

The Schola Cantorum also established a model choir school with places for ten young boys.[26] D'Indy, Bordes, and Guilmant, its masters, were having an influence on choir schools in Paris and in the provinces, "particularly the one in Rouen, directed at that time by Canon Bourdon."[27] It bears parenthetical noting that the work of these men was a logical extension of the ultramontanist reforms in France, and that it preceded by some nine years the promulgation of the like-minded *Tra le sollecitudini* by Pius X. More will be said about the document below.

But the revival of Gregorian chant had two major obstacles. The first of these was the difficulty of restoring an authentic performance practice. The second was that the nineteenth century's musical worldview was now essentially diatonic. Gregorian modality was foreign to the modern ear of Europe, implying that it was imposed on Catholic congregations rather artificially, which is one reason that it was rejected at Sainte Clotilde.

For two or three years, from 1904 to 1907,[28] Maurice Emmanuel (1862–1938) was *maître de chapelle* at Sainte Clotilde and in that capacity was Tournemire's colleague. There he introduced Gregorian chant and polyphony to the well-heeled congregation and conducted a choir of men and boys, just one year after Pius X issued his *motu proprio*. His congregation was eventually able to sing three different plainsong ordinaries: Mass IV (*Fons bonitatis*), Mass VIII (*Missa angelorum*), and Mass XI (*Orbis factor*).[29] Emmanuel's choir alternated with the congregation in the singing of the *Kyrie* and *Credo* from the ordinary, and they also sang abbreviated propers.

But chant did not receive a very cordial response from the congregation. The curé of the parish remarked that "Monsieur Emmanuel may be a great artist, but he gives us boring music without letup."[30] As the Gregorian and polyphonic repertoire was thought too serious, the pastor terminated Emmanuel for his efforts.

It took most of the nineteenth century for musicians and scholars to explore the old chant books, making many false starts as to performance practice. The four-line staff, the neumes, and their accompanying signs having long ago given way to modern notation, their meaning and interpretation were not immediately apparent. In fact, the earliest attempts at interpreting them followed not the practices of the medieval era, but those of the nineteenth century. In the early stages of the reform, the practice of Gregorian chant in France was heavy, slow, and tedious, either sung in four parts or accompanied by the organ in rigid diatonic harmony.

Louis Vierne gave this description of plainsong accompaniment at the time he was a student of Franck at the Conservatoire:

Existing since the inception of the organ class, it consisted of a note-for-note accompaniment of a liturgical chant in the upper voice; the chant then became the bass in whole notes, not transposed, accompanied by three upper parts in a sort of academic florid counterpoint. The whole notes then passed into the top voice, transposed a fourth higher, receiving in their turn a "florid" academic accompaniment. Nothing was more formalized than that counterpoint—strict without being exactly so, crammed with retarded fifths, seventh chords prolonged with fifths, and sequences—in a word, with all that is forbidden in written counterpoint. It was "traditional," and Franck could not change anything. In those bygone days, one did not hesitate to accompany each neume with a chord, an effect about as artistic as if it were applied to *bel canto* vocalizes. Not until Guilmant's time did we see the disappearance of this erroneous procedure and its replacement by the normal accompaniment of Gregorian chant and its paraphrased commentary. What a revelation and what a relief![31]

For over a century, theorists sought to influence the performance practice of plainsong. In 1855, Louis Niedermeyer published his modal method of accompanying chant, *Traité théorique et pratique de l'accompagnement du plain-chant.* Written in collaboration with Joseph d'Ortigue, the effort met with strong resistance.[32] Théodore Dubois wrote his *Petit Traité pour apprendre à accompagner le plain-chant, à la basse ou à la partie supérieure (à l'usage des personnes qui savent peu ou pas l'harmonie),*[33] intending it, as the title indicates, even for use by persons with no knowledge of harmony. In 1913 Maurice Emmanuel published his *Traité de l'accompagnement modal des psaumes.*[34]

Duruflé's immediate predecessors in the practice of church music, especially Guilmant, Gigout, and Tournemire, made notable strides toward a sacred sound in church music and to the restoration of plainsong. In 1884 Guilmant published *Les Soixante Interludes dans le tonalité grégorienne*, the year after Dom Joseph Pothier's edition of the *Liber gradualis* came out from Solesmes. But of all his works promoting chant, the most influential was his *L'Organiste liturgiste*, Op. 65, a series whose last issue was published in 1899, in which chant-based organ music came into its own.[35] Gigout published *Chants du graduel et du vespéral romains* (ca. 1880), *Interludes grégoriens* (1884), *Cent Pièces brèves grégoriennes* (1888), *Album grégorien* (1895), and *Quatre Pièces grégoriennes* (1918). Tournemire advanced the cause through his improvisations and in his published organ works, especially in his massive series of organ suites, *L'Orgue mystique*. He was the first prominent Parisian organist to interpret on such a scale Gregorian chant according to the then new Solesmes principles of supple rhythm. He visited Solesmes to study the performance of chant by the monks.[36]

In addition to Dupré's *Symphonie-Passion* (1924), Tournemire's *L'Orgue mystique* (begun by 1920 when Duruflé was studying with him), and Duruflé's own *Prélude, adagio et choral varié sur le Veni Creator* (1930), there were the Gregorian-inspired works of Daniel-Lesur, Gaston Litaize, André Fleury, Georges Robert, and Jean Langlais.[37]

One cause for the disdain with which the chapter of Notre-Dame cathedral held Louis Vierne was the lingering secular character of many of his improvisations and compositions, and of his too-little use of Gregorian chant, even into the fourth decade of the twentieth century.[38] He did play Bach, of course, and was renowned for the quality of his service-playing, but Vierne embraced the tradition of the picturesque, even if in an incontestably more sophisticated vein than the playing of Lasceux at Saint Étienne-du-Mont and of Lefébure-Wély at Saint Sulpice.

Some consensus on the singing of chant gathered ultimately around the Benedictine monks at Saint Peter's monastery in Solesmes, in the département of Sarthe. Founded originally in 1010, the community was not reestablished after the Revolution until 1833, when Dom Prosper Guéranger settled there with five other priests.[39] Guéranger became abbot of the monastery and spearheaded the controversial, but ultimately successful, reforms in liturgy and music.

The systematic study of the origins and development of chant began with the Solesmes publication of the first volume of *Paléographie musicale* in 1889 under the direction of Dom Mocquereau. All earlier efforts were superseded by this and by the succeeding scholarship of the Benedictines, who sought to strip plainsong of its diatonic accretions, to free it of inappropriate practices, and to promote their belief that the authentic rhythm of chant was to be found in the free rhythm of its two-note and three-note groupings.

The rhythmic theory of the Solesmes method[40] provoked more controversy than any of its other features and is a subject of debate to this day. According to Solesmes, the archlike rise of the arsis and the fall of the thesis comprise an unmetered period, contrasting sharply with diatonic music of the west from the baroque period on. In the latter the measure and its bar lines predominate, each beat being strictly ordered according to an internal hierarchy. By contrast, the Solesmes method lacked a regular pulse, and was intimately tied to the pronunciation and stress of the language it bore. The Solesmes method was unsuitable to a pronunciation of Latin as if it were French; only with the adoption of a universal Italian pronunciation did the Solesmes method have any real chance of success.

On November 22, 1903, Pope Pius X issued his *motu proprio* entitled *Tra le sollecitudini*, which called for a restoration of the church's legacy of plainsong, the codification of her official chant books, the teaching of a basic chant repertoire to congregations so that they could sing the ordinary of the mass themselves, and the establishment of choirs at those cathedrals and basilicas capable of singing the chant propers and choral polyphony. This seminal document sought to counter the invasion of secular music into the worship of the church, as well as to solidify the incremental gains of plainsong and inculcate a universal performance practice.

According to the *motu proprio*, the following were to be among the guiding principles for music in the church:

2. Sacred music must . . . eminently possess the qualities which belong to liturgical rites, especially holiness and beauty, from which its other characteristic, universality, will follow spontaneously. It must be holy, and therefore avoid everything that is secular, both in itself and in the way in which it is performed. It must really be an art, since in no other way can it have on the mind of those who hear it that effect which the Church desires in using in her liturgy the art of sound. But it must also be universal in this sense, namely, that although each country may use in its ecclesiastical music whatever special forms may belong to its own national style, these forms must be subject to the proper nature of sacred music, so that it may never produce a bad impression on the mind of any stranger who may hear it.[41]

The pope's *motu proprio* gave wholehearted support to modern works composed for the liturgy, provided they accord with liturgical law.

5. The Church has always recognized and encouraged all progress in the arts, and has always admitted to the service of her functions whatever is good and beautiful in their development during different centuries, as long as they do not offend against the laws of her liturgy. Hence more modern music may also be allowed in churches, since it has produced compositions good and serious and dignified enough to be worthy of liturgical use. Nevertheless, since modern music has become chiefly a secular art, greater care must be taken, when admitting it, that nothing profane be allowed, nothing that is reminiscent of theatrical pieces, nothing based as to its form on the style of secular compositions.[42]

Soon after the publication of the *motu proprio*, the monks of Solesmes, at the request of the Vatican, published the so-called typical editions of the *Antiphonale*

(1905) and the *Graduale* (1908), replacing the editions of these books previously published by Pustet in Ratisbonne (1870).[43]

As individual bishops became persuaded of the authority of the Solesmes method, they implemented its use in their own dioceses. In Rouen, the two archbishops who reigned during Duruflé's chorister years—Archbishop Edmond-Frédéric Fuzet and Archbishop Louis-Ernest Dubois—ensured his exposure to the method. Both men had high expectations for ecclesiastical chant in the cathedral and the diocese. Fuzet instructed the superiors of his major and minor seminaries to see to it that the seminarians received serious training in music and ordered the provision of a manual.[44]

Despite its formal ratification by Rome, the Solesmes method continued to meet with resistance, even among the most prominent organists in Paris, Charles-Marie Widor among them. While Widor commended the Benedictines for their colossal scholarship, he considered the presentation of their source material uncritical. He viewed the older syllabic approach to the hymns and antiphons[45] superior to the melismatic vocalizes of Solesmes. The latter had "too many ornaments, too many accents, too many notes," in his view, whose complexity and archaic notation, coupled with the rhythmic theories of Solesmes, made them unsuitable for the average parish.[46] He wrote: "The rhythmical freedom of Gregorian chant clashes with our stern metronomic time. What task requires more delicate handling than the transcription into modern notation of a vocal Gradual or of an Alleluia? The transcriber is reduced to the necessity of verbal explanations: quasi recitativo, rubato, expressivo, a piacere, etc."[47]

Widor was ill equipped to find a solution to this problem in a way that equaled the success of the methods used later by Duruflé, who fully understood how the Solesmes method could be made compatible with modern notation and meter. Widor at least took the question of chant seriously enough to make inquiries of the Vatican about the rhythmical signs that Solesmes had added to the 1905 *Kyriale*. Cardinal Merry del Val asked Dom Pothier of Solesmes to explain the symbols to Widor.[48]

Some Parisian parishes that had not already done so established choirs of men and boys, like the one at Saint Étienne-du-Mont. Later on, other parishes formed mixed adult choirs having similar purposes, some of which, like those at the Madeleine and Saint Eustache, and the one based at Saint Gervais, eventually achieved local renown.

As a result of the *motu proprio*, a spate of new choral music, much of it to be sung *a cappella*, was composed in the spirit of Renaissance polyphony. Much of this music was derivative at best and little of it survives, but it was taken seriously at the time. Duruflé's four motets, though they were composed much later, are pristine examples of twentieth-century works in Renaissance dress, and they represent the spirit and the letter of the *motu proprio* to a superior degree. Likewise, the *Requiem* and the *Messe "Cum jubilo"* were Duruflé's effort to make significant contributions to progress in the liturgical arts and to modern music, as the *motu proprio* envisaged them, all the while avoiding the profane and theatrical qualities shunned by the document. The impersonal and objective character of his writing also lent to his works a certain anonymity that was in keeping with historic church tradition.

By an odd reversal of fortune, the secular sphere that had successfully invaded the church during the nineteenth century found itself, at the turn of the twentieth century, being influenced by developments in church music; plainsong was appearing in orchestral works, some of which had religious themes, but some of which were frankly secular. Lili Boulanger's *Pour les Funérailles d'un soldat*, for example, includes a direct quotation from the *Dies irae*. In the first part of his *Rédemption*, Gounod quotes the *Vexilla regis* and the *Stabat mater*. Both Dukas and d'Indy quoted the *Pange lingua* in secular works. D'Indy wrote twenty-four Gregorian canticles under the title *Pentecosten* (1928). Fauré, Ravel, and Dukas all experimented with modality in their otherwise diatonic, secular compositions, and so would Poulenc and Messiaen.

In Italy, Ottorino Respighi wrote several instrumental works whose titles betray their debt to plainsong, such as his *Concerto gregoriano* for violin and orchestra (1921) and *Tre Preludi sopra melodie gregoriane* (1921). His popular *Pines of Rome* quotes the Gregorian *Sanctus* that features in Duruflé's *Messe "Cum jubilo."*[49]

The influence of plainsong and modality upon Claude Debussy has been underappreciated. Until he was nineteen years old, Debussy returned often to Cannes, on the Côte d'Azur, where he had lived with his aunt. He regularly heard Gregorian chant during the services he frequented at the cathedral.[50] He even visited Solesmes, on August 5, 1893.[51] Some of his works show its influence, especially the later ones. *Le Martyre de Saint-Sébastien*, first performed in Paris in 1911, had "no tangible imitation of ancient forms, [but] the music makes frequent use of Gregorian modes."[52] The general effect of his Sonata No. 1, for violoncello and piano (1915), is "modal and slightly medieval."[53] In his opera *Pelléas et Mélisande* (1892–1902), "the feeling of tonality is largely negatived [*sic*] by the shifting character of his chord successions."[54] In fact, Debussy's discovery of Renaissance polyphony, while living in Rome, affected him deeply. He became fond of Palestrina and Orlande de Lassus, whose works he heard sung also by the Chanteurs de Saint Gervais. A colleague met Debussy one day "as he came out of the church of Saint-Gervais with his eyes aflame and the fervid words 'Voilà la musique!' "[55]

The influence of plainsong in Erik Satie's works is seen in his *Ogives*, the *Gnossiennes*, the four *Préludes*, the *Danses gothiques*, and the *Messe des pauvres*. In his three *Gymnopédies* he suspends a modal Gregorian-like melody over a swaying ostinato bass. But a particular case can be made for the direct lineage of one of Satie's later and more secular works, the *Trois Poèmes d'amour* (1914), from the Easter sequence *Victimae paschali laudes*. The first poem has several keen melodic resemblances to the chant, but the most conspicuous is Satie's setting of the words *Tout doux, ma chère belle* to a virtually exact quote of the sequence melody, where the words are *Christus innocens Patri.*[56]

Several documents were issued by the Holy See after *Tra le sollecitudini* (1903), further to regulate the reforms of sacred music. *Divini cultus* (1928), *Mediator Dei* (1947), and *Musicae sacrae disciplina* (1955) promoted plainsong, Renaissance polyphony, and such modern music as had a distinctly ecclesiastical and sacred character. In thus reinforcing the *motu proprio* throughout Duruflé's career as a composer, these documents gave him the additional incentive and the rationale to persist in his musical style, his ethos and methodology, and his Catholic worldview, well into the 1960s, after which they came to be thought old-fashioned and were succeeded by a new call for "musical relevance" in the church.

Exactly when the movement came to an end is an arguable point. Books promoting the Solesmes method were published as late as 1960,[57] suggesting that the reforms were still vital until then. Duruflé noted: "In his study dealing with Gregorian chant in France, Benoit Neiss reminds us that the period from 1950 to 1960 could be called the golden age of Gregorian chant in France. At that time Gregorian chant was becoming ever more widely sung."[58] And since the Second Vatican Council's *Constitution on the Sacred Liturgy* is widely regarded as the successor to *Tra le sollecitudini* and to the documents issued in its train, the end of the plainsong revival can with merit be dated at 1963, the year of its promulgation. Even though the constitution insisted that Gregorian chant and polyphony continued to enjoy pride of place in the Roman liturgy, its concession to vernacular languages and music effectively spelled the end to Latin-texted plainsong.

The heyday of the plainsong revival, therefore, was coterminous with the ubiquity of the Solesmes method, extending roughly from 1903 to 1963, almost exactly the period from Duruflé's birth until the time he wrote his last major work, the *Messe "Cum jubilo,"* in 1966. Duruflé's toil not only paralleled the last half century of the reform, but was representative of its ultimate aspirations.

By the 1920s, the stage for Duruflé had thus been set by the reforming movement that reestablished plainsong and polyphony as the treasury of church music par excellence. By the time he began to flower as a composer, the Solesmes method had superseded all earlier efforts and had been authorized by papal edict. Although he never had the occasion to train a choir in the subtleties of chant or to write a treatise on the subject, Duruflé would exercise his refined compositional sensibilities to give Gregorian chant a contemporary use, both reflecting the warm reception Pius X gave to modern music in the church, demonstrating the relevance of chant to modern harmony, and eschewing the profane theatricality of the past, of which Duruflé proved himself eminently capable. In so doing, he not only brought to full flower the modern implications of the Solesmes method, and introduced the sacred and the secular into a unique accommodation of each other, but he was thus the last great partisan of a movement which, though it looked to the past, could be called progressive and even revolutionary. The sad irony is that Duruflé's success at composing music properly sacred for the church was trumped in the second half of the twentieth century by another period of decline, in which the church's inclination to musical recidivism triumphed through another round of tunes all too similar to those that had failed in the nineteenth century.

# Chapter Sixteen

# The Vichy Commissions

In the late 1930s, before the Second World War began, the grave economic conditions in France had become a serious concern of the government. In an effort to ameliorate the situation, the Administration des Beaux-Arts began awarding commissions to composers in 1938, giving them an incentive to work. The official title of the commissions program was "Commandes exceptionnelles aux artistes vivants et compositeurs de musique en vue de lutter contre le chômage."[1] It was indeed a radical notion on the part of the Third Republic to institute such a program in response to the worsening economy.[2]

The first commissions[3] were awarded, in 1938, to Elsa Barraine, Yvonne Desportes, Charles Koechlin, Paul Le Flem, Georges Migot, Darius Milhaud, and Germaine Tailleferre, among a total of twelve who were commissioned to write either a symphonic work, a ballet or opera in one act, or an opera or similar work in three acts.

In 1939, another eight composers were commissioned to write either a symphonic poem, a ballet, an opera or similar work, or incidental music for a dramatic work. Eugène Bozza and Claude Delvincourt were among them.

In the first half of 1940, prior to the June invasion of Paris by the Germans, only two commissions were awarded. They went to Alfred Bachelet, for a symphonic poem, and to Henri Hirschmann, for an opera or similar work.

The new Vichy regime, formally established in July 1940 after France's defeat by Germany, continued the program of commissions established by the now displaced Third Republic. It spent a considerable amount of money to relieve the severe unemployment in France, awarding a total of eighty-one commissions throughout the war to composers needing financial incentive to produce new works. Because the Vichy government took music seriously for its propaganda value, it generally restricted its awards to composers who upheld the conservative, antimodernist, and pro-Catholic sentiments of the regime.[4]

The government offered 10,000 francs for a symphonic poem, 20,000 francs for a symphony, and 30,000 francs for an opera or similar work. The monetary awards for the commissions were not intended to be generous, but were large enough merely to free the composer to devote his or her time to the composition for as long as needed, roughly six to twelve months.

The first Vichy awards were given on May 16, 1941. Composers Louis Aubert, Tony Aubin, Louis Beydts, and Jeanne Leleu were commissioned to write operas

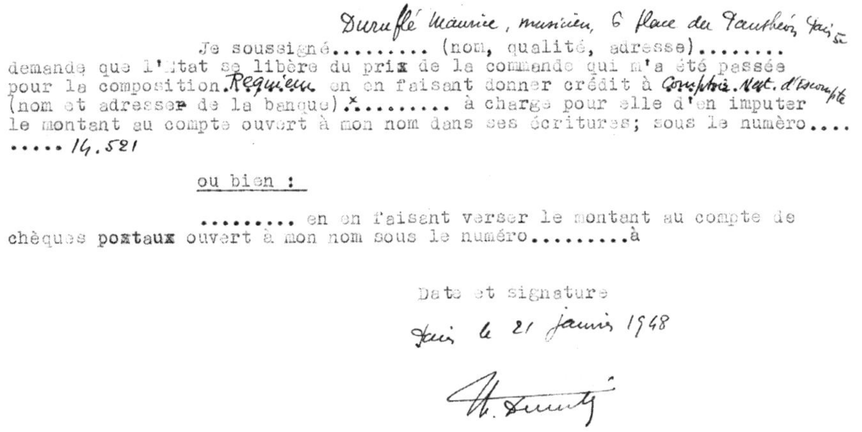
Duruflé Maurice, musicien, 6 place du Panthéon, Paris 5e

Je soussigné........ (nom, qualité, adresse).......
demande que l'Etat se libère du prix de la commande qui m'a été passée pour la composition. Requiem en en faisant donner crédit à Comptoir Nat. d'Escompte (nom et adresse de la banque).......... à charge pour elle d'en imputer le montant au compte ouvert à mon nom dans ses écritures; sous le numèro.... ..... 14.521

ou bien :

......... en en faisant verser le montant au compte de chèques postaux ouvert à mon nom sous le numéro.........à

Date et signature

Figure 16.1. Duruflé's formal request for payment from the French government upon the completion of the *Requiem*. Dated January 21, 1948. From the Archives nationales.

or similar works, and Ermend-Bonnal and Lucien Haudebert symphonies of at least three movements. Henri Challan, Yvonne Desportes, Pierre Lantier, Gaston Litaize, and Maurice Duruflé were commissioned to write symphonic poems.[5]

Duruflé took some six years to complete his work, far longer than was anticipated by the authorities. The war had ended by then, and a new French government had replaced the Vichy regime. On January 21, 1948, Duruflé submitted a certificate to the Administration des Beaux-Arts of the new Fourth Republic, indicating that he had completed his commission by writing the *Requiem* and requesting payment of the agreed amount. Duruflé was one of few composers whose submitted certificate indicated the name of the piece that fulfilled the commission, thus leaving no doubt as to which piece he had composed under commission (see Fig. 16.1).[6]

Duruflé was ultimately paid 30,000 francs, instead of the contracted 10,000 francs, for writing what proved to be the greatest composition of his career. The *Requiem* is, moreover, the most famous work of all 103 works commissioned under the program between 1938 and 1945, and it is the only one that remains in the repertory today.

That the amount Duruflé received was larger than the agreed amount was probably a token of the severe economic climate. During the war, inflation skyrocketed such that between 1939 and August 1944, wages rose by 63 percent. But prices rose by 180 percent.[7] Inflation continued unabated after the war as well.

So by the time Duruflé was paid, in 1948, 30,000 francs was not a lot of money. Consider, by way of comparison, that André Malraux's new novel *Le*

*Musée imaginaire* was selling in bookstores at that time for the prohibitive cost of 2,500 francs, a tenth of the average family's income of 25,000 francs per month (the minimum salary for gas and electric workers was a paltry 6,587 francs per month). Young American soldiers were living and studying on the left bank under the GI Bill of Rights, and their $20 weekly allowance was just enough to live on.[8] But despite the unrelenting hardship of most of the French, some few had money to spare. The well-off could buy an opossum coat at a smart shop on the Champs-Élysées for 42,500 francs.

Exactly how Duruflé justified submitting a requiem mass in fulfillment of a commission for a symphonic poem is quite another question. As a genre, the symphonic poem is an orchestral work having extramusical themes that are either poetic, literary, pictorial, or realistic, but not, as a rule, religious. It usually consists of a single movement, in contrast to the symphony. A nine-movement choral work with liturgical purposes simply does not fit the description. Whether the government authorities cared could well be doubted, under the circumstances. A requiem came more easily for Duruflé, because the basic materials for a requiem already existed, namely, the Gregorian chants themselves and his earlier effort to set them as an organ suite.

Among the composers awarded commissions by the government, Duruflé was not the only one to provide a work that stretched the musical definitions. Jean-Jacques Grunenwald, later to become organist at Saint Sulpice, wrote *Bethsabée*, a "biblical poem for orchestra" upon commission for a symphonic poem.[9] Henri Goublier composed *Le Jugement dernier* on commission for an operetta. Georges Hugon, on commission for a chamber music piece, wrote *Chant de deuil et d'espérance*, "an oratorio for soloists, chorus, narrator and orchestra."[10] Marcel Mirouze, commissioned to write an opera or similar work, submitted the religious opera *Geneviève de Paris*.[11] And while all of the genres of commission required multiple instrumentalists—usually an orchestra, but occasionally a chamber group—Alexandre Cellier wrote *Églises et paysages*, a suite for solo organ (Heugel 1952).[12]

The *Requiem* is Duruflé's only major work known to have been written on commission. The fact that he accepted the commission when his only steady income was from his church position and from the royalties from his few compositions, with limited additional income accruing from his work as house organist for the Société des Concerts—at a time when the national economy was in grave disarray—suggests that he did so, in part, for the income. If the fee he received for the commission was modest, the royalties from this work eventually proved considerable.[13]

It was typical for the postwar government to honor the contracts made by the Vichy regime. In doing so, the new administration as much as declared the commissioned composers innocent of collaboration with the Germans. If Duruflé had written his work as speedily as most of the other composers did, he would have been paid by the Vichy government. To have been paid instead by the new government further freed Duruflé from the implication of having been a sympathizer.

In addition to the commissions program initiated by the Third Republic, the Vichy government established a project of its own, to record an Anthology of Contemporary Music representing works of modern French composers. The set consisted of forty discs at 78 rpm, each with a total duration of about nine minutes playing time. Duruflé's *Tambourin*, the third movement from his *Trois Danses*, was performed by the Orchestre Lamoureux, under the baton of Eugène Bigot, and was recorded for the anthology in 1944 by the Association française d'action artistique. The set also contained works by Jean Françaix, Georges Hugon, Henri Rabaud, Guy Ropartz, Florent Schmitt, Paul Pierné, Alexandre Cellier, Charles Koechlin, Tony Aubin, Noël Gallon, Claude Delvincourt, Jacques de la Presle, Georges Dandelot, Max d'Ollone, Marcel Dupré (the Intermezzo from Concerto for organ and orchestra, Op. 31), Jehan Alain (*Introduction, thème et variations* for instrumental quintet), and Olivier Messiaen (*Les Offrandes oubliées*).[14]

The author has found no evidence suggesting that, after the war, the commissions and recordings were construed as awards for collaborating with Vichy. It cannot be inferred that by accepting his commission and permitting the recording of his *Tambourin*, Duruflé was a sympathizer with the Vichy regime. Like countless others in occupied France, he was simply trying to make an honest living under desperate economic and political circumstances.

French nationalism played a prominent role in the arts both before, during, and after the war. The musician-painter Georges Migot, for instance, linked the passion of Christ with the passion of France in a dozen intensely dramatic paintings he produced. Following the war, Marcel Dupré composed his *La France au Calvaire*, which depicts France on Calvary, begging the forgiveness of Christ for her sins. Likewise, the numerous masses and oratorios commemorating Joan of Arc, particularly Honegger's *Jeanne d'Arc au bûcher*, were at once religious and nationalistic.[15] A song from the époque of the Second World War reflected this sentiment: "Catholique et français toujours."

Though Duruflé's *Requiem* is dedicated to the memory of his father and was constructed as a liturgical work, it was heard by his countrymen in 1947 as an obsequy for France. The fact that all of the earliest performances of the work occurred elsewhere than in churches allowed connotations such as these. Internal features of the work have been taken, by some critics, to suggest that Duruflé intended the work as a nationalistic statement. Leslie A. Sprout, for instance, writes that the *Requiem* fulfilled the objectives of Vichy's arts administrators and met the expectations of postwar audiences.

Despite its not having been completed until 1947, the *Requiem* fully embodied the vision of French contemporary music that the Vichy Administration was working so hard to promote: a repertoire that was respectful of national traditions and deferential to the achievements of predecessors, especially those active at the turn of the century. The prominence accorded to religious music by Vichy, particularly if it were written by Conservatoire-trained organists, had made Duruflé a logical choice to receive a commission.[16]

Claiming that Duruflé intentionally used the full resources of the orchestra to give the *Requiem* military overtones of defiance and victory whenever the text referred to liberation or thanksgiving, Sprout reads too much into the score. She writes:

> In the *Sanctus* in particular, imitative repetitions of the words "Hosanna in excelsis" are accompanied by an extended fanfare. The aural effect is that of a military parade approaching from afar: voices enter one by one to repeat the acclamation as steady drumbeats support muted trumpet calls that grow louder and louder. The entire orchestra erupts to join the full chorus, now singing together, as the trumpets complete their calls to victory. . . . Duruflé's *Requiem* is thus a mixture of musical associations, from the sounds of defiance and military triumph to studious, even self-effacing respect for the music of the Catholic liturgy. . . . More intriguing is the fact that this very dual nature was uniquely appropriate for the representation of the joy and sorrow experienced by the French at the conclusion of the war.[17]

At the same time, Sprout concedes that the *Requiem* bears no textual references having the specificity of, for instance, "the *maréchaliste* narrative in [André] Gailhard's *Ode à la France blessée*, on the one hand, and [Paul] Éluard's Resistance poetry in Poulenc's *Figure humaine*, on the other. In addition, the moderation of the victorious moments by the chant, if anything, added to the work's postwar appeal."[18]

Referring to the *In paradisum* and its quiet, ethereal ending, Sprout concludes: "At the end of the war there was something about a trumpet-and-drums symphonic finale that would not ring true,"[19] and concurs that Duruflé's instincts were right in composing a *Requiem* instead of a *Te Deum*. "Four years of defeat and occupation by a foreign power were coming to a close, and while the French . . . might call it Liberation, even the most outspoken politician dared not refer [to] it as Victory."[20]

In view of the postwar secrecy shrouding the commission, it is no surprise that Duruflé denied any nationalism in his *Requiem*. He wrote that his "goal was to write a religious work intended for the church. Besides, the very origin of the themes would have justified and even imposed this purpose."[21]

Of course, if the *Requiem* had to satisfy for a symphonic poem, an orchestra would be a necessity. But even if its length and orchestral breadth suggest a concert hall, there is nothing in the work that is, in itself, alien to the nature and mood of the liturgical text. Trumpet blasts and drumbeats, so foreign to the text of the *In paradisum*, hardly constitute a military parade anywhere else in this work for that matter, including in the Hosanna in excelsis, a text that composers have always supported with the full force of the orchestra or organ. Moreover, given the genesis of the *Requiem* as an organ suite, a fact evidently unknown to Sprout, her case for any intended nationalism in the work is weak.

To what extent Duruflé may or may not have factored nationalistic sentiment into the *Requiem* remains a delicate question. Although the piece is demonstrably a statement of faith (generally adhering to then current liturgical laws), it is brilliantly vague about whatever nationalistic sentiment it may harbor, enough so, at least, that any doubts about Duruflé's intentions remain moot. While Sprout offers no foundation for her judgment that "Duruflé intended from the start that his *Requiem* be a concert work," the fact remains that all of the *Requiem*'s earliest performances were indeed given on the radio and in concert halls, not in churches.

In any case, it is unassailable that the *Requiem* was received in the postwar years as an utterance of French mourning. Jörg Abbing attests that one cannot rule out the possibility, in the postwar years, of hearing in the work the horror and sacrifice of the war years, but he notes that Duruflé did not write the *Requiem* as a response to the Second World War.[22] The fact that for the radio premiere the *Requiem* was programmed alongside two works entitled *In Memoriam*, one by Alexandre Tansman and another by László Lajtha, and broadcast on the eve of All Souls Day, suggests that the billing as such was intended as a national memorial. Given the success with which this essentially sacred work stirred nationalistic sentiment in the late 1940s and early 1950s, the case can reasonably be made that the *Requiem* represented the same uneasy alliance of church and state after the war that Joan of Arc had represented in the years before and during the war.

The facts of the Vichy commissions did not come to light until the early 2000s. While the scientific study of the cultural life of France during the Second World War had begun in the early 1980s, it centered on literature, the plastic arts, theater, and cinema. Music was ignored until the formation in 1995 of an interdisciplinary group of historians and musicologists that worked within the framework of the Institut de recherche sur le patrimoine musical en France (IRPM), and in collaboration with the Institut d'histoire du temps présent (IHTP). Both groups were functions of the Centre national de la recherche scientifique.

In January of 1999, IRPM and IHTP hosted a colloquium at the Paris Conservatoire on Musical Life in France during the Second World War. One fruit of the colloquium was the book entitled *La Vie musicale sous Vichy* (2001), edited by Myriam Chimènes, which contained contributions from more than twenty writers. A highly regarded musicologist, Ms. Chimènes received an award from the Académie des Beaux-Arts for her book.

One of the book's chapters, "Les Commandes de Vichy: Aube d'une ère nouvelle" (The Vichy Commissions: Dawn of a New Era), was written by Leslie A. Sprout.[23] It is here that the fact of Duruflé's commission from the Vichy government was first published. Because Chimènes's book was addressed primarily to musicologists and historians, rather than to the organ and choral world, let alone the general public, the response among organists was accordingly contained.

Nevertheless, the disclosure caught the attention of the Duruflé Association. The secretary of the association, Alain Cartayrade, obtained the address of Sprout with the intention of writing to condemn her work.[24] He never wrote to her, but the near skirmish provided a glimpse of the vehement public stance the association in particular and French organists in general would soon take.

This author published two articles in *The American Organist*,[25] in 2002, extending Sprout's research to the international organ and choral community. In response, Frédéric Blanc, then president of the Duruflé Association, flatly denied that the *Requiem* was commissioned by Vichy, pointing to the existence of an unpublished orchestral work in Duruflé's archives marked "Commande de l'État."[26] The existence of this manuscript was unknown until that time and remains a mystery. Blanc raised the existence of this score as "proof" that the *Requiem* was *not* commissioned by Vichy. His disclosure only roused further questions.

The French response eluded many Americans. Even though the author's articles stated categorically that Duruflé's loyalties were never in doubt, the disclosure of his having accepted the commission was tantamount, in the French view, to declaring Duruflé a collaborator. Their reaction typifies what has been called the Vichy syndrome, the French amnesia surrounding the painful records of the Second World War.

It has never been easy to distinguish collaboration from mere accommodation, and Duruflé's case is no exception. While the historian Philippe Burrin provides a clear delineation between the two, and describes three types of accommodation, no such schema is easy to apply in ambiguous instances. Structural or necessary accommodation, as he calls the first type, was absolutely essential if there was to be any hope for a stable economy and dependable public services. The second type, which he calls opportunist collaboration, involves some desire for closer ties or agreement with the occupiers. While this second type of accommodation occasionally provides moral or material assistance to the occupiers, it is not prompted primarily by political or ideological motives, though these are present in a limited or diffuse form. The third type, while political in the widest and deepest sense of the word (even though the motivation is mixed), is still to be distinguished from collaboration as such. In the case of Duruflé and most of the other composers who accepted commissions, their accommodation of Vichy stands somewhere between the structural type and the opportunist type. Myriam Chimènes wrote, "As in all circles, a minority resisted, another minority collaborated, and the majority accommodated."[27]

Many musicians were active in the Resistance, including conductors familiar to Duruflé, among them Paul Paray, Charles Münch,[28] and Roger Désormière.[29] The Front national des musiciens, a resistance organization specifically for musicians, distributed a clandestine periodical urging the performance of forbidden works.[30] Francis Poulenc was active in this group, but he was also a member of the government's Comité Cortot. In 1943 he composed the cantata *Figure humaine* and published it clandestinely.

Another organization was founded in 1940 by Robert Bernard, the Association de musique contemporaine, whose aim was "to collaborate in rehabilitating the values of French music of the past and the present, and to honor the memory of all those musicians who—for several reasons, and with divergent methods and aesthetic ideals—have enriched our musical heritage and secured for French music a prominent role in our era."[31]

According to Leslie Sprout, Bernard believed that "the current crisis made it necessary for such a society to focus not on the discovery of new talents—the usual practice of any new music society—but instead on the presentation of a comprehensive picture of the country's shared musical heritage."[32]

The organization fostered a new spirit of consensus among the members of once competing societies, among them the Société nationale de musique, of which Duruflé was a member, and Triton, for which he performed in 1937. The concerts presented by the association sought to balance the best of French music from before 1918 with the finest music of the present day. As Sprout writes, "The solid values of music composed before the First World War would not only provide a foundation for the future, but would also contribute to the shared goals necessary for the formation of a New French School."[33]

Florent Schmitt was named honorary president of the association, whose roster included over twenty composers, among them Georges Auric, Tony Aubin, Henri Barraud, Louis Beydts, Claude Delvincourt, Georges Dandelot, Henri Sauguet, Jean Rivier, Marcel Delannoy, Francis Poulenc, André Jolivet, Jean Françaix, Alexander Tcherépnin, and Maurice Duruflé. The conductor Charles Münch was also a member.

To determine how postwar opinion might have viewed the political implications of the commissions awarded by Vichy, we need only consider the aims and goals of the postwar purge, whose primary targets were intellectuals and writers, not composers. As a group, composers were spared by the fact that their imprecise message, or ambiguous text, lacked ideological content and political persuasion, especially where a sung text was not involved. Consequently, composers benefited from some indulgence by the purge, because, " 'the work of art not being governed by the same codes of readability,' they were not sanctioned for aesthetic reasons, but for their attitude."[34] Indeed, musicians in general were excluded, virtually by definition, from the class of intellectuals judged by the purge to have accommodated or collaborated with the enemy. There would be no cause for questioning a requiem.

Even though Vichy did not define an acceptable aesthetic, the work of the most avant-garde composers was frowned upon, because it represented a breach with traditional French culture, and in some quarters may even have been

judged subversive. But the avant-garde compositions of Messiaen were not considered threats to French culture and identity, as were the writings of philosophers and essayists, partly because, if his compositions were musically modernist,
they were theologically faithful to historic Catholic creed.

Likewise, while Arthur Honegger was a member of Les Six, and as such was
out of favor with Vichy, his oratorio *Jeanne d'Arc au bûcher* (1939) endeared him
to the authorities, as we have seen, the heroine being that religious and political symbol of French unity par excellence. The work was even performed in
Vichy, in 1941, at the Grand Casino.

Composers who favored more traditional styles, such as Duruflé, Daniel-
Lesur, Litaize, Grunenwald, and Langlais, were by definition protected from the
purge, as Vichy looked favorably upon their work for its continuity with traditional French values.

The musical statements of Duruflé, as found in his *Requiem*, were evidently not
subjected to scrutiny after the war. Leslie Sprout writes, "As for the [*Requiem*'s]
close connections with Vichy, there was little incentive in the years following the
war for anyone to draw attention to such details"[35] as any pro-Vichy sentiments
that might be lurking in the pages of the score.

Some composers, nevertheless, were avowed promoters of the Vichy agenda.
André Gailhard's commissioned works, *La Française: Hymne au Maréchal* and *Ode
à la France blessée*, clearly reflected the values and aspirations of the regime. And
a small number of musicians actually served as its employees, among them
Jacques Benoist-Méchin,[36] Alfred Cortot,[37] and René Dommange, all of whom
fell from favor after the war.

Duruflé's friend and publisher, René Dommange (b. 1888), was a pianist and
the cousin of the publisher Jacques Durand. He joined the Durand firm in 1920
and was made a partner in 1921, becoming its musical director in 1928. He served
as vice-president of the Association syndical des compositeurs et éditeurs de
musique until 1929. He joined the Indépendants d'union républicaine et
nationale, and was a signatory of the "motion des dix-sept" of July 7, 1940, which
declared itself in favor of a policy of collaboration. Faithful to Maréchal Pétain to
the end, Dommange militated within the Amis du Maréchal and the
Rassemblement pour la Révolution nationale, and was named the director responsible for the Comité d'organisation des industries et commerces de la musique.
Until 1941 he presided over the Comité national de propagande pour la musique.

Late in 1941, Dommange was among the delegation of French composers,
musicologists, critics, performers, and administrators who accepted all-
expenses-paid invitations to a weeklong celebration in Vienna marking the
sesquicentennial of the death of Mozart. Hosted by Reichsminister Goebbels,
the event drew Germany's finest orchestras, singers, and conductors for sixty-five
concerts attended by delegations of musicians and officials from annexed countries and nineteen foreign countries, along with high-ranking officials from Nazi
Germany.[38] The French guests suffered reprisals after the war.

Other musicians of Duruflé's acquaintance played unambiguous roles during the Occupation. Henri Rabaud, for instance, who had been director of the Conservatoire since 1920, was president of Vichy's Comité professionel des auteurs dramatiques, compositeurs et éditeurs de musique. His successor at the Conservatoire, Claude Delvincourt, belonged to the Comité Cortot, and from December 1941 headed the Comité national de propagande pour la musique.[39]

Some musicians, however, used their official functions as a cover for their subversive activities, Delvincourt being a case in point. Though a member of the Comité Cortot, he took an active role in the Resistance within the Front national des musiciens, perhaps as early as September 1941, and until at least the end of 1942, welcoming clandestine meetings at the Conservatoire.[40] He also established the Orchestre des cadets du Conservatoire, comprising eighty musicians, and with it a choir of fifty singers, which became a symbol of the Conservatoire's resistance, even if it had to obey the orders of the occupiers.

The stance of some resisting musicians, however, such as Jacques Ibert, was unequivocal. Ibert resigned his post as director of the Villa Medici, abandoning all institutional responsibility during the Occupation. Paul Paray and Felix Raugel fled to the free zone in the south, while Joseph Bonnet and Nadia Boulanger left the country.[41]

Considering the various ways in which French musicians dealt with the moral dilemma of the Vichy era—from fleeing France altogether, and participating in the Resistance and in clandestine activity, to performing in Germany and holding positions of authority in the Vichy government—merely to have accepted a commission, by comparison, can be judged for what it was: an accommodation by which a working composer accepted the financial incentive to produce a new work in a grave economic climate. The fact that Duruflé composed the *Requiem* on commission from the Vichy government in no way implicates him of crimes against his country. It only adds to the rich complexity of the genesis of this, his most masterful work, about which more will be said in the following chapter.

# Chapter Seventeen

# *The* Requiem

Duruflé's greatest composition, the *Requiem*, Op. 9, completed in September 1947,[1] enjoys a reputation as one of the undisputed masterpieces of the twentieth-century choral repertoire. The single piece most responsible for establishing his fame worldwide, it continues to enjoy frequent performances in the West and the East alike. Reviewers have described it as softly luminous, sumptuous, suffused with a tender radiance, of a noble and restrained eloquence and a sweet and serene light, a work of scrupulous craft and exquisite sensibility, having beautiful unity and real grandeur.

For a long time Duruflé had been seduced by the beauty of the Gregorian chants from the Mass for the Dead. He said:

> At first I formed the project of writing a Suite for organ on these themes, each of whose sections would have been able to be adapted to the different phrases of the liturgical office. After I had finished two of them (the *Sanctus* and the *Communion*),[2] it seemed to me that it was difficult to separate the Latin words from the Gregorian text to which they are so intimately connected. It was thus that the Suite for organ was transformed into something that was more important and that called naturally for choirs and orchestra. This is how I came to write this work.[3]

## Composition

Duruflé composed the piece during the day on the Elke upright piano at his mother's home in Louviers, and in the evening would refine his work on the organ in the church.[4]

Duruflé has been credited as the first to compose a requiem based upon the chants of the Gregorian *Missa pro defunctis*,[5] but he was, in fact, not the first.[6] In his nine-movement *Missa pro defunctis* for six voices (SSATTB), the Renaissance composer Tomas Luis da Vittoria incorporated the Gregorian cantus verbatim, assigning it to the second soprano part throughout. Vittoria's setting lacks parts that Duruflé included, namely, the *Pie Jesu* and the *In paradisum*. But insofar as it lacks the *Dies irae*, Vittoria's setting is similar to Duruflé's. Whether Duruflé knew of this work is a matter of conjecture. In any case, Duruflé's is the first such setting since the Renaissance.

Feeling some anxiety about the rhythmic subtleties of plainsong, Duruflé sought technical advice about the Solesmes interpretation of Gregorian rhythms from Auguste Le Guennant, the eminent liturgist and theologian and an excellent musician, who authored the several volumes of *Précis de rythmique grégorienne: D'après les principes de Solesmes.*[7] Duruflé explained:

> I could not find better advice. [Le Guennant] explained to me the theory of the interpretation of the Benedictines of Solesmes, the placement of the rhythmic ictus, not necessarily on the tonic Latin accent, but more readily on the last syllable of the word. Consequently, the strong beat of our modern measure coinciding naturally with the ictus because of the concordance of the rhythmic support (thesis), this strong beat is considerably lightened, because it no longer supports the tonic Latin accent. It no longer has this heaviness, this monotony of our modern first beat, always weighty, always regularly accentuated. In this interpretation of the Gregorian rhythm, there remain only weak beats, so to speak. The marvelous Gregorian line and the Latin text take on a suppleness and a lightness of expression, a reserve and an ethereal gentleness that free it from the compartmentalizing of our bar lines. Besides, the irregular alternation of binary and ternary groups, based on a unit of invariable value, gives the musical rhythm a life, a density, and a constant recurrence.[8]

In his conception of the work, Duruflé kept firmly in mind the style of the Gregorian themes, while for the form of each of the nine sections he confined himself to the forms suggested by the liturgy itself, developing or interpreting these only when the idea contained in the Latin text allowed for it.[9]

In the version of the work for organ and large orchestra, Duruflé retained the normal composition of the orchestra, but with a predominance of the violas and divided cellos. The organ plays a strictly episodic role, intervening not to support the choirs, but only to emphasize particular expressive passages or to represent the calm detachment of the hereafter as over against the human sonorities of the orchestra.[10]

Sometimes the work respects the Gregorian text in its entirety, while the orchestra only supports it or comments on it, and sometimes the Gregorian is completely eliminated. Duruflé did whatever he could to reconcile the plainsong rhythms with the demands of modern meter, the Latin accent occasionally falling on a weak beat, giving the piece a greater freedom and suppleness.[11] In several passages, the Gregorian line is slightly ornamented; often it is not ornamented at all, but is simply given a rhythm and harmonized. Some of the developments are constructed on elements completely foreign to the chant, which however respect its modal character as much as possible.[12]

Duruflé constructs much of Opus 9 around the building blocks of the Solesmes two-note and three-note rhythmic units, which he exploits to the fullest. In the *Requiem* these groupings often dictate the meter, but the pulse is felt more as uplift than downbeat, a concept that goes against the grain of virtually all diatonic music, thus challenging singers and conductors alike. Peter G. Jarjisian suggests "that the conductor should strive to feel the impulse coming out of the beat, rather than thrusting into it."[13] But we see it also in his superimposition of duples and triples, and in the meter changes that throw off our expectation of metrical regularity and a too-earthly beat, effectively relieving much of the work of any heavy, accented pulse (there are conspicuous exceptions). Some critics have noted that Duruflé's use of triplets is alien to the steady eighth and quarter-note rhythms of plainsong (i.e., in modern notation).[14] While this is true, Duruflé's purpose, rather, was to simulate the lightness of chant by undermining a beat through cross-rhythms.

The most remarkable instance of this is the first word of the *Sanctus*, where the stressed syllable *Sanct-* falls (rises) on (from) a short, weak note while the unstressed syllable *-tus* falls on a long note. Likewise, in the phrase *et lux perpetua luceat eis*, at rehearsals 9 and 10, accented syllables are placed on weak beats, and vice versa. The *Liber usualis* specifies that the light, arsic character of the Latin accent is to be retained even when it coincides with the rhythmic ictus of a note grouping.

Central to Duruflé's construction not only of medium and long phrases, but of the entire opus, are this arsis and thesis fundamental to the typical Gregorian phrase. The *Pie Jesu* is so organized that everything before rehearsal 58 is arsic and everything after it thetic. Furthermore, Jarjisian has perceptively shown how the magnificent *Hosanna in excelsis*, spanning measures 24–55 of the *Sanctus*, and emerging from a quiet harmonic turbulence to the excited grandeur of fanfares at measure 50, represents the conceptual middle of Duruflé's entire Opus 9, everything before it the arsis, and everything after it the thesis.[15]

The genius of the *Requiem* lies in the way the modal "harmony" merely implied in the purely horizontal, medieval melodies spreads vertically, at Duruflé's urging, and reaches our ears as a twentieth-century structure. Faithful to his own epoch, Duruflé uses block chords in parallel motion reminiscent of Debussy and Ravel.[16] His occasional shifts of harmonic center by a third reflect Debussy, Ravel, and Fauré alike.[17]

Duruflé never made any reference to the fact that the incentive to enlarge and orchestrate the organ suite was a commission from the Vichy government. It is likely that the commission for a symphonic poem helped convince him that the organ suite could be transformed into a larger work to good effect. He completed the work nearly two and a half years after his father's death on February 5, 1945,[18] and dedicated it to his memory.

Some sources recount that the commission came from Durand—certainly through his friend René Dommange—but that it came to him while he was already at work on the organ suite.[19] Given Dommange's concurrent positions with Durand and Vichy, it is reasonable to assume that the commission from Vichy would be honored by Durand virtually de facto. Duruflé's version of the story is thus compatible with the Vichy commission.

Duruflé's family and devotees, as well as the Duruflé Association, denied that the *Requiem* was written on commission from the Vichy government, basing their argument on the assumption that because the work is dedicated to his father, he must have started it some time after his father's death. But Duruflé could well have begun work on the piece before his father's death—the fact needs no further proving—later deciding to dedicate it to his father. The inscription of a piece does not necessarily disclose the incentive for its composition. At the same time, it is entirely possible that a dedication of the piece never occurred to Duruflé until after his father's death. In any case, his father's death certainly inspired his continued work on the composition, which was already four years in the making after he received the commission.

## First Performances and Reception

Duruflé submitted his completed score to the reading committee of the radio for their consideration.[20] They accepted the work and the first performance of the *Requiem* was broadcast to a national (not merely a Parisian) audience over French radio, on November 2, 1947, on the observance of All Souls Day,[21] the day on which the Roman Catholic Church prays for the dead in purgatory. The performance took place at Salle Gaveau. On the same program were the Sixth Symphony, "In memoriam" (1944), a four-movement work composed by the Polish composer Alexandre Tansman (1897–1986) in memory of those who had died for France, and *In memoriam*, by the Hungarian composer László Lajtha (1892–1963). Roger Désormière conducted the large Orchestre national, with the Chœurs de la radio (Yvonne Gouverné, director), soloists Hélène Bouvier (whom Duruflé did not know personally, but whose voice was exactly what he was looking for[22]) and Camille Maurane.[23] Henriette Roget played the organ.[24]

The radio performance was announced in *Le Monde* neither as a premiere nor as a major musical event, and no mention was made of its being a commission. Indeed, the announcement of the broadcast appeared in small print, among the regular announcements of upcoming radio broadcasts. The critics did later note the work's being a premiere, but they made no reference to its being a commission.

A review by Clarendon (Bernard Gavoty), appearing in *Le Figaro* on November 8, compares Duruflé's work with that of Fauré:

> Because he is an organist—which is an indelible blemish—we do not sufficiently know that Duruflé is a marvelously gifted composer. He writes little, but he signs only pages of the first order, where there are manifest a scrupulous craft and an exquisite sensibility. He is the Fauré of the organ. And precisely at the moment of writing a *Requiem*, his first care was to move away as much as possible from the inimitable and discouraging model that the *Requiem* of Fauré suggests to composers. He kept only its Gregorian ambiance; or rather, like Fauré, but very differently, he attempted and succeeded at a savory compromise between the austerity of the lines of the plainchant and the unobtrusive delight of a modern harmonization. A well-placed seventh chord weakens the

rigor of the Gregorian monotony and gives the illusion of a rose that blossoms suddenly on a bare branch.[25]

Another review, by Henriette Roget (it is peculiar that a musician involved in the performance should write a review of it) appeared in *Les Lettres françaises* on November 27. Identifying the *Requiem* as "an intense expression of its era," Roget writes:

> The work of Maurice Duruflé pertains no more to tomorrow than to today or yesterday: it bears a permanent character which is communicated by the immutability of the faith that enlivens it. Constructed by pious hands, this score is outside of time. Inspired by the Gregorian, it is the expression of a belief rather than the voice of a man.
>
> If the *Requiems* of Mozart, Berlioz, or Fauré instruct us very exactly on the state of soul of their authors in the face of death, if the *Requiem* of Verdi is the cry of a people at a specific era, Duruflé's Mass brings a great peace, an absolute serenity, as anonymous as the collective impetus to which we owe our cathedrals. . . .
>
> The orchestration and the choral writing are precisely what they should be.
>
> Finally, a work essentially of the church which is neither sweetened nor plaintive and which bears the mystical spark that César Franck had revived after the end of the too excited spirit of the eighteenth century and the physical turmoil of romanticism.[26]

The first concert performance of the *Requiem* was presented at the Palais de Chaillot nearly two months after the radio broadcast, on December 28, 1947, by the Chorale Yvonne Gouverné, with soloists Hélène Bouvier and Charles Cambon, and organist Henriette Roget, along with the Orchestre Colonne under the direction of Paul Paray. The work was performed alongside the *Rédemption* of Franck and the Piano Concerto of Schumann.

A brief and hesitant review that appeared in *L'Ordre*, on December 30—after noting the incongruity of presenting a *Requiem* during the Christmas season— had little to say, other than that the work, "skillfully and dramatically paraphrasing the liturgical prose, . . . recalling the Franckian element in its totality, a restrained pathos that reached the imposing, attests to a classic solidity of high quality, free of vulgarity, showing the fruits of long study, with all the license of an acceptable modernism."[27]

On November 14, 1948, the *Requiem* was performed again, this time by Concerts Pasdeloup, with the Chorale Brasseur, under the baton of Pierre Dervaux. The concert was reviewed by Clarendon in *Le Figaro*, in which he again draws a comparison with Fauré:

> I add that Maurice Duruflé is today one of the best French musicians—and we barely have enough of his caliber. He is the most authentic heir of the Fauré tradition, this tradition made of elegance, of modesty, and of effective sobriety. Duruflé is, moreover, an organist as was Fauré, and their familiarity with plainchant raises certain stylistic parallels between the two composers. They are, both of them, "voluptuous Gregorianists," as our Reynaldo Hahn said of the composer of *La Bonne Chanson*. More obviously than

Fauré, Duruflé uses the liturgical language, cites certain textual motifs and uses a harmonic system whose modal simplicity daringly espouses the refinements of contemporary writing. Like Fauré's *Requiem*, Duruflé's offers the surprise of many shimmering chords that appear suddenly from the Gregorian aridity, just as a flower blossoms by chance in the desert sand. What a lot of devices concealed by a magician's hand in these discreet and fervent pages![28]

The *Requiem*s by Duruflé and Fauré contrast sharply with earlier, more wrathful settings by Mozart/Süssmayer, Berlioz, and Verdi, in large part because they omit the sequence *Dies irae*,[29] which, with its depictions of the gloom and terror of the last judgment, reinforces the fear of God and the eternal punishment of the deceased.

But it is not merely in the omission of the *Dies irae* that the two settings are alike. Both divide the lower strings to obtain a darker timbre. Both also include settings of the *Pie Jesu* and the *In paradisum*, which reinforce the loving-kindness of God and the peacefulness of paradise. Neither movement appears in the settings by Mozart, Berlioz, or Verdi.

In both scores, the *Pie Jesu*—which is, in fact, the final couplet of the sequence text *Dies irae*—is not positioned after the tract, where the sequence properly occurs. Instead, Fauré and Duruflé postponed it until after the *Sanctus*. While the liturgy does not specify the singing of a *Pie Jesu* between the *Sanctus* and the *Agnus Dei*, the *motu proprio* of 1903 allowed a motet to be sung after the *Benedictus*,[30] during the silent recitation of the canon by the priest, and that is probably where the two composers intended it to be sung (even though the *Pie Jesu*, as the two men set it, is not a motet as such, but rather more of an aria).

Gwilym Beechey points out that in Duruflé's setting of the *Pie Jesu*

> there may be an unconscious reminiscence . . . of Princess Eboli's aria, *O mia Regina*, in Act IV of Verdi's *Don Carlos*, which is also in A flat major, and which has a slightly similar melodic and rhythmic basis to Duruflé's theme here. Duruflé's movement is perhaps a little too simple and straightforward in its rhythm to make a memorable impact in spite of its melodic and harmonic attractiveness. The intensity of the climax between Figures 48 and 50 seems to call perhaps for a little stronger rhythmic activity.[31]

The *Dies irae* is not alone responsible for the depiction of a wrathful God in the requiem; the same imagery appears in other movements. In Duruflé's setting of the *Domine Jesu Christe*, for instance, the choir pleads, at a *forte*, that the departed be freed from the jaws of the lion, and that they not be swallowed up by hell or fall into darkness. And in the *Libera me*, the baritone sings the text *Dies illa, dies irae, calamitatis et miseriae*, in effect retaining the words otherwise lost by the omission of the sequence, while the choir asks to be freed from everlasting judgment by fire. Duruflé himself acknowledged the presence of terror in his work.[32]

Fauré and Duruflé both link the *Introit* and the *Kyrie* because in the pre–Vatican II requiem mass, the first segues into the latter, nothing else intervening between the two.[33] Both settings are unique in this regard, suggesting that both composers were writing more for a liturgical context than for a concert. Duruflé, however, separates the *Agnus Dei* from the *Lux aeterna*, which are also contiguous in the ritual; this suggests the very opposite.

But there are distinct differences between the two settings as well. Duruflé's orchestra is considerably larger than that of Fauré, especially compared to the latter's original version. Fauré excluded the *Benedictus* altogether,[34] whereas Duruflé included it with the *Sanctus*,[35] choosing to treat them as a unit. In thus restoring the original and ancient unity of these texts, Duruflé effectively made his *Sanctus-Benedictus* a little less practical for use in the Tridentine rite, because of their combined length, perhaps implying that he had a concert venue in mind for the performance of the *Requiem*. By the same token, his approach anticipated, by nearly twenty years, the mass of the Second Vatican Council, in which the unity of the sung *Sanctus-Benedictus* was restored.

Fauré also excluded the communion, *Lux aeterna*, which Duruflé and Mozart retained. The *Libera me*, which is sung for the absolution of the deceased during the burial, is added by Verdi, Fauré, and Duruflé alike. The latter two composers were the first to include settings of the *In paradisum*, which is sung as the body is borne from the church.

Fauré's setting of the requiem has been described correctly as having a liturgical quality and a modal character. This accounts for Reynaldo Hahn's having called him "the voluptuous Gregorianist," a moniker that Bernard Gavoty said could be applied to Duruflé as well.[36] But Fauré's setting has incorrectly been characterized as being based on Gregorian chant, which it is not. In this regard Duruflé's setting is unique in the history of post-Renaissance requiems.

Alec Robertson observes that, compared to Fauré's setting, Duruflé's style "is not so pure," a critique that has some merit.

> It would not be difficult to write it off, on a superficial view, as a pastiche of Fauré's *Requiem*. . . . There are echoes of the harmonies of Debussy, Ravel, and Dukas, but if these on paper suggest a work less integrated than that of Fauré, the result in performances puts the matter in a more favourable perspective. There is a personal quality that surpasses these influences and unifies the disparate elements.[37]

Felix Aprahamian makes a similar observation:

> Plain-chant and polyphony, dominant ninths and the orchestra of Debussy—without the evidence of an actual performance, Duruflé's *Requiem* might appear to be a hotch-potch. But it is the absolute unification in a very personal manner of these seemingly disparate elements that constitutes Duruflé's chief claim to be taken seriously as a composer.[38]

And likewise Gwilym Beechey:

> For some performers and listeners the Op. 9 *Requiem* may not be as original in con-
> ception, mood and content as they might have wished or expected, and the music of
> older French composers may have influenced it to too great an extent. For some tastes
> the work may be too restrained and quiet, and the *Libera me* movement may not be so
> striking in its context as the similar movement in the Fauré *Requiem*. Nonetheless the
> overall impression of Duruflé's work in performance is one of deep religious feeling
> and commitment, and it reveals a fluent creative mind that is full of sensitivity to vocal
> and instrumental colour.[39]

Nevertheless, Duruflé himself denied being influenced by the *Requiem* of
Fauré:

> I do not think I was influenced by Fauré, contrary to the opinion of certain musical critics,
> who, anyway have never given any explanation concerning their viewpoint. I have sim-
> ply tried to surround myself with the style suitable to the Gregorian chants as well as
> the rhythmic interpretation of the Benedictines of Solesmes.[40]

One of the more arresting facts about the reception of the *Requiem* in North
America is that, after the *Requiem* of Fauré, it is only the second French choral
work that holds a place in the standard repertory among the much more numerous English, Italian, and German works such as Bach's *Magnificat* or Mass in
B Minor, Handel's *Messiah*, Vivaldi's *Gloria*, Brahms's *Ein Deutsches Requiem*,
Mendelssohn's *Elijah*, and Mozart's *Requiem*, to name a few examples. That both
of the French works happen to be requiems is also noteworthy.[41] A case could be
made for a third French choral work, Théodore Dubois's *Sept Paroles du Christ*,
by virtue of its immense popularity in North America earlier in the twentieth
century, but the work lacks the stature of the works by Fauré and Duruflé. In
France it was never as popular as the two requiems.

Certainly the choral tradition in France has always been mediocre, a fact that
advances our reverence for Duruflé's work, insofar as it succeeded in such a climate. As far back as the reopening of the Paris Conservatoire, on October 22,
1796, for example, the director Bernard Sarrette delivered a merciless depiction
of the state of vocal music in France, blaming the church's choir schools for the
poor condition of music education and performance across the land.

> Singing, such an essential part of music, has always been taught badly in France: the
> *maîtrises* of the cathedrals were the only schools that existed for this purpose under the
> former government, and it seems that the goal of these establishments, created and
> maintained for the service of worship, whose principal need was to fill an immense
> space with voluminous sound, forced the choir directors to show them only how to sing
> loudly, a method that naturally tended to exclude nuance and expression. We cannot
> speak here about these former schools of song and declamation, now disenfranchised,
> or their restricted boundaries and bad institutions, ill equipped to allow their skilled
> professors any appreciable reform in the manner of singing.[42]

Early in the twentieth century Albert Schweitzer wrote an article for *Die Musik* entitled "Why It Is So Difficult to Organize a Good Chorus in Paris."[43] Schweitzer identified the Société des Concerts du Conservatoire, the Concerts Colonne, and the Schola Cantorum as having the best choirs, but he wrote that none of them had any real success. He noted that French choral singers had little sense of ensemble.

> Everyone brings to the rehearsals his full personality; he does not become a member of the chorus, a stop that the director pulls, but remains Mr. So-and-So, or Mrs. So-and-So, who wants to be recognized as such. The modern Frenchman has an instinctive anxiety about anything that is called discipline; he sees in it nothing but a submission that is unworthy of a free being. The higher conception, that discipline means the natural expression of the individual in a society united for a purpose, is in all circumstances foreign to the French spirit. He sees first of all in discipline the sacrifice of freedom and personal worth.[44]

First-hand descriptions of Parisian church choirs early in the century are rare. The few critiques that do exist, like those of the writer Joris-Karl Huysmans (1848–1907), command our attention for their assessment of plainsong and choral music as they were sung in the churches of Paris around the turn of the century. "Most choirs," he wrote, in the persona of Durtal, "when they intone [plainsong], like to imitate the rumbling and gurgling of water-pipes, others the grating of rattles, the creaking of pulleys, the grinding of a crane, but, in spite of all, its beauty remains unextinguished, dulled though it be by the wild bellowing of the singers."[45]

At Sainte Clotilde, Durtal thought: "The psalmody, at least, is upright, and has not . . . lost all shame," but he still "encountered dance music and profane tunes, a worldly orgie [*sic*]."[46] At Notre-Dame, "the voices of the choir boys always wanted mending; they broke, while the advanced age of the basses made them hoarse."[47]

But Durtal declared that "St. Étienne-du-Mont . . . was worse still; the shell of the church was charming, but the choir was an offshoot of the school of Sanfourche, you might think yourself in a kennel, where a medley pack of sick beasts were growling."[48] As for the churches on the right bank, "they were worthless, plain chant was as far as possible suppressed, and the poverty of the voices was everywhere ornamented with promiscuous tunes."[49]

In the early 1920s, when Duruflé was able to hear many of the choirs in question, *The American Organist* published articles by Paul De Launay, Marshall Bidwell, Hugh McAmis, and G. Criss Simpson, in which they made cursory observations about the choirs at several Paris churches.[50] Not a single prominent church escaped their criticism, but the two parish choirs that made a name for themselves among concertgoers during Duruflé's lifetime were those of Saint Eustache and the Madeleine, both on the right bank. Choirs not associated with churches, such as the radio choir and the Chorale Yvonne Gouverné, fared better still.

Despite the prevailing choral climate, Duruflé's *Requiem* continued to be performed by various choirs in Paris every November through 1950, but according to Gwilym Beechey, performances of the work were relatively infrequent for some time thereafter.[51]

The *Requiem* was first performed in the United States on February 24, 1952,[52] at Calvary Episcopal Church, New York City, under the direction of Jack Ossewaarde, with Frederick Swann as organist.[53] Seth Bingham wrote afterward, in what proved to be an understatement, that the work "seems destined to achieve many performances and win a wide circle of friends in this country."[54] The British premiere of the *Requiem* was presented in the same year by the City of Birmingham Choir and Orchestra, at Birmingham Town Hall, with conductor David Willcocks.[55] It was presented in England again, by the Liverpool Philharmonia in 1953, with Nicolai Malko conducting and Duruflé at the organ.

## Versions of the *Requiem* and Its Publication

Duruflé provided four versions for the accompaniment: large orchestra and organ; reduced orchestra and organ; solo organ; and solo piano. The version for large orchestra calls for the usual complement of strings, plus four horns, three trumpets, three trombones, a tuba, two flutes, a piccolo, two oboes, an English horn, two clarinets, one bass clarinet, two bassoons, four timpani, cymbals, a bass drum, gong, celesta, harp, and organ. Anticipating that there would be occasions when an organ is not available, Duruflé made orchestral provision so that the piece can be performed without one. The inclusion of bass drum, cymbals, and timpani was contrary to liturgical law then in force—another indication that Duruflé's earliest intended venue for the work was the concert hall. The reduced version calls for the strings and retains the three trumpets, the four timpani, and the harp, but these instruments are all ad libitum. The version for solo organ includes the cello solo for the *Pie Jesu*, but it is ad libitum.

The three versions were published in a different order, however: first came the version for solo organ (1948); then the version for organ and large orchestra (1950); and lastly the version for organ and reduced orchestra (1961). The chronology of their publication has often led to a mistaken chronology of their composition.

The version for solo organ is the one most commonly used, because, despite its formidable technical demands, it is the easiest and the least expensive to mount.[56] The fourth version, for piano accompaniment,[57] still unpublished, would be useful in situations where even an organ is unavailable. It would also allow a further analysis of Duruflé's approach to transcription and reduction, and would be useful for rehearsals. Needless to say, however, for actual performance a piano accompaniment would be no match for the organ version, to say nothing of the orchestral versions.

It is futile to try to determine which version of the *Requiem* is the most authentic. As Claude Costa has written, "It is useless to embark upon inevitably subjective classifications that seek to determine the most authentic version."[58] And François Sabatier compares the version for large orchestra with the version for organ: "The fact remains that the original version calls upon the orchestra and that the second is content with the organ only in the absence of the latter. . . . That said, the instrument with pipes sounds marvelous and is not treated as a simple reduction of the orchestra."[59]

It bears noting that Duruflé did not consider the versions for reduced orchestra and organ solo as transcriptions of the version for large orchestra, but rather as reductions,[60] a telling distinction of some importance, as it reflects how Duruflé perceived the various means and intentions of transferring a musical idea from one medium to another. We do not know exactly how he distinguished the act of transcription from the act of reduction.

In any case, of the three published versions, Duruflé preferred the original version for large orchestra, which was used for the two premieres in 1947. The version for organ and reduced orchestra was his next favorite, because he believed it gave the illusion of a complete orchestra and is more interesting to the audience than the version for organ alone.[61] In the composer's note in the score for reduced orchestra, Duruflé writes that the organ version

> was done with a practical purpose. Indeed, it is rarely possible to gather together in a church the choirs, the organ and a complete orchestra. On the other hand, the reduction for organ alone seems insufficient in certain parts of the *Requiem* where the expressive timbre of the strings stands out. At the same time, this intermediary formula allows a lightening of the organ part in blending it or in opposing it to the other instruments.
>
> There was anticipated the possible addition, in total or in part and by order of priority, of a harp, of 2 or 3 trumpets and of 2, 3, or 4 timpani, according to the circumstances. Certain pieces can content themselves with the organ and a string quartet, for example: *Agnus Dei, Lux aeterna*. Others demand at least 2 first violins, 2 seconds, 2 violas, 2 cellos, 2 double basses, for example: *Domine Jesu Christe, Libera me*. In these two pieces, more numerous strings will be even preferable owing to the balance of sound, above all if there is the addition of trumpets and timpani. The same in the *Sanctus*. On the whole, the part of the double bass was deliberately reduced, the sound of this instrument blending with the basses of the organ with difficulty.
>
> To sum up, here is the minimum composition of strings for each piece:
> *Introit*: double string quartet*
> *Kyrie*: double string quartet*
> *Domine Jesu Christe*: double string quintet
> *Sanctus*: string quintet (It is possible to do without the double bass.)
> *Pie Jesu*: cello solo
> *Agnus Dei*: string quartet
> *Lux aeterna*: 2 violins and 1 viola
> *Libera me*: double string quintet

*In Paradisum*: double string quintet* (A 3rd first violin is wished for at No. 100 if there is a double quartet.)

Usually, the slight differences of the string quintet have been indicated for a minimum number of 22 instrumentalists (6–6–4–4–2). When trumpets are lacking, the part has been noted on the organ part (in small notes).

So as not to exceed the duration permitted in the course of the celebration of the mass, there has been allowed a cut in the *Sanctus* at rehearsal 46. For the same reason, the *Introit* can easily be separated from the *Kyrie* and be performed alone while adding a *point d'orgue* [fermata] on the 3rd beat of the last measure.

In the *Domine Jesu Christe* from rehearsal 34 to rehearsal 36, in the *Libera* from rehearsal 93 to rehearsal 94, and at the beginning of the *In Paradisum* up to rehearsal 101, it will be preferable to have a small group of sopranos sing, or better, a children's choir.

*It is possible, in a pinch, to content oneself with a string quartet. A version in this sense has been indicated in the score and the material.

On his tours of North America, Duruflé consented to the performance of extracts from the *Requiem*, specifying several options for a performance in Toledo, Ohio in 1966. One option featured the *Introit* and *Kyrie*, the *Pie Jesu*, and the *Agnus Dei*; another featured the *Introit*, the *Pie Jesu*, and the *Agnus Dei*; and the third featured the *Sanctus*, the *Pie Jesu*, and the *Agnus Dei*. For a performance in New Bedford, Massachusetts, in 1971, he suggested the *Domine Jesu Christe*, the *Pie Jesu*, and the *Lux aeterna*.[62] Despite his early disdain for it, Duruflé evidently became fond of the *Pie Jesu*, which he included in all four options.

It is remarkable that the organ part is scored not for a three-manual instrument, but for an ample but otherwise typical two-manual French-style organ, that is, a grand orgue, récit, and pedal. For the récit, Duruflé calls for the usual complement of fonds 8′ and 4′, flûtes at 8′, 4′, and 2′, mixtures, reeds 8′ and 4′. For the grand orgue he requires ample fonds 8′ and 4′, including a salicional, flûtes 8′ and 4′, and a flûte harmonique 8′, with mixtures and a bourdon 16′, but no reeds. Apart from a single exception, the only stops specified for the pedal are the bourdons 8′ and 16′, a flûte 8′, and, at the end of the Pie Jesu, a bourdon 32′. Only in the version for reduced orchestra does he also call for reeds 16′, 8′, and 4′ in the single pedal line at a place where, in the organ-only version, he writes instead for double pedal, the right foot playing at the octave. For the *Domine Jesu Christe*, in the organ-only version, the solo line is assigned to the principal 8′ on the grand orgue, but he suggests a clarinette as an alternative, implying the desirability of a third manual division, such as a positif, where the clarinette is often found. At the same place in the version for reduced orchestra, however, he specifies a récit clarinette, or, in lieu of it, an hautbois, with the accompaniment played by the violas in the orchestra. In the reduced orchestral version he specifies a dulciana where he had asked for a salicional in the organ-solo version. But in neither version does he call for any reeds in the grand orgue.

Whereas the organ plays almost as prominent a role in the version for reduced orchestra as it does in the version for solo organ, in the version for large orchestra it plays a decidedly subsidiary role. With few exceptions, even its solo passages are usually mere background, often only doubling the orchestra or the voices, and only rarely having any thematic importance. There are long passages where the organ is silent, and when it does play, it often fulfills the function that the organ usually fills in orchestral works, providing body and mass behind the orchestra, playing mostly larger note values. In this version, the organ does not appear in the *Introit* at all. It plays at the beginning of the *Kyrie*, and in several passages of the *Domine Jesu Christe* and the *Libera me* it accompanies the chorus, without the orchestra. At the end of the *In paradisum* the Gregorian melody is played by a flute on the organ, over the chorus and orchestra. The version for large orchestra therefore presents none of the technical demands that the organist faces in the other two versions.

Throughout his American tours Duruflé consistently requested that the two brief passages for baritone solo in the third and eighth movements be sung by the entire bass section, or by the bass and tenor sections together (both movements go up to an F), not by a soloist. The rationale he usually supplied was that, unlike the mezzo-soprano solo in the *Pie Jesu*, those for the baritone were too brief to justify the expense of a professional soloist. Duruflé wrote the following note in the published score: "The baritone solo being of too short a duration, it is preferable to have it sung by the ensemble of tenors and basses (*Domine Jesu Christe* and *Libera me*)." For a few occasions on tour he asked that the *Pie Jesu* be sung by a children's choir instead of a mezzo-soprano.[63] But for the recording of the *Requiem* by Robert Shaw and the Atlanta Symphony Chorus and Orchestra, the *Pie Jesu* is sung by the women's chorus, a practice that was not condoned by Duruflé.[64]

Duruflé's insecurity as a composer is nowhere better documented than with regard to the *Requiem*. He obtained the advice of Jean Gallon and Noël Gallon, and consulted with Nadia Boulanger,[65] "whose severity of judgment always attracted me, although this severity was sometimes terrible."[66] She considered the *Requiem* weak and made some suggestions to him.[67] In a letter to her, dated December 11, 1947, in which he invited her to attend the public premiere, Duruflé mentioned, "I did not have time to redo the middle of my *Offertoire*, but I will recast it entirely next month in the way you indicated to me." In several other letters Duruflé acknowledged his debt to her because it was for the *Requiem*, he said, that the Holy See raised him to knighthood in the Order of Saint Gregory the Great.[68] In 1957, she wrote complimentary words to him following a performance of the *Requiem*, which he heard from the audience. He replied on July 13, 1957, "I was profoundly moved by your very touching letter. This *Requiem* is nevertheless very modest music. I am happy for this occasion to express to you again all my gratitude for the wonderful advice you gave me at the time when I was working with difficulty on this music. It is indeed thanks to you that I was able to overcome my troubles."[69]

On the other hand, the *Requiem* might never have been completed without the urging of Marcel Dupré, who is reported to have liked the piece very much.[70]

Maurice went to Dupré in order to show him his *Requiem*, and Dupré said (as [he had] already before, concerning the Suite and other compositions he had brought with him, in order to hear his opinion), "This music is perfect." Maurice then answered disbelievingly that this or that spot, perhaps, was, in fact, somewhat unsuccessful, but in time Dupré knew how to deal with Duruflé's self doubt, and said only, jokingly: Oh, don't come by any further with your own compositions.[71]

But Duruflé's doubts persisted and he originally intended to retract the work from publication. Marie-Claire Alain remembered him saying, "Oh what a disaster that I let this work be published! The *Pie Jesu* is a complete failure! . . . an unsuccessful and detestable work."[72] As it turned out, the *Requiem* is one of few works that Duruflé did not subject to continual revision over the years, for his later preference for the baritone section to replace the solos never led to a revised edition.

The fact that the original version of the *Requiem*, the one technically specified by the commission, is accompanied by a large orchestra, makes it a departure from some of the prescriptions of the *motu proprio* of 1903:

15. Although the proper music of the Church is only vocal, nevertheless the accompaniment of an organ is allowed. In any special case, within proper limits and with due care, other instruments may be allowed too, but never without special leave from the Bishop of the Diocese, according to the rule of the *Cæremoniale Episcoporum.*
16. Since the singing must always be the chief thing, the organ and the instruments may only sustain and never crush it.
17. It is not lawful to introduce the singing with long preludes, or to interrupt it with *intermezzi.*
. . .
19. The use of the piano-forte is forbidden in churches, as also that of all noisy or irreverent instruments, such as drums, kettledrums, cymbals, triangles and so on.
20. Bands are strictly forbidden to play in church, and only for some special reason, after the consent of the Bishop has been obtained, may a certain number of specially-chosen wind instruments be allowed, which must be carefully selected and suitable to their object; and the music they play must always be reverent, appropriate, and in every way like that of the organ.[73]

While the spirit of the *Requiem* is liturgical, its length, its manipulation of a few texts, and its orchestral accompaniment theoretically banned it from liturgical use, if the *motu proprio* was to be observed jot and tittle. Duruflé took some liberties with the text, delivering, for example, the entire phrase *Sanctus, Sanctus, Sanctus Dominus Deus Sabbaoth* three times instead of the prescribed once, a practice at odds with the *motu proprio.*[74] Likewise, he presents the text *Agnus Dei, qui tollis peccata mundi, dona eis requiem* more than the prescribed three times. These features may help to explain why the earliest performances of the work occurred not in churches, but on the radio and in concert halls.

Mme Duruflé did not often disclose personal memories of her husband. But in an interview during the last year of her life, she said: "And now I will entrust to you what I have never said yet to anyone. My husband confessed to me that he had wept several times while writing the *Requiem*. That touched me very deeply. Certainly in the *Agnus Dei* or the *In paradisum* the theme is so sensitive, and so eloquent, that it does not surprise me that he broke down in tears."[75]

The last performance of the *Requiem* given in the presence of the composer was that on April 25, 1980 by the Chorale Colbert, conducted at Saint Étienne-du-Mont by Éliane Chevalier.[76] It was subsequently performed for the public funeral of Duruflé at Saint Étienne-du-Mont.

# Chapter Eighteen

# The Musical History of Saint Étienne-du-Mont

The church of Saint Étienne-du-Mont,[1] originally called Sainte Geneviève-du-Mont, stands on the highest hill in Paris south of the Seine, behind the Panthéon. It was established there as a dependency of the rich and powerful Abbaye Sainte-Geneviève (founded from Abbot Suger of Saint Denis, in 1146). It received official status as a parish from Pope Honorius III in 1222, and eventually was surrounded by the numerous colleges of the Latin quarter. After the Reign of Terror, when the church was designated a Temple of Theophilanthropy, Saint Étienne-du-Mont was reopened to worship in 1802, and since 1803 has housed a shrine containing the relics of Sainte Geneviève, the patroness of Paris. Through the centuries the church has been the focus of Catholic devotion during times of pestilence, famine, and war.

Until the second half of the twentieth century, the church had a relatively undistinguished musical pedigree, a remarkable fact in view of its long history. Indeed, through 1929, when Duruflé was named its titular organist, the musical tradition of the parish was probably average, at best. And because of the vicissitudes of the church's *grand orgue* during the first half of the twentieth century, Duruflé could not fully make his distinct mark on the church's music until after 1956. The musical renown of Saint Étienne-du-Mont is thus the direct result of Maurice Duruflé's tenure there.

There is no available information regarding the musicians of Saint Étienne-du-Mont from its founding in 1222 through the first three centuries of its independence. Beginning in the sixteenth century, however, the names of organists Florent Moret, Nicolas Cohanet, and Philippe Racquet are recorded during the hundred-year construction of the present building.[2] The list of titular organists shown in table 18.1 represents an amalgamation of several sources and makes no attempt to reconcile apparent discrepancies.

A contract dated March 25, 1635, describing the exhaustive duties of the organist for Saint Étienne-du-Mont, was certainly the one awarded to Marin Deslions, the first titular in the newly completed church.[3]

Jean Buterne was organist at the chapel of Louis XIV, in Versailles, and was known for his improvisations. An agreement dated August 15, 1705, names

Figure 18.1. Plan de Turgot (1734–39), engraved by Louis Bretez; detail, showing Saint Étienne-du-Mont (just below center, to left), adjacent to the Abbey of Sainte Geneviève and surrounded by colleges. Photograph courtesy of the Bibliothèque historique de la Ville de Paris.

Table 18.1. Titular Organists of Saint Étienne-du-Mont

| | |
|---|---|
| ca. 1564 | Florent Moret |
| ca. 1576 | Nicolas Cohanet |
| to 1636 | Philippe Racquet[a] (d. August 1636) |
| 1636–1672 | Marin Deslions |
| 1666–1679 | Charles Deslions |
| 1672–1673 | Girard Jollain |
| 1674–1726 | Jean Buterne (d. 1727) |
| from 1705 | Antoine Barthélemy la Vergne |
| 1726–1774 | Claude-Nicolas Ingrain |
| 1774–1819 | Guillaume Lasceux |
| 1819–1827 | un Sieur Baron |
| from 1827 | Baron fils |
| 1824–1853 | Gabriel Gauthier (1808–53; blind) |
| 1853–1888 | Louis Lebel (blind) |
| 1888–1894 | Georges Syme (blind) |
| 1894–1924 | Alexandre Dantot (blind) |
| 1924 | Rémy Clavers (blind) |
| 1924–1929 | Gaston Singery (1893–1942; blind) |
| 1929–1975 (1986) | Maurice Duruflé |
| 1953–1999 | Marie-Madeleine Duruflé-Chevalier, co-titular with her husband |
| 1975–1989 | Sarah Soularue, suppléant to the Duruflés |
| 1989–1992 | Sarah Soularue, co-titular with Mme Duruflé |
| from 1997 | Thierry Escaich and Vincent Warnier, co-titulars |

[a]Philippe's brother Balthasar (d. 1630) was organist of Saint Germain-l'Auxerrois. Philippe's nephew, Balthasar's son, was the composer and harpsichordist Charles Racquet (d. 1664), organist of Notre-Dame from 1618 to 1643.

Antoine Barthélemy la Vergne the successor to Buterne, whose *suppléant* he had been until that year.[4]

Charles Deslions was a composer but none of his works survive.[5] And of the works that may have been composed by the church's other organists of this time, there are none in the repertory and no manuscripts are known to exist. The master organists of the French classic period—Nicolas Lebègue, Jacques Boyvin, Louis Marchand, Pierre Du Mage, Louis-Nicolas Clérambault, Francois Couperin, Nicolas de Grigny—had no colleague their equal at Saint Étienne-du-Mont. Compared with Saint Gervais just across the Seine, for instance, where the Couperin family were organists for nearly 250 years of this era, Saint Étienne's musical life was of little consequence.

Guillaume Lasceux (1740–1831) was named *maitre de chapelle* at Saint Étienne-du-Mont in 1769, before being named titular organist in 1774. With his appointment as organist, Saint Étienne-du-Mont had its first titular of any repute. Indeed he was one of the better Parisian organists at the turn of the century, although his musical legacy is of dubious merit.

Lasceux deplored the decadence of the organ after the Revolution, but his work curiously only hastened it. He composed a number of short liturgical pieces, fugues, and noël variations without pedal, including some based on plain-song. His collections include the *Journal de pièces d'orgue* (1771 or 1772), *Nouvelles Pièces d'orgue* (ca. 1782), *Nouveau Recueil de pièces d'orgue* (1784), *Nouvelle Suite de pièces d'orgue* (1810), *Noëls pour orgue,* and *Douze Fugues* (1820). In his illustrated "Essai de théorique et pratique sur l'art de l'orgue" (1809, unpublished), he lists the stops of the organ, gives instruction in their combination, and warns that the art of organ playing is disappearing from France "for two reasons: it keeps one from teaching the piano, and it pays too poorly." This work and his "Annuaire de l'organiste" (1819, unpublished), which contains a storm piece for the *Judex crederis* from the *Te Deum,* are invaluable sources of information about the forms, styles, and performance practice of early nineteenth-century organ music.

Lasceux reclaimed his church post after the Revolution. Counting his tenures as choirmaster and as organist, Lasceux was employed at Saint Étienne-du-Mont for a total of fifty years. According to Félix Raugel, there remained several "brilliant representatives of the old French school," prior to the Revolution, that is, whose reputation drew crowds. He lists Saint Étienne-du-Mont, along with Saint Sulpice, Saint Merry, and Saint Germain-des-Prés, among the churches where such playing could still be heard.[6]

Lasceux was followed in 1819 by Baron *père*.[7] The organist Adolphe Adam, composer of the popular noël *Minuit, chrétiens* (1847), known variously as *Noël d'Adam, Cantique de noël,* or *O Holy Night,* and of the ballet *Giselle,* occasionally substituted for Baron *père,* who was succeeded in turn by his own son, in 1827.[8]

By 1820 three Paris churches (Saint Étienne-du-Mont, Saint Médard, and Saint Nicolas-des-Champs) were employing blind organists for a month at a time. Beginning with the appointment of Gabriel Gauthier, Saint Étienne-du-Mont had blind organists for the next hundred years.[9] The early nineteenth-century custom in many Paris churches of playing a *Te Deum* on the eve of the patron saint's day was dying out in Gauthier's day, and the last occurrence of the tradition may have been the performance he gave at Saint Étienne-du-Mont in 1850.[10]

Another example demonstrates the low level to which the parish music had fallen during the nineteenth century. On Easter day in 1838 the French political leader and writer, the Comte de Montalembert (1810–70),[11] attended benediction at Saint Étienne-du-Mont. He recognized the melody of a drinking song co-opted for use during the service. Associated with the tune were these words: "My friends, when I'm drinking I'm happier than a king." Gauthier, the organist, objected to the use of the song, but he considered it hardly less profane than the melody they usually used.[12]

The blind Louis Lebel, organist from 1853 to 1888, was also the professor of organ at the Institut des jeunes aveugles. He studied organ with Lemmens and was Louis Vierne's first organ teacher.

Alexandre Dantot was Saint Étienne-du-Mont's titular organist at the same time he was teaching solfège to Jean Langlais at the Institut des jeunes aveugles. As a student at the Conservatoire, Langlais occasionally substituted for Dantot at Saint Étienne-du-Mont.

Rémy Clavers (1891–1940) followed Dantot for a brief tenure in 1924. Clavers obtained the *premier prix* in organ in 1912, then was named titular at Saint Antoine des Quinze-Vingts. He studied organ with Alexandre Guilmant, but he also played and taught violin.

Gaston Singery followed Clavers in 1924. He studied with Vierne, Widor, André Gédalge, and Louis Diémer, and received the *premier prix* in 1918 in Gigout's organ class. He was Gigout's *suppléant* both at Saint Augustin and at the Conservatoire; he and Duruflé undoubtedly knew each other at the school. A graduate of the Institut de jeunes aveugles, Singery composed pieces for piano, harmonium, and organ, some songs, a sonata for piano and violin, and another for piano and violoncello. After leaving Saint Étienne-du-Mont, he went to the church of Notre-Dame Auxiliatrice in Clichy. He also taught the Conservatoire organ class on an interim basis in 1924, between the tenures of Gigout and Dupré.

Singery was better known as a pianist than as an organist. He performed piano concertos with Paris orchestras and he accompanied singers in recital, receiving consistently favorable reviews for his virtuosic performances of piano works by Liszt and Chopin, for instance, and for the performance of his own transcription of extracts from Wagner's operas.[13] Critics commended his "bright musical intellect and solid technique."

There was a brief interim between Singery and Duruflé, when an amateur organist named Henri de Chantérac was nearly appointed to the post at Saint Étienne-du-Mont, in 1929. A banker by trade, Chantérac acquired some wealth while working at the Compagnie financière. The Union des maîtres-de-chapelle et organistes reproached him for assuming professional church music posts in the city, and he was at the point of accepting the position at Saint Étienne-du-Mont, without pay, when the organization issued its reprimand.[14] In 1937 he became organist and *maître de chapelle* at Saint Bernard-de-la-chapelle, Paris, and remained there for many years.[15]

When the post at Saint Étienne-du-Mont became vacant after the uproar over Chantérac, there was no competition, if the existence of letters of recommendation is any indication. Charles-Marie Widor wrote to the curé on October 4, 1929,[16] identifying Duruflé as "my former student (at the Conservatoire) . . . a consummate musician . . . remarkable performer." Charles Tournemire wrote two days later, on October 6, saying that Duruflé had been his replacement at Sainte Clotilde for the past ten years, and describing him as "the most brilliant subject of our national school." In an undated letter that identified Duruflé as "an applicant for the post of organist," Louis Vierne wrote to the curé: "He is one of my best students, a virtuoso, admirable, remarkable improviser, an excellent musician. I consider him one of the best organists of this time, and by employing him you are acquiring one of the future glories of the French organ. . . . Moreover, he is a charming young man, of high morals, endowed with an excellent character and perfect sentiments." Even the parish's organ technician, Paul Koenig, writing on September 19, recommended Duruflé to the curé. He probably thought better of having done so after he lost his contract with the parish under Duruflé's titularship.

In a report on the organ at Saint Étienne-du-Mont, compiled by Félix Raugel and Marcel Dupré, probably in 1936, and contained in a dossier at the Département des orgues of the Monuments historiques, in Paris, the date of Duruflé's appointment as titular is given as October 1929.[17] The timing at the year's end may well account for the fact that many sources give 1930 for Duruflé's appointment.[18] It is possible that he was unable to free himself from his obligations in Louviers until after Christmas.

It is not known exactly when Duruflé moved from his apartment on the right bank to the one on the left bank, in closer proximity to his new post, except that he was living at 8, rue Dupuytren during the 1931–32 season. It is possible that he moved there in 1930, right after assuming his new appointment. It is likewise conceivable that he moved there only upon his marriage to Lucette Bousquet, which took place in 1932. In any case, soon into his tenure at the church he relocated to his new apartment on rue Dupuytren, in the sixth arrondissement, a few doors south of the boulevard Saint Germain and just west of boulevard Saint Michel. Duruflé occupied this dwelling until 1938. By December of that year he had moved to the eighth-floor of 6, place du Panthéon,[19] directly across the square from the church (see Fig. 18.2), to a small and modest roof-top apartment, with a music room that enjoyed a spectacular vista of the Seine and Notre-Dame below, with Montmartre and Sacré-Cœur in the distance. The tiny room contained a piano and, in time, his three-manual organ. Those who studied with Duruflé recall the ride part way up in a simple caged elevator and the walk up the last two flights of stairs. He lived there for forty-eight years, until his death.

Apart from his tenure as titular at Notre-Dame in Louviers, Duruflé never held a post as titular organist anywhere but at Saint Étienne-du-Mont. For forty-six years he worked steadily at this single parish. After he married Marie-Madeleine Chevalier, in 1953, he shared his duties as titular with her. He ceased playing the organ for mass after 1975.[20]

Duruflé's duties at the church were, at first, typical of those of most titular organists; that is, he played solo organ repertoire and improvisations at the prelude, the offertory, the elevation, the communion, and the *sortie*, using the gallery organ. Although he was not hired as the *organiste du chœur*, he had to use the organ in the choir for about eighteen years while the *grand orgue* was out of commission.

The archives accounting for the *maîtres de chapelle* and *organistes du chœur* at Saint Étienne-du-Mont are sketchier than they are for the titulars. The approximate list shown in table 18.2 has been collated from disparate sources.

Figure 18.2. The home of the Duruflés, place du Panthéon, top floor left, partially obscured. Photograph by the author.

Table 18.2. *Maîtres de chapelle* and *organistes du chœur* at Saint Étienne-du-Mont

| | |
|---|---|
| until 1705 | Antoine Barthélemy la Vergne, *suppléant* to Buterne |
| 1723–1726 | Claude-Nicolas Ingrain |
| 1769–1774 | Guillaume Lasceux |
| ? | Juste-Adrien de La Fage, *maître de chapelle* |
| 1830–1833 | Jacques Claude Adolphe Miné (1796–1854), *organiste du chœur* |
| ? | Xavier Croizier, *maître de chapelle* |
| ca. 1927 into the 1940s | Bernard Loth, *maître de chapelle* |
| 1950s | Mme Murcier, *maître de chapelle* |

Juste-Adrien de La Fage, a musicologist, published twenty-nine motets "collected or composed for the use of the parish church of Saint Étienne-du-Mont." La Fage is credited as the first in Paris to introduce an *orgue de chœur* for the accompaniment of plainchant. The organ in question, by John Abbey, was installed in the choir of the church in 1829. Described as an "awful little positif," the instrument of three and a half "very ugly ranks" was subsequently moved to the lady chapel at Saint Roch by a curé transferred there from Saint Étienne-du-Mont, the same man who had the instrument built in the first place.[21] Some years prior to Duruflé's tenure, a two-manual, fourteen-stop pneumatic organ by Puget was installed on the north side of the choir, replacing the Abbey. It served for all liturgical functions during the period that the gallery organ was out of commission, but "was damaged during World War II by sandbags intended to protect the stone jubé" adjacent to it.[22] Duruflé referred to it as "a poor bagpipe."[23]

Jacques Claude Adolphe Miné was choir organist at Saint Étienne-du-Mont and at Saint Roch, and then became titular organist at Chartres Cathedral. He published many collections of service music and three organ methods.

Bernard Loth attended the Maîtrise Saint-Évode in Rouen as a youth, and studied voice at the Schola Cantorum before being appointed to Saint Étienne-du-Mont. He was the founder of Les Amis de Henri Expert et de la musique ancienne. Like Duruflé, Loth occasionally accompanied Les Petits Chanteurs à la Croix de Bois. He was a member of L'Union des maîtres-de-chapelle et organistes.[24]

The choral tradition at Saint Étienne-du-Mont has probably always been mediocre. At any rate, the parish choir of men and boys,[25] with Bernard Loth as the *maître de chapelle*, achieved no particular renown among the choirs of Paris. Indeed, throughout Duruflé's tenure the parish choir was never included in performances or recordings of his compositions, nor is he known to have composed anything for them. In 1937, however, to mark the anniversary of the Armistice, the choir did sing Loth's *Requiem* mass for soloists, choirs, organ, harp, and string orchestra, a work verging on oratorio, for which Duruflé was the organist. At least the event achieved notice in the journal *Musique et Liturgie*.[26]

The parish occasionally hosted major choral concerts and premieres. On November 11, 1927, a performance of the Berlioz *Requiem*, under the direction of Gabriel Pierné, was given at the church during a solemn high mass by the chorus and orchestra of Concerts Colonne, and Chorale Amicitia, in memory of the war dead.[27] The concert was a fund-raiser for the church's organ. And in 1929 the Vienna Choir Boys, with singers from the Vienna Opera Chorus, sang the Mozart *Coronation Mass* there, with instrumentalists from the Société des Concerts du Conservatoire.

During holy week of 1938, Francis Poulenc attended the first performance of Milhaud's cantata *Les Deux Cités* for unaccompanied chorus, which was sung at the church by Les Petits Chanteurs à la Croix de Bois. The performance inspired Poulenc to compose his *Quatre Motets pour un temps de pénitence*, which he wrote on commission from Abbé Maillet, director of the choristers. The motets were premiered by his choir at Saint Étienne-du-Mont in 1939.

Duruflé's income from the church was very modest. A mere one and a half years into his tenure, he wrote to the curé, asking for an increase in pay.

My salary of 2400F per year represents an average of about 20F per service. I play 44 masses at 11 o'clock during the year:
1) 40 Sundays, from October 1 to June 1 inclusive;

2) 4 feasts (Ascension, All Saints, Christmas, Assumption).
This comes to 44 noontime masses.
Will you accept a base of 20F45 for the noontime mass, which will be for the year an increase of 20F45 × 44 = 900F, being an increase of 900/12 = 75F per month.[28]

Between his acceptance of the post, in 1929, and the installation of the new *grand orgue*, in 1956, Duruflé flourished as a composer. He completed his Opus 4 on *Veni Creator*, he composed the *Suite*, the *Trois Danses*, the *Andante et Scherzo* for orchestra, the *Prélude et fugue sur le nom d'ALAIN*, and, most importantly, the *Requiem*. It was the most fruitful period of his life as a composer, demonstrating his tenacity in the face of hardship. The fact that until 1943 he was living almost totally on his meager salary as a church musician would suggest that his urge to compose may have been prompted by the need to supplement his income. In that year he was named professor at the Conservatoire and began earning a second salary.

For the first decade or so after the new organ was installed, Duruflé felt his work supported by the parish clergy. This support eroded with the regrettable musical changes wrought by his priests after the Second Vatican Council. His relationship with some of them was tenuous at best, and conflicted at worst. In 1964 he embarked upon overseas concert tours and recording projects that restored some of the musical satisfaction lost from his church work.

After her husband's death, in 1986, Mme Duruflé continued as the church's primary titular organist, but was assisted in various capacities by several other organists, sometimes as *suppléants* and sometimes as co-titulars. These included Sarah Soularue, her American protégé, whom she met on one of her earlier tours of the United States,[29] and Hervé Morin, who wrote a dissertation on her husband's music but died by his own hand in September of 1996, at the age of thirty-three.[30] She was later assisted by Thierry Escaich and Vincent Warnier,[31] who began as co-titulars during her final years and succeeded her after her death.

Figure 19.1. The organ at Saint Étienne-du-Mont, view from the choir. Photograph by the author.

# Chapter Nineteen

# The Organs at Saint Étienne-du-Mont

The present organ at Saint Étienne-du-Mont, completed in 1956, was not simply one installation among many by its builder. Those involved in the effort clearly believed, in the beginning, that it would be a routine enterprise. But the design, construction, and installation of the instrument became a complicated saga of so many trials, missteps, and disputes that it took eighteen years to complete.

Very little is known about the organs at Saint Étienne-du-Mont prior to the seventeenth century, and their succeeding history is complex. It is known that the church had an organ in 1517,[1] and that Jehan d'Argillières, an organist and builder of organs and harpsichords, did repairs on it in 1573–75,[2] while the new church was still under construction and while Nicolas Cohanet was organist. According to at least one account, two fairly mediocre organs preceded the organ of 1636.[3]

On January 22, 1631, five years after the church's dedication, a contract for a new organ and organ case was signed by the churchwardens of the parish.[4] Jehan Buron, a master woodworker, was contracted to design and construct an organ case. Pierre Le Pescheur, an organ builder whose house adjoined the church, was hired to construct the organ itself.[5]

Buron began work on the case immediately, because it had to be completed the following year. The case he built is often cited as the most beautiful in Paris. Norbert Dufourcq was more effusive, describing it as "one of the most perfect masterpieces of seventeenth-century European woodwork."[6]

Le Pescheur's organ of four manuals (forty-eight notes) and pedal (thirty-two notes), with thirty-four stops, was installed in 1636.[7] Very little of this organ remains in the current instrument. A restoration and enlargement of the organ, necessitated by a fire that destroyed much of the instrument, was begun by Nicolas Somer in 1760, and remained unfinished upon his death. In 1777 François-Henri Clicquot rebuilt the reeds, added an hautbois to the positif, another hautbois to the récit in place of the trompette, and a bombarde 16′ to the pedal.[8] The instrument was one of the rare organs[9] spared during the ensuing Revolution, but not without some damage. In 1807, care of the organ was entrusted to Pierre Dallery.

In 1832, the choir organist Jacques Claude Miné, who played the "awful little positif" by John Abbey, prepared a report on the condition of the *grand orgue* and recommended its thorough restoration. In 1833 Abbey certified that the stop knobs had been sawed off and six ranks stolen, and submitted a precise description of the surviving thirty-five stops. Abbey was hired to provide new bellows and a new récit wind chest and swell box; to remove and restore the mechanism, clean and repair the stops on the grand orgue and positif, restore the stops of the pédale, récit, and écho; and to replace the wooden pipes of the bombarde and trompette with tin pipes. He was also to add a prestant and six pipes for the hautbois and the flûte on the récit, a wooden bourdon for the grand orgue, extend the flûte ouverte up to 4′, and restore the exterior of the pipes of the montre. Abbey's work was accepted by the church's *conseil de fabrique* on December 20, 1833.

Only thirty years later, in 1862, another revision was deemed urgent, and the following year Aristide Cavaillé-Coll was charged with the work. Cavaillé-Coll retained the pipes of the 51-note positif and most of the remaining old pipework, added a bombarde 16′ to the grand orgue, reduced to three the number of manuals (he removed the écho division), and constructed a new 42-note récit expressif. The organ thus revised had thirty-nine stops,[10] with the positif playable from the bottom manual, the grand orgue from the middle. Four organists played the inaugural recital on April 26, 1863: César Franck, Auguste Durand, the blind titular Louis Lebel, and Charles Hesse.

In 1873 Cavaillé-Coll did further work on the organ and was given charge of its maintenance.[11] Care for the organ subsequently passed to Charles Mutin until 1908. At the request of Alexandre Dantot, the church engaged Théodore Puget of Toulouse in 1911 to extend the pédale to thirty notes and extend the récit through the lowest octave. In 1922 Puget installed an electric blower.[12]

In the 1920s, Paul-Marie Koenig, the nephew of Charles Mutin, was restoring organs in the area more or less successfully. The changes that were made to the instrument, first by Puget and then by Paul-Marie Koenig, were of doubtful merit—Louis Vierne called the organ "a horrible cuckoo."[13] In 1928 Koenig began a complete restoration of the instrument, and by the time Duruflé assumed his duties as organist, the 54-stop[14] organ was in a lamentable state. Duruflé wrote in his memoirs that a "restoration" was under way by a clumsy worker. The mechanism was undependable[15] and the sonority mediocre, despite a few fine stops. He advised the curé to seek an evaluation from a commission comprising Vierne, Tournemire, and Marchal, whose severe report was delivered in 1932 to the Département des Beaux-Arts of the city of Paris, which would be responsible for some of the financing.[16] Despite the charges in the report, Koenig continued working on the organ until at least 1935.

The commission reported[17] that Koenig had established no well-determined plan before he began the restoration. His new récit was oddly disposed on two chests, each under separate expression, and the two parts did not speak simultaneously. Leaks appeared on each manual. The two notes added at the top end of each manual were badly joined to the existing chests, causing an unacceptable shaking of the wind and a sagging of the pitch. Because of these defects, the commission found it impossible to render an account of the organ's voicing. Despite these drawbacks, they found some beautiful colors on the instrument, among them the eighteenth-century quint (viz. nasard), tierce, cromorne, and trompette, and the flûte harmonique, montre, and plein jeu by Cavaillé-Coll.

In 1932, Albert Alain, the father of Jehan Alain, wrote to the curé, recommending that Duruflé oversee the voicing by Koenig. Charles-Marie Widor also wrote, telling the curé of Koenig's incompetence and urging that the work be stopped.[18] On December 1, 1934, Duruflé himself wrote to the curé, contesting that the organ was now worse than it had been five years earlier.[19]

A subsequent "Étude d'un projet de reconstruction du grand orgue de Saint Étienne-du-Mont," dated probably 1936,[20] conducted by Felix Raugel and Marcel Dupré, determined that the organ should be completely rebuilt. They recommended that the irreparable mechanical action be replaced by an electro-pneumatic system,[21] for the following reasons: (1) the slider chests were in a good state, and could be adapted to an electro-pneumatic system without additional cost; (2) the console could be removed to a side gallery, where "the organist will hear the whole organ perfectly"; (3) doing so would free the interior of the case, making room for the écho division removed by Cavaillé-Coll, thus returning the instrument to its eighteenth-century disposition.

Raugel and Dupré gave their specification for an organ of fifty-nine stops. (See Appendix C, p. 272) The specification included an adjustable crescendo pedal, a combination action, and a generous supply of couplers at 16', 8', and 4', as well as unisons off. The specification with the revised pedal brought the number of stops to sixty-five.

Having already provided the Directeur général des Beaux-Arts with the names of several possible builders, Dupré wrote on July 12, 1938 giving three additional names: Gloton in Nantes, Jacquot in Ramberviller, and Roethinger in Strasbourg. On his advice,[22] the contract was awarded to Joseph Beuchet of Gloton, later to be named Debierre-Gloton, and later still Beuchet-Debierre. On August 4, 1938, the builder was asked to submit a bid for an organ of sixty-six (not sixty-five) stops on four manuals.

Joseph Beuchet (1904–70) was the grandson of Louis Debierre, an organ-builder in Nantes, and was one of the directors of the Cavaillé-Coll firm after it had been bought by the Pleyel piano company. Beuchet repaired and enlarged the organ at Notre-Dame in 1931.

The firm submitted its bid on November 5, 1938.[23] The contract was approved, in January of 1939, for a total of 400,000 francs, of which 75,000 would come from the parish and 325,000 from the city of Paris.

The work of dismantling the organ began on April 17, 1939, with the new organ estimated to be finished in a year's time. Work was suspended with the declaration of war in September, but resumed again in October.

At the beginning of 1940, however, the firm was requisitioned for the production of armament, and work was suspended again. A meeting in February 1941 considered the conditions under which work would resume, and ratified changes in the project. In a report from the organ builder, dated August 25, 1941, a plan to cut into the large molding around the rose window above the organ was forbidden, thus necessitating "a complete reshaping of the project."[24] As a result, the fourth manual division, referred to as the solo in the report, would be removed from the main case and relocated to a chamber in the south tower, above the staircase to the tribune, thus suggesting its being reconceived as an écho division.[25] There it had plenty of room and excellent acoustics, according to Duruflé's later estimation, and an interior gothic window opening onto the south aisle of the church, making it an ideal location. The relocation of the écho left room for a more complete récit.

The report alludes to otherwise unspecified "damages caused to the instrument and to the builder on the occasion of measures of the Défense Passive." The report also notes that Norbert Dufourcq had replaced Félix Raugel on the commission, who had relocated to the free zone (in the south of France). Dufourcq recommended adding 2′ doublettes to the grand orgue and the pedal. The changes and repairs thus described, plus four more stops on the écho, would add 200,050 francs to the original bid of 400,000 francs. The city of Paris agreed to pay only an additional 125,000 francs, leaving the parish to provide the balance.

In the absence of any formal authorization from the city for the builder to proceed with all the aforementioned changes, work in the factory proceeded at a much reduced pace for a full year. The builder feared that still further changes would be ordered, and did not want to redo work already completed. Moreover, the firm reported "circumstances consequent upon the Occupation, the requisition of personnel, the reduction of the motor force, and some contingencies of raw materials, etc." that further jeopardized any continuing work.

If that were not enough, the city of Nantes, in September 1943, underwent aerial bombardment. While the organ factory was practically unharmed, the means of production were diminished as a result of the halt to the city's economy, and the fact that "certain categories of personnel" were subjected to a forced evacuation. Work on the organ again came to a virtual standstill.

A meeting on December 8, 1944[26] admitted all the modifications to the original bid, as well as the transfer to the positif of the old 8′ hautbois from the écho; the addition of bourdons 8′ and 16′ and a voix humaine to the écho, and a basson 8′ to the pédale; and the replacement of the old façade pipes by a new polished façade.

For the next two years and three months, the architect conducted a thorough study to determine the design of an iron girder in the shape of a double T that would have to be fit beneath the tribune in order to support the added weight of the new organ. In the process, the determination was made that an iron corset would have to be constructed to support and tighten the positif case on the rail. The architectural study was not completed until April 1947.

At a meeting in June, Beuchet pointed out that the weight of the organ (around thirty tons) would itself suffice to hold the organ securely in place, a fact that was said to have escaped the architect's notice. A subsequent meeting by the architect and the builder would determine the need for the iron corset.

In late 1944 and early 1945, Duruflé requested the addition of a percussion stop called Cloches cathédrale for the écho; and bassons 4′ and 16′, and a tierce 6⅗′ (extension) for the pédale.

In a letter dated June 19, 1945, the city of Paris adopted all the requested tonal and architectural changes, and urged Beuchet to proceed with the work. The factory promptly resumed work on the instrument, including the repair of the four keyboards ruined in the train station during the bombardment of Nantes.

In December, Beuchet was ordered to suspend the work. In January 1946 he was told that the city was unable to permit the completion of the work as a whole, and that the project would have to be done in stages, the first costing between 1,800,000 and 2,000,000 francs, an amount to be shared by the parish, the city, and the state.

The various reports and minutes, to date, make little mention of the stoplist or how it grew between 1939 and 1945. But in a codicil to his third report, dated 1946, Beuchet provided a schema summarizing the changes made during that time period.

A progress report on the finances of the project appeared in Beuchet's fifth report, dated May 20, 1948.[27] The first stage would cost 3,708,082 and the second 2,162,049, for a total of 5,870,131 francs.

In 1950, some six years after the need for it first became clear, an immense steel girder in the form of a double T (ten meters long, .80 meters high and .25 meters wide) was installed to support the organ. With its installation it became difficult for the organist to pass from the tribune to the console in the adjacent alcove. So a quarter-circle stone passage was constructed around the square pillars astride the organ case, allowing passage to the console.[28]

The constitution of the organ in its finished state[29] reflects a vast enlargement over the "Étude" of 1936. There were fifty-four stops in the case prior to the restoration. Because the new organ had been enlarged to eighty-three real stops,[30] all but fifty-six of them had to be located outside the case, namely those from the pédale that were installed below the tribune, and those in the écho. The depth of the case being relatively shallow, all of the pedal bourdons and flûtes (32′, 16′, 8′, 4′, 2′, quints, tierces, and septième) were placed beneath the tribune, above and to both sides of the main west entrance into the church. All of the pedal principals and reeds were in the usual place in the case, on the same level as the grand orgue. The old wind chests for the grand orgue and the pédale were retained, but their treble ends were extended. New wind chests were built for the positif, récit, and écho.

Duruflé found the original location of the manual and pedal pistons on the console unsatisfactory, so he asked to have them repositioned. The original 129 tilting stop tablets—both stop tabs and couplers—he ordered replaced with new ones because he was not happy with the appearance of the ones provided by Beuchet-Debierre. The pedal contacts did not meet his expectations either, and for their alteration they had to be returned to the factory.[31]

The voicing of the organ was entrusted to Henri Yersin, who encountered one problem after another. Because the wind pressure was to be lower than that of the previous organ, the old pipes that were retained had to be reworked in Nantes. The voicing of the new pipework began in January 1954 and ended not until February 1956, taking an exceptionally long two years. One of the causes for the delays arose when the wind was found to be unstable on all four manuals. Duruflé believed that for an organ this size Beuchet should have known to include wind stabilizers in the design from the beginning. These corrective measures were effective for the récit, but less so, in Duruflé's view, for the écho, the positif, and especially the grand orgue.

The task of voicing the forty-four new stops into satisfactory cohesion with the thirty-nine old stops was not easy. Duruflé wanted the positif to have a more classic voicing, and to some extent also the écho, but the récit and grand orgue were to retain their more romantic voicing, though without compromising their overall blend. Four years after the organ was completed, Duruflé wrote, "On the four manuals, only one had been voiced in the classic style and the three others in a style rather more romantic, but with little success."[32] The concept was naive, to be sure. Duruflé judged the écho very successful, and he favored that division above the others.[33] But with the positif, which he wanted to be a replica of the écho in its classical aesthetic, he had several reservations.

On the grand orgue there were problems with blend and balance, the prestant being too heavy. Duruflé was displeased with the pipes added by Beuchet at the upper end of the cornet, and he felt Beuchet's altering of the harmonic flûte left its mid-range thick and its upper range less singing than it should be. Problems with blend and stylistic ethos marred the récit as well.

All of the mixtures on the organ were new. Duruflé did not like the way they grew weaker toward the upper end, just the reverse of what he wanted for polyphony, for the singing quality of the soprano, and for the tutti where they should strengthen the treble reeds at exactly the place where they began falling off, at middle C. Moreover, their thinness and spikiness in the upper end prevented any blend with the foundations.

Duruflé thought the écho, surrounded by hard stone walls, had a remarkably expressive quality. But the récit, he believed, lacked that distant, mysterious sonority that he considered necessary for the works of Franck. As a result, the inside walls of the box were lined with an insulating material called *isorel* (the registered trademark for a hardwood product) and *laine de verre* (glass wool) in common use at the time. Duruflé believed that its expressive potential was greater than could be achieved from the same thickness of wood.

It did not help matters that Duruflé's taste in organ design was evolving from a more romantic bent to a more neoclassic one, in such a way that the voicing of the instrument was, in his view, "an immense failure." Beuchet's Parisian voicer, Jacques Picaut,[34] did some revoicing, but Duruflé was not happy with the results. Moreover, Duruflé was publicly critical of Beuchet's misjudgments about the scaling.[35] Even after several revoicings beyond 1956, the instrument still lacked cohesion.

The placement of the console in the north alcove was not as successful as anticipated, a fact that should have surprised no one. From that location, the distant C-side of the organ, to the south, was less audible than the closer C-sharp side. Duruflé asked Beuchet to voice the C-side louder, to the advantage of the organist, but he wisely refused to do so. Duruflé discovered that the problem could be ameliorated somewhat by turning the console at an angle[36] (see Fig. 19.2).

Because of Duruflé's reservations about the instrument, there was no formal inauguration.[37] But in June of 1956, Duruflé and his wife presented a recital on it for Les Amis de l'Orgue.[38] Jean-Louis Coignet[39] attended the concert and remembered his disappointment: "The church was packed—which does not help!—and the organ sounded remote and high-pitched (a typically neoclassic sound!): the finest division was the Écho. Full organ was quite disappointing and did not bear any similarity with the organ in Notre-Dame (still in a close to original state, at that time . . . !)."[40]

In his memoirs Duruflé wrote: "Despite real qualities, the general aesthetic did not satisfy me. The sonority lacked character. Too much nicking on the pipes, some scales a little big, many tuning slots. All of this gave thickness to the timbre. Besides, the treble was too weak, the bass too heavy."[41] The parish clergy consented to a revoicing in 1958, only two years after the organ was finished.[42] Mme Duruflé referred to this work as a restoration and confessed to her disappointment with the organ's sharp and acidic tone.[43]

In 1972 Duruflé obtained permission from the city of Paris "to replace the zinc pipes with pipes of tin, take another look at all the scales and the progressions, and touch up the overall voicing."[44] The work was begun on March 1974, by Jacques Bertrand of the Gonzalez-Danion firm.[45] Bertrand reduced the wind pressures, lightened the bass and brightened the treble. The $2\frac{2}{3}'$ quint, considered of little use, was replaced by a large two-rank fourniture having a 16′ resultant. The cornet on the grand orgue was returned to its own mounted channel board. The reeds were furnished with thinner tongues, giving them a lighter and brighter color. The unit basson in the pedal was extended to 32′ pitch, but, for want of space, there are no pipes in the lowest octave. And a trompette en chamade was added above the récit box. The work was completed in October

Figure 19.2. Maurice and Marie-Madeleine at the organ of Saint Étienne-du-Mont. Photograph by Seeberger, courtesy of the American Guild of Organists.

1975. Duruflé was pleased with the results,[46] and wrote that the voicing was "carried out magnificently by Bertrand. The ensemble is no longer recognizable. It is now remarkable."[47] Even so, Duruflé was not immediately happy with the sound of the 32' reed. He asked Bertrand, "Tell me, dear friend, when are you going to add the resonators?"[48]

Duruflé covered much of the cost of the work himself, paying four and a half million old francs from his personal resources.[49] But the Beuchet-Debierre firm lost money on the job as well.[50]

Despite his satisfaction with the work of Bertrand, Duruflé was never fully happy with the instrument. "Saint Étienne-du-Mont is a beautiful organ," he once said, "but it is not perfect. An organ is rarely perfect." He considered the voicing of the organ "heavy and without poetry"[51] and thought the treble too weak. Duruflé still considered the organ at Notre-Dame "the most beautiful, without a doubt."

The instrument nevertheless garnered considerable renown. In 1957, it received international attention during the Troisième congrès international de musique sacrée that was held in Paris, an event of enormous proportion about which more will be said shortly. On July 7, Duruflé was the organist for per-formances of his *Requiem* and of *Psaume XLVII* of Schmitt at Saint Étienne-du-Mont. The concert was broadcast via radio the following day to a national audience.[52]

A final restoration and revoicing took place in 1992, six years after Duruflé had died, this time by Bernard Dargassies.[53] Mme Duruflé confided in him that she and her husband "had always found the instrument pale, despite beautiful qual-ities and already excellent earlier work. . . . What must be done," she asked, "to have an instrument at once grand, refined, and colorful?"[54] Dargassies's work achieved the desired result, so that the organ had finally become the instrument Duruflé always wanted.[55] Mme Duruflé announced, "The organ became superb again!" She reinaugurated the instrument on November 16, 1992.[56]

There is not another organ in Paris more closely identified with its titular than the one at Saint Étienne-du-Mont. The organs at Sainte Clotilde, Notre-Dame, and Saint Sulpice were renowned as artifacts of Cavaillé-Coll. While the Gonzalez organ at Saint Merry reflected the neoclassic aesthetic of its titular, Norbert Dufourcq, and the van den Heuvel at Saint Eustache that of Jean Guillou, it is only at Saint Étienne-du-Mont that the organ is identified more with its titular than with its builder or voicers. The instrument is, indeed, the fruit of Duruflé's own aesthetic.

# Chapter Twenty

# *Durufle as Organist and Teacher*

With his wife, Marie-Madeleine, Maurice Duruflé was arguably the last great proponent of the French romantic school of organ playing. An uncompromising artist, he performed with impeccable virtuosity, and with the same eloquent lyricism, the same poetry, and the same sense of nobility and grandeur for which his predecessors were renowned. Moreover, his supple playing exhibited a controlled sensitivity and an apollonian personality that neither intruded upon the works he played, nor distracted attention from their composers' purposes.

Despite his early technical prowess, it took a longer time for Duruflé to achieve the personality for which his playing would later be known. One of his earliest recitals in Paris to be reviewed, if not the first, was the one he shared with Jenny Joly on April 20, 1928, under the auspices of Les Amis de l'Orgue. He was twenty-six years old. The reviewer [M. P.] wrote that Duruflé

> certainly can be counted among the good organists who possess a technique that is as sure as it is impeccable. It appears, however, that to become a perfect performer he will have to acquire still other qualities, especially in the area of sensitivity. Translating too literally the pages he performs, which leads him to leave his personality aside, M. Duruflé does not always draw sufficiently from the musical phrase the elasticity inherent in it, which gives it its true meaning: too often, and especially in the *Cantabile*, as well as in the *Troisième Choral* of Franck, the melodic line seems fixed in an inflexible stiffness under his fingers, at the same time that its articulation proved to have an unfortunate dryness.[1]

As he matured, Duruflé objected to such rigid performances and believed that the interpreter's personality should be evident in the playing. He also acknowledged that at some point every student must wean himself from his teacher and develop his own interpretive style. He said, "I think that the student, at a certain time in his life, is no longer a student. He is his own teacher, if you will, and his personality develops. At that moment, he has only to listen to his own instincts. He has no need to study with this one or that one who will influence him in the matter of style."[2] Music, he believed, was not fixed. "Just as when you give a concert you never play the same piece in the same manner. It depends on the acoustics, the instrument. It depends on your mood at the moment. We are all obliged to take these differences into account."[3]

Exactly how Duruflé came to approach freedom at the console can be assessed to a convincing degree by understanding the freedom with which he believed the works of César Franck should be played. Duruflé held that one must play Franck (as well as Vierne) with nuance. While "we have no idea of the freedom with which Franck played his own pieces," as writes Marie-Louise Jaquet-Langlais, and doubt there was ever "one single tradition of Franck interpretation among French organists,"[4] Duruflé took a clear position on the subject, and followed the example of his teacher Tournemire, who had studied organ with Franck.

Jaquet-Langlais identifies four Franck traditions, each of which claimed it represented the true tradition: (1) that of Tournemire, reflecting his book on Franck; (2) that of Guilmant-Pierné-Dupré (contained in the Dupré edition [Bornemann 1955]); (3) that of Mahaut-Marchal-Tournemire-Langlais; (4) and that of Tournemire-Duruflé (following Duruflé's edition of Franck's *Trois Chorals* [Durand, 1973]). The fact that Tournemire appears in three of the four camps, more frequently than any other interpreter, suggests that Tournemire's authority has been perceived as central. The second tradition, that of Dupré, is contrary to Tournemire's, and it is through a comparison of these two that we come to appreciate Duruflé's contribution to the discussion. Duruflé learned the freedoms of Franck from his study of Franck's works with Franck's student Tournemire, on Franck's instrument at Sainte Clotilde, thus giving him some authority in their performance practice.

In the preface to his 1973 edition of the *Trois Chorals*, Duruflé wrote:

> Lastly, concerning the general interpretation of this music, it is certain that one must bring to it a wide-awake sensitivity, but a sensitivity the measure of which must ceaselessly be controlled. Even though it is delicate and even dangerous to give too precise indications in this realm, which remains personal, I have allowed myself, without striking anything out of the original edition, to add a few notes in brackets concerning tempo, dynamics, and certain *ritenuto's, a tempos, poco animandos* [emphasis in the original], which are obviously only suggestions. They were pointed out to me by my Master Charles Tournemire, who was a pupil of Franck.

On the basis of the Duruflé edition, and of the priority due the opinion of Tournemire, it can safely be assumed, as Daniel Roth has said, that Franck "played with remarkable freedom."[5] Similarly, what distinguished Duruflé's approach to interpreting Franck from that of Dupré was that the latter played with an unwavering beat, and a strictness lacking flexibility, while Duruflé came to play with the lyrical nuance of a sensitive poet, without exceeding the constraints of good taste.

Unlike Dupré's edition of the Franck chorals, Duruflé's made no changes in the text of the original Durand edition (1891). Dupré's sweeping editorial changes were useful in many regards and his edition provides an instructive secondary resource, but many of his changes disregard Franck's original text. One may well assume that Duruflé intended his edition as a corrective to Dupré's. One may also theorize that without Duruflé's edition, Franck performance practice would still be dictated by the concepts of Dupré.

Duruflé's approach to touch, and the pressing conundrum of legato, was unambiguous. In his edition of the chorals, he wrote:

> On the subject of phrasing, it goes without saying that the general style will be that of absolute legato in all expressive sections, which does not exclude, on the contrary, the many breaths in the exposition of the themes. One must, from this point of view, rely on the phrasing slurs indicated by the composer, without it always being necessary to have the harmonies participate in these breaths, except after perfect cadences and certain ends of phrases. In the latter case, a comma has been added to the text. Often the soprano alone must breathe, since a single phrase is generally composed of several different sections which it would always be regrettable to separate one from the other; this risks removing all the spirit from the melodic line.

Not only in the works of Franck, but for the playing of his own works Duruflé insisted on a very exacting legato except where otherwise noted, even to the point of demanding precisely legato thumb glissandos.[6] He called for a moderate approach to articulation, specifying a gradation of touches, from fully detached to legato, and giving his style a fluidity and nuance of expression unknown to the Dupré school of organ playing. In this regard, it was said by Pierre Labric that "to hear Dupré was to hear a great organist; to hear Duruflé was to hear a great musician."[7]

Moreover, Duruflé's approach to touch at the organ was unique. Marie-Claire Alain, wrote:

> [He] was the only one of my professors to explain and demonstrate the nature of touch at the organ. It was he who made me understand the importance of note values and how they are held, the relation of one note to another within the concept of a musical line. Refuting the much too pervasive idea that the organ is not an expressive instrument, he gave the basis for a way of handling the keyboards that I had always sensed the need for but I never dared realize without a guide. Under the hands of great organists, I heard the organ discourse but did not know how they arrived at this result. Thanks to Duruflé, I began to find my own personality at the keyboard, with the aid of my touch, my tactile and intellectual awareness, to be able to master the complex art of expressive articulation.[8]

To say that Duruflé insisted on a rigorous legato in the performance of his own works, therefore, is not to imply that the player should never use a non-legato touch (his scores usually, but not always, indicate when he wants something besides legato), as the above quotations suggest. It simply means that when Duruflé wanted legato, he wanted a rigorous legato.

Nor is it to imply that Duruflé never lifted his hands between phrases. There are numerous instances in his works where he wanted a break between phrase markings. More often than not, however, he preferred that phrases be linked by a careful legato; indeed, without an indication to the contrary, one faithfully assumes legato. Unfortunately, Duruflé did not always indicate in the score where he wanted such breaks and where he did not. Caesura marks between phrases, and markings articulating individual notes, began to appear in later editions. But in most instances, whether to break between phrases, or not, had to be learned privately from the man himself. Frustrating as it is for the performer, Duruflé changed his mind on many of these issues, sometimes even in the middle of a single lesson.[9]

At the same time, however, it will be of interest to organists that, in his edition of Franck's *L'Organiste* (1957), Duruflé provided precise instructions as to how much time is given to the silence between repeated notes. In a moderate or fast tempo, he wrote, the first note loses half its value. In a slow tempo, the note loses only a quarter of its value. A dotted note loses the value of the dot. In a ternary meter (in 3/8, for example) the dotted note loses the value of an eighth note. When a unison is produced with a held note, the held note must be released immediately before the unison. In chords, common notes are to be tied. Individual notes or chords having tenuto marks lose a quarter of their value. When Franck writes a slur over two notes having dots above them, which Duruflé says has a particular significance in piano writing, at the organ it ought to be treated as a *louré*. To what extent Duruflé followed his own instructions in the performance of other organ music is another matter altogether, given the wide latitude he recommended in matters of articulation.

In his earliest years as an organ teacher, Duruflé taught the kind of articulation described immediately above, which was also typical of Marcel Dupré's approach. According to one of Duruflé's earliest American pupils, Marilyn Mason, who studied with him when he was teaching at Fontainebleau, probably in 1948, "He insisted on all repeated notes being given half their value, and would say, 'Un, deux, un, deux,' with the 'un' being the note and the 'deux' being the rest."[10] In later years he grew less rigid in his approach.[11]

Duruflé exerted all possible influence over the way other organists interpreted his music. Although when he said that "to interpret means many things; it means a certain freedom in the phrase," he was answering the question as to whether performers of his works should "take liberties in the rhythm, to make nuances," and in practice he did not generally appreciate a player's taking liberties with his music. As Mme Duruflé herself confirmed, "there are some liberties that [he does] not like."[12]

In the first editions of the *Prélude et fugue sur le nom d'ALAIN*, for instance, Duruflé specified an imperceptible accelerando from measure 69 to the end: "Animer peu à peu, insensiblement, jusqu'à la fin." In subsequent editions this indication was removed because Duruflé grew to dislike the effect of nervousness about it and objected to the accelerando. Why speed up, he asked in an interview, when in general terms speeding up is considered a fault?[13] His wife concurred:

"There was so little difference on the metronome, you don't feel it. Just by the dynamism you do it." But, she said, "if you take the second fugue as you say, slowly, the end lacks enthusiasm." In eliminating the instruction to speed up, Duruflé thus presented the performer with an insoluble problem. The player, he said, will "speed up without meaning to. So I left it to the organist to press ahead. He will always speed up (laughs)." Likewise, although he objected to a rubato at the end of the *Toccata* from the *Suite,* Op. 5, he consented to "a little rubato, if you wish."[14] Duruflé's position on such matters was typically evasive.[15]

In general terms, Mme Duruflé insisted:

> It is necessary to be very faithful to what he wrote, and, above all, not to want to add anything to it or to change anything in the score. In these cases he got angry. Even for registrations, he had rather precise ideas. For tempos, crescendos, and accelerandos, he was quite opposed to "free" interpretations of his indications. . . .
>
> He was very meticulous in his writing; it is for this reason that it is not necessary to add anything to it. Everything is written. When he indicates a tempo, an effect, it is always necessary to execute it with a certain discretion. He himself was very fussy in his own interpretations. They were well adjusted and fulfilling, without excesses. He said that it was not necessary to speed up, but to play "in a kindly manner." But all these words and explanations do not take the place of listening to recordings of his works by him and myself, if I may say so; anyway, I was never permitted to produce my interpretations if he was not in agreement.[16]

At the same time, in teaching his own works to his students, Duruflé suggested not only registration alternatives,[17] but the addition of staccatos and rests in various places, as many as fifty or so throughout his œuvre. He also suggested registration alternatives, as, for instance, the addition of a mixture for the final reprise of the main theme in the *Scherzo.*[18]

Of his skill at registration, Norbert Dufourcq wrote of Duruflé that he retained certain formulas of registration used by his predecessors, "registrations that were judicious and poetic, and never extreme."[19] But in unique passages, his registrations were beautifully conceived, and more colorfully orchestrated than the norm.

The registrations that Duruflé provided for his earliest organ compositions, especially the *Scherzo,* imply a late nineteenth-century Cavaillé-Coll aesthetic, whereas his later works, and the later editions of his early works, imply a growing neoclassic aesthetic, with its multiple mixtures, clear principal choruses, octave couplers, and the registrational devices made possible by an electric console.

The theory has been advanced that the registration indications of the *Sicilienne* and the first edition *Scherzo* reflect a direct relationship to the organ Duruflé knew in Louviers, and that those of the *Prélude, adagio et choral varié sur le Veni Creator* and the *Suite* (except for the *Sicilienne*) reflect a direct relationship to the organ he inherited at Saint Étienne-du-Mont. While instructive, the theory is uncompelling.[20] Duruflé wrote the *Scherzo,* after all, some seven years after he began commuting to Paris and had surely already been exposed to the emerging neoclassic aesthetic. Nor is there evidence enough to demonstrate such a relationship between his work on *Veni Creator* and the unfortunate 1928 rebuilding of the organ as Duruflé knew it at Saint Étienne-du-Mont. What one can say with merit is that Duruflé's registrations, and his subsequent editions, reflect his gradual departure from a romantic aesthetic to a neoclassic one. It is only natural that his early works should reflect the character of the instruments he knew.

Furthermore, Duruflé did not write for particular instruments. Mme Duruflé confirmed that "he wrote his works with an ideal organ in mind,[21] remembering his favorites from Normandy and Paris, rather than for [Saint Étienne-du-Mont] in particular."[22] His concept of that ideal organ changed gradually over the years, from the romantic to the neoclassic.

One might assume that, given Duruflé's strictness about how his works were to be performed by organists, and his wife's faithfulness to his wishes, the pair's performances of his works would be virtually indistinguishable. But this was not the case. Herndon Spillman noted that upon close listening one could hear a "tremendous difference in the way Maurice Duruflé played his music versus his wife."[23] The most conspicuous difference was her electrically rhythmic playing as contrasted with his more lyrical playing.

Duruflé's inflexibility, if you will, in the performance of his organ works, did not obtain under all circumstances. When the Duruflés first saw the enormous five-manual console at Riverside Church in New York, for example, Frederick Swann, the church's organist and the organist for the upcoming performance of the *Requiem*, could see the consternation on Duruflé's face, and the excited and joyful expression on Madame's face. Duruflé nevertheless proved receptive to the increased potential and greater flexibility that the larger, more complex American console offered the performer. Swann tells what happened:

> I was terrified because I had added many things from the orchestra score that were possible because of the colorful Riverside organ, complete with devices such as Pedal Divide. At one point in the *Agnus Dei* I had a bass line going in the pedal, [a] cushioning chord in the left hand, a right hand melody, plus another "thumbed" down line on a 2nd manual PLUS another melody going on the upper part of the pedal board through the Pedal Divide. He stopped the rehearsal and they both came charging to the console, and he wouldn't continue until I demonstrated what I was doing. She was delighted, and although I feared he would say "STOP IT!"—he actually smiled and said "Très bon!"[24]

Liturgical improvisation has made the French organ school famous. Duruflé held that one must have an excellent grasp of harmony and be a composer in order to be a good improviser. One must know the classic forms and their evolution, he believed, be good at analysis, and have a prodigious technique. One must also "know orchestration, because the organ and the orchestra have certain points in common."[25] His private organ student, Marie-Claire Alain, indicated:

> His improvisation lessons derived quite naturally from his harmony instruction. It was thus that I found my fingers instinctively following the successions of chords favored in our harmony exercises. Even after fifty years, I find myself using them in my liturgical improvisations. He helped me to discipline my style so that I could adapt it to the molds of "academic" improvisation that had to remain musical, according to him.[26]

Duruflé occasionally improvised in concert, but commonly improvised at mass, generally for the *entrée* and the *sortie*. His improvisations were said by many to have been identical to his own style of formal composition.[27] Duruflé was like Louis Vierne in this regard, but was unlike Tournemire, whose improvisations Duruflé considered of greater inspiration than his written *L'Orgue mystique.*

Duruflé valued improvisation as an indispensable skill for organists in liturgical churches, for functions of indeterminate duration, and he considered Gregorian chant the virtually sole source of themes.[28] Among the themes he used were the *Ave maris stella* for feasts of the Blessed Virgin Mary, *Parce, Domine* for Lent, and the *Veni Creator* for Pentecost. But he also improvised on noels for the Christmas season and used the *Marche des rois* for Epiphany.[29] He particularly enjoyed improvising in alternation with the choir and the *orgue de chœur*, especially at vespers. Unfortunately, there are no known (authorized) recordings of his liturgical improvisations.[30]

Duruflé held that Bach ought to constitute the foundation of every organist's repertoire, and he "played Bach with a great seriousness."[31] He thought the works of Bach had a suitable place in the Roman Catholic liturgy, if carefully chosen, and cited the *Orgelbüchlein* as the source of much useful repertoire.[32] He liked to play *Nun komm, der Heiden Heiland*, BWV 599, for Advent; various chorales on the *Gloria* for Christmas; *Das alte Jahr vergangen ist*, BWV 614, for the beginning of January; *Christ, unser Herr, zum Jordan kam*[33] for the baptism of Christ; *O Mensch, bewein' dein' Sünde gross*, BWV 622, and *O Lamm Gottes, unschuldig*, BWV 618, for Lent; and the Saint Anne triple fugue (Fugue in E flat, BWV 552) for Trinity Sunday, as well as preludes and fugues, fantasies, and sonatas that can be adapted to the liturgy, including the Toccata and Fugue in D Minor, BWV 565.

In Duruflé's view, French classic works were appropriate for the service as well, but he believed that, apart from de Grigny and François Couperin, French classic works did not enjoy a musical value equal to Bach.[34] His custom was to play published repertoire during the offertory and the communion of the mass, drawing on works by Clérambault, Claude-Bénigne Balbastre, Jean François Dandrieu, Lebègue, Jean Huré, Dupré (including *Le Chemin de la croix*), Litaize, Fleury, and Messiaen, among others. He played his own fugue on the name ALAIN for the feast of Christ the King.[35]

The Duruflés' approach to Bach is documented in the recordings they made between November 1963 and July 1965, which featured the preludes, toccatas, fantasies, and fugues of Bach (BWV 531–66, 572, 578, 582) on the 1956 Gonzalez organ of the cathedral in Soissons.[36] Mme Duruflé played the more technically demanding works on the recordings, including the Toccata in F, BWV 540, for instance, the Prelude and Fugue in D, BWV 532, and the Fantasy and Fugue in G Minor, BWV 542. Duruflé himself gave rousing performances as well, of the Fugue in A Minor, BWV 543, for example.

Their playing is reasonable, elegant, colorful, and technically compelling, with an insistent rhythmic vitality and energy, with registrations that reinforce the formal architecture of the works, and with a variety of articulation that ranges from legato to rather detached, all in the service of musicality. Duruflé's approach to playing Bach was thought of highly enough in the 1960s that he played an all-Bach recital on the organ at Saint Donat in 1962, and another for Paris Radio in 1964; he participated in a Festival Bach et l'École française at Saint Merry in 1967, and played for Bach Festivals at London's Westminster Abbey and the Église des Carmes in Brussels, both in 1969.[37]

The approach taken by him and his wife for the playing of Bach soon came to be discounted as old-fashioned—for their changes of registration and manuals that were more frequent than became the norm, for instance, for playing legato, as well as for their use of expression boxes, their use of reeds on fugue expositions (reflecting French classic practice), their use of the brash bombardes, and their use of dramatic dynamic ranges. While this style was not all that unusual in the 1960s, by the 1980s their approach had clearly been discarded by the early music movement, particularly by its more extreme adherents. So when the Duruflés' Bach performances were reissued on compact disc, in 1996, critics noted that their style was contrary to authentic performance practice, which Mme Duruflé called "tout staccato." In her view, there was never a reason to play the organ as if it were a harpsichord, and in Bach, she said, "it is sensitivity that determines quality."[38] Her husband expressed the same sentiment: "Today, for example, there's a manner of playing the organ that I don't like at all. They play very detached. . . . I find that they go too far with articulation. . . . There are some who detach all the notes. I find that a right balance between detached and legato is necessary."[39] By the end of the twentieth century, the Duruflés would be partially vindicated in their style of playing Bach, when the extremes of the neo-baroque movement gave way to moderating influences, particularly in the matter of articulation, registration, and freedom of expression.

It is of singular interest that on October 31, 1943, when he was forty-one, Duruflé was one of two harpsichordists to perform Bach's *Art of Fugue*, BWV 1080, in a concert with the Société des Concerts du Conservatoire, under the direction of Charles Münch. As mentioned earlier, his partner was the Swiss harpsichordist Marguerite Roesgen-Champion (1894–1976), who had trained as a pianist. The fact that the work was the only piece on the program suggests that the performance was more or less complete, and that some movements were performed by the orchestra. Duruflé's being the house organist for the Société may well explain why he was offered the engagement, rather than for any particular expertise he had demonstrated as a harpsichordist, or for his stylistic approach to Bach. This appears to be the only documented instance of Duruflé's playing solo harpsichord in a public context.

The Duruflés exhibited a similar disregard for the tenets of a historic performance practice of French classic works. He was convinced that there was no such thing as inégalité.[40] Otherwise, he believed, the composers of the period would have indicated as much.[41] It bears noting, however, that for their recording of French classic works, which they produced in 1969, they chose not the organ at Saint Étienne-du-Mont, or that in Soissons, both of which were tonally equipped for the task, but the organ at Saint Sauveur in Le Petit-Andely, constructed in 1674 by Robert Ingout, apparently believing that neoclassic organs did not trump historic organs for the playing of early music.

Duruflé considered piano study essential preparation for the organist,[42] and the Bach keyboard works were, in his view, the pianist's *vade mecum*. He accepted only organ students who could demonstrate a solid foundation in piano playing, making no distinction between a technique suited to the piano and one suited to the playing of Bach on the organ. On at least one occasion, for example, he declined to accept a student who had not studied Bach's *Well-Tempered Clavier*.[43] Duruflé himself was an excellent pianist[44] and had some experience as a pianist performing chamber music.[45] A former student of Duruflé, Rolande Falcinelli, commented that there were two personalities who attracted her to the world of the organ: Duruflé and Fleury. Lured not only by their great talent as organists, she appreciated that they were also wonderful pianists.[46]

Duruflé believed that organists ought to get away from their own instruments occasionally and listen to something besides organ music. He recommended hearing symphony concerts because they help the organist to develop a sense of color at the organ.[47] His position as organist for the Société des Concerts for over thirty years gave him a great deal more orchestral experience than most organists have.

Duruflé believed there was no point in playing from memory. He did not do so himself, as a rule, and he did not expect it of his students.[48] The story is told of a performance he played at the Palais de Chaillot, when he walked on stage carrying under each arm some large cardboard on which were glued the pages of his scores, whereupon "the public, astonished at such an entrance onto the stage, could not hold back a surge of sympathy as if the artist had arrived in overalls to start up the immense machine that was slowly moving forward from the back of the stage."[49] At the same time, his pieces were usually memorized, as for a particular concert when, because of insufficient light, he played Debussy's *Rhapsodie* for piano practically from memory.[50]

Duruflé considered his wife's playing superior to his own. He told Lilian Murtagh so in 1963. While it is difficult and ultimately fruitless to argue style, his was elegant and lyrical while hers was rhythmically intense. With her formidable technique she was able to play with "that remarkable 'internal flame' so well known by her audiences."[51]

In 1970 the Duruflés performed at Chester Cathedral in England, to inaugurate the 1969–70 rebuild of the organ. The cathedral organist, Roger Fisher, said he learned a great deal from them by the way they prepared for the recital.

> On two evenings they worked from 6 pm to 1 am on registration alone, playing effects to one another until they were quite satisfied. Monsieur in addition spent six hours sitting at a desk reading his scores—"revisé," he said, although he must have played them countless times before! Madame, on the other hand, practiced for nine hours "without the sound"—she was not content until her fingers found their way instinctively to all the right notes, and not content until the touch of the organ, together with the feel of the swell pedals was totally comfortable.[52]

Fisher recounted Mme Duruflé's facility with the swell pedal. "Her performance of Vierne's Naïades was supple, totally secure and elegant, with control of the swell pedals which rivaled that of Harold Darke, whose subtlety was legendary."[53]

The couple's recitals were not always perfect, they did not always agree with each other on registration, and occasionally the peculiarities of an organ befuddled them. In Chester, Duruflé was playing his *Choral varié sur le Veni Creator* when Mme Duruflé pushed a piston that caused a slight hiccup in the sound. "Order was soon restored and he took it all very calmly, but Madame was very puzzled until I explained the difficulty. Her face lit up as she exclaimed 'Ah! Le doobler poosh!'"[54]

Duruflé did not teach organ at the Paris Conservatoire, except when he was substituting for Marcel Dupré, and although, at least in the beginning, he took few private students outside the Conservatoire, he managed over a period of some forty years to have taught organists from Paris and the provinces, from Germany, the Netherlands, Scandinavia, the United States, Australia, and elsewhere.

One of Duruflé's earlier French students was André Levasseur, a former *maîtrisien* of Saint-Évode, who studied with him between 1945 and 1947. Levasseur's lessons took place on the tubular-pneumatic *orgue de chœur* at Saint Étienne-du-Mont, at a time when the electricity was undependable and the organ in the tribune still unavailable. He studied mostly Bach and Franck, along with some of the twenty-four works of Louis Vierne in free style, but he studied none of the French classic composers. Duruflé used the Bornemann edition of the Bach works, edited by Marcel Dupré, but did not insist on Dupré's fingerings.[55] Another private organ pupil, Henri Bert, said that Duruflé respected without qualification the rules imposed by Dupré concerning slurred (*liées*) and detached notes, trills, and ornaments.[56]

Even without having generated a school of disciples as such, Duruflé's former students, those who studied harmony with him and others who studied the organ with him, and with Mme Duruflé, represent a living memorial to their legacy. Among Duruflé's prominent French students were Marie-Claire Alain, Suzanne Chaisemartin, Daniel Roth, Jean Guillou, Philippe Lefèbvre, Pierre Cochereau, Odile Pierre, Félix Moreau, and André Jorrand. Among his European pupils were Günther Kaunzinger, Hans Fagius, and Dorothy de Rooij.[57] The Australian Edward Theodore was one of Duruflé's few former students to have recorded the complete organ works, making his document an important source for other performers.

Among Duruflé's earliest American students was Robert Burns King, who worked with him beginning in February 1962, and again from January to July in 1964, studying his compositions as well as his reconstitutions of the Tournemire improvisations, many pieces by Vierne, and occasionally pieces by Bach, Couperin, Franck, and others. Also among Duruflé's first North American students were Ralph Kneeream, Marilyn Mason, and Herndon Spillman, the last-named being the first ever to record Duruflé's complete organ works.[58] Lynn Davis and Susan Ferré also studied with Duruflé, as did Donald Wilkins,[59] Reginald Lunt, Sarah Soularue, Kurt Lueders, Rodger Vine, Charles Bradley, as well as Fred Gramann and the eminent Canadian harpsichordist and musicologist Kenneth Gilbert. Dennis Keene[60] and Jesse Eschbach studied with Mme Duruflé, as did Rodger Vine.

If any of Duruflé's students could lay claim to being his protégé, it was Pierre Cochereau (1924–84), who won first prize in Duruflé's harmony class at the Conservatoire in 1946. Marie-Madeleine Duruflé reported that Cochereau was one of her husband's most brilliant pupils.[61] Early in Cochereau's career, when he was organist at Saint Roch, Duruflé promoted him as a skilled improviser, and he supported him after he became Léonce de Saint-Martin's successor at Notre-Dame in 1955. Duruflé was in the audience at the cathedral on February 27, 1970, when Cochereau played what some considered his greatest recital, improvising a *Prélude, adagio et choral varié* on a seventeenth-century noël, thus paying homage to Duruflé, whose own similarly-titled work on *Veni Creator* followed the same grand lines.[62] In 1962 Cochereau became director of the Conservatoire de musique in Nice.

Cochereau's unique harmonic idiom was said to have issued essentially from Debussy and Ravel (the use of the tritone, for instance), through Dukas (the use of the augmented fifth and the whole-tone scale) and Duruflé (Gregorian-inspired modality).[63] His music is almost always tonal, with elements of bitonality and modality, and with many added notes. Cochereau was also influenced by Duruflé's use of dense, compact chords.[64] Although he rarely played written works during the services at Notre-Dame, one of the few he did play was the *Prélude et fugue sur le nom d'ALAIN.*[65] Cochereau died in 1984, preceding Duruflé in death by two years.

Duruflé's last American pupil was Rodger Vine, who studied both with him and with Mme Duruflé from 1971 to 1973. He studied with Duruflé again in

September of 1978, and therefore had the rare opportunity of studying with him both before and after the accident. Mme Duruflé said that he had become a "brilliant virtuoso with a volcanic technique." In 1977 he played the complete organ works of Duruflé at Old South Church in Boston on the occasion of Duruflé's seventy-fifth birthday, and in 2004 he presented the first concert performance of Duruflé's Fugue in C Minor at the Arlington Street Church, also in Boston.

Jörg Abbing interviewed several of Duruflé's former organ students, and in his book *Maurice Duruflé: Aspekte zu Leben und Werk* he wrote: "From nearly all of these students I have obtained the illuminating information that Duruflé was an extremely exact yet always endearing and humble teacher, who continually concerned himself with an objective tone with his students and from whom one could notice his joy in teaching."[66]

# Chapter Twenty-One

# *Duruflé and Organ Design*

The organs that Duruflé heard and played during his formative and early adult years were all products of the romantic aesthetic of Cavaillé-Coll, John Abbey, Merklin-Schütze, and others of their ilk from the nineteenth century. His first compositions, such as the first edition of the *Scherzo*, betray this influence. He had little, if any, early exposure to the French classic organ of the eighteenth century, or to the eighteenth-century organs of Germany. In the course of his career, however, he came to see the artistic value of both the classic and romantic models. Over the years he wrote many articles on organ design and served as consultant for a number of both new organs and organ restorations. In 1941 he was appointed to the advisory committee of the Commission des orgues, which had been established in 1933 by the French government's Service des monuments historiques.[1]

Duruflé had great respect for the work of Cavaillé-Coll, and he wrote with admiring detail, as we have seen, of the Cavaillé-Coll organs at Sainte Clotilde and Notre-Dame. For one of his recordings he used the little-known, rebuilt Cavaillé-Coll at Notre-Dame d'Auteuil in Paris (1966).[2] In 1949, Duruflé said that "Notre-Dame, Saint Sulpice, and Saint Eustache are for me the most beautiful and the most complete of the organs in the capital."[3] The organ at Saint Sulpice issued from Cavaillé-Coll, while the instrument at Saint Eustache was built by Victor Gonzalez (1932), whose work will be described shortly.

Despite his respect for Cavaillé-Coll, Duruflé favored the addition of mixtures to brighten the Cavaillé-Coll at Notre-Dame, a work carried out under Pierre Cochereau's titularship. While he considered it one of the most beautiful organs ever built, he thought it heavy in the bass. "One had to be careful, nevertheless, not to use a thick registration, for the Pleins Jeux did not have the brilliancy that one might desire."[4] Cochereau added mixtures and other stops, drastically altering the instrument Vierne knew. Duruflé liked many of the changes: "The organ previously lacked a bit of clarity. It was a little bit heavy. The added mixtures help to brighten the sound."[5]

On the other hand, Duruflé thought the changes made by Tournemire on the organ at Sainte Clotilde were ill-conceived. "It was Maison Beuchet who did [the work]. From the point of view of the workmanship it was very well done. But from the point of view of the voicing, you can disagree. It doesn't blend very well with the former organ."[6]

Soon after moving to Paris, Duruflé was exposed to the pioneering work of organ builder Victor Gonzalez (1877–1956), a former employee of Cavaillé-Coll, who introduced the neoclassic organ design in the early 1920s. In 1896, Gonzalez worked with Cavaillé-Coll in the shop on avenue de Maine, and then studied early organ building in Germany and Austria.[7] In 1922 he established a firm in Malakoff, and then built a new establishment in the Paris suburb of Châtillon-sous-Bagneux, in 1930. Louis Vierne considered Gonzalez "the foremost voicer of our time."[8]

Gonzalez believed there were excesses in romantic organ building that tended to imitate orchestral colors at the expense of the true organ character of the classic period. He believed that mixtures could be added without renouncing the contributions of Cavaillé-Coll, but it would be necessary to lighten the foundations, and to clarify and lighten the reeds, alterations that would assure the tonal cohesion of the ensemble. Wind pressures would have to be reduced. Gonzalez was inspired by the impassioned playing of the early and classic works, and by the refined registrations and the care for detail exhibited in the playing of André Marchal, who, with his former pupil, the musicologist Norbert Dufourcq, took a leading role with Gonzalez in the revival of French classic organ building. Gonzalez adopted the system of electro-pneumatic action, allowing a uniformly light key action, with a supple and silent touch, and the instantaneous changing of stops.

In a homage to Gonzalez after his death, Duruflé outlined his qualifications and influence, and the characteristics of a neoclassic organ.

> He opted boldly for the return to lowered pressures, to pipes with tuning slots or cut to length, with low mouths and without nicking for principals 16–8–4–2 and pleins-jeux. The color then takes on this discreet brilliance, this delightful freshness of naturally emitted sound, without effort. Thanks to low wind pressures, to scales and halving ratios exactly calculated so as to find their right point of balance, the different stops of the organ blend marvelously. The fundamentals and the mixtures, both simple and composé, are mixed (incorporated) so as to form only one sound, achieving the ideal conjunction of transparence and fullness.[9]

Duruflé became an advocate of the neoclassic organ because he saw the wisdom of new instruments designed to play all periods of organ literature, Franck as well as Bach.[10] He was fond of Gonzalez's restoration of the Merklin at Saint Eustache (1932), for example, under the supervision of Joseph Bonnet, as well as Gonzalez's instruments at Saint Merry (1946) and the Soissons cathedral (1956). The instrument at Saint Étienne-du-Mont, rebuilt under Duruflé's direction by Beuchet-Debierre, followed neoclassic lines, as we have seen. From these successes he argued that contemporary organs of neoclassic design would succeed the romantic organ that Cavaillé-Coll had brought to perfection,[11] retaining especially his harmonic flûtes, a well-furnished pedal, and an expressive récit with its battery of reeds and undulating ranks.[12] The neoclassic organ, he wrote, should have an adjustable combination action, sixty-one notes on the manuals and thirty-two in the pedal, with pipes speaking without excessive chiff, and enclosed in a case.[13] He advocated that the manuals be ordered, from bottom to top: grand orgue, positif, and récit, each manual having a coupler to the pedal. There should also be a sub-octave coupler from the récit to the grand orgue.[14]

Comparing organs that are suitable for playing Bach with those suitable for playing Franck, Duruflé specified that Bach's counterpoint and architectonic grandeur can be played to good effect upon a wide variety of organs, if carefully registered. Franck's works, however, rely on the timbre and romantic quality of the stops and the expressive character of the swell box. Otherwise, he believed, they lose much of their musical substance and interest.[15]

As to whether neoclassic organs should be saved and preserved, the proponent of historic organs and historic performance practice, Marie-Claire Alain, declared, "And how, absolutely!" Insisting that the repertoire written for the neoclassic organ deserves to be played on instruments intended for it, she said: "When we think of Duruflé, Messiaen, Alain, Fleury, Langlais, Litaize, who are played all over the world, and who have defended this style of organ, and when we think that people would want to destroy the organs for which they composed! We have to save them and indeed restore them."[16]

Despite his predilection for the neoclassic organ—he said that "if it is well voiced, the organ will not lack character"—Duruflé ascribed to the view that authentic performances require historic organs rather than modern eclectic ones. "If . . . you want 'authentic' sounds for a recording, you can go play an original Cavaillé-Coll, Schnitger or Clicquot."[17]

As to whether French organ builders should resort to the designs and methods of the German baroque, Duruflé explained: "The return to the traditional sources of French classic techniques in the spirit and limit to which Victor Gonzalez has restored or constructed his instruments is clearly sufficient. I don't think that in France it is necessary to go elsewhere."[18]

Despite his appreciation for electric action, when he was asked, in 1961, whether he preferred mechanical, electro-pneumatic, or electric action, Duruflé replied, without equivocation, "mechanical action without any doubt. Beginning with a certain number of manuals and stops, electric action [is necessary] if the mechanical system risks rendering the manuals too heavy."[19] For recital instruments, Duruflé considered a combination action essential, and held that a church organ of thirty or more stops should be so equipped.[20] At the same time he believed that the expression pedal for the récit ought to remain mechanical, there being nothing more detestable than an electric mechanism that is never subtle.[21]

Though he avowed historic instruments for authentic performances, Duruflé had little patience with the historicist movement in the construction of new instruments, which began to influence French organ building in the late 1950s. "Some are . . . happy with unequal temperament and cuneiform bellows. The more shaking of the wind there is, the happier they are. I cannot stand shaky wind."[22]

Recalling the historic organs in Poitiers, Marmoutier, and Ebersmünster as authentic examples of the finest in classical organ building, Duruflé noted that, far from being dominated by mixtures, they had a "just proportion of foundations 8′ and 4′ and mixtures that blend marvelously." One never hears an aggressive mixture or a crackling at the attack. Instead, "the plenum 8-4 with mixtures is . . . calm, balanced, of an incomparable nobility."[23]

In the case of historic organs in need of restoration, Duruflé, in general terms, respected their integrity of design without inappropriately imposing the neo-classic aesthetic upon them. He was one of two consultants, for instance, for the restoration of the organ at the collegiate church of Notre-Dame d'Espérance in Montbrison, in the region of Rhône-Alpes. The instrument was originally constructed by the Alsatian builder Louis Callinet, but was romanticized in 1870 by Merklin. Even with its mixed pedigree, the organ was designated an *orgue historique* in 1972, making it eligible for a serious restoration. Upon Duruflé's advice, the firm of Dunand de Villeurbanne restored the instrument to its original specification of forty-six stops on three manuals and pedal.[24]

Under certain conditions, Duruflé recommended electric action for what he himself described as authentic historic instruments. In too many cases, he wrote, old organs had been designated historic instruments merely for their old dilapidated mechanisms and collapsing pipework. Such was not the case, in his judgment, with the organ at the cathedral in Angoulême, whose remaining old pipework qualified the organ for designation as a historic instrument. But because its inaccessible mechanism was in an irreparable state, he recommended an electro-pneumatic action rather than a new tracker mechanism. Moreover, its fifty-five stops and three manuals were too many to allow for a light and supple mechanical action.[25] Its manuals were extended from fifty-four to sixty-one notes, thus requiring the construction of a new console and new wind chests. This historic instrument became, in Duruflé's words, "an entirely new organ."[26]

In the late 1950s Duruflé commissioned Gonzalez to construct an organ for his apartment.[27] He was fond of the organ in the home of André Marchal's son-in-law, and the Gonzalez organ in his own apartment is said to have been influenced by it. In fact Duruflé went with tape measure in hand to take measurements of critical features.[28] Duruflé's instrument was finally installed in 1967, but not without considerable difficulties.

Construction was begun on the console before Duruflé had informed his landlord about the planned instrument. The man vetoed the project, so the unfinished console remained in a corner of the shop for a long while before the organ was finally completed for the church in Le Locle, Switzerland. In the absence of a practice instrument, Mme Duruflé did her pedal practice on the design she traced on a piece of linoleum.

Upon the death of the landlord, Duruflé resurrected the project. The récit and the positif were to have their own boxes, but the reeds, distributed among the various divisions, were to stand in an enclosure of their own, controlled by its own expression pedal. He also wanted the largest space possible between the black notes.

It looked at first as though the chore of hoisting the hundred-kilogram console by hand up eight floors would necessitate notching the plaster walls so the corners of the console would clear. But the console still would not pass the last little hallway. So instead the workers rigged a scaffolding on the balcony, up to the height of the kitchen window, and used the ladder that Duruflé kept as a fire escape. The ladder allowed them to slide the console over the scaffolding, then through the kitchen window, and from there into the music room.[29]

The voicing of the instrument was the result of a close collaboration between Duruflé and the voicer, Jacques Bertrand, but it took several years to complete, partly because of the Duruflés' tours and other projects in the Gonzalez shop. Duruflé asked Bertrand to replace the too narrowly scaled plein jeu on the grand orgue (at Duruflé's expense) and to add a larigot to the positif. But his desire to add a dessus de cornet was abandoned because it would entail winding a chest near the ceiling in an opposite corner of the room. Other problems and challenges were solved more or less easily.

The completed instrument was warm and gently voiced, and had excellent action, a combination mechanism, and no chiff.[30] It must have satisfied Duruflé, because Mme Duruflé told Bertrand that she was happy that, with the new instrument, her husband had resumed improvising again, something he had not done for a long time (see Fig. 21.1).

Later in life, Duruflé confessed to an abhorrence of electronic organs, but in the early 1930s he was taken by an experimental instrument called the *orgue électronique des ondes*. Patented by Armand Givelet and Édouard Éloi Coupleaux, the device had two short manuals and a pedal clavier, and was composed of seven hundred vacuum oscillator tubes that produced seventy notes and ten different timbres.[31] Duruflé played it numerous times during 1932, and even played it for two inaugural events in Paris, one on October 26 with Louis Vierne and M. Béché and another on October 27 with Béché alone.[32] In effect the predecessor of the Hammond organ, the device was short-lived; Duruflé's regard for such instruments changed with time.

For his first American tour, in 1964, Westminster Choir College inquired whether Duruflé would consent to play an Allen electronic organ for a festival taking place while he was in the country.[33] Duruflé did not participate. Again in 1969 he was asked about playing a Rodgers electronic organ with the El Paso Symphony and for a recital in Fanwood, New Jersey. He declined in both instances, partly because he assumed American organists disapproved of them and he did not want to appear to be taking a position contrary to prevailing American opinion.[34]

After his tours of North America, Duruflé wrote that the most well-known organs in the United States were those, first of all, by Aeolian-Skinner, and then those by Möller, Austin, Schlicker, Casavant, and Noehren. He described particular

Figure 21.1. Maurice and Marie-Madeleine Duruflé at the organ in their apartment. Photograph by Seeberger, courtesy of the American Guild of Organists.

instruments in some detail, but he found the organs in perfect working order, unlike the organs in France. Singling out the Aeolian-Skinner at Saint Thomas Church in New York City, with its newly installed French reeds, as the one he and Mme Duruflé particularly appreciated, he called it the most remarkable of those in the city. He also commended the celebrated Aeolian-Skinner at the Riverside Church, calling it a grand cathedral organ, of the symphonic style, with limitless possibilities. Likewise he admired the Schlicker at the First Congregational Church in Los Angeles. But from a very different design perspective, he also noted both the successful von Beckerath at Saint Paul's Roman Catholic Cathedral in Pittsburgh, "an authentic masterwork" despite its heavy action, and the Flentrop at Saint Mark's Episcopal Cathedral in Seattle, of exceptional construction and voicing, but with the same mechanical detriment.[35]

Despite having favorites among romantic and neoclassic instruments, Duruflé thus enjoyed a wide swath of organ styles and idiomatic aesthetics, ranging from French classic, north German baroque, French romantic, and French and American neoclassic instruments of the twentieth century. The breadth of his taste stands in sharp contrast to the more limited taste of so many organists of the late twentieth century.

# Chapter Twenty-Two

# *The Church in Transition*

The liturgical document *Sacrosanctum Concilium*, promulgated in 1963 by the Second Vatican Council, was a natural extension of the *motu proprio* of 1903 and of subsequent documents issued by the Holy See. What it had to say about Gregorian chant, polyphony, and the pipe organ had already been said before. But at the same time, the council fathers authorized worship in vernacular languages set to indigenous music. Whether it was by a stroke of genius that the church's bishops sanctioned the coexistence of these two, or merely reticence, is not for us to debate here. But in France, as elsewhere, they did not coexist very well.

In April 1969 the Holy See promulgated its *Novus Ordo Missae*, the *New Order of Mass*, fulfilling the demands of the council for a reformed liturgy. The complete missal of Paul VI appeared, in Latin, in 1970, and translations into the vernacular appeared soon thereafter.

While the more centrist French bishops sought at first to toe the conciliar line, maintaining the tradition while exploring new vernacular possibilities, the lower ranks of the clergy, inspired by a radical new secularism, had little investment in the Latin Gregorian tradition, which, in the event, was unable to withstand the emergence of vernacular translations and musical idioms that were widely regarded with suspicion by professional musicians.

One could argue that, in France, the council brought the church's music full circle. As popular forms of music had prevailed in the French church during the nineteenth century, so would they prevail again in the second half of the twentieth. Duruflé flourished between these two periods of musical secularism. The triumph of plainsong, of polyphony, and of truly liturgical organ playing, in the first half century of his life, represented for Duruflé the victory of a transcendent, hieratic worldview over the secular and popular aberrations ushered in by the nineteenth century. Their demise in the 1960s meant more than the loss of a well-regarded musical tradition; it was also an assault on the worldview that gave his life meaning.

As a centrist, Duruflé was not opposed to the reforms outlined in *Sacrosanctum Concilium*. What he opposed was the way he felt the French clergy disposed of the past, demeaned their congregations, and introduced trivial musical fare into the liturgy. But because he was so vociferously opposed to what he considered the clerical misinterpretations of the council's dictates, he was labeled a reactionary, even by an otherwise informed organ world. The truth was rather more complex than that. Even though Duruflé actively promoted the Latin liturgical and musical traditions in the decade following the council, his writings, as we shall see, prove his receptivity to vernacular forms such as chorales and hymns, whose value had been tested for four hundred years by Protestants.

The controversy can also be attributed to a difference of understanding between the so-called regular clergy, that is, those bound by their rule to the common recitation (or singing) of the divine office, such as the Benedictines, and the diocesan clergy, who were not so bound. Whereas the latter were suspicious of hieratic art forms, and thus took a more populist view of the reforms (based on an immanent view of the relationship of the divine to the human), the Benedictines had less reason to bother themselves with the parish renewal of Christian art as it was being promoted in the 1960s and later, because, for them, the medieval forms continued to suffice. Duruflé was clearly a proponent of the approach espoused by the Benedictines.

During the week of July 1–8, 1957, the Troisième congrès de musique sacrée convened in Paris to address topics of universal concern; the conference attracted experts in liturgy and music from all over the world.[1] Fourteen hundred delegates attended from France and Europe, Africa, the Americas, Asia, and Oceania, and choirs from all over Catholic France and Europe sang concerts and services in the churches and concert halls of Paris, Versailles, and Reims.

The congress gave particular attention, and its full support, to Pius XII's 1955 encyclical on sacred music, *Musicae sacrae disciplina*, maintaining the strict position that Gregorian chant and sacred polyphony were the supreme treasures of the Roman Catholic church and that they should be maintained at all cost.[2] At the same time the congress took a serious look at wide-ranging threats to that patrimony. It was one of the last triumphal displays of the historic Tridentine liturgy and of the music associated with it, before the convening of the Second Vatican Council only five years later.

Lecture topics at the congress ran the gamut from the most arcane historical and musicological studies to rather more mundane matters touching on the practice of church music. The lecturers thus provided a bird's-eye view of the contrary movements at play around the world, some of them conservative and others progressive, and a glimpse at how the council would soon deal with the same issues. The most intractable problem the congress grappled with was that of congregational participation.

The congress enjoyed a wide visibility before the general public. Many of the concerts and services reached the homes of listeners all over the country, via radio broadcast to regional or national audiences. The opening ceremony at Notre-Dame, for example, was broadcast live over national radio, as were the performances of the Palestrina *Missa "Aeterna Christi munera"* from the cathedral later in the week, and the concluding concert, a program of contemporary religious music by the Orchestre national and the radio choirs, at Saint Étienne-du-Mont on July 8. The latter concert featured Duruflé's *Requiem*, Henry Barraud's *Te Deum* (1956), and Florent Schmitt's *Psaume XLVII*. Duruflé was the organist.

On December 4, 1963, the Second Vatican Council promulgated its document *Sacrosanctum Concilium*, known also by its English title, *The Constitution on the Sacred Liturgy*. It was the first of the council's sixteen documents, a dramatic pronouncement whose directives about the liturgy and its music made a serious attempt at compromise. Duruflé was wont to point out that this document was passed almost unanimously by the council fathers: 2,147 bishops, archbishops, and cardinals voting in favor, with only four opposed.

"To promote active participation," reads the document, "the people should be encouraged to take part by means of acclamations, responses, psalms, antiphons, hymns, as well as by actions, gestures and bodily attitudes."[3] And, "since the use of the vernacular . . . may frequently be of great advantage to the people, a wider use may be made of it, especially in readings, directives and in some prayers and chants."[4]

As for the church's traditional instrument, the document declared that "the pipe organ is to be held in high esteem," as its sound adds to the splendor of the church's ceremonies and uplifts people's minds to God and higher things.[5] But it also allowed other instruments provided they are suitable for sacred use, accord with the dignity of the temple, and truly contribute to the edification of the faithful.[6]

At the same time, the document stipulated that "the use of the Latin language . . . is to be preserved in the Latin rites,"[7] and that "care must be taken to ensure that the faithful may also be able to say or sing together in Latin those parts of the Ordinary of the Mass which pertain to them."[8] Moreover, it insisted that "the treasury of sacred music is to be preserved and cultivated with great care." Choirs were to be assiduously developed, especially in cathedrals, while ensuring that the faithful be able to participate.[9] Article 116 of the document declared that Gregorian chant should be given pride of place, but that other kinds of music, especially polyphony, are by no means excluded.[10]

The bishops of the council thus steered a politically safe, but ambiguous middle course between competing interests, probably realizing, and perhaps fearing, that in sanctioning contrary positions they were preparing the ground for conflict over language and music in the church for decades to come. Most of the clergy in Paris, and elsewhere for that matter, saw the wisdom of a vernacular liturgy with little need to maintain Latin plainsong. They set themselves at staunch odds with most of the church's greatest musicians, despite the ambiguities in the document that might have allowed compromise, if such a thing were possible in that adversarial climate.

In January of 1964 Paul VI issued his *motu proprio* entitled *Sacram liturgiam*, which forbade the hasty introduction of the vernacular and ordered that all translations be approved by Rome. The bishops of several countries expressed their displeasure with the pope, and the French hierarchy made it clear that it would proceed with the vernacular no matter what Rome thought. In reply, Rome made fifteen changes to the original version of the *motu proprio* so that the French hierarchy and any other hierarchy inclined to introduce the vernacular at once would not be breaking the law.

Four months later, on May 20, 1964, the French episcopate, through its designee Maurice Rigaud, issued its own directives on sacred music for the churches of France.[11] The Commission de musiciens experts advising the bishops on the subject included the organists Jean Langlais, Gaston Litaize, Jean Bonfils, Édouard Souberbielle, and Maurice and Marie-Madeleine Duruflé, as well as the priests Joseph Gelineau and Lucien Deiss. Also added to the roster were Jacques Chailley,[12] director of the Schola Cantorum; Auguste Le Guennant, director of the Institut grégorien; and the Benedictine Dom Jean Claire from Solesmes, among other clergy and choir directors. The commission signed a plea for the retaining of chant.[13]

If their course was decidedly more pastoral, the bishops nevertheless specified: " 'pastoral' will not be understood to mean mediocre. Under cover of 'pastoral necessity' we do not have to content ourselves with mediocrity or platitudes." The bishops summarized their purposes in these three points: (1) they wanted quality, and they had taken counsel from a committee of professional musicians to ensure it; (2) while they wanted congregational music in French, they also wanted a place for Latin chant, whether it be the ordinary or the proper; and (3) they wanted a more active participation by the faithful. In unmistakable terms they insisted that "the Schola and the organ will continue to take their traditional role in liturgical celebrations." Where possible, they wanted scholas to sing the old and the modern, French and Latin repertoire alike. Noting that many organs had been silenced, they supported a "discreet recall" of the organ that would be consistent with its role in the liturgy. Finally, the bishops ordered that "every musical composition on the approved liturgical texts must be approved by the Comité épiscopal de musique sacrée," aided either by the Comité de musiciens experts, or by diocesan or regional authorities. Duruflé was in agreement with the position taken by the bishops, except for their merely "discreet recall" of the organ.

At a joint meeting of the Comité épiscopal de musique sacrée and of the Commission des musicians-experts, on November 24, 1964, Msgr. Rigaud, president of the committee, asked Duruflé to prepare a report on "La Fonction et place de l'orgue en accompagnateur et en soliste."[14] Duruflé drew the attention of the bishops to relevant articles in the conciliar constitution. He also pointed out that many fine organs across France had been restored at the expense of the Services des Beaux-Arts of the national government and the city of Paris.[15]

In his "L'Orgue dans la nouvelle liturgie," Duruflé laid out the underlying issues he believed at stake. Ordering his comments on points five and six, on the organ and silence, respectively, of the "Note pastorale sur le chant et la musique dans la célébration de la Messe," dated April 10, 1965, he wrote that the French directives, in effect, suppressed the traditional use of the *grand orgue* during sung masses. The organ was still technically permitted to play (1) shortly before mass; (2) at the offertory, after the antiphon has been sung; (3) during the canon, but only in certain (unspecified) cases, and then only a discreet piece to sustain the silence; (4) during the communion for interludes between sung versets; and (5) after the blessing or final hymn. But Duruflé objected that (1) the music before mass was often played to empty seats; (2) a choral piece and silence were other alternatives for the offertory; (3) silence was preferred during the canon; (4) for communion the norm would be a balance between silence and the singing of vulgar musical platitudes; and (5) the *sortie* would have to be short because the so-called dialog mass would begin shortly.[16] In effect, the *grand orgue*, whose function had never been to accompany singing, would now begin accompanying the congregation.

Duruflé drafted a public declaration to be read at the Fifth International Church Music Congress in Chicago and Milwaukee, August 21–26, 1966,[17] which was signed by Souberbielle, Litaize, Raugel, Grunenwald, Langlais, Demessieux, and Dufourcq, among others. In it he remarked: "We are very far from Article 116 of the Constitution, which recognized that Gregorian chant as the proper chant for the liturgy, all things being equal, should occupy first place."[18]

As a member of the national commission for sacred music, Duruflé began taking a more public and active role in the reforms than was his custom and ease, setting before the general public and the music profession his insightful and well-reasoned views in the debate.[19]

At the same time, he became active in a new lay organization called Una Voce,[20] founded on December 19, 1964, which sought to promote the Tridentine Latin mass as contained in the pre–Vatican II *Missale Romanum* (1962) of Pope John XXIII. The International Una Voce Federation, currently with affiliates in over two dozen countries, enjoys the support of Pope Benedict XVI and works to safeguard and promote the use of Latin Gregorian chant and sacred polyphony without severing its ties to Rome. It has brought influence to bear upon the highest levels of the Vatican hierarchy, such that the Tridentine rite has become authorized under certain circumstances to be determined by local bishops. But to date it has had limited impact upon the global achievements of the vernacular liturgy.[21]

The first president of Una Voce in France was Amédée de Vallombrosa, who was also vice-president of the country's Union des maîtres-de-chapelle et organistes.[22] After Vallombrosa's death in 1968, Henri Sauguet became the new president and would remain so for more than twenty years. The members began meeting at a location rented for them on rue de Rome, near the Conservatoire, chosen in part for its symbolic reference to the heart of Roman Catholicism.

Other members of the group included Canon Calle, the chief of protocol for the services at Notre-Dame; Simone Wallon, conservator for the department of music at the Bibliothèque nationale de France; Édouard Souberbielle, professor at the Schola Cantorum and titular organist at the Église des Carmes on rue de Vaugirard; and Maurice Duruflé, among others.

But the articles that Duruflé began writing for the Catholic press were more centrist in tone. In *La Croix*, the newspaper for the archdiocese of Paris, on December 13, 1968, he set forth remarkably balanced and tolerant views,[23] even welcoming congregational singing in French. The direction of the new chants[24] lately composed for the French texts, he wrote, "has often been confided to inexpert and clumsy hands." The dismissal of choir directors was a mistake, he wrote, because choirs are "indispensable for leading the collective singing."

Duruflé noted the musical poverty of the new melodies and described them as caricatures of Gregorian chant. He credited congregations with better musical instincts than was usually accorded them. "It is not by degradation that we will obtain the support of the masses. The liturgy ought to educate, cultivate, and not pamper bad taste and ignorance. It will bring insult to the level of intelligence and culture of the majority of the faithful to believe them incapable of understanding what *Kyrie eleison, Sanctus,* and *Agnus Dei* mean."[25]

Duruflé brought his keen sense of language to bear in assessing the French translations of the Latin texts. He was not at all certain that the people would appreciate the "monstrous mélange" of two languages in the phrase *Hosanna au plus haut des cieux* from the *Sanctus.*[26] He wondered whether some of the French texts should be recited, not sung, particularly when "high mass no longer exists and all masses are now standardized."[27] The solemn tone for the collects, for instance, so "perfectly suited to the Latin by virtue of the nobility of the language, and of the 'music' detachable from it, does not lend itself to the French text." He lamented also "our grotesque *Saint, Saint, Saint*" as the vernacular replacement for the Latin *Sanctus, Sanctus, Sanctus.*[28] To use a "sonic garb" that was not intended for it, he wrote, risks ridicule and comedy. He wrote in 1966, "I shall confess to you frankly that I do not feel myself the least bit inclined to write music for 'Saint, Saint, Saint!' "[29] The Latin, he believed, had a hieratic and sacred resonance that the French would never have. Composers, he concluded, cannot do their work until they have definitive translations that have the same poetic and rhythmic qualities required of any literary text that is set to music.

The reformers blamed the church's composers for their failure to cooperate in the process of setting the new texts to music. In 1969 Duruflé wrote that what they expect of composers is to devise a body of repertoire that pretends to replace Gregorian chant. All of the qualities required of this new repertoire already exist in plainsong, he wrote, "So why suppress it?"[30]

Duruflé held to the hope that the proper of the mass would continue to be sung by choirs, as the public could still hear it through radio broadcasts on Sunday mornings. Even if the proper is in unison and is relatively easy to sing, he wrote, congregations lack the vocal facility and the familiarity with solfège to be able to sing it themselves.

With a theological insight that was rare among musicians during the debate, Duruflé asked why choirs should be opposed to congregations. "We must not forget that the parish choir is part of the people. It is an emanation of it, a delegation."[31] When the choir sings, he added, the congregation gives its momentarily silent assent, which is as spiritually valuable as if it were singing the proper itself. In churches that had no choir, Duruflé believed the best solution for the proper lay in the chorales and the *mélodies populaires*—hymns—whose musical value in Protestant worship he found to be incontestable. Few musicians or clergy were as receptive as Duruflé was to borrowing from the hymn and chorale tradition of Anglicans and Lutherans. He wrote: "At least with the marvelous chorales that J. S. Bach introduced in his Cantatas and his Passions, we will have music of quality that is easy for people to sing because their melodic line is simple and clearly designed. The experiment made in this area among Protestants is favorably conclusive."[32]

Regarding the ordinary of the mass, Duruflé agreed with article 54 of the conciliar constitution, that the congregation should be able to sing it in Latin. He identified several Gregorian ordinaries that were known and loved by many congregations, for example, Mass XVII for Advent and Lent, Mass XI (*Orbis factor*), and Mass IX (*Cum jubilo*), as well as the *Missa angelorum* and the popular mass of Dumont.[33]

Duruflé wrote another article for *La Croix* in reply to an item that *Le Figaro* published on July 11, 1968, which announced that jazz was now permitted in the church.[34] Quoting a pronouncement made by Pope Paul VI on October 13, 1966, Duruflé rebutted the false claim of *Le Figaro*, noting that nothing manifestly secular was to be admitted to sacred worship.

In the same article Duruflé noted further that what is appropriate for one race of people at worship is not necessarily appropriate for another, a position that would soon become common among progressives. Negro spirituals, which he said "degenerated very quickly into a New Orleans jazz style," have a place among North American blacks, for whom the tradition has meaning. But imposing spirituals upon French congregations is as illogical, he wrote, as imposing Gregorian chant upon the blacks of North America. He quoted from articles 54 and 61 of the post-conciliar instruction from the Vatican entitled *Musicam sacram* (March 5, 1967), which said that composers should take account of the particular character of each people, combining it with a sense of the sacred.

The issue came to a head for Duruflé on February 13, 1969, with a service that took place at Saint Germain-des-Prés. The service was "animated" by a priest, with music by a jazz orchestra. Duruflé wrote that the organist for the occasion,

settling down before his electronic mini-instrument, drew out of it dreadful, hypertrophic sounds, epileptic tremolos, jerky, convulsive rhythms, terrifying barks, a veritable foretaste of the music of hell. Then, for an hour and a half, there followed on the platform Marc Laférière and his "Dixieland," the "Swingers," and the negro-totems. . . . This spectacle was truly sensational. "We must pray with joy," we were told over the microphone. Then, in "the ambiance of joy" thus created, where the smoke of cigarettes replaced that of incense, . . . the chaplain of the variety show struck up a song in French in a blues rhythm.[35]

In the spring of that year, the Duruflés attended a jazz mass in one of the chapels at Saint Étienne-du-Mont. After the service, Mme Duruflé was visibly upset by the experience. In a loud voice her husband expressed his outrage over what he considered a scandalous travesty, upon which a vicar of the church several times called him a *voyou* within earshot of bystanders.[36]

The lopsided course actually taken by the reforms in France was the result of a double tragedy. The first was that too many professional musicians equipped to adapt the church's musical heritage to the vernacular liturgy did not think their congregations capable of artful music, no matter how simple it be, and few composed examples of it. The second tragedy was that those least equipped for the writing of music in a French vernacular idiom, namely the priests and musical amateurs who were impassioned by the worthy goal of vernacular music, took up the task themselves. Believing that artfulness was elitist, they produced a rash of sincere, ephemeral tunes, thus contributing another chapter to the history of tawdry *art saint-sulpice.*

If Duruflé offered in public his sound musical suggestions for the new liturgy, in private he could see there was little hope of a reasonable balance. Two years after publishing his articles in *La Croix,* he wrote to his American manager, Lilian Murtagh, mentioning the "liturgical revolution and anarchy imposed on French organists, which suppresses all interest in [their] participation in the services."[37]

In 1978 he gave an assessment of the situation after the council:

> The experiments attempted during these last twelve years have often been the pretext for the introduction of unbearably vulgar songs. This new music, played with the accompaniment of guitars and drums, which was introduced into our sanctuaries for the express reason of attracting crowds, has done just the opposite. The error in calculation has turned out to be monumental. People have deserted their parishes in order to attend Sunday masses in places that have maintained the cult of beauty, the only thing that counts when it comes to glorifying God. Numerous examples could be given from the Parisian churches. The most spectacular is certainly Notre-Dame, where nine or ten thousand worshippers attend the sung masses each Sunday.[38]

In a 1983 interview for France-Culture, Duruflé's venom was barely concealed: "After Vatican II, Gregorian chant was done away with and this was carried out in a way that was completely brutal in relationship to what the council said. The angry reason that was given for drowning this dog was that it was old-fashioned, outmoded music that most people did not understand."[39]

The slow disintegration of the worldview that had given purpose, direction, and meaning to Maurice Duruflé's career in the church was now assured. He had been an engaged partisan of the progressive nineteenth-century reforms, and a proponent of the principles set forth by Pius X in 1903, and to that extent he was a man of his time. But proving himself incapable of withstanding the new tide of trivial music that flooded the church sixty years later, he thus became disenfranchised from the church, a profoundly disillusioned man. As one critic has written:

> It cannot be stressed too much the despair [the Duruflés] both felt at the musical-liturgical revolution that occurred in France in the aftermath of Vatican II. No sensitive visitor could fail to be aware of how culturally disinherited they felt to be creating magnificent, plainsong-inspired improvisations . . . when the plainsong had been expunged from the service and replaced by banal jingles. They knew that the sun had set on a great live tradition.[40]

After writing his *Messe "Cum jubilo,"* in 1966, Duruflé effectively stopped composing. And with his retirement from the Conservatoire, four years later, he severed his half-century connections with another institution that, together with the church, had nurtured his identity and career. What remained for him, therefore, was the more active concertizing that he undertook through his tours of North America.

# Chapter Twenty-Three

# *The North American Tours*

Duruflé began touring when he was about twenty years old. While his earliest tours took him to Normandy and later to the Côte d'Azur, he eventually concertized in England, Germany, Switzerland, Belgium, Holland, Austria, Spain, North Africa, the former Soviet Union (USSR), Canada, and the United States.

Duruflé made his first trip to England to perform for the Organ Music Society in 1938, and returned under their aegis in September 1949. After his marriage to Marie-Madeleine Chevalier, in 1953, he shared many of his tours with her. In 1968 he conducted "*Cum jubilo*" in London, and in 1969[1] and 1970 he and Mme Duruflé played joint recitals in the Royal Festival Hall. In 1970 they also performed at Chester Cathedral. In the same year, Mme Duruflé played Vierne's Third Symphony at Westminster Abbey as part of a series that featured the complete symphonies of Vierne in observance of the centenary of the composer's birth. In 1971 the couple performed at King's College, Cambridge, then again at Royal Festival Hall, this time for a performance of the *Requiem* presented by the London Bach Choir and the New Philharmonia Orchestra on February 5, with David Willcocks conducting and Mme Duruflé playing the organ.

In North Africa the couple performed at the Tunis cathedral (1954), and at Rabat and Casablanca (1958). They subsequently made two tours of the Soviet Union, in 1965 and 1970.[2] On their first tour, from November 11 to 29,[3] which was arranged through the Service des relations culturelles de Paris, they played seven recitals to capacity audiences, appearing in Moscow and Leningrad (Russia), at the Riga Dom (Latvia), at Philharmonic Hall in Tallinn (Estonia), and in Baku (Azerbaijan).

A review of their performance on the Cavaillé-Coll organ at the Bolshoi Conservatory appeared in the journal *Sovetskaya Muzyka*, the reviewer noting that the arrival of the couple was anticipated with much excitement. The titles of all the pieces printed in their programs "had been 'purged' by the soviets of all religious allusions," so that *Variations sur un noël* became "Variations sur un thème populaire."[4]

In Leningrad they performed in Philharmonic Hall, on a tubular pneumatic, a rather poor organ from Walcker (1903), as Duruflé recounted it.[5] "We were subjected there to one of our more cruel agonies, all the more cruel in that the console *en fenêtre* is perched . . . on a breathtakingly high podium 2.5 meters wide by 2 meters high and completely lacking a railing."[6] He was seized by vertigo and "it was in permanent anguish that I participated in this concert." His wife, he wrote, "always calm and imperturbable, achieved her usual success."[7]

In Riga they performed in the former cathedral, which the soviets had transformed into a state museum and concert hall "for the artistic education of workers." The 125–rank mechanical-action Walcker had no combination devices, requiring "at least two organists to manage to overcome this monster."[8]

The couple encountered major inconveniences and insults on their trip to Baku on the Caspian Sea. After their flight was cancelled, they tried to rest on mattresses in the Moscow airport waiting room. At midnight they were driven to the French embassy back in the city, where they had to sit on their suitcases at the bottom of the service stairs until morning. They played their recital in the hall of the conservatory on a 1963 baroque-style instrument by the East German builder Hermann Eule. Although the organ had a beautiful sound, its manuals were ordered, bottom to top: grand orgue, récit, and positif, and the swell box opened by pushing the pedal with the heel, and closed by pushing with the toe.[9]

The Duruflés' second tour of the Soviet Union took place in October of 1970,[10] when they performed in Leningrad, at the Riga Dom, in Vilnius (Lithuania), and at the Tchaikovsky Conservatory in Moscow. Duruflé wrote to Lilian Murtagh, "Interesting trip, but life is quite sad. We much prefer the U.S.A. There is no comparison."[11]

It was through their tours of North America that Duruflé's compositions became etched in the memory of a much broader audience than he had hitherto known and Mme Duruflé was introduced to an enthusiastic public that had never heard of her.

The couple were represented on their North American tours[12] by Lilian Murtagh of the Colbert-LaBerge Concert Management. Karen McFarlane succeeded her in the management, after Murtagh's death in 1976, and was Murtagh's equal in her solicitude for them.[13]

The first tour originated with a letter from Lilian Murtagh, dated January 6, 1963, on behalf of the committee planning the 1964 convention of the American Guild of Organists, slated for the week of June 22 in Philadelphia. The letter was addressed to Maurice alone, and it invited him to play a solo recital at the Philadelphia Academy of Music. Mme Duruflé was still virtually unknown in the United States and she was not invited to perform.

Duruflé was not satisfied with the terms they proposed. He asked if they would also program his *Requiem*. The committee declined, saying Britten's *War Requiem* was already scheduled.[14] They countered with the offer of a commission and premiere, but Duruflé declined, saying there was risk of not finishing the work in time.[15]

The convention committee agreed to pay his round-trip travel expenses between Paris and Philadelphia, as well as his hotel expenses for the week, plus a stipend of $300. Duruflé still thought the offer modest, and asked if they would schedule several additional concert dates for him, to make the trip more worthwhile.[16] Murtagh explained that the committee's offer was identical to that made with Anton Heiller in the summer of 1962 for the Los Angeles convention. She tried to help Duruflé appreciate that the committee's proposal was "a most generous offer," but this time specified an additional stipend of $200.[17] She offered to sign a contract guaranteeing at least $750 in gross fees (including the $300 from the convention itself). Murtagh indicated that New York's Riverside Church and the University of Michigan wanted him for recitals, and Union Theological Seminary wanted him for a master class.[18] The convention committee also invited him to serve as an adjudicator for the improvisation contest, the first such competition to be held at a national AGO convention.[19] Regarding the participation of Marie-Madeleine, Lilian repeated that the committee wanted him to play, and him alone.[20] She wrote, "I think you may not realize the importance of the engagements that have been arranged. . . . You could not hope for a more distinguished introduction to this country."[21]

The program that Duruflé sent to Murtagh the following December included three pieces to be performed by his wife, who "plays the organ *better than I* [emphasis in the original]."[22] She was scheduled to play Bach's Prelude and Fugue in D, BWV 532,[23] Tournemire's *Victimae paschali laudes*, and her husband's *Prélude et fugue sur le nom d'ALAIN*, out of the total of seven works on the program. They flew to Philadelphia by way of New York on June 22, 1964.[24]

But Duruflé injured his back on what Mme Duruflé called "one of these 'flying' machines," and had to use two canes to walk. Robert Burns King, who was just then finishing his studies with Duruflé in Paris, attended the convention and was called to assist. He tells the story:

> I went right away to the Duruflés' room [at the Bellevue-Stratford Hotel] where he was in bed in great pain. The doctor was called, and when he arrived it was necessary for me to translate what he said regarding treatment and medication. (My French was far from perfect, but it was superior to the English of the Duruflés, who knew none. Anyway, they needed help and I was glad to be available.) Mme Duruflé and I discussed what was to be done about the concert that they were to share, and she decided that she would play the entire program as it was printed, and perform the pieces he had planned to play in addition to hers.[25]

Mme Duruflé played the entire recital by herself, on June 25, on the Aeolian-Skinner organ at the Academy of Music, before the largest convention audience to date.[26] The *Diapason* reported:

> There was no high feeling of anticipation as the announcement was made that Marie-Madeleine Duruflé-Chevalier would play the entire recital. What happened to the audience within the first minute of that recital is something we have never seen duplicated. It was as if an electric shock had run from one end of the historic hall to another as the audience realized that here indeed was the unquestioned highest point of the entire convention. A season-long tour for this gracious lady could easily have been booked at

the intermission. We wonder if any French organist has made such an auspicious American debut since Marcel Dupré.[27]

A reviewer in *The American Organist*, Robert Lodine, wrote:

The regret that M. Duruflé had a back disability which prevented his playing was soon forgotten as the program played by Madame Duruflé-Chevalier quickly set the Academy of Music figuratively on fire. Many felt that this was the most exciting playing of the week; and on one of the best organs. Her Bach D major Prelude and Fugue was all virtuosity in the old Dupré tradition—breathtaking not only in speed but in rhythmic vitality. The fugue is assuredly a showpiece and there was no doubt of that when Mme. Duruflé had finished. She was as able and musical in the little things (a Bach chorale transcribed by her husband, Couperin, Clérambault and Vierne) which she tossed off with dash and abandon; a bit of brusque, careless quality only made for excitement and refreshment. The Tournemire improvisation reconstructed by M. Duruflé from a recording was a tonic for those who think of Tournemire only in the dreamy style of L'Orgue Mystique. . . . Bravo, Mme. Duruflé![28]

Robert Burns King tells the story from his own perspective:

She opened the program with the Bach Prelude and Fugue in D Major. Because the pedals are so different on American organs, she brushed a couple of notes on the first page unintentionally, but by the time she had finished the prelude there was no question left about her technique, musicianship, and ability. When she lit into the fugue at a truly virtuosic tempo, people held their breaths! And she went through it with a liveliness of rhythm and speed that few had ever heard. After this first piece, the entire crowd stood and shouted "bravo." . . . Her performance of the Duruflé *Variations on "Veni Creator"* and the *Prelude and Fugue on Alain* showed how the strong personality of a performer can shine through without doing one bit of damage to the composer's intent. . . .

She could have booked an entire tour from that receiving line, and as a result of it, Duruflé's music was much more often taught and played in the United States than it had been before.[29]

It was history in the making. Duruflé took a bow at the end, leaning on his canes. He recovered enough to be able to honor the remaining engagements of the tour,[30] but his back was susceptible to stress for the remainder of his life.

After the convention, the Duruflés continued to Ann Arbor, Michigan, for a master class[31] and a recital at Hill Auditorium of the University of Michigan, on June 28. In Pittsburgh they played a recital at Saint Paul's Roman Catholic Cathedral, then went to New York City.

On July 2, Maurice conducted a performance of the *Requiem* at St. Paul's Chapel of Columbia University, in a concert by the Asylum Hill Oratorio Choir[32] from Hartford, Connecticut, sponsored by the Alumni Association of Union Theological Seminary, for the closing event of its seventh annual workshop (June 29–July 2).[33] The original plan was for the work to be accompanied by a large professional orchestra, with organ, but owing to financial constraints and space limitations, the solo organ version was used instead, and was played by Mme Duruflé.[34]

They went to Akron, Ohio, and then returned to New York for a recital at the Riverside Church, where Frederick Swann, who had established an "on paper" relationship with the Duruflés, was the organist.[35] Karen McFarlane drove them around Manhattan in her Volkswagen and joined them for dinner at Swann's home, where Mme Duruflé fell in love with Swann's cat Alleluya, her favorite of the many cats Swann had over the years.[36]

At Riverside, the Duruflés were quite taken at the sight of the console, but, according to Swann, in divergent ways. "I will always remember their reaction when they first saw the Riverside console. He: not looking pleased, with hand raised to forehead (or was he just overwhelmed?)—'Oh, mon Dieu.' She: BROAD smile, rubbing her hands together over and over, and purring 'Hmmmm.' She couldn't wait to 'get at it'!"[37]

Their first tour was a stunning introduction to the United States. Americans recalled their sometimes comical teamwork at the console, with the assistant adding a stop to the player's dismay, and the player making a lightning-fast cancellation of the stop just drawn. What their audiences did not know was that Mme Duruflé often did not know which pieces she would be playing until they arrived at a new venue and her husband would tell her, "You're going to play this, this, and this."[38] Mme Duruflé told how, on one occasion, he was about to play the *Prélude et fugue sur le nom d'ALAIN*, but turned to her and said, "Oh, why don't you go ahead and play!" And so she simply played.[39]

The Duruflés made their return transatlantic crossing on the France, the longest ocean liner in the world at the time, when the great era of transatlantic steamship travel was in its decline. Their crossing from New York to Southampton proved rough and noisy for the Duruflés because their cabin in tourist class was just above the ship's propellers.[40]

For their second and longest American tour, from September 16 to November 16, 1966—which was sold out within a short time after its announcement—the Duruflés arrived in New York on September 14. From there they flew to their first engagement, in Buffalo, New York, and continued to Akron, Ohio; Fort Wayne, Indiana; Toledo, Ohio; Independence, Missouri; Saint Louis; Milwaukee; Northwestern University in Evanston, Illinois; Seattle; Oakland and San Diego, California; Charlotte, North Carolina; New Brunswick, New Jersey; New York City (Saint Thomas Church)[41]; the National Shrine of the Immaculate Conception in Washington, DC; Lancaster, Pennsylvania; Dallas (Southern Methodist University, where he played the Poulenc Organ Concerto and the Saint-Saëns Organ Symphony); Sewanee, Tennessee; Elon, North Carolina; Pittsburgh (Saint Paul's Roman Catholic Cathedral); Philadelphia (First Baptist Church)[42]; the Hammond Museum in Gloucester, Massachusetts; and finally Hartford, Connecticut.

In Saint Louis, Missouri, the Duruflés made a recording on the Aeolian-Skinner Organ at Christ Church Cathedral[43] for the King of Instruments series. On side one, Mme Duruflé played her husband's Opus 4 in its entirety, along with two works by Clérambault. On side two, Duruflé played the *Prélude* in E-flat Minor, from Opus 5, his reconstructions of Tournemire's improvisation on the *Te Deum* and the *Petite Rapsodie*, and *Le Banquet céleste* of Messiaen.

Without Duruflé's prior knowledge, or that of his manager, the presenters in Akron disseminated publicity materials announcing that Duruflé would conduct a performance of the Poulenc *Gloria*. Lilian Murtagh sent him an urgent telegram on July 17, 1966, asking for his consent after the fact. She expressed her hope that he would agree to do it, inasmuch as "it would create a very embarrassing situation for everyone if this now had to be changed." But the very next day Duruflé wired a telegram saying "impossible conduire gloria poulenc regrets." In a letter the same day he wrote, "Really, I am not a *professional* orchestral conductor. I can conduct only my own works: *Requiem, Trois Danses.*"[44]

While his conducting has been described as hardly textbook, Duruflé nonetheless elicited the quality and affect he wanted from his choirs and orchestras. He conducted his own works, including the *Trois Danses*, the *Requiem*, and *Messe "Cum jubilo,"* but never conducted the works of other composers. Besides declining to conduct the *Gloria* of Poulenc, he refused to conduct the same composer's *Litanies à la Vierge noire* at Riverside Church in New York, preferring that Frederick Swann conduct, saying "I am a very bad conductor."[45]

The review by Charles Crowder in *The Washington Post* of the Duruflés' performance at the National Shrine in Washington, DC, appeared under the headline: "Organ Recital Is So Dazzling It Will Be Discussed for Years." Crowder wrote:

> It was one of those evenings that immediately prompts the keener listening apparatus to switch on. A direct communication with the core of the musical matter rang through in the first few seconds. . . .
> For both Duruflés are superb musicians first, organists second . . . [ellipsis in the original] and is this not the case of all great artists? . . .
> Mrs. Duruflé's [*sic*] played with the kind of speed that would come hard to a seasoned pianist or harpsichordist. Yet she not only played fast, but made music of glowing beauty while doing it.
> The program was a triumph. . . . [Mme Duruflé] even left the impression in Tournamire's [*sic*] Fantasia [*sic*] on "Ave Maris Stella" that the instrument itself was not capable of doing all that she intended.
> Duruflé himself plays in a broad, stately manner. . . . The Franck Fantasie [*sic*] in A Major was a masterpiece of noble statement. . . .
> It's a safe bet that most of those organists there last night will cancel their luncheon appointments to stay put and practice tomorrow.[46]

Their third North American tour was considerably shorter than the second. Appearing first at the International Congress of Organists in Montreal, on August 30, 1967, where they performed at the Cathédrale Marie Reine-du-Monde, they continued to Houston and Dallas, Texas, and thence to Tempe, Arizona; Colorado Springs; Elkhart, Indiana; the Riverside Church in New York (the *Requiem* was conducted by Duruflé and accompanied by Frederick Swann); Haddonfield, New Jersey; and ended with recording sessions at the National Shrine in Washington, DC, on September 28 and 29.

Their fourth American tour, in September and October of 1969, took them to Fort Wayne, Indiana, on September 16, then to Burlington, North Carolina; Indianapolis; Minneapolis; Evanston, Illinois; San Antonio; Wichita; El Paso; San Francisco; San Diego; Urbana, Illinois; Miami; the Riverside Church in New York City; Holland, Michigan; Baltimore; and Washington, DC.

Anticipating this tour, three New York City churches vied for the opportunity to host a performance of the *Messe "Cum jubilo"* with the Duruflés: the Church of Saint Paul the Apostle (just south of Lincoln Center), where Father Foley directed a distinguished boychoir; the Riverside Church, where Frederick Swann was organist; and Saint Thomas Episcopal Church, where William Self was the organist. Lilian Murtagh advised the Duruflés that Saint Paul's and Riverside "have good choirs," but that Saint Thomas "has a much less adequate choir." The performance of "*Cum jubilo*" took place at Riverside.[47]

Duruflé had a recurrence of his back trouble in 1970 that required surgery early in 1971, when he was sixty-nine years old. When he returned home from the hospital, on April 3, he anticipated a month of rest before resuming his normal activities.[48] But by mid-August, just six weeks before their fifth tour was to begin, he still had back pain and was not sure he could make the trip. He believed he would never get well again and considered having Marie-Madeleine make the tour alone.[49]

As it turned out, they made the fifth tour together. It was an exhausting two-month-long trip and was Duruflé's last. They appeared in Washington, DC, on October 2, 1971, then went to Norfolk, Virginia; Columbus, Ohio; Baltimore; Saint Thomas Church in New York City; Trenton, New Jersey; Lancaster, Pennsylvania; Ann Arbor, Michigan; New Orleans; Houston; Tulsa; Fort Worth; the First Congregational Church in Los Angeles; Palo Alto, California; Portland, Oregon; Chicago; Milwaukee; Boys Town, Nebraska; Grand Rapids, Michigan; then to Birmingham, Alabama; Newtonville, Massachusetts; Hartford, Connecticut; and lastly, on December 7, New Bedford, Massachusetts.[50]

The tour was not without mishap. In Portland, Marie-Madeleine became ill and had to be taken to a hospital, forcing them to miss their concert there on November 17.[51] And in Milwaukee, Maurice was the victim of a robbery, three items of value having been stolen from their room at the Continental Hotel.[52]

After the 1971 tour, Duruflé greatly curtailed his public appearances. Like the earlier tours, the sixth, proposed for the spring of 1974, was to have been a joint venture. But the planning was jeopardized throughout by Maurice's medical problems and, in the end, by the sudden news that their apartment building would be sold, forcing them to move. In July of 1972, Duruflé had surgery on his foot for a serious abscess caused by a doctor's use of a contaminated needle. He stayed in a clinic for a month, and spent the rest of the summer at home in a chair. Then he developed phlebitis, for which prolonged sitting, standing, and lying down are ill-advised. He walked with a cane, and it took at least six months before he could play the organ normally.[53] In mid-November he was still recuperating,[54] but by February of 1974 he was unable to play the organ at all, because of the surgery. And his brother Henri died in March. Duruflé nevertheless agreed to a sixth North American tour, for May of 1974, and said it would be the last, just as he had said of the fifth.[55]

Duruflé's foot did not heal properly. He thought he might be able to play one piece on each recital of their 1974 tour, and conduct the *Requiem*, but that Marie-Madeleine would have to play the greater part of the recitals.[56] By September of 1973 he was not sure whether he would be able to play, and said he would decide two months later, on the advice of his new surgeon.[57] By November he doubted he could make the trip at all,[58] and in December he had decided not to try, but thought he would delay making a final decision until a month before the tour.[59]

In January 1974, Mme Duruflé wrote to Murtagh canceling the tour. In November her husband started having intense dizzy spells that forced him to cancel his appointments and take to his bed. And on the morning she wrote the letter, she and Maurice learned that their apartment building would be sold sometime between Easter and July, and that they would have to move in the spring. A tour would be impossible.[60]

Despite this decision and Mme Duruflé's letter to Murtagh, Maurice subsequently reopened the possibility that he might go, and said he would make a final decision a month before the tour was scheduled to begin. Murtagh was insistent that he could not delay a decision that late, and demanded to know immediately and finally whether Marie-Madeleine would make the tour alone, or whether the tour would be cancelled altogether.[61] On January 25, 1974, Duruflé wrote that his wife would make the tour alone.[62]

A month later Marie-Madeleine wrote privately to Murtagh that her husband's health was not bad, but that his morale was not good.[63] At the end of March, Maurice was very anxious about her tour, imagining she would be robbed and killed at least once in every hotel.[64] Nevertheless Duruflé hoped his wife would be able to leave as planned on the 18th. But he advised Murtagh that if he had to have surgery, his wife's tour might have to be cut short.[65]

The tour went along as planned, but not without stress for the couple. Mme Duruflé left Paris in a state that troubled her husband. He wrote to Murtagh that his wife's doctor told him that "her nervous state was abnormal and that she needed a lot of rest."[66] Murtagh responded that everything was going well and promised to call his wife at least once a week.[67]

In the end, Marie-Madeleine completed a successful solo tour of the United States, performing in Bayshore, Long Island, on April 21, then in Hartford,

Miami, Los Angeles, Phoenix, Palo Alto, Corpus Christi, Lincoln, Lansing, Toronto, Washington, DC, and lastly in Lancaster, Pennsylvania. After returning to Paris, Marie-Madeleine sent a thank-you note to Murtagh, saying, among other things, "I found Maurice in good form, rather better than before my departure."[68]

Almost immediately upon her return to Paris, they began discussing a tour for 1975.[69] But on December 4, 1974, Mme Duruflé wrote to Murtagh to say that her husband would not make the trip, and a month later she announced she would not go either. Duruflé cited his poor health, his dizzy spells, and their worry that he and Marie-Madeleine might have to move out of their apartment during the month of the tour.[70] There was no tour, and all discussion of future tours became irrelevant at the end of May, when they had their automobile accident.

North Americans did not seem to understand the severity of their injuries. At the end of 1977, Duruflé's leg still hurt a great deal, and would require further surgery, and Mme Duruflé still had to have hip replacement surgery.[71] Her husband would never return to North America, but he presented a recital for Les Amis de l'Orgue (his first after the accident) at Saint Étienne-du-Mont, on May 11, 1977.[72] André Fleury and Mme Duruflé shared the program with him. Duruflé's last public recital took place in Granville, in 1979, where they had gone to recuperate after the accident; he performed to an audience of over five hundred people. Mme Duruflé played as well.[73]

Duruflé's North American recitals always followed a predictable four-part format, except when the *Requiem* or the *Messe "Cum jubilo"* was also on the program:

I Bach's Prelude and Fugue in D, BWV 532, or Handel's Concerto in A, or occasionally Dupré's transcription of Handel's Second Concerto in B-flat
II Excerpts from the French classical repertoire, and/or a lesser work by Buxtehude or Bach
III Several major French romantic works, especially by Franck, Vierne, Tournemire, or, less frequently, either Dupré's Variations sur un noël or his Deux Esquisses
IV Works by Duruflé

Except at venues where they had already performed, the only other Bach works they ever played to open their recitals were the Vivaldi-Bach Concerto in G, BWV 592, Dupré's transcription of Bach's *Sinfonia* from Cantata 146, the Trio in G Major, BWV 1027a,[74] and only rarely the Partita in E Minor, BWV 770. They never programmed a trio sonata, a major chorale, or any of the other fantasies or preludes and fugues. On her solo tours Mme Duruflé did play the two chorals that her husband had transcribed from Bach cantatas, sometimes even as encores.

They frequently paired single movements by Clérambault and Couperin, and sometimes the *Coucou* or the G-major *Noël* of Daquin, but they never programmed any other early French works, nor a complete suite or hymn, such as those by Titelouze or de Grigny.

The piece by Franck that Duruflé programmed most frequently was the *Choral* in B Minor, and after it the *Fantaisie* in A. Only rarely did he play the *Choral* in A Minor, and never the *Choral* in E Major, or any other Franck works.

The only work of Widor that Duruflé ever programmed was the *Allegro* from the *Grande Symphonie*, as he called it, which Marie-Madeleine performed. They included Vierne's written compositions only rarely, and then only the Toccata and Naïades from *Pièces de Fantaisie*, which were always played by Mme Duruflé, and the improvised *Méditation*, which he was always the one to play. He never played any part of Vierne's Sixth Symphony.

From Tournemire's recorded improvisations, Duruflé nearly always programmed either the *Victimae paschali laudes* or the *Ave maris stella*, both of which were always played by his wife. He occasionally programmed the *Petite Rapsodie improvisée* instead, but never the *Te Deum* or the *Cantilène improvisée*. And he never programmed the *Triple Choral* or anything from *L'Orgue mystique*.

Furthermore, Duruflé never programmed works by Gigout, Guilmant, Saint-Saëns, Alain, Fleury, Litaize, Langlais, Demessieux, or Messiaen. Besides the Dupré *Variations sur un noël* and the *Deux esquisses* that Mme Duruflé played on their joint tours, for her solo tour in 1974 she also programmed *La Fileuse* from his *Suite bretonne*. She never played anything by Demessieux.

Duruflé never programmed an improvisation for his North American recitals.[75] Whether he ever improvised an encore is difficult to ascertain. After her husband's death, Mme Duruflé began programming improvisations.

The only post-baroque Germanic repertoire they played were two Schumann etudes in the form of a canon, two chorals of Brahms, Mozart's Fantasy in F Minor, and Liszt's *Ad nos ad salutarem undam*.[76]

Of his own works, Duruflé never programmed the *Prélude* or the *Adagio* from his triptych on *Veni Creator*, but played only the *Choral varié*, believing that the complete work was too long for audiences.[77] Nor did he program the *Sicilienne* or the *Toccata* from the *Suite*, but played only the *Prélude*. In other words, he played neither Opus 4 nor Opus 5 in its entirety in North America.[78] Nor did he program the *Introit* for Epiphany, or the *Fugue sur le thème du carillon des heures de la cathédrale de Soissons*.

Duruflé accepted none of the commissions offered him in North America. His earliest refusal on this side of the Atlantic was probably the commission offered him in 1963 by the committee planning the 1964 national convention of the American Guild of Organists in Philadelphia. For the 1970 national convention, in Buffalo, New York, Duruflé was offered "a generous commission to compose a piece in the vein of the *Requiem* or the *Quatre Motets*. He would not consider it."[79] What was perhaps the last commission offered him was one proposed by Philip Brunelle in 1981.[80] But Duruflé declined.[81]

# Chapter Twenty-Four

# *The Man Duruflé*

Maurice Gustave Duruflé was a complex man. Of a dark and brooding temperament, he had a keen intellect, a breadth of character, a penetrating soul, and a rich cultural aptitude. Though short as to physical stature and retiring by nature, he had the disposition of a great man. And though his musical and spiritual imagination were vast, they were not prolific.

Duruflé's music reveals an important dimension of his personality, a dimension that would otherwise remain invisible, thus rendering him even more complex than at first glance. Many have noted how his gloomy constitution was so different from the luminous character of his music. Even those who knew him well believed that he had little resemblance to his music.[1] One cannot know Duruflé without knowing his music.

Duruflé was modest. Even late in his life, when one might expect his recital career to have inured him to accolade, he remained self-effacing and sheepishly acknowledged compliments from admirers. When asked by one of his harmony students to present his *Requiem* or his organ works during class, out of his sense of modesty he refused categorically. In the introductory remarks for an article, written when he was seventy-eight years old, he asked the reader's pardon for his audacity in referring to his own *Requiem*, detestable as it is, he wrote, to speak of oneself.[2]

But Duruflé was not merely modest; he was also shy. Taciturn and disinclined to speak, as Marie-Claire Alain wrote, "He was timid and he spoke little. He hesitated to open his thoughts. . . ."[3] And yet his timidity did not cower under threat. It did not prevent his speaking his mind on matters important to him, writing for professional organ journals and for the secular and religious press, or declaring his position on contentious issues. Even so, he would blush like an adolescent when defending an idea or personal sentiment.[4]

Duruflé always went to his lessons and classes dressed in a suit, white shirt, and tie,[5] even for private lessons in his own home, befitting his sense of formality and his respect for his students. He bore himself with a cultured demeanor. But on other occasions—for meetings, for instance—he seemed to put no stock in appearances, wearing "gabardine of an indeterminate grey, almost always with a sort of knitted scarf, caramel in color and rather shapeless, around his neck."[6]

Some thought Duruflé aloof. Marie-Claire Alain wrote, "Some found him distant even though he was only preoccupied with the essential. However, when [one became] closer to him, he could be very warm."[7] The words he once used to describe organ sound could well have been used of himself: "cold, distant, inaccessible, an impenetrable realm."[8] But though he was private to the point of stiffness, some say even secret to a fault, and from that perspective unapproachable and virtually inaccessible, he was nevertheless available when he was needed. His phone number—Danton 457—was listed in the telephone book throughout his career.

Although "radiating a physically robust, strong and balanced person,"[9] Duruflé's body motions were sometimes nervous or uncomfortable, and he did not have a relaxed demeanor.[10] He even made reference to his own "frightful awkwardness."[11] Sometimes he was distracted or absent-minded, "sensitive and fragile."[12] At the same time, Duruflé was amiable with his pupils and was known to greet them at school and at home with "Bonjour, mon ami."

Duruflé was indeed a private man. Jean Guillou said: "He was . . . protected by several thick walls that denied any access to his sensitive personality. Also when he appeared outwardly friendly, even cordial, as a person Maurice Duruflé remained hidden, unapproachable, perhaps even anxious."[13]

Despite his serious demeanor, Duruflé was not unemotional. He told his wife Marie-Madeleine that when he was writing the *Requiem* he was sometimes brought to tears by its melodies.[14] He was even subject to outrage. A priest of Saint Étienne-du-Mont once scoured the church for statues, ancient objects, and other legacies of the past, with a view toward disposing of them. In telling of how he colluded with the sacristan in saving a discarded old antiphonary from possible destruction, Duruflé released his fury over iconoclasm and sacrilege.[15] Likewise, a colleague serving with Duruflé on the French church's national commission on music recalled a man sometimes given to sudden outbursts.[16]

Duruflé had few close friends outside his dearest colleagues and his wife's family, and several of his closest relationships were marked by turmoil. Mme Duruflé did her best to facilitate a rapprochement between her husband and his brother Henri, but without avail. After the death of their mother, Henri's anger at Maurice precluded their ever seeing each other again.[17] Toward the end of his life, Henri left instructions that Maurice was not to be told of his death. When Henri died in 1974, his son Paul honored that wish and did not tell his uncle. Maurice later reproached his nephew for complying with Henri's wishes.[18]

Whether Maurice chose to walk away from bad relationships, or was simply inept at resolving them, his failed first marriage and his estrangement from his brothers were sources of pain for him. And they betrayed a personality that was ill at ease with conflict. Some of his Conservatoire students do not remember him fondly.

All of Duruflé's close friends were from within the circle of church and Conservatoire, including especially Gaston Litaize and André Fleury. To the latter Duruflé often said, "You are my best friend!"[19] Jean Langlais had "always expressed thanks for the help and friendship given him by other students at the

Conservatoire, some in his classes, some older . . . [and] Maurice Duruflé" among them.[20] He had great admiration for his harmony professor Jean Gallon, and was a friend of the Russian Irène Aïtoff, the vocal coach and pianist who trained the better choirs for major performances in Paris. He was particularly close to the priest and organist Henri Doyen. He and his wife were close friends of René Dommange and his wife Lola, occasionally visiting them at their country home in the Vaucluse.[21]

Duruflé was truly a master composer and organist. The craft, the precision, the economy, and the intellectual mastery discernible in his best works are above reproach. But he declined to be called "maître." It was common practice in France for a pupil thus to show his regard for a teacher, but Duruflé had "a horror of this style of bootlicking."[22] "Oh no," he was quoted as saying, "call me Monsieur."[23]

He was an exacting perfectionist whose high standards exceeded his perceived grasp. Some considered him an always worried, pathological perfectionist.[24] Most of his acquaintances saw a pessimistic streak in him. To whatever other causes one may attribute his refusal to produce only about a dozen opus numbers, his over-severe estimation of his ability lay at the heart of it. Mme Duruflé believed he was too severe with himself, and toward the end of his life he wished he had written more music, and, by implication, been less severe with himself. With the wisdom of age he could admit that it did not have to be an impediment to creative expression, or a renouncing of his standards, that his vision exceeded his reach.

Despite his self-assured, articulate, and vociferous opinions about matters of import to him, whether they were liturgical proprieties or varieties of articulation at the keyboard, he was uncertain and hesitant about his compositional prowess. That he repeatedly sought the technical advice of others may have been a function of his truly wanting to know the opinion of people he respected, but it may also have been a function of his fundamental insecurity, of a need for approval. About his lack of self-confidence there can be little doubt. His self-effacement was surely an amalgam of his innate insecurity and of whatever doubts he may have harbored about the quality of his work. At the same time, however, he had little need to please, or to ingratiate himself with his colleagues, or to curry the favor of others.

By virtue of his rarefied life in the halls of academe and the tribunes of churches, Duruflé was, perhaps, naive about the modern world, unwilling or unable to grapple with new perspectives as they became the increasingly dominant forces guiding the waning century. This is perhaps one cause for his indecisiveness. Certainly he was sensitive to the ambiguities of life and art, and he was characteristically Norman in his evasive response to questions, saying "maybe yes, maybe no," when grey, as often as not, was closer than black or white to the truth. Daniel Roth attributed this pattern to Duruflé's "great carefulness in judgment. The people of Normandy often answer a concrete question with 'possibly but possibly also not.' When a colleague asked him, for example: 'How do you find the composer X?' Duruflé answered cautiously, 'And you?' "[25]

Jean Guillou described Duruflé's labored and hesitant manner: "He would struggle for the right expression, sometimes taking back what was just said. Sometimes plagued by conscience in order thus to achieve the desired solution. . . . A man of retraction, of pains of conscience, of hesitation, a person who also repeatedly questioned himself over the thousand 'possibilities.' . . ."[26]

Rather than impose an opinion on a student, for instance, he was more inclined to lead by suggestion, to ask questions that the student would then answer, becoming, as it were, a student of his student. "Do you think this is better?" or "What do you think about it?" Whether this approach was actually a function of his teaching method, or a token of his indecisiveness and his reluctance to declare himself, can be debated. Certainly he was unsure of himself.[27]

One day Claude Terrasse played Duruflé's *Toccata* for him. Duruflé gave him "some very interesting, very intelligent instructions; he noted just a few things. When he had finished, he made me take up the whole thing again, and he told me absolutely the opposite!!"[28]

Duruflé was driven not by ego needs, or by self-aggrandizement, but by a deep-felt quest for the kind of artistic perfection that is inseparable from the life of the spirit. All matters of ecclesiastical orthodoxy and theological fashion aside, Duruflé was endowed with a keen aptitude for spiritual things that stood above the vicissitudes of the changing church. The pursuit of the beautiful was, for him, a gesture of the soul, not merely a function or an exercise of musical giftedness, or even of liturgical necessity. This is, perhaps, what Mme Duruflé meant in saying that he had *une âme grégorienne*, a Gregorian soul.

The innateness of this spiritual giftedness notwithstanding, it was inexorably linked to a type of Catholicism, and its liturgical practice, that was deeply akin to the hieratic, the mystical, and the transcendent, as opposed to populism, the vernacular, and the imminent. Indeed, the genius of Maurice Duruflé was that his innately spiritual temperament was fully receptive to and expressive of the kind of Catholicism whose full-flower and waning were contemporary with his own growing up, his adulthood, and the decline of his final twenty years, so much so that one may say that his temperament perfectly expressed the years of peak and decline in the music of twentieth-century French Catholicism.

Although he was described by Jacques Bertrand as "generous and selfless," Duruflé was sometimes accused of stinginess by some of his Conservatoire students who thought him miserly because he rode his bicycle to the Conservatoire instead of taking the metro.[29] He was thought parsimonious by some, and others thought him evasive, irascible, avaricious, and greedy. But he was lavish in acknowledging his gratitude for the work done for him by organ builders over the years, giving them sizeable gifts upon the completion of major stages of work.[30] And he gave enormous sums of his own money to improve the organ at Saint Étienne-du-Mont.[31]

Asked if Duruflé had a sense of humor, one of his early students replied succinctly and without hesitation, No. Others, discovering his personality at a deeper level, appreciated "sometimes, his sense of humor."[32] One acquaintance described his laughter as reserved and his smiles measured. His nephew Paul said he had "an excellent sense of humor that appeared in his drawings and his stories."[33] Still others saw him as sometimes deadpan, but capable of humor, particularly, one might imagine, when a practical joker, like Xavier Darasse, tried cheering up the class behind his back. The story is told that, while serving on a jury with Flor Peeters, Duruflé said to him, " 'My goodness, you speak French, Flemish, German, English—and play the organ besides!' When he noted that he didn't like a piece, and Flor said, 'But, Maurice, you must give a reason,' he replied: 'All right. I don't like it *at all!*' "[34]

Bernard Dargassies, as a young apprentice organ builder, noted how rare were those who saw Duruflé laugh, and was glad to have had the privilege. While attending to some repairs on Duruflé's studio organ, he found himself pinned behind the console. Mme Duruflé pulled him by the head, while her husband pushed from the other end, both of them overwhelmed with laughter.[35] And there was the time Duruflé arrived at class one day having just heard a contemporary work on the radio: three pieces, each dedicated to a note held on a wind instrument, sliding a quarter tone higher at the end than at the beginning. Duruflé's description of the work was extremely funny.[36]

He was reportedly delighted when his harmony class, in 1952, organized a fiftieth birthday reception for him at the home of one of his pupils, at which he sat at the piano and regaled them with the popular bawdy song from his home town, *Sur la Route de Louviers*.[37] And one day he borrowed a table organ to show the students of his harmony class, and surprised them by playing "Waltz of the Roses," eliciting giggles from the classroom.[38]

Duruflé's life-long association with the church must not be equated or confused with his personal life of faith. If such comparisons are valid, one may safely say that Mme Duruflé was a more devout believer than her husband showed himself to be, an opinion held by a long-time intimate acquaintance of theirs.[39] Nevertheless one cannot deny that Duruflé's improvisations and compositions had their source and their summit in a climate of belief. And to that extent it may be said that his work as a liturgical organist "becomes a real meditation. There is not merely an auditory delight, as refined as it might be, and God knows that Maurice Duruflé was refined, but an interior elevation that disposes the heart and spirit of others to the infinite encounter, to the radiance of divine contact."[40]

Duruflé thought of himself as *sportif*. He enjoyed bicycling and swimming. A close acquaintance of his, in pointing out that Duruflé did all the driving, not his wife, attributed to him a certain machismo.[41] He was a do-it-yourselfer, a handyman, having at his home a well-stocked collection of tools. When it came to the rigors of international touring, however, he wrote that he did not have "an excessive taste for adventure."[42]

He had a pronounced knack for fine cuisine and he practiced his culinary skills whenever he was given the opportunity, as when, on several occasions, he prepared lunch in his spare apartment for the crew from Gonzalez organ builders, waiting on them at an improvised table which he had set in the small music room. (He and Mme Duruflé ate in the kitchen, there being too little space at the table.)[43]

But ordinarily the Duruflés entertained outside their home[44] because their apartment was too small to accommodate guests. One of their favorite dining establishments was on the boulevard Saint-Michel, just beyond the Luxembourg Gardens. Occasionally seen walking arm in arm along the boulevard to dinner,[45] the couple were affectionate with each other, he referring to her by the term of endearment *ma grosse poulette*.[46]

Duruflé never published his political views. It is known that he took little interest in politics,[47] although he took elections seriously and made sure that his wife voted in presidential elections when she was out of the country. Whatever Duruflé may have thought about Pétain, Vichy, and de Gaulle is unknown, unlike some of his colleagues and family members, whose political views are no longer secret.[48]

For the last twenty-two years of his life, Duruflé contended with practically unrelieved medical problems. He was hospitalized in a clinic in Neuilly for pleurisy, probably in 1945.[49] The back ailment he suffered in 1964 at the beginning of his first U.S. tour recurred in 1970.[50] In 1972, as we have seen, he had surgery on his foot for an abscess, and playing the organ was still difficult for him two years later. The healing process was so slow that it contributed to his decision not to make the 1974 U.S. tour with his wife. In the same year, 1974, he suffered the recurrence of a urinary infection. In 1975 he was experiencing bouts of severe dizziness that his doctors were unable to alleviate.[51] His recovery after the automobile accident was a very long process. Toward the end, he grew increasingly confused and needed constant attention, leaving Mme Duruflé in an exhausted state. He would repeat the same simple questions over and over again within brief time spans.[52] But he retained an uncanny memory for music and matters related to music, and it was only on this subject that he could focus his thoughts and speak with perfect clarity.[53]

When it became necessary to provide him with professional care, Duruflé was taken to the Clinique médicale du Val de Seine, in Louveciennes—situated on the river Seine, a half hour west of Paris and only a few kilometers north of Versailles—where round-the-clock medical assistance was available to him. There Maurice Duruflé died, on June 16, 1986, at age eighty-four. Mme Duruflé wrote, "Surely, the auto accident was one of the causes for his assaulted health, perhaps even for his death. The doctor certified, as the cause of death, 'mort naturelle.' "[54]

The formal announcement of his death identified six survivors: his wife, her sister and their parents, his nephew Paul Duruflé, and his cousin Robert Guéry.

News of his death reached American organists who were assembled at that time in Detroit, Michigan, for the biennial national convention of the American Guild of Organists. Daniel Roth, a featured recitalist at the convention, improvised an elegy to the memory of his maître, before a plenary audience of organists in Detroit's Ford Auditorium.

In Paris a requiem mass was said in the presence of close family members shortly after his death, for which the organ was silent. The public memorial mass was delayed until October 11, when "a throng of admirers from the ranks of his parishioners, colleagues and former students gathered to hear the *Requiem*, sung this time in his own memory."[55] He was buried in Ménerbes, in the same grave that now holds also his wife, her sister Éliane, and their parents Auguste and Suzanne.

# Appendix A

# *Maurice Duruflé*

## *Complete Œuvre*

Abbreviations
MD       Maurice Duruflé
MMD      Marie-Madeleine Duruflé
SEM      Saint Étienne-du-Mont

## Original Works: Student Years

Untitled work in four parts, on a *basse donnée* by M. J. Morpain, in open score with four clefs.
Composed for the men's harmony competition in 1924; published that year by Heugel.

*Pastorale pour orgue*
Duruflé played this piece for the examination in composition on January 26, 1926; unpublished.

*Pièce pour orgue sur le thème du Credo*
Submitted for the examination in composition on May 12, 1926; unpublished.

*Scherzo,* Op. 2. See below.

*Méditation pour orgue*
Duruflé played this piece for the examination in composition on January 26, 1927; unpublished.

*Pièce pour orgue*
Based on a theme by Raoul Lapavia; written for the examination in composition on April 26, 1927; unpublished.

Fugue in C Minor
Composed in 1928 on a subject by Henri Rabaud, in open score with four clefs, for the competition in fugue; published that year by Heugel under the title *Fugues à 4 parties des élèves ayant remporté le premier prix aux Concours de Fugue (Année 1928).*

*Pièce pour orgue*
Written on a given theme for the examination in composition on May 8, 1928; unpublished.

## Original Works: Published Works and Works with Opus Numbers

Op. 1   *Tryptique: Fantaisie sur des thèmes grégoriens* (1927; revised 1943)
for organ; ded.: Louis Vierne; unpublished

Op. 2    *Scherzo* (1926, 1928)
    ded.: Charles Tournemire; publ.: 1929, Durand; premiere: March 15, 1928, by
    André Fleury, at the Hôtel Majestic

Op. 3    *Prélude, récitatif et variations* (1928)
    for flute, viola, and piano; ded.: Jacques Durand; publ.: 1929, Durand; premiere:
    January 12, 1929, for the Société nationale de musique, by Marcel Moyse, Maurice
    Vieux, and Jean Doyen, at Salle Pleyel

Op. 4    *Prélude, adagio et choral varié sur le Veni Creator* (1926, 1930) [*Choral varié*, 1926;
    *Prélude* and *Adagio*, 1930]
    for organ; ded.: Louis Vierne; publ.: 1931, Durand; premiere: May 16, 1931 for the
    Société national de music, by MD, at the Salle du Conservatoire

Op. 5    *Suite: Prélude, Sicilienne, Toccata* (1932–33)
    for organ; ded.: Paul Dukas; publ.: Durand, 1934; premiere of the Prélude February
    22, 1932, by MD, at Saint Merry; premiere of the entire work January 23, 1935, by
    Geneviève de la Salle, at Saint François-Xavier, Paris

Op. 6    *Trois Danses* (1932) for orchestra (*Divertissement, Danse lente, Tambourin*)
    ded.: Paul Paray; publ.: (miniature score) 1939, Durand; premiere: January 18,
    1936, by Orchestre Colonne, dir. Paul Paray, Théâtre du Châtelet
        Transcription of *Tambourin*, for piano solo (1961); publ.: 1962, Durand
        Transcription of all three movements for one piano, four hands; publ.: 1996,
        Durand
        Transcription of all three movements for two pianos; publ.: 1996, Durand
        Transcription of all three movements for piano; publ.: 1997, Durand

Op. 7    *Prélude et fugue sur le nom d'ALAIN* (1942)
    for organ; ded.: Jehan Alain; publ.: 1943, Durand; premiere: December 26, 1942,
    by MD, at Palais de Chaillot

Op. 8    *Andante et Scherzo*
    for orchestra
        *Scherzo* (1940); ded.: none; publ.: 1947, Durand; premiere: November 17,
        1940, by Société des Concerts du Conservatoire, dir. Charles Münch
        *Andante* (1950); ded. Henri Tomasi; publ.: 1955, Durand; premiere:
        January 14, 1952, by Orchestre national, dir. Henri Tomasi
        *Scherzo*, miniature score; publ.: 1947, Durand
        *Andante*, miniature score; publ.: 1955, Durand

Op. 9    *Requiem* (1947)
    for orchestra, chorus, solos; ded.: his father; publ.: 1948, Durand; premiere:
    November 2, 1947, on French radio, Orchestre national, the Chœurs de la Radio
    (dir. Yvonne Gouverné), dir. Roger Désormière, Salle Gaveau, with organist
    Henriette Roget; First concert performance, December 28, 1947, by Orchestre
    Colonne, the Chorale Yvonne Gouverné, dir. Paul Paray, with organist Henriette
    Roget, at Palais de Chaillot
        Version for solo organ; publ.: 1948, Durand
        Version for large orchestra and organ; publ.: 1950, Durand
        Miniature score; publ.: 1950, Durand
        Version for reduced orchestra and organ; publ.: 1961, Durand

Op. 10   *Quatre Motets sur des thèmes grégoriens* (1960)
    for voices
        Ubi caritas, no. 1, Tota pulchra es, no. 2, Tu es Petrus, no. 3, Tantum ergo, no. 4
        ded.: Auguste Le Guennant; publ.: 1960, Durand; premiere: May 4, 1961, by
        Chorale Stéphane Caillat, at Saint Merry

Op. 11 *Messe "Cum jubilo"* (1966)
>> ded.: MMD; premiere: December 18, 1966, by Orchestre Lamoureux, the Chorale Stéphane Caillat, dir. Jean-Baptiste Mari, at Salle Pleyel
>>> Version for organ; publ.: 1961, Durand
>>> Version for reduced orchestra and organ; publ.: 1967, Durand
>>> Version for large orchestra and organ; publ.: 1972, Durand (There is no miniature score.)

Op. 12 *Fugue sur le thème du carillon des heures de la cathédrale de Soissons* (1962)
>> ded.: Henri Doyen; publ.: 1962, Éditions de la Procure du Clergé. Second edition by Europart-Music; premiere: June 6, 1964, by MD, at the Soissons cathedral

Op. 13 *Prélude sur l'Introït de l'Épiphanie* (1961)
>> for organ; publ.: early 1960s, Éditions de la Schola Cantorum; premiere: May 4, 1961, by MD, at Saint Merry

Op. 14 *Notre Père* (1977)
>> ded.: MMD
>>> Version for unison voices and organ; publ.: 1977, Durand
>>> Version for SATB choir *a cappella*; publ.: 1978, Durand

Op. posth. *Méditation* (circa 1964)
>> for organ; publ.: 2002, Durand

## Unpublished Original Works without Opus Numbers

*Adagio*, composed by Duruflé as the middle movement for the Handel *Organ Concerto* in A Major, Op. 7, no. 2, performed September 1967, by the Duruflés, at the National Shrine of the Immaculate Conception, Washington, D.C.

*Sicilienne* [1945?], probably from *Suite*, Op. 5 for organ; transcription for small orchestra; unpublished

## Unpublished Transcriptions for Organ

T.G. Albinoni, *Adagio*
J. S. Bach, *Aria*
Gabriel Fauré, *Prélude* to *Pelléas et Mélisande* (dedicated to Princess Edmond de Polignac)
G.F. Handel, *Largo*
J.-A. DePlanes, *Intrada*
Caix d'Hervelois, *Plainte*

## Prefaces, Orchestrations, Editions, Registrations, Reductions, Reconstitutions, and Transcriptions of Works by Other Composers

Johann Sebastian Bach
> *Werde munter, mein Gemüthe* (*Réjouis-toi, mon âme*) from Cantata 147: *Herz und Mund und Tat und Leben.*
>> Transcribed for organ by MD; publ.: 1943, Leduc/Bornemann; premiere: December 26, 1942, by MD, at Palais du Chaillot

*Ertödt uns durch dein' Güte (Mortifie-nous par ta Bonté)* from Cantata 22: *Jesus nahm zu sich die Zwölfe*
  Transcribed for organ by MD; publ.: 1951, Bornemann
*Wachet auf, ruft uns die Stimme* from Cantata 140: *Wachet auf, ruft uns die Stimme*
  Transcribed for orchestra by Duruflé; unpublished
Chorales for organ (1942, 1945): *Nun komm, der Heiden Heiland* (BWV unknown); *Nun freut euch, lieben Christen gmein* (BWV 734 or 755); *O Lamm Gottes, unschuldig* (BWV 656); *In dir ist Freude* (BWV 615)
  Transcribed for orchestra by MD; unpublished; three of the works were performed on December 23, 1944, Société des Concerts du Conservatoire, dir. Charles Münch, in a program featuring the works of Bach, at the Théâtre des Champs-Élysées
César Franck
  *L'Organiste*, for organ or harmonium, volume 1 of œuvres complètes for organ
    Edited, fingered, and registered for organ by MD; publ.: 1957, Durand
  *Les Trois Chorals*, volume 4 of *Œuvres complètes* for organ
    Revisions and annotations by MD; publ.: 1973, Durand
Jules Mouquet
  *Deuxième Rapsodie en sol mineur* (1914)
  *Cortège en la mineur* (1916)
    Registrations by MD; both publ.: 1953
Francis Poulenc
  Concerto for organ
    Registration in consultation with MD; ded.: Princess Edmond de Polignac; publ.: 1939, Salabert; miniature score; publ.: 1939
Charles Tournemire
  *Triple Choral*, Op. 41 (1910)
    Révision et annotations par MD; publ.: 1962, Schola Cantorum
  *Cinq Improvisations* (in two volumes)
      Reconstituted by Duruflé from recordings made at Sainte Clotilde
      Ded.: Charles Tournemire; publ.: 1958, Durand
      *Cantilène improvisée* (September 1930), vol. 1
        Premiere: April 7, 1956, by MMD, at Saint Merry; and June 7, 1956, by MD, at SEM
      *Fantaisie-Improvisation sur l'Ave maris stella* (October 1930), vol. 2
        Premiere: June 3, 1958, by MMD, at SEM
      *Choral-Improvisation sur le Victimae paschali laudes* (October 1930), vol. 2
        Premiere: June 3, 1958, by MMD, at SEM
      *Petite Rapsodie improvisée* (November 1931), vol. 1
        Premiere: January 22, 1957, by MD, at Palais de Chaillot
      *Improvisation sur le Te Deum* (March 1932), vol. 1
        Premiere: April 7, 1956, by MMD, at Saint Merry; and June 7, 1956, by MD, at SEM
Louis Vierne
  *Soirs le: étrangers*, Op. 56 (1928)
    For violoncello and piano; orchestration by MD (1943)
      Publ.: 1928, Lemoine; premiere: May 18, 1938, by Paul Bazelaire, cello, and Bernard Gavoty, piano, in the salons of La Revue musicale, Paris. Premiere of Duruflé's version for orchestra: April 23, 1944, by Concerts Pasdeloup, under the direction of Jean Clergue, with cellist Georges Schwartz, at Salle Gaveau
  *La Ballade du désespéré*, Op. 61 (1931) lyric poem for orchestra and soprano
      "Orchestration de Maurice Duruflé d'après les indications de l'auteur."

Photocopy of the manuscript is in the Bibliothèque nationale de France (Gr. Vma G40), 1947. Version for tenor and orchestra or piano
Ded.: Madeleine Richepin; publ. 1945, 1963, Salabert; premiere: April 8, 1945, Concerts Lamoureux, under the direction of Eugène Bigot, with Marcelle Bunlet, soprano, at Salle Pleyel
*Trois Improvisations* reconstituted by Duruflé from recordings made at Notre-Dame, preface by Madeleine Richepin
    *Marche épiscopale* (December 1928)
    *Méditation* (December 1928)
    *Cortège* (December 1928)
    Publ.: 1954, Durand; premiere: April 5, 1954, by MD, at Sainte Clotilde

## Compositions in Pedagogical Works

Marcel Mule
    *Traits difficiles: Répertoire du Conservatoire National de Musique de Paris tirés d'œuvres symphoniques et dramatiques pour tous instruments; recueillis par Marcel Mule pour saxophone alto; 2e fascicule*
    Eight measures from Duruflé's Tambourin appear as example 8, page 2; publ.: 1943, Leduc
Various Composers
    *64 Leçons d'harmonie offertes en Hommage à Jean Gallon par ses Elèves. Professeur honoraire au Conservatoire National de Musique par ses élèves prix d'Harmonie entre 1919 et 1948. Préface de Claude Delvincourt*
    A piece based on a chant donné, by Duruflé (pages 52–53); publ.: February 1953, Durand; reprinted in L'Orgue: Cahiers et mémoires, no. 45 (1991): 21
Catherine Meyer Garforth
    *Cours progressif de déchiffrage: Débutant à élémentaire pour le piano*
    Preface by Duruflé; publ.: 1984, Mâcon: Éditions Robert Martin

# Appendix B

# *Discography*

## *Works by Maurice Duruflé and Other Composers Recorded by Maurice Duruflé and Marie-Madeleine Duruflé*

Abbreviations
CD       Compact disc
HMV      His Master's Voice
MD       Maurice Duruflé
MHS      Musical Heritage Society
MMD      Marie-Madeleine Duruflé-Chevalier
ORTF     Office de Radiodiffusion-télévision française
SEM      Saint Étienne-du-Mont

## Compositions by Maurice Duruflé, Recorded by the Duruflés

*Requiem*
> Orchestre des Concerts Lamoureux, MD, conductor; Chorale Philippe Caillard,
>    Chorale Stéphane Caillat, Philippe Caillard, chef des choeurs; MMD, organ
> Rec. at Saint Étienne-du-Mont, Paris, November 1958
> Erato LDE 3098; Epic LC3856; Epic 1256; MHS 1509 (1973)
> Awarded the *Grand prix du disque*, 1959

*Requiem*
*Prélude, adagio et choral varié sur le Veni Creator*
*Prélude* and *Sicilienne*, from the *Suite*, Op. 5
> Orchestre des Concerts Lamoureux, MD, conductor; Chorale Philippe Caillard,
>    Chorale Stéphane Caillat; MMD, organ
> CD Erato 4509-96952-2 (1958); Erato Ultima 3984-24235-.

**Musique sacrée du 20ème siècle**
*Requiem* (1958)
*Messe "Cum jubilo"* (1971)

*Quatre Motets sur des thèmes grégoriens* (1965)
    Orchestre des Concerts Lamoureux, Orchestre national de l'ORTF, MD, conductor;
        Chorale Stéphane Caillat; MMD, organ
    Rec. at Maison de la Radio, Paris
    CD Erato 06301 79362

*Messe "Cum jubilo"* (1971)
*Quatre Motets sur des thèmes grégoriens* (1965)
*Trois Danses* (1968)
    Orchestre national de l'ORTF, MD, conductor; Chorale Stéphane Caillat; MMD, organ
    Rec. at Maison de la Radio, Paris
    Erato 70502; Erato 4509-98526-2; MHS 1819 (1974)
    This recording was reissued on CD with the *Prélude et fugue sur le nom d'ALAIN*
        and the *Scherzo*, Op. 2: Erato Ultima 3984-24235-2

**Anthology of Contemporary Music**
*Tambourin*, from *Trois Danses*
    Eugène Bigot, conductor
    A project of the Secrétariat général des Beaux-Arts and the Association française
        d'action artistique of the Vichy government
    Eleventh recording in a series of forty (1944)
    This recording may have been taken from a private, noncommercial recording
        made of a concert in 1938 with Bigot and the Concerts Lamoureux

*Messe "Cum jubilo"* (1971)
*Quatre Motets* (1965)
*Trois Danses* (1968)
*Scherzo* (1963)
*Prélude et fugue sur le nom d'ALAIN* (1963)
    Orchestre national de l'ORTF, MD, conductor; Chorale Stéphane Caillat; MMD,
        organ
    Rec. at Saint Étienne-du-Mont, Paris; Cathedral of Saint Gervais and Saint
        Protais, Soissons
    Erato CD 4509-98526-2

**L'Orgue français: L'Époque contemporaine**
Maurice Duruflé, Pièces pour orgue
*Prélude, adagio et choral varié sur le Veni Creator* (MD at Soissons)
*Prélude*, from *Suite*, Op. 5 (MD at Soissons)
*Sicilienne*, from *Suite*, Op. 5 (MD at SEM)
*Scherzo*, Op. 2 (MMD at SEM)
*Prélude et fugue sur le nom d'ALAIN* (MMD at Soissons)
    MD and MMD, organ
    Rec. at Saint Étienne-du-Mont, Paris; Cathedral of Saint Gervais and Saint Protais,
        Soissons, 1961–62
    Pro Columbia [JP] OS-428; Erato 4509-96952-2 (1973); Erato EDO 245; MHS
        999 (1969)
    Awarded the *Grand prix du disque*, 1962

**Berühmte Organistinnen**
*Prélude et fugue sur le nom d'ALAIN*
 MMD, organ
 Rec. at Saint Étienne-du-Mont, Paris
 CD Organ-Schott 7006-2 (1992)

**Orgues et organistes français du XXe siècle (1900–1950)**
*Scherzo*, Op. 2 (Phonothèque INA PHD 85024331; December 9, 1947)
*Prélude et fugue sur le nom d'ALAIN*, Op. 7 (PHD 86037761; March 5, 1953)
 MD, organist
 Rec. at Institut des jeunes aveugles, Paris
 EMI 5 74866 2 (2002); CD 2004

# Compositions by Other Composers, Recorded by the Duruflés

Fauré, *Requiem*, Op. 48
Monteverdi, *Madrigals*
 Ensemble vocal et instrumental; Nadia Boulanger, conductor; MD, organ
 Rec. at Salle Gaveau, Paris
 EMI: CDH 7 61025 2 (October 11–13, 1948)

Fauré, *Requiem*, Op. 48
 Orchestre des Concerts Lamoureux, Jean Fournet, conductor; Chorale Élisabeth
 Brasseur; MD, organ
 Epic LC 3044; Philips PHCP 5111; Philips 438 970-2 (July 1953)

Fauré, *Requiem*, Op. 48
 Chanteurs de Saint Eustache et orchestre, André Cluytens, conductor; MD, organ
 Rec. at the Church of Saint Roch, Paris, September 14, 16–17, 1950
 EMI C04512809; EMI [JP] EAB-5014: LP; Columbia FCX108 (UK Columbia
 33CX 1145); Reissued on Testament SBT 1240 (2002)

Arthur Honegger, *Une Cantate de Noël*
 Orchestre de la Société des Concerts du Conservatoire, Georges Tzipine, conductor;
  Chorale Élisabeth Brasseur; Les Petits Chanteurs de Versailles (Dir. P. Béguigné);
  MD, organ
 Rec. at Saint Eustache, Paris
 EMI (Trianon) C04512171 (33 rpm); Telefunken HT 7/8; Columbia FCX 336

Arthur Honegger, *Une Cantate de Noël*
 Orchestre des Concerts Lamoureux, Paul Sacher, conductor; Chorale Élisabeth
  Brasseur; Les Petits Chanteurs de Versailles; MD, organ
 Philips N00749R

Arthur Honegger, *Le Roi David*
 Orchestre national de l'ORTF, Arthur Honegger, conductor; Chorale Élisabeth
  Brasseur; MD, organ

Rec. at the Church of Saint Roch, Paris
Telefunken HT 7/8; Ducretet-Thomson LPG 8342/43

Poulenc, Concerto for organ
Poulenc, *Gloria*
    Orchestre national de l'ORTF, Georges Prêtre, conductor; Choral Yvonne
      Gouverné; MD, organ
    Rec. at Saint Étienne-du-Mont, Paris, February 1961
    EMI C06912102; EMI CDC7477232; Columbia FCX882; Angel S 35953; CD
      August classics

Poulenc, Concerto for organ
    Orchestre philharmonique de l'ORTF, Pierre Michel Le Conte, conductor; MD,
      organ, March 21, 1960

Poulenc, *Concerto champêtre*
Poulenc, Concerto for Two Pianos
Poulenc, Concerto for Organ
    Société des Concerts du Conservatoire, Pierre Dervaux, conductor; MD, organ
    EMI Classics 7243 5 62647 2 4

**Cello Arias**
Tommaso Giovanni Albinoni, *Adagio
Johann Sebastian Bach, *Grave, *Aria, and *Adagio* (from Toccata, Adagio and Fugue in C
    Major)
Louis Caix d'Hervelois, *Plainte*
Jean-Antoine Desplanes, *Intrada*
George Frideric Handel, *Largo
Jean Huré, *Air*
Édouard Lalo, *Chant russe*
Guiseppe Tartini, *Adagio*
    *transcriptions by Maurice Duruflé
    André Navarra, violoncello; MD, organ
    Rec. at Notre-Dame d'Auteuil, Paris, 1966
    Pacific-Vogue Counterpoint: CMC20 18

Johann Sebastian Bach, *Préludes, Toccatas, Fantaisies, et Fugues* for organ, BWV 531–566,
572, 578, 582
    MD and MMD, organ
    Rec. at Cathedral of Saint Gervais and Saint Protais, Soissons, November 1963–July 1965
    EMI 489173 2; HMV FALP811; EMI 7243 4 89173 2 4 (1996) on 5 CDs

Johann Sebastian Bach, [Works for organ], BWV 565, 578, 615
Johann Sebastian Bach, Two chorals transcribed by MD:
*Werde munter, mein Gemüthe* [*Jésus, que ma joie demeure*], BWV 147
*Ertödt uns durch dein' Güte* [*Mortifié-nous par ta bonté*], BWV 22
    MD, organ
    Rec. at Saint Étienne-du-Mont, Paris
    Erato (1957)

**Actus Tragicus**
Johann Sebastian Bach, Cantata 106: *Gottes Zeit ist die allerbeste Zeit*, BWV 106
> Les Chanteurs de Saint Eustache and instrumental ensemble, Émile Martin,
> conductor; MD, organ
> Pathé PDT239

**Bach Organ Music from Soissons Cathedral**
Prelude and Fugue in G Major, BWV 550
Toccata and Fugue in F Major, BWV 540
Prelude and Fugue in D Minor, BWV 554
Prelude and Fugue in A Minor, BWV 543
Fantasie and Fugue in A Minor, BWV 561
Prelude and Fugue in B-flat Major, BWV 560
> MD and MMD, organ
> Angel S-36507

Louis-Claude Daquin, *Noëls*, Nos. 1, 9, 10, 11 (MMD)
Louis-Claude Daquin, *Le Coucou* (MMD)
Louis-Nicolas Clérambault, *Suite du deuxième ton* (MMD)
Louis-Nicolas Clérambault, Extracts from *Suite du premier ton* (MMD)
François Couperin, *Messe des couvents* (MD)
Nicolas de Grigny, *Veni Creator* (MD)
Nicolas de Grigny, *Pange lingua* (MD)
> MD and MMD, organ
> Rec. at Saint Sauveur, Le Petit-Andely (organ by Robert Ingout, 1674)
> EMI C063 10545 (1969); INA Mémoire vive IMV039 contains the *Récit de tierce
> en taille* from Couperin's *Messe des couvents*.

*Les Grandes Toccatas pour orgue*
François Couperin, Offertoire, from the *Messe des couvents* (MD)
Louis Clérambault, Caprice sur les grands jeux, from the *Suite du deuxième ton* (MMD)
> MD and MMD, organ
> Saint Sauveur, Le Petit-Andely
> CD EMI 767 291-2 (1969); EMI France 7649154

*The Historical Saint Thomas Organ Series II*
*Aeolian-Skinner Series II*
François Couperin, *Récit de tierce en taille*, from *Messe pour les couvents* (MD)
François Couperin, *Dialogue sur la trompette*, from *Messe pour les paroisses* (MD)
César Franck, *Fantaisie in A Major* (MD)
George Frideric Handel, Organ Concerto in A Major, Op. 7, no. 2 (MD)
Maurice Duruflé, *Prélude*, from *Suite*, Op. 5 (MD)
Franz Liszt, *Fantasy and Fugue on "Ad nos, ad salutarem undam"* (MMD)
> MD and MMD, organ
> Recorded live at a concert sponsored by the New York City Chapter of the
> American Guild of Organists, October 18, 1966, Saint Thomas Church, New
> York City
> API Records 9003-2; reissued on CD: August Productions

**François Couperin: Enregistrements historiques** (1944–1977)
containing keyboard works performed on organ, piano, or harpsichord
with two arias for tenor
François Couperin: *Tierce en taille*, from *Messe pour les Couvents* (MD)
    Rec. at Saint Étienne-du-Mont, Paris, December 27, 1947
    INA: IMV 039; Abeille CD

**Quatre Versets d'un Motet**
(Extrait du tome XI des *Œuvres Complètes* de François Couperin)
    Chorale Yvonne Gouverné; Gisèle Peyron, soprano; MD, organ
    L'Oiseau-Lyre OL92

*Seconde Leçon de ténèbres*
François Couperin, *Seconde Leçon des ténèbres*
    Lise Daniels, soprano; Jules Lemaire, violoncello; MD, organ
    L'Oiseau-Lyre OL43 (1942)

*L'Orgue français: Vierne and Tournemire*
Tournemire, *Cantilène improvisée* (MD at SEM)
Tournemire, *Petite Rapsodie improvisée* (MD at SEM)
Tournemire, *Fantaisie-Improvisation sur l'Ave maris stella* (MMD at Soissons)
Tournemire. *Choral-Improvisation sur le Victimae paschali laudes* (MMD at Soissons)
Vierne, *Carillon de Westminster*, from Op. 54 (MD at Soissons)
Vierne, *Andantino*, from Op. 51 (MD at Soissons)
Vierne, *Impromptu* (MMD)
Vierne, *Final* from Third Symphony (MMD at Soissons)
    Rec. at Saint Étienne-du-Mont, Paris, 1960 and Cathedral of Saint Gervais and
        Saint Protais, Soissons, 1961
    Erato EJA13; Erato CD 2564 60593 2; Westminster WST-17134 (1967); MHS 1016
    Awarded the *Prix du Conservatoire*, 1962–63

*The Organs of the National Shrine*
Johann Sebastian Bach, *Herr Gott, nun schleuss den Himmel auf*, BWV 617 (MD)
Dietrich Buxtehude, *Fugue à la gigue in C Major*, BuxWV 174 (MD)
George Frideric Handel, Organ Concerto in A Major, Op. 7, no. 2, transcribed for two
    organs by Duruflé; *Adagio* by Duruflé (MD and MMD)
Robert Schumann, Canon in B Minor, Op. 56, no. 5 (MD)
Tournemire, *Choral-Improvisation sur le Victimae paschali laudes* (MMD)
Duruflé, *Prélude et fugue sur le nom d'ALAIN* (MMD)
    MD and MMD, organ
    Rec. at the National Shrine of the Immaculate Conception, Washington DC,
        September 1967
    Westminster WST-17138: LP; Gothic CD G49107 (1999); Westminster Gold Series
        WGS 8116

*Messe de minuit*
Marc-Antoine Charpentier, *Messe de minuit sur les Noël*
    Orchestre Jean-François Paillard, Louis Martini, conductor; Chorale des Jeunesses
        musicales de France; MD, organ
    Columbia [JP] OS-939-R: LP; Erato STE 50083 (1961)

**Maurice Duruflé and Marie-Madeleine Duruflé**
**King of Instruments Series**
Duruflé, *Prélude, adagio et choral varié sur le Veni Creator* (MMD)
Duruflé, *Prélude*, from *Suite*, Op. 5 (MD)
Olivier Messiaen, *Banquet céleste* (MD)
Louis Clérambault, *Basse et dessus de trompette* (MMD)
Louis Clérambault, *Caprice sur les grands jeux* (MMD)
Tournemire, *Petite Rapsodie improvisée* (MD)
Tournemire, *Improvisation sur le Te Deum* (MD)
>    MD and MMD, organ
>    Rec. at Christ Church Cathedral, Saint Louis, MO, September 1966
>    Aeolian-Skinner AS 322

*Pour célébrer Mozart*
Wolfgang Amadeus Mozart, *Misericordias Domini*, K. 222
Wolfgang Amadeus Mozart, *Jubilate*, K. 117
Wolfgang Amadeus Mozart, *Sancta Maria, Mater Dei*, K. 273
Wolfgang Amadeus Mozart, *Alma Dei Creatoris*, K. 277
Wolfgang Amadeus Mozart, *Regina coeli*, K. 276
>    Soloists, chorus and orchestra of L'Anthologie Sonore; Felix Raugel, conductor;
>        MD, organ
>    Everest SDBR 3191 (1967)

Camille Saint-Saëns, Symphony No. 3 in C Minor
>    Orchestre de la Société des Concerts du Conservatoire, George Prêtre, conductor;
>        MD, organ
>    Rec. at Saint Étienne-du-Mont, Paris, 1963
>    ANGEL S 35924; EMI: C 069 10606; EMI 5 74637 2 CD

Camille Saint-Saëns: Symphony No. 3 in C Minor
>    Orchestre des Champs-Élysées, Ernest Bour, conductor; MD, organ
>    Rec. at Salle Gaveau, Paris, 1955
>    Ducrétet-Thomson TOM 4511; Ducrétet-Thomson 270 C 054

*[Psaume XLVII, Op. 38]*
Florent Schmitt, *Psaume XLVII*, Op. 38
>    Orchestre de la Société des Concerts du Conservatoire, Georges Tzipine, conductor;
>        Chorale Élisabeth Brasseur; MD, organ
>    Rec. at Palais de Chaillot, Paris, June 1952
>    EMI 5 85204 2; 2 CDs; Pathé Marconi 33FCX171

*Les Angélus*
Vierne, *Les Angélus*, Op. 57, for voice and organ
>    Hélène Bouvier, mezzo-soprano; MD, organ
Vierne, Sonata in B Minor for Violoncello and Piano, Op. 27
>    Geneviève Martinet, violoncello;
>    Jean Doyen, piano
>    Odéon ODX176

Fred Barlow, *Ave Maria*
    MD, organ
    Erato (1960)

**Concert: Marie-Madeleine Duruflé**
George Frideric Handel, Concerto No. 2 in B-flat Major
Antonio Vivaldi, *Larghetto from the Concerto in D Minor
Louis-François Clérambault, *Récit de nasard*
Dietrich Buxtehude, *Fugue ut modale*, BuxWV 174
Johann Sebastian Bach, Prelude and Fugue in D Major, BWV 532
Felix Mendelssohn, Allegretto from Sonata No. 4
Robert Schumann, Canon in B Minor, Op. 56, no. 5
César Franck, *Cantabile*
Vierne, *Naïades*
Tournemire, *Choral-Improvisation sur le Victimae paschali laudes*
Duruflé, *Prélude et fugue sur le nom d'ALAIN*
    *transcriptions by MMD
    MMD, organ
    Rec. at Notre-Dame des Carmes, Pont-L'Abbé, June 1990
    Notre-Dame des Carmes Association, CD

**Orgues de Paris**
Duruflé, *Prélude et fugue sur le nom d'ALAIN*
    MMD, organ
    Rec. at Saint Étienne-du-Mont, Paris, December 1991
    Erato (1992)

**Marie-Madeleine Duruflé à Saint Eustache, Paris**
César Franck, Choral in A Minor
Vierne, *Méditation*
Vierne, *Naïades*
Tournemire, *Choral-Improvisation sur le Victimae paschali laudes*
Marcel Dupré, *Cortège et Litanie*
Schumann: Canon in B Minor, Op. 56, no. 5
Duruflé, *Prélude et fugue sur le nom d'ALAIN*
Chopin, Etude in C-sharp Minor
Marie-Madeleine Duruflé: *Improvisation*
    Rec. at Saint Eustache, Paris, July 1, 1993
    Festivo CD 6941 772 (live)

**Exultate Deo Adjutari Nostro**
Louis-François Clérambault, *Motet: Exultate Deo adjutari nostro*
    Orchestre philharmonique de Paris, Eugène Bigot, conductor; Chorale universitaire
      de Paris; MD, organ
    Chant du Monde LDX-S-8190 (1957)

# Note

In the (undated) press material sent to sponsors prior to one of their North American tours, reference was made to the Duruflés' recording on Pathé-Marconi of works by Franck, Vierne, Widor, and French composers of the eighteenth century. No further information is available about this recording.

Duruflé himself never recorded the *Andante et Scherzo*, Op. 8, but it was recorded by the BBC Concert Orchestra, under the direction of Murray Stewart (London, 1986).[1]

Duruflé did not record *Hommage à Jean Gallon* (also referred to as *Chant donné*), but it has been recorded by organists Pierre Pincemaille (at Saint Joseph, Bonn-Beuel), Stefan Schmidt (Saint Peter, Dusseldorf), and Piet van der Steen (Saint Bavo, Haarlem).[2]

In preparation: INA *Mémoire vive*, two CDs at the organ of the Institut des jeunes aveugles and the Maison de la radio.[3]

[1] Reisinger, "Limited Musical Output," 9n16.
[2] Ibid., 12.
[3] See Alain Cartayrade, "Discographie," *Bulletin* 3 (June 2003): 64.

Appendix C

# Stoplists of Organs Important to the Careers of Maurice and Marie-Madeleine Duruflé

## 1. Cathédrale Saint Véran, Cavaillon[1]

Ch. Royer 1653; Frère Isnard 1782; Mader of Marseille 1868; Ruche de Lyon 1932

**Grand Orgue**

Bourdon 16
Montre 8
Bourdon 8
Gambe 8
Prestant 4
Doublette 2
Grosse Fourniture
Dessus de Cornet
Trompette 8
Clairon 4

**Récit**

Flûte harmonique 8
Kéraulophone 8
Voix céleste 8
Flûte 4
Flûte 2
Trompette 8
Basson hautbois 8

**Pédale**

Soubasse 16

[1]Jacques Bertrand, "Cathédrale de Cavaillon: Reconstruction du Grand Orgue," *Bulletin* 4 (June 2004): 48.

## 2. Notre-Dame, Louviers (Disposition in 1940)[1]

Clicquot; Daublaine/Callinet 1843; Abbey 1887; restoration by Convers 1926

| Grand Orgue | Positif | Récit (expressif) | Pédale |
|---|---|---|---|
| Montre 16 | Flûte 8 | Flûte 8 | Contrebasse 16 |
| Bourdon 16 | Bourdon 8 | Cor de nuit 8 | Soubasse 16 |
| Montre 8 | Salicional 8 | Gambe 8 | Bourdon 8 |
| Flûte harmonique 8 | Unda maris 8 | Voix céleste 8 | Flûte 8 |
| Violoncelle 8 | Prestant 4 | Flûte 4 | Bombarde 16 |
| Gambe 8 | Flûte douce 4 | Octavin 2 | Trompette 8 |
| Prestant 4 | Nazard $2\frac{2}{3}$ | Piccolo 1 | |
| Dulciana 4 | Doublette 2 | Quinte $2\frac{2}{3}$ | |
| Doublette 2 | Clarinette 8 | Tierce $1\frac{3}{5}$ | |
| Cornet V | Trompette 8 | Cor anglais 16 | |
| Plein jeu III | | Voix humaine 8 | |
| Basson 16 | | Hautbois 8 | |
| Trompette 8 | | Trompette 8 | |
| Clairon 4 | | | |

[1]Abbing, *Duruflé*, 507.

## 3. Notre-Dame, Louviers[1]

1941–1942, 1961–1974, Beuchet-Debierre, reflecting work done under the direction of Maurice Duruflé
manuals 56 notes; pédale 32 notes

**Grand Orgue**

Montre 16
Bourdon 16
Montre 8
Flûte harmonique 8
Viole de gambe 8
Bourdon 8
Prestant 4
Dulciane 4
Doublette 2
Cornet V
Plein-jeu III
Cymbale III
Basson 16
Trompette 8
Clairon 4

**Positif**

Flûte 8
Bourdon 8
Salicional 8
Prestant 4
Flûte douce 4
Doublette 2
Nasard $2\frac{2}{3}$
Tierce $1\frac{3}{5}$
Plein-jeu IV
Trompette 8
Clarinette 8

**Récit (expressif)**

Flûte traversière 8
Cor de nuit 8
Viole de gambe 8
Voix céleste 8
Flûte octaviante 4
Octavin 2
Quinte $2\frac{2}{3}$
Tierce $1\frac{3}{5}$
Fourniture IV
Voix humaine 8
Basson-Hautbois 8
Bombarde 16
Trompette harmonique 8
Clairon 4

**Pédale**

Soubasse 32
Contrebasse 16
Soubasse 16
Flûte 8
Bourdon 8
Flûte 4
Bombarde 16
Trompette 8
Clairon 4

[1]SAF, 269, 271.

## 4. Jules Haelling

Salon Organ[1]
Cavaillé-Coll-Mutin

**Grand Orgue**

Bourdon 16
Diapason 8
Flûte 8
Octave 4

**Récit**

Cor de nuit 8
Viole da gamba
Voix céleste 8
Flûte 4
Basson 8
Plein jeu

**Pédale**

Bourdon 16

[1]Hugh McAmis, "Our Paris Letter," *American Organist* 7 (September 1924): 534.

# 5. Sainte Clotilde[1]

Cavaillé-Coll 1859
manuals 54 notes; pédale 27 notes

| Grand Orgue | Positif | Récit (expressif) | Pédale |
|---|---|---|---|
| Montre 16 | Bourdon 16 | Flûte harmonique 8 | Soubasse 32 |
| Bourdon 16 | Montre 8 | Bourdon 8 | Contrebasse 16 |
| Montre 8 | Bourdon 8 | Viole de gambe 8 | Basse 8 |
| Bourdon 8 | Flûte harmonique 8 | Voix céleste 8 | Octave 4 |
| Flûte harmonique 8 | Gambe 8 | Basson-hautbois 8 | Bombarde 16 |
| Viole de gambe 8 | Unda maris 8 | Voix humaine 8 | Basson 16 |
| Prestant 4 | Prestant 4 | Flûte octaviante 4 | Trompette 8 |
| Octave 4 | Flûte octaviante 4 | Octavin 2 | Clairon 4 |
| Quinte 2⅔ | Quinte 2⅔ | Trompette 8 | |
| Doublette 2 | Doublette 2 | Clairon 4 | |
| Plein jeu VI[2] | Plein jeu II-V | | |
| Bombarde 16 | Trompette 8 | | |
| Trompette 8 | Cromorne 8 | | |
| Clairon 4 | Clairon 4 | | |

[1] Jesse Eschbach, *Aristide Cavaillé-Coll: A Compendium of Known Stoplists*, vol. 1 (Paderborn: Verlag Peter Ewers, [2003]), 175. This is the most authoritative account of the organ as it existed at the time of the inaugural recital, which followed Cavaillé-Coll's original completion of the organ by a full year and a half. Originally it had only 40 stops and 25 pedal notes. By the time of the inaugural, the instrument had been enlarged to the 46 stops listed above, and the pédale had been expanded to 27 notes. Weidner (*Tournemire*, 9) cites the specification as provided him by Flor Peeters, who owned the original console after it was replaced by the new one, and it is identical to that given above, apart from a single variance in nomenclature: the Fourniture VI on the grand orgue is identified by Peeters as a Plein-jeu VI. For a history of the instrument, see also Rollin Smith, *Toward an Authentic Interpretation of the Organ Works of César Franck* (New York: Pendragon Press, 1983), chap.5. Jesse Eschbach writes: "We have never had the complete story of the 1859 Cavaillé-Coll at Ste-Clotilde. With the exception of proposals, there is no complete report available in any archives, church or state. The earliest accounts of this organ come from Tournemire, and his titularate followed the 1891 restoration by Cavaillé-Coll" (Eschbach, e-mail message to author, March 6, 2005). See also Fenner Douglass, *Cavaillé-Coll and the French Romantic Tradition* (New Haven, CT: Yale University Press, 1999), 141.

[2] The composition of this stop has been a matter of dispute (see Jaquet-Langlais, "Organ Works of Franck," 167). Marie-Claire Alain claimed there were five ranks in the Plein-jeu; Duruflé and Tournemire claimed six; Langlais claimed seven. During a restoration in 1983, six ranks were found, but a seventh had been silenced.

## 6. Notre-Dame Cathedral[1]

Cavaillé-Coll 1868
manuals 56 notes; pédale 30 notes

**Grand chœur**

Principal 8
Bourdon 8
Prestant 4
Quinte $2\frac{2}{3}$
Doublette 2
Tierce $1\frac{3}{5}$
Larigot $1\frac{1}{3}$
Septième $1\frac{1}{7}$
Piccolo 1
Tuba magna 16
Trompette 8
Clairon 4

**Grand Orgue**

Violonbasse 16
Bourdon 16
Montre 8
Flûte harmonique 8
Viole de gambe 8
Bourdon 8
Prestant 4
Octave 4
Doublette 2
Fourniture II–V
Cymbale
  harmonique II–V
Basson 16
Basson-hautbois 8
Clairon 4

**Bombarde**

Principal-basse 16
Soubasse 16
Principal 8
Flûte harmonique 8
Grosse quinte $5\frac{1}{3}$
Octave 4
Grosse tierce $3\frac{1}{5}$
Quinte $2\frac{2}{3}$
Septième $2\frac{2}{7}$
Doublette 2
Grand cornet II–V
Bombarde 16
Trompette 8
Clairon 4

**Positif**

Montre 16
Bourdon 16
Flûte harmonique 8
Bourdon 8
Salicional 8
Unda maris 8
Prestant 4
Flûte douce 4
Doublette 2
Piccolo 1
Plein jeu harmonique
  III–VI
Clarinette basse 16
Cromorne 8
Clarinette aiguë 4

**Récit (expressif)**

Quintaton 16
Flûte traversière 8
Quintaton 8
Viole de gambe 8
Voix céleste 8
Flûte octaviante 4
Dulciana 4
Nasard $2\frac{2}{3}$
Octavin 2
Cornet harmonique
  III–V
Bombarde 16
Trompette 8
Basson-hautbois 16
Clarinette 8
Voix humaine 8
Clairon 4

**Pédale**

Principal basse 32
Contre basse 16
Soubasse 16
Grosse quinte $10\frac{2}{3}$
Flûte 8
Violoncelle 8
Grosse tierce $6\frac{2}{5}$
Quinte $5\frac{1}{3}$
Septième $4\frac{4}{7}$
Flûte 4
Contre bombarde 32
Bombarde 16
Basson 16
Trompette 8
Basson 8
Clairon 4

[1]Eschbach, *Cavaillé-Coll*, 292–93.

## 7. Studio organ of Louis Vierne

Cavaillé-Coll-Mutin 1926

| Grand Orgue | Récit | Pédale |
|---|---|---|
| Montre 8 | Cor de nuit 8 | Soubasse 16 |
| Flûte harmonique 8 | Gambe 8 | |
| Prestant 4 | Voix céleste 8 | |
| | Flûte douce 4 | |
| | Nazard $2\frac{2}{3}$ | |
| | Hautbois-basson 8 | |

[1]Duruflé, "Interview with Duruflé [Baker]," 60.

## 8. Église Reformée de l'Étoile[1]

Cavaillé-Coll 1874; Mutin-Cavaillé-Coll 1917

**Grand Orgue**

Bourdon 16
Montre 8
Flûte harmonique 8
Salicional 8
Bourdon 8
Prestant 4
Plein jeu
Trompette 8

**Positif (expressif)**

Principal 8
Cor de nuit 8
Viola 4
Flûte 4
Nazard $2\frac{2}{3}$
Quarte de nazard 2
Tierce $1\frac{3}{5}$
Basson-hautbois 8

**Récit (expressif)**

Quintaton 16
Flûte harmonique 8
Gambe 8
Voix céleste 8
Flûte 4
Octavin 2
Plein jeu
Basson 16
Trompette 8
Cromorne 8
Clairon 4

**Pédale**

Contrebass 16
Soubasse 16
Flûte 8
Bourdon 8
Basson 16

[1]From a brochure at the church.

## 9. Hôtel Singer-Polignac: Atelier of the Princess Edmond de Polignac[1]

Cavaillé-Coll 1892
manuals 56 notes; pédale 30 notes

**Grand Orgue (expressif)**

Montre 8
Bourdon 8
Flûte harmonique 8
Prestant 4
Flûte à cheminée 4
Basson 16
Trompette 8
Clairon 4

**Récit (expressif)**

Flûte harmonique 8
Viole de gambe 8
Voix céleste 8
Flûte octaviante 4
Octavin 2
Plein-Jeu III
Basson et Hautbois 8
Clarinette 8

**Pédale**

Soubasse 16
Flûte 8

# 10. Saint Étienne-du-Mont[1]

Pierre Le Pescheur 1631–1636
The first organ built for the new church; destroyed by fire on the night of July 23, 1760

| Grand Orgue, 48 notes[2] | Positif | Cornet (separate manual)[3] | Écho | Pédale, 29 notes |
|---|---|---|---|---|
| Montre 16 | Bourdon 8 | Cornet | Cornet | Flûte 8 (4) |
| Bourdon 16 | Montre 4 | | | Trompette 8 |
| Montre 8 | (Flûte 4) | | | |
| Bourdon 8 | Nasard $2\frac{2}{3}$ | | | |
| Prestant 4 | Doublette 2 | | | |
| Flûte 4 | Larigot $1\frac{1}{3}$ | | | |
| Nasard $2\frac{2}{3}$ | (Tierce $1\frac{3}{5}$) | | | |
| Doublette 2 | Fourniture III | | | |
| Flûte 2 | Cymbale III | | | |
| Tierce $1\frac{3}{5}$ | Cromorne 8 | | | |
| Flageolet 1 | | | | |
| Fourniture VI | | | | |
| Cymbale IV | | | | |
| Cornet | | | | |
| Trompette 8 | Two tremulants | | | |
| Clairon 4 | Rossignol | | | |
| Cromorne 8 | | | | |
| (Voix Humaine 8) | | | | |

[1]Dufourcq, Livre de l'orgue 1:586, 3:103. Dufourcq indicates that (Nicolas?) Le Pescheur did some work also in 1602, quoting Brossard, Musiciens de Paris. In 1628 an organ from the church of Saint Gervais, on the right bank, was moved to Saint Étienne-du-Mont and placed just inside the west door.

[2]Dufourcq, Livre de l'orgue 3:178. No explanation is given for the several parentheses. Felix Raugel gives a rather different specification for the organ by Le Pescheur.

[3]This clavier played a cornet standing on a separate wind chest hidden in the bottom of the case. See Dufourcq, Livre de l'orgue 3:114.

## 11. Saint Étienne-du-Mont[1]

Clicquot 1777

| Grand Orgue, 48 notes | Positif, 48 notes | Récit, 33 notes | Écho, 36 notes | Pédale, 32 notes |
|---|---|---|---|---|
| Montre 16 | Montre 8 | Cornet | Bourdon 8 | Flûte 16 |
| Bourdon 16 | Bourdon 8 | Hautbois | Flûte 4 | Flûte 8 |
| Flûte 8 | Prestant 4 | | Trompette 8 | Flûte 4 |
| Bourdon 8 | Nasard $2\frac{2}{3}$ | | | Bombarde 16 |
| Flûte allemande 4 | Doublette 2 | | | Trompette 8 |
| Prestant 4 | Tierce $1\frac{3}{5}$ | | | Clairon 4 |
| Grosse tierce $3\frac{1}{5}$ | Larigot $1\frac{1}{3}$ | | | |
| Nasard $2\frac{2}{3}$ | Fourniture | | | |
| Quarte de nasard 2 | Cymbale | | | |
| Doublette 2 | Hautbois 8 | | | |
| Tierce $1\frac{3}{5}$ | Trompette 8 | | | |
| Grand cornet | Clairon 4 | | | |
| Fourniture | | | | |
| Cymbale | | | | |
| 1re Trompette 8 | | | | |
| 2e Trompette 8 | | | | |
| Voix humaine 8 | | | | |
| Clairon 4 | | | | |

[1]Ebrecht, *Duruflé*, 209. Ebrecht gives no source for this specification.

# 12. Saint Étienne-du-Mont[1]

Cavaillé-Coll 1863

| Grand Orgue, 54 notes | Positif, 52 notes (first manual)[2] | Récit (expressif), 42 notes | Pédale, 27 notes |
|---|---|---|---|
| Montre 16 | Montre 8 | Bourdon 8 | Sousbasse 16 |
| Bourdon 16 | Dessus de flûte 8 (39 notes) | Salicional 8 | Flûte 8 |
| Montre 8 | Bourdon 8 | Voix céleste 8 | Bombarde 16 |
| Dessus de flûte 8 (harmonique, 30 notes) | Prestant 4 | Flûte octaviante 4 | Trompette 8 |
| Bourdon 8 | Nasard 2⅔ | Octavin 2 | Clairon 4 |
| Gambe 8 | Doublette 2 | Trompette 8 | |
| Prestant 4 | Tierce 1⅗ | Hautbois 8 | |
| Octave 4 | Fourniture III | Voix humaine 8 | |
| Doublette 2 | Cymbale III | | |
| Plein jeu III–VI | Trompette 8 | | |
| Cornet V | Cromorne 8 | | |
| Bombarde 16 | Clairon 4 | | |
| Trompette 8 | | | |
| Clairon 4 | | | |

[1]Eschbach, *Cavaillé-Coll*, 229. See also Raugel, Grandes Orgues, 25–26; idem, "Saint Étienne-du-Mont"; and Claude Noisette de Crauzat, *Cavaillé-Coll* (Paris: La Flûte de Pan, 1984), 130.
[2]Eschbach, *Cavaillé-Coll*, does not show the Montre 8 on the Positif, or the Dessus de flûte 8, but instead lists a Salicional 8 (thirty-eight notes) and Unda maris 8 (thirty-two notes).

## 13. Saint Étienne-du-Mont, 1932[1]

Reflecting the work of Théodore Puget and Paul-Marie Koenig

**Grand Orgue, 54 notes**

Montre 16
Bourdon 16
Montre 8
Flûte harmonique 8
Gambe 8
Bourdon 8
Flûte creuse 8
Prestant 4
Doublette 2
Plein jeu VI
Cornet V
Bombarde 16
Trompette 8
Clairon 4

**Positif, 54 notes**

Salicional 8
Unda maris 8
Principal 8
Bourdon 8
Prestant 4
Bourdon 4
Nazard $2\frac{2}{3}$
Doublette 2
Fourniture III
Sesquialtera II
Cromorne 8
Trompette 8

**Récit (expressif), 54 notes**

Quintaton 16
Cor de chamois 8
Flûte 8
Gambe 8
Voix céleste 8
Salicet 4
Flûte 4
Nazard $2\frac{2}{3}$
Octavin 2
Tierce $1\frac{3}{5}$
Plein jeu III
Trompette 8
Cor [sic] 8
Basson-hautbois 8
Voix humaine 8
Clairon 4

**Pédale, 30 notes**

Soubasse 32
Soubasse 16
Contrebasse 16
Quinte $10\frac{2}{3}$
Dolce 8
Flûte 8
Flûte 4
Bombarde 16
Trompette-quinte $10\frac{2}{3}$
Trompette 8
Clairon 4
Carillon III

[1]Source: Félix Raugel and Marcel Dupré, "Étude d'un projet de reconstruction du grand orgue de Saint Étienne-du-Mont," [1936?], Dossier: Saint Étienne-du-Mont, Département des orgues, Monuments historiques, 3 rue de Valois, Paris.

## 14. Saint Étienne-du-Mont

Specification for an organ of 59 stops proposed by Felix Raugel and Marcel Dupré, 1936
Unbuilt

| Grand orgue, 61 notes | Positif, 61 notes | Récit expressif, 73 notes | Écho, 61 notes | Pédale (revised),[1] 32 notes |
|---|---|---|---|---|
| Montre 16 | Principal 8 (flûte timbre) | Quintaton 16 | Quintaton 8 | Bourdons 32, 16 (en dédoublement) |
| Bourdon 16 | Salicional 8 | Diapason 8 | Principal italien 4 | Principal 16 |
| Montre 8 | Bourdon 8 | Flûte ouverte 8 | Doublette 2 | Bourdon 8 |
| Flûte harmonique 8 | Prestant 4 | Cor de nuit 8 | Terciane II (Tierce 1³⁄₅ and Larigot) | Flûte 8 |
| Bourdon 8 | Flûte à cheminée 4 | Gambe 8 | Cymbale III | Principal 8 |
| Gros Nasard 5¹⁄₃ | Nasard 2²⁄₃ | Voix céleste 8 | Hautbois d'écho 8 | Flûte 4 |
| Prestant 4 | Quarte de Nasard 2 | Flûte 4 | Chalumeau 4 | Principal 4 |
| Flûte 4 | Tierce 1³⁄₅ | Nasard 2²⁄₃ | | Quinte 10²⁄₃ |
| Quinte 2²⁄₃ | Fourniture III | Octavin 2 | | Grande fourniture V (résultante de 16) |
| Doublette 2 | Cymbale III | Tierce 1³⁄₅ | | Bombarde 16 |
| Plein jeu VI | Cromorne 8 | Piccolo 1 | | Trompette 8 |
| Cornet V | Trompette 8 | Plein jeu IV | | Clairon 4 |
| Bombarde 16 | Clairon 4 | Basson hautbois 8 | | |
| Trompette 8 (en chamade) | | Voix humaine 8 | | |
| Clairon 4 | | Bombarde acoustique 16 | | |
| | | Trompette 8 | | |
| | | Clairon 4 | | |
| | | Clarinette 8 | | |

[1] The original specification for the pedal included Bourdons 32′, 16′, 8′ (extensions), Flûtes 16′, 8′, 4′ (extensions), Principals 8′, 4′, (2²⁄₃′ [undecipherable] extensions), Quinte 10²⁄₃′, Grande fourniture V (16′ resultant), and reeds 16′, 8′, 4′.

## 15. Saint Étienne-du-Mont[1]

Gloton de Nantes (Beuchet-Debierre) 1956
manuals 61 notes (récit 73 pipes), pédale 32 notes

| Grand Orgue | Positif | Récit (expressif) | Écho (expressif) | Pédale |
|---|---|---|---|---|
| Montre 16 | Principal 8 | Quintaton 16 | Dulciane 16 | Soubasses 32, 16, 8 (unit) |
| Bourdon 16 | Flûte creuse 8 | Principal italien 8 | Principal 8 | Principal 16 (from the Montre 16 on the G.O.) |
| Montre 8 | Bourdon à cheminée 8 | Gambe 8 | Gemshorn 8 | Flûte 16 |
| Principal 8 | Prestant 4 | Cor de nuit 8 | Bourdon 8 | Principal 8 |
| Flûte harmonique 8 | Flûte ouverte 4 | Voix céleste 8 | Unda maris 8 | Flûte 8 |
| Bourdon 8 | Nasard $2\frac{2}{3}$ | Fugara 4 | Principal 4 | Principal 4 |
| Prestant 4 | Doublette 2 | Flûte 4 | Flûte conique 4 | Flûte 4 |
| Flûte à cheminée 4 | Tierce $1\frac{3}{5}$ | Nasard $2\frac{2}{3}$ | Doublette 2 | Doublette 2 |
| Quinte ouverte $2\frac{2}{3}$ | Larigot $1\frac{1}{3}$ | Quarte de nasard 2 | Sesquialtera II | Flûte 2 |
| Doublette 2 | Septième $1\frac{1}{7}$ | Tierce $1\frac{3}{5}$ | Plein jeu IV | Fourniture IV |
| Fourniture IV | Piccolo 1 | Fourniture IV | Trompette 8 | Grosse quinte bouchée $10\frac{2}{3}$ |
| Cymbale III | Plein jeu IV | Cymbale III | Clairon 4 | Grosse tierce $6\frac{3}{5}$ |
| Cornet III–V | Cromorne 8 | Bombarde acoustique 16 | Hautbois 8 | Grosse septième $4\frac{4}{7}$ |
| Bombarde 16 | Trompette 8 | Trompette harmonique 8 | Régale 8 | Quinte ouverte $5\frac{1}{3}$ |
| Trompette 8 | Clairon 4 | Clairon 4 | Pédale d'écho: | Tierce $3\frac{1}{5}$ |
| Clairon 4 | Chalumeau 4 | Clarinette 8 | bourdons 16, 8 unit | Nasard $2\frac{2}{3}$ |
|  |  | Basson-hautbois 8 |  | Bombarde 16 |
|  |  | Voix humaine 8 |  | Trompette 8 |
|  |  | Trémolo |  | Clairon 4 |
|  |  |  |  | Bassons 16, 8, 4 |

[1]Source: Duruflé, "Restauration du grand orgue Saint Étienne-du-Mont," 48.

## 16. Saint Étienne-du-Mont[1]

Orgue de chœur
Théodore Puget, 1902
tubular pneumatic; manuals 56 notes; pédale 30 notes

**Grand Orgue**

Bourdon 16
Principal 8
Flûte harmonique 8
Salicional 8
Prestant 4
Trompette 8

**Récit (expressif)**

Cor de nuit 8
Viole de gambe 8
Voix céleste 8
Flûte octaviante 4
Plein jeu IV
Basson-hautbois 8

**Pédale**

Soubasse 16
Basse 8

[1]Ebrecht, *Duruflé*, 210.

## 17. The Cathedral of Saint Gervais and Saint Protais, Soissons[1]

Gonzalez 1956

**Grand Orgue**

Montre 16
Quintaton 16
Montre 8
Diapason 8
Flûte harmonique 8
Bourdon 8
Prestant 4
Flûte à cheminée 4
Quinte $2\frac{2}{3}$
Doublette 2
Fourniture V
Cymbale IV
Cornet V
Bombarde 16
Trompette 8
Clairon 4

**Positif**

Montre 8
Flûte creuse 8
Bourdon 8
Salicional 8
Prestant 4
Flûte douce 4
Nazard $2\frac{2}{3}$
Quarte de nazard 2
Tierce $1\frac{3}{5}$
Larigot $1\frac{1}{3}$
Plein jeu III
Cymbale II
Trompette 8
Cromorne 8
Clairon 4

**Récit (expressif)**

Bourdon 16
Principal 8
Flûte harmonique 8
Cor de nuit 8
Gambe 8
Voix céleste 8
Principal 4
Flûte 4
Nazard $2\frac{2}{3}$
Flageolet 2
Tierce $1\frac{3}{5}$
Piccolo 1
Plein jeu V
Cymbale IV
Bombarde 16
Trompette 8
Hautbois 8
Régale 8
Clairon 4

**Pédale**

Flûte 32
Soubasse 32
Principal 16
Flûte 16
Soubasse 16
Principal 8
Flûte 8
Bourdon 8
Principal 4
Flûte 4
Flûte 2
Plein jeu V
Cornet IV
Bombarde 16
Trompette 8
Clairon 4
Clairon 2

[1]Abbing, *Duruflé*, 514

## 18. Organ in the Duruflé apartment[1]

Gonzalez 1967

**Grand Orgue**

Flûte à fuseau 8
Prestant 4
Doublette 2
Plein jeu III
Cromorne 8
Trompette 8
Chalumeau 4

**Positif**

Bourdon 8
Flûte 4
Nasard 2⅔
Quarte 2
Tierce 1⅗
Larigot 1⅓
Régale 8
Chalumeau 4

**Récit (expressif)**

Principal 8
Dulciane 8
Unda maris 8
Principal 4
Cymbale III
Régale 8
Trompette 8
Clairon 4

**Pédale**

Soubasse 16
Soubasse 32
Bourdon 8
Flûte conique 4
Flûte 2
Trompette 8
Clairon 4
Régale 8
Cromorne 8
Chalumeau 4

[1]Stoplist obtained by the author during a visit to the Duruflé apartment.

# 19. An ideal organ

Proposed by Maurice Duruflé[1]
Unbuilt

**Grand Orgue**

Principal 16
Bourdon 16
Principal 8[2]
Bourdon 8
Flûte 8
Octave 4
Flûte 4
Doublette 2
Cornet V
Grosse fourniture II
Plein-jeu V (or VI)
Cymbale IV
Bombarde 16
Trompette 8
Clairon 4
Régale 8

**Positif[3]**

Principal 8
Bourdon 8
Flûte 8 (optional)
Praestant 4
Flûte 4
Nasard 2⅔
Doublette 2
Tierce 1⅗
Larigot 1⅓
Piccolo 1
Fourniture IV
Cymbale III
Cromorne 8
Trompette 8
Clairon 4
Chalumeau 4

**Récit**

Quintaton 16
Cor de nuit 8
Dulciane 8
Voix céleste 8
Flûte 8 (optional)
Flûte 4
Gemshorn 4
Quarte de nasard 2
Dessus de cornet (optional, to dialog
  with the Cromorne)
Sesquialtera II
Plein-jeu IV
Trompette 8
Hautbois 8
Voix humaine 8
Clairon 4

**Pédale (all stops are independent)**

Soubasse 32
Soubasse 16
Flûte 16
Grosse quinte 10⅔ (optional)
Octave 8
Bourdon 8
Flûte 8
Grosse tierce 6⅗ (optional)
Octave 4
Flûte 4
Bombarde 32
Basson 16
Basson 8
Trompette 8
Clairon 4

[1] Duruflé, "Orgue français," 86–88.
[2] Duruflé recommended two principals at 8′ pitch, a lighter one to be used with the principal chorus, and a second to be used with the fonds 8.
[3] Duruflé recommended at least two 8′ flues.

# Notes

## Introduction

1. The title of this unusual work is a play on words. At that time, the Palais royal had a Café mécanique which featured a conveyor-belt system that automatically brought customers their drinks. A similarly automated café, with the same name, was established in the Palais royal in 1785, where a dumb-waiter emerged at the center of the table to deliver the customer's order.

2. Noel Riley Fitch, *Sylvia Beach and the Lost Generation: A History of Literary Paris in the Twenties and Thirties* (New York: W. W. Norton), 239.

3. During the Second World War Benoist-Méchin had strong ties with the German government and served as a junior minister in the Vichy administration.

4. The Beach Papers at Princeton University contain no reference to Duruflé and no correspondence between Duruflé and Beach (Margaret M. Sherry, reference librarian, e-mail to the author, February 12, 2001).

5. Regina M. Sweeney, *Singing Our Way to Victory: French Cultural Politics and Music during the Great War* (Middletown, CT: Wesleyan University Press, 2001), 3.

6. Sylvie Bausseron Ragucci, of Rouen, e-mail to the author, October 29, 2002.

7. Sylvia Kahan, e-mail to the author, December 11 and 13, 2001. Kahan is the author of *Music's Modern Muse: A Life of Winnaretta Singer, Princesse de Polignac* (Rochester, NY: University of Rochester Press, 2003).

## Chapter One

1. Many of the following details about Louviers are taken from *Louviers*, produced by the Société d'Études diverses de Louviers et de sa Région (Louviers: Librairie "A la Page" H. Fontaine, 1999).

2. The Duruflé house is pictured in the book *Louviers*, pp. 48 and 84, in the block of buildings on the right, but is not identified as such.

3. A number of sources give 1903 incorrectly as Duruflé's year of birth. Philippe Robert is correct in tracing the error to the "Autographe des musiciens," a preparatory piece for the *Dictionnaire biographique français contemporain*, 2nd ed. (Paris: Pharos, 1954). See Philippe Robert, "Maurice Duruflé: Sa vie, son œuvre" (Diss., Université de Liège, 1979), 5. In preparation for the second edition of the work, the editor of the *Autographe des musiciens* sent questionnaires to composers whose biographies were to be included. The form submitted by Duruflé, however, though signed by him, was filled out by his wife, Marie-Madeleine, who listed 1903 incorrectly as his birth date. The penmanship is unmistakably hers.

4. Paul Duruflé, letter to author, March 14, 2002.

5. Ibid.

6. Sweeney, *Singing*, 36.

7. Little is known of Charles Duruflé's work. For the Duruflé centenary exposition in Louviers, in 2002, the curator of the town museum, Mlle Laurence Reibel, researched his architectural work, but with little result. All she found was a Plan de la Ville de Louviers drawn by him in 1934, which was mounted for the exposition.

8. Maurice Duruflé, "Mémoires," *L'Orgue: Cahiers et mémoires*, no. 45 (1991-I): 5. This and many details from the following account of Duruflé's youth are taken from his "Souvenirs," published in Duruflé, *Maurice Duruflé: Souvenirs et autres écrits*, ed. Frédéric Blanc (Paris: Séguier, 2005), 15–58 (hereafter identified as *SAE*), excerpts of which were earlier published as "Mémoires," cited at the beginning of this note. The "Souvenirs" are hereafter referred to as "Souvenirs [1976]." Material from *Maurice Duruflé: Souvenirs et autres écrits* is used by permission.

9. Henri Dumont (1610–84) was *maître de chapelle* at the Chapelle royale in Versailles during the reign of Louis XIII. See Paul Huot-Pleuroux, *Histoire de la musique religieuse des origines à nos jours* (Paris: Presses universitaires de France, 1957), 232.

10. Duruflé, "Souvenirs [1976]," 20.

11. Ibid.

12. The report card (from the Duruflé Papers) was on exhibit at the Musée municipal for the centenary exposition.

13. Sweeney, *Singing*, 30.

14. Duruflé, "Mémoires," 8.

15. Bernard Delaporte et al., *La Maîtrise Saint-Évode de la Cathédrale de Rouen* (Anciens Élèves de la Maîtrise Saint-Évode, [after 1993]), 22.

16. Laurent Ronzon, "Maurice Duruflé et le Conservatoire de Paris: Sa formation et son enseignement, 1920–1970" (Diss., Université de Paris: 1996), 13. Before the Revolution the name *psallette* was also used for the choir schools.

17. Paul Duruflé made this conjecture in a letter to the author, March 14, 2002.

18. Ibid.

19. Duruflé, "Souvenirs [1976]," 21.

20. Ibid., 22.

21. Ibid.

22. This is the word used by Paul Duruflé, in the letter of March 14, 2002, in reference to his father's godmother. The word *marraine* enjoyed some ambiguities during World War I. "The images of wife, fiancée, 'pen pal/godmother' (*marraine*), and prostitute overlapped along a continuum" (Sweeney, *Singing*, 98). "Charitable organizations first developed the concept of *marraines* or godmothers in early 1915 to assist those soldiers without families or whose families lived in the occupied territories. The system asked the *marraines* to send letters and gifts to the front to help maintain morale" (ibid., 117).

23. Henri's son Paul thus remembered his father's account (Paul Duruflé, e-mail message to author, February 10, 2002).

24. He married and had four children, three of them dying in 1935, 1977, and 1981. Only his son Paul survived into the twenty-first century.

25. Paul Duruflé, e-mail message to author.

26. Ibid.

# Chapter Two

1. Many of the details recounted below are taken from the following sources: Delaporte, *Maîtrise Saint Évode*; Francis Pinguet, *Les Écoles de la musique divine* (Lyons: Éditions à cœur joie, 1987); André Levasseur, "La Maîtrise Saint-Évode: Les organistes de la cathédrale de Rouen," *L'Orgue normand* 26 (second semester 1993): 6–11; and Christian Goubault, "La Musique à Rouen du VIIIe siècle à nos jours," *Revue internationale de musique française* 4 (January 1981): 83–92. The classic history of the school is *Histoire de la Maîtrise de Rouen*, by Abbé Collette and A. Bourdon (Rouen: Cagniard, 1892), which was issued under the same title in a new edition by Francis Pinguet in 2000.

2. For a history of the musical establishments of the French church, see Bernard Dompnier, ed., *Maîtrises et chapelles aux XVIIe et XVIIIe siècles: Des institutions musicales au service de Dieu* (Clermont-Ferrand: Presses universitaires Blaise-Pascal, 2003).

3. Ronzon, "Duruflé," 14.

4. The *maîtrise* remained Rouen's premier music school until the Conservatoire national de région was established there in 1945 (ibid.).

5. See G. Panel, *Démographie et statistique médicale, Ville de Rouen, 1918* (Rouen: Cagniard, 1919), 13–14, 18.

6. Bernard Delaporte, "En Hommage à Maurice Duruflé," *La Voix de St Évode*, no. 13 special (May 2002): 1; and conversations the author had in Rouen with three former choristers: Bernard Delaporte, Francis Pinguet, and André Levasseur (January 15, 2002). "Their story of an unsterile razor spreading infections is quite reasonable" (e-mail message to author, from Michael S. Lehrer, MD, Clinical Assistant Professor, Department of Dermatology, Hospital of the University of Pennsylvania, December 20, 2004).

But according to his nephew, Paul Duruflé, Maurice had severe headaches as an adolescent, and his hair loss was more likely the direct consequence of experimental electroshock therapy administered as treatment. "Some metal plates on his head burned his scalp and left large scars, which my uncle hid, as much as possible, by a wig which he changed according to his age" (Paul Duruflé, letter to author, March 14, 2002). M. Duruflé admitted the possibility that the headaches may well have been the result of an infection caused by an unsterile razor.

7. Ronzon, "Duruflé," 14. Philippe Robert indicates he also studied English, but this seems unlikely.

8. Ibid., 22.

9. Delaporte, "Hommage," 2.

10. Duruflé, "Souvenirs [1976]," 22–23.

11. Duruflé, "Mémoires," 8.

12. Duruflé to Francis Pinguet, February 13, 1970.

13. Duruflé, "Souvenirs [1976]," 23.

14. Delaporte, *Maîtrise Saint-Évode*, 17.

15. An earlier student of Haelling, Maurice Desrez, went to Paris for study with Guilmant. In 1902(?), Desrez wrote to Haelling that at his first lesson with Guilmant, the latter could see by the way he held his hands and feet that he was a student of Haelling, and that he was of Guilmant's school.

16. Delaporte, *Maîtrise Saint-Évode*, 22.

17. In addition to the *Chanson des maîtrisiens*, Haelling composed a Prélude in C-sharp Minor for organ (Leduc, 1902), *Hymne à l'épée* (Ledru, 1896), *Ariette de mai* for piano (Hamelle, 1913), *Inviolata* (Hamelle, 1914), *Ave Maria* (Hérelle), and *Panis Angelicus* (Éd. de la Schola).

18. Ronzon, "Duruflé," 14.

19. He published a pedagogical work for organists: Henri Beaucamp, *École de la pédale* (Senart, 1925).

20. Delaporte, "Hommage," 2.

21. Duruflé, "Souvenirs [1976]," 22.

22. Ronzon, "Duruflé," 15.

23. Duruflé, "Souvenirs [1976]," 23–24.

24. Duruflé, "Mémoires," 8.

25. Ample details about the *Christus vincit* are given in Pinguet, *Écoles de la musique divine,* 125–26.

26. The instrument was inaugurated on March 2, 1860, by Jacques-Nicolas Lemmens.

27. The instrument was destroyed in the German bombardments of 1944. The eleven-stop organ in the choir today was built in 1895 by Aristide Cavaillé-Coll for the residence of Albert Dupré. His son Marcel gave the instrument to the cathedral to replace the one destroyed during the war. André Levasseur, a *maîtrisien* at the time, helped haul the pipes from the Dupré home to the cathedral by handcart, and proudly held notes while the organ was tuned and revoiced for the larger space (Levasseur, interview); see also Levasseur, "Maîtrise Saint-Évode," 10.

28. Duruflé, "Mémoires," 11.

29. In 1945, Olivier Messiaen and his future wife Yvonne Loriod played his *Visions de l'Amen* for two pianos in the Salle des États (Pinguet, *Écoles de la musique divine,* 118–19).

30. Ronzon, "Duruflé," 16.

31. Duruflé, "Souvenirs [1976]," 25.

32. Robert, "Duruflé: Sa vie, son œuvre," 9; the composition is reproduced in ibid., 98–99; and in Duruflé, "Mémoires," 12–13. In 1953 Jules Lambert conducted a performance of Duruflé's *Requiem* by La Cantate at Notre-Dame in Louviers, with Duruflé playing the organ.

33. Prior to the installation of the *grand orgue*, Camille Saint-Saëns accompanied the services at Saint Sever from a piano (Information from a flyer at Saint Sever).

34. In his memoirs Duruflé wrote that he was a chorister at the *maîtrise* for six years, that is, until some time in 1918.

35. Robert, "Duruflé: Sa vie, son œuvre," 9, quoting information given him by Lambert in 1979. Saint André had a *grand orgue* by Cavaillé-Coll-Mutin. Pierre Labric told Ronald Ebrecht, in interviews between 1985 and 2002, that neither Saint Sever nor Saint André had "interesting organs" (Ronald Ebrecht, ed., *Maurice Duruflé 1902–1986: The Last Impressionist* [Lanham, MD: Scarecrow Press, 2002], 158).

36. Robert, "Duruflé: Sa vie, son œuvre," 8. The following information is contained in *SAE,* 245.

37. Duruflé, "Souvenirs [1976]," 39.

38. Duruflé, "Mémoires," 11. For the stoplist, see Appendix C, p. 260. Charles Tournemire oversaw work done on the organ in 1926 by Cavaillé-Coll-Convers and he played the inauguration on October 17, 1926, sharing the bench with Duruflé. The instrument was damaged during the bombardments on June 10, 1940. Between July 1941 and June 1942, the firm Debierre-Gloton from Nantes restored the organ under Duruflé's direction. The instrument was inaugurated on June 14, 1942, by Duruflé, with the assistance of the titular, Simonne Bouvier. Two stops were added in 1961 and 1962. See Olivier Soularue, "L'Orgue de l'église Notre-Dame de Louviers," in Ville de Louviers, *Hommage à Maurice Duruflé,* a commemorative brochure published for the centenary observance of Duruflé's birth (2002). See stoplist Appendix C, p. 261.

39. *Dictionnaire des églises de France*, vol. 4, *Ouest et Île-de-France* (Paris: Robert Laffont, 1966), s.v. "Louviers." Cardinal Melchior de Polignac (1661–1742) was an ancestor of Prince Edmond-Melchior de Polignac (1834–1901), whose wife, Winnaretta Singer (1865–1943), commissioned Francis Poulenc's Organ Concerto, which Duruflé premiered in her palace. Duruflé may never have known the Polignac connection between the organ in Louviers and the commission of the concerto.

40. Information provided by Olivier Soularue, the husband of Sarah Soularue, for the centenary exposition at the Hôtel de Ville in Louviers, in 2002.

41. *SAE*, 238.

42. A list of less prominent alumni is found in Delaporte, *Maîtrise Saint-Évode*, 28.

43. Francis Pinguet to author, February 5, 2002, quoting a letter from Paul Paray to Pinguet.

44. Delestre wrote the book *L'Œuvre de Marcel Dupré* (Paris: Éd. "Musique sacrée," 1952).

45. Ronzon, "Duruflé," 60, quoting a letter from Pierre Villette to Ronzon.

# Chapter Three

1. Jörg Abbing, *Maurice Duruflé: Aspekte zu Leben und Werk* (Paderborn: Verlag Peter Ewers, 2002), 32.

2. Ibid., 29.

3. Timothy J. Tikker, "My Studies of Tournemire's Music with Jean Langlais," in *Ch. Tournemire in Saint Paul: On the Occasion of the Fiftieth Anniversary of His Death* (St. Paul, MN: Institute for Critical Studies of Organ Music, 1989), 44, quoting Jean Langlais.

4. Abbing, *Duruflé*, 38.

5. Robert, "Duruflé: Sa vie, son œuvre," 11.

6. Duruflé, "Souvenirs [1976]," 26.

7. Because the organ at Sainte Clotilde had been supplied with an electric blower in 1918, it would have been convenient for Tournemire to teach there (Raymond F. Weidner, "The Improvisational Techniques of Charles Tournemire as Extracted from His Five Reconstructed Organ Improvisations" [PhD diss., Michigan State University, 1983], 10). But Duruflé does not mention having taken his lessons at the church.

8. Duruflé, "Souvenirs [1976]," 26.

9. Ibid., 26–27.

10. Ibid., 27.

11. Charles Tournemire, *Précis d'exécution de registration et d'improvisation à l'orgue* (Paris: Max Eschig, 1936), 102.

12. Ibid.

13. Tikker, "Tournemire's Music," 43, quoting Langlais.

14. Duruflé, "Souvenirs [1976]," 30–31.

15. Duruflé, "My Recollections of Tournemire and Vierne," trans. Ralph Kneeream, *American Organist* 14 (November 1980): 54.

16. Duruflé, "Souvenirs [1976]," 28.

17. Henri Doyen, *Mes Leçons avec Louis Vierne* (Paris: Éditions de musique sacrée, 1966), 44.

18. Ibid., 92.

19. Duruflé, "An Interview with Duruflé by George Baker," in *SAE*, 210. Despite its English title, the published interview is in French. Hereafter the interview will be referred to as "Interview with Duruflé [Baker, French]," which should be distinguished from the heavily edited translation of the interview that appeared first in English as "An Interview with Maurice Duruflé," in *The American Organist* 14 (November 1980): 57–60. Hereafter the latter is referred to as "Interview with Duruflé [Baker]." The English version contains outright errors and misrepresents a number of points given in the original French. Some of these will be noted in course.

20. Doyen, *Mes Leçons*, 44, quoting Norbert Dufourcq, *La Musique d'orgue française: De Jehan Titelouze à Jehan Alain* (Paris: Librairie Floury, 1949), n.p. An exact contemporary of Duruflé, Henri Doyen (1902–88) was a chorister in the *maîtrise* at Notre-Dame Cathedral, Paris, when Vierne was the organist. After being ordained a priest, he became organist and *maître de chapelle* at the cathedral in Soissons, where a neoclassic organ by Gonzalez was installed under his supervision in 1956. A composer as well (he wrote *Sicilienne* and *In paradisum* for organ), several of his compositions have been recorded. He also wrote a monograph titled *Les Orgues de la cathédrale de Soissons* (Soissons: Author, 1956).

21. Duruflé, "Interview with Duruflé [Baker]," 58.

22. Doyen, *Mes Leçons*, 45.

23. Ronzon, "Duruflé," 55. André Fleury wrote that Tournemire never played for vespers (except on big feast days), nor for weddings or funerals (André Fleury, "Entretien avec André Fleury," by Kurt Lueders, *Bulletin* 4 [June 2004]: 67. Originally published in *La Flûte harmonique* 63/64 [1992]: n.p.).

24. Duruflé, "Souvenirs [1976]," 28–29.

25. Duruflé continued substituting for Tournemire until at least 1929. On October 6 of that year, Tournemire wrote to the curé at Saint Étienne-du-Mont recommending Duruflé for the post that was vacant there, adding that Duruflé had been assisting him for ten years, and implying that he was still doing so (letter at the Archives Historiques de l'Archevêché de Paris: Saint Étienne-du-Mont; 2D Biens Mobiliers: Dossier sur les orgues de l'Église Saint Étienne-du-Mont et audition d'orgue). In a letter written on June 27, 1930, regarding a recital he would be playing at Sainte Clotilde, Lynnwood Farnam thanks Tournemire for giving him the name of his assistant, who was now Daniel-Lesur. It is likely that Duruflé's tenure as Tournemire's assistant ended about the time he took the post at Saint Étienne-du-Mont.

26. Duruflé, "Souvenirs [1976]," 30. For stoplist see Appendix C, p. 262.

27. Duruflé, "Interview with Duruflé [Baker, French]," 205.

28. Ibid., 31.

29. Duruflé, "My Recollections," 56.

30. Ann Labounsky, *Jean Langlais: The Man and His Music* (Portland, OR: Amadeus Press, 2002), 106.

31. Duruflé, "My Recollections," 55.

32. Georges Jacob (1877–1950) studied organ with Guilmant at the Conservatoire, and composition with Widor; he subsequently studied organ also with Vierne. He succeeded Joseph Bonnet as organist of the Société des Concerts du Conservatoire, a post which Duruflé would hold following Jacob's departure. Jacob was vice-president of the Union des maîtres-de-chapelle et organistes, an organization to which Duruflé would later belong. Jacob had an *orgue de salon* which he allowed Vierne to use for teaching until Vierne purchased one of his own in 1926. Vierne taught Henri Doyen at Jacob's residence, and probably also Duruflé. Note: in "Interview with Duruflé [Baker]," Baker incorrectly gives Jacob's first name as Jean (p. 58).

# Chapter Four

1. The address is recorded on Duruflé's military register dated about 1920 (photocopy provided to the author by Mlle Laurence Reibel).

2. The well-known piano teacher Marie Dhéré lived next door to Duruflé at 50, rue de Douai through the 1920s and 1930s (letter from Jean-Claude Ibert, the son of Jacques Ibert, to M. Wesley Roberts, quoted by Roberts in e-mail message to author, February 25, 2005). By a remarkable coincidence, Dhéré was giving lessons to the ten-year old Marie-Madeleine Chevalier, beginning in October 1931, when her family moved from Provence to advance her musical formation in Paris; this raises the possibility that her future husband was still living next door.

3. Boulanger could well have learned about Duruflé much earlier from her long-time assistant Annette Dieudonné, who was his fellow student in Gigout's organ class. Dieudonné taught harmony, counterpoint, solfège, and fugue to her students before they advanced to work with Boulanger herself.

4. Jérôme Spycket, *Nadia Boulanger* (Paris: Lattès, 1987), 84.

5. Éliane Chevalier, interview by author, Paris, January 21, 2001.

6. Duruflé, "Interview with Duruflé [Baker]," 57.

7. National Institute for Blind Youth, located at 56, boulevard des Invalides.

8. Rollin Smith, *Louis Vierne: Organist of Notre-Dame Cathedral* (Hillsdale, NY: Pendragon Press, 1999): 265.

9. Ibid., 660–61. Smith writes that Vierne moved to his new apartment in 1921, but 1920 seems more likely because Duruflé met Vierne in that apartment prior to entering the Conservatoire in October of 1920.

10. Doyen, *Mes Leçons*, 12.

11. Duruflé, "Interview with Duruflé [Baker]," 58. In the original French version of his interview of Maurice Duruflé, however, there is no mention of Duruflé's having taken lessons at Notre-Dame. Baker added the phrase "as well as to Notre-Dame" in his English translation. In any event, the organ at the cathedral was not practical as a teaching instrument until 1924, when it was equipped with an electric blower.

12. Duruflé, "Interview with Duruflé [Baker]," 60. Includes specification; see Appendix C, p. 265.

13. Duruflé, "Souvenirs [1976]," 31–32.

14. Marie-Louise Jaquet-Langlais, interview by author, Paris, January 24, 2001. Jaquet-Langlais was a former student and the second wife of Jean Langlais.

15. Duruflé, "Interview with Duruflé [Baker]," 58.

16. Ibid.

17. Duruflé, "Souvenirs [1976]," 32.

18. Doyen, *Mes Leçons*, 112.

19. Claude Rostand, "Le *Requiem* de Maurice Duruflé," *Revue internationale de musique* (Winter 1950): 267.

20. See William J. Peterson, "Lemmens, His *École d'orgue*, and Nineteenth-Century Organ Methods," in *French Organ Music from the Revolution to Franck and Widor*, ed. Lawrence Archbold and William J. Peterson (Rochester, NY: University of Rochester Press, 1995), 85.

21. Duruflé, "Souvenirs [1976]," 40.

22. Mes Leçons, 10; Doyen quotes Vierne.

23. Ibid., 41.

24. Program notes by Duruflé for the concert presented by former Vierne pupils at Notre-Dame Cathedral, April 7, 1970.

25. Doyen, *Mes Leçons*, 18.

26. Ibid., 17.

27. Ibid., 21.

28. Also known as the *Fantasia* in G Major, this work is more often referred to today in France by its French title, reflecting its French influence.

29. Doyen, *Mes Leçons*, 27.

30. Probably symphonies six through nine (Louis Vierne, "Mes Souvenirs," in Smith, *Vierne*, 105).

31. Of Widor's works, Henri Doyen studied only the Andante-cantabile from the Fourth Symphony with Vierne, and the Allegro from the Sixth Symphony (Henri Doyen, *Mes Leçons*, 78).

32. Duruflé, "Interview with Duruflé [Baker, French]," 206.

33. Duruflé, "Souvenirs [1976]," 40.

34. Abbé J. Muset-Ferrer, "Quelques Souvenirs sur Louis Vierne," in *In Memoriam Louis Vierne, 1870–1937: Souvenirs suivis d'un hommage à sa carrière, son enseignement, par ses confrères, élèves et amis* (Paris: Desclée de Brouwer, 1939), 139.

35. He visited once, intending to hear the monks sing, but because he was being escorted by a female friend wearing short sleeves, and whose arms were therefore bare, he was denied entrance.

36. Doyen, *Mes Leçons*, 92.

37. Vierne, "Mes Souvenirs," 195.

38. Ibid.

39. Maurice Duruflé, "Mes Souvenirs sur Tournemire et Vierne," *L'Orgue*, no. 162 (1977): 6.

40. Smith, *Vierne*, 291. Duruflé, in "Interview with Duruflé [Baker]," gives the same period, as does *L'Orgue*, no. 32 (December 1937): 9. But in "Interview with Duruflé [Baker, French]," 206, Duruflé says he started in 1927 and continued "to [Vierne's] death in 1937, it's possible." See also Duruflé, "Souvenirs [1976]," 38; and Duruflé, "Mes Souvenirs sur Tournemire et Vierne," 6. The Duruflé Association also gives 1927 (see also Duruflé, "Mémoires," 1).

41. Duruflé, "Souvenirs [1976]," 39–40.

42. Ibid., 40. For stoplist see Appendix C, p. 264.

43. Brigitte de Leersnyder, interview by author, Saint Paul, MN, July 30, 2003.

44. Jean Guérard, *Léonce de Saint-Martin à Notre-Dame de Paris, 1886–1954* (Paris: Éditions de l'officine, 2005), 64.

45. This date is at variance with other sources, as given above.

46. Ibid., 65.

47. Duruflé, "Interview with Duruflé [Baker]," 58.

48. Vierne, "Mes Souvenirs," 13.

# Chapter Five

1. Archives nationales, Conservatoire de musique, Aj37 532–34 and 537.

2. André Marchal (1894–1980), blind from birth, studied at the Institut des jeunes aveugles and was a pupil of Eugène Gigout at the Paris Conservatoire. He became Gigout's assistant at the Conservatoire and at Saint Augustin. Titular organist at Saint

Germain-des-Prés (1915–45) and at Saint Eustache (1945–63), he concertized extensively in Europe, England, the United States, and Australia. In 1930 he played most of Bach's organ works in ten recitals at the Cleveland Museum of Art. His influence as a teacher was paramount, as he taught at the American Academy in Fontainebleau, and he counted many distinguished organists among his former pupils.

3. Jacqueline Englert-Marchal, "André Marchal and His Contributions to the Neo-Classic Movement," *American Organist* 28 (February 1994): 56.

4. Duruflé's nine other classmates were Messieurs Le François, Eyzat, Stiegler, Fournier, and Mailbé, and Mlles Dieudonné, Mercier, Blanchot, and Renée-Madeleine Drouineau.

5. *The New Grove Dictionary of Music and Musicians*, 2nd ed., ed. Stanlie Sadie and John Tyrrell (London: Macmillan, 2001).

6. Fannie Edgar Thomas, *Organ Loft Whisperings: The Paris Correspondence of Fannie Edgar Thomas to "The Musical Courier," New York, 1893–1894*, ed. Agnes Armstrong (Altamont, NY: Sticut Tuum Productions, 2003), 92.

7. Norbert Dufourcq, "Eugène Gigout (1844–1925)," *L'Orgue: Cahiers et mémoires*, no. 27 (1982): 18.

8. Albert Schweitzer, "The Art of Organ Building and Organ Playing in Germany and France," in Charles R. Joy, *Music in the Life of Albert Schweitzer* (New York: Harper, 1951), 165–66; first published in *Deutsche und französische Orgelbaukunst und Orgelkunst* (Leipzig: Breitkopf und Härtel, 1906).

9. Ibid., *Schweitzer*, 169–70, quoting Schweitzer, "Organ Building."

10. Ibid., 171–72, quoting Schweitzer, "Organ Building."

11. Duruflé, "Souvenirs [1976]," 33. In 1994, Mark D. Bailey provided a different perspective: "Duruflé's comments about repertoire are intriguing considering the number of journal reports from 1885 to 1911 that praise Gigout's students for performing a wide body of literature on their recitals" ("Eugène Gigout and His 'Course for Organ, Improvisation, and Plainchant,'" *American Organist* 28 [March 1994]: 78). André Fleury said that "Gigout liked Mendelssohn very much" ("Entretien," 70).

12. Duruflé, "Interview with Duruflé [Baker]," 58.

13. André Fleury (1903–95), an exact contemporary of Duruflé, was *suppléant* to Eugène Gigout at Saint Augustin and to Charles Tournemire at Sainte Clotilde. He was named titular organist at Saint Augustin in 1930 and subsequently moved to Dijon, where he became a professor at the Conservatoire in 1949, and held the post at the cathedral there until 1971. Upon his return to Paris, he was named co-titular at Saint Eustache with Jean Guillou, but was also organist at Saint Louis Cathedral in Versailles and a professor of organ at the Schola Cantorum.

14. Rulon Christiansen, "Hommage à Louis Vierne: A Conversation with André Fleury," *American Organist* 21 (December 1987): 60.

15. Fleury, "Entretien," 70.

16. Duruflé, "Mes Souvenirs sur Tournemire et Vierne," 1.

17. Duruflé, "Souvenirs [1976]," 33.

18. Duruflé, "Mes Souvenirs sur Tournemire et Vierne," 5; Duruflé, "Interview with Duruflé [Baker]," 57.

19. Duruflé, "Interview with Duruflé [Baker]," 58.

20. Duruflé, "L'Orgue français de l'an 2000," *L'Orgue*, no. 160–61 (1976–77): 81–82.

21. The *premier accessit* is an award of merit, roughly equivalent to honorable mention. The awards, in ascending order of distinction, are the *2e accessit*, *1er accessit*, *2e prix*, and *1er prix*. The details concerning the examinations, competitions, and prizes are taken from two sources: *Annuaire officiel du Conservatoire national de musique et de déclamation:*

*Distribution des prix pour les cours d'études, 1920–1928*, and Archives nationales, Conservatoire de musique, série Aj37, nos. 189, 190, 303, 312, 2, and 532–34.

22. Duruflé, "Souvenirs [1976]," 34.

23. Gallon's daughter was married to the sculptor Léon Sévérac, who produced busts of Duruflé and of Mme Duruflé, which are pictured on the front and back covers of Ebrecht, *Duruflé*.

24. Duruflé, "Souvenirs [1976]," 34.

25. Ibid.

26. Olivier Messiaen received the *second prix*.

27. Duruflé, "Souvenirs [1976]," 35.

28. Félix Moreau made a cursory reference to Duruflé's having been a student of "the great fugist" André Gédalge (1856–1926), who taught counterpoint and fugue at the Conservatoire ("Maurice Duruflé, l'homme et le pédagogue," *Bulletin* 2 [June 2002]: 32). Moreau meant simply that Duruflé belonged to the school of Gédalge.

29. Duruflé, "Souvenirs [1976]," 35–36. Caussade was married to a former student of his, the composer and pianist Simone Plé.

30. In classes in piano accompaniment, students learned to play from figured bass, to improvise appropriate accompaniments for given melodies, to transpose at sight into a different key a score for piano and voice of a lyric work, to sight-read unpublished piano pieces, and to play at sight piano reductions from the open scores of orchestral works.

31. Duruflé, "Souvenirs [1976]," 35.

32. Ibid.

33. Olivier Messiaen won the *second prix*.

34. Messiaen won the *premier prix*.

35. *Ménestrel* 89 (September 30, 1927): 408.

36. Duruflé, "Interview with Duruflé [Baker, French]," 205. Frédéric Blanc and Éliane Chevalier were unaware that Duruflé had studied with Widor until the author told them so in January 2001.

37. *Annuaire officiel du Conservatoire national*, vols. 1925–26, 1926–27.

38. Andrew Thomson, *The Life and Times of Charles-Marie Widor, 1844–1937* (Oxford: Oxford University Press, 1987), 87.

39. Smith, *Vierne*, 66.

40. Thomson, *Widor*, 87. The author has seen no other reference to Ganay.

41. *Courrier musical et théâtral* 31 (February 1, 1929): 85.

42. Ibid. 29 (July 15–August 1, 1927).

43. Thomson, *Widor*, 52.

44. Ibid., 88.

45. Vierne, "Mes Souvenirs," 65.

46. Thomson, *Widor*, 55.

47. Vierne, "Mes Souvenirs," 113–14.

48. Henriette (Puig-)Roget (1910–92) entered the Paris Conservatoire when she was nine years old, winning six *premiers prix*. An organ student of Tournemire, she substituted for him at Sainte Clotilde. In 1934 she was named organist at the Oratoire du Louvre in Paris, remaining in the post until 1979. She also had a career as pianist with French radio from 1935 to 1979. Beginning in 1957 she taught piano accompaniment at the Paris Conservatoire. Roget played the organ for the radio premiere of Duruflé's *Requiem*.

49. Blind from birth, Gaston Litaize (1909–91) was a close friend of Duruflé. At the Paris Conservatoire, where he studied organ with Marcel Dupré, he won *premiers prix* in organ and improvisation, fugue, and composition. He was named organist at Notre-Dame de la

Croix de Ménilmontant in 1930, and in 1946 he was named organist at Saint François-Xavier in Paris.

50. This is not to be confused with the *Méditation* he composed around 1964.

51. "An exceptional work in any genre" composed by a young musician during the year (Léonie Rosenstiel, *The Life and Works of Lili Boulanger* [London: Associated University Presses, 1978], 85). When Lili Boulanger received the *Prix Lepaulle* in 1913, *Le Ménestrel* described it as "a particularly flattering award" (Rosenstiel, *Lili Boulanger*, 68).

52. John Richard Near, "The Life and Work of Charles-Marie Widor" (DMA diss., Boston University, 1985), 283.

53. Georges Favre, *Paul Dukas: Sa vie, son œuvre* (Paris: La Colombe, 1948), 37.

54. Duruflé, "Souvenirs [1976]," 35.

55. Ibid., 36.

56. There is no correspondence between Dukas and Duruflé among the Duruflé Papers (Éliane Chevalier, e-mail message to author, May 11, 2001).

57. Favre, *Paul Dukas*, 22, quoting Pierre Lalo's review of Dukas's *Symphonie* in *Le Temps*, 1902.

58. Denise Mayer and Pierre Souvtchinsky, eds., *Roger Désormière et son temps: Textes en hommage* (Monaco: Éditions du Rocher, 1966), 13.

59. Association Elisabeth et Joachim Havard de la Montagne, "Musica et Memoria," http://www.musimem.com/.

60. Georges Favre, *L'Œuvre de Paul Dukas* (Paris: Durand, 1969), 80, quoting an article of October 12, 1901.

61. Ibid., 81, quoting an article of May 28, 1892.

62. The words of Gustave Samazeuilh, quoted in Vincent d'Indy, *Emmanuel Chabrier et Paul Dukas: Conférence prononcé le 8 Avril 1920 aux Concerts historiques Pasdeloup*, foreword by Samazeuilh (Paris: Heugel, 1920), 14.

63. Duruflé, "Interview with Duruflé [Baker, French]," 204.

64. Ibid.

65. Abbing, *Duruflé*, 73, quoting *Olivier Messiaen: Meditationen über Musik*. Film documentary on the occasion of the eightieth birthday of Oliver Messiaen, shown on December 8, 1988 (ARD television network, Germany).

66. Duruflé, "Souvenirs [1976]," 36.

67. Ibid., 48.

68. This is probably the same *Scherzo* that Duruflé had written under Tournemire's guidance in 1926, a fact that is not surprising in view of Duruflé's penchant for revisiting earlier works. What is surprising, however, is that Duruflé submitted a two-year-old work for the examination.

69. Labounsky, *Langlais*, 93.

70. Published in Favre, *Œuvre de Dukas*.

71. After he completed his studies with Dukas, Duruflé would occasionally drop by the class to show his works to the students; see Kathleen Thomerson, *Jean Langlais: A Bio-Bibliography* (New York: Greenwood Press, 1988), 22, quoting Jean Langlais.

72. Ronzon, "Duruflé," 28. Herndon Spillman claims in his dissertation that Duruflé studied music history with Maurice Emmanuel ("The Organ Works of Maurice Duruflé," [DMus diss., Indiana University, 1976], 6). The author has seen no other reference to this.

73. Civil records from the Hôtel de Ville, Louviers. The marriage was announced in *L'Orgue*, no. 12 (December 1932).

74. Civil records from the Hôtel de Ville, Louviers.

75. Except where noted, all details regarding Lucette Bousquet are drawn from the following sources: correspondence from her son, Patrick Bousquet, to Paul Duruflé, February 26, 2002; Paul Duruflé, letters to author, March 14, 2002, April 19, 2002, and August 4, 2002; Patrick Bousquet to author, May 16, 2002; the civil records of Lucette Bousquet from the Hôtel de Ville, Louviers; and Dossier 1C in the marriage records from Saint Étienne-du-Mont, in the Archives historiques de l'Archevêché de Paris.

76. Frédéric Wurtz, e-mail message to author, June 11, 2002.

77. Ibid.; and Katia Labèque, e-mail message to author, November 25, 2003.

78. Bousquet's son Patrick reported to Paul Duruflé (letter of February 26, 2002) that she taught at the Paris Conservatoire, but Bousquet's name appears nowhere on rosters of the piano faculty, as, for example, in Emmanuel Hondré, ed., *Le Conservatoire de musique de Paris: Regards sur une institution et son histoire* ([Paris]: Association du Bureau des étudiants du Conservatoire national supérieur de musique de Paris, 1995). Nor are there references to her at the BnF, or in the Paris Conservatoire documents, Aj37, housed at the Archives nationales. She may have served as *suppléant* to someone who was on the faculty.

79. Maurice Duruflé to Nadia Boulanger, December 22, 1938 (BnF NLa 68, letter 199). It has yet to be determined when the couple began a formal separation.

80. André Levasseur, who studied organ and harmony with Duruflé between 1945 and 1947, recounted, however, that Duruflé was living alone at the time (Levasseur, interview).

81. Jean Langlais knew Duruflé's first wife well (Jaquet-Langlais, interview). Mme Jaquet-Langlais surmised that Bousquet might still be alive. Indeed, she was still alive, and was still teaching piano until she suffered a cerebral hemorrhage only a few years earlier.

82. Civil records for Maurice Duruflé and Lucette Bousquet in the Hôtel de Ville, Louviers.

83. Dossier 1C in the marriage records from Saint Étienne-du-Mont, Archives historiques de l'Archevêché de Paris. The longstanding rumor that Bousquet was a bigamist appears unfounded, and the official grounds for the annulment by the church, as stipulated on the ecclesiastical decree, do not include bigamy. Paul Duruflé called the rumor "absolutely unlikely" (Paul Duruflé to author, August 2, 2002).

84. Whether or not Lucette was ever known as Mme Duruflé, after the divorce she used her family name. It was as Lucette Bousquet that she was known by the Duruflé family and by her students, some of whom, at least, did not know she was ever married to Maurice Duruflé. It is curious that her son Patrick used his mother's surname instead of his father's.

85. When the exposition on Duruflé was mounted at the Hôtel de Ville in Louviers, in 2002, Frédéric Blanc, then president of the Duruflé Association, refused to allow the posting of photographs of Bousquet.

# Chapter Six

1. Duruflé, "Souvenirs [1976]," 38.

2. For stoplist see Appendix C, p. 266.

3. In his memoirs Duruflé gave a somewhat different repertoire list and wrote that the pieces had to be played from memory (ibid.). But on November 1, 1928, *Le Courrier musical et théâtral* announced that performance from memory would not be required (vol. 30, p. 630).

4. Ronzon, "Duruflé," 30.

5. D'Indy substituted for Widor, who was ill ("La Vie de l'orgue en France, 1928–1929," *Bulletin Semestriel des Amis de l'Orgue*, no. 1 [June 1929]: 3).

6. "Les Amis de l'Orgue," *Revue liturgique et musicale* (1928): 40.

7. Vierne, "Mes Souvenirs," 193.

8. Joseph Ermend-Bonnal, *Suite pyrénéenne*, published by Lemoine.

9. Letter, Tournemire to Ermend-Bonnal, June 12, 1930 (BnF NLa 122 [5]).

10. Duruflé, "Soixante Années au service de l'orgue," *L'Orgue*, no. 201–4 (1987): 46. A renowned musicologist, Dufourcq was one of the founders of Les Amis de l'Orgue, and at the time of his death in 1990 had been organist at Saint Merry for sixty-seven years.

11. P. M., "Prix des 'Amis de l'Orgue,'" *Ménestrel* 92 (June 27, 1930): 297.

12. Pierre Denis, ed. "Concours des Amis de l'Orgue, 1927–1987," *L'Orgue*, no. 201–4 (1987): 58; Smith, *Vierne*, 671.

13. The jury's autographed manuscript designating Duruflé as laureate was reproduced in *L'Orgue*, no. 201–4 (1987): 56–57.

14. Jesse Eschbach, "In Memoriam Maurice Duruflé, 1902–1986," *American Organist* 21 (July 1987): 46n, quoting Éliane Chevalier.

15. "Le Prix Blumenthal," *Courrier musical et théâtral* 24 (October 1, 1922): 286.

16. Eschbach, "In Memoriam Maurice Duruflé," 44.

17. Armand Machabey, "Galerie de quelques jeunes musiciens parisiens: Maurice Duruflé," *L'Information musicale* (December 4, 1942): n.p.; and Armand Machabey, *Portraits de trente musiciens français* (Paris: Richard-Masse, 1949), 70.

18. *Revue musicale* 17 (July–August 1936). Daniel Roth conjectured that the award was for Duruflé's 1935 performance of Vierne's Sixth Symphony (interview by author, Paris, January 19, 2001).

19. In her handwritten additions to Claude Chamfray, "Chronology of Maurice Duruflé," *Courrier musical de France* 29 (1st trimester 1970): 51, Mme Duruflé gave 1956 as the date (in collection of the author).

20. Ibid.

21. M. G., "Discographie," *Musique et Liturgie* 72 (November–December 1959): 16.

22. Norbert Dufourcq, "Les Disques d'orgue," *L'Orgue*, no. 105 (January–March 1963): 37; the recording is Erato–Jardin des Arts EJA 13.

23. "Onorificenze," *Acta Apostolicae Sedis* 54 (February 28, 1962): 123.

24. Hyginus Eugene Cardinale, *Orders of Knighthood, Awards and the Holy See*, ed. Peter Bander van Duren (Gerrards Cross, England: Van Duren Publishers, 1984), 54; and James Van der Veldt, *The Ecclesiastical Orders of Knighthood* (Washington, DC: Catholic University of America Press, 1956), 50–51.

25. Duruflé to Nadia Boulanger, BnF NLa 68, letter 201, December 11, 1947; NLa 68, letter 205, July 13, 1957; NLa 68, letter 207, December 18, 1961.

26. Chamfray, "Chronology," 51.

# Chapter Seven

1. A former organ student of Gigout, the pianist Alexandre Georges directed the *maîtrise* at Sainte Clotilde from 1877, when César Franck was titular organist there.

2. Vierne to the Archbishop of Paris, March 3, 1929 (Archives de Notre-Dame de Paris), quoted in Abbing, *Duruflé*, 78. Rollin Smith relates that the letter was written with regard to a position at Saint Pierre-du-Gros-Caillou (*Vierne*, 669).

3. More will be said about this appointment in the chapter on the musical history of Saint Étienne-du-Mont.

4. Smith, *Vierne*, 428. See a complete account of Vierne's death and the succession in Béranger de Miramon Fitz-James, "Sur la Mort et la succession de Louis Vierne," in *In Memoriam Louis Vierne*, 216–21.

5. Smith, *Vierne*, 290–91. Saint-Martin had previously been organist at Théâtre-Cinéma des Champs-Élysées (see *Le Courrier musical et théâtral* 32 [March 1, 1930]).

6. Smith, *Vierne*, 428.

7. Duruflé's pulling stops for Vierne was what they called "la cuisine" (Duruflé, "Interview with Duruflé [Baker]," 58).

8. Smith, *Vierne*, 421.

9. Duruflé, "Souvenirs [1976]," 41.

10. *SAE*, 66, quoting Duruflé, "Louis Vierne," *Bulletin trimestriel de l'Union des maîtres-de-chapelle et organistes* 24 (October 1937).

11. Labounsky, *Langlais*, 103.

12. This and subsequent details regarding Madeleine Richepin were provided by Allen Hobbs, telephone conversation with author, November 30, 2000; and by Éliane Chevalier and Frédéric Blanc, interviews by author, Paris, January 18, 2001.

13. Madeleine Richepin died on June 10, 1962 (Hobbs, telephone conversation with author, February 19, 2001).

14. Foreword by Allen Hobbs, in Smith, *Vierne*, xix.

15. "Les Candidats à la succession de Louis Vierne," *L'Orgue*, no. 32 (December 1937): 9–10. Mme Jaquet-Langlais maintained that Langlais and Litaize agreed that Duruflé should get the position, and consented to a competition with the intention of withdrawing their names (Jaquet-Langlais, interview). Olivier Latry, an organist at Notre-Dame, Paris, said that Vierne had recommended Duruflé to the clergy (Latry, interview, Paris, January 23, 2001). Duruflé's nephew, Paul, wrote that "a prominent figure came 'to advise my uncle not to apply for the succession'—Léonce de Saint-Martin had more support than competence, by virtue of his fortune, it appears" (letter to author, May 29, 2002). In "Entretien avec François-Henri Houbart," *L'Orgue: Cahiers et mémoires*, no. 34 (1985): 6, Gaston Litaize asked Houbart about Vierne. Houbart said that "after his funeral, on the advice of Bérenger de Miramon, we had, Langlais and I, sent our application to the archpriest with the intention of justifying the competition, waiting to withdraw it at the last moment to leave the field free to Maurice Duruflé, knowing the secret desire of Vierne to see this great artist succeed him."

16. Les Amis de Léonce de Saint-Martin gave June 14 as the date of his nomination by the chapter (*Bulletin de l'Association des Amis de Léonce de Saint-Martin* 16–17 [June 1978]: 20).

17. Smith, *Vierne*, 432.

18. Robert Bernard, "Louis Vierne," *Revue musicale* 18 (October 1937): 287–88.

19. Some sources incorrectly cite November 4 as the date of his death. His body was discovered on the fourth and the coroner's report indicated he had been dead for twenty-four hours (Weidner, "Tournemire," 7, quoting *Grove's Dictionary of Music and Musicians*, 5th ed., s.v. "Charles Tournemire," by Gustave Ferrari).

20. Labounsky, *Langlais*, 104, quoting Langlais, "Charles Tournemire," trans. Labounsky, *Bulletin de Sainte Clotilde* (1949).

21. Labounsky, *Langlais*, 106.

22. Marie-Louise Jaquet-Langlais, *Ombre et lumière: Jean Langlais 1907–1991* (Paris: Éditions Combre, 1995), 118–20.

23. After Ermend-Bonnal's death, in 1944, Langlais was again the only candidate for the post, to which he was appointed by the archbishop and the curé, without a competition (Labounsky, *Langlais*, 108).

24. Albert Bertelin, article in *La Petite Maîtrise*, April 1939; repr. in *Bulletin de l'Association des Amis de Léonce de Saint-Martin* 16–17 (June 1978): 24–26.

25. Vierne himself had substituted for Sargent beginning in February of 1900, some two months before the latter's death (See Vierne's "Mes Souvenirs," 219, 221).

26. In his memoirs, Louis Vierne wrote that there were ninety-eight candidates, of whom about ten made the short list, and that because of the intrigues to which the clergy of Notre-Dame were being subjected by "certain applicants," a competition would be necessary. Besides Vierne, five contestants were heard by the jury (see ibid., 219–20).

27. Bertelin was mistaken. Vierne himself served on the jury that named Henri Lambert to the post at the basilica of Saint Denis, on July 28, 1896, and on the jury that named Joseph Bonnet to the post at Saint Eustache, on March 23, 1906. See Smith, *Vierne*, 112, 148.

28. The directive appeared first in *Semaine religieuse*, April 17, 1943, and was reprinted in *L'Orgue*, no. 42 (January–March 1947).

# Chapter Eight

1. André Fleury et al., "Souvenirs," in "Charles Tournemire (1870–1939)," *L'Orgue: Cahiers et mémoires*, no. 41 (1989-I): 16.

2. The two premieres were thus identified in the review, but the Molto adagio is actually the Offertoire from the Suite for Christmas, dated December 13, 1927, which is numbered 3, not 35. The same error is found in Joël-Marie Fauquet, *Catalogue de l'œuvre de Charles Tournemire* (Geneva: Minkoff, 1979), 41.

3. *Courrier musical et théâtral* 30 (May 15, 1928): 368.

4. See J. Stan, "Un Concert à la Cathédrale," *L'Éclaireur de Nice et du sud-est*, March 5, 1931.

5. "Échos et nouvelles," *Ménestrel* 94 (Dec 9, 1932): 508.

6. "Échos et nouvelles," *Ménestrel* 95 (Dec 8, 1933): 484.

7. "Programme établi par Charles Tournemire (Document aimablement communiqué par Daniel Lesur)," handwritten note, *L'Orgue*, no. 201–4 (1987): 28–29; Fleury, "Souvenirs," 12; Labounsky, *Langlais*, 78.

8. M. P., "*L'Orgue mystique*," *Ménestrel* 94 (May 6, 1932): 202.

9. Norbert Dufourcq, in "Soixante Années au service de l'orgue," *L'Orgue*, no. 201–4 (1987): 19; Dufourcq gives the date as 1931 instead of 1930.

10. Smith, *Vierne*, 671. Smith also reports that on January 23, 1930, Duruflé and Madeleine Richepin performed the premiere of Vierne's *Quatre poèmes grecs*, Op. 60, composed in 1930 for voice and piano (ibid., 670). The author has found no other evidence that Duruflé played for this recital. Vierne accompanied Richepin for a performance of the work for the Société nationale de musique, on January 23, 1932 (see *Le Courrier musical et théâtral* 34 [February 15, 1932]: 101).

11. "L'Association des Amis de l'Orgue: Son activité, son diffusion, 1937–1957," *L'Orgue*, no. 83 (April–September 1957): 1.

12. "Concerts données par Les Amis de l'Orgue," *L'Orgue*, no. 160–61 (October 1976–March 1977): 14–17.

13. Including the competitions in 1935, 1936, 1939, 1953, 1957, 1963, and 1965 (see Pierre Denis, "Concours," 59, 60, 62).

14. Audition de M. Louis Vierne avec le concours de M. Maurice Duruflé [recital program], Notre-Dame, Paris, June 3, 1935, reprinted in *L'Orgue*, no. 47 (1992-I): 73–75. Bernard Gavoty gives 1934 in *Louis Vierne: La vie et l'œuvre* (Paris: Buchet/Chastel, 1980), 315, an error found in other sources as well. See, for example, Smith, *Vierne*, 719 and 567. On p. 719 Smith incorrectly gives the date of Duruflé's premiere as 1934; it appears correctly as 1935 on p. 567.

15. Smith, *Vierne*, 295, quoting Vierne "Mes Souvenirs."

16. Lynnwood Farnam was organist at the Episcopal Church of the Holy Communion in New York City, and was highly regarded among French organists. He championed their music and "was the first to record Vierne's organ music in any medium" (Smith, *Vierne*, 565).

17. Roquebrune is near Menton, the easternmost town on France's Mediterranean coast (the Côte d'Azur).

18. Gavoty, *Vierne*, 153.

19. *SAE*, 67, quoting Duruflé, "Louis Vierne."

20. See Smith, *Vierne*, 566–67. Weinrich was a student of Farnam at the Curtis Institute.

21. *Courrier musical et théâtral* 34 (May 15, 1932): 301.

22. Ibid. 34 (December 1, 1932): 441.

23. Duruflé assisted Rollin Smith on a project for *The American Organist* to publish a final compilation of textual corrections for Vierne's six symphonies (Smith, *Vierne*, 719, 721).

24. Duruflé to Smith, July 3, 1970, quoted in ibid., 567.

25. Duruflé, "Interview with Duruflé [Baker]," 58.

26. A. F., "Organ Recital Notes," *Musical Times* 90 (October 1949): 356. The reviewer wrote that Duruflé's performance of "Dupré's 'Cortège et Litanie' . . . reminded us of the days when [Dupré] first came to England, when we thought we had found a new master, little dreaming that his output would degenerate into a series of steely machines each more mechanical than the other."

27. Pierre Denis, "L'Activité des Amis de l'Orgue: Saison 1963–1964," *L'Orgue*, no. 112 (October–December 1964): 108.

28. Kamiel d'Hooghe, "Flor Peeters: 4 juillet 1903–4 juillet 1986," *L'Orgue*, no. 207 (July–September 1988): 15.

29. Lilian Murtagh to Duruflé, June 17, 1963. As it turned out, he did not serve on the jury.

30. *SAE*, 252–53.

31. Duruflé, "L'Orgue de Deauville," *L'Orgue* no. 82 (1957): 16–17.

32. Duruflé, "La Restauration du grand orgue de la cathédrale d'Angoulême," *L'Orgue*, no. 119 (1966): 107.

33. Paul Duruflé to author, March 14, 2002; and Éliane Chevalier, e-mail message. The PTT was the postal and telecommunications service of France, for which Duruflé played recitals as early as 1936.

34. Information provided by Olivier Soularue for the Duruflé exposition in Louviers (2002).

35. Paul Duruflé to author, March 14, 2002.

36. Robert O. Paxton, *Vichy France: Old Guard and New Order, 1940–1944* (New York: Alfred A. Knopf, 1972), 348.

37. Paul Duruflé to author, August 4, 2002.

38. According to Paul Duruflé, Léonce de Saint-Martin had been labeled a collaborator (Paul Duruflé to author, April 19, 2002 and May 29, 2002).

39. Paul Duruflé to author, April 19, 2002. Saint-Martin remained in the cathedral post until his death in 1954.

40. Antony Beevor and Artemis Cooper, *Paris After the Liberation, 1944–1949* (New York: Penguin Putnam, 1994), 62–63. Accounts of this astonishing event differ, and the truth is difficult to assess. Paul Duruflé's version is one often told, namely, that the armed men opened fire over the crowd in the cathedral with blanks, causing no damage to the stonework. M. Duruflé conjectures that it was less an assassination attempt than an attempt to sow panic among the crowd. Access to the organ tribune is now by way of the south tower; in those years the organist used the steps in the north tower.

41. Paul Duruflé to author, March 14, 2002.

42. Duruflé lost his mother on December 13, 1950 (Éliane Chevalier, interview).

43. Duruflé uses this description of his cold apartment.

44. Duruflé to André Fleury, probably 1945, reprinted in *SAE*, 78.

45. The following account of Duruflé's association with Janine Solane is taken from Solane, [Hommage à Maurice Duruflé], *Bulletin* 2 (June 2002): 35–36.

46. By Joseph Noyon.

47. It is not known whether this is from BWV Anh. 78, or BWV 431, 432, or 641.

48. In 1938 he accompanied the ensemble on tours to Berlin and Spain (BnF NLa 37, Letter 298; and Norbert Dufourcq, "Panorama de la musique d'orgue française au XXe siècle," [part 3], *Revue musicale* 20 [August–November 1939]: 107–8).

# Chapter Nine

1. This and the immediately following orchestral engagements are listed in *SAE*, 249–51.

2. The facts of these performances are given in *SAE*, 248–49.

3. Columbia FCX 336.

4. Chamfray, "Chronology," 51, and Machabey, *Portraits*, 70.

5. The Société did not record any of Duruflé's works. The orchestra was dissolved in 1967 to be succeeded by the Orchestre de Paris.

6. This and the following information about Société concerts that involved the organ are taken from D. Kern Holoman, "The Société des Concerts du Conservatoire (1828–1967)," http://hector.ucdavis.edu/sdc/.

7. The Société des Concerts recorded this piece with the Chorale Yvonne Gouverné, under director Charles Münch, for which Duruflé may have been the organist (Voix de son maître DB 5135/7 and FJLP 5026).

8. In 1901 Florent Schmitt (1870–1958) was named the first titular organist at the church of Saint Lambert-de-Vaugirard, where he remained for twenty years. He was a member of Société musicale indépendante from its founding in 1909. A renowned music critic, especially for the journal *Le Temps* (1919–39), he was director of the Conservatoire in Lyons from 1922–24, where he also taught harmony.

9. Michel Duchesneau, *L'Avant-Garde musicale et ses sociétés à Paris de 1871 à 1939* (Liège: Mardaga, 1997), 334.

10. Duruflé, "Souvenirs [1976]," 49.

11. "Questionnaire envoyé en 1936 par Bérenger de Miramon à des jeunes organistes français," *L'Orgue*, no. 201–4 (1987): 24.

12. Duruflé, "L'Orgue" (1941, unpublished?), reprinted in *SAE*, 77.

# Chapter Ten

1. Andrew Thomson, "Pure Invention," *Choir and Organ* 10 (July–August 2002): 50.

2. Ravel dedicated his *Pavane pour une infante défunte* to Princess Polignac.

3. Gigout occasionally performed for the musicales the princess hosted in the music room of her mansion (Thomas, *Whisperings*, 67).

4. He was also a poet, a composer, and a member of the *comité* of the Schola Cantorum. He died in 1901.

5. For an account of the commission for the organ concerto, see Jeanice Brooks, "Nadia Boulanger and the Salon of the Princesse de Polignac," *Journal of the American Musicological Society* 46 (Fall 1993): 454–64.

6. Carl B. Schmidt, *The Music of Francis Poulenc: A Catalogue* (Oxford: Clarendon Press, 1995), 281.

7. According to Brooks ("Boulanger," 457), the story was more complex than Françaix recounted. He actually began writing an organ suite for the princess at the same time Poulenc accepted the commission for the concerto. On October 6, 1934, Polignac wrote to Boulanger, "Will the works of Jean Françaix and of Poulenc be for organ and small orchestra, as I hope, with an organ part that isn't too difficult? I know nothing about it— I'm delighted that Françaix has agreed to write something for me" (translation by Brooks). In November, the princess wrote to Boulanger, telling her that Françaix had finished the first movement of his organ suite.

8. Another version of the story is that the idea originated with Poulenc himself. In a series of radio interviews with Claude Rostand, between October 1953 and April 1954, Poulenc said, "It is I who proposed writing an organ concerto to Princess Edmond de Polignac" (Poulenc, *Entretiens avec Claude Rostand* [Paris: René Julliard, 1954], 115). Poulenc noted that some of these "commissions" were more in the manner of long-term suggestions, his patrons leaving him "completely free as to the choice of subject, form, the duration of the work, etc."

Poulenc considered writing for the organ long before he composed the concerto. In the spring of 1923 he wrote to Comte Étienne de Beaumont, saying that he intended to write an organ sonata that summer for Beaumont's wife. Apparently nothing ever came of this work.

9. Francis Poulenc, *Correspondance, 1910–1963*, ed. Myriam Chimènes (Paris: Fayard, 1998), 397.

10. Ibid., 398.

11. Ibid., 247. According to the usual terms of the princess's commissions, the composer was free to sell the piece to a publisher (Brooks, "Boulanger," 454).

12. Benjamin Ivry, *Maurice Ravel: A Life* (New York: Welcome Rain Publishers, 2000), 110.

13. Poulenc drew from the concerto in composing his opera *Les Dialogues des Carmélites*, in which the first prioress's theme is "an agitated melody from the Organ Concerto" (Benjamin Ivry, *Francis Poulenc* [London: Phaidon Press, 1996], 179).

14. Poulenc, *Correspondance*, 414.

15. Archives Poulenc, quoted in Poulenc, *Correspondance*, 417.

16. Ibid., 419.

17. Poulenc is referring to his choral work for treble voices and organ, *Litanies à la Vierge noire*.

18. Ibid., 428.

19. Ibid., 434.

20. Kahan, *Polignac*, 346, quoting a letter from Françaix to Boulanger, December 6, 1937 (BnF NLa 71:111).

21. Poulenc, *Correspondance*, 462–63.

22. Ibid., 463–64.

23. The princess had renounced the role of organ soloist.

24. From a private collection, quoted in Poulenc, *Correspondance*, 463.

25. Kahan, *Polignac*, 351.

26. Poulenc, *Correspondance*, 466. Sylvia Kahan reports the existence of a manuscript of the concerto "in a different family archive," whose location she would not disclose. The score contains no registration indications or pencil markings of any sort. "My best guess is that all decisions about registration were made by Nadia Boulanger, and that these decisions were made after Poulenc had already given the ms. to [Polignac]" (Kahan, e-mail message to author, December 13, 2001).

27. Brooks, "Boulanger," 463, referring to a letter of Lewis to Boulanger, July 5, 1938 (BBC Written Archives Centre, Nadia Boulanger Artist File I). According to the usual terms of a commission by the princess, a new work could not be performed anywhere for six months after the salon premiere without the permission of the princess; Brooks, "Boulanger," 454, quoting a letter from Polignac to Markevitch, February 7, 1931.

28. Poulenc, *Correspondance*, 472.

29. "The Hôtel Singer-Polignac contains a sumptuous mirrored music room, the grand salon, which seats approximately two hundred. . . . In addition, there was a second music room, called the 'atelier' because the princess used it for painting; it belonged to an already existing structure that she had owned since the early 1890s. When the hôtel was built, the house containing the atelier was annexed onto it, retaining, however, its separate entry on a side street. Somewhat smaller than the salon, the atelier contained two pianos and an organ by Cavaillé-Coll; it was used for smaller-scale performances as well as for concerts that required the organ" (Brooks, "Boulanger," 422).

30. For the stoplist, see Appendix C, p. 267. The Princess de Polignac bequeathed the organ to her nephew, Comte Jean de Polignac. After his death, his widow, Marie-Blanc de Polignac, gave the organ in 1952 to the Maison diocésaine d'accueil in merville, in the north of France (Marie-Odile Andrade, of the Fondation Singer-Polignac, e-mail message to author, September 2, 2003).

31. The fees Polignac paid to her performers were low compared with those paid by concert halls (Brooks, "Boulanger," 432). On December 22, Duruflé wrote to Boulanger acknowledging receipt of the check she had sent him for 1000 francs (BnF NLa 68. Letter 198). In a postscript to this letter, Duruflé tells Boulanger of his new address: 6 place du Panthéon, in the fifth arrondissement. This is the earliest of the eighteen letters (nos. 198–215) written by Duruflé to Boulanger that are contained in the Boulanger correspondence at the BnF.

32. By this time, *Le Figaro* was more interested in the cinema than in salon concerts (Kahan, e-mail message).

33. December 1938.

34. Schmidt, *Poulenc*, 281, quoting the special number of *Revue musicale* 19 (December 1938), entitled *Hommage à Maurice Ravel*, iv.

35. Kahan, e-mail message.

36. Ibid. There were notable exceptions, including Vladimir Horowitz, Arthur Rubinstein, and Clara Haskil, as Kahan points out (e-mail message).

37. Ibid.

38. It would also be interesting to know whether Boulanger or the princess heard the premiere of *Trois Danses*, or subsequent performances of it.

39. Maurice Duruflé, "Poulenc's *Organ Concerto*," trans. Rollin Smith, *Music* 8 [July 1974]: 22; and idem, "*Le Concerto pour orgue et orchestre à cordes de Francis Poulenc*," *L'Orgue*, no. 154 (1975): 40. The tubular pneumatic organ of thirty-six stops and two enclosed divisions had a faulty wind supply and its pipes did not speak properly into the hall (Michael Murray, *Marcel Dupré: The Work of a Master Organist* [Boston: Northeastern University Press, 1985], 56).

40. BnF NLa 37. Letter 297, reprinted in *SAE*, 68.

41. Sylvia Kahan indicates erroneously that Marcel Dupré was the organist (Kahan, *Polignac*, 353).

42. Duruflé, "Poulenc's *Organ Concerto*," 22; and idem, "*Concerto pour orgue*," 40. Reviews appeared in the journals *Le Guide du concert*, *Le Ménestrel*, and *Le Monde musical*.

43. Dufourcq, "Panorama de la musique d'orgue française," 107–8.

44. Harry Halbreich, "Concerto pour orgue, orchestre à cordes et timbales," Disque Erato (1970), reprinted in *Bulletin* 4 (June 2004): 30.

45. Poulenc, *Correspondance*, 475.

46. Ibid.

47. Poulenc, *Entretiens*, 115.

48. Duruflé, "*Organ Concerto*," 22, and idem, "*Concerto pour orgue*," 40.

49. Abbing, *Duruflé*, 96.

50. Duruflé, "*Organ Concerto*," 22.

51. This meeting at Saint Étienne-du-Mont apparently took place at the ailing organ, before its dismantling in April 1939.

52. Ivry, *Poulenc*, 110.

53. Duruflé, "*Organ Concerto*," 22; and idem, "*Concerto pour orgue*," 40.

54. BnF NLa 37. Letter 298.

55. Duruflé owned two copies of the organ score (Éditions R. Deiss, 1939). Frédéric Blanc published the "Notes pour l'interprétation du Concerto pour orgue d'après les exemplaires personnels de Maurice Duruflé, à partir des annotations de Francis Poulenc et de Maurice Duruflé," in *Bulletin* 4 (June 2004): 45–47. The annotations, by Poulenc and Duruflé alike, include dynamic markings, tempo markings, registration indications, swell shade indications, legato phrasings, and keyboard indications.

56. French Radio recorded a performance of the work by the ORTF on March 21, 1960, with Pierre Michel Le Conte conducting and Duruflé as organ soloist (*Bulletin* 4 [June 2004]: 44).

57. Poulenc, *Correspondance*, 975. Henri Hell wrote the liner notes for the recording.

58. Ibid., 977.

59. Duruflé, "*Organ Concerto*," 22; and idem, "*Concerto pour orgue*," 40. Other sources, including Myriam Chimènes, indicate that Poulenc was present for the recording (see Poulenc, *Correspondance*, 976).

60. Angel S35953.

61. Marie-Madeleine Duruflé-Chevalier, "Entretien avec Marie-Madeleine Duruflé," by Frédéric Denis, *Bulletin* 3 (June 2003): 14. Originally printed in *Organ: Journal für die Orgel* 2 (April 7, 1999). Also available at http://www.multimania.com/frdenis/durufle.html.

62. Letter probably from the Duruflé Papers. It is reprinted in *Bulletin* 4 (June 2004): 39.

63. Hell, *Poulenc*, 154–55.

64. The British premiere was conducted in 1944 by Horace Hawkins, organist of Chichester Cathedral (Thomson, *Widor*, 69).

65. Allen Hughes, "A Tribute to Francis Poulenc," *Music* 8 (July 1974): 20.

# Chapter Eleven

1. Duruflé and Marcel Dupré shared a recital at Saint Étienne in Caen in 1944 (*SAE*, 253).

2. Duruflé, "Souvenirs [1976]," 45–46.

3. Marie-Claire Alain, "Hommages," *Bulletin* 2 (June 2002): 9.

4. Marie-Claire Alain, "Introduction: Maurice Duruflé," trans. Ebrecht in his *Duruflé*, xiv.

5. Marie-Claire Alain, "Entretien avec Marie-Claire Alain, Le Pecq, décembre 2003," ed. Frédéric Blanc, *Bulletin* 4 (June 2004): 4.

6. Suzanne Chaisemartin, interview by author, Paris, January 19, 2001.

7. Minutes of the 184th meeting of the Conseil supérieur de l'enseignement, April 9, 1937, in Archives nationales, cote Aj37, carton 520, dossier 1c; and minutes of the 186th meeting of the same body, on October 12, 1937, Archives nationales, cote Aj37, carton 480, dossier 6c (quoted in Ronzon, "Duruflé," 54).

8. The class in question was established in 1798, the second oldest of the several classes in harmony.

9. Duruflé, "Souvenirs [1976]," 46.

10. Ronzon, "Duruflé," 61.

11. Mme Duruflé, conversation with Rodger Vine, Boston, June 1990, reported by Vine, e-mail message to author, March 4, 2005.

12. Ronzon, "Duruflé," 38.

13. Abbing, *Duruflé*, 402–3, quoting Jean Guillou.

14. Quoted in Pierre Pincemaille, "Maurice Duruflé," liner notes for Pincemaille's CD recording *Maurice Duruflé: Intégrale de l'œuvre pour orgue*, Beuel Motette 12541.

15. Ronzon, "Duruflé," 75.

16. Ibid., 71.

17. Duruflé, "Souvenirs [1976]," 46–47.

18. Ibid., 40–44.

19. Henri Bert, [Hommage], *Bulletin* 2 (June 2002): 11.

20. Ronzon, "Duruflé," 71.

21. Marie-Claire Alain studied harmony, organ performance, and improvisation with Duruflé from 1944 to 1950.

22. Alain, "Entretien," 3.

23. Roth to Abbing, August 7, 1992, quoted in Abbing, *Duruflé*, 113–14.

24. Ronzon names ninety-six students, but the actual number is slightly larger than that because documents for the two academic years 1947–49 are not available. Marie-Madeleine Chevalier was never a member of his harmony class.

25. Duruflé-Chevalier, "Entretien," 11.

26. Ibid.

27. Duruflé, letter to the director of the Conservatoire, Claude Delvincourt, dated July 6, 1951, Archives nationales, cote Aj37, carton 488, dossier 5, quoted in Ronzon, "Duruflé," 66.

28. The women were tested separately from the men in those years.

29. Ronzon, "Duruflé," 67.

30. Duruflé, "Réflexions sur la musique liturgique," *L'Orgue*, no. 174 (April–June 1980): 3–4.

31. Ronzon, "Duruflé," Annexe no. 1, Tableaux nos. 1–3, pp. 99–111.

32. Duruflé to Murtagh, May 11, 1970.

## Chapter Twelve

1. Except where noted, the following account of the life of Marie-Madeleine Chevalier is gleaned from the following sources: Duruflé-Chevalier, "Entretien"; Marie-Madeleine Duruflé-Chevalier, "Les Organistes français d'aujourd'hui: Marie-Madeleine Chevalier-Duruflé"; Pierre Denis, "Les Organistes français d'aujourd'hui: Marie-Madeleine Chevalier-Duruflé," *Bulletin* 3 (June 2003): 3–5, first published in *L'Orgue*, no. 90 (April–June 1959): 33–37; Éliane Chevalier, "Marie-Madeleine Chevalier-Duruflé," *Bulletin* 3 (June 2003): 15–22, which appears in a free English translation by Ronald Ebrecht, in Ebrecht, *Duruflé*, 181–93; Éliane Chevalier, interview by author; Éliane Chevalier to author, May 11, 2001; Éliane Chevalier, "Extraits des souvenirs familiers d'Éliane Chevalier," *Bulletin de l'Association des Amis de l'art de Marcel Dupré* 19 (Spring 2001), also available at http://www.adevnet.fr/mdupre/bull19-2.htm, and reprinted as "Marie-Madeleine Chevalier-Duruflé et Marcel Dupré," in *Bulletin* 3 (June 2003): 15–22; Éliane Chevalier, liner notes for *Marie-Madeleine Duruflé Memorial* compact disc (Festivo 6941 772), recorded live, Saint-Eustache, Paris, July 1, 1993.

2. Dhéré was the first piano teacher of Jacques Ibert (1890–1962).

3. Éliane Chevalier, "Chevalier-Duruflé," 16. The future proved otherwise.

4. For the stoplist, see Appendix C, p. 259.

5. Including Franck's *L'Organiste* and works of Handel, Daquin, and Couperin.

6. Duruflé-Chevalier, "Chevalier-Duruflé," 33–34.

7. Ibid., 34.

8. Éliane Chevalier, "Chevalier-Duruflé et Dupré," 22.

9. Dupré made a note for himself concerning his interview with Marie-Madeleine. "Audition with the little Marie-Madeleine Chevalier who came from her Provence: *adventurous* [téméraire] *and exceptionally gifted!* [emphasis in the original]" (Éliane Chevalier, "Chevalier-Duruflé," 18). And this: "May 10, 1939—received the little Marie-Madeleine Chevalier arrived from her Vaucluse. . . . Adventurous, very talented, ready for my class" (ibid., 23).

10. Duruflé-Chevalier, "Chevalier-Duruflé," 34.

11. Her sister Éliane joined her shortly thereafter.

12. Éliane Chevalier, "Chevalier-Duruflé et Dupré," 23.

13. Jeanne Marie-Madeleine Demessieux was born on February 13, 1921, less than three months before the birth of Jeanne Marie-Madeleine Chevalier, in Montpellier, which is not far from Marseilles, where Chevalier was born. Like Chevalier, she was a stunning improviser and played Bach's Fugue in D (BWV 532) at lightning speed (Clarence H. Barber, "Some Observations on Paris Organists Visited by American," *American Organist* 38 [July 1, 1947]: 15). Demessieux became organist at Église Saint-Esprit in 1933, when she was twelve years old, and remained in that post until her nomination to the Madeleine, in 1962. She toured North America in 1953, 1955, and 1958, and produced sixteen recordings, including the complete works of Franck, recorded at the Madeleine. She published eight major organ works. See Graham Steed, "Dupré and Demessieux: The Master and the Pupil," *American Organist* 13 (March 1979): 42–43.

14. Duruflé-Chevalier, "Chevalier-Duruflé," 34. Maurice Duruflé was an admirer of Demessieux, and was quoted as saying, "Next to Jeanne Demessieux, we play the pedal like elephants" (Christiane Trieu-Colleney, *Jeanne Demessieux: Une Vie de luttes et de gloire*. [{Avignon}: Presses Universelles, 1977], 186).

15. Eschbach, e-mail message to author, March 18, 2005.

16. Trieu-Colleney, *Demessieux*, 231. Unfortunately, Mme Duruflé published nothing else about her studies with Demessieux.

17. Éliane Chevalier, "Chevalier-Duruflé et Dupré," 23. Her fellow pupils at Meudon and the Conservatoire included Éliane Lejeune, Micheline Lagache, Suzanne Chaisemartin, Jeanne Joulain, Pierre Labric, Françoise Renet, Jean Costa, and Jean Bonfils.

18. Marcel Dupré, "Notes de concours et examens d'orgue au Conservatoire National Supérieur de Musique, 1922–1956." These are Dupré's critiques of the competitions and examinations of the organ class, but they include the final year of Eugène Gigout and the first years of Rolande Falcinelli (BnF, Rés. Vm dos. 56 [1–3]).

19. Olivier Messiaen also substituted for Dupré's organ class on occasion (See Rolande Falcinelli, "Entretien avec Rolande Falcinelli, 1er Mai 2002, Pau," by Frédéric Blanc, *Bulletin* 4 (June 2004]: 9), as did Marcel Lanquetuit (See Marie-Louise Girod, "Entretien avec Marie-Louise Girod, Paris, janvier 2004," by Frédéric Blanc, *Bulletin* 4 [June 2004]: 18).

20. Dupré, "Notes de concours et examens d'orgue." Marie-Claire Alain won second prize.

21. Éliane Chevalier, "Chevalier-Duruflé," 18.

22. Duruflé-Chevalier, "Entretien," 11.

23. Another source reports that Éliane Chevalier did not move to Paris until 1947, following her sister by two years.

24. Frédéric Blanc, "Hommage à Pierre Cochereau pour le 20e anniversaire de sa disparition," *Bulletin* 4 (June 2004): 82.

25. Cochereau also studied organ with Duruflé, in 1942 (Abbing, *Duruflé*, 128).

26. Yvette Carbou, ed., *Pierre Cochereau: Témoignages* (Bourg-la-Reine: Éditions Aug. Zurfluh, 1999), 34.

27. Association Élisabeth et Joachim Havard de la Montagne, "Musica et Memoria." She was at Saint Bernard-de-la-chapelle in 1949–50.

28. She played there in 1974 and in the summer of 1990.

29. Most details of the festival are found in Marcel Paponaud, "Festival de Lyon (1953)," *L'Orgue*, no. 69 (October–December 1953): 124–25, reprinted in *Bulletin* 3 (June 2003): 25–26. See also "Les Festivals en France: Lyon-Charbonnières," *Revue musicale*, no. 222 (June 20–July 10, 1953): 73–75.

30. Widor was born in Lyons in 1844.

31. Alain [Allen] Hobbs, "Post-scriptum," in "Charles-Marie Widor (1844–1937)," *L'Orgue: Cahiers et mémoires*, no. 40 (1988-II): 47; Duruflé-Chevalier, "Chevalier-Duruflé," 34; Duruflé-Chevalier, "Entretien," 12; Éliane Chevalier, "Chevalier-Duruflé," 2.

32. Paponaud, "Festival de Lyon," 125; Éliane Chevalier, liner notes; Denis, "Marie-Madeleine Chevalier-Duruflé," 4; Duruflé-Chevalier, "Entretien," 12. The prestige of this international competition seems to have been as great as it was short-lived. The author has seen no mention of it after that date.

33. Mme Duruflé shared this information with Joyce Painter Rice in June 1990 (Rice, telephone conversation with author, May 4, 2005).

34. Mme Duruflé shared this information with Jesse Eschbach and Rodger Vine, Boston, June 1990 (Eschbach and Vine, e-mail messages to author, March 19, 2005).

35. Mme Duruflé, conversation with Joyce Painter Rice, Boston, June 1990 (Rice, interview with author, Boston, January 18, 2004).

36. The marriage was announced in "Échos," *L'Orgue*, no. 69 (October–December 1953): 126. Duruflé was hardly unique in marrying one of his students. Several of his friends and colleagues at the Conservatoire also married former students, including Tournemire, Langlais, and Messiaen.

37. He played the *orgue de chœur* for the service, the new organ in the tribune being unfinished.

38. Mme Duruflé, conversation with Joyce Painter Rice in June 1990 (Rice, telephone conversation).

39. Ibid.

40. "Principaux concerts: Marie-Madeleine Duruflé en solo de 1933 à 1997 et Joint-Récitals avec Maurice Duruflé de 1953 à 1979," *Bulletin* 3 (June 2003): 52.

41. Denis, "Marie-Madeleine Chevalier-Duruflé."

42. According to Éliane Chevalier, the work has been recorded in France, Japan, and the United States (Chevalier, "Chevalier-Durufle," 4).

43. Éliane Chevalier, "Chevalier-Duruflé," 19.

44. The work was recorded in 1992 by the vocal ensemble Ars Musicae, under the direction of Claude Carrot, for a CD entitled *Musique vocale française* (Solstice SOCD 113).

45. Murray, *Dupré*, 222, quoting "Hommage à Marcel Dupré," *Courrier musical de France* 14 (1966): 113.

46. Denis, "Marie-Madeleine Chevalier-Duruflé," 35.

47. The dismissal pronounced by the priest at the end of mass.

48. Duruflé-Chevalier, "Chevalier-Duruflé," 35.

49. Mme Duruflé shared this information with Joyce Painter Rice in June 1990 (Rice, telephone conversation).

50. Jean-Martin Chevalier, "Hommage à Marie-Madeleine," *Bulletin* 3 (June 2003): 33.

51. Duruflé's account of the accident appears in a letter he wrote to André Fleury on January 4, 1976, reprinted in *SAE*, 58–59.

52. Mme Duruflé told Marie-Claire Alain, who relayed it to Wolfgang Reisinger, March 14, 2002 (see Wolfgang Reisinger, "Maurice Duruflé's Limited Musical Output: Implications for Contemporary Performers" [DMA diss., University of Kansas, 2003], 11).

53. Mme André Longueverne, interview by author, Ménerbes, January 18, 2003. Duruflé told Rodger Vine that any other doctor would have amputated both of his legs (Vine, telephone interview by author, December 2, 2002).

54. Thalassotherapy is a form of treatment for the human body that uses the therapeutic virtues of seawater and seaweed.

55. Duruflé to Murtagh, March 11, 1976.

56. Duruflé to Murtagh, April 28, 1976. (In this letter Duruflé wrote that they had spent about twelve million francs.) The Duruflés had the option of receiving the insurance settlement in a single sum, or on a monthly basis. They chose the former and, in so doing, were able to put the accident behind them, at least to some degree. The settlement made them more financially secure than they had ever been previously. After her husband died, Mme Duruflé said she would never have to worry about money again. (Mme Duruflé, conversation with Rodger Vine, Boston, 1990 [Vine, telephone conversation with author, December 2, 2002]).

57. Ms. Soularue had auditioned with the Duruflés during their visit to Boys Town, Nebraska in 1971.

58. Mme Duruflé shared this information with Joyce Painter Rice in June 1990 (Rice, telephone conversation).

59. Duruflé to Murtagh, April 28, 1976; Éliane Chevalier, "Chevalier-Durufle," 3.

60. Dennis Keene, "Madame Duruflé Returns to the United States," *American Organist* 23 (October 1989): 18.

61. McFarlane to Mme Duruflé, June 8, 1977. In this letter McFarlane quotes Jean Langlais, who said Mme Duruflé's recent recital was magnificent. Langlais dedicated his *Kyrie "Orbis Factor" du Livre œcuménique* to Mme Duruflé.

62. McFarlane to the Duruflés, September 10, 1977.

63. Dennis Keene, "The Duruflé Album," liner notes for compact disc of the *Requiem, Messe "Cum jubilo,"* and *Notre Père*, Delos International DE 3169 (1995), 6.

64. Ronzon, "Duruflé," 58, and Abbing, *Duruflé*, 141.

65. Telephone interview with Vine by the author, December 2, 2002.

66. Conversation with Abbing, December 7, 2001, quoted in Abbing, *Duruflé*, 140.

67. Mme Duruflé to Boulanger, January 14, 1978 (BnF NLa. 68. Letter 197).

68. Mme Duruflé to McFarlane, November 28, 1979.

69. Mme Duruflé to author, August 9, 1994.

70. McFarlane to the Duruflés, September 10, 1977.

71. Letter of April 15, 1986.

72. Mme Duruflé to McFarlane, November 19, 1986.

73. Letter dated November 10, 1986.

74. Mme Duruflé to McFarlane, November 19, 1986.

75. Letter from Mme Duruflé dated January 23, 1987, probably to McFarlane.

76. Mme Duruflé was reluctant at first, because she doubted the instrument capable of a serious recital. She finally consented, but not before trying out the cymbals and other sound effects (Bernard Dargassies, [Hommage], *Bulletin* 2 [June 2002]: 21).

77. Éliane Chevalier, "Chevalier-Durufle," 3.

78. During January of 2002 a retrospective similar to the one that took place in New York, but on a smaller scale (no orchestras were involved), was sponsored in Paris and Louviers by the Duruflé Association, in observance of the centenary of Duruflé's birth. A commemorative brochure was also published for this retrospective.

79. This was the first time she played all three movements of this work in North America.

80. The concerts were recorded by J. Michael Barone for Minnesota Public Radio's organ series *Pipedreams*. A video of the concerts was also produced.

81. Letter dated August 1, 1989.

82. Richard Dyer, "Duruflé's Bold Technique Weaves in Fantasy, Color," Concert review, *Boston Globe*, undated news clipping in the McFarlane Papers.

83. She said she would not accept master classes while on tour, because they did not allow work in depth, and, oddly, she preferred not to play her husband's works or to accompany the *Requiem* or the *Messe "Cum jubilo."*

84. In the early stages of planning for this tour, Mme Duruflé was slated for a performance at the Cathedral of Saint John the Divine in New York (McFarlane to Mme Duruflé, April 17, 1991), but it never took place.

85. Swann was organist at the Crystal Cathedral from 1982 to 1998.

86. Frederick Swann, e-mail message to author, August 10, 2003.

87. McFarlane to Mme Duruflé, April 24, 1992.

88. McFarlane to Mme Duruflé, February 2, 1994.

89. Eschbach, e-mail message to author, March 18, 2005.

90. Duruflé-Chevalier, "Entretien," 12.

91. Quoted in Anthony Tommasini, "Marie-Madeleine Duruflé, 78, an Organist," *New York Times* (October 12, 1999), reprinted in *Bulletin* 3 (June 2003): 43.

92. Vine, e-mail message to author, March 19, 2003.

93. Duruflé-Chevalier, "Entretien," 14.

94. Blanc, [Hommage à Marie-Madeleine Duruflé], *Bulletin* 3 (June 2003): 31–32.

95. Vine, "Souvenirs," *Bulletin* 3 (June 2003): 44.

96. Jesse Eschbach, "Madame Duruflé, le professeur," *Bulletin* 3 (June 2003): 34.

97. Roger Fisher, "Marie-Madeleine Duruflé: A Reminiscence," *Organists' Review* 86 (February 2000): 36; reprinted in *Bulletin* 3 (June 2003): 35–36.

98. Vine, interview by author, Boston, February 6, 2004. Mme Duruflé was not the first to play Chopin on the organ. Louis-James Lefébure-Wély played several of Chopin's works on the organ during the composer's funeral at the Madeleine in 1849.

99. Ibid.

100. Swann, e-mail message to author, August 10, 2003.

101. Vine, "Souvenirs," 44.

102. Founded by T. Tertius Noble, Saint Wilfred's club provided social occasions for New York City's elite organists.

103. George Decker, e-mail message to author, February 27, 2001. The serpent was a stop in the choir division.

104. Mme Duruflé to McFarlane, February 2, 1996.

105. Her mother, Suzanne Chevalier-Rigoir, had died only the year before.

106. Jeffrey Crane, e-mail message to author, n.d.

# Chapter Thirteen

1. Duruflé, "Interview with Duruflé [Baker, French]," 215–16.

2. Quoted in Robert Kent Nelson, "The Organ Works of Maurice Duruflé," *Music* 11 (July 1977): 35.

3. Canon Jehan Revert (the *maître de chapelle* of Notre-Dame Cathedral), "Homélie," preached at Duruflé's funeral, printed in *L'Orgue*, no. 201–4 (1987): 93–95.

4. Huot-Pleuroux, *Musique religieuse*, 272, 320.

5. Alain, "Entretien," 4.

6. Falcinelli, "Entretien," 10.

7. Alain, "Introduction," xiv; translation by Ebrecht.

8. Alain, "Entretien," 4.

9. Abbing, *Duruflé*, 347, quoting correspondence from Mme Duruflé to Abbing, n.d.

10. Duruflé, "Interview with Duruflé [Baker, French]," 227.

11. Duruflé, "Réflexions," 4, quoted in Ronzon, "Duruflé," 77.

12. Maurice Duruflé, "Interview of Maurice Duruflé," by Pierre Cochereau, Notre-Dame, Paris, September 28, 1973, trans. Susan Spillman, in liner notes for the CD *Duruflé: Herndon Spillman*, organist, recorded May 21–27, 1973 (Titanic Records TI-200), n.p.

13. Ibid.

14. Ibid.

15. Ned Rorem, *Lies: A Diary, 1986–1999* (Washington, DC: Counterpoint, 2000), 179. Seth Bingham would have taken exception to Rorem's verdict, writing that in the *Requiem* "there are no prettified tunes" ("Duruflé's *Requiem* Marked by Elegance and Warm Humanity," *Diapason* 44 [March 1, 1953]: 18).

16. Duruflé, "Réflexions," 4, quoted in Ronzon, "Duruflé," 78.

17. Bernard Gavoty, *Les Français: Sont-ils musiciens?* (Paris: Éditions du Conquistador, 1950), 102.

18. Dated November 1947, and quoted in Delaporte, "Hommage," 2.

19. Marie-Claire Alain, "Introduction: Maurice Duruflé," xiv.

20. Duruflé, "Interview with Duruflé [Baker, French]," 217.

21. Ibid.

22. He did, however, transcribe an orchestral work by Fauré in a version for organ.

23. Duruflé, "Souvenirs [1976]," 37.

24. Duruflé, "Interview with Duruflé [Baker, French]," 219.

25. Introductory notes for Rogg's organ piece entitled *Hommage à Maurice Duruflé* (Lemoine).

26. Duruflé, "Interview with Duruflé [Baker]," 59. In the original French interview of Duruflé by Mr. Baker, Duruflé did not actually say that Debussy was less of an influence than Ravel. He said "Yes, above all Ravel, and Debussy naturally" ("Interview with Duruflé [Baker, French]," 217).

27. Ibid.

28. Blanc, interview by author.

29. Duruflé, "Souvenirs [1976]," 37.

30. Spillman, "The Organ Works of Maurice Duruflé," 38.

31. Haig Mardirosian, "Maurice Duruflé 1902–1986," *American Organist* 37 (July 2003): 56.

32. Edward Lockspeiser, *Debussy: His Life and Mind* (London: Cassell, 1962), 17.

33. Quoted in James Wierzbicki, "Impressionism," St. Louis *Dispatch*, July 22, 1990; available at http://pages.sbcglobal.net/jameswierzbicki/impressionism.htm.

34. Michel Fleury, *L'Impressionisme et la musique* (Paris: Fayard, 1996), 112.

35. Ebrecht, *Duruflé*, vi; translation by Ebrecht.

36. Mardirosian, "Duruflé," 56.

37. Ibid.

38. Ibid.

39. See Steven Lee Cooksey, "Impressionistic Aspects of Twentieth-Century French Organ Literature" (PhD diss., Washington University, 1972); Harald Rise, "Impressionism and the Organ: A Study of Impressionistic Aspects of Organ Works by Maurice Duruflé" (Dr. Art, Norwegian University of Science and Technology, 2001); and Wolfgang Reisinger, "Neoklassizistische, spätromatische und impressionistische Einflüsse auf das Werk von Maurice Duruflé" (Doctoral diss., Universität für Musik und darstellende Kunst, Vienna, forthcoming in 2007).

40. Jörg Abbing makes a passing reference to it in *Duruflé*, 350, as does Andrew Thomson in "Invention," 50.

41. François Lesure and Richard Langham Smith, eds., *Debussy on Music* (New York: Alfred A. Knopf, 1977), 31.

42. Stefan Jarocinski, *Debussy, Impressionism and Symbolism*, trans. Rollo Myers (London: Eulenburg Books, 1976), 104–5.

43. Jarocinski does not specify whether Debussy was referring to BWV 1048 or BWV 1049 (ibid.).

44. Ibid., 104. See also Françoise Gervais, "La Notion d'arabesque chez Debussy," *Revue musicale*, no. 241 (1958): 3–22.

45. Prince Poniatowski, *D'un siècle à l'autre* (Paris, 1948), quoted in Lesure and Smith, *Debussy*, 31.

46. Gervais, "Notion d'arabesque," 10–12.

47. Bingham, "Duruflé's *Requiem*," 18.

48. Abbing, *Duruflé*, 34.

49. Bingham, "Duruflé's *Requiem*," 18.

50. "To Hear the *Requiem* of Maurice Duruflé (1902–1986) as a Theologian: Discovering in a Work of High Musical Composition the Exercise of an Understanding of Faith in the Mystery of the Last Ends," Institut Catholique de Paris, 2003.

51. Duruflé, "Requiem," *L'Orgue: Cahiers et mémoires*, no. 45 (1991): 59.

52. Quoted in Roger Nichols, *Messiaen* (London: Oxford University Press, 1975), 8.

53. Conspicuous exceptions are found in the early works *Le Banquet céleste* and *Apparition de l'Église éternelle.*

54. Huot-Pleuroux, *Musique religieuse*, 320.

55. Felix Aprahamian, "Maurice Duruflé and His Requiem," *Listener* (April 11, 1957) 613.

56. Ibid.

57. Roger Nichols, "Maurice Duruflé," *Choir and Organ* 4 (May 1996): 30.

58. *L'art saint-sulpice* refers to tawdry religious art issuing from the numerous shops in the neighborhood of Saint Sulpice where plastic statues and their ilk were sold. Rostand extends its meaning to tawdry religious music.

59. Poulenc, *Entretiens*, 114. Poulenc "did not miss a concert of works by Duruflé" (Daniel Roth, "In Memoriam Maurice Duruflé," *Bulletin* 2 [June 2002]: 33).

60. Ronzon, "Duruflé," 78.

61. Ebrecht, "Ties That Bind," in *Duruflé*, 159, quoting Lesure, *Claude Debussy* (Paris: Klincksieck, 1994), 66–67.

62. Pierre Pincemaille, "L'Improvisateur à Notre-Dame," in Carbou, *Cochereau*, 303.

63. Duruflé, "Interview of Duruflé [Cochereau]," n.p.

64. Duruflé, "Interview with Duruflé [Baker, French]," 217.

65. Ibid.

66. Debussy wrote and published a piece for organ titled *Sarabande* (Édition Jobert), but his prelude and fugue for organ remain unpublished. See François Lesure, *Catalogue de l'œuvre de Claude Debussy* (Geneva: Minkoff, 1977); and John Henderson, *A Directory of Composers for Organ.* 2nd ed. (Swindon, Wiltshire: John Henderson Ltd.: 1999), 141.

67. Englert-Marchal, "Marchal," 59.

68. Duruflé, "Souvenirs [1976]," 48.

69. Quoted in Pincemaille, "Duruflé."

70. Duruflé, "Interview with Duruflé [Baker]," 59.

71. Ibid.

72. Marcel Belvianes, "[Review]," *Ménestrel* 95 (June 23, 1933): 259. The quotation is taken from Belvianes's review of the performance by Geneviève de La Salle of Duruflé's variations on *Veni Creator* on June 16, 1933 at the Schola Cantorum.

73. Christoph Martin Frommen, Liner notes for the recording of the complete organ works of Duruflé by Stefan Schmidt (Aeolus AE-10211 EAN: 4026798102111).

74. Contrast *Poèmes pour MI*, written by Messiaen for Claire Delbos, and Langlais' *Virgo Dei Genitrix*, with its veiled reference to Ann Labounsky (See Labounsky, *Langlais*, 273).

75. See the fifth movement of his *Cinq méditations sur l'apocalypse.*

76. Rostand, "*Requiem*," 269.

77. Charles Münch, *I Am a Conductor*, trans. Leonard Burkat (New York: Oxford University Press, 1955), 18.

78. Duruflé, "My Recollections," 55.

79. Duruflé, "Interview with Duruflé [Baker, French]," 219.

80. Olivier Soularue, "Maurice Duruflé, un artiste engagé," in *Hommage à Maurice Duruflé*, a commemorative brochure published by the Ville de Louviers for the centenary observance of Duruflé's birth (2002), n.p.

81. Duruflé, "Entretien avec Maurice Duruflé par Claude Chamfray," *Guide du concert et du disque* (December 14, 1956); reprinted in *SAE*, 94.

82. Pierre Denis, "Les Organistes français d'aujourd'hui: Maurice Duruflé," *L'Orgue*, no. 50 (January–March 1949): 5. See also Aprahamian, "Requiem," 613.

83. Once, when urged by Rodger Vine to write an organ concerto, Duruflé replied that Poulenc had already written a great one (Vine, telephone interview by author, December 2, 2002).

84. Ibid.

85. See Lionel Rogg (*Hommage à Maurice Duruflé*), David Hurd (*On the Name Maurice Duruflé*), Philippe Lefèbvre (*Prélude et Fugue*), and Craig Penfield (*Étude artistique*).

# Chapter Fourteen

1. As we shall see, two other academic works were published, in 1924 and 1928, namely an untitled work on a *basse donnée* by J. Morpain (1924) and a fugue in C Minor (1928), but not in performance editions.

2. Éliane Chevalier, e-mail message.

3. The author learned of the work in 2004 through an anonymous correspondent in Paris.

4. Rodger Vine gave its first concert performance at the Arlington Street Church in Boston on December 5, 2004. The Duruflé Association has demonstrated no knowledge of the piece.

5. See the website of the Duruflé Association, on the page titled Les Œuvres de Maurice Duruflé: Œuvres inédits: http://www.france-orgue.fr/durufle/index.php?zpg=drf.mmm.oeu.

6. "Interview with Duruflé [Baker, French]," 221.

7. Duruflé, "Souvenirs [1976]," 35.

8. Fleury gave the musicologist Philippe Robert a photocopy of the score he used for the premiere (Philippe Robert, e-mail message to author, September 19, 2002).

9. See Robert, "Duruflé: Sa vie, son œuvre," 29.

10. Archives nationales. Conservatoire de musique. Aj37 532–34.

11. Subsequent editions of the *Scherzo* were published in 1942, 1951, 1962, 1969, and 1971.

12. When Pierre Cochereau studied the *Scherzo* with Duruflé in the 1940s, the composer not only changed entire measures, but he "changed entire pages" (Duruflé, "Interview with Duruflé [Baker, French]," 220).

13. Fleury had already presented the *Scherzo* in a performance in 1927 at Notre-Dame du Rosaire, but for unknown reasons that performance has not been considered the premiere. *La Revue musicale* published a review of this recital by Norbert Dufourcq (10 [July 1, 1929]: 159), in which he identifies this performance of the *Scherzo* as its premiere.

14. Norbert Dufourcq, "Discours de Monsieur Norbert Dufourcq," *L'Orgue*, no. 208 (October–December 1988): 33. *Le Courrier musicale et théâtral* took no note of the premiere.

15. Ebrecht, *Duruflé*, 161n11.

16. Nelson, "Organ Works," 32. For an analysis of the hierarchical rhythmic structures in the *Scherzo*, see Marie Rubis Bauer, "The Large Beat," in Ebrecht, *Duruflé*, 65–85.

17. Chamfray, "Chronology," 51; Robert, "Duruflé: Sa vie, son œuvre," iv; Gwilym Beechey, "The Music of Maurice Duruflé," *Music Review* 32 (May 1971): 148.

18. Duruflé, "Souvenirs [1976]," 35. Rodger Vine studied the work with the composer, who acknowledged being touched by the opportunity, as he was so unaccustomed to teaching it (Vine, telephone interview).

19. Machabey, "Galerie," n.p.

20. *Courrier musical et théâtral* 32 (March 15, 1930): 194.

21. Ian Wells, "Maurice Duruflé, 1902–1986," *Organists' Review* 82 (November 1996): 293. See also Murray, *Dupré,* 224.

22. Reviews of the *Prélude, récitatif et variations* appeared in *Chantecler,* by P. O. Terroud (January 19, 1929); *Le Figaro,* by R. Brussel (January 24, 1929); and *Paris-Soir,* by L. Aubert (January 29, 1929).

23. *Courrier musical et théâtral* 31 (May 15, 1929): 332.

24. Jean Doyen taught piano at the Conservatoire from 1941 to 1977.

25. *SAE,* 250.

26. Thomson, "Pure Invention," 51.

27. Norbert Dufourcq, "In Memoriam: Maurice Duruflé," *L'Orgue,* no. 201–4 (1987): 91.

28. Beechey, "Duruflé," 149.

29. Philippe Robert, e-mail message, quoting Fleury's comments about Robert's 1979 dissertation. Fleury also wrote *Versets sur le "Veni Creator."*

30. Poster for the concert, reproduced in Société d'études diverses, *Louviers,* 69.

31. Philippe Robert, e-mail message to author, quoting Fleury's comments on Robert's dissertation. Fleury wrote further, "I can speak with knowledge because [Duruflé] played it at my wedding [on August 29] in 1928. He recast it several times, in particular to give it a brilliant conclusion."

32. Without access to the manuscripts, it is impossible to determine how the variations Duruflé performed in Louviers differed from the *Choral varié* finally published with Opus 4. Duruflé made many changes after the first edition was published.

33. The guidelines for the competition were published October 1, 1929 in *Le Courrier musical et théâtral,* vol. 31, 526.

34. In Tournemire's *Triple choral* each section segues into the next, justifying the singular title.

35. The frequent practice of having a schola sing the Gregorian verses between the variations, approximating alternatim praxis, finds its authority in the recording that Duruflé and his wife made in 1969. After the *Andante religioso* is sung verse 1: *Veni Creator Spiritus;* after the *Poco meno lento,* verse 2: *Qui diceris Paraclitus;* after the *Allegretto,* verse 6: *Per te sciamus da Patrem;* and after the *Andante espressivo,* verse 7: *Deo Patri sit gloria,* with the Amen.

36. Subsequent editions of the *Prélude, adagio et choral varié sur le Veni Creator* were published in 1931, 1941, 1945, 1951, 1956, 1960, 1963, 1965, 1969, and 1971. Duruflé made changes even after the latest edition was published.

37. Some sources incorrectly give 1933 (see Chamfray, "Chronology," 51).

38. Subsequent editions of the Op. 5 *Suite* were published in 1945, 1949, 1955, 1959, 1961, 1965, 1967, and 1970.

39. Nigel Simeone, *"Dear Maître Tournemire . . .": Charles Tournemire's Correspondence with Felix Aprahamian and His Visit to London in 1936,* Bangor Monographs in Musicology (Bangor: University of Wales, 2003), 8.

40. Dufourcq, *Musique d'orgue,* 206.

41. Vierne's Sixth Symphony was published in 1931.

42. Thomson, "Pure Invention," 51.

43. Beechey, "Duruflé," 150.

44. Vine, telephone interview by author, December 2, 2002.

45. *SAE,* 250.

46. Armand Machabey refers to the transcription for orchestra of the *Sicilienne* (rather surprisingly, in view of the fact that it was never published) in "Galerie," n.p.

47. Beechey, "Duruflé," 151.

48. "Interview with Duruflé [Baker, French]," 218.

49. Ibid.

50. Rodger Vine studied the piece with Duruflé in September 1978.

51. Vine, e-mail message to author, December 12, 2002.

52. Duruflé-Chevalier, "Entretien"; Duruflé, "Interview with Duruflé [Baker]," 59.

53. Marilyn Mason indicated that Duruflé specified some cuts, probably in 1948 (Marilyn Mason, "Conversations with Marilyn Mason," by Lorenz Maycher, *American Organist* 39 [July 2005]: 66). Robert Kent Nelson wrote that Duruflé recommends omitting measures 120–34 and the penultimate measure (Nelson, "Organ Works," 34). Duruflé also suggested that the first chord in the left-hand part and the high c in the pedal part of measures 100 and 101 be changed from a quarter note to two eighth notes. The low F of the chord may be tied (ibid.).

54. Duruflé, "Interview with Duruflé [Baker]," 59.

55. Vine, e-mail message to author, December 9, 2002.

56. See, for example, Craig R. Whitney, *All the Stops: The Glorious Pipe Organ and Its American Masters* (New York: Public Affairs, 2003), 148–49, 210. Having discovered the music of Duruflé in 1949, Frederick Swann wrote that he believes he was among the very first to play the *Suite* in America ("Souvenirs sur Maurice et Marie-Madeleine Duruflé," *Bulletin* 2 [June 2002]: 39).

57. Referring to the *Requiem*, Bingham wrote, "In musical language it even differs radically from Duruflé's own much-played *Suite* for Organ, Op. 5" ("Duruflé's *Requiem*," 18).

58. George Butler, e-mail message to Rodger Vine, September 28, 2004, forwarded to the author.

59. Duruflé, "Souvenirs [1976]," 43.

60. Édouard Dujardin (1861–1949) was a novelist, poet, playwright, journalist, and professor of the history of religion. Enrolled briefly at the Paris Conservatoire, he was a friend of Debussy and Dukas, and of the symbolist poet Stéphane Mallarmé.

61. Duruflé, "Souvenirs [1976]," 44.

62. Chamfray, "Chronology," 51. Abbing dates the work to 1929 (*Duruflé*, 76).

63. Chamfray, "Chronology," 51, and Eschbach, "Maurice Duruflé," 44. Chamfray erroneously gives 1935 for the first performance (Robert, "Duruflé: Sa vie, son úuvre," iv).

64. Liner notes to the recording of *Trois Danses* on Musical Heritage Society MHS 1819, printed in an English translation.

65. Rostand, "*Requiem*," 267.

66. Machabey, *Portraits*, 70.

67. Beechey, "Duruflé," 151.

68. See Jean-Philippe Mousnier, *Paul Paray* (Paris: L'Harmattan, 1998), 72.

69. The second volume (p. 2, example 8) includes eight measures of the E-flat alto saxophone part from *Tambourin*, the passage beginning at the *Tempo primo* after rehearsal 19.

70. Chamfray, "Chronology," 51. In January 1962 Duruflé gave a copy to the pianist Robert Casadesus (1899–1972). The score is housed in the BnF, Archives Robert et Gaby Casadesus, Vm Casadesus 000241; it is inscribed "au grand Robert Casadesus en amical souvenir. M. Duruflé. janvier 1962." This score contains no pencil markings of any sort, and it appears it was never used for practice or performance.

71. François Porcile refers to the premiere of a four-hand piano version played by Jehan Alain and his brother Olivier (*La Belle Époque de la musique française* [Paris: Fayard, 1999], quoted in Reisinger, "Limited Musical Output," 2).

72. Duruflé, "Interview with Duruflé [Baker, French]," 221.

73. Ibid. It is instructive to note that Duruflé referred to the piano versions as transcriptions rather than reductions.

74. The two-piano version of the *Trois Danses* was published in 1996.

75. Stagebill, March 1989, concert program, 17. The couple played the European premiere of the two-piano version at the Salle Gaveau the following year (Loumbrozo, interview by author, New York, April 15, 1994).

76. Loumbrozo, interview, quoting Éliane Chevalier.

77. This recording of the two-piano version, on Cybelia CY824, was never distributed commercially, but was issued in 1997 on Phoenix PHCD 135.

78. Marie-Madeleine Duruflé, liner notes to the CD Phoenix PHCD 135, 3.

79. Both versions are undated and appear without opus numbers.

80. Leslie Kandell, "Marie-Madeleine Duruflé," *Musical America* 110 (1990): 65.

81. Loumbrozo, interview.

82. Reisinger, "Limited Musical Output," 10.

83. William Whitehead, e-mail message to author, June 19, 2005. Mr. Whitehead performed the transcription at Southwell Minster, England, on October 19, 2005, and recorded it on Chandos Records CHAN 10315.

84. Robert, "Duruflé: Sa vie, son œuvre," iv; Nelson, "Organ Works," 32–33; and Chamfray, "Chronology," 51.

85. "Interview with Duruflé [Baker, French]," 222.

86. Elsewhere spelled Petit Puy.

87. "L'Appel aux morts: Jehan Alain," *Revue musicale* 22 (February–March 1946): 53.

88. "Association des Amis de l'Orgue," 3.

89. Subsequent editions of the *Prélude et fugue sur le nom d'ALAIN* appeared in 1947, 1958, 1963, 1965, 1967, 1969, and 1970. By the mid-1970s Duruflé had made several more changes in the score.

90. Beechey, "Duruflé," 151. Langlais used a musical alphabet in *Voluntary Sainte-Marie-Madeleine* (1969) and *Voluntary Sainte-Trinité* (1969). Jörg Abbing points out that Duruflé's spelling of ALAIN is similar to Messiaen's piano piece *Mode de valeurs et d'intensités*, no. 2 from *Quatre études de rhythme*, 1949–50 (see Abbing, *Duruflé*, 284).

91. Abbing, *Duruflé*, 286.

92. Ivry, *Ravel*, 62.

93. Frommen, Liner notes (Aeolus AE-10211).

94. Frederick Swann believes he "was among the very first in America to play . . . the *Prélude et fugue sur le nom d'Alain*" (Swann, "Souvenirs," 39).

95. Alain, "Entretien," 5.

96. Ebrecht, *Duruflé*, 162n.

97. Chamfray, "Chronology," 51; Machabey, *Portraits*, 70.

98. Probably Cantata no. 56: *Ich will den Kreuzstab gerne tragen*.

99. The program does not specify whether the work was BWV 1068 or 1069.

100. From the printed program, reproduced in Duruflé, "Mémoires," 28.

101. A. F., "Organ Recital Notes," 356.

102. Duruflé to Marie-Madeleine Chevalier, September 22, 1950, quoted in *SAE*, 50.

103. Tomasi was a fellow student of Duruflé in the class of Georges Caussade at the Conservatoire, and a recipient of the *Prix Halphen* in 1926, the year before Duruflé was named recipient of the prize. He was a brilliant orchestral conductor but his focus was on theater; he was awarded the Prix de Rome in 1927.

104. René Dumesnil, [Review of *Andante et Scherzo*], *Le Monde*, January 27, 1954.

105. Duruflé to Marie-Madeleine Chevalier, September 22, 1950, quoted in *SAE*, 50.

106. Blanc, interview.

107. Bernard Gavoty, "Les Concerts symphoniques," *Opéra* (February 13, 1952); reprinted in *Bulletin* 3 (June 2003): 78.

108. Ibid. See also Bernard Gavoty, "Musiques rassurantes," *Paris Comœdia* (February 3, 1954); reprinted in *Bulletin* 3 (June 2003): 78–79.

109. Blanc, interview.

110. Mme Duruflé, conversation with author, Saint Paul, Minnesota, May 25, 1992. Despite its inherent difficulties, the work has been transcribed by several organists.

111. Robert, "Duruflé: Sa vie, son œuvre," v; Chamfray, "Chronology," 51; Nelson, "Organ Works," 32; Beechey, "Duruflé," 146. For an analysis of the motets, see Jeffrey Reynolds, "On Clouds of Incense," in Ebrecht, *Duruflé*, 108–14. Le Guennant served as *maître de chapelle* at Saint Pierre-du-Gros-Caillou, Notre-Dame du Rosaire, and Notre-Dame de Clignancourt, all in Paris.

112. Stéphane Caillat, e-mail message to author, March 19, 2001. Also Chamfray, "Chronology," 51.

113. Duruflé, "Souvenirs [1976]," 49.

114. See *Liber Usualis*, no. 780 (1964), 675.

115. This attribution is today contested by some scholars who suggest that Aquinas may have edited material from earlier sources.

116. Paul Dukas makes an allusion to the *Pange lingua* in his Sonata for piano (1901).

117. A lesser number of congregations sang the *Ubi caritas*, but few sang the plainsong *Tota pulchra es* or the *Tu es Petrus*.

118. It was also sung on Corpus Christi as the hymn for second vespers (see *Liber Usualis*, 957) and for the procession following mass (ibid., 950.).

119. Wells, "Duruflé," 292.

120. Jeffrey Reynolds suggests incorrectly that Duruflé could have composed a *Credo* if he had chosen to ("On Clouds of Incense," 115), and that because he did not, it would simply be recited. The reason Duruflé did not set the creed for the *Messe* is that it is not used in the Gregorian *Cum jubilo*.

121. Duruflé to Boulanger, April 14, 1966, BnF NLa. 68, letter 211.

122. See the current *Graduale Romanum* (1974), where *Cum jubilo* is designated more explicitly for the greater solemnities and feasts of Mary.

123. Pierre Denis, "L'Activité des Amis de l'Orgue: Saison 1967–1968," *L'Orgue*, no. 128 (October–December 1968): 150.

124. Ibid., and Caillat, e-mail message.

125. Thomson, "Pure Invention," 51.

126. Éliane Chevalier, e-mail message.

127. Duruflé to Murtagh, February 3, 1969.

128. Quoting the liner notes by Carol de Nys for the first German recording of the work (Duruflé—Missa Cum jubilo und Goller-Missa in honorem B.M.V. de Loreto, Kammerchor der Kirchenmusikschule Gregoriushaus, Aachen; under the direction of Hans-Josef Roth, recorded May 1986); reprinted in Abbing, *Duruflé*, 134.

129. Reynolds, "On Clouds of Incense," 115–16.

130. Abbing, *Duruflé*, 220, 224.

131. Stephen Walsh, [Review of *Messe "Cum jubilo"*], *Musical Times* 109 (August 1968): 760.

132. Duruflé to McFarlane, July 24, 1968.

133. Nicholas Kaye to author, March 30, 2005. Mr. Kaye was director of the society for many years.

134. John Morehen, [Report on the performance of *Messe "Cum jubilo"*], *Musical Times* 109 (July 1968): 656.

135. Duruflé to Murtagh, February 10, 1971.

136. Duruflé to Murtagh, March 29, 1969, with regard to the performance of the mass at Riverside Church in New York City.

137. Duruflé to Swann, March 29, 1969.

138. See, for example, Wells, "Duruflé," 292.

139. Henri Doyen, "In memoriam . . . ," *L'Organiste* 50 (June 1962): n.p.

140. Chamfray, "Chronology," 51.

141. Robert, "Duruflé: Sa vie, son œuvre," v; Nelson, "Organ Works," 32; and Beechey, "Duruflé," 147, give 1960?—including the question mark—for the publication date. Mme Duruflé included no date in her handwritten additions to Chamfray, "Chronology," 51.

142. Abbing, *Duruflé*, 132.

143. *Music* 11 (July 1977): 36–37.

144. The chant appears in the *Liber Usualis*, 459, and the *Graduale Romanum*, 56. Ian Wells observes that the piece can also be used for the common of feasts of the Blessed Virgin Mary, whose introit, *Salve sancta Parens*, is set to virtually the same melody as *Ecce advenit* (Wells, "Duruflé," 292. See *Liber Usualis*, 1263).

145. Éliane Chevalier, "Chevalier-Duruflé et Dupré," 24.

146. Reynolds, "On Clouds of Incense," 117.

147. Philippe Robert designates it opus 12 ("Duruflé: Sa vie, son œuvre," v.).

148. Keene, "Duruflé Album," 14.

149. Handwritten notes added by Mme Duruflé to Chamfray, "Chronology," 51, in the possession of the author.

150. Martin Anderson, "Marie-Madeleine Duruflé," *The Independent*, October 20, 1999; reprinted in *Bulletin* 3 (June 2003): 30–31.

151. Wells, "Duruflé," 293.

152. Reynolds, "On Clouds of Incense," 116–17.

153. Blanc, interview.

154. *SAE*, 239. Also see the website of the Duruflé Association, under the section titled Les Œuvres de Maurice Duruflé, where Mr. Blanc identifies his performance of the work at Notre-Dame as its premiere.

155. See *Bulletin* 3 (June 2003): 93–94.

156. It appeared again in *L'Orgue: Cahiers et mémoires*, no. 45 (1991), on p. 21, in a hand-written two-staff performance edition by Philippe Robert, which was also reproduced in Abbing, *Duruflé*, 312.

157. Abbing, *Duruflé*, 309–11.

158. Reisinger, "Limited Musical Output," 13–14.

159. In his recording of the complete organ works of Duruflé, Pierre Pincemaille identi-fied his recording of this work as a premiere (Pincemaille, "Duruflé").

160. This opinion is shared by Brigitte de Leersnyder (conversation with author, Saint Paul, MN, July 30, 2003).

161. The bound photocopy of the manuscript in the BnF appears to be in Duruflé's hand (Gr. Vma G40).

162. From Duruflé's "Le Compositeur," 151, quoted in Smith, *Vierne*, 520.

163. Vierne went on to write what was truly his last work, the *Messe basse pour les défuncts*, Op. 62.

164. BnF has a 1945 photocopy of the manuscript of Duruflé's orchestration.

165. The manuscript is BnF Ms. 18198.

166. Murger was also the author of *La Vie de bohème*, the source of the libretto for Puccini's opera *La Bohème*.

167. Other sources give November 17, 1928, January 1929, or 1930 (See Duruflé, "Interview with Duruflé [Baker]," 60). In her introduction to Duruflé's published transcriptions, Madeleine Richepin indicates that the recordings were made in 1930. EMI's 33 rpm reissue of the original 78 rpm recording lists no date for the original recordings, but indicates that *Cortège* was issued in October 1929 (Odéon 166149), while *Marche épiscopale* and *Méditation* (Odéon 171074) were issued in January 1930.

168. Jean-Pierre Mazeirat to Rollin Smith, January 27, 1997, quoted in Smith, *Vierne*, 513.

169. Jörg Abbing notes that there is an obvious harmonic error in the recording of this piece, which Duruflé corrects in the published score: p. 2, third system, second measure, last chord (Abbing, *Duruflé*, 316).

170. Smith, *Vierne*, 514–15, quoting Henri Doyen, *Mes Leçons*, 51–52.

171. *SAE*, 90, quoting Duruflé to Marie-Madeleine Chevalier, April 2, 1953.

172. Nelson, "Organ Works," 32; Beechey, "Duruflé," 147, 152.

173. The date "avril 1954" is printed at the end of the published edition, indicating that is when Duruflé completed the transcriptions.

174. Gwilym Beechey gives only 1930 ("Duruflé," 152), as do Weidner ("Tournemire," 12) and others.

175. *Rapsodie*, without the *h*, is an alternative spelling for the more common *rhapsodie*.

176. *Cantilène improvisée* was released in September 1930; *Fantaisie-Improvisation sur l'Ave maris stella* and the *Choral-Improvisation sur le Victimae paschali laudes* in October 1930; *Petite Rapsodie improvisée* in November 1931; and the *Improvisation sur le Te Deum* in March 1932. All of the recordings were distributed in France. *Cantilène improvisée* and *Choral-Improvisation sur le Victimae paschali laudes* were also distributed in Germany, and *Cantilène improvisée* was distributed in the United States. The latter was listed in 1937 as number 95048 on the Brunswick-Polydor label, in the "Hall of Fame Series" (see Weidner, "Tournemire," 13). In 1981[?], the improvisations by Vierne and Tournemire were reissued on compact discs by La Voix de son maître under the title "Orgues et organistes français en 1930" (EMI 2C153-16411/5).

177. Bernard Schulé, "Soixante Années au service de l'orgue," *L'Orgue*, no. 201–4 (1987): 20.

178. In 1979 Duruflé said that Mme Tournemire had control of the original discs and that her authorization would be required for the recordings to be reedited for sale on a commercial label. Duruflé said he did not believe Tournemire made any other recordings of his improvisations ("Interview with Duruflé [Baker, French]," 213).

179. Henri Doyen, *Mes Leçons*, 52.

180. This is the name Tournemire's students gave to their professor. A *tournebroche* is a rotating spit.

181. *SAE*, 110–11, quoting Duruflé to André Fleury, May 5, 1955.

182. Duruflé, "Interview with Duruflé [Baker, French]," 212.

183. "Principales Œuvres données en première audition à Paris aux concerts des Amis de l'Orgue," *L'Orgue*, no. 160–61 (October 1976–March 1977): 22–23.

184. Some sources indicate, in error, that Duruflé himself premiered all five works.

185. Charles Tournemire, *Cinq Improvisations pour orgue*, reconstitution and introduction by Maurice Duruflé (Éditions Durand, 1958).

186. Raymond Weidner, e-mail message to author, December 4, 2001.

187. Conversation between Marie-Madeleine Duruflé and Joyce Painter Rice, Boston, June 1990, recounted by Painter Rice in an interview by the author, Boston, January 18, 2004.

188. Mme Duruflé, conversation with Joyce Painter Rice, Boston, June 1990, quoted by Painter Rice in e-mail message to author, August 5, 2005.

189. Duruflé, "Souvenirs [1976]," 28n.

190. Quoted in Simeone, *"Dear Maître Tournemire,"* 37.

191. Ibid., quoting Tournemire to Aprahamian, February 6, 1936.

192. Felix Aprahamian, telephone interview by author, January 6, 2001.

193. From the program notes by Felix Aprahamian for Alan Harverson's recital at the Festival Hall on February 16, 1966, for which he performed Tournemire's *Te Deum* (Beechey, "Duruflé," 152–53). See "L'Art d'improvisation" by Tournemire in *Listener* (February 19, 1936).

194. James David Christie, interview by author, Saint Paul, MN, October 28, 2002.

195. Duruflé-Chevalier, "Entretien," 13.

196. Photocopy of Tournemire's manuscript in the collection of the author. The work was first performed by Joseph Bonnet, March 19, 1911, at Saint Eustache, Paris.

197. Denis, "L'Activité 1963–1964," 108.

198. Carlton T. Russell, "Franck's *L'Organiste* Reconsidered," *American Organist* 53 (February 1970): 12.

199. Volume 4 of Franck's *Œuvres complètes pour orgue* (Paris: Durand, 1973). This edition is not to be confused with the "Édition originale" (see Marie-Louise Jaquet-Langlais, "The Organ Works of Franck: A Survey of Editorial and Performance Problems," trans. Matthew Dirst and Kimberley Marshall, in Archbold and Peterson, *French Organ Music*, 151).

200. Jaquet-Langlais, "The Organ Works of Franck," 151.

201. Duruflé, "My Recollections," 55.

202. Jaquet-Langlais, "Œuvre d'orgue de Franck," 8, 18.

203. Jesse Eschbach points out, however, that the *Final*, Op. 21, does require 16′ stops in the récit. This evidence suggests that Franck thought generically, and not always specifically in terms of the organ at Sainte Clotilde (Eschbach, e-mail message to author, March 18, 2005).

204. The BWV number is unspecified. Bach wrote several settings of this chorale.

205. The source does not specify whether it is BWV 734 or 755.

206. Blanc was performing the work in public recitals as early as 2004. It remained unpublished as of 2005.

207. Published in 1953 by Lemoine under the title *Deux pièces*.

208. Mâcon: Éditions Robert Martin.

209. As we have seen, however, after her husband's death Mme Duruflé gave a photocopy of Duruflé's transcription of *Trois Danses* for two pianos to Rémy Loumbrozo and his wife Arianna Goldina.

210. Blanc, interview. Not everyone will agree that the publication of these works is in the best interest of the legacy of Maurice Duruflé, who surely had reasons of his own for not publishing them.

211. Duruflé-Chevalier, "Entretien," 13.

212. Duruflé emulated Tournemire in this regard. With his orchestral works, Tournemire usually wrote a piano version first, with the orchestral version sometimes following a year or so later. For Tournemire's first, second, fourth, and eighth symphonies he wrote full piano reductions for performance (Ruth Sisson, "Charles Tournemire, 1870–1939," *American Organist* 23 [December 1989]: 57).

213. Duruflé, "Interview of Duruflé [Cochereau]," n.p.

214. Frommen, Liner notes (Aeolus AE-10211).

215. Felix Aprahamian, "Requiem," 613.

216. Ebrecht, *Duruflé*, xii, quoting conversations between Duruflé and Jean Guillou.

217. Reisinger, "Limited Musical Output," 6.

218. From Marcel Dupré's *Philosophie de la musique* (1949; Tournai, Belgium: Collegium Musicum, 1984), quoted in Pincemaille, "Duruflé," 18.

# Chapter Fifteen

1. Duruflé was not the first to do so. While he was a student at the Conservatoire, an article by Louis Fleury boldly proposed a relationship between the rhythms of plainsong and those of jazz ("Réflexions sur le rythme du plain-chant et du jazz-band," *Courrier musical et théâtral* 26 [November 1, 1924]: 516–17).

2. Smith, *Vierne*, 528.

3. Abbé Poisson, "New method for learning Plainchant. Printed by order of His Eminence, His Grace, Cardinal de la Rochefoucault, Archbishop of Rouen. Particularly for use in his diocese"(Rouen: Labbey, 1789).

4. Jean Lebeuf, "Historic and practical treatise on ecclesiastical chant: With the directory containing the principles and rules following the present usage in the diocese of Paris and other [dioceses]" (Paris: Herissant, 1741).

5. Orpha Ochse, *Organists and Organ Playing in Nineteenth-Century France and Belgium* (Bloomington: Indiana University Press, 1994), 131.

6. Thomson, *Widor*, 18.

7. Ochse, *Organists*, 131.

8. Robert L. Tuzik, ed., *How Firm a Foundation: Leaders of the Liturgical Movement* (Chicago: Liturgy Training Publications, 1990), 20.

9. Huot-Pleuroux, *Musique religieuse*, 245.

10. "Observations on Music for Large Orchestra Introduced in Several Churches and . . . on the Admission of Musicians from the Opera in These Churches."

11. Huot-Pleuroux, *Musique religieuse*, 300.

12. James H. Johnson, *Listening in Paris: A Cultural History* (Berkeley: University of California Press, 1995), 259. Similarly, the conductor Charles Münch wrote that "I consider my work a priesthood, not a profession" (Münch, *Conductor*, 9).

13. Johnson, *Listening in Paris*, 269, quoting Donald Geoffrey Charlton, *Secular Religions in France, 1815–1870* (London: Oxford University Press, 1963), 36.

14. Johnson, *Listening in Paris*, 269, quoting Ralph P. Locke, "Liszt's Saint-Simonian Adventure," *19th-Century Music* 4 (Spring 1981), 221.

15. *L'Artiste* 1st series, vol. 3 (1832): 164, quoted in Johnson, *Listening in Paris*, 269.

16. Jean-Michel Nectoux, "French Archives: Music in the Archives of Paris Churches," *19th-Century Music* 7 (Fall 1983): 101.

17. See Jesse Eschbach, "Paris, Bibliothèque Nationale, MS 8707: A New Source for Franck's Registrational Practices and Its Implications for the Published Registrations of His Organ Works," in Archbold and Peterson, *French Organ Music*, 115.

18. Huot-Pleuroux, *Musique religieuse*, 312, quoting *La Tribune de Saint Gervais*, 1897. Gounod's "Fathers of the Church" is a reference to the ecclesiastical writers from the end of the fourth century whose authority on doctrinal matters carry particular weight.

19. *Catholic Encyclopedia* (1913), s.v. "Ecclesiastical Music," quoting Richard Wagner, *Gesammelte Werke* 2: 337.

20. Robert, "Duruflé: Sa vie, son œuvre," 6.

21. Alexandre Choron, "The Complete Body of Church Music for Two Choirs, with Organ ad libitum, without Orchestra, Chosen from Among the Best Works of the Greatest Masters" (Paris, 1829).

22. Duruflé's organ teacher, Eugène Gigout, performed with this choral ensemble in 1900, under the direction of Vincent d'Indy, and in 1911 at the home of Édouard de Laheudrie (Norbert Dufourcq, "Correspondances," in "Eugène Gigout, 1844–1925," *L'Orgue: cahiers et mémoires*, no. 27 [1982]: 9, 12).

23. Huot-Pleuroux, *Musique religieuse*, 323.

24. Robert, "Duruflé: Sa vie, son œuvre," 6, quoting Joseph Samson, *La Polyphonie sacrée en France des origines à nos jours* (Paris: Schola Cantorum, 1953), 128.

25. Ochse, *Organists*, 220.

26. Ibid., 221.

27. Robert, "Duruflé: Sa vie, son œuvre," 6.

28. Some sources give 1906.

29. Labounsky, *Langlais*, 372n22, quoting Daniel-Lesur.

30. Henri Doyen, *Mes Leçons*, 43.

31. Vierne, "Mes Souvenirs," 42–43.

32. Ochse, *Organists*, 134.

33. "A Little Treatise for Learning to Accompany Plainchant, in the Bass or the Upper Part, for the Use of Persons Who Know Little or No Harmony."

34. As late as the 1950s, the quarrel about chant accompaniment continued, with the medieval scholar Jacques Chailley insisting that chant was meant to be sung unaccompanied and that any accompaniment only disfigures it (Huot-Pleuroux, *Musique religieuse*, 44–45, quoting Chailley, *Histoire musicale du moyen âge* [Paris: Presses universitaires de France, 1950], 45).

35. For a thorough study of this work, see Edward Zimmerman and Lawrence Archbold, " 'Why Should We Not Do the Same with our Catholic Melodies?': Guilmant's *L'Organiste liturgiste*, op. 65," in Archbold and Peterson, *French Organ Music*, 201–47.

36. Sisson, "Tournemire," 58. He made his first contact with Solesmes in 1927, and had several conversations with Dom Joseph Gajard and Dom Charles Letestu, the abbey organist (see Bernadette Lespinard, "*L'Orgue mystique* de Charles Tournemire," *L'Orgue: Cahiers et mémoires*, no. 139 bis (1971): 4.

37. Norbert Dufourcq, "Jouer de l'orgue à l'èglise catholique?" *L'Orgue*, no. 199 (July–September 1986): 4–5.

38. Allen Hobbs, telephone conversation, February 19, 2001.

39. On July 1, 1901, the anticlerical Third Republic passed legislation against religious congregations, precipitating the exile of the Benedictines from Solesmes. The monks moved to the Isle of Wight and were not able to return to Solesmes until 1922.

40. See Dom Joseph Gajard, *The Solesmes Method: Its Fundamental Principles and Practical Rules of Interpretation*, trans. R. Cecile Gabain (Collegeville, MN: Liturgical Press, 1960).

41. Robert F. Hayburn, *Papal Legislation on Sacred Music, 95 A.D. to 1977 A.D.* (Collegeville, MN: Liturgical Press, 1979), 224.

42. Ibid., 225.

43. The use of the Vatican edition was generally binding from September 25, 1905.

44. Ch. Cordonnier, *Monseigneur Fuzet, Archevêque de Rouen* (Paris: Beauchesne et ses Fils, 1948), 358.

45. Such as the antiphons *Beatus vir*, *Puer nobis*, and *Haec dies*, and the hymns *Ave maris stella* and *Lauda Sion*, all of which appear in his organ works.

46. Thomson, *Widor*, 68, quoting Charles-Marie Widor, "Le Plainchant de Solesmes," 1904, an unpublished manuscript in the Archives de la maison diocésaine, Paris. Widor referred to the Benedictines as the Malédictins (see Pinguet, *Écoles de la musique divine*, 113n), but he nevertheless requested the Gregorian requiem for his own funeral (see Thomson, *Widor*, 94).

47. Quoted in Sisson, "Tournemire," 60.

48. Hayburn, *Papal Legislation*, 276.

49. It appears in the second movement, assigned to a solo tromba interna, and is among the classic trumpet solos of the orchestral repertoire.

50. Julia d'Almendra, "Les Modes grégoriens dans l'œuvre de Claude Debussy" (Diss., Institut Grégorien de Paris, 1947−1948), 62.

51. Dom Clément Jacob, "Erik Satie et le chant grégorien," *Revue musicale*, no. 386−87 (1985): 92, quoting from the thesis of Almendra.

52. Oscar Thompson, *Debussy: Man and Artist*, an unabridged and corrected republication of the original 1937 edition (New York: Dover Publications, 1967), 352.

53. Ibid., 338.

54. Ibid., 350.

55. Ibid., 75.

56. See Léon Guichard, "Erik Satie et la musique grégorienne," *Revue musicale* 17 (November 1936): 334−35.

57. Such as Gajard's *Solesmes Method*, mentioned above.

58. Interview with Duruflé during a program on France-Culture dedicated to him and his work. Some of his remarks were printed in *Una Voce* (France) 111 (July–August 1983) and reprinted in "Maurice Duruflé on Church Music since Vatican II," trans. Virginia A. Schubert, *Sacred Music* 110 (1983): 15.

# Chapter Sixteen

1. "Extraordinary commissions to living artists and composers of music toward combating unemployment," as translated by Leslie A. Sprout in "Music for a 'New Era': Composers and National Identity in France, 1936–1946" (PhD diss., University of California, Berkeley, 2000), 20. The French is found in Myriam Chimenes, *La Vie musicale sous Vichy* (Brussels: Éditions Complexe, 2001), 157.

2. The following account of the commissioning of Duruflé's *Requiem* is based on Sprout, "New Era," 354–60, 386; and idem, "Les Commandes de Vichy, aube d'une ère nouvelle," in Chimènes, *Vichy*, 160, 176–77. Sprout's work on this subject can hardly be overestimated. Her research has opened up areas of study that were unknown before the writing of her dissertation and the chapter.

3. The archival sources for the commissions program were difficult to piece together, "owing, on the one hand, to the initial tenuousness of the program in the 1938 budget, and on the other, to the fact that Vichy era documents have only recently been made available to researchers" (Sprout, "New Era," x). The key sources exist in two separate locations at the Archives nationales in Paris. The first, in the legislative files of the Administration des Beaux-Arts (F21 5305: Musique, Législation [2]: Œuvres commandées aux compositeurs de musique, Arrêtés originaux, 1938–1944), "consists of the

decrees announcing the final lists of composers for each year from 1938 to 1950 (1942 is missing)"; the second (F21 5150: Musique et Spectacles, Comptabilité, Engagements ou ordonnements, Exercice 1947, Chapitre 547, Commandes à des artistes musiciens) "contains the receipts of payments to composers in the records of the Administration's accounting department, confirms and updates the original decrees." The author acknowledges Sprout's generosity in providing the specific identities and locations of the files (Sprout, e-mail message to author, October 28, 2002).

4. Messiaen was an exception to this rule.

5. Later in 1941, commissions were awarded to Georges Dandelot, Henri Dutilleux, Jean-Jacques Grunenwald, Pierre Maillard-Verger, Amédée Gastoué, and André Gailhard. In 1942, commissions were given to organists Alexandre Cellier, André Jolivet, Jean Langlais, Paul Pierné, and Elsa Barraine, among others. In 1943, the commissions were awarded to Georges Hugon, Georges Dandelot, Henri Sauguet, Jean Françaix, Charles Koechlin, Gustave Samazeuilh, Paul Le Flem, and Daniel-Lesur, among others. Three of the fourteen commissions awarded in 1944 went to Robert Planel, Francis Casadesus, and Marcel Landowski. And four of the fifteen commissions awarded in 1945 went to Charles Koechlin, Tony Aubin, Elsa Barraine, and Jean-Jacques Grunenwald.

6. The certificate signed by Duruflé is found in the Archives nationales (Exercice 1947: Commandes à des artistes musiciens, Comptabilité, engagements ou ordonnements, 1938–1950, Spectacles et musique, Beaux-Arts) and is cited in Sprout, "New Era," 386.

7. Jean-Pierre Patat and Michel Lutfalla, *A Monetary History of France in the Twentieth Century*, trans. Patrick Martindale and David Cobham (New York: St. Martin's Press, 1990), 92, 103.

8. Beevor and Cooper, *Paris*, 419.

9. Sprout, "New Era," 385, 387.

10. Ibid., 393, 395.

11. Ibid., 379, 381.

12. Ibid., 391.

13. In the 1980s, the single most lucrative French composition was Maurice Ravel's *Boléro*. But Duruflé's *Requiem* reported the largest licensing and rental fees of any work from a living French composer (Pinguet to author, April 10, 2002). Current figures are available from the Société des auteurs, compositeurs et éditeurs de musique (SACEM).

14. Sprout, "New Era," 234–38, and 409–11. Her source: Série Guerre 1939–1945, Vichy, État français, Service des Œuvres, Radio: dossier général, 1940–44 (See Sprout, "New Era," 411). Duruflé's *Tambourin* appears on disc AA.11.

15. Charles-Marie Widor composed *Jeanne d'Arc*, a mimed legend, for soloists, choirs, harps, orchestra, fanfares, drums, etc.

16. Sprout, "New Era," 360.

17. Ibid., 356, 359.

18. Ibid., 360.

19. Ibid., 362.

20. Ibid., 355.

21. Maurice Blanc, "Le Requiem de Maurice Duruflé," *Musique et Liturgie* 18 (November–December 1950): 10.

22. Abbing, *Duruflé*, 165.

23. Sprout, "Commandes de Vichy."

24. Cartayrade wrote to Chimènes to obtain Sprout's address (Sprout, e-mail message to author, October 28, 2002).

25. James Frazier, "Maurice Duruflé: A Centenary," parts 1 and 2, *American Organist* 36 (November 2002): 58–65; 36 (December 2002): 51–53.

26. See Frédéric Blanc's letter to the editor, *American Organist* 37 (March 2003): 16, 18.

27. Chimènes, *Vichy*, 28.

28. Münch's substantial earnings helped finance the Resistance. His country house was an important way station for prisoners escaping from the Germans (Münch, *Conductor*, xxviii).

29. Désormière took care of Milhaud's effects when the latter left Paris in 1940, paid his rent during the Occupation, and prevented the loss of his piano when the rest of his furniture was liquidated (Mayer and Souvtchinsky, *Désormière*, 28). He also defended Jacques Rouché, director of the Paris Opéra, "unable to bear the fact that he was unjustly suspected" (Ibid., 28–29, quoting Milhaud).

30. Chimènes, Introduction, in *Vichy*, 28.

31. Quoted in Sprout, "New Era," 217, translation by Sprout.

32. Ibid.

33. Ibid., 219.

34. Chimènes, Introduction, 30.

35. Sprout, "New Era," 360.

36. Benoist-Méchin was blacklisted for his writings and for having served as secretary of state for Franco-German relations. Sentenced to a life of forced labor, he was released in 1954 (Beevor and Cooper, *Paris*, 162).

37. The renowned pianist held a number of high-level posts in the Vichy government. On December 30, 1943, he was named president of the Comité professionnel de l'art musical et de l'enseignement musical libre de la musique, known simply as the Comité Cortot. Six days later Marcel Dupré was designated president of the commission on the organ and church music (Chimènes, *Vichy*, 41). One of Cortot's greatest faults was to have performed in Germany, as did Les Petits Chanteurs à la croix de bois, the boychoir that Duruflé sometimes accompanied. In 1943 the choir performed in Vichy.

38. Chimènes, "Alfred Cortot et la politique musicale du gouvernement de Vichy," in *Vichy*, 30; Sprout, "New Era," 362. Claude Delvincourt, Marcel Dupré, and Germaine Lubin declined the invitation (ibid.). An earlier trip, in 1941, would have included Marcel Dupré and Marcel Delannoy, but it never progressed beyond the planning stages (Philippe Burrin, *France under the Germans: Collaboration and Compromise*, trans. Janet Lloyd [New York: New York Press, 1996], 349).

39. Chimènes, "Introduction," 26.

40. Ibid., 29.

41. However, "One can indeed believe that [Boulanger] always showed a strong admiration for maréchal Pétain" (Spycket, *Boulanger*, 124).

## Chapter Seventeen

1. Éliane Chevalier, interview; Gwilym Beechey, "Maurice Duruflé and his *Requiem*," *Music Review* 32 (May 1971): 92.

2. Maurice Blanc, "Requiem," 10. Ronald Ebrecht erroneously identified the second piece as the *Libera me* (Ebrecht, *Duruflé*, 89n3).

3. Maurice Blanc, "Requiem," 10. Duruflé recalled having begun this work in 1945 (Duruflé, "Souvenirs [1976]," 47), but an earlier date is more likely, considering that he received the commission in 1941.

4. Éliane Chevalier, interview.

5. Settings of the requiem mass always include the ordinary of the mass (but without the *Gloria in excelsis* or the *Credo*) as well as the proper, because it is the latter that conveys the sentiments of the mass for the dead.

6. The musicologist Philippe Robert wrote, erroneously, "In all the history of the polyphonic *Requiem*, that of Maurice Duruflé is the first to have cited textually the elements of the Gregorian model" ("La Place de Maurice Duruflé dans l'histoire de la musique," in Ville de Louviers, *Duruflé*, n.p.).

7. Paris: Institut grégorien, 1948, 1953.

8. Duruflé, "Souvenirs [1976]," 47–48.

9. Maurice Blanc, "Requiem," 10–11.

10. Ibid., 11.

11. Ibid.

12. Ibid.

13. Peter G. Jarjisian, "The Influence of Gregorian Chant on Maurice Durufle's 'Requiem,' op. 9" (DMA diss., University of Wisconsin–Madison, 1991), 119.

14. See, for instance, ibid., 53.

15. Ibid., 82–84.

16. Ibid., 53, quoting Robertson, *Requiem*, 124.

17. Jarjisian, "Duruflé's 'Requiem,'" 72.

18. Éliane Chevalier, liner notes, 2.

19. Jarjisian, "Durufle's *Requiem*," 46; Aprahamian, "Requiem," 613; Beechey, "*Requiem*," 89. None of these writers cites a source. Alec Robertson suggested that the *Requiem* "was the result of a commission from his publishers to compose a suite of organ pieces based on plainsong themes from the Mass of the Dead but, on the death of his father it became, in extended form, a Requiem" (*Requiem: Music of Mourning and Consolation* [London: Cassell, 1967], 123).

20. Ibid., 49.

21. Where possible, Duruflé urged the performance of the *Requiem* at "an opportune occasion," and "the best," he wrote, "is certainly the time of All Saints," November 1. It is the companion feast with All Souls Day, which falls on November 2 (Duruflé to M. Savoye, general secretary for the Société des Concerts, May 17, probably 1951; BnF Bob20363, letter 132).

22. Duruflé, "Souvenirs [1976]," 49.

23. Chamfray, "Chronology," 51; Duruflé-Chevalier, "Entretien"; Machabey, *Portraits*, 72.

24. *SAE*, 254. Elsewhere Duruflé wrote that he himself was the organist (Duruflé, "Souvenirs [1976]," 49).

25. Clarendon [Bernard Gavoty], "Le *Requiem* de Duruflé," *Le Figaro*, November 8, 1947, n.p.

26. Henriette Roget, "La Musique," *Les Lettres françaises*, November 27, 1947, n.p.

27. Ch. Pons, "*Le Requiem* de M. Duruflé," *L'Ordre*, December 30, 1947, n.p.

28. Clarendon [Bernard Gavoty], "Le *Requiem* de Duruflé," *Le Figaro*, November 19, 1948, n.p.

29. The *Dies irae* was the proper sequence appointed to be sung after the tract and before the gospel prior to the reforms of the Second Vatican Council. It is no longer used.

30. The 1903 *motu proprio* also specified that "It is . . . permitted, after the Offertory of the mass has been sung [at a solemn mass], to execute during the time that remains a brief motet to words approved by the Church." Prior to Vatican II, therefore, the *Pie Jesu* could be sung *ad libitum* immediately after the proper offertory chant, or immediately after the *Benedictus*, or during communion.

31. Beechey, "*Requiem*," 91.

32. "It is often dramatic, or filled with resignation, or hope or terror" (Duruflé, "Requiem," 57).

33. Evidently unaware of this liturgical fact, Jeffrey Reynolds writes, "Duruflé like Fauré chose to combine these two separate texts into one introductory prayer on behalf of both the living and the dead" ("On Clouds of Incense," in Ebrecht, *Duruflé*, 94). Reynolds also erroneously writes that the *Hostias et preces tibi* "is the moment in the Mass when, at the elevation of the host, the mystical act of transubstantiation occurs" (ibid., 97). Rather, the transubstantiation is held to occur at the words of the priest over the bread, *Hoc est enim corpus meum* (For this is my body) and at the words over the chalice, *Hic est enim calix sanguinis mei* (For this is the chalice of my blood).

34. Alec Robertson states incorrectly that "the same sections are set." See Robertson, *Requiem*, 123.

35. In settings of the ordinary prior to the Second Vatican Council, the *Benedictus* was delayed until after the consecration. As a single movement, Duruflé's *Sanctus-Benedictus* at once looked backward to earlier centuries, and was also ahead of its time, in that the practice was restored by the council. In his Messe *"Cum jubilo,"* the two are separate movements.

36. Clarendon [Gavoty], "*Requiem* de Maurice Duruflé," n.p.

37. Robertson, *Requiem*, 123.

38. Aprahamian, "Requiem," 613.

39. Beechey, "*Requiem*," 89.

40. Reynolds, "On Clouds of Incense," 89, quoting Duruflé to Charles Lewis, November 8, 1971.

41. One may wonder why the oratorio did not fare better in Catholic France. The genre had its origin in Catholic Italy, where Saint Philip Neri (1515–95) formed a community of priests called the Fathers of the Oratory and established a building called an oratorio, where services of a popular character were held. Marc-Antoine Charpentier (1634–1704) composed so-called *histoires sacrées*, but he had no successors. Through Johann Mattheson (1681–1764) the oratorio became identified with Protestant worship in Germany and was fully exploited by Handel and Bach.

The once popular *Psaume XLVII* of Schmitt unfortunately did not survive the test of time. And why a work like Dupré's sophisticated and well-crafted *De profundis*, a nine-movement psalm for soloists and chorus with organ or orchestral accompaniment, should remain virtually unknown is a mystery.

42. Constant Pierre, *B. Sarrette et les origines du Conservatoire national de musique et de déclamation* (Paris: Librairie Delalain Frères, 1895), 183.

43. Vol. 9, no. 19, n.d. The article is reprinted in Joy, *Schweitzer*, 48–56, under the title "The Chorus in Paris."

44. Ibid., 53.

45. Joris-Karl Huysmans, *En Route*, trans. C. Kegan Paul (New York: E. P. Dutton, 1920), 10.

46. Ibid., 64–65. Durtal made this observation some nine years before Maurice Emmanuel became *maître de chapelle*. Under the direction of Jules Meunier, Tournemire called them "the screamers" (Labounsky, *Langlais*, 78).

47. Huysmans, *En Route*, 43.

48. Ibid.

49. Ibid., 44.

50. See Paul De Launay, "Charles Marie Widor," *American Organist* 3 (August 1920): 278; Marshall Bidwell, "Organ Music in Paris Cathedrals: III, Widor and Saint Sulpice," *American Organist* 5 (October 1922): 419–20, 422, 424; idem, "Organ Music in Paris

Churches: IV, St. Eustache and La Madeleine," *American Organist* 5 (November 1922): 467–68, 472; G. Criss Simpson, "A Second Organistic Pilgrimage: An American Organist Again Gives His Impressions of Europe after an Absence of Several Seasons at Home," *American Organist* 12 (October 1929): 597–99; idem, "Paris as I Saw It," *American Organist* 10 (October 1927): 262; idem, "Organ Music in Paris Churches: VI, Reims and La Trinité," *American Organist* 6 (February 1922): 76, 78; and Hugh McAmis, "Paris Pictures," *American Organist* 8 (February 1925): 81.

51. Beechey, "*Requiem*," 92. The *Requiem* was performed at Notre-Dame, Paris, for the 1996 funeral of French President François Mitterand (Paul Duruflé to author, September 23, 2002). Paul Duruflé told the author about rumors in France that the *Requiem* was performed for the funeral of President John Fitzgerald Kennedy. It was not, but stories have occasionally been told of people hearing the Gregorian *Missa pro defunctis* and thinking it was the Duruflé *Requiem*.

52. Bingham gives the year 1951 in his article, "Organ Personalities: Duruflé," *American Organist* 46 (October 1963): 13.

53. Frederick Swann, e-mail message.

54. Bingham, "Duruflé's *Requiem*," 18.

55. See http://www.bach-cantatas.com/Bio/Willcocks-David.htm.

56. In June 1952, Seth Bingham met with Duruflé in Paris, and had the "rare privilege to go over his Requiem with the composer and to compare the orchestra score with the organ arrangement" (Bingham, "Duruflé's *Requiem*," 18.).

57. Abbing, *Duruflé*, 174.

58. Liner notes for the recording of the *Requiem* by the Ensemble vocal de Neuwird, directed by B. Kämpf (Motette CD 50241), quoted in François Sabatier, [Untitled], *L'Orgue*, no. 221 (January–March 1992): 49.

59. Sabatier, [Untitled], 49.

60. Duruflé, "Interview with Duruflé [Baker, French]," 219.

61. Duruflé to Murtagh, March 4 and 22, 1964.

62. Duruflé to Murtagh, September 18, 1971.

63. Bert, [Hommage], 12.

64. Shaw conducted the *Requiem* in Minneapolis, MN shortly before his death, and assigned the movement to the entire alto section instead of a soloist. In his dissertation, Peter Jarjisian writes that Duruflé suggested doing so ("Durufle's *Requiem*," 120). But Mme Duruflé wrote, "I hope that this execution was truly *exceptional*, for my husband never asked for such a grouping. He wanted a *soloist* [emphasis in the original]" (Letter to author, August 9, 1994).

65. Duruflé was like Vierne in this regard, who wrote, "Until 1907 I did not write one page without showing it to the maître [Widor]" (Vierne, "Mes Souvenirs," 105).

66. Ibid., 49.

67. Blanc, interview.

68. BnF NLa 68 (201), December 11, 1947; NLa 68 (205), July 13, 1957; NLa 68 (207), December 18, 1961.

69. Duruflé to Boulanger, BnF NLa 68 (205).

70. Nelson, "Organ Works," 32.

71. Letter from Marie-Madeleine Duruflé, probably to Jörg Abbing, July 21, 1992, quoted in Abbing, *Duruflé*, 84–85.

72. Alain, "Entretien," 4. Duruflé would be alarmed over how the *Pie Jesu* came to be used after his death. Robert Shaw's 1987 Telarc recording of the work, with the Atlanta Symphony Orchestra, is quoted at the beginning of pop singer Michael Jackson's song *Little*

*Susie*, on the recording entitled *History* (dated 1995, with copyright clearance noted thus: "© 1948 Éditions Durand [SACEM/ASCAP]").

73. Hayburn, *Papal Legislation*, 229.

74. The *motu proprio* prescribes, in paragraph 8, that "it is not lawful to change either the words or their order"; and in paragraph 11, that the parts of the mass "must represent in the music the unity of their text" (Hayburn, *Papal Legislation*, 226–27.).

75. Duruflé-Chevalier, "Entretien."

76. Éliane Chevalier, "Chevalier-Duruflé," 20.

# Chapter Eighteen

1. Saint Stephen-on-the-Mount.

2. Civil records about artists and artisans living and working in Paris from 1535 to 1792 are found in the Actes d'état civil, and are contained in the Fichier Laborde in the BnF. The work of Marquis Léon de Laborde, a member of the Institut, who was named Garde général des archives de l'empire in 1857 and died in 1869, the Fichier Laborde consists of 66,080 file cards arranged alphabetically. It includes the civil records of organists and other musicians for nearly 250 years of the Ancien régime. Yolande de Brossard (in *Musiciens de Paris, 1535–1792: Actes d'état civil d'après le fichier Laborde de la Bibliothèque Nationale* [Paris: Éditions A. et J. Picard, 1965]) culls the musicians from the collection, including organists. For a variety of reasons the Fichier Laborde is not exhaustive. The listing of organists at Saint Étienne-du-Mont given in table 18.1, therefore, is not a complete account. Norbert Dufourcq (in *Le Livre de l'orgue français, 1589–1789*, 5 vols. [Paris: Éditions A. et J. Picard, 1971]) deals with roughly the same period. John Henderson (in *Composers*), and Corliss Richard Arnold (in *Organ Literature: A Comprehensive Survey*, 2nd ed. [Metuchen, NJ: Scarecrow Press, 1984]) document later centuries.

3. Archives nationales, Minutier Central, XVIII, Reg. 193, fol. 337. Reprinted in Norbert Dufourcq, "La Contribution à l'histoire des orgues parisiennes à la fin du règne de Louis XIII," *L'Orgue: Dix années au service de l'orgue français: 1927–1937* (1937): 52–54.

4. Dufourcq, *Le Livre de l'orgue*, 1:596.

5. See ibid., 4:58.

6. Félix Raugel, "Orgues et Organistes," *Courrier musical et théâtral* 24 (January 1, 1922): 66.

7. Havard de la Montagne reports that Baron *père* was choir accompanist at Saint Vincent-de-Paul from 1814 (see http://musicaetmemoria.ovh.org/st-vincent-dp.htm#besozzi).

8. Havard de la Montagne reports that Baron *fils* was choir organist at Saint Vincent-de-Paul from 1827 to 1830 (ibid.). This is incompatible with the dates given above, where Baron *fils* is shown as having become titular at Saint Étienne-du-Mont in 1827.

9. Labounsky, *Langlais*, 31. See also Sébastien Durand's "Les Aveugles et l'école d'orgue française: Un siècle d'orgue à l'Institut national des jeunes aveugles, 1820–1930" (Doctoral diss., Université de Nancy, 2000). The work was later published under the same title (Lille: A.N.R.T., 2003).

10. Ochse, *Organists*, 130.

11. Montalembert vigorously promoted a regard and taste for medieval art. He was concerned about the deteriorating condition of Notre-Dame and denounced the ignorant restorations conducted by government architects.

12. Henri Bachelin, "L'Orgue de tribune et les organistes en France," *Ménestrel* 91 (November 8, 1929): 475. This is one of a series of articles published weekly from October 11 through November 22, 1929.

13. *Courrier musical et théâtral* 24 (July 1922): 242; 25 (January 15, 1923): 34; 25 (April 1, 1923); and 26 (March 15, 1924).

14. Association Élisabeth et Joachim Havard de la Montagne, "Musica et Memoria."

15. Jesse Eschbach believes Chantérac was the last official titular at Saint Bernard. Eschbach himself played for Saturday masses there in 1978, the first time the organ had been heard since the early 1960s. On one occasion the very elderly monsignor said to him: "Look, there used to be a young lady, a blonde, who came to replace our organist. She played fast and loud. Her name was Mlle Chevalier" (Eschbach, e-mail message to author, March 18, 2005).

16. The following letters are held at the Archives historiques de l'Archevêché de Paris: Saint Étienne-du-Mont; 2D Biens mobiliers: Dossier sur les orgues de l'Église Saint Étienne-du-Mont et audition d'orgue.

17. Duruflé wrote that he was named to Saint Étienne-du-Mont in 1929 (Duruflé, "Souvenirs [1976]," 38).

18. The announcement of Duruflé's appointment did not appear in the *Bulletin semestriel des Amis de l'Orgue* until June 1930 (p. 4). Mme Duruflé gives October 1930 in "Les Grandes-Orgues de Saint Étienne-du-Mont et son role dans la liturgie," in *Bulletin* 3 (June 2003): 8; first printed in *Journal paroissial de Saint Étienne-du-Mont*, 181–82 (September and November 1984). While this date is incorrect, the conflation of October with 1930 may be the understandable result of her confusing an October appointment with an actual start in 1930.

19. On January 11, 2002, the city of Paris placed a plaque at 6, place du Panthéon, to mark the hundredth anniversary of Duruflé's birth. It reads:

> The composer
> Maurice Duruflé
> and the organist Marie-Madeleine Duruflé
> lived in this building
> from 1930 to 1999.

The first date, 1930, is incorrect by a wide margin. The Duruflé Association, which made the arrangements with the city to install the plaque, assumed that Duruflé moved to place du Panthéon shortly after he began his duties at Saint Étienne-du-Mont. The fact is that he continued living on rue Dupuytren until 1938 and moved to place du Panthéon in that year (see the certificate of Duruflé's marriage to Marie-Madeleine Chevalier, in the Archives historiques de l'Archevêché de Paris: Saint Étienne-du-Mont, dossier 1C).

20. Eschbach, e-mail message to author, March 18, 2005.

21. A. de Vallombrosa, "Les Orgues de Chœur à Paris," *L'Orgue*, no. 58–59 (January–June 1951): 36.

22. Ebrecht, *Duruflé*, 166n, quoting a letter from the prefect to the Beaux-Arts (April 15, 1941), Dossier Saint-Étienne. Ebrecht reports that Beuchet repaired the instrument after the war (referring to "L'Activé [*sic*] des factueurs [*sic*]," *L'Orgue*, no. 43 [April–June 1947]: 44).

23. Duruflé, "Souvenirs [1976]," 43. For stoplist see Appendix C, p. 274.

24. Loth's brother Georges, who trained as a chorister at the *maîtrise* of the Rouen Cathedral, had been organist of Notre-Dame de Lorette in Paris, and was organist at Sacré-Cœur on Montmartre in 1902–3.

25. Parish records indicate that during the Second World War there were "enfants de chœur" who were paid for their services. See Archives historiques de l'Archevêché de Paris. Saint Étienne-du-Mont, 2Er Journal Générale 1921–32 and 1943–50.

26. A. V., "Une Messe de Requiem," *Musique et Liturgie* 5 (March–April 1938): 103.

27. "Les Grandes Orgues de l'Église Saint Étienne-du-Mont," *Courrier musical et théâtral* 29 (October 15, 1927): 489; "Échos et Nouvelles," *Ménestrel* 89 (October 1927): 423; G. S., "Le *Requiem* de Berlioz à Saint Étienne-du-Mont," *Ménestrel* 89 (November 18, 1927): 474.

28. Letter dated March 16, 1931 (Archives historiques de l'Archevêché de Paris: Saint Étienne-du-Mont; 2D Biens Mobiliers: Dossier sur les orgues de l'Église Saint Étienne-du-Mont et audition d'orgue).

29. Soularue's tenure as titular was brief because of a disagreement with the clergy (Abbing, *Duruflé*, 145–46).

30. Eschbach, e-mail message to author.

31. Warnier was co-titular at the cathedral in Verdun before assuming the post at Saint Étienne-du-Mont.

## Chapter Nineteen

1. Bachelin, "Orgue de Tribune," 438.

2. Dufourcq, *Le Livre de l'orgue* 1:135–36. D'Argillières was from a family of organists and organ builders active in Normandy and the Île-de-France from 1557 to 1620. In 1570 he completed repairs on the organ of Sainte Chapelle in Paris.

3. Duruflé-Chevalier, "Grandes-Orgues," 8.

4. The complete contract appears verbatim in Dufourcq, "Contribution," 51–52.

5. Dufourcq, *Le Livre de l'orgue* 1:586, 3:103. Details of the following account of the organ's history are taken from Duruflé, "La Restauration du grand orgue de Saint Étienne-du-Mont," *L'Orgue*, no. 90 (1959): 47; Félix Raugel, "Du second au troisième grand orgue de Saint Étienne-du-Mont," *L'Orgue*, no. 90 (1959): 38–44; Pierre Hardouin, "Du Premier Grand Orgue de Saint Étienne-du-Mont, à l'achèvement du second," *L'Orgue*, no. 87 (July–September 1958): 73–83.

6. Dufourcq, *Le Livre de l'orgue* 2:89–91; and Pierre Hardouin, "Les Grandes Orgues de Saint Étienne-du-Mont, à Paris," *L'Orgue*, no. 76 (July–September 1955): 83–88.

7. For the stoplist of the organ in 1636, see Appendix C, p. 268.

8. Nelson, "Organ Works," 31; Duruflé, "Restauration du grand orgue Saint Étienne-du-Mont," 47; Arthur Lawrence, "An Organ Tour of Paris," *American Organist* 27 (December 1993): 72; Dufourcq, *Le Livre de l'orgue* 1:353. The specifics appear in Félix Raugel, *Les Grandes Orgues des églises de Paris et du département de la Seine* (Paris: Librairie Fischbacher, 1927), which was quoted in the "Étude d'un projet de reconstruction du grand orgue de Saint Étienne-du-Mont [1936?]." The latter was written by Raugel and Marcel Dupré, and is contained in the dossier on Saint Étienne-du-Mont in the Département des orgues, Monuments historiques, 3 rue de Valois, Paris; copy in the possession of the author.

9. See Appendix C, p. 269.

10. For the stoplist of the organ in 1863, see Appendix C, p. 270.

11. In 1894, the writer Lucien Descaves dedicated an entire chapter of his novel *Les Emmurés* (Paris: Tresse et Stock) to the organ of Saint Étienne-du-Mont as constituted by Cavaillé-Coll.

12. Smith, *Vierne*, 350.

13. Vierne, "Mes Souvenirs," 195. For stoplist see Appendix C, p. 271.

14. This number of stops was mentioned in the report signed by Vierne, Tournemire, and Marchal.

15. Duruflé's friend Gaston Litaize managed to play a recital there on March 19, 1931 (Ebrecht, *Duruflé*, 166n26, quoting "L'Activité de nos organistes," *L'Orgue*, no. 8 [December 1931]: 9).

16. Duruflé, "Souvenirs [1976]," 42.

17. Except where noted, the following assessment of the organ is taken from the "Étude d'un projet de reconstruction du grand orgue de Saint Étienne-du-Mont [1936?]"; see also Duruflé, "Restauration du grand orgue Saint Étienne-du-Mont." The "Étude" is the first of several formal reports submitted to the Service des monuments historiques. It contains three sections: (1) "Résumé historique de l'instrument," much of which is quoted from the article on Saint Étienne-du-Mont in Raugel's book (1927), contains the stoplist for the organ as it existed in 1911; (2) "Dernier Projet de restauration [1928] de M. Paul-Marie Koenig" describes the state of the organ after Koenig's work on it and gives the stoplist as it existed in 1932; (3) "État actuel et project de reconstruction" gives the commission's recommendations regarding the system of transmission, and the stoplist for a new organ of fifty-nine stops, showing also the old stops to be kept or completed. Subsequent reports were submitted by Debierre-Gloton, the first on August 25, 1941, a second on June 30, 1944, and a third on February 7, 1946. The second and third reports are contained in the dossier of the Département des orgues; the first is not. There must have been subsequent reports from the organ builder, inasmuch as the organ was not finished for another ten years after the third report was filed, but these do not appear in the dossier.

18. These letters are in the Archives historiques de l'Archevêché de Paris, Saint Étienne-du-Mont, 2D Biens Mobiliers: Dossier sur les orgues de l'église Saint Étienne-du-Mont et audition d'orgue.

19. Ibid.

20. Dupré wrote a letter on April 29, 1936, to the Directeur général des Beaux-Arts, in Paris, agreeing to provide his study of the needed repairs of the organ "in the briefest time possible."

21. In the letter that Duruflé wrote to the curé in December 1934, complaining of Koenig's work, he gave his rationale for recommending electro-pneumatic key and stop action in the new instrument, instead of mechanical action, and reported that Vierne had supported placing the console in the side gallery.

22. Georges Danion, [Hommage], 18–19.

23. According to the report of Debierre-Gloton dated June 30, 1944.

24. Reference to this point is made in Beuchet's "Second Rapport."

25. The fourth division had already been identified as an écho in the 1936 proposal of Raugel and Dupré. Éliane Chevalier told Ronald Ebrecht that Duruflé paid for the écho division but she could not remember its cost (Ebrecht, *Duruflé*, 179n56, quoting interviews with her between March and August 2001).

26. A statement from the city of Paris, dated February 10, 1945, which quoted details from the minutes of the meeting of 1944, was quoted in the organ builder's third report.

27. Quoted in a letter dated May 25, 1949, from the Ministère de l'éducation nationale, Direction de l'architecture, to the Directeur d'architecture, contained in the dossier in the Département des orgues.

28. Éliane Chevalier told Ronald Ebrecht that Duruflé paid 200,000 francs from his own resources to cover the cost of the balustrade (Ebrecht, *Duruflé*, 179n56, quoting interviews with Chevalier, March–August 2001).

29. The following details are taken from Duruflé, "Restauration du grand orgue Saint Étienne-du-Mont."

30. For the stoplist of the organ in 1956, see Appendix C, p. 273.

31. Latry, interview.

32. Duruflé to Donald Metz, September 18, 1960.

33. Blanc, interview.

34. Danion, [Hommage], 19.

35. Duruflé, "Restauration du grand orgue Saint Étienne-du-Mont," 52.

36. Latry, interview.

37. Duruflé, "Souvenirs [1976]," 43.

38. "L'Association des Amis de l'Orgue, 1937–1957," 5.

39. Jean-Louis Coignet was tonal director for the Canadian firm Casavant Frères and expert-organier for the city of Paris.

40. Jean-Louis Coignet to author, June 18, 2004.

41. Duruflé, "Souvenirs [1976]," 43.

42. Duruflé-Chevalier, "Entretien."

43. Duruflé, "Interview with Durufleé [Baker], 59.

44. Duruflé, "Souvenirs [1976]," 43.

45. Mme Duruflé to Murtagh, September 17, 1974.

46. Jacques Bertrand, "L'Orgue de salon de Maurice Duruflé," *Bulletin* 2 (June 2002): 15.

47. Duruflé, "Souvenirs [1976]," 43.

48. Coignet to author, March 29, 2004.

49. Bertrand, "Orgue de salon," 14. According to Georges Danion, Duruflé, "wanting everything to be perfect, personally paid the additional costs to repair the Positif wind chest and several stops, for a total cost of 45,000 francs" (*Bulletin* 2 [May 2002]: 19).

50. Latry, interview.

51. Duruflé, "Interview with Duruflé [Baker]," 59.

52. *Actes du troisième congrès international de musique sacrée, Paris—1er—8 juillet 1957: Perspectives de la musique sacrée à la lumière de l'encyclique Musicae sacrae disciplina.* (Paris: [Éditions du congrès], 1959), 716, 720.

53. Blanc, interview.

54. "grandiose, délicat et fruité." Dargassies, [Hommage], 21.

55. Blanc, interview, quoting Mme Duruflé. "Flooding and humidity is [*sic*] a recurrent problem in this organ (dead pigeons stop gutters that hence overflow)" (Coignet to author, June 18, 2004).

56. *SAE*, 107.

# Chapter Twenty

1. M.P., [Review], *Ménestrel* 90 (April 27, 1928): 185.

2. "Interview with Duruflé [Baker, French]," 227.

3. Ibid., 216.

4. Jaquet-Langlais, "Organ Works of Franck," 170.

5. Daniel Roth, "Some Thoughts on the Interpretation of the Organ Works of Franck, on His Organ, and on the Lemmens Tradition," trans. David Gramit, in *French Organ Music*, ed. Archbold and Peterson, 195.

6. Vine to author, December 3, 2002.

7. Quoted in Ebrecht, *Duruflé*, x.

8. Alain, Introduction, xiii–xiv, trans. Ebrecht.

9. Vine, interview by author, Boston, February 6, 2004.

10. Mason, "Conversations," 66.

11. Vine, e-mail message to author, June 20, 2005.

12. Duruflé, "Interview with Duruflé [Baker, French]," 216.

13. Ibid., 219.

14. Ibid., 216–17. By contrast, Duruflé is not known to have regretted the *Animando poco a poco* in the *Adagio* on *Veni Creator*, where the quarter note accelerates from 60 to 100 in the course of six measures (pp. 24–25).

15. The author encountered the same evasiveness over this point when he studied the work with Mme Duruflé.

16. Duruflé-Chevalier, "Entretien." Virgil Fox took liberties with Duruflé's music, even adding measures. Mme Duruflé said, "You know what he does at the beginning of my husband's *Sicilienne*? He adds two measures of solo pedal, and he always does it with such enthusiasm. He's so sincere, so generous that you want to forgive him completely. He's a good friend." Her husband added, "Possibly from the point of view of registration he does some things that aren't always very pleasing. He will pull the tremolo with the cornet for example" (Duruflé, "Interview with Duruflé [Baker, French]," 220).

17. Vine, telephone conversation with author, December 2, 2002.

18. Vine, e-mail message to author, March 3, 2005.

19. Alain Pâris, *Dictionnaire des interprètes et de l'interprétation musicale au XXe siècle* (Paris: Éditions Robert Laffont, 1995), s.v. Duruflé.

20. See Ronald Ebrecht, "Ties That Bind," in Ebrecht, *Duruflé*, 157–79.

21. See stoplist in Appendix C, p. 277.

22. Lawrence, "Organ Tour," 72.

23. Herndon Spillman, "As the Master Wanted," in Ebrecht, *Duruflé*, 155.

24. Frederick Swann, e-mail message to author, August 10, 2003.

25. Duruflé, "Interview with Duruflé [Baker]," 59.

26. Alain, Introduction, xiv.

27. Günther Kaunzinger said that Duruflé's "improvisations were like his compositions: perfected in form. The harmonic language which he used was that of his works" (Abbing, *Duruflé*, 377, quoting an interview of Kaunzinger by Abbing, *Musica Sacra* [1996]: 381–85). Rodger Vine made the same observation (telephone interview with author, December 2, 2002).

28. Duruflé, "Questionnaire posé aux organistes français," *L'Orgue*, no. 100 (October–December 1961): 106. Éliane Chevalier told Wolfgang Reisinger that Duruflé's "improvisations were entirely based upon chant themes, sounding very much like his compositions" (Reisinger, "Limited Musical Output," 23).

29. Duruflé-Chevalier, "Grandes-Orgues," 9.

30. Mme Duruflé wrote: "What a pity there are no recordings!" (Ibid.)

31. Duruflé-Chevalier, "Entretien."

32. Duruflé, "Questionnaire," 106.

33. The source does not specify whether it is BWV 684 or BWV 685.

34. Duruflé, "Questionnaire," 106.

35. Duruflé-Chevalier, "Grandes-Orgues," 9.

36. For stoplist see Appendix C, p. 275. Jean-Jacques Grunenwald recorded the complete works of Bach on this instrument between 1957 and 1962, finishing his project the year before the Duruflés began theirs.

37. *SAE*, 260, 261, 263, and 264.

38. Duruflé-Chevalier, "Entretien."

39. Duruflé, "Interview with Duruflé [Baker, French]," 227–28.

40. Ibid.

41. Reisinger, "Limited Musical Output," 11.

42. *L'Orgue*, no. 201–4 (1987): 23.

43. Vine, telephone interview by the author, December 2, 2002.

44. Alain, "Hommages," 10.

45. Alain, Introduction, xiv.

46. Falcinelli, "Entretien," 9.

47. Duruflé, "Questionnaire," 106.

48. Bert, [Hommage], 11.

49. Bernard Lechevalier, *Le Cerveau de Mozart* (Paris: Éditions Odile Jacob, 2003), 48.

50. Jean-Marc Cochereau, [Hommage], *Bulletin* 2 (June 2002): 17. The writer is the son of Pierre Cochereau.

51. Keene, "Madame Duruflé," 18.

52. Fisher, "Marie-Madeleine Duruflé," 36.

53. Ibid.

54. Ibid., 35–36. Double touch is a device by which a deeper pressing of the key, against a stronger spring, will cause the stops drawn on a coupled manual to sound. In this way an inner line, for instance, can be brought out. It is found mostly on British organs.

55. Levasseur told the author that Dupré's student Jean Bonfils provided some of the fingering in the Bach editions (Levasseur, interview).

56. Bert, [Hommage], 11.

57. Professor of organ at the conservatories in Maastricht and Zwolle, and organist at the church of the Augustinians in Eindhoven, Dorothy de Rooij studied organ with Albert de Klerk, Maurice Duruflé, and Luigi Tagliavini. She concertized in Europe and the United States, and recorded several discs of early music on historic organs of Portugal.

58. The recording was awarded the *Grand Prix du disque* in 1975. A comparison of Theodore's and Spillman's interpretations would be instructive.

59. Wilkins studied with Duruflé at the American Academy in Fontainebleau just after World War II (Labounsky, *Langlais*, 375).

60. Dennis Keene obtained a doctoral degree from Juilliard School of Music and became organist and choirmaster of the Church of the Ascension, in New York City, where he established the professional choral ensemble Voices of Ascension.

61. Carbou, *Cochereau*, 33.

62. Jean-Marc Cochereau, quoted in ibid., 302. The performance was recorded (FYCD 118).

63. David Briggs, quoted in Carbou, *Cochereau*, 269.

64. Pierre Pincemaille, "L'Improvisateur," in Carbou, *Cochereau*, 303.

65. François Sabatier, [Hommage à Cochereau], in Carbou, *Cochereau*, 362.

66. Abbing, *Duruflé*, 110.

# Chapter Twenty-One

1. "Les Monuments historiques au service des orgues de France," *L'Orgue: Bulletin trimestriel*, no. 8 (April–September 1962): 52.

2. Blanc, interview. The organ was altered in 1937–38 by Gloton-Debierre.

3. Denis, "Les Organistes: Maurice Duruflé," 4.

4. Duruflé, "My Recollections," 56.

5. Duruflé, "Interview with Duruflé [Baker]," 59.

6. Duruflé, "Interview with Duruflé [Baker, French]," 223.

7. The following account is based on Duruflé's article, "Orgue français," 81–89.

8. Smith, *Vierne,* 277, quoting Vierne's memoirs.

9. Duruflé, [Hommage à Victor Gonzalez], *L'Orgue,* no. 81 (October–December 1956): 108–9.

10. Duruflé, "Quelques Tendances de la facture d'orgue française contemporaine," *L'Orgue,* no. 97 (1961): 8.

11. Duruflé, "Orgue français," 82.

12. Soularue, "Duruflé," n.p.

13. Duruflé, "Interview with Duruflé [Baker]," 59–60.

14. Duruflé, "Orgue français," 86. See also the fairly thorough statement that Duruflé wrote in 1941, which remained unpublished until it appeared in 2005 in *SAE,* 71–77.

15. Duruflé, "My Recollections," 55.

16. Alain, "Entretien," 5.

17. Duruflé, "Interview with Duruflé [Baker]," 60.

18. Duruflé, "Questionnaire," 105.

19. Ibid.

20. Ibid.

21. Duruflé, "Orgue français," 85.

22. Duruflé, "Interview with Duruflé [Baker]," 59.

23. Duruflé, "Quelques Tendances," 6.

24. See "Les Orgues de la Collégiale Notre-Dame d'espérance à Montbrison," http://montbrisorgue.chez.tiscali.fr/historique.htm.

25. Duruflé, "Restauration du grand orgue Angoulême," 108.

26. Ibid., 110.

27. Except where noted otherwise, the following account of the construction of the *orgue de salon* is taken from Bertrand, "Orgue de salon," 12–16. See also Danion, [Hommage].

28. David Liddle, telephone conversation with author, December 27, 2000.

29. Duruflé said, "When I saw my piano going up to the eighth floor at the end of a cable, I was terrified thinking that the cable could break. I never wanted to relive that" (Paul Duruflé to author, September 23, 2002, quoting his uncle).

30. Blanc, interview. For stoplist see Appendix C, p. 276.

31. See the Web site: 120 Years of Electronic Music, http://www.obsolete.com/120_years/machines/orgue_des_ondes/index.html.

32. [Fréderic Blanc], "Concerts de Maurice Duruflé de 1917 à 1977 et Joint-Récitals avec Marie-Madeleine Duruflé de 1953 à 1979," in *SAE,* 249–50.

33. Murtagh to Duruflé, November 25, 1963.

34. Duruflé to Murtagh, February 3, 1969.

35. Duruflé, "U.S.A.—U.R.S.S.," *L'Orgue,* no. 122–23 (1967): 191–93; and "Nouvelle Tournée aux U.S.A.: Souvenirs," *L'Orgue,* no. 141 (1972): 31–34.

# Chapter Twenty-Two

1. This account is drawn from *La Musique sacrée au IIIème congrès international de musique sacrée—Paris, Juillet 1957* (Paris: *Revue musicale,* n.d.) and *Actes du troisième congrès.*

2. The same view would be espoused six years later by the Consociatio Internationalis Musicae Sacrae, an organization established by Pope Paul VI on November 22, 1963, for

the promotion of sacred music, less than a month before the council published the Constitution on the Sacred Liturgy.

3. Austin Flannery, ed., *Vatican Council II: The Conciliar and Post Conciliar Documents* (Northport, NY: Costello Publishing, 1977), 11.

4. Ibid., 13.

5. Ibid., 33.

6. Ibid.

7. Ibid., 13.

8. Ibid., 18.

9. Ibid., 32.

10. Ibid., 32–33.

11. "Directives de l'Épiscopat français sur la musique sacrée," *Musique et Liturgie*, no. 99 (July–September 1964): 33–34.

12. From 1969 to 1974 Chailley was president of the Consociatio Internationalis Musicae Sacrae, and in 1971 he was named an "expert musical."

13. See Gérard Seneca, "Les Musiciens laïcs plaident pour le chant grégorien," *L'Intransigeant*, January 8, 1967.

14. "The function and place of the organ as accompanist and as soloist." The title of the report indicates that a distinction is made therein between the solo role of the *grand orgue* and the accompanimental role of the *orgue de chœur*. In his article "L'Orgue dans la nouvelle liturgie," in *L'Orgue*, no. 115 (1965): 143, Duruflé summarizes his report to the bishops.

15. Ibid.

16. Ibid. 141–43.

17. The *Requiem* of Duruflé was performed during the congress, by the Roger Wagner Chorale, from Los Angeles, on August 26, 1966, at the Milwaukee Auditorium. See Johannes Overath, ed., *Sacred Music and Liturgy Reform after Vatican II: Proceedings of the Fifth International Church Music Congress, Chicago-Milwaukee, August 21–28, 1966* (Rome: Consociatio Internationalis Musicae Sacrae, 1969), 211.

18. Labounsky, *Langlais*, 228, quoting "Aspects de la France," *Le Figaro* (August 18, 1966).

19. Duruflé was appointed by the Vatican to serve on a commission to assist in the renewal of religious music, but he left the commission on realizing that the committee's ideas of reform were very different from his own (See Manuel Rosenthal, [Hommage], *Bulletin* 2 [June 2002]: 33).

20. This account is taken from Jacques Dhaussy, "Maurice Duruflé: Économie de paroles et art de la suggestion," *Bulletin* 2 (June 2002): 22–23.

21. The continuing strength and growth of the archconservative Una Voce and of the Latin Mass occasionally attract surprisingly wide notice. On Sunday, May 12, 1996, over four thousand worshippers gathered at Saint Patrick's Cathedral in New York City, to participate in a Pontifical Tridentine Mass. The event was described by religious editor Peter Steinfels as "one of the most important dates in the history of the restoration of the Traditional Mass in the United States and, for that matter, in the entire world." In his review of the event (*New York Times*, May 13, 1996), Steinfels wrote: "It cannot be justly said that the Tridentine Mass is a 'fringe' phenomenon, or in any way 'unfaithful' to the mission of the Church."

22. In January 1965, Jeanne Demessieux became a co-vice-president with Vallombrosa (Trieu-Colleney, *Demessieux*, 40). On July 2, 1988, Pope John Paul II issued a *motu proprio* entitled *Ecclesia Dei*, which authorized the public celebration, under certain conditions, of

the so-called Tridentine mass as it appears in the missal of 1962. The action would have pleased Duruflé.

23. Duruflé, "L'Expérience des nouveaux chants liturgiques en français," *La Croix*, December 13, 1968, 2. See also Duruflé's articles "Une Table ronde sur la musique religieuse," *L'Orgue*, no. 130 (1969): 33–37; "La Masse silencieuse du clergé," *L'Orgue*, no. 134 (1970): 49–51; "Orgue dans la nouvelle liturgie," 141–43; and "Réflexions," 1–5.

24. The French word *chant*, and the Latin word *cantus* which it translates, can be translated into English either as *chant* or *song*, words that have very different connotations. The ubiquitous use of *song* has effectively abandoned the very concept of chant. Furthermore, its current use in reference to all genres—from a psalm, a *Sanctus*, a hymn, an anthem, a canticle, and an acclamation, to "Here comes the bride"—has diminished the distinctions among these different forms.

25. Duruflé, "L'Expérience," 2.

26. The Latin is *Hosanna in excelsis*, which is translated into English as *Hosanna in the highest*.

27. The principle that every Sunday mass should include congregational singing for at least the most important parts of the liturgy became the expectation after the council. The former distinctions between low mass and high mass were correspondingly diminished.

28. Duruflé, "Orgue français," 85.

29. *SAE*, 140, quoting Duruflé, "Pourquoi je n'écrirai pas de messe en français," *Le Monde*, December 29, 1966.

30. Duruflé, "Table ronde," 161.

31. Duruflé, "Expérience," 2.

32. Ibid.

33. Duruflé, "Réflexions," 3.

34. Duruflé, "La Musique de jazz à l'Église," *La Croix*, October 18, 1968.

35. Duruflé, "L'Opinion d'un musicien d'église sur les messes en jazz," *Journal musical français* 180 (May 1969): 15.

36. B. G. "Messes en jazz," quoted in Duruflé, "Opinion," 14. The word *voyou* does not have an apt equivalent in English. It translates, roughly, lout or crook. On one of their North American tours, the Duruflés heard jazz performed at Preservation Hall in New Orleans (see Duruflé, "Nouvelle Tournée," 33–34).

37. Duruflé to Murtagh, January 9, 1970.

38. Labounsky, *Langlais*, 231, quoting *Sacred Music* 106 (Summer 1979): 25, which in turn quotes the French review *Una Voce* 83 (November–December 1978).

39. Some of Duruflé's comments were printed in *Una Voce* (France) 111 (July–August 1983) and reprinted in his "Maurice Duruflé on Church Music since Vatican II," trans. Virginia A. Schubert, *Sacred Music* 110 (Fall 1983): 15.

40. Nicholas Kaye to author, March 30, 2005.

# Chapter Twenty-Three

1. Basil Ramsey, "Recitals," *Musical Times* 110 (May 1969): 529.

2. Duruflé was not the first western organist officially invited to perform in the USSR. His student Pierre Cochereau enjoyed that distinction (see Carbou, *Cochereau*, 16).

3. Details of their tour of the Soviet Union in 1965 are taken from L. Royzman, "Slushaya Organistov" ["Listening to the Organists"], *Sovetskaya Muzyka* 30 (February 1966): 84–87; and letters from the Duruflés to Lilian Murtagh, March 2 and December 5, 1965.

4. Duruflé, "Souvenirs [1976]," 51.

5. Duruflé, "U.S.A.—U.R.S.S.," 194.

6. Ibid. In his memoirs Duruflé wrote that the platform was five or six meters high (*SAE*, 55).

7. Ibid.

8. Duruflé, "U.S.A.—U.R.S.S.," 194–95.

9. Ibid., and Duruflé, "Souvenirs [1976]," 58.

10. Duruflé to Murtagh, January 9, 1970. Duruflé always wrote to his manager in French (translations by author), while his manager always wrote in English.

11. Letter of November 13, 1970.

12. The following details of the North American tours are drawn from the McFarlane Papers.

13. The name of the agency was later changed to Karen McFarlane Artists.

14. As it turned out, the Verdi *Requiem* was performed instead, to the memory of the recently assassinated President John Fitzgerald Kennedy.

15. Duruflé to Murtagh, February 26 and March 22, 1963; Murtagh to Duruflé, March 14, 1963.

16. Duruflé to Murtagh, April 18, 1963.

17. Murtagh to Duruflé, March 14 and April 11, 1963; Duruflé to Murtagh, March 22, 1963.

18. Duruflé declined to accept the master class because he did not speak English (Duruflé to Murtagh, October 29, 1963).

19. As it turned out, Seth Bingham substituted for the ailing Duruflé.

20. Duruflé to Murtagh, July 6, 1963; Murtagh to Duruflé, November 25, 1963.

21. Murtagh to Duruflé, November 18, 1963.

22. Duruflé to Murtagh, December 1, 1963.

23. Mme Duruflé's teacher Jeanne Demessieux occasionally played the fugue for an encore (see Barber, "Paris Organists," 15).

24. Duruflé to Murtagh, May 13, 1964.

25. Robert Burns King, quoted in Éliane Chevalier, "Marie-Madeleine," 188.

26. Duruflé-Chevalier, "Entretien"; 1964 itinerary (McFarlane Papers). The program actually played was slightly different from what had been planned.

27. Frank Cunkle, "Biennial National Convention: Philadelphia, 1964," *Diapason* 657 (August 1964): 37.

28. Robert Lodine, "TAO Report on AGO Biennial Convention, Philadelphia, June 22–26," *American Organist* 47 (August 1964): 23.

29. Robert Burns King, quoted in Éliane Chevalier, "Marie-Madeleine," 188–89.

30. Eschbach, "Duruflé," 45.

31. Duruflé did not like giving master classes, and he gave master classes on few contemporary French composers.

32. Albert Russell was the organist and choirmaster of the church.

33. Seth Bingham, "Recitals and Concerts," *American Organist* 47 (August 1964): 5.

34. Murtagh to Duruflé, March 15 and May 8, 1964.

35. Murtagh to Duruflé, March 15, 1964; Duruflé to Murtagh, March 22, 1964. Swann was organist at the Riverside Church from 1957 to 1982.

36. The Duruflés stayed with Swann on a subsequent tour. Upon learning at the airport that Alleluya had died, Mme Duruflé's "tears began to flow and she excitedly motioned Maurice (who was gathering luggage) with a wail: 'Oh, Maurice! Alleluya is dead'. You must compose a Little Requiem for Alleluya!" (Swann, e-mail message).

37. Ibid.

38. Duruflé-Chevalier, "Entretien."

39. Related to Abbing by Frédéric Blanc, October 4, 2001, quoted in Abbing, *Duruflé*, 124.

40. Duruflé to Murtagh, September 7, 1966; Mme Duruflé to Murtagh, July 15, 1964.

41. "This recital . . . gave many a first opportunity to hear the most recent revisions made to the St. Thomas organ—the new swell division done by the Gilbert F. Adams Organ Co., of NYC" (Grady Wilson, William Tufts, et al., "Recitals and Concerts," *American Organist* 49 [December 1966]: 8).

42. Surprised that he was not asked to conduct, Duruflé declined to play the organ for this performance of the *Requiem*, leaving the task to his wife (Duruflé to Murtagh, May 24 and June 17, 1966; Murtagh to Duruflé, May 31, 1966).

43. Aeolian-Skinner AS 322 stereo.

44. Duruflé to Murtagh, July 18, 1966.

45. Duruflé to Swann, March 29, 1969, in McFarlane Papers.

46. Charles Crowder, "Organ Recital Is So Dazzling It Will Be Discussed for Years," *Washington Post*, October 22, 1966.

47. Murtagh to Duruflé, October 29, 1968.

48. Duruflé to Murtagh, April 3, 1971.

49. Duruflé to Murtagh, August 12, 1971.

50. A live recording of this concert, which took place at Saint Joseph's Church, became available commercially in the United States in 2005. It contains performances of several works which either do not appear on any of the Duruflés' other recordings, or appear on recordings that are out of print.

51. Murtagh to the Duruflés, February 23, 1972.

52. Duruflé to Murtagh, February 8, 1972.

53. Duruflé to Murtagh, November 15, 1972.

54. Ibid.

55. Duruflé to Murtagh, February 24, 1973.

56. Duruflé to Murtagh, July 9, 1973.

57. Duruflé to Murtagh, September 24, 1973.

58. Duruflé to Murtagh, November 20, 1973

59. Murtagh to the Duruflés, December 14, 1973; Duruflé to Murtagh, December 24, 1973.

60. Mme Duruflé to Murtagh, January 6, 1974.

61. Murtagh to the Duruflés, January 22, 1974.

62. The Duruflés to Murtagh, January 25, 1974.

63. Mme Duruflé to Murtagh, February 28, 1974.

64. Mme Duruflé to Murtagh, March 30, 1974, from a train in Avignon.

65. Duruflé to Murtagh, April 4, 1974.

66. Duruflé to Murtagh, April 23, 1974.

67. Murtagh to Duruflé, May 4, 1974.

68. Mme Duruflé to Murtagh, June 4, 1974.

69. Mme Duruflé to Murtagh, June 25, 1974.

70. Duruflé to Murtagh, February 3, 1975. The Duruflés never did have to move out of their apartment.

71. Mme Duruflé to McFarlane, October 24, 1977.

72. Bertrand, "Orgue de salon," 15.

73. Duruflé, "Mémoires," 3.

74. The trio is Bach's transcription of the fourth movement from his first sonata for viola da gamba and harpsichord, BWV 1027 (Duruflé to Murtagh, September 18, 1971).

75. Duruflé did occasionally improvise for recitals in Europe (Abbing, *Duruflé*, 364–65).

76. Marie-Madeleine Duruflé recorded the Liszt *Ad nos* (Aeolian-Skinner Series II [Historical Saint Thomas Organ Series II], API Recores 9003-2) as did Jeanne Demessieux (Decca LXT 2773). It was a favorite of both women (see Trieu-Colleney, *Demessieux*, 231–32).

77. Vine, e-mail message to author, December 16, 2002. Mme Duruflé performed the complete work on the recording she made jointly with her husband on the Aeolian-Skinner organ at Christ Church Cathedral in Saint Louis, in 1966.

78. Apart from Mme Duruflé's recording of it in Saint Louis.

79. John Hofmann, e-mail message to author, November 27, 2002. In his capacity as the Buffalo Chapter's Dean and Program Chairman, in 1968, Hofmann conveyed the chapter's offer to Duruflé.

80. February 20, 1981. Copy in the possession of Philip Brunelle.

81. Duruflé to Brunelle, March 17, 1981, and August 18, 1981.

# Chapter Twenty-Four

1. Interviews of Frédéric Blanc, Olivier Latry, and Marie-Louise Jaquet-Langlais.

2. Duruflé, "Réflexions sur la musique liturgique," *L'Orgue*, no. 174 (April–June 1980): 1.

3. Alain, Introduction, xiv.

4. René Saorgin, [Untitled], *Bulletin* 2 (June 2002): 35.

5. Vine, telephone interview with the author, December 2, 2002.

6. Dhaussy, "Économie," 22.

7. Alain, Introduction, xiv.

8. Duruflé, "Poulenc's *Organ Concerto*," 22.

9. Jean Guillou, quoted in Abbing, *Duruflé*, 401–2.

10. Vine, telephone interview with author, December 2, 2002.

11. Duruflé, "My Recollections," 54.

12. Paul Duruflé to author, March 14, 2002.

13. Quoted in Abbing, *Duruflé*, 401–2.

14. Duruflé-Chevalier, "Entretien."

15. Bertrand, "Orgue de salon," 14.

16. Moreau, "Duruflé," 32.

17. Paul Duruflé to author, May 29, 2002.

18. Paul Duruflé to author, March 14, 2002.

19. Frédéric Blanc, "In Memoriam André Fleury," *Bulletin* 4 (June 2004): 65.

20. Thomerson, *Langlais*, 4.

21. Éliane Chevalier, interview. Lola Dommange was a singer.

22. Jacques Bertrand, quoting Duruflé, in "Orgue de salon," 15.

23. Rolande Falcinelli, "Hommage à Maurice Duruflé," *Bulletin* 2 (June 2002): 24.

24. See, for example, Jeanne Joulain, "Quelques Souvenirs," *Bulletin* 3 (June 2003): 41.

25. Interview of Daniel Roth by Jörg Abbing, August 7, 1992, quoted in Abbing, *Duruflé*, 13–14.

26. Quoted in Abbing, *Duruflé*, 403–4.

27. Blanc, interview.

28. Ibid.

29. Bertrand, "Orgue de salon," 14.

30. Ibid.

31. Ibid.

32. Alain, "Hommages," 9.

33. Paul Duruflé to author, March 14, 2002.

34. Francis P. Schmitt, *Church Music Transgressed: Reflections on "Reform"* (New York: Seabury Press, 1977), 105.

35. Dargassies, [Hommage], 20.

36. Roth, "In memoriam," 33.

37. Bert, [Hommage], 11.

38. Alain, "Entretien," 4.

39. Longueverne, interview.

40. Duruflé, "Mémoires," 63, quoting from the homily delivered by Canon Jehan Revert at the memorial mass for Maurice Duruflé.

41. Longueverne, interview.

42. Duruflé, "Souvenirs [1976]," 50.

43. Bertrand, "Orgue de salon," 14.

44. Vine, telephone interview by author, December 2, 2002.

45. Ibid. The restaurant no longer exists.

46. *Ma petite poulette*, literally "my little chicken," is a common term of endearment, such as "darling" or "sweetheart." *Ma grosse poulette* is a play on the literal words, *grosse* meaning "big" or "fat."

47. Paul Duruflé to author, April 19, 2002.

48. Marie-Madeleine's father had been a royalist in his earlier years, and was a supporter of Pétain during the war (Longueverne, interview).

49. Duruflé to André Fleury, probably in 1945, excerpts quoted in *SAE*, 78.

50. Murtagh to the Duruflés, June 5, 1970.

51. Duruflé to Murtagh, February 3, 1975.

52. Vine, conversation with Mme Duruflé, Boston, June 1990, forwarded by Vine, e-mail message to author, August 5, 2005.

53. Mme Duruflé shared this information with Joyce Painter Rice and Rodger Vine, Boston, June 1990. Information relayed by Painter Rice, conversation with author, Boston, January 18, 2004, and e-mail messages to author, August 4 and 5, 2005.

54. Abbing, *Duruflé*, 141, quoting Mme Duruflé to Abbing, December 18, 1991.

55. Eschbach, "Duruflé," 46.

# Bibliography

## Abbreviations

*Bulletin*  *Bulletin* of the Association Maurice et Marie-Madeleine Duruflé.
SAE  Duruflé, Maurice. *Maurice Duruflé: Souvenirs et autres écrits.* Edited by Frédéric Blanc. Paris: Séguier, 2005.

## Primary Materials, Archives, and Unpublished Interviews

Archives historiques de l'Archevêché de Paris. Saint Étienne-du-Mont.
Archives nationales. Administration des Beaux-Arts.
  F21 5305. Musique. Législation. (2): Œuvres commandées aux compositeurs de musique. Arrêtés originaux. 1938–44;
  F21 5150. Musique et Spectacles. Comptabilité. Engagements ou ordonnements. Exercice 1947. Chapitre 547. Commandes à des artistes musiciens; Minutier Central, XVIII, Reg. 193, fol. 337.
Archives nationales. Conservatoire de musique.
  Série Aj37, nos. 189; 190; 303; 312,2; 480; 488; 520; 532–34.
Bibliothèque nationale de France. Actes d'état civil. Fichier Laborde.
———. Notes de concours et examens d'orgue au Conservatoire national supérieur de musique, 1922–1956. Marcel Dupré's critiques of the competitions and examinations of the organ class, including the final year of Eugène Gigout and the first years of Rolande Falcinelli. BnF Rés. Vm dos. 56 (1–3).
Blanc, Frédéric. Interview by author. Paris, January 18, 2001.
Chaisemartin, Suzanne. Interview by author. Paris, January 19, 2001.
Chevalier, Éliane. Interview by author. Paris, January 21, 2001.
Christie, James David. Interview by author. Saint Paul, MN, October 28, 2002.
Delaporte, Bernard. Interview by author. Rouen, January 14, 2002.
Hobbs, Allen. Telephone conversations with author. November 30, 2000, and February 19, 2001.
Hôtel de Ville, Louviers. Civil records.
Jaquet-Langlais, Marie-Louise. Interview by author. Paris, January 24, 2001.
King, Robert Burns. "Random Thoughts from Marie-Madeleine during Our Visit, November 1989." Burlington, NC.
Latry, Olivier. Interview by author. Paris, January 23, 2001.
Leersnyder, Brigitte de. Conversation with author. Saint Paul, MN, July 30, 2003.
Levasseur, André. Interview by author. Rouen, January 14, 2002.
Longueverne, Mme André. Interview by author. Ménerbes, January 18, 2003.

Loumbrozo, Rémy. Interview by author. New York, April 15, 1994.

McFarlane Papers. Correspondence between the Duruflés and their American managers, Lilian Murtagh and Karen McFarlane, 1963–97, with itineraries, programs, reviews, and miscellaneous items. Cleveland, OH.

Monuments historiques. Département des orgues. Saint Étienne-du-Mont.

Palmer, Larry. "Letters from Salzburg: A Music Student in Europe, 1958–1959." Dallas, TX.

Pinguet, Francis. Interview by author. Rouen, January 14, 2002.

Rice, Joyce Painter. Interview by author. Boston, January 18, 2004.

——. Telephone conversation with author. May 4, 2005.

Roth, Daniel. Interview by author. Paris, January 19, 2001.

Vine, Rodger. Interview by author. Boston, February 6, 2004.

——. Telephone conversation with author. December 2, 2002.

## Published Books, and Articles in Journals and Newspapers

Abbing, Jörg. *Maurice Duruflé: Aspekte zu Leben und Werk.* Paderborn: Verlag Peter Ewers, 2002.

*Actes du troisième congrès international de musique sacrée, Paris—1er–8 juillet 1957: Perspectives de la musique sacrée à la lumière de l'encyclique Musicae sacrae disciplina.* Paris: [Éditions du congrès], 1959.

Alain, Marie-Claire. "Entretien avec Marie-Claire Alain, Le Pecq, décembre 2003." By Frédéric Blanc. *Bulletin* 4 (June 2004): 2–8.

——. "Hommages." *Bulletin* 2 (June 2002): 9–10.

——. "Introduction: Maurice Duruflé." Translated by Ronald Ebrecht. In Ebrecht, *Duruflé,* xiii–xv.

Almendra, Julia d'. "Les Modes grégoriens dans l'œuvre de Claude Debussy." Diss., University of Paris, 1947.

*The American Organist,* May 1919–August 2005.

"Les Amis de l'Orgue." *Revue liturgique et musicale* (1928): 38–40.

Anderson, Martin. "Marie-Madeleine Duruflé." *The Independent,* October 20, 1999. Reprinted in *Bulletin* 3 (June 2003): 30–31.

——. "Marie-Madeleine Duruflé-Chevalier, 1921–1999." *Choir and Organ* 8 (March–April 2000): 10.

*Annuaire officiel du Conservatoire national de musique et déclamation: Distribution des prix pour les cours d'études, 1920–1928.*

"L'Appel aux morts: Jehan Alain." *La Revue musicale* 22 (February–March 1946): 53.

Aprahamian, Felix. "Maurice Duruflé and His Requiem." *Listener* (April 11, 1957): 613.

Archbold, Lawrence, and William J. Peterson, eds. *French Organ Music from the Revolution to Franck and Widor.* Rochester, NY: University of Rochester Press, 1999.

Arnold, Corliss Richard. *Organ Literature: A Comprehensive Survey.* 2nd ed. Metuchen, NJ: Scarecrow Press, 1984.

*L'Artiste.* 1st series, vol. 3 (1832).

"L'Association des Amis de l'Orgue: Son activité, son diffusion, 1937–1957." *L'Orgue,* no. 83 (April–September 1957): 1–10.

Association Élisabeth et Joachim Havard de la Montagne. "Musica et Memoria." http://www.musimem.com/

Aubert, Louis. [Review of *Trois Danses*]. *Journal*, January 21, 1936. Reprinted in *Bulletin* 3 (June 2003): 75.

———. [Review of *Prélude, récitatif et variations*]. *Paris-Soir*, January 29, 1929.

Audition de M. Louis Vierne avec le concours de M. Maurice Duruflé [recital program]. Notre-Dame, Paris, June 3, 1935. Reprinted in *L'Orgue*, no. 47 (1992-I): 73–75.

Bachelin, Henri. "L'Orgue de tribune et les organistes en France." *Le Ménestrel* 91 (November 8, 1929): 473–76.

Bailey, Mark D. "Eugène Gigout and His *Course for Organ, Improvisation, and Plainchant.*" *American Organist* 28 (March 1994): 76–79.

Barber, Clarence H. "Some Observations on Paris Organists Visited by American." *American Organist* 38 (July 1, 1947): 15.

Bauer, Marie Rubis. "The Large Beat." In Ebrecht, *Duruflé*, 65–85.

Beaucamp, Henri. *École de la pédale.* Paris: Senart, 1925.

———. *La Maîtrise Saint-Évode de Rouen (1881–1935).* Rouen: Édition Lainé, 1936.

Beechey, Gwilym. "Maurice Duruflé and His *Requiem*, op. 9." *Musical Opinion* 105 (December 1981): 89, 91–92.

———. "The Music of Maurice Duruflé." *Music Review* 32 (May 1971): 146–55.

———. "Organ Recitals by French Organists in England." *Organ* 195 (January 1970): 108–17.

Beevor, Antony, and Artemis Cooper. *Paris After the Liberation, 1944–1949.* New York: Penguin Putnam, 1994.

Belvianes, Marcel. [Review]. *Le Ménestrel* 95 (June 23, 1933): 259.

Bernard, Robert. "Louis Vierne." *La Revue musicale* 18 (October 1937): 287–88.

Bert, Henri. [Hommage]. *Bulletin* 2 (June 2002): 10–12.

Bertelin, Albert. Article in *La Petite Maîtrise*, April 1939.

Bertrand, Jacques. "Cathédrale de Cavaillon: Reconstruction du grand orgue." *Bulletin* 4 (June 2004): 47–51.

——— "L'Orgue de salon de Maurice Duruflé." *Bulletin* 2 (June 2002): 12–14.

Bidwell, Marshall. "Organ Music in Paris Cathedrals: III, Widor and Saint Sulpice." *American Organist* 5 (October 1922): 419–20, 422, 424.

———. "Organ Music in Paris Churches: IV, St. Eustache and La Madeleine." *American Organist* 5 (November 1922): 467–68, 472.

Bingham, Seth. "Duruflé's 'Requiem' Marked by Elegance and Warm Humanity." *Diapason* 44 (March 1, 1953): 18.

———. "Organ Personalities: Duruflé." *American Organist* 46 (October 1963): 13–14.

———. "Recitals and Concerts." *American Organist* 47 (August 1964): 5.

Blanc, Frédéric. "Concerts de Maurice Duruflé de 1917 à 1977 et Joint-Récitals avec Marie-Madeleine Duruflé de 1953 à 1979." In *SAE*, 249–50.

———. [Hommage à Marie-Madeleine Duruflé]. *Bulletin* 3 (June 2003): 31–32.

———. "Hommage à Pierre Cochereau pour le 20e anniversaire de sa disparition." *Bulletin* 4 (June 2004): 82–89.

———. "In Memoriam André Fleury." *Bulletin* 4 (June 2004): 65.

———. [Letter to the editor.] *American Organist* 37 (March 2003): 16, 18.

Blanc, Maurice. "Le Requiem de Maurice Duruflé." *Musique et Liturgie* 18 (November–December 1950): 10–11. Reprinted in *SAE*, 83–87.

Bonnet, Joseph. "*L'Orgue mystique* par Charles Tournemire." *Revue liturgique et musicale* (1929–30): 110.

Boschot, Adolphe. [Review of *Trois Danses*]. *L'Écho de Paris*, January 20, 1936. Reprinted in *Bulletin* 3 (June 2003): 75–76.

Bret, Gustave. "M. Maurice Duruflé, organiste et compositeur, obtient aux concerts Colonne un très beau succès." *L'Intransigeant*, January 24, 1936. Reprinted in *Bulletin* 3 (June 2003): 72.

Brooks, Jeanice. "Nadia Boulanger and the Salon of the Princesse de Polignac." *Journal of the American Musicological Society* 46 (Fall 1993): 415–68.

Brossard, Yolande de. *Musiciens de Paris, 1535–1792: Actes d'état civil d'après le fichier Laborde de la Bibliothèque nationale*. Paris: Éditions A. et J. Picard, 1965.

Brussel, Robert. "Œuvres nouvelles: *Trois Danses* de M. Maurice Duruflé." *Le Figaro*, January 20, 1936. Reprinted in *Bulletin* 3 (June 2003): 69.

———. [Review of *Prélude, récitatif et variations*]. *Le Figaro*, January 24, 1929.

*Bulletin de l'Association des Amis de Léonce de Saint-Martin* 16–17 (June 1978): 20–26.

Burrin, Philippe. *France under the Germans: Collaboration and Compromise*. Translated by Janet Lloyd. New York: New York Press, 1996. First published in 1995 as *La France à l'heure allemande, 1940–1944*.

"Les Candidats à la succession de Louis Vierne." *L'Orgue*, no. 32 (December 1937): 9–10.

Cantrell, Scott. "Louis Vierne: His Life and Works." *American Organist* 14 (November 1980): 42–49.

Capdevielle, Pierre. [Review of *Trois Danses*]. *Le Monde musical* (January 31, 1936). Reprinted in *Bulletin* 3 (June 2003): 73.

Carbou, Yvette, ed. *Pierre Cochereau: Témoignages*. Bourg-la-Reine: Éditions Aug. Zurfluh, 1999.

Cardinale, Hyginus Eugene. *Orders of Knighthood, Awards and the Holy See*. Edited and revised by Peter Bander van Duren. Gerrards Cross, England: Van Duren Publishers, 1984.

Cartayrade, Alain. "Discographie." *Bulletin* 3 (June 2003): 63–64.

"Catalogue des œuvres [of Marie-Madeleine Duruflé]." *Bulletin* 3 (June 2003): 62.

Chailley, Jacques. *Histoire musicale du moyen-âge*. Paris: Presses universitaires de France, 1950.

Chamfray, Claude. "Chronology of Maurice Duruflé." *Le Courrier musical de France* 29 (1st trimester 1970): 51–52. With additions in the hand of Marie-Madeleine Duruflé; in the possession of the author.

Charlton, Donald Geoffrey. *Secular Religions in France, 1815–1890*. London: Oxford University Press, 1963.

Chassain-Dolliou, Laetitia. *Le Conservatoire de Paris ou les voies de la création*. Paris: Gallimard, 1995.

Chevalier, Éliane. "Extraits des souvenirs familiers d'Éliane Chevalier." *Bulletin de l'Association des amis de l'art de Marcel Dupré* 19 (Spring 2001). Reprinted as "Marie-Madeleine Chevalier-Duruflé et Marcel Dupré," *Bulletin* 3 (June 2003): 22–25. Also at http://www.adevnet.fr/mdupre/bull19-2.htm

———. Liner notes for *Marie-Madeleine Duruflé Memorial*. Compact disc, Festivo 6941 772. Recorded live at Saint Eustache, Paris, July 1, 1993.

———. "Marie-Madeleine Chevalier-Duruflé." *Bulletin* 3 (June 2003): 15–22. Originally delivered as an address at a conference commemorating Marie-Madeleine Duruflé-Chevalier, May 8, 2000, Cathedral of the Holy Trinity, Paris. First published, in English translation by Edward Tipton, as "Marie-Madeleine," in Ebrecht, *Duruflé*, 181–93.

———. "Marie-Madeleine Chevalier-Duruflé et Marcel Dupré." *Bulletin* 3 (June 2003): 22–25.

Chevalier, Jean-Martin. "Hommage à Marie-Madeleine." *Bulletin* 3 (June 2003): 32–33.

Chimènes, Myriam, ed. *La Vie musicale sous Vichy*. Brussels: Éditions Complexe, 2001.

Christiansen, Rulon. "Hommage à Louis Vierne: A Conversation with André Fleury." *American Organist* 21 (December 1987): 60–64.

"Chronique." *Revue liturgique et musicale* (1929): 199.

Clarendon [Bernard Gavoty]. "Le *Requiem* de Duruflé." *Le Figaro*, November 8, 1947.

———. "Le *Requiem* de Duruflé." *Le Figaro*, November 19, 1948.

Cochereau, Jean-Marc. [Hommage]. *Bulletin* 2 (June 2002): 17.

Collette, Abbé, and Adolphe Bourdon. *Histoire de la maîtrise de Rouen.* Rouen: Cagniard, 1892.

———. *Histoire de la maîtrise de Rouen.* New ed. Edited by Francis Pinguet. Paris: L'Harmattan, 2000.

———. *Notice historique sur les orgues et les organistes de la Cathédrale de Rouen.* Rouen: E. Cagniard, 1894. Reprinted in *La Vie musicale dans les provinces françaises*, vol. 3, 225–51. Geneva: Minkoff Reprint, 1974.

"Concerts données par Les Amis de l'Orgue." *L'Orgue*, no. 160–61 (October 1976–March 1977): 14–17.

"Concours des Amis de l'Orgue," *L'Orgue*, no. 160–61 (October 1976–March 1977): 21.

"Les Concours des Amis de l'Orgue." *Revue liturgique et musicale* (1930): 24.

Cooksey, Steven Lee. "Impressionistic Aspects of Twentieth-century French Organ Literature." PhD diss., Washington University, 1972.

Cordonnier, Ch. *Monseigneur Fuzet, Archevêque de Rouen.* Paris: Beauchesne et ses Fils, 1948.

*Le Courrier musical et théâtral.* January 1, 1922–July 1, 1930.

Crauzat, Claude Noisette de. *Cavaillé-Coll.* Paris: La Flûte de Pan, 1984.

———. *L'Orgue français.* Paris: Éditions Atlas, 1986.

Cross, F. L., ed. *Oxford Dictionary of the Christian Church.* Oxford: Oxford University Press, 1974.

Crowder, Charles. "Organ Recital Is So Dazzling It Will Be Discussed for Years." *Washington Post*, October 22, 1966.

Cunkle, Frank. "Biennial National Convention: Philadelphia, 1964." *Diapason* 55 (August 1964): 31–39.

Dambly, Paul. [Review of *Trois Danses*]. *Le Petit Journal*, January 20, 1936. Reprinted in *Bulletin* 3 (June 2003): 70.

Danion, Georges. [Hommage]. *Bulletin* 2 (June 2002): 18–19.

Dargassies, Bernard. [Hommage à Maurice Duruflé]. *Bulletin* 2 (June 2002): 19–22.

Delaporte, Bernard. "En Hommage à Maurice Duruflé." *La Voix de St Évode: Bulletin de Liaison des Anciens Maîtrisiens de St-Évode*, no. 13 special (May 2002).

——— et al. *La Maîtrise Saint-Évode de la Cathédrale de Rouen.* Anciens élèves de la Maîtrise Saint-Évode, [after 1993].

De Launay, Paul. "Charles Marie Widor." *American Organist* 3 (August 1920): 278.

Delestre, Abbé R. "La Chorale de la Cathédrale de Rouen." *Musique et Liturgie* 28 (July–August 1952): 12.

———. *L'Œuvre de Marcel Dupré.* Paris: Édition "Musique sacrée," 1952.

Denis, Pierre. "L'Activité des Amis de l'Orgue: Saison 1963–1964." *L'Orgue*, no. 112 (October–December 1964): 106–8.

———. "L'Activité des Amis de l'Orgue: Saison 1967–1968." *L'Orgue*, no. 128 (October–December 1968): 150–51.

———. "L'Activité des Amis de l'Orgue: Saison 1969–1970." *L'Orgue*, no. 136 (October–December 1970): 134–35.

Delestre, Abbé R., ed. "Concours des Amis de l'Orgue, 1927–1987." *L'Orgue*, no. 201–4 (1987): 55–70.

Delestre, Abbé R. "Les Organistes français d'aujourd'hui: Marie-Madeleine Chevalier-Duruflé." *Bulletin* 3 (June 2003): 3–5. First published in *L'Orgue*, no. 90 (April–June 1959): 33–37.

———. "Les Organistes français d'aujourd'hui: Maurice Duruflé." *L'Orgue*, no. 50 (January–March 1949): 3–6.

Descaves, Lucien. *Les Emmurés*. Paris: Tresse et Stock, 1894.

Dézarnaux, Robert. "*Trois Danses* de M. Maurice Duruflé." *La Liberté*, January 21, 1936. Reprinted in *Bulletin* 3 (June 2003): 67–68.

Dhaussy, Jacques. "Maurice Duruflé: Économie de paroles et art de la suggestion." *Bulletin* 2 (June 2002): 22–23.

*Dictionnaire des églises de France*. Vol. 4, *Ouest et Île-de-France*. Paris: Robert Laffont, 1966.

"Directives de l'Épiscopat français sur la musique sacrée." *Musique et Liturgie* 99 (July–September 1964): 33–34.

Dompnier, Bernard, ed. *Maîtrises et chapelles aux XVIIe et XVIIIe siècles: Des institutions musicales au service de Dieu*. Clermont-Ferrand: Presses universitaires Blaise-Pascal, 2003.

Douglass, Fenner. *Cavaillé-Coll and the French Romantic Tradition*. New Haven, CT: Yale University Press, 1999.

Doyen, Henri. "In memoriam . . . ," *L'Organiste* 50 (June 1962): n.p.

———. *Mes Leçons avec Louis Vierne*. Paris: Éditions de musique sacrée, 1966.

———. *Les Orgues de la cathédrale de Soissons*. Soissons: Author, 1956.

Duchesneau, Michel. *L'Avant-Garde musicale et ses sociétés à Paris de 1871 à 1939*. Liège: Mardaga, 1997.

Dufourcq, Norbert. "La Contribution à l'histoire des orgues parisiennes à la fin du règne de Louis XIII." *L'Orgue: Dix années au service de l'orgue français, 1927–1937* (1937): 48–54.

———. "Correspondances," in "Eugène Gigout, 1844–1925." *L'Orgue: Cahiers et mémoires*, no. 27 (1982): 2–29.

———. "Discours de Monsieur Norbert Dufourcq: An address to Les Amis de l'Orgue." *L'Orgue*, no. 208 (October–December 1988): 32–37.

———. "Les Disques d'orgue." *L'Orgue*, no. 105 (January–March 1963): 36–37.

———. "Eugène Gigout (1844–1925)." *L'Orgue: Cahiers et mémoires*, no. 27 (1982): 3–29.

———. "In Memoriam: Maurice Duruflé." *L'Orgue*, no. 201–4 (1987): 91–92.

———. "Jouer de l'orgue à l'église catholique?" *L'Orgue*, no. 199 (July–September 1986): 3–8.

———. *Le Livre de l'orgue français, 1589–1789*. 5 vols. Paris: Éditions A. and J. Picard, 1971.

———. "Mode et facture d'orgues, II." *L'Orgue*, no. 101 (January–March 1962): 1–7.

———. *La Musique d'orgue française: De Jehan Titelouze à Jehan Alain*. Paris: Librairie Floury, 1949.

———. "Notre numéro '100.'" *L'Orgue*, no. 100 (October–December 1961): 89–90.

———. "Les Orgues de Saint-Eustache de Paris du XVIe siécle a nos jours: Un grand organier contemporain, Victor Gonzalez." *La Revue musicale* 13 (September–October 1932): 205–11.

———. "Panorama de la musique d'orgue française au XXe siècle" (part 3). *La Revue musicale* 20 (August–November 1939): 103–16.

———. [Review of 1927 Performance of the *Scherzo* by André Fleury]. *La Revue musicale* 10 (July 1, 1929): 159.

Dufourcq, Norbert. "Soixante Années au service de l'orgue." *L'Orgue*, no. 201–4 (1987): 17–19.

Dufourcq, Norbert. *Visites diffusées des églises Saint Sulpice, Sainte Eustache, Sainte Clotilde et Notre-Dame de Paris, avec le concours de MM. Dupré, Joseph Bonnet, Charles Tournemire et Louis Vierne.* Paris: Secrétariat général des Amis de l'Orgue, 1936.

Dumesnil, René. [Review of *Andante et Scherzo*]. *Le Monde,* January 27, 1954. Reprinted in *Bulletin* 3 (June 2003): 78.

Durand, Sébastien. "Les Aveugles et l'école d'orgue française: Un siècle d'orgue à L'Institut national des jeunes aveugles, 1820–1930." Doctoral diss., Université de Nancy, 2000. Published Lille: A.N.R.T., 2003.

Duruflé, Maurice. "Ce que les Grands Maîtres compositeurs et organistes français pensent de notre croisade." *SAE,* 65. First published in *L'Orgue,* no. 30–31 (June–September 1937).

———. "Le Compositeur." In *In Memoriam Louis Vierne,* 151–53. Reprinted in *SAE,* 69–71.

———. "*Le Concerto pour orgue et orchestre à cordes* de Francis Poulenc." *L'Orgue,* no. 154 (1975): 40–42.

———. Edition and preface for César Franck's *L'Organiste.* Paris: Durand, 1957.

———. "Une Enquête sur Schoenberg et sur ses théories." *SAE,* 88–89. First published in *Le Guide du concert* (June 13, 1952).

———. "Entretien avec Maurice Duruflé par Claude Chamfray." *Le Guide du concert et du disque* (December 14, 1956). Reprinted in *SAE,* 94.

———. "Entretien de Maurice Duruflé avec Pierre Cochereau." Notre-Dame, Paris, September 28, 1973. By Pierre Cochereau. On LP recording *Maurice Duruflé: L'Œuvre d'orgue intégral, interprété par Herndon Spillman,* recorded May 21–27, 1973 (RCA FY 002/003).

———. "L'Expérience des nouveaux chants liturgiques en français." *La Croix,* December 13, 1968.

———. "Hommage à Bérenger de Miramon Fitz-James." *SAE,* 89. First published in *L'Orgue,* no. 64 (July–September 1952).

———. [Hommage à Victor Gonzalez]. *L'Orgue,* no. 81 (October–December 1956): 108–10. Reprinted in *SAE,* 91–92.

———. "Interview of Maurice Duruflé." By Pierre Cochereau. Notre-Dame, Paris, September 28, 1973. English translation by Susan Spillman. Liner notes for the CD recording *Duruflé: Herndon Spillman,* recorded May 21–27, 1973 (Titanic Records TI-200).

———. "An Interview with Maurice Duruflé." By George Baker. *American Organist* 14 (November 1980): 57–60. Altered and abridged from the original French, in *SAE,* 203–28.

———. "An Interview with Maurice Duruflé by George Baker" [in French]. *SAE,* 203–28. First published in English, altered and abridged, in *American Organist* 14 (November 1980): 57–60.

———. [Introduction to *Les Trois Chorals* of César Franck]. Révision et annotations de Maurice Duruflé. Paris: Durand, 1973.

———. "Jeunes organistes français en 1936: Réponse au questionnaire envoyé par Béranger de Miramon." *L'Orgue,* no. 201–4 (1987): 23–24. Reprinted in *SAE,* 63–64.

———. "Louis Vierne." *SAE,* 65–67. First printed in *Bulletin trimestriel de l'Union des maîtres-de-chapelle et organistes* 24 (October 1937).

———. "La Masse silencieuse du clergé." *L'Orgue,* no. 134 (1970): 49–51.

———. "Maurice Duruflé on Church Music since Vatican II." Translated by Virginia A. Schubert. *Sacred Music* 110 (1983): 15. First published in *Una Voce* (France) 111 (July–August 1983).

Duruflé, Maurice. *Maurice Duruflé: Souvenirs et autres écrits.* Edited by Frédéric Blanc. Paris: Séguier, 2005.

———. "Mémoires" [extracts]. *L'Orgue: Cahiers et mémoires,* no. 45 (1991-I): 4–11.

———. "La Musique de jazz à l'Église." *La Croix,* October 18, 1968.

———. "Mes Souvenirs sur Tournemire et Vierne." *L'Orgue,* no. 162 (1977): 1–7. Translated by Ralph Kneeream as "My Recollections of Tournemire and Vierne." *American Organist* 14 (November 1980): 54–57.

———. "Note de l'auteur." In *Messe "Cum jubilo"* for organ and reduced orchestra. Paris: Durand, 1971.

———. "Nouvelle Tournée aux U.S.A.: Souvenirs." *L'Orgue,* no. 141 (1972): 31–34.

———. "L'Opinion d'un musicien d'église sur les messes en jazz." *Journal musical français* 180 (May 1969): 14–16.

———. "L'Orgue" ([published?], 1941). Reprinted in *SAE,* 71–77.

———. "L'Orgue dans la nouvelle liturgie." *L'Orgue,* no. 115 (1965): 141–43.

———. "L'Orgue de Deauville." *L'Orgue,* no. 82 (1957): 16–17.

———. "L'Orgue français de l'an 2000." *L'Orgue,* nos. 160–61 (1976–77): 81–89.

———. "Où allons-nous?" *L'Orgue,* no. 145 (1973): 1–3.

———. "Poulenc's *Organ Concerto.*" Translated by Rollin Smith. *Music* 8 (July 1974): 22.

———. "Pourquoi je n'écrirai pas de messe en français." *Le Monde,* December 29, 1966.

———. [Preface to *Cinq Improvisations* by Charles Tournemire]. Paris: Durand [1958]. Reprinted in *L'Orgue,* no. 92 (1959): 126.

———. "Quelques Tendances de la facture d'orgue française contemporaine." *L'Orgue,* no. 97 (1961): 5–8.

———. "Questionnaire posé aux organistes français." *L'Orgue,* no. 100 (October–December 1961): 91–92, 105–6.

———. "Réflexions sur la musique liturgique." *L'Orgue,* no. 174 (April–June 1980): 1–5.

———. "Reflexões sobre a musica liturgica." *Canto Gregoriano* 24 (1981): 13–18. First published in *Revue de l'orgue,* 173.

———. "Réponse au questionnaire J. S. Bach." *L'Orgue,* no. 55 (1950). Reprinted in *SAE,* 79–82.

———. "Requiem." *L'Orgue: Cahiers et mémoires,* no. 45 (1991): 57–59.

———. "La Restauration du grand orgue de la cathédrale d'Angoulême." *L'Orgue,* no. 119 (1966): 107–10.

———. "Restauration du grand orgue de Notre-Dame de Louviers (1941–1942)." *L'Orgue: Cahiers et mémoires,* no. 45 (1991): 52–54.

———. "La Restauration du grand orgue de Saint Étienne-du-Mont." *L'Orgue,* no. 90 (1959): 47–52.

———. "Révision et annotations" of Charles Tournemire's *Triple Choral. Orgue et Liturgie* 54 (1962).

———. "Soixante années au service de l'orgue." *L'Orgue,* no. 201–4 (1987): 46–51.

———. "Souvenirs" (1976). In *SAE,* 15–58.

———. "Souvenirs sur les Amis de l'Orgue." *L'Orgue* no. 201–4 (1987): 46–47. Reprinted in *SAE,* 228–29.

———. "Souvenirs sur Tournemire et Vierne." *L'Orgue,* no. 162 (1977): 5–10.

———. "Une Table ronde sur la musique religieuse." *L'Orgue,* no. 130 (1969): 33–37.

———. "U.S.A.—U.R.S.S." *L'Orgue,* nos. 122–23 (1967): 191–96.

Duruflé-Chevalier, Marie-Madeleine. "Entretien avec Marie-Madeleine Duruflé." By Frédéric Denis, April 7, 1999. In *Bulletin* 3 (June 2003): 11–14. Originally printed in *Organ: Journal für die Orgel* 2 (April 7, 1999).

Duruflé-Chevalier, Marie-Madeleine. "Les Grandes-Orgues de Saint Étienne-du-Mont et son role dans la liturgie." In *Bulletin* 3 (June 2003): 7–11. First printed in *Journal paroissial de Saint Étienne-du-Mont* 181–82 (September and November 1984).

———. [An Interview with Marie-Madeleine Duruflé-Chevalier]. By J. Michael Barone. Minnesota Public Radio, May 25, 1992.

———. "Marie-Madeleine Chevalier-Duruflé." Interview by Pierre Denis. *L'Orgue*, no. 90 (April–June 1959): 33–37.

———. "Pierre Cochereau, 1924–1984: Témoignages." *L'Orgue: Cahiers et mémoires*, no. 42 (1989-II): 27–28.

Dyer, Richard. "Duruflé's Bold Technique Weaves in Fantasy, Color." Concert review. *Boston Globe*, undated news clipping in McFarlane Papers.

Ebrecht, Ronald. [Letter to the editor]. *American Organist* 37 (March 2003): 18, 20.

———, ed. *Maurice Duruflé, 1902–1986: The Last Impressionist*. Lanham, MD: Scarecrow Press, 2002.

"Échos." *L'Orgue*, no. 69 (October–December 1953): 126.

Englert, Giuseppe-Giorgio. [Hommage à Victor Gonzalez]. *L'Orgue*, no. 81 (October–December 1956): 110–11.

Englert-Marchal, Jacqueline. "André Marchal and His Contributions to the Neo-Classic Movement." *American Organist* 28 (February 1994): 54–59.

Eschbach, Jesse. *Aristide Cavaillé-Coll: A Compendium of Known Stoplists*. Vol. 1. Paderborn: Verlag Peter Ewers, [2003].

———. "In Memoriam Maurice Duruflé, 1902–1986." *American Organist* 21 (July 87): 44–46.

———. "Madame Duruflé, le professeur." *Bulletin* 3 (June 2003): 33–35.

———. "Paris, Bibliothèque Nationale, MS 8707: A New Source for Franck's Registrational Practices and Its Implications for the Published Registrations of His Organ Works." In Archbold and Peterson, *French Organ Music*, 103–17.

F., A. "Organ Recital Notes." *Musical Times* 90 (October 1949): 356, 359.

Falcinelli, Rolande. "Entretien avec Rolande Falcinelli, 1er Mai 2002, Pau." By Frédéric Blanc. *Bulletin* 4 (June 2004): 8–12.

———. "Hommage à Maurice Duruflé." *Bulletin* 2 (June 2002): 24.

Fauquet, Joël-Marie. *Catalogue de l'œuvre de Charles Tournemire*. Geneva: Éditions Minkoff, 1979.

Favre, Georges. *L'Œuvre de Paul Dukas*. Paris: Durand, 1969.

———. *Paul Dukas: Sa vie, son œuvre*. Paris: La Colombe, 1948.

"Les Festivals en France: Lyon-Charbonnières." *La Revue musicale* (June 20–July 10, 1953): 73–75.

Fisher, Roger. "Marie-Madeleine Duruflé: A Reminiscence." *Organists' Review* 86 (February 2000): 36. Reprinted in *Bulletin* 3 (June 2003): 35–36.

Fitch, Noel Riley. *Sylvia Beach and the Lost Generation: A History of Literary Paris in the Twenties and Thirties*. New York: W. W. Norton, 1985.

Flannery, Austin, ed. *Vatican Council II: The Conciliar and Post Conciliar Documents*. Northport, NY: Costello Publishing, 1977.

Fleury, André. "Entretien avec André Fleury." By Kurt Lueders. *Bulletin* 4 (June 2004): 65–76. Originally published in *La Flûte harmonique* 63–64 (1992).

——— et al. "Souvenirs." In "Charles Tournemire (1870–1939)." *L'Orgue: Cahiers et mémoires*, no. 41 (1989-I): 13–14, 16.

Fleury, Louis. "Réflexions sur le rythme du plain-chant et du jazz-band." *Le Courrier musical et théâtral* 21 (November 1, 1924): 516–17.

Fleury, Michel. *L'Impressionisme et la musique.* Paris: Fayard, 1996.

Fragny, Robert de. "De Quelques Nouveautés [Review of *Andante et Scherzo*]." *Vie musicale,* January 14, 1952. Reprinted in *Bulletin* 3 (June 2003): 77.

Frazier, James. "In Gregorian Mode." In Ebrecht, *Duruflé,* 1–64.

———. "Maurice Duruflé: A Centenary." Parts 1 and 2. *American Organist* 36 (November 2002): 58–65; 36 (December 2002): 51–53.

Frommen, Christoph Martin. Liner notes for the recording of the complete organ works of Duruflé by Stefan Schmidt. Aeolus AE-10211 EAN: 4026798102111.

G., M. "Discographie." *Musique et Liturgie* 72 (November–December 1959): 16.

Gajard, Dom Joseph. *The Solesmes Method: Its Fundamental Principles and Practical Rules of Interpretation.* Translated by R. Cecile Gabain. Collegeville, MN: Liturgical Press, 1960.

Gavoty, Bernard. "Les Concerts symphoniques [Review of *Andante et Scherzo*]." *Opéra* (February 13, 1952). Reprinted in *Bulletin* 3 (June 2003): 77–78.

———. "L'Événement musical de la semaine [Review of *Andante et Scherzo*]." *Paris Comœdia* (February 3, 1954). Reprinted in *Bulletin* 3 (June 2003): 78–79.

———. *Les Français: Sont-ils musiciens?* Paris: Éditions du Conquistador, 1950.

———. *Louis Vierne: La vie et l'Œuvre.* Paris: Buchet/Chastel, 1980. Updated from the first edition published by Albin Michel, 1943.

———. "Musiques rassurantes." *Paris Comœdia,* February 3, 1954. Reprint in *Bulletin* 3 (June 2003): 78–79.

Gervais, Françoise. "La Notion d'arabesque chez Debussy." *La Revue musicale* 241 (1958): 3–22.

Gigout, Eugène. *Avertissement* (May 1920) to his revised edition of Lemmens's *École d'orgue.*

Girod, Marie-Louise. "Entretien avec Marie-Louise Girod, Paris, janvier 2004." By Frédéric Blanc. *Bulletin* 4 (June 2004): 15–19.

Goubault, Christian. "La Musique à Rouen du huitième siècle à nos jours." *Revue internationale de musique française* 4 (January 1981): 83–92.

*Graduale Romanum Sacrosanctae Romanae Ecclesiae de Tempore et de Sanctis.* Abbaye Saint-Pierre de Solesmes. Tournai: Desclée et Co., 1974.

"Les Grandes Orgues de l'Église Saint Étienne-du-Mont." *Le Courrier musical et théâtral* 29 (October 15, 1927): 489.

Guérard, Jean. *Léonce de Saint-Martin à Notre-Dame de Paris, 1886–1954.* Paris: Éditions de l'officine, 2005.

Guichard, Léon. "Erik Satie et la musique grégorienne." *La Revue musicale* 17 (November 1936): 334–35.

Guillou, Jean. "Maurice Duruflé." *Bulletin* 2 (June 2002): 27.

Halbreich, Harry. "Concerto pour orgue, orchestre à cordes et timbales." Disque Erato (1970). Reprinted in *Bulletin* 4 (June 2004): 30.

Hardouin, Pierre. "Du Premier Grand Orgue de Saint Étienne-du-Mont, à l'achèvement du second." *L'Orgue,* no. 87 (July–September 1958): 73–83.

———. *Le Grand Orgue de Notre-Dame de Paris.* Tours: Barenreiter, 1973.

———. "Les Grandes Orgues de Saint Étienne-du-Mont, à Paris." *L'Orgue,* no. 76 (July–September 1955): 83–88.

Hartman, James B. [Review of] "Maurice Duruflé, 1902–1986: The Last Impressionist." *Diapason* 94 (May 2003): 13–14.

Hayburn, Robert F. *Papal Legislation on Sacred Music, 95 A.D. to 1977 A.D.* Collegeville, MN: Liturgical Press, 1979.

Hays, William. "André Marchal: 1894–1980." *American Organist* 15 (January 1981): 54–55.

Hell, Henri. *Francis Poulenc: Musicien français*. Paris: Fayard, 1978.

Henderson, Archibald Martin. "Personal Memories of Vierne." *Musical Times* 95 (June 1954): 318.

Henderson, John. *A Directory of Composers for Organ*. 2nd ed. Swindon, UK: John Henderson, 1999.

"Les Heures musicales et liturgiques de Saint Merry." *L'Orgue*, nos. 160–61 (October 1976–March 1977): 19–20.

Himonet, André. "A travers les Grands Concerts—*Trois Danses* de M. Duruflé (Colonne)— Premières auditions à la Société nationale." *L'Ami du peuple*, January 21, 1936. Reprinted in *Bulletin* 3 (June 2003): 69–70.

Hirschfeld, Gerhard, and Patrick Marsh. *Collaboration in France: Politics and Culture during the Nazi Occupation, 1940–1944*. New York: Berg Publishers, 1989.

Hobbs, Alain [Allen]. "Post-scriptum." In "Charles-Marie Widor, 1844–1937." *L'Orgue: Cahiers et mémoires*, no. 40 (1988-II): 47.

Holoman, D. Kern. *The Société des Concerts du Conservatoire, 1828–1967*. Berkeley: University of California Press, 2004. See also http://hector.ucdavis.edu/sdc/.

Hondré, Emmanuel, ed. *Le Conservatoire de musique de Paris: Regards sur une institution et son histoire*. [Paris]: Association du bureau des étudiants du Conservatoire national supérieur de musique de Paris, 1995.

Hooghe, Kamiel d'. "Flor Peeters: 4 juillet 1903–4 juillet 1986." *L'Orgue*, no. 207 (July–September 1988): 11–19.

Houbart, François-Henri. "Entretien avec François-Henri Houbart." *L'Orgue: Cahiers et mémoires*, no. 34 (1985): 1–7.

Hughes, Allen. "A Tribute to Francis Poulenc." *Music* 8 (July 1974): 20–21.

Huot-Pleuroux, Paul. *Histoire de la musique religieuse des origines à nos jours*. Paris: Presses universitaires de France, 1957.

Huysmans, Joris-Karl. *En Route*. Translated by C. Kegan Paul. New York: E. P. Dutton, 1920. The original French edition was published in 1895.

Ibert, Jacques. [Review of *Trois Danses*]. *Marianne*, January 29, 1936. Reprinted in *Bulletin* 3 (June 2003): 70.

Imbert, Maurice. "Les Concerts symphoniques." *Journal des débats*, January 22, 1936. Reprinted in *Bulletin* 3 (June 2003): 69.

———. [Review of *Trois Danses*]. *L'Art musical*, January 24, 1936. Reprinted in *Bulletin* 3 (June 2003): 71–72.

*In Memoriam Louis Vierne, 1870–1937: Souvenirs suivis d'un hommage à sa carrière, son enseignement, par ses confrères, élèves et amis*. Paris: Desclée de Brouwer, 1939.

Indy, Vincent d'. *Emmanuel Chabrier et Paul Dukas: Conférence prononcé le 8 Avril 1920 aux concerts historiques Pasdeloup*. Foreword by Gustave Samazeuilh. Paris: Heugel, 1920.

Irving, Margaret. "A French Program on a French Kind of Organ." November 16, 1966. Unidentified news clipping in McFarlane Papers, Cleveland, OH.

Ivry, Benjamin. *Francis Poulenc*. London: Phaidon Press, 1996.

———. *Maurice Ravel: A Life*. New York: Welcome Rain Publishers, 2000.

Jacob, Dom Clément. "Erik Satie et le chant grégorien." *La Revue musicale* 386–87 (1985): 90–99.

Jaquet-Langlais, Marie-Louise. "L'Œuvre d'orgue de César Franck et notre temps." *L'Orgue*, no. 167 (July–September 1978): 5–41.

———. *Ombre et lumière: Jean Langlais, 1907–1991*. Paris: Éditions Combre, 1995.

Jaquet-Langlais, Marie-Louise. "The Organ Works of Franck: A Survey of Editorial and Performance Problems." Translated by Matthew Dirst and Kimberly Marshall. In Archbold and Peterson, *French Organ Music*, 143–88.

Jarjisian, Peter G. "The Influence of Gregorian Chant on Maurice Durufle's 'Requiem,' op. 9." DMA diss., University of Wisconsin, Madison, 1991.

Jarocinski, Stefan. *Debussy, Impressionism and Symbolism*. Translated by Rollo Myers. London: Eulenburg Books, 1976.

Johnson, James H. *Listening in Paris: A Cultural History*. Berkeley: University of California Press, 1995.

Joulain, Jeanne. "Quelques Souvenirs." *Bulletin* 3 (June 2003): 41.

*Journal de Rouen*, April 4–May 31, 1912.

Joy, Charles R. *Music in the Life of Albert Schweitzer*. New York: Harper, 1951.

Jutten, Odile. "L'Évolution de l'enseignement de l'improvisation à l'orgue au conservatoire." In *Le Conservatoire de Paris: Deux cents ans de pédagogie, 1795–1995*. Edited by Anne Bongrain and Alain Poirier. Paris: Buchet/Chastel, 1999.

Kahan, Sylvia. *Music's Modern Muse: A Life of Winnaretta Singer, Princesse de Polignac*. Rochester, NY: University of Rochester Press, 2003.

Kandell, Leslie. "Marie-Madeleine Duruflé." *Musical America* 110 (1990): 65.

Kasouf, Edward J. "Louis Vierne and His Six Organ Symphonies." PhD diss., Catholic University of America, 1970.

Keene, Dennis. "The Duruflé Album." Liner notes for recording of the *Requiem*, *Messe "Cum jubilo,"* and *Notre Père*. Delos International DE 3169, 1995.

———. "Madame Duruflé Returns to the United States." *American Organist* 23 (October 1989): 18.

———. Program notes for a performance of the *Requiem*. New York City, November 6, 1998.

Labounsky, Ann. *Jean Langlais: The Man and His Music*. Portland, OR: Amadeus Press, 2000.

Laigue, A.-L. de, et al. *Le Mystère chrétien dans l'église Saint Étienne-du-Mont: Art, culture et foi*. Paris: Saint Étienne-du-Mont, 1995.

Lalo, Pierre. [Review of Dukas's *Symphonie*.] *Le Temps*, 1902. Quoted in Favre, *Paul Dukas: Sa vie, son œuvre*.

Langlais, Jean. "Charles Tournemire." *Bulletin de Sainte Clotilde*, 1949.

Laparra, Raoul. "Chez Colonne." *Le Matin*, January 20, 1936. Reprinted in *Bulletin* 3 (June 2003): 75.

Lawrence, Arthur. "An Organ Tour of Paris." *American Organist* 27 (December 1993): 70–73.

Lechevalier, Bernard. *Le Cerveau de Mozart*. Paris: Éditions Odile Jacob, 2003.

Le Flem, Paul. "En première audition: Trois Danses." *Comœdia*, January 20, 1936. Reprinted in *Bulletin* 3 (June 2003): 66–67.

Le Guennant, Auguste. *Précis de rythmique grégorienne: D'après les principes de Solesmes*. Paris: Institut grégorien, 1948–54.

Lemmens, Jacques-Nicolas. *École d'orgue basé sur le plain-chant romain*. Brussels: Chez l'Auteur, 1862.

Lescroart, Yves. *Rouen: La Cathédrale Notre-Dame*. Paris: Éditions du Patrimoine, 2000.

Lespinard, Bernadette. *"L'Orgue mystique* de Charles Tournemire." *L'Orgue: Cahiers et mémoires*, no. 139 bis (1971).

Lesure, François. *Catalogue de l'œuvre de Claude Debussy*. Geneva: Minkoff, 1977.

———. *Claude Debussy*. Paris: Klinksieck, 1994.

Lesure, François, and Richard Langham Smith, eds. *Debussy on Music.* New York: Alfred A. Knopf, 1977.

Levainville, J. *Rouen pendant la guerre.* New Haven, CT: Yale University Press, 1926.

Levasseur, André. "La Maîtrise Saint-Évode: Les organistes de la cathédrale de Rouen." *L'Orgue normand* 26 (second semester 1993): 6–11.

*Liber Usualis Missae et Officii pro Dominicis et Festis cum Cantu Gregoriano ex Editione Vaticana Adamussim Excerpto et Rhythmicis Signis in Subsidium Cantorum a Solesmensibus Monachis,* No. 780. Tournai: Desclée et Co., 1964.

Liner notes for the recording of the *Requiem* by the Ensemble vocal de Neuwird, directed by B. Kämpf (Motette CD 50241). Quoted in François Sabatier, [Untitled], *L'Orgue,* no. 221 (January–March 1992): 49.

"Liste des orgues construites par la Maison Cavaillé-Coll." *La Flûte harmonique* 25 (1983): 15–30.

Litaize, Gaston. "Maurice Duruflé, mon ami." *L'Organiste* 195 (1987): 3–5.

Locke, Ralph P. "Liszt's Saint-Simonian Adventure." *19th-Century Music* 4 (1981): 209–27.

Lockspeiser. Edward. *Debussy: His Life and Mind.* London: Cassell, 1962.

Lodine, Robert. "The Duruflés in Evanston." *Diapason* 57 (November 1966): 25.

———. "TAO Report on AGO Biennial Convention, Philadelphia, June 22–26 [1964]." *American Organist* 47 (August 1964): 18–26.

Lueders, Kurt. "L'Œuvre d'Aristide Cavaillé-Coll à Paris." Supplement to *La Flûte harmonique* (2nd trimester 1978): 25.

Machabey, Armand. "Galerie de quelques jeunes musiciens parisiens: Maurice Duruflé." *L'Information musicale,* December 4, 1942.

———. *Portraits de trente musiciens français.* Paris: Richard-Masse, 1949.

Mallet-Richepin, Madeleine. [Introduction to *Trois Improvisations* by Louis Vierne], reconstituted by Maurice Duruflé. Paris: Durand, 1954.

Mansart, Édouard. "Histoire de la Maîtrise Saint-Évode pendant les années de la première guerre mondiale." Rouen: unpublished, 1989.

Mardirosian, Haig. "Maurice Duruflé, 1902–1986." *American Organist* 37 (July 2003): 56–59.

Mason, Marilyn. "Conversations with Marilyn Mason." By Lorenz Maycher. *American Organist* 39 (July 2005): 66–67.

"Maurice Emmanuel et son temps, 1862–1938." *Revue internationale de musique française* 11 (June 1983): 8–55.

Mayer, Denise, and Pierre Souvtchinsky, eds. *Roger Désormière et son temps: Textes en hommage.* Monaco: Éditions du Rocher, 1966.

McAmis, Hugh. "Our Paris Letter." *American Organist* 7 (September 1924): 534.

———. "Paris Pictures." *American Organist* 8 (February 1925): 81.

Mender, Mona. *Extraordinary Women in Support of Music.* Lanham, MD: Scarecrow Press, Inc., 1997.

*Le Ménestrel.* March 5, 1927–March 16, 1934.

Meyer-Garforth, Catherine. *Cours progressif de déchiffage pour le piano: Débutant à élémentaire.* Preface by Maurice Duruflé. Mâcon, France: Éditions Robert Martin, 1984.

Miramon Fitz-James, Béranger de. "Sur la Mort et la succession de Louis Vierne." In *In Memoriam Louis Vierne,* 216–21.

Montagne, Joachim Havard de la. *Mes Longs Chemins de musicien.* Paris: L'Harmattan, 1999.

"Les Monuments historiques au service des orgues de France." *L'Orgue: Bulletin trimestriel* 8 (April–September 1962).

Moreau, Félix. "Maurice Duruflé, l'homme et le pédagogue." *Bulletin* 2 (June 2002): 31–32.

Morehen, John. [Report on the performance of *Messe "Cum jubilo"*]. *Musical Times* 109 (July 1968): 655–56.

Mousnier, Jean-Philippe. *Paul Paray.* Paris: L'Harmattan, 1998.

Münch, Charles. *I Am a Conductor.* Translated by Leonard Burkat. New York: Oxford University Press, 1955.

Murray, Michael. *French Masters of the Organ.* New Haven, CT: Yale University Press, 1998.

———. *Marcel Dupré: The Work of a Master Organist.* Boston: Northeastern University Press, 1985.

Muset-Ferrer, Abbé J. "Quelques Souvenirs sur Louis Vierne." In *In Memoriam Louis Vierne,* 139. Quoted in Smith, *Vierne,* 474.

*Music.* July 1974–July 1977.

*La Musique sacrée au IIIème Congrès international de musique sacrée—Paris, Juillet 1957.* Paris: Revue musicale, n.d.

Near, John Richard. "The Life and Work of Charles-Marie Widor." DMA diss., Boston University, 1985.

"Nécrologie de Maurice Duruflé." Translated by Robert Burns King. *American Organist* 20 (October 1986): 14, 16. First published in *Le Monde* (June 25, 1986).

Nectoux, Jean-Michel. "French Archives: Music in the Archives of Paris Churches." *19th-Century Music* 7 (Fall 1983): 100–103.

Nelson, Robert Kent. "The Organ Works of Maurice Duruflé." *Music* 11 (July 1977): 31–37.

Nichols, Roger. "Maurice Duruflé." *Choir and Organ* 4 (May 1996): 30–31.

———. *Messiaen.* Oxford Studies of Composers 13. London: Oxford University Press, 1975.

Ochse, Orpha. *Organists and Organ Playing in Nineteenth-Century France and Belgium.* Bloomington: Indiana University Press, 1994.

*Olivier Messiaen: Meditationen über Musik.* Film documentary on the occasion of the 80th birthday of Olivier Messiaen, shown on December 8, 1988. ARD Television Network, Germany.

"Onorificenze." *Acta Apostolicae Sedis* 54 (February 28, 1962): 122–23. (*Acta Apostolicae Sedis* is the official monthly gazette of the Holy See and the Vatican City State.)

Overath, Johannes, ed. *Sacred Music and Liturgy Reform after Vatican II: Proceedings of the Fifth International Church Music Congress, Chicago-Milwaukee, August 21–28, 1966.* Rome: Consociatio Internationalis Musicae Sacrae, 1969.

P., M. [Review]. *Le Ménestrel* 90 (April 27, 1928): 185.

———. "Prix des 'Amis de l'Orgue.'" *Le Ménestrel* 92 (June 27, 1930): 297.

Panel, G. *Démographie et statistique médicale, Ville de Rouen, 1918.* Rouen: Cagniard, 1919.

Paponaud, Marcel. "Festival de Lyon (1953)." *L'Orgue,* no. 69 (October–December 1953): 124–25. Reprinted in *Bulletin* 3 (June 2003): 25–26.

Pâris, Alain. *Dictionnaire des interprètes et de l'interprétation musicale au vingtième siècle.* Paris: Éditions Robert Laffont, 1995.

*Paroissien romain contenant la messe et l'office pour les dimanches et les fêtes,* no. 800. *Chant grégorien extrait de l'édition vaticane et signes rythmiques des Bénédictins de Solesmes.* Tournai: Desclée et Cie, n.d.

Patat, Jean-Pierre, and Michel Lutfalla. *A Monetary History of France in the Twentieth Century.* Translated by Patrick Martindale and David Cobham. New York: St. Martin's Press, 1990.

Paxton, Robert O. *Vichy France: Old Guard and New Order, 1940–1944.* New York: Alfred A. Knopf, 1972.

Pendleton, E. J. "France: New Compositions Hold Center Stage in Paris." *Musical America* 70 (January 15, 1950): 26–27, 46.

Perrelet, Robert. "Homélie." Preached at the funeral of Maurice Duruflé. *L'Orgue: Cahiers et mémoires*, no. 45 (1991): 60–61.

Peterson, William J. "Lemmens, His *École d'orgue*, and Nineteenth-Century Organ Methods." In Archbold and Peterson, *French Organ Music*, 51–100.

Pierre, Constant. *B. Sarrette et les origines du Conservatoire national de musique et de déclamation*. Paris: Librairie Delalain Frères, 1895.

Pincemaille, Pierre. "L'Improvisateur à Notre-Dame." In Carbou, *Cochereau*, 273–318.

———. "Maurice Duruflé." Liner notes for the CD recording *Maurice Duruflé: Intégrale de l'œuvre pour orgue*. Beuel Motette 12541.

Pinguet, Francis. *Les Écoles de la musique divine*. Lyons: Éditions à Cœur Joie, 1987.

Pons, Ch. "*Le Requiem* de M. Duruflé." *L'Ordre*, December 30, 1947.

Porcile, François. *La Belle Époque de la musique française*. Paris: Fayard, 1999.

Poulenc, Francis. *Correspondance, 1910–1963*. Edited by Myriam Chimènes. Paris: Fayard, 1998.

———. *Entretiens avec Claude Rostand*. Paris: René Julliard, 1954.

"Principales Œuvres données en première audition à Paris aux concerts des Amis de l'Orgue." *L'Orgue*, no. 160–61 (October 1976–March 1977): 22–23.

"Principaux Concerts: Marie-Madeleine Duruflé en solo de 1933 à 1997 et Joint-Récitals avec Maurice Duruflé de 1953 à 1979." *Bulletin* 3 (June 2003): 51–62.

"Quelques programmes de concerts [of Marie-Madeleine Duruflé]." *Bulletin* 3 (June 2003): 48–51.

"Questionnaire envoyé en 1936 par Bérenger de Miramon à des jeunes organistes français." *L'Orgue*, nos. 201–4 (1987): 24.

Ramsey, Basil. "Recitals." *Musical Times* 110 (May 1969): 529.

Raugel, Felix. "Du Second au Troisième Grand Orgue de Saint Étienne-du-Mont." *L'Orgue*, no. 90 (1959): 38–44.

———. *Les Grandes Orgues des églises de Paris et du département de la Seine*. Paris: Librairie Fischbacher, 1927.

———. "Orgues et organistes." *Le Courrier musical et théâtral* 24 (January 1, 1922): 66.

Reisinger, Wolfgang. "Maurice Duruflé's Limited Musical Output: Implications for Contemporary Performers." DMA diss., University of Kansas, 2003.

———. "Neoklassizistische, spätromatische und impressionistische Einflüsse auf das Werk von Maurice Duruflé." Doctoral diss., Universität für Musik und darstellende Kunst, Vienna, forthcoming in 2007.

"Répertoire de Marie-Madeleine Duruflé." *Bulletin* 3 (June 2003): 46–47.

Revert, Jehan. "Homélie." Preached at the funeral of Maurice Duruflé. *L'Orgue*, nos. 201–4 (1987): 93–95; and in *L'Orgue: Cahiers et mémoires*, no. 45 (1991): 62–64.

*La Revue musicale*. 1927–88.

Reynolds, Jeffrey. "In Memoriam: Maurice Duruflé." *Choral Journal* 27 (April 1987): 17.

———. "On Clouds of Incense." In Ebrecht, *Duruflé*, 87–119.

Rise, Harald. "Impressionism and the Organ: A Study of Impressionistic Aspects of Organ Works by Maurice Duruflé." Dr. Art, Norwegian University of Science and Technology, 2001.

Robert, Philippe. "Maurice Duruflé: Sa vie, son œuvre." Diss., Université de Liège, 1979. Part of the dissertation was later published as "Maurice Duruflé: Sa vie, son œuvre religieuse." *L'Orgue: Cahiers et mémoires*, no. 45 (1991): 14–46.

Robert, Philippe. "La Place de Maurice Duruflé dans l'histoire de la musique." In Ville de Louviers, *Hommage à Maurice Duruflé*, n.p.

Robertson, Alec. *Requiem: Music of Mourning and Consolation.* London: Cassell, 1967.

Roget, Henriette. "La Musique." *Les Lettres françaises* (November 27, 1947).

Ronzon, Laurent. "Maurice Duruflé et le Conservatoire de Paris: Sa formation et son enseignement, 1920–1970." Diss., Université de Paris, 1996.

Rorem, Ned. *Lies: A Diary, 1986–1999.* Washington, DC: Counterpoint, 2000.

Rosenstiel, Léonie. *The Life and Works of Lili Boulanger.* London: Associated University Presses, 1978.

Rosenthal, Manuel. [Hommage]. *Bulletin* 2 (June 2002): 33.

Rostand, Claude. "Le *Requiem* de Maurice Duruflé." *Revue internationale de musique* (Winter 1950–51): 266–73.

Roth, Daniel. "In Memoriam Maurice Duruflé." *Bulletin* 2 (June 2002): 33–34.

———. "Some Thoughts on the Interpretation of the Organ Works of Franck, on His Organ, and on the Lemmens Tradition." Translated by David Gramit. In Archbold and Peterson, *French Organ Music,* 189–98.

Roussel, Gaston. "Le Rôle exemplaire des maîtrises de cathédrale." *La Revue musicale,* no. 239–40 (1957): 263–66.

Royzman, L. "Slushaya Organistov." *Sovetskaya Muzyka* 30 (February 1966): 84–87.

Russell, Carlton T. "Franck's *L'Organiste* Reconsidered." *American Organist* 53 (February 1970): 12.

S., G. "Le *Requiem* de Berlioz à Saint Étienne-du-Mont." *Le Ménestrel* 89 (November 18, 1927): 474.

Sabatier, François. [Hommage à Cochereau]. In Carbou, *Cochereau,* 355–64.

———. "Les Orgues de Maurice Duruflé." *L'Orgue: Cahiers et mémoires,* no. 45 (1991): 47–50.

———. [Untitled]. *L'Orgue,* no. 221 (January–March 1992): 49.

Samson, Joseph. *La Polyphonie sacrée en France des origines à nos jours.* Paris: Schola Cantorum, 1953.

Saorgin, René. [Untitled]. *Bulletin* 2 (June 2002): 34–35.

Sauvlet, Emmanuel. "Les Six Symphonies pour orgue de Louis Vierne." *L'Orgue: Cahiers et mémoires,* no. 47 (1992-I).

Schmidt, Carl B. *The Music of Francis Poulenc: A Catalogue.* Oxford: Clarendon Press, 1995.

Schmitt, Florent. [Review of *Trois Danses*]. *Feuilleton du temps,* February 15, 1936. Reprinted in *Bulletin* 3 (June 2003): 73–74.

Schmitt, Francis P. *Church Music Transgressed: Reflections on "Reform."* New York: Seabury Press, 1977.

Schulé, Bernard. "Soixante Années au service de l'orgue." *L'Orgue,* nos. 201–4 (1987): 20.

Schweitzer, Albert. "The Art of Organ Building and Organ Playing in Germany and France." In Joy, *Schweitzer,* 138–76. First published in *Deutsche und französiche Orgelbaukunst und Orgelkunst* (Leipzig: Breitkopf und Härtel, 1906).

Schwemmer, Marius. *Das Orgelwerk Maurice Duruflés im Orgelunterricht: Ein Beitrag zur Form, Ästhetik und Technik.* Marburg: Tectum-Verlag, 2003.

Seneca, Gérard. "Les Musiciens laïcs plaident pour le chant grégorien." *L'Intransigeant,* January 8, 1967.

Simeone, Nigel. *"Dear Maître Tournemire . . .": Charles Tournemire's Correspondence with Felix Aprahamian and His Visit to London in 1936.* Bangor Monographs in Musicology. Bangor: University of Wales, 2003.

Simpson, G. Criss. "Organ Music in Paris Churches: V, Sainte Clotilde—Sacré Cœur—St. Gervais." *American Organist* 6 (January 1923): 15, 16, 19.

———. "Organ Music in Paris Churches: VI, Reims and La Trinité." *American Organist* 6 (February 1923): 76, 78.

Simpson, G. Criss. "Paris as I Saw It." *American Organist* 10 (October 1927): 262.

———. "A Second Organistic Pilgrimage: An American Organist Again Gives His Impressions of Europe after an Absence of Several Seasons at Home." *American Organist* 12 (October 1929): 597–99.

Sisson, Ruth. "Charles Tournemire, 1870–1939." *American Organist* 23 (December 1989): 56–64.

Smith, Rollin. *Louis Vierne: Organist of Notre-Dame Cathedral.* Hillsdale, NY: Pendragon Press, 1999.

———. *Toward an Authentic Interpretation of the Organ Works of César Franck.* New York: Pendragon Press, 1983.

Société d'Études diverses de Louviers et de sa Région. *Louviers.* Louviers: Librairie "A la Page" H. Fontaine, 1999.

Solane, Janine. [Hommage à Maurice Duruflé]. *Bulletin* 2 (June 2002): 35–36.

Sordet, Dominique. [Review of *Trois Danses*]. *Action française,* January 24, 1936. Reprinted in *Bulletin* 3 (June 2003): 67.

Soularue, Olivier. "Maurice Duruflé, un artiste engagé." In Ville de Louviers, *Hommage à Maurice Duruflé,* n.p.

———. "L'Orgue de l'église Notre-Dame de Louviers." In Ville de Louviers, *Hommage à Maurice Duruflé,* n.p.

Spillman, Herndon. "As the Master Wanted." In Ebrecht, *Duruflé,* 121–55.

———. "Hommage à Maurice Duruflé." *Bulletin* 2 (June 2002): 37–39.

———. "The Organ Works of Maurice Duruflé." DMus diss., Indiana University, 1976.

Sprout, Leslie A. "Les Commandes de Vichy, aube d'une ère nouvelle." In Chimènes, *Vichy,* 157–81.

———. "Music for a 'New Era': Composers and National Identity in France, 1936–1946." PhD diss., University of California, Berkeley, 2000.

Spycket, Jérôme. *Nadia Boulanger.* Paris: Lattès, 1987.

Stan, J. "Un Concert à la cathédrale." *L'Éclaireur de Nice et du sud-est,* March 5, 1931.

Steed, Graham. "Dupré and Demessieux: The Master and the Pupil." *American Organist* 13 (March 1979): 42–43.

Steinfels, Peter. [Review of Tridentine Mass at St. Patrick's]. *New York Times,* May 13, 1966.

Swann, Frederick. "Souvenirs sur Maurice et Marie-Madeleine Duruflé." *Bulletin* 2 (June 2002): 39.

Sweeney, Regina M. *Singing Our Way to Victory: French Cultural Politics and Music during the Great War.* Middletown, CT: Wesleyan University Press, 2001.

Terroud, P. O. [Review of *Prélude, récitatif et variations*]. *Chantecler,* January 19, 1929.

Thomas, Fannie Edgar. *Organ Loft Whisperings: The Paris Correspondence of Fannie Edgar Thomas to "The Musical Courier," New York, 1893–1894.* Edited by Agnes Armstrong. Altamont, NY: Sticut Tuum Productions, 2003.

Thomerson, Kathleen. *Jean Langlais: A Bio-Bibliography.* New York: Greenwood Press, 1988.

Thompson, Oscar. *Debussy: Man and Artist.* An unabridged and corrected republication of the original 1937 edition. New York: Dover Publications, 1967.

Thomson, Andrew. *The Life and Times of Charles-Marie Widor, 1844–1937.* Oxford: Oxford University Press, 1987.

———. "Pure Invention." *Choir and Organ* 10 (July–August 2002): 50–52.

Tikker, Timothy J. "My Studies of Tournemire's Music with Jean Langlais." In *Ch. Tournemire in Saint Paul: On the Occasion of the Fiftieth Anniversary of His Death,* 43–48. St. Paul, MN: Institute for Critical Studies of Organ Music, 1989.

Tommasini, Anthony. "Marie-Madeleine Duruflé, 78, an Organist." *New York Times* (December 10, 1999).

Torroud, P. O. [Review of *Prélude, récitatif et variations*]. *Chantecler,* January 19, 1929.

Tortolano, William. "Maurice Duruflé, 1902–1986." *Journal of Church Music* 29 (April 1987): 22–23.

Tournemire, Charles. "L'Art de l'improvisation." *Listener* (February 19, 1936).

———. *Cinq Improvisations pour orgue.* Reconstitution and introduction by Maurice Duruflé. Paris: Durand, 1958. The introduction was also published in *L'Orgue,* no. 92 (1959): 126.

———. *Précis d'exécution de registration et d'improvisation à l'orgue.* Paris: Max Eschig, 1936.

Trieu-Colleney, Christiane. *Jeanne Demessieux: Une Vie de luttes et de gloire.* [Avignon]: Presses universelles, 1977.

Tuzik, Robert L., ed. *How Firm a Foundation: Leaders of the Liturgical Movement.* Chicago: Liturgy Training Publications, 1990.

V., A. "Une Messe de Requiem." *Musique et Liturgie* 5 (March–April 1938): 103.

Vallombrosa, A. de. "Les Orgues de Chœur à Paris." *L'Orgue,* no. 58–59 (January–June 1951): 35–45.

Van der Veldt, James. *The Ecclesiastical Orders of Knighthood.* Washington, DC: Catholic University of America Press, 1956.

"La Vie de l'orgue en France, 1928–1929." *Bulletin Semestriel des Amis de l'Orgue,* no. 1 (June 1929): 3.

Vierne, Louis. "Memoirs of Louis Vierne; His Life and Contacts with Famous Men." Translated by Esther E. Jones. *Diapason* (October–November 1938).

———. "Mes Souvenirs." In Smith, *Vierne,* 7–319.

Ville de Louviers. *Hommage à Maurice Duruflé.* Published in conjunction with the centenary exposition at the Musée municipal, 2002.

Ville de Paris. *Inspection générale des beaux-arts, Paris 1943: Arts, lettres.* Paris: Presses universitaires de France, 1943.

Vine, Rodger. "Souvenirs [de Marie-Madeleine Duruflé]." *Bulletin* 3 (June 2003): 43–45.

Vinteuil, Roger. [Review of *Trois Danses*]. *Le Ménestrel* 98 (January 24, 1936). Reprinted in *Bulletin* 3 (June 2003): 71.

Walsh, Stephen. [Review of *Messe "Cum jubilo"*]. *Musical Times* 109 (August 1968): 760.

Weidner, Raymond F. "The Improvisational Techniques of Charles Tournemire as Extracted from His Five Reconstructed Organ Improvisations." PhD diss., Michigan State University, 1983.

Wells, Ian. "Maurice Duruflé, 1902–1986." *Organists' Review* 82 (November 1996): 292–94.

Whitney, Craig R. *All the Stops: The Glorious Pipe Organ and Its American Masters.* New York: Public Affairs, 2003.

Widor, Charles Marie. "Le Plainchant de Solesmes." Unpublished manuscript, 1904, in the Archives de la maison diocésaine, Paris.

Wierzbicki, James. "Impressionism." *St. Louis Dispatch,* July 22, 1920. Available at http://pages.sbcglobal.net/jameswierzbicki/impressionism.htm.

Wilson, Grady, William Tufts, et al. "Recitals and Concerts." *American Organist* 49 (December 1966): 8, 12.

Zimmerman, Edward, and Lawrence Archbold. " 'Why Should We Not Do the Same with Our Catholic Melodies?': Guilmant's *L'Organiste liturgiste,* op. 65." In Archbold and Peterson, *French Organ Music,* 201–47.

# *Index*

# Eastman Studies in Music

*Maurice Duruflé: The Man and His Music* is a new biography of the great French organist and composer (1902–86), and the most comprehensive in any language. Written by James E. Frazier, himself an organist and noted authority on Duruflé's life and work, this book traces Duruflé's musical formation as an impressionable chorister at the cathedral in Rouen; his studies with Charles Tournemire and Louis Vierne and at the Paris Conservatoire; and his subsequent career as performer, composer, and Conservatoire professor. Frazier also examines the career and contributions of Duruflé's wife, the formidable organist Marie-Madeleine Duruflé-Chevalier.

Duruflé brought the church's unique language of plainsong into a compelling liaison with the secular harmonies of the modern French school as typified by Debussy, Ravel, and Dukas.

Frazier's book reveals the genesis and early history of each of Duruflé's works, including the fact that his widely loved masterpiece—the *Requiem* Op. 9 for soloists, chorus, organ, and orchestra—was composed on commission from the Vichy government. The book describes the conflicted circumstances, particularly the turbulent relationship of the French church with French secularism and nationalism, under which Duruflé composed what proved to be one of the greatest choral works of the twentieth century.

Because Duruflé was the greatest musician in the eight-hundred-year history of the church of Saint Étienne-du-Mont in Paris, the book provides the most thorough account extant of its musicians and its organs, including the organ that Duruflé himself designed according to the neoclassic principles that he espoused, and whose design and construction spanned two decades.

Frazier, drawing on the accounts of those who knew Duruflé personally as well as on his own detailed research, offers a broad sketch of this modest and elusive man, whom some considered a pathological perfectionist, but who is widely recognized today for having created some of the greatest works in the organ repertory—and the masterful *Requiem*.

James E. Frazier holds advanced degrees in organ, sacred theology, and sacred music from the Hartt School of Music (University of Hartford), Yale University Divinity School, and Yale Institute of Sacred Music. He was organist and director of music at Trinity Episcopal Church in Hartford (1974–81) and is currently organist and director of music at the Episcopal Church of Saint John the Evangelist in Saint Paul, Minnesota. He concertizes widely and has taught at Saint John's University in Collegeville, Minnesota.

"The compositions of Maurice Duruflé succeed brilliantly in piercing the soul. Duruflé himself, by contrast, was legendary in his reticence and discretion. James Frazier provides readers with the most comprehensive overview yet to be written—objective yet sympathetic—of Duruflé's life and music. Through this study, we also learn of the rich culture that nurtured the arts in the first half of the twentieth century. Essential reading for performers and concertgoers alike."

—Jesse Eschbach, DMA, Professor of Organ, University of North Texas

"A rich and detailed biography of Duruflé, one in which so many vital strands of his time and place—the sacred role of the organ in the liturgy, the impact of liturgical reforms, the secular role of the organ in concertos and symphonies, educational institutions and in particular life at the Paris Conservatoire, the backdrop of a turbulent political scene, and many more—come together effectively and impressively. And Marie-Madeleine Duruflé, without whom Duruflé's story would have been so different, finally receives the attention she has long deserved. Written with admiration and respect, yet adhering to the highest standards of scholarship and fairness, his work is a model for biographies in music."

—Lawrence Archbold, co-editor of *French Organ Music from the Revolution to Franck and Widor* (University of Rochester Press)